A White Preacher's Message

*Let us work together
to keep the dream alive.*

A White Preacher's Message on Race and Reconciliation

Based on His Experiences Beginning with the Montgomery Bus Boycott

ROBERT S. GRAETZ

NewSouth Books
Montgomery | Louisville

NewSouth Books
P.O. Box 1588
Montgomery, AL 36102

Library of Congress Cataloging-in-Publication Data

Graetz, Robert S., 1928-
A white preacher's message on race and reconciliation : based on his experiences beginning with the Montgomery bus boycott / Robert S. Graetz.
p. cm.
Includes index.
ISBN-13: 978-1-58838-190-3
ISBN-10: 1-58838-190-0
1. Montgomery (Ala.)--Race relations. 2. African Americans--Civil rights--Alabama-
-Montgomery. 3. Civil rights movements--Alabama--Montgomery--History--20th
century. 4. United States--Race relations. 5. Graetz, Robert S., 1928- 6. Civil rights
workers--Alabama--Montgomery--Biography. 7. Lutheran Church--Alabama--Mont-
gomery--Clergy--Biography. I. Title.
F334.M79.N435 2006
323.1196'073076147--dc22

2006017107

Design by Randall Williams
Printed in the United States of America

TO JEANNIE

Contents

Foreword

LIVES OF COMMITMENT

BY JOHN LEWIS

With all that I have experienced in the past half century, I can still say without question that the Montgomery bus boycott changed my life more than any other event before or since. I have been reminded of this all through this excellent memoir by the Reverend Robert Graetz, who with his wife, Jeannie, was in the forefront of the boycott.

Montgomery was just fifty miles away from where I grew up in rural Alabama. I'd been there only once myself, on a day trip I took by train in my seventh-grade year. But my parents and my neighbors knew Montgomery. Our minister lived there. Most of my teachers were from there. Even though we lived far out in the Alabama woods, we were connected to Montgomery in many ways. We were part of the place. And when that young minister, the Reverend Dr. Martin Luther King, Jr., in his role as the president of a group called the Montgomery Improvement Association, launched a black boycott of the buses after the arrest of Rosa Parks, we felt we were a part of that as well.

Robert Graetz was an active member of the board of directors of the Montgomery Improvement Association and he was the minister of a Montgomery African American church during the boycott. Even his home was bombed—twice.

You can appreciate that I was more than a little surprised to learn all this about Reverend Graetz when I met him in later years and saw that he was a white man. What an amazing thing it was that a white man would be the pastor of a black congregation in Alabama in 1955 and that he and his family would live in a black neighborhood and they would all be completely committed to the goals and principles of the bus boycott and the larger civil rights movement. The book you are now reading explains where this commitment came from, and shows how Bob and Jeannie Graetz have lived lives dedicated to bringing about what Dr. King called the "beloved community."

The Montgomery boycott went on for more than a year, and I followed it almost every day, either in the newspapers or on radio. This was riveting. It was real. This wasn't just talk. This was action. And it was a different kind of action from anything I'd heard of before. This was a fight, but it was a different way of fighting. It wasn't about confrontation or violence. Those fifty thousand black men and women in Montgomery were using their will and their dignity to take a stand, to resist. They weren't responding with their fists; they were speaking with their feet.

There was something about that kind of protest that appealed to me, that felt very, very right. I can see in Reverend Graetz's account of his life that he felt the same way. We may not have started out as practitioners of nonviolence or passive resistance, but when shown the way by the eloquent example of Dr. King, we knew instinctively that nonviolence was not only the right strategy but also the right way to live.

Over the years that followed, I left rural Alabama and went off to school and then I got totally involved in the civil rights movement, from the sit-ins to the freedom rides to the voter registration campaigns. My journey, which I tell about in my own memoir, *Walking with the Wind*, eventually took me to the U.S. Congress, where I am proud to serve today. But over the years I have stayed involved with many of the people who worked with me in various phases of the movement. And I have stayed committed to the principles which were put into motion back in Montgomery and that influenced me so much when I was a young boy.

In the pages of Reverend Graetz's memoir, you see where his journey took him and his life partner, Jeannie Graetz. You see that the journey of a black youngster from the woods of Alabama to the U.S. Congress is not all that different from the journey of a white youngster from West Virginia who grew up to become a minister committed to the same principles of equal justice and civil rights.

I believe in my heart that we need to read and understand stories like those told in this book. We need to understand that people of courage, conscience, and commitment are still willing to spend their lives dedicated to the brotherhood of mankind. As I learned in my work, and as Bob Graetz clearly learned in his, the Beloved Community is nothing less than the Christian concept of God on earth.

Believers in the Beloved Community insist that it is the moral responsibility of men and women with soul force, people of goodwill, to respond and to struggle nonviolently against the forces that stand between a society and the harmony it naturally seeks.

This book shows that the Reverend Robert Graetz has done that with his life. In fact, he is still doing it.

John Lewis is a member of the U.S. Congress from the Fifth District of Georgia. The former chairman of the Student Non-Violent Coordinating Committee, he is internationally known for his courage during the civil rights movement.

Preface

A Jubilee Year

In the Torah (the first portion of the Hebrew scriptures) God commanded his people to set aside every fiftieth year as a Year of Jubilee. It was to be a time of restoration. Any land that had been bought was to be returned to its previous owners. The purchasers had merely paid for the use of the land for a given period of time until the next Jubilee Year. Those who had been sold into bonded servitude were to be freed. It was God's desire that no Hebrews be allowed to remain in permanent servitude. "You shall proclaim liberty throughout the land to all its inhabitants" (Leviticus 25:10). God seemed to be saying, "No matter how much things have gotten out of kilter, let's put them all back into their proper order."

Whether the ancient Hebrews ever observed the Year of Jubilee as instructed in Leviticus is a matter for discussion among theologians, but the God-given concept is still fitting for us today. Fifty years is long enough. If you took something that wasn't yours, even if it was fifty years ago, it's time to give it back.

We are presently in the midst of a series of fifty-year celebrations of events of the twentieth century Civil Rights Movement: The 1954 U.S. Supreme Court decision, *Brown v. Board of Education,* and its follow-up decision in 1955, which ruled segregation in the public schools to be unconstitutional. The murder of Emmett Till in Money, Mississippi, in 1955, for whistling at a white woman. The Montgomery Bus Boycott of 1955–56, which led to the desegregation of municipal transportation. The Birmingham Campaign to break down racial barriers in public accommodations and jobs in the early 1960s, including the bombing of the Sixteenth Street Baptist Church. The Selma Voting Rights Campaign marked by the Bloody Sunday march on March 7, 1965. And others. For the next decade and more we'll be celebrating jubilees of the triumphs and tragedies of the modern Civil Rights Movement.

Whether by accident or by design, we seem also to have entered into a different and regrettably fitting pattern of honoring the "foot soldiers" of the movement—by bringing to trial those suspected of committing mayhem, assault, and even murder against movement participants or sometimes innocent bystanders. In most of those recently reopened cases, trials were held long ago, but at the time the defendants were handily acquitted by all-white juries, even in some cases where the perpetrators had confessed to their crimes and bragged about them.

In 1991, I completed (with the full participation of my wife, Jeannie) a brief book about our experiences during the Montgomery Bus Boycott. It was first published as *Montgomery: A White Preacher's Memoir*, and later republished as *A White Preacher's Memoir: The Montgomery Bus Boycott*. In the years following, we have often shared memories with other people who took part in that world-changing movement, in which we were privileged to share, despite our tender years and our white skins. During such reminiscing, our memories of the events of that time have been sometimes enlightened, sometimes corrected. In the first portion of this new volume, as we review our years in Montgomery, 1955–58, we have expanded our account of the boycott to include both the new information and our new understandings of the events.

In 1992 our nation marked, not a fiftieth, but a five-hundredth anniversary of another event which also impacted the entire world, the arrival of Christopher Columbus in what was later referred to as "The New World." During the anniversary, that event was variously celebrated by some as a daring achievement which brought great and lasting rewards to many, and by others as the invasion of an occupied land and the beginning of the virtual destruction of those who had occupied it for millennia.

In the sixty-five synods of the Evangelical Lutheran Church in America, of which Jeannie and I are a part, the 1992 Columbus quincentennial was noted in an introspective manner. Most of our synods used the theme "Remembrance, Repentance, and Renewal" for their annual meetings that year. I had the privilege of preaching at the closing worship service for the Southern Ohio Synod. In my message, I reflected on our U.S. history of oppression of Native Americans, African-Americans, homosexuals, women, the Irish, and a long list of ethnic, national, religious, and otherwise "different" groups.

In recent years I have noted an increasingly active debate about the results of the Civil Rights Movement. There are voices (mostly white), which proclaim that we have resolved most of our racial conflicts and should be ready to put "race" behind us as an issue, turning to other "more pressing" problems. Other voices (mostly black) proclaim the movement to have been largely a failure, with many African-Americans being in just as miserable a condition as they were fifty years ago. I am frequently asked which group is right. And my answer is always, "Both!" In this volume I review the fifty years since the momentous events occurred in Montgomery, pointing out both our successes and our failures, as well as my appraisal of the directions we need to move in to continue the momentum begun more than fifty years ago.

One of the most remarkable aspects of our experiences during the half-century of the movement has been the broadening of our understanding of "civil rights." Our eyes had so narrowly focused on the oppression of African-Americans that we scarcely noticed how badly we were treating the women who worked side-by-side with men in the movement. In the years that have followed, our attention has been drawn to the oppression of many groups within our society, including the handicapped, the aged, members of minority faith groups (such as Muslims), and Appalachians. In Chapter Eight I call attention to some of the special problems relating to poor people. And in Chapter Ten I focus on the mistreatment of the homosexual community, an oppressed group about which there has been considerable disagreement among the traditional supporters of the Civil Rights Movement. I argue that the consequences of our either accepting or oppressing the gay community will give even more credence to Dr. King's oft-stated truism that *"Injustice anywhere is a threat to justice everywhere."*

It can scarcely have escaped the attention of any serious, or even casual, observer of the Civil Rights Movement that the last few decades have brought a virtual flood of biographies, travel guides, and other books dealing with this subject. Our own bookshelves groan under the weight of several hundred volumes on the history and culture of African-Americans and the modern Civil Rights Movement. Why, then, do we dare to add another book to that accumulation?

The answer is that we believe we have a unique perspective on the movement in this country. We are European-Americans who have lived in African-American communities and served African-American Lutheran congregations in the North, South, East, and West. We have been active participants in the Movement, placing our lives and our livelihoods on the line alongside our African-American sisters and brothers. And we have been at it for a long time. In December 2000 we were back in Montgomery for the forty-fifth anniversary celebrations of the Montgomery Bus Boycott. In a conversation with Kweisi Mfume, then-president and CEO of the NAACP, I said to him, "You need to know that I first joined the

NAACP in 1948." He looked at me with surprise and exclaimed, "That's the year I was born!"

In addition, we have been involved in campaigns for almost all of the oppressed groups in our society. As we have moved from seeking full citizenship for African-Americans, to giving women an equal role in our society, to working for what has come to be called "gay rights," we have noticed that much of the opposition rhetoric is the same—just substituting the names of different oppressed groups. The same specious arguments we heard for the exclusion of black people have been proffered to keep women in an inferior status and gays and lesbians in the role of societal outcasts. In our minds all of these campaigns are part of the one movement to achieve Dr. King's dream of the "Beloved Community," where all people accept and respect each other with love, regardless of the differences which now divide us.

As we read one new book after another in the civil rights genre, it is fascinating to realize how fallible is human memory. Even active participants in key civil rights events differ in their memories of those events. So it should come as no surprise if we hear readers of this volume say, "No, it didn't happen that way." That does not trouble me. These are my memories and Jeannie's. These are our observations and evaluations. And these are our prescriptions for future action.

"Action" must be the key word. It is time to resurrect that 1992 church theme of "Remembrance, Repentance, and Renewal." We who are European-American heterosexual males, especially, must be honest about our own histories, and about what has been the impact of our thoughts, words, and actions on the lives of those who have suffered because of our ancestors. Furthermore, as I will contend in this volume, we must accept the reality of what I refer to as "white privilege," as well as the corollary reality that historically we have been the recipients of resources that had been wrongfully removed from non-European-Americans. I will then contend that the acceptance of those realities requires us to move on through the steps of "repentance" and "renewal," if we are to achieve the dream of Martin Luther King, Jr., that all peoples will one day live together peacefully in what he called the "Beloved Community."

Acknowledgments

I am deeply grateful to Dr. Janice R. Franklin, director of the Levi Watkins Learning and Resource Center at Alabama State University, in Montgomery, Alabama, and to her entire staff. Our total collection of papers and artifacts is in the process of being transferred to that ASU library, where it will become a permanent collection at their National Center for the Study of Civil Rights and African-American Culture. The Center's staff provided us with invaluable assistance as we did research in our papers during the writing of this book, as well as giving us much-needed support services. Over the past decade, as we have brought our civil rights pilgrimage groups to Montgomery, Dr. Franklin and her associates have been most generous in providing speakers and other resource people to educate and enlighten our pilgrims.

We are grateful also to the staff of the Amistad Center at Tulane University, in New Orleans, Louisiana, for allowing us access to the Preston Valien Papers relating to the Montgomery Bus Boycott. Those papers provided us with valuable insights into the events of that historic time that we had not had access to before.

Many thanks also to our editor and longtime good friend, Randall Williams. We have appreciated his encouragement, support, and valuable suggestions as this volume was taking shape. And we look forward to working with him on other publishing adventures in the future.

I also want to express my profound appreciation to those masses of unknown and unnamed people often referred to as the "foot soldiers" of the Civil Rights Movement. These are the true heroes and sheroes. I salute those who were willing to sacrifice their lives, their livelihoods, and all that they possessed, not for themselves, but, in the words of labor leader Mr. E. D. Nixon, "for the children coming on!"

Finally, there is only one person without whose total and generous involvement this book would not have been possible. That is my wife, Jeannie. She has served not only as my primary editor, but also as questioner, reminder, exhorter, organizer, and quintessential partner in this endeavor. Had it not been for her absolute refusal, she deservedly would have been listed as coauthor.

As these words are written, we are in our fifty-fifth year of married life. We'll be celebrating that anniversary in Montgomery, Alabama, during the observance of the fiftieth anniversary of the celebrated bus boycott. Through good times and bad, our relationship has remained a partnership. We see our lives and our ministry as a series of adventures directed by God, into whose hands we have entrusted our present days and our unknown future.

It is with profound gratitude that I dedicate this volume to the one human being who has meant the most to me during my entire adult life, without whose presence and support my ministry could not have been as full and rewarding as it has been, the one person with whom I am looking forward to growing old, to my dearest wife, Jeannie. I love you with all my heart. And I thank God for you.

A White Preacher's Message

Chapter 1

WHY AM I (STILL) HERE?

After all that I have been through, I keep asking myself the question, "Why am I still here?" As I reflect on the first fifty years of the modern civil rights movement, one of the most remarkable realities to me is that I am still alive and able to report it and to tell my story. Quite frankly, I didn't expect to be. I have vivid memories of some of our discussions in the Montgomery Improvement Association Board of Trustees meetings. During those long, difficult months of the bus boycott and its follow-up actions, Dr. King would remind us, "If you're not ready to sacrifice your life for this cause, you have no business sitting on this board." We all believed that some of us were going to die. That was the reality that we lived with day after day. Though it was never spoken aloud, we were all aware that Dr. King would be the prime target. We also knew, for a variety of reasons, that I too was likely to be high on the list of targets. I was the only white member of the board. Since my very presence was a novelty to the press corps, my picture appeared much too often in local and out of town newspapers. Most significantly, Jeannie and I had the audacity to live in a black neighborhood and to consider ourselves totally part of "black" Montgomery.

Our lives and those of our children were constantly threatened in anonymous letters and phone calls. We assumed that most of the threats were meant merely as intimidation, in hopes of frightening us into leaving Montgomery. However, we took all the threats seriously, and for good reason. When our car was vandalized in January 1956, the front tires were carefully slashed on the inside, where the damage would not be noticed. The cuts were just deep enough not to flatten the tires until they heated up after a long drive. The vandals must have hoped that one or both tires would blow out when I was on the road.

In those days I made frequent car trips out of Montgomery. Early on I discovered to my dismay that not only did many of our opponents know what car I drove, but I was frequently followed. It did not take long for me to learn alternate routes to the places I normally drove, and I never used the same route twice in a row. Nevertheless, knowing I was a target, each time I said good-bye to Jeannie and the children when leaving home, I was very much aware that I might not come back. Jeannie, on the other hand, always "knew" that God would not allow anything bad to happen. To this day she remembers her shock when the second bomb exploded at our house. She says she was mad at God for allowing the Klan to throw bombs at our house again, this time with children inside!

I had taken Dr. King's warnings seriously about the danger all of us faced; and I was determined to be faithful to the commitment I had made, though it might cost me my life. I fully expected that I would not survive. Whatever our differing expectations, Jeannie and I learned to live our lives one day at a time.

Montgomery never became a "Bombingham," the nickname given to Birmingham, Alabama, after a long string of bombings there of African American homes, businesses and churches. But bombings were plentiful enough in Montgomery, beginning on January 30, 1956, less than two months after the beginning of the bus boycott. The first target, as was to be expected, was the home of Dr. King and his family. Another early target was Mr. E. D. Nixon, a courageous labor leader and one of my all-time heroes, who had spent his entire life fighting racism.

On August 25, 1956, and again on January 10, 1957, our home was the target of bombs, each estimated to contain two or three sticks of dynamite. The first had landed more than forty feet from the house; so the damage to the structure (and to our neighbors' homes) was minimal. The second time, however, the bombers had put more strength into their throw, landing the bomb just a few feet from our front door. That door and all of our front windows were shattered, as were the windows of the B. T. Knox family next door. The roof of our house was raised several inches. Our living room floor was covered with broken glass and plaster dust; the kitchen floor was littered with broken dishes and smashed pots and pans and groceries, as our cupboards had disgorged their contents. Nothing had been spared!

The August bombing had taken place while we were out of town. We had spent the previous week at Highlander Folk School in Monteagle, Tennessee, at a workshop dealing with racial desegregation. Mrs. Rosa Parks, our neighbor and good friend, had come with us to the workshop. We still remember the shock we experienced, knowing that we could be the victims of such a cowardly attack. But no great damage was done. And the bombing served to strengthen our relationship with the African American community. Now they all knew we were with them in the "movement."

The January attack was totally different. Our family was home at the time, with a nine-day-old baby! And the bomb exploded at 2:00 AM, jolting us all out of a sound sleep. Minutes later, as I and our neighbors stood outside assessing the damage, we heard sounds that seemed to be other explosions. We soon learned that four churches and two homes had been bombed in Montgomery that night. Ours was the first.

All of us who had gathered in front of our house kept stumbling over something in the driveway, which turned out to be another bomb that had not exploded! That device contained eleven sticks of dynamite and a container of TNT, all taped to a TV antenna which had served as a handle for throwing the bomb! As stunned as we were, we were still alive. The demolitions experts told us that the bomb that did not explode would have leveled the entire neighborhood. We and many of our neighbors would have been killed.

THE SERIES OF MY REMARKABLE EXPERIENCES of escaping death predates Montgomery by several years. In the summer of 1949, I worked in the green pea harvest in Idaho. It was just after my junior year at Capital University, in Columbus, Ohio. A national Lutheran youth gathering had been scheduled for late that summer in Pullman, Washington. To entice more young men to attend, planners had lined up jobs for students from several Lutheran colleges across the country. We were promised $1 an hour for twelve-hour shifts, seven-day weeks, with free housing. All we had to do was get there.

As it turned out, the pea growers had had a bad spring, with well-below-normal rainfall. By the beginning of summer, they knew their crops were going to be much smaller than they had anticipated. But commitments had been made, and travel plans had been arranged, so on we came from our various parts of the country, several hundreds of us, to take those promised jobs. We learned when we arrived in Lewiston, Idaho, that at most we would be working two or three days a week in the harvest. I was fortunate enough to pick up an occasional day's labor picking cherries, or filling in at the local cannery or frozen foods plant, packaging peas. When the harvest ran out, many of my compatriots gave up and went home. Because I still wanted to attend the youth gathering, I bummed around looking for odd jobs.

I had the good fortune to link up with another Capital University student, Dan Mathes, with whom I later roomed when we got back to school. Since Dan had a car, we were able to go more places to find work, though all the jobs we had were short-lived and dangerous. We signed on at a building construction site and were given the task of digging out what would become the bottom of an elevator shaft. Our fellow workers told us that all of them had refused to do that particular job, deeming it unsafe. When the large hole was completely dug and the form was set into place for pouring concrete, our foreman discovered that one corner needed another inch or two of dirt removed to level the form. Since I was smaller than Dan, I was lowered into the narrow space between the form and the dirt wall, some seven or eight feet deep. As I finished digging, Dan saw the ground begin to give way. He yanked me out of that trap by my arm, just as the bank collapsed! I probably would not have survived the cave-in.

We also got jobs on a road-construction crew, where the road builders had set up a rock crusher at the bottom of a limestone hill. Rocks formed by blasting away the side of the hill were then crushed into gravel for the roadway. Boulders would occasionally get hung up on the hillside, requiring someone to work them loose so they could roll down the hill into the crusher. I was assigned to dislodge one particularly large boulder. As I pried loose the rocks that were holding it up, the stone suddenly broke loose, roaring down the hill. I narrowly missed being crushed to death.

When we finally got to the youth gathering, Dan and I were early enough to volunteer to help with the setting up. I was assigned to attach a banner to the wall high above the stage. To reach the spot, I had to stand on a box on top of a chair perched on a narrow ledge. After all the close calls I'd had, I'm not sure why I agreed to that assignment; except that no one else was volunteering to do it. By the end of the summer, I reflected long and hard about the many times that God had given me special protection. Truly his angels had carried me in their hands.

Those memories of God's special care came back to me some

five years later. In the fall of 1954, as an "old married couple" with more than three years behind us, Jeannie and I were returning from Los Angeles, California, where I had served for two years as a student pastor. We brought with us our two children, Margee, not quite two, and Bobby, about six months, who had both been born in Los Angeles. We were going back for my final year at what is now Trinity Lutheran Seminary, in Columbus, Ohio. That year, 1954-55, turned out to be perhaps the most difficult year in our lives. For a variety of reasons, we had to move several times during those months. Jeannie also had a series of medical emergencies, including hospitalization for an ectopic (tubal) pregnancy. I got so far behind in my studies that we finally moved Jeannie and the children back with her parents in Pennsylvania, while I moved in with my sister and her husband, Suzanne and Bill Deutschmann. Working a nearly full-time job to pay the bills, I tried to do two semesters of schoolwork in one during the time that was remaining. (Incidentally, the only time I saw my family during that second semester was Easter Sunday; so we knew precisely when our third child, Dianne, was conceived!) It was only thanks to the grace and generosity of my professors that I was able to graduate on time. One of them wrote to me during the Montgomery Bus Boycott, assuring me that what I had accomplished there made up for what I had not completed in class.

In many conversations during that year, Jeannie and I tried to figure out why God was allowing us to endure such misfortune. We kept coming back to the same answer. God must be preparing us for some difficult task that we could not handle without special training. Jeannie made a wonderful "discovery" in 1 Corinthians 10:13, "There hath no temptation taken you but such as is common to man: but God is faithful, who will not suffer you to be tempted above that ye are able; but will with the temptation also make a way to escape, that ye may be able to bear it." (KJV) The true eye-opener for Jeannie was the realization that in more modern translations the word "temptation" appears as "testing." God was testing us to be sure we were ready for what lay ahead! Sure enough, in June 1955 we arrived in Montgomery, Alabama, a mere six months before the beginning of the bus boycott.

AGAIN I FEEL COMPELLED to ask, "Why am I (still) here?" I am sure I have a better grasp on the answer now than I did fifty-five years ago, or even fifty. During the intervening years I have had hundreds of opportunities to speak and to preach, write, and teach about the civil rights movement. Jeannie and I never turn down an opportunity to appear in a classroom, from pre-school to graduate school. We now believe we are here to continue to share the message with the generations following us, the ones whom our labor leader friend, Mr. E. D. Nixon, used to refer to as the "Children Coming On."

During the last ten years or so, we have led a number of groups on what we call "civil rights pilgrimages." We visit the sites of major civil rights events and introduce our groups to people who participated in those early activities, who then tell their own stories of their involvement. We walk across the Edmund Pettus Bridge in Selma, Alabama, site of "Bloody Sunday" in 1965. We take our people to the Sixteenth Street Baptist Church in Birmingham, where four girls were murdered with a bomb on a Sunday morning in 1963. We travel to the church in Montgomery that was served by Dr. King, as well as the site of his entombment in Atlanta. We tour the Rosa Parks Museum in Montgomery. We visit the Trinity Lutheran Church parsonage, our old home, and show where the bombs exploded, with the official Alabama Historical Tree planted in one of the spots. And we explain how we too took part in those activities. The most frequent comment we hear from our participants is "A life-changing experience!"

Jeannie and I believe we have a God-given challenge to continue to tell our stories and to share our lives, as do other participants in the movement who are still able to do so. Both African Americans and European Americans need to be reminded of their histories and of how their ancestors related to one another. We keep in mind the maxim that if we do not remember our history, we shall be doomed to repeat it. Only as we face our past openly and honestly, can we work up the courage to address and correct the wrongs that have been committed by one people against another. So God leads us to share our memories, in order that we may be in a position to be mediators and reconcilers. We feel God has given us the unique privilege of standing with one foot in the black community and one foot in the white. It may not be comfortable; but that is where we are. And until God tells us it is time to slow down, we intend to keep pressing ahead with our witness.

Chapter 2

THE LONG ROAD
TO MONTGOMERY

Jeannie and I followed a circuitous path to reach Montgomery, Alabama, and to become part of the modern civil rights movement. When I had grown up in West Virginia, the schools were totally segregated. Black and white people lived in separate neighborhoods, where we had little contact with one another. The dirtiest and most difficult and dangerous jobs were reserved for blacks. I had little personal knowledge about African Americans (probably referring to them as "colored people" then), and even less awareness of the problems they faced. That awareness did not hit me until the year 1948, when I was a junior at Capital University in Columbus, Ohio.

Even my choice of Capital was somewhat foreordained by my name. There was a long tradition of Robert Graetzes serving as Lutheran clergy. My great-grandfather, Gottlob Wilhelm Robert Grätz, arrived in the United States from Germany in 1844, as a young man in his twenties, enrolling in the Lutheran Seminary of the Ohio Synod, in Columbus. One of his sons, another Robert, my grandfather's brother, also later served as a Lutheran minister. And my own father, the first male child of my grandfather and grandmother, was appropriately named Robert.

When Dad was a small child, he had to have a growth removed

The author as a boy in West Virginia at about ages two and eight.

from the back of his neck, a most dangerous operation in the early days of the twentieth century. Grandfather, a life-long devout Lutheran, prayed for his son's health and safety. "God," he said, "if you will spare his life, I will dedicate him to your service as a minister." Dad recovered with no complications; and his future was determined. Or so Grandpa thought. Dad, however, had other ideas about his future. After suffering through two years as a pre-theological student at Capital University, he transferred to Ohio State University, also in Columbus, and graduated as a chemical engineer!

Grandpa had failed with his own son. But I had been named Robert, Jr. So I was also fair game. Dad had really wanted to give me a different name. Making me a "junior" was Mother's idea. Failing to resolve the argument, they came up with a compromise. If I arrived before my due date, Dad had the naming honors. Afterward, it was Mother's choice. Though Mother was glad to win the contest, she certainly wasn't happy that I was almost a month late. Just under two years later, Mother had a daughter, Suzanne, my only sibling. She and I are today dearest friends. She married Bill Deutschmann, one of my best buddies and a classmate in college and seminary, who also became a Lutheran minister. Bill has since passed away.

From the time I was quite small, Grandpa was preparing me for the Lutheran ministry. He taught me German any time he had a chance. In his mind, I am certain, all proper Lutheran ministers had to speak German. As a matter of fact, when my Dad was growing up, no English was allowed in his home. If a playmate slipped and said something in English, he was kicked out of the house. Dad told me many times that in his home there were eleven commandments. The first, and most important, was, "Sprecht Deutsch!" (Speak German!)

Grandpa encouraged me to read the Bible and to be active in church. And by the time I was in elementary school, he was talking with me as often as he could about my becoming a minister. For years I wavered between ministry and medicine. But by September of 1946, when I registered at Capital, I signed on as a pre-theological student.

German was still important to me. I wanted to be able to read the old German theological volumes that had been passed down to me from my great-grandfather, including a Bible printed in 1704! (I also have the shaving mug that traveled with my great-grandfather on the sailing ship that brought him across the Atlantic. I have used it a few times, along with an antique straight razor!) My plans were sidetracked, however. For two years I studied German under a professor who taught us little more than drinking songs and other fun things. (We learned to chant the German alphabet as a football cheer!) When I started my third year of the language under a different professor, he informed me within a few days that I would never make it in German. I should choose another major—immediately!

Halfway through my college years by then, my choices were somewhat limited. Capital, however, offered a conglomerate Social Science major, with a wide range of courses in that broad field. The student was allowed to choose one subject for concentrated studies. Several courses that I had already taken would be counted toward the major. And I opted for a concentration in sociology. It seemed as good a choice as any. I dropped my German and signed up for a sociology course from Dr. Karl Hertz. For one assignment in the course I was required to write a term paper on a subject of my own choosing.

That gave me a chance to focus on a personal agenda. In my high school I had had several good Jewish friends. In our senior year, when we were all announcing to one another that we had been accepted at this college or that one, I found out that most major colleges in the United States had "Jewish quotas." Only a certain limited number of Jews would be admitted into each incoming class. My friends had to be really good to get into the schools of their choice. I determined to use my paper to expose this discriminatory practice.

I began searching through microfilms of the *New York Times* and other significant newspapers, looking for references to racial or ethnic discrimination. And I found what I was looking for. Though it was not often brought up in public discussion, there were indeed "Jewish quotas." But I found a great deal more than what I was looking for, coming across references to people named Heman Marion Sweatt, Ada Sipuel Fisher and others. They were African Americans who were also trying to get into colleges. But there were no "Negro quotas" in the schools they tried to enter. The schools were all white, and intended to remain that way. I borrowed Caesar's phrase when crossing the Rubicon for the title of my paper. Caesar said, "The die is cast." My term paper was entitled "The Caste is Dyed—Black."

According to the early draft of the paper which I recently discovered tucked away in a filing cabinet, most of my writing dealt with details of court cases regarding Negroes attempting to enter colleges and statistics about Jewish quotas, which were sometimes as low as 0 percent! But I also included a quote from an author whose name is not in my notes:

> Truth is not nearly so strong a motivation as opinion. There were no witches in New England, but the unfortunate victims of fanatical persecution were none the less martyred. "We live by faith," but we kill by prejudice. "Faith is the substance of things hoped for," but prejudice is the substance of things feared; and one is as real and as dynamic as the other.

I added,

> So real is the fear of minority groups in America that the resulting prejudice has made a myth of the concept of equality in education.

In my Preface I stated,

> In this paper I have endeavored to show how deeply rooted in our educational system is this problem of racial and religious discrimination in admissions practices at our colleges and universities. I hope that in reading this paper, others may be moved to give their support to a drive to secure genuine educational equality in America.

The paper closed with these words:

Perhaps in another decade, a few of the resolutions of the Association of American Colleges and other organizations will be translated into practical actions, and we will see the beginning of the end of racial and religious prejudice in colleges and universities. We must all work and pray for the time when the myth of educational equality will be a part of America's "glorious" past.

(The board of the National Education Association had voted unanimously to condemn school segregation, on May 11, 1943!)

Within that next decade, the civil rights movement did indeed blossom into its fullness. The Montgomery Bus Boycott had been successfully carried out and had been reported around the world. Martin Luther King, Jr., had become one of the most recognized names on the planet. The inequitable nature of our nation's "inglorious" past had been fully exposed. The battles had been joined, in the North as well as the South.

The die was certainly cast for me. I had crossed my Rubicon. A typical new convert, I turned my full attention to matters that related to my newfound calling. Because I was so moved by my experience in Dr. Hertz's class, the following semester I took three more courses from him. He turned out to be the most difficult professor I ever studied under, and probably the very best. Within weeks, I had also organized a Race Relations Club on the campus.

I joined the Columbus chapter of the NAACP, traveling by streetcar over to Mount Vernon Avenue, the heart of the black business district, to attend meetings. My recollection is that we met in a room over the Pythian Theatre. Becoming a membership recruitment volunteer, I solicited memberships from all my friends on campus. But my most vivid memory from that time was the experience of meeting Walter White, then the national head of the NAACP. I had read his book, *A Man Called White*, and was moved

The author, front row, second from left, with the Capital University Race Relations Club, which he organized in 1948.

by his courage and tenacity. Addressing our gathering, Mr. White told us that one of the most hopeful indicators for improvement in race relations in this country was the growing involvement of white people in the movement. I was "busting my buttons." Since I was the only white person in the room, I knew he was talking about me. About a year after that, he would also be talking about another Capital student named Jeannie Ellis, who would later become Jean Ellis Graetz.

Jeannie's pathway to the movement was somewhat different from mine. She had grown up with an intense desire to learn about people who were different from herself. In her own small community of East Springfield, Pennsylvania, west of the city of Erie and close to the Lake Erie shoreline, most of the people looked pretty much like her, though they had roots in many European countries. But

Bob Graetz's seminary graduating class, 1955. He is second from right on the first standing row.

Jeannie was an avid reader. She learned a great deal about people of other cultures and other nationalities through the books that she devoured. During the last years of World War II, after her high school graduation and before she started at Capital, Jeannie worked at the General Electric plant in Erie. In her desire to meet new (different) people, she made friends with an African American co-worker, inviting her to the Ellis home in East Springfield. Jeannie has memories of both her parents and her new friend being a little uncomfortable, not knowing quite how to relate to one another. That was the kind of gutsy thing that Jeannie was likely to do. And that gutsy spirit is what got her to Capital.

Living on a farm with four sisters and no brothers, Jeannie knew that her contributions at home were important to the family. But she had her heart set on going to college, even though she knew that her parents, especially her Dad, would have opposed her if they had known of her plans. The only reason for a "girl" to go to college was to get a husband, according to Dad Ellis. There were plenty of eligible young men in the area. "Besides," her father told her, "if you have enough money to go to college, you ought to start a grocery store in East Springfield instead. We really need one." But once Jeannie put her mind to something, as many of us would learn over the years, there was no turning her back. In September 1949, Jeannie Ellis became a student at Capital University. She did not know it yet, but her die was cast also.

The following February 12, a Saturday, Jeannie and I had our first date, at a picnic-retreat of the Luther League, our Lutheran youth group. In the midst of the throng of students, Jeannie and I were in our own little world all day, as we talked and shared our lives. Walking the mile back to the campus in the rain, we turned down all offers for rides. Our newfound love was all the covering we needed. A friend who had briefly dated Jeannie had warned me not to try to kiss her on our first date, but I ignored his advice. From that point on, we were inseparable. The following summer, I made my first visit to Jeannie's home and fell in love with her family, too. On Sunday, June 10, 1951, we were married in the Ellis family's home congregation, The Federated Church, East Springfield, Pennsylvania.

In the meantime, on another rainy Saturday the previous October, Jeannie and I had spent the day piling up pavement bricks along the side of an empty lot on East Long Street in Columbus. The excavating company was due there the following week to prepare the land for a group of volunteer mission builders. That fall they constructed a building for St. Philip Lutheran Church, an almost totally black congregation that I would later serve as pastor, and with which we retain a strong relationship to this day. (On August 22, 2004, I was awarded the title "Pastor Emeritus" of St. Philip.)

Above, Capital University yearbook photos of Bob Graetz and Jean Ellis.

Right, the Graetzes' wedding photo, June 10, 1951, at her home church in Pennsylvania.

By the fall of 1952 I was ready for my internship, a year of on-the-job training under the supervision of a seasoned pastor. It happened that there was a small congregation in the Los Angeles area, mostly black, that was served at that time by a lay leader. The lay leader wanted to attend our seminary in Columbus for a year, so he could be ordained.

We had very few African American pastors in the Lutheran Church in those days, not enough to fill all the pulpits of our largely black congregations. Our denomination required a full college and seminary training for its pastors. And the elementary and secondary schools attended by Negro youngsters, north and south, were a poor excuse for a proper education. The children were ill prepared to enter schools of higher learning. Any white pastors who were interested in serving black congregations were snatched up in a hurry. Since that lay leader, Bob Trygstad, expected to return to Los Angeles a year later, the church officials would not consider calling a different pastor to serve Community Lutheran Church for that short a time. A student would have to suffice. Thus began my on-the-job training. Except that there was no pastor there to train me. I was the pastor! A neighboring pastor met with me once in a while to check on me and to make suggestions.

Community Lutheran Church was located in the midst of a large tract development south of the city of Los Angeles. Hundreds of homes had been built on what used to be a farm, all originally intended for white families. By the time we arrived there in the summer of 1952, black people had occupied most of the homes in our immediate neighborhood, with the changeover moving slowly southward. A minor race riot broke out not far from our house after two African American families moved onto a new block. I had my baptism of fire, learning firsthand how to work to achieve racial reconciliation. At the time we lived in that part of Los Angeles County, the area known as "Watts" was limited to South Central L.A.

By the time of the Watts Riot in 1965, the concept had changed, and our neighborhood was considered to be part of Watts. Some of the rioting took place not far from our former church.

With no other church buildings nearby, that congregation truly became a "community" church. The membership grew from about seventy-five to one hundred and fifty while we were there; while the Sunday School swelled to more than five hundred, with two sessions back-to-back at the church, and a third in two side-by-side double garages in an adjacent neighborhood. I could not have survived without the presence of a roaming parish worker named Thelma Tollefson, an angel in disguise who directed all of our educational activities. One of the women at Community Lutheran, Mrs. Doris Holman, a leader at the church in the 1950s, is still active. We have recently been in contact with her. Not long ago we were invited back for a big anniversary celebration. The pastor serving Community when we returned was Fred Wimberly, who had been one of my faithful teenage assistants during the time when I was a student pastor!

In January 1956, after the Montgomery Bus Boycott had begun, we received the following letter from Community Lutheran:

Dear Pastor Graetz,

We, the Community Lutheran Church, whom you served not too long ago, have been keeping abreast of these changing times and the wonderful part you are doing to help all people in the United States to realize that together we stand or together we fall.

We also realize that this cannot be accomplished without cost, so, here enclosed in a check (collected at door) for the amount of $25.05—no strings attached. You may use it where it is most needful; to you, or your congregation.

May the Lord bless you and family, keep you and give you

peace, is our prayer. In Jesus' name and for his sake. Amen.

Yours very truly,

Community Lutheran Church

Jeannie and I learned some things about ourselves while in California. Our awareness of racial differences became less acute. Some of the little boys near our house climbed to the roof of our garage one day; and Jeannie chased them off. When she told me that evening about the incident, I asked, "Were they white or black?" Jeannie thought for a moment, and then replied, "I didn't notice!" We also learned the importance of relaxing and not taking life too seriously. We began a pattern of playing a game each evening before we went to bed. In those days it was usually gin rummy. We believe this practice helped to keep us centered during some of our more difficult years. We have kept up that pattern for more than fifty years! (Now we have dozens of games that we play. The loser from the night before chooses the next game that we play.)

That one year at Community turned into two years, when the lay leader discovered he could not be ordained with only one year of seminary study. The delay meant that our two oldest children were born in California. Margaret Ellen (now Meta Ellis) was born on November 3, 1952. Robert III, who later called himself Ray, followed on March 13, 1954. Both of them later moved back to their birth state. Meta now lives in the "high desert" in Southern California. Ray lived mostly in the San Francisco area until his untimely death from the complications of AIDS on June 21, 1991.

By the fall of 1954 we were back in Columbus for my last year of seminary studies, a most difficult year. And by the time we arrived in Montgomery in June of 1955, we knew we were survivors. We were certain that God was doing something special with our lives. We just didn't know what it was. In less than six months we would find out!

Civil War and Civil Rights — This photo is from the 1940s, but downtown Montgomery had not changed appreciably when the Graetzes arrived in June 1955. This view looks east up Dexter Avenue toward the state capitol. The Court Square fountain in the foreground dominates the area where slave auctions were once held. In 1861, the first building on the far right was the telegraph office from which the message was sent to fire on Fort Sumter, thus beginning the Civil War. The Montgomery Fair department store, where Rosa Parks worked, is not in this photo, but would have been just behind the first building on the far left. Mrs. Parks would have boarded her bus on December 1, 1955, just to the left of the fountain, thus beginning the modern Civil Rights Movement.

Chapter 3

ROCKING THE CRADLE!

Montgomery, Alabama, was known as "The Cradle of the Confederacy." On Goat Hill, at the highest point of Dexter Avenue, which is the main street of the downtown district, stands the Alabama state capitol building, a beautiful and imposing structure, presiding over the commercial and political life of the state's capital city. A star is imbedded in the marble floor at the top of the long stairway from the street, just outside its main doorway. The inscription on that star tells us that it was on this very spot that Jefferson Davis took his oath of office as President of the Confederate States of America on February 18, 1861. Alabama had formally seceded from the Union just a few weeks before, on January 7.

There is a "must-see" for tourists just inside that main doorway—a magnificent cantilevered two-story double spiral staircase, believed to be designed and constructed by a slave, Horace King! Mr. King was also noted as a bridge-builder, whose works are still in existence in several parts of Alabama and Georgia.

At the bottom of the hill, at the other end of Dexter Avenue, stands an a large ornate cast-iron water fountain fed by an artesian well, marking the spot once occupied by a slave auction block. The telegram that started the Civil War was sent from the Winter Building, standing next to the fountain. With that message, President Davis had ordered the firing on Fort Sumter, a military base in South Carolina occupied by Union forces.

In between, just one short block from the capitol building, a double stairway leads to the main entrance of a simple brick building, constructed in 1885. Next to the sidewalk a sign used to identify this building as the Dexter Avenue Baptist Church. A few years ago, however, its members renamed it "Dexter Avenue *King Memorial* Baptist Church." This congregation has the distinction of being the only one that Dr. Martin Luther King, Jr., served as its presiding pastor. (When he moved to Atlanta in January 1960, he began serving as co-pastor under his father, who remained as presiding pastor of Ebenezer Baptist Church.)

Soon after Jeannie and I arrived in Montgomery, nearly a century after the Civil War, we were informed that that conflict should be referred to as "The War Between the States." We also learned something else about that war. Lee may have surrendered. The Confederacy may have been dissolved. The bloody battlefields may have been turned into memorial parks. But the South had not yet given up! Ninety years had not been nearly long enough for this vanquished people to fully regain their dignity and self-respect. Though the war was over, the struggle continued on.

Slavery had been legally abolished. But it had been replaced with a system of servitude that, for many poor African Americans, was little better. Sharecroppers lived on land owned by "the Man." They borrowed money from him for seed and for their personal needs, sold their crops back to him, and relied on him to keep honest and accurate records of their dealings. But somehow they never "came out," which meant paying off their debt in full. How often did they hear the refrain at harvest time, "Well, George, if you'd have had just another half-bale of cotton, you'd have come out." As long as they owed money to "the Man," they were bound to the land.

Poor white people, especially in rural areas, fared little better than their black neighbors. Both groups were at the mercy of the wealthy plantation owners and cotton processors and merchants.

The shared poverty of poor whites and blacks should have forced them to support one another in order to survive. But because it served the purposes of white business and political leaders to keep both groups poor, those leaders made certain that poor whites were always thrown the sop of racial superiority. It was the only prop for their self-esteem. They may not have had wealth, fame, education, or power, but they always "knew" they were better than their black neighbors.

The threat of the loss of racial supremacy was even used to thwart labor union organizing in the South. I recall overhearing a conversation between two white men in downtown Montgomery, who were discussing a vote in the plant where one of them worked. The workers had just voted not to organize a union at the plant. The man who worked there said to his friend, "I know it's costing me a dollar an hour not to have the union, but it's worth it to keep the niggers out."

To add insult to injury, the 1901 Constitution of Alabama had imposed a poll tax on all voters in the state, which was as much a burden on poor whites as it was on poor blacks.

In the cities the pattern was different from that of rural areas, but just as demeaning. When we arrived in Montgomery, we learned that you could hire a maid or a "yard boy" (which could refer to a sixty-year-old man) for $2 to $3 a day for full-time work! And everyone in our African American community knew of people who had gotten better jobs, working side-by-side with white people, where those white workers received perhaps double what was being paid to their fellow laborers who happened to be black. Most African Americans were vulnerable, living from hand to mouth, not owning their own homes. The upper-class black community was small indeed, consisting of a few professional people like doctors, schoolteachers and administrators, and some of the pastors.

In those days every social interaction was subject to the segregation laws. Black and white people were not allowed to be together in any meaningful way. In the "white" theaters, black patrons sat only in separate balconies. African Americans were not allowed in "white" restaurants. They had to order their food at the back door as "take-out." Shopping for clothes in stores, they were not allowed to try them on. (There is a wonderful story from Martin Luther King's youth, when his father marched him out of a shoe store, after they were refused service in the "white" section of the store.) There were separate "white" and "colored" drinking fountains, rest rooms, and bus and train waiting rooms, if, indeed, such facilities were available to African Americans at all. Black travelers needing fuel would first inquire about rest rooms. If there were none available for them, they would purchase their gas elsewhere.

In white communities there were nice public parks, some with swimming pools and other normal facilities. The so-called "parks" in black neighborhoods were usually nothing more than vacant lots. (In my journal at Trinity Lutheran Church, there is an entry for August 12, 1957, noting that I and our youth group were "asked to leave King Hill Park, continued at Madison Park.") Most libraries were open to whites only. Black citizens wanting to read library books often had to order them through their local schools, all totally segregated, of course. Those schools gave the lie to the "separate but equal" doctrine that had been established by the United States Supreme Court in its 1896 *Plessy v. Ferguson* decision. Though totally separate throughout the South, they were in no way equal. School buildings in black communities tended to be poorly constructed and poorly furnished. Discarded schoolbooks that were no longer wanted by white schools were sent to the black schools. Rural black children frequently had to walk miles to school, while they watched white students ride by in buses. In the aftermath of the Supreme Court's 1954 *Brown v. Board of Education* decision, declaring school segregation unconstitutional, some new schools had been hastily constructed for black students. Political leaders hoped to keep schools "separate" longer by finally making them "equal."

Jeannie was pregnant with our third child when we arrived in

Bob with the three Graetz children who lived through the boycott: Dianne, in his arms, and Bobby and Margee.

Alabama in June of 1955. Her obstetrician in Columbus had referred her to a doctor in Montgomery. She was surprised to learn
that her new doctor, who was white, served both black and white
patients. But she was appalled by the arrangement. White moth-
ers-to-be came in through the front door into the regular waiting
room. Black patients entered from the back into a separate, smaller
room. Jeannie was never comfortable going to that doctor. When
he and his staff learned that we were involved in the bus boycott,
they treated her as if she really didn't belong in their office. One
nurse, she felt, was especially mean to her. Jeannie remembers that
nurse hurting her physically and giving her a stern lecture every
time she came in for a checkup. (To his credit, that doctor had the
courage to come by our house to check on his patient when our
house was bombed.) Jeannie and I never adapted well to the system
of segregation, with all of its restrictive laws. We tried very hard
never to patronize or make use of any segregated facilities.

Beyond the laws, there were customs that were just as demeaning,
if not more so. Blacks meeting whites on the sidewalk were expected
to step into the gutter while they passed. The use of courtesy titles
was required when black people spoke to white, but prohibited
in the other direction. The laws and customs were all designed to
reinforce the perception that European Americans were superior to
African Americans. America indeed had its own caste system.

Many segregated facilities could be avoided if one chose to. But
the black citizens of Montgomery generally could not avoid the
segregated seating pattern on the buses. Most African Americans did
not own automobiles. Their only options for traveling to work were
the city buses or walking. Unfortunately, however, the treatment of
black passengers was more demeaning on the buses than in most
other venues of the segregated society. While a few drivers—all the
drivers were white, of course—did treat their African American
passengers with dignity and respect, many seemed to have chosen

this profession largely to give them opportunities to harass black passengers. Constituting less than half of Montgomery's population, black citizens accounted for about 70 to 75 percent of its bus riders. White people tended to ride the buses for convenience; black people out of necessity.

During the bus boycott, I heard hundreds of stories about drivers cursing and threatening black riders, and using abusive racial slurs. Black passengers would often board the bus and pay their money at the front, then be required to dismount and enter by the back door. (They were always required to ride in the back of the bus, of course.) It was not unusual for a driver to pull away before all of his black passengers had re-entered the bus at the rear. One blind man caught his foot in the rear door as he tried to board, falling and hurting himself as the driver pulled away.

The front ten seats were always reserved for white passengers, even if there were none on board. If a larger number of white people got on, and no seats were available, the front row of black passengers was required to relinquish their seats. People were arrested from time to time for refusing to yield. Among them were two young children, ages ten and twelve, who were visiting from New Jersey. Not knowing any better, they sat beside white passengers near the front of the bus, refusing to give up their seats when ordered to. On August 20, 1950, Private First Class Thomas Edward Brooks, a World War II veteran dressed in his army uniform, boarded a Cloverdale bus. He first refused the driver's order to pay his fare at the front, then board through the back door of the bus. When the driver then told him to get off the bus, Brooks would not do so without getting his money back. In the ensuing fracas, PFC Brooks was shot in the back and killed by a Montgomery policeman who had come to the driver's aid. The coroner ruled it "justifiable homicide."

In 1955 alone, two teenaged young women had been arrested

Claudette Colvin, left, and Mary Louise Smith (recent photo) were both arrested in 1955 before Mrs. Parks.

for refusing to give up their seats to white passengers, though neither had been sitting in the section reserved for whites. The first was fifteen-year-old Claudette Colvin, in March. The second was eighteen-year-old Mary Louise Smith, in October. Both were found guilty. Over the months and years, more and more black bus riders had chosen to avoid the problems altogether and were walking to work or wherever else they needed to go.

Truly the black people of Montgomery disliked their bus-riding experiences at least as much as any other aspect of segregation. People complained regularly to city and bus company officials. A group of courageous women called the Women's Political Council had threatened for years that they would call for a boycott of the city's buses if conditions did not improve. The WPC had been organized in 1946 under the leadership of Mrs. Mary Fair Burks, head of the English department at Alabama State College. The chair of the Council in 1955 was Mrs. Jo Ann Robinson, also a professor of English at Alabama State, and a friend of ours. The college was state-supported, which created its own set of hurdles for activists like Profs. Burks and Robinson.

Before organizing the WPC, Mrs. Burks and another woman had first tried to join the League of Women Voters, but had been turned down because they were black. Interestingly, while the Montgomery LWV was not inclusive, it would not have been surprising for it to have been, since a significant number of Southern white women within the organization had worked for years to ameliorate the evils of segregation.

Dr. Robinson was one of a handful of people who took advantage of every opportunity to ease the racial burdens on Montgomery's black citizens. In her book, *The Montgomery Bus Boycott and the Women Who Started It,* she notes that the boycott leadership initially called for an adjustment in the system of segregation on buses, not an end to it. But she adds, "The WPC, however, knew all the

Alabama State College professors Mary Fair Burks, left, and Jo Ann Robinson, were leaders of the Women's Political Council.

time that black Americans were working for integration, pure and simple." We first met Jo Ann in a meeting of the Montgomery Council on Human Relations, one of the few places where white and black people could come together on the basis of mutual acceptance and respect. Some years earlier, the Ford Foundation had provided funding for the establishment of a new organization called the Southern Regional Council, based in Atlanta, Georgia. The purpose of the SRC was to develop councils on human relations in all the southern states, whose purpose, in turn, was to create local councils in major cities in those states. Those local councils provided what were often the only safe sites for black and white people to work together constructively on racial problems. The full-time director of the Alabama Council on Human Relations was Rev. Robert Hughes, a Methodist minister who lived in Montgomery. He and his wife Dottie became good friends of ours.

After the boycott began, an even greater degree of courage was required to participate in the MCHR. Police would stand outside of our meeting places, very ostentatiously writing down the license numbers of all who entered, in an obvious attempt to intimidate us.

Alabama State College was a fruitful source of leaders and participants in the civil rights movement. Prof. James E. Pierce was a colleague of Profs. Burks and Robinson. He taught political science and was a very active member of the Alabama Council on Human Relations, where we saw him often. Pierce may have acquired his courage by growing up in Lowndes County, the most heavily African American county in Alabama, and probably the most thoroughly oppressed. During the early days of the Montgomery Bus Boycott, Prof. Pierce was regularly selected to be a member of the negotiating teams that met often, though fruitlessly, with the city and bus company officials. Not long after we left Montgomery in 1958, we learned that the governor had caused several professors at Alabama

Two of the strongest leaders in Montgomery were E. D. Nixon, left, and Rufus Lewis. They were also rivals.

State to be fired from their positions.

Another friend of ours, Mr. Rufus Lewis, scarcely had time to take part in the MCHR because of his many other involvements. (He was usually called "Coach Lewis," because he had once coached football at Alabama State.) With a passion for voter registration, Lewis often attempted to inspire young people by reminding them that "a voteless people is a hopeless people," and "your power is at the ballot box." His ownership of the Ross-Clayton Funeral Home enabled him to spend time working with the Citizens Steering Committee, which focused on getting people registered to vote. Mr. Lewis also owned the Citizens Club, a nightclub for Negroes, located on the West Side of Montgomery. Only registered voters were allowed to patronize the club!

Because of the long-standing rivalry between Lewis and E. D. Nixon, however, the boycott threatened to unravel before it even began. Many thought there could be a contest between the two for leadership of the newly organized Montgomery Improvement Association. Mr. Lewis was a leader of the "classes" on the East Side of Montgomery; Mr. Nixon, of the "masses," who tended to live on the West Side. We, our church, Mrs. Parks, and Mr. Nixon were all on the West Side. The issue was resolved when Mr. Lewis nominated Dr. Martin Luther King, Jr., to be the first president of the MIA.

(The "classes" included many of the faculty and administrators of Alabama State College, as well as the handful of other professionals and business people in the African American community. As a group they had a powerful impact on efforts to achieve racial progress in Montgomery. Without their full support, it would not have been possible to find enough cars to make up the carpool to keep the boycott going, nor the money to pay for ongoing expenses.)

During the bus boycott, Coach Lewis served as chairman of the Transportation Committee, which recruited drivers for the car pool and developed a very efficient system of routes that served us well during the year of the boycott. In the early 1970s, Lewis was elected to the Alabama House of Representatives; later he was appointed by President Jimmy Carter as the first black U.S. marshal in Montgomery.

Among the older black leaders in Montgomery was Rev. Solomon S. Seay, whom Dr. King called "the spiritual father of the Movement." In 1948 he had begun serving as pastor of Mt. Zion A.M.E. Zion Church in Montgomery. In his memoir, *I Was There by the Grace of God,* Dr. Seay recalls that he was involved with an interracial group of Christian ministers, and also with the Alabama Council on Human Relations. He notes that the white people with whom he associated were working for gradual, rather than revolutionary, change.

Most white people are unaware of the prejudice that exists in many African American communities based on darkness or bright-

Rev. Solomon S. Seay and Mrs. A. W. West. Hers, incidentally, is a photo from when she was one of the persons indicted for supporting the boycott. Those arrests were a badge of honor in the community.

ness of skin color, an attitude obviously learned from slave-holders. Brighter skin is often deemed to be more acceptable. Rev. Seay's dark complexion, and his lack of concern about it, led to some humorous exchanges. At a planning committee session in 1957, meeting in the living room of Mrs. A. W. West, our hostess brought in a tray filled with cups of coffee, some with cream and some without. One member of our group walked across the room to pick up the last cup on the tray. Seeing it was black, he said, "I'm not going to drink that. It might turn my skin dark." After the laughter died down, Seay pushed his ample frame out of his overstuffed chair to get the coffee. "Well," he said, "it won't hurt me none!"

In the summer of 1958, when Mr. Clifford Tyree had come from Columbus, Ohio, to visit us, prior to our leaving to serve his congregation in Columbus, he attended a mass meeting presided over by Rev. Seay. Seay announced to the assembled crowd, "There is someone sitting in the front row tonight, who is from the congregation that is taking the Graetzes from us." From my seat on the platform I could see the entire balcony stand to see our visitor. Rev. Seay laughed and assured them, "Oh, don't worry. He looks just like me." They all laughed and sat back down.

Not long before Rev. Seay died in 1988, at the age of eighty-nine, we visited him in Montgomery. He was staying at the home of his daughter, who is a physician. Preparing to leave at the end of our visit, I said, "I'd like to pray for you before we go." My good friend replied, "I'd like that. Please pray for my peaceful passing." Not long after that, he slipped peacefully away. Incidentally, Rev. Seay's oldest son, Solomon, Jr., studied law and later became a partner with Fred Gray, the lead attorney for the MIA. The younger Seay was involved in many civil rights cases in Alabama.

There is an African American family that needs special recognition, Mr. and Mrs. Arlam and Johnnie Carr and their son, Arlam, Jr. The Carr family was involved in civil rights activities long before the bus boycott; and Mrs. Carr was called a boycott "organizer" by Fred Gray. Not long after the U.S. Supreme Court's *Brown v. Board of Education* decision, Mr. and Mrs. Carr decided to attempt to enroll their son in a white school. That determination eventually led to a court suit filed May 11, 1964, *Carr v. Montgomery County Board of Education*. Just two and a half months later, Judge Frank M. Johnson ordered Montgomery to admit eight black students to formerly all-white schools. Arlam Jr., enrolled in Sidney Lanier High School, from which he graduated in 1968. Clifford and Virginia Durr, a white couple who had supported the movement for years, lived across the street from Lanier. Knowing how frightening the experience might be for those new students, they told Arlam that he and the other black students should use their house as a sanctuary.

Mr. Carr died in 2005 at age ninety-five; Mrs. Carr turned

Above, two of the great ladies of civil rights history: Rosa Parks, left, and Johnnie Carr, at the fortieth anniversary of the Montgomery Bus Boycott, in 1995.

Right, Virginia and Clifford Durr were among the few white Montgomerians who stood publicly for civil rights and civil liberties in the 1950s and 1960s.

ninety-five in January 2006 and at this writing was still going strong. She has been president of the Montgomery Improvement Association since 1967, is deeply involved in every positive program in Montgomery working for reconciliation, and travels all over the country making speeches. She tells her own story in a delightful book, *Johnnie: The Life of Johnnie Rebecca Carr.*

Another black citizen who had regularly registered his protests about the harsh treatment on the buses was Mr. E. D. Nixon, a tall, muscular, dark-skinned man, with a deep, resounding voice, who was as fearless as any person I have ever met. Born in 1899, and with only a fourth-grade education, Mr. Nixon was spurned by some of the younger, better-educated leaders in the city. He was a railroad man, an active member of the Brotherhood of Sleeping Car Porters, and president of its Montgomery chapter since 1938. He had also served as president of the Montgomery chapter of the National Association for the Advancement of Colored People, as well as the Alabama NAACP. Among the active members of the Montgomery chapter was a man named Mr. Raymond Parks, who had risked his life by working to free a group of nine young men, called the "Scottsboro Boys," who had been wrongfully convicted of raping two white women in 1931. Mr. Parks brought his young wife, Mrs. Rosa Parks, to an NAACP meeting. She remembers joining and being elected secretary on the same night.

In his role as NAACP president, Mr. Nixon was often called upon to intercede with public officials on behalf of citizens who had been ill-treated by the police or by someone else in authority. Many times he was asked to get people out of jail, often putting up the bond money himself. Attempting to change the balance of political power, Nixon also organized a voter registration campaign. And he was president of the Progressive Democratic Association, dedicated to improving the lot of African Americans. Courageously breaking new ground, Mr. Nixon was the first African American to run for public office in Montgomery since Reconstruction! Amazingly, he garnered more than 42 percent of the vote in 1954, in an attempt to win a seat on the Montgomery County Democratic Executive Committee. African American voters had only been allowed to vote in the Democratic primary since 1946. By 1955, it was reported that 1,774 of Montgomery's 28,097 registered voters were black. Statewide they numbered about 5 percent of the electorate.

Black people in Montgomery were amazed by Mr. Nixon's courage as he challenged mayors, police chiefs, and anyone else who needed to be confronted on behalf of his people. Attorney Fred Gray, who was to become the lead counsel for the Montgomery movement, said that Mr. Nixon "was the key to the history of the African American struggle for first class citizenship and equal rights in Alabama." We, too, were impressed with our good friend, who lived just around the corner from us. We considered him to be one of our all-time heroes. As would be expected, Mr. E. D. Nixon was among those who regularly appealed for more humane treatment of black bus-riders.

Ironically, it would be the arrest of Mr. Nixon's own secretary on December 1, 1955, that would trigger the Montgomery Bus Boycott and the beginning of the modern civil rights movement. We had met Mrs. Parks soon after we arrived in Montgomery in June 1955. She lived across the street from us in the Cleveland Court apartments. Serving as advisor to the NAACP Youth Council, she often met with them in our church building, just a few feet from her front door.

Quiet, dignified, almost withdrawn, Mrs. Parks did not seem to us to be the kind of person who would not only allow herself to be arrested, but would also be willing for her case to become the basis of a legal challenge to Alabama's system of racial segregation. We learned after the boycott began that a driver named J. F. Blake had put her off a city bus twelve years earlier. She had refused to obey his order to pay her fare at the front, then get off the bus and enter by the rear door. After that incident, Mrs. Parks always looked to see who was driving before entering her bus. Whenever Mr. Blake was in the driver's seat she waited for the next bus.

We also learned that in the summer of 1955 she had gone to the Highlander Folk School in Monteagle, Tennessee, to attend a two-week workshop on school desegregation. Mrs. Virginia Durr, a liberal white activist who later became one of our closest friends, had secured a scholarship to allow her friend to attend. It was during that workshop that Mrs. Parks determined she would never again give up her seat on the bus! (Just a year later, in August 1956, we took Mrs. Parks with our family to another workshop at Highlander!)

On the Saturday after her arrest, she described to me the events of December 1. Mrs. Parks was tired that afternoon, having worked long hours as a tailor's assistant at the Montgomery Fair Department Store during their pre-Christmas rush. And she was carrying several packages. In her fatigued state she neglected to check to see who was driving her bus that day. As it turned out the same James Blake was in the driver's seat. It was clear from Mrs. Parks's later actions, however, that her tiredness was much more than physical. She was emotionally and spiritually tired of a system that had demeaned and devalued her for the more than forty-two years she had lived. She was more than ready to do whatever she could to put an end to that system.

(That bus, #2857, was used in Montgomery from 1954 through 1971. After sitting in a farm field for thirty years, it was found, reconditioned, and brought to the Henry Ford Museum in Dearborn, Michigan. Another bus that had been in operation in 1955 was acquired by a member of a group called One Montgomery, which gave it to the Montgomery Improvement Association, which donated it to become an exhibit in the Rosa Parks Museum, dedicated in 2000 on the forty-fifth anniversary of Mrs. Parks's arrest. And yet another two buses from that era were purchased by the city of Montgomery, the parts of which were used to recreate as closely as possible a 1955 city bus. That bus now runs a downtown route, stopping at several civil rights sites.)

Incidentally, we had always heard that driver J. Fred Blake had gone to his death still a bitter racist man. But we were delighted to be disabused of that notion recently. Jeannie and I attended a gathering at Alabama State University to honor the first Negro drivers who had been hired to drive Montgomery's buses, now a group of older retired men. We were amazed to hear one of the African American drivers describe his good relationship with Blake. The Negro driver had become president of the bus drivers' local union, with Blake serving as secretary under him. Fred Blake was totally supportive and cooperative. He had made a complete turnaround long before his death! His reason for refusing to give interviews about his earlier actions was that he considered them to be based on a belief he no longer espoused. He wanted to leave the past behind him.

My white skin had undoubtedly caused some delay in my being told about Mrs. Parks's arrest. Though the members of our congregation trusted and accepted me totally, the black community in general did not know me that well. I found out later than most of Montgomery's African American ministers had received phone calls, alerting them to a planned one-day boycott of the city's buses set for the following Monday. On Saturday, December 3, I received a phone call from Pastor Bill Griffen, a fellow Lutheran and good friend (who happened to be African American). Bill was in the process of organizing a new congregation in Montgomery. He had gotten word that a woman had been arrested and a boycott had been announced; but he didn't have much more information. Knowing that my neighbor Mrs. Parks would be aware of what was happening, I called her to get more details. What a shock it was to find out that our mild-mannered friend was the one who had been arrested! Shortly after our conversation, someone brought us one of the flyers that were being distributed in the black neighborhoods of Montgomery.

> Don't ride the bus to work, to town, to school, or any place Monday, December 5.
>
> Another Negro woman has been arrested and put in jail because she refused to give up her bus seat.
>
> Don't ride the buses to work, to town, to school, or anywhere on Monday. If you work, take a cab, or share a ride, or walk.
>
> Come to a mass meeting Monday at 7:00 P.M., at the Holt Street Baptist Church for further instructions."

This flyer had been circulated by a group of ministers and lay leaders, who had hurriedly organized themselves in the last day or two. The Women's Political Council had already announced the coming boycott. Dr. Robinson and some of her students had gone to the Alabama State College campus the Thursday night after Mrs. Parks's arrest. They wrote their own flyer, a longer one, and cranked out tens of thousands of copies during the night. By morning the flyers were passed along to members of the WPC, who carried them all over Montgomery. After announcing the arrest, Dr. Robinson's flyer said,

> This has to be stopped. Negroes have rights, too, for if Negroes did not ride the buses, they could not operate. Three-fourths of the riders are Negroes, yet we are arrested, or have to stand over empty seats. If we do not do something to stop these arrests, they will continue. The next time it may be you, or your daughter, or mother.

Professor Robinson spoke from personal experience. In 1949 she had boarded a city bus, heading for the airport to begin her Christmas vacation. Only two passengers were on the bus when she entered, a white woman near the front, and a black man in the back. She took a seat in the fifth row from the front of the bus, well behind the ten seats always reserved for white people. But the driver, apparently deciding she was too far forward for a black person, told her to move back. Failing to move quickly enough, she was ordered to leave the bus. She never forgot her feeling of total humiliation. (Incidentally, Professor Robinson proved her commitment to the movement by driving six hours a day in the car pool, 6– 8 AM, 1–2 PM, and 5–8 PM, all as an unpaid volunteer! She was also a member of the team that attempted to negotiate with city and bus company officials, as well as playing an active and enthusiastic role in many other aspects of the boycott and other programs, before she was forced to leave her position at Alabama State.)

Now that we knew what the black citizens of Montgomery were planning, Jeannie and I had a difficult decision to make. What part should we play in the boycott, if any? Since my "race relations awakening" in 1948, I had developed a reputation for being something of an activist. Our Lutheran Church officials had been more sensitive than I had been about the delicate relationship between a white pastor and a black congregation in the racially segregated Deep South. Several church executives at the national and district level, both offices located in Columbus, had called me in for a meeting before we traveled to Alabama. They lectured me sternly about the dangers we might be facing. And they made me promise to focus on being a pastor and not to start any trouble in Montgomery. I still believe I kept my promise!

Jeannie and I did a lot of praying on Saturday, December 3. What should I, as pastor of Trinity Lutheran Church, do about the boycott? It didn't take long for us to realize that, if our members were going to be involved in this one-day boycott, we should be also. The next morning I urged the worshipers at Trinity to stay off the buses on Monday. I would be on the road starting early Monday morning. They should call the parsonage if they needed a ride to work. Once again, for Jeannie and me, the die was cast!

Early that Monday morning, as I had promised, I was in our car cruising the streets of Montgomery. I picked up people at random, delivering them to all parts of the city. And I couldn't believe what I was seeing. These were not the same downcast, hopeless people I had observed during the almost six months we had lived in Montgomery. There was a new spring in their step and a bright, confident countenance on their faces. As many people reflected later, this was a "new Negro" that I was observing! They seemed to inspire one another as they walked purposefully to work, smiling, looking like they owned the world. And, for the first time in their lives, they really did.

By mid-morning the crowds on the streets had thinned out; so I headed for the courthouse in downtown Montgomery, where Mrs. Parks's trial was set to take place. To my dismay, I had no choice but to use a segregated facility if I wanted to observe the proceedings. Though the "colored" section of the courtroom was packed, with a large crowd waiting outside, the "white" side had plenty of seats available. Trying to be as unobtrusive as possible, I slipped into a spot about halfway back. I wasn't there long. The trial ended almost as soon as it began. Mrs. Parks was quickly found guilty of violating the segregation law and fined $10 plus court costs, a total of $14. Her attorney, Fred Gray, announced that he would file an appeal. And it was over. But not really. It had only begun.

In a matter of hours the crowds would be gathering at Holt Street Baptist Church, just a few blocks from our home and church. Mr. Robert Dandridge, one of the older members of Trinity, had suggested on Sunday morning that we go to the mass meeting together. It was fitting that Mr. Dandridge should accompany me to that gathering. Born in Lowndes County, just to the west of Montgomery, he was part of a family that was known for its independent spirit. Lowndes County was located in the "Black Belt," so-called for its rich soil and also for the presence of large numbers of Negroes. This had been, and still was, prime land for raising cotton. And where there was cotton, there had to be large numbers of slaves to make the enterprise profitable. White residents made up some 20 percent of the population of Lowndes County; but they maintained a firm grip on all the sources of power. Only a handful of African Americans were allowed to vote. (Some scholars insist there were none.) The economy and the political structures were totally controlled by European Americans.

But the Dandridge family was different. They had acquired their land when slavery had been abolished, as a gift from their former master. There were some relatively "kind-hearted" slave-owners who had divided their plantations among their faithful slaves when they ceased being slaves. Mr. Dandridge was old enough to have grown up hearing stories from the slave days; and he had indeed inherited his family's boldness and free spirit.

In later months my life was constantly in danger, because many white people of the Ku Klux Klan mentality knew my car and my visage. The church council at Trinity told me I should always have someone with me when I made my frequent trips out of town. Some of our men were a little uneasy about riding along. But never Mr. Dandridge! Whenever I needed him, he was ready.

A husky, dark-skinned man with a booming bass voice, Mr. Dandridge loved to attend evening worship services all over town in African American churches. Normally he would head straight for the choir section as soon as he arrived, where his presence was always welcomed. He was universally loved and respected, not only for his warmth and his good singing voice, but also for his well-known courage.

On the evening of December 5, I was doubly glad to have my faithful church member with me. When we reached the Holt Street Baptist Church, we couldn't believe our eyes. Though we had arrived well before the scheduled beginning time of 7 PM, it was obvious that we were way too late. The church sanctuary had long since filled up. The balcony, basement, classrooms and hallways were jammed with people. And a large crowd was gathering outside, ready to listen to the proceedings on loudspeakers that had been hastily installed. Long before 7 PM, the streets were filled for several blocks in every direction. Newspaper reporters estimated the crowd to be five thousand people, one-tenth of Montgomery's black population!

Mr. Dandridge knew better than I did the importance of my being physically present in that building at that historic moment. So he led the way through the crowd, greeting people by name and excusing himself, until he had gotten us inside, into the basement of the church. Hymns and prayers had been going on for some time, seemingly spontaneous. Soon, however, the leaders whom we could not see from our vantage point were at the front of the auditorium; and the real service was underway. I could not recognize many of the voices of those who spoke, most of whom I had not yet met. But there was one speaker whose voice I, and people all around the world, would soon know very well. Though this speaker was not introduced by name at the mass meeting, Mr. Dandridge affirmed my assumption that it was the Rev. Martin Luther King, Jr., who had been pastor at the Dexter Avenue Baptist Church for just over a year. I recalled having met him at a meeting of the Montgomery Council on Human Relations, which had been held in the basement of his church.

The crowd was on fire that night, especially when Dr. King

This was the typical joyous attitude of the boycott mass meetings.

spoke. He praised Mrs. Rosa Parks as "one of the finest citizens of Montgomery," who had bravely refused to give up her seat to a white man. Reviewing the history of brutal treatment of African Americans on Montgomery's buses, he declared that Negroes had been "humiliated, intimidated, oppressed," and that "we are here this evening because we are tired." Dr. King reminded his listeners that our only weapon was a peaceful protest, not the physical violence of the Ku Klux Klan nor the economic violence of the White Citizens Council.

Declaring that we were totally justified in what we were doing, King sang out, "If we are wrong, the Supreme Court of this nation is wrong! If we are wrong, the Constitution of the United States is wrong! If we are wrong, God Almighty is wrong . . . and justice is a lie!" With each line, the roar of the crowd grew more intense. He spoke what was clearly in their minds when he declared that "we are determined . . . to fight until justice runs down like water," a quote from the Old Testament prophet Amos that came to be associated with the message of this modern-day prophet.

Rising to new oratorical heights, Dr. King was near the end of his message. "When the history books are written in the future," he declared, "somebody will have to say, 'There lived a race of people, a *black people,* fleecy locks and black complexion, a people who had the moral courage to stand up for their rights; and they thereby injected a new meaning into the veins of history and civilization!'" In the months that followed, we often heard speakers echo that thought: "Let the history books record that there was a people in Montgomery, Alabama, a *black people* . . ."

When Dr. King had finished, Mrs. Parks was introduced to the crowd. The ovation she received would have been excessive for a Hollywood star or a visiting head of state. But she was their new star, who had dared to stand up against all the heads of government and commerce. And she had emboldened them to do the same. There would be no turning back.

The real business of the evening came somewhat as an anticlimax. Rev. Ralph Abernathy read the three demands that had been drawn up during the day by a group of pastors and lay leaders who had organized themselves as the Montgomery Improvement Association. Those demands were: 1) an end to the demeaning treatment of Negroes on the buses. 2) a new form of segregated seating, wherein blacks would fill seats from the back, and whites from the front, with the line being drawn wherever the groups met, and *no one being required to give up a seat to someone from the other race.* 3) Negro drivers to be hired for the routes that carried all or mostly African American passengers. The "protest" would continue until the demands were met. (We refused to use the word "boycott" in order to avoid being charged with violating a state anti-boycott law.) The vote on the demands was unanimous, as was the decision to continue the protest until we had achieved what we sought. The new organization that would provide leadership for the boycott would be called the Montgomery Improvement Association. Dr. Martin Luther King, Jr., had already been elected as president of the newly formed group.

In retrospect we can see that our "demands" were so mild they hardly justified that label. Since we were not attacking segregation itself, the national office of the NAACP at first refused to support our efforts. (Less than two months later, however, a suit was filed in federal court directly challenging the segregation laws.) But that was no concern to the five thousand black citizens of Montgomery gathered that evening at the Holt Street Baptist Church. Regardless of the language or the label, they knew that what we had accomplished that day was the beginning of a revolution. It was a new day! There was a new Negro! And we were more than observers; we were participants! As Mr. Dandridge and I left the church building that evening, someone shook my hand, asking me, "Did you enjoy the meeting?" Before I could speak, Mr. Dandridge interjected, "Enjoy it! He's part of it!" And indeed I was.

The Graetz children doing a little desegregating of their own with some of their playmates.

Chapter 4

'Ain't Gonna Let Nobody Turn Me 'Round'

Everyone knows the theme song of the civil rights movement, "We Shall Overcome." Who is there in this entire nation, whose heart has even a spark of the love of justice, who has not crossed arms and joined hands with those on either side to sing the words,

> We shall overcome;
> We shall overcome;
> We shall overcome someday;
> Oh, deep in my heart I do believe,
> We shall overcome someday!

After the first stanza, the succeeding words would match the local scene and circumstances. "No more Bull Connor," etc. But there were many movement songs, some adapted from old beloved hymns. And the hymns themselves were sung over and over, now with new meaning. There is one song, however, that seemed most appropriate to characterize the spirit of black Montgomery during the bus boycott:

> Ain't gonna let nobody turn me 'round,
> Turn me 'round, turn me 'round;

Ain't gonna let nobody turn me 'round;
Keep on a-walking; keep on a-talking;
Marching up to Freedom's Land.

From the moment the boycott was announced, there seemed to be no doubt that nobody was going to turn Montgomery's African Americans 'round. It was as if the entire population had been simply waiting for someone to give the signal. In the days between December 1 and December 5, everyone wondered how effective the planned one-day withdrawal of service could possibly be. Even Dr. King had said privately he believed a sixty percent response should be considered to be a success. No one anticipated that the call to boycott would be heard and followed by nearly one hundred percent of the African American community! On Monday, December 5, only a dozen or so black riders were seen on the buses all day long.

That afternoon's edition of the *Alabama Journal* reported:

> At 5:30 AM today the big yellow busses of the Montgomery City Lines began pulling into Court Square to pick up passengers. Generally a swarm of Negro passengers are waiting at the stop for the busses to take them to the railroad shops, private homes, laundries, factories, and jobs throughout the city . . . Negroes were on almost every corner in the downtown area silent, waiting for rides or moving about to keep warm, but few got on busses.

That same issue of the paper reported, "At least one white man was carrying Negroes in his automobile and parked in the downtown area until he got a load." The reporter had obviously seen me driving, as I did every day for weeks. The boycott's Transportation Committee assigned me to an early morning schedule.

That first day's success so buoyed up the black people of Montgomery, it was almost a foregone conclusion that they would vote unanimously on Monday evening to continue the boycott until their demands were met. They could not know how long they would have to walk and share rides. Nor could they know what kinds of opposition white Montgomery would array against them. But they knew full well, from their own experience and from the stories that had been handed down since slave days, what kinds of brutality white people were capable of. Indeed, some of those stories were not that ancient. Fourteen-year-old Emmett Till was brutally murdered in Mississippi on August 28, 1955, a little over three months before the boycott began. An all-white jury acquitted his self-confessed murderers.

The murder of young Till was very much on the minds of Montgomery's boycotters. It sharpened our awareness of a reality that we faced often in the months that followed. There would surely be retaliation for our actions. And some of us might even die before we had achieved our goal. But the black citizens of Montgomery would not allow even the threat of death hinder to them from their march toward freedom.

The police harassment began in a hurry. On the first day of the boycott, a young man named Fred Daniels was arrested and charged with preventing a black woman from boarding a bus. I attended his trial, to observe how he would be treated. It turned out he was helping a lady friend across the street. Before long it became a common experience for boycott drivers to be stopped by the police on all sorts of charges. On January 26, Dr. King himself was arrested. The charge—driving thirty miles an hour in a twenty-five mph zone.

In spite of the danger, more than two hundred volunteer drivers signed up during the first week of the boycott. They picked up passengers at forty-two locations in the morning in black neighborhoods and forty-eight points in shopping centers and downtown locations in the evening. There were also "transfer" points, such as Dean's Drug Store and Posey's Parking Lot in downtown Montgomery, both black-owned, where carloads could be gathered who were going to the same white neighborhoods. Remarkably, dozens of white housewives drove to shopping centers and other places to pick up their domestic workers. Much to the chagrin of white political leaders, these women became a very necessary component of our transportation system.

We recently met the daughter of a white airman who had been stationed at Maxwell Air Force Base in Montgomery in the 1950s. She told us that both her dad and her mom had also been volunteer drivers in the boycott; though we never met them at that time.

Beginning on December 8, there was a series of unfruitful meetings between boycott leaders and city and bus company officials. Though the pattern of seating "demanded" by the Montgomery Improvement Association was being used in other southern cities, including Mobile, Alabama, local officials declared it to be a violation of Alabama law.

On December 7, I sent the first of several letters to members of the all-white Montgomery Ministerial Association, asking for their help in communicating the truth about what was happening in our city. As I later learned, to my dismay, those ministers who were friendly and supportive of what we were doing never remained long in their congregations. Most of the so-called "liberal" pastors were dismissed from their pulpits as soon as the congregations were aware of their support for us. Unfortunately, most of the white pastors were not sympathetic to our cause in the first place.

Monday, December 19, marked my first contact with the police in Montgomery. I had parked legally by a meter near Dean's Drug Store, at the corner of Monroe and Lawrence streets downtown. Soon I had a load of five women needing transportation to Normandale, a popular shopping mall in an all-white section of town. As I crossed Dexter Avenue, just a few blocks away from the drug store, I heard a siren and pulled to the curb, wary and fearful. The man who appeared beside my door announced, "I'm Sheriff Mac Sim Butler; and you're under arrest!" With that, he ordered me to follow him back to the county courthouse, where he dismissed my passengers and brought me into a deputy's office. Picking up a phone, he called a judge's office. I could hear only his side of the conversation. "Hello, this is Mac Sim Butler. I've got a man in here who was hauling niggers . . . Yes, but this is a white man!"

By the time I was released, I discovered that my erstwhile passengers had raced back to Dean's Drug Store and reported my plight. Doc Rich Harris, the druggist, had already arranged for money to be brought to the county jail, to bail me out as soon as I had been imprisoned. He knew, even better than I did, that I probably would not have survived the experience. I would have been placed in the all-white part of the jail, where I am certain I had few friends.

Though the sheriff now knew my face, most white people still did not. On January 6 I felt safe enough to attend a meeting of the White Citizens Council, a group which most of us considered to be an "uptown" version of the Ku Klux Klan. I checked carefully to find a seat near the back and close to an exit. If I had been discovered, I intended to vacate the premises immediately! At the gathering, I heard a state senator harangue the crowd about how badly Montgomery's black citizens were acting. And I witnessed Police Commissioner Clyde Sellers's public acceptance of membership in the WCC. I didn't trust him after that, though he did promise me special police protection on at least two occasions. Eighteen days later, Mayor W. A. Gayle and Commissioner Frank Parks announced that they too had joined the White Citizens Council. By the first of March, the membership of the Montgomery chapter had grown to twelve thousand.

Even if the sheriff had not stopped me in December, my involvement in the movement would not have remained hidden much longer. On January 7 I got a call from Tom Johnson, a reporter for the *Montgomery Advertiser.* He wanted to talk with me about my role in the boycott. In his investigative article, printed on Tuesday, January 10, he explained that I "hauled as many as 40 to 50 passengers a day, while driving some 50 miles." I was grateful that Tom made it clear that I accepted no money from my passengers. Early that morning, long before the newspapers hit the streets, we got our first call in response, obviously from an employee at the *Advertiser.* My log says, "Jan. 10, 2:15 AM—White man who seemed to be drunk. Demanded that I come and give him taxi service like what has been furnished to the dark complected people. Suggested that we set up car pool for white people so can save the ten-cent fare. Refused to give name but called himself Roger." That was the beginning of a long string of nasty, threatening, and harassing phone calls and letters over the next few years.

Just two days later, on January 12, our car was vandalized. Both front tires had been slashed with a number of cuts, on the inside where they would not be noticed. The cuts were not deep enough to flatten the tires immediately; but under stress, such as on a long drive out of town, they could have blown out. The vandals undid themselves, however, by putting sugar in our gas tank, spilling some on the ground below the fuel cap, where I could see it. The damage to the tires was discovered only when mechanics put the car on a hoist to remove and clean the gas tank. A courageous white mechanic called me aside to tell me secretly about the tires. That man probably prevented an accident or worse.

After we filed a claim for replacing the tires and cleaning the gas tank, our auto insurance policy was cancelled. Our agent tried several other companies, finally informing us that no other company would cover us. Eventually we received coverage under Alabama's "assigned-risk" plan. Each company operating in the state had to take a percentage of people like us that no one wanted to cover.

The city tried a new tactic a little more than a week later. Officials called in three little-known ministers for a "conference." These were men who had nothing much to do with the Montgomery Improvement Association. Working out some sort of an "agreement" with the three, city officials planned to announce on Sunday that both sides had accepted a compromise, bringing an end to the boycott. If any sizeable number of boycotters believed the reports and returned to the buses the following week, the movement could have collapsed. The wire services began disseminating the story on Saturday night. Fortunately for us, Carl Rowan, an African American reporter for the *Minneapolis Tribune*, who had been in Montgomery only two weeks before, read one of the wire stories and called Dr. King for more details, With the ruse exposed, it was not difficult for boycott leaders to spread the word through the marvelously effective "grape-vine" in the black community. By Monday morning, everyone knew that the story they had read in Sunday's paper was a hoax. The boycott continued uninterrupted.

White leaders were so angry over their failure they called off all negotiations. Mayor Gayle warned white people that there was much more at stake than the seating pattern on the buses. "What they are after is the destruction of our social fabric," he declared. And he was right!

Our own attention was diverted from the movement for a time in early 1956. Our second daughter (and third child), Dianne Elaine Graetz, was born on January 24. We always figured that God knew we had special needs in that tense time. Dianne was a sweet, easy-going, and pleasant baby from the day she was born. Full of smiles and laughter, we called her "Our Little Sunshine Girl."

January 30 marked the beginning of another new technique by our opponents, when the first bomb was thrown at the home of

Dr. King and his family. By this time we knew that the dangers we had casually discussed early on were deadly serious. As I later told author David Garrow, "All of us on the board [of the Montgomery Improvement Association] discussed the fact that we knew that some of us were going to die, we just didn't know who and when." The Ku Klux Klan, with its history of cowardice and violence, was not about to allow a group of African Americans (that would not be the term they would use) and their allies to change "our way of life."

When Dr. King's house was bombed, a huge crowd of African Americans gathered in Jackson Street in front of the parsonage, many of them armed. It was an especially dangerous situation, since most of the white leadership of Montgomery had assembled on Dr. King's front porch. Mayor W. A. Gayle, Police Commissioner Clyde Sellers, Fire Chief R. L. Lampley, and others were examining the bomb damage.

Joe Azbell, city editor of the *Montgomery Advertiser,* later told me, "Dr. King saved our lives. All of us white people who were there would have been killed by that mob if King had not stopped them." Dr. King had been hurriedly brought back from the Monday evening mass meeting at the First Baptist Church (where Rev. Ralph Abernathy was pastor). He rushed into his home, checking on his wife and new baby, Yolanda, as well as Mrs. King's friend, Mrs. Mary Lucy Williams, all of whom had stayed in the King parsonage while Dr. King was at the mass meeting. While he was inside reassuring himself about his family, the crowd in the street grew in numbers as well as in the level of their anger. In their minds, the officials on the porch were some of their worst enemies. Before Dr. King came back out, Commissioner Sellers stepped inside to ask him if would say a few words to calm the crowd. In King's book, *Stride Toward Freedom,* he describes the scene:

> In this atmosphere I walked out to the porch and asked the

crowd to come to order. In less than a moment there was complete silence. Quietly I told them that I was all right and that my wife and baby were all right. "Now let's not become panicky," I continued. "If you have weapons, take them home; if you do not have them, please do not seek to get them. We cannot solve this problem through retaliatory violence. We must meet violence with nonviolence. Remember the words of Jesus: 'He who lives by the sword will perish by the sword.' I then urged them to leave peacefully. "We must love our white brothers," I said, "no matter what they do to us. We must make them know that we love them. Jesus still cries out in words that echo across the centuries: 'Love your enemies; bless them that curse you; pray for them that despitefully use you.' This is what we must live by. We must meet hate with love. Remember," I ended, "if I am stopped, this movement will not stop, because God is with the movement. Go home with this glowing faith and with this radiant assurance." (*Stride Toward Freedom,* M. L. King, Jr.; Harper & Bros. Pub. 1958; p. 137-138)

It has been reported that someone in the crowd began singing "Amazing Grace." And the crowd quietly dispersed. FBI agent Woodrow Draut, who would soon become our primary contact with the Bureau, told me later that he and several other agents were mixed in with the crowd, observing the situation. He assured me that the accounts about the weapons in the hands of the mob were not exaggerated. Before King spoke, he feared a terrible outbreak of violence.

This incident was obviously quite disturbing to the white leadership. Commissioner Sellers immediately promised to do everything necessary to apprehend the bombers; and a reward was soon offered. The Montgomery police guarded our house throughout that night. Only two nights later, however, a small bomb was thrown in front of the home of Mr. E. D. Nixon, just two blocks from our house.

But on that very day, February 1, 1956, we added a new tactic of our own. Attorney Fred Gray filed a suit in federal court, known as *Browder v. Gayle*. The suit challenged both Montgomery's and Alabama's bus segregation laws and asked for an injunction against police harassment of the bus boycott's car pool. Mrs. Aurelia Browder, a black Montgomery housewife, and four other women filed suit against Mayor W. A. Gayle and others. All of the women had been arrested or harassed on the city's buses. Within days, under pressure from the white community, one of the women announced that she had not hired Attorney Gray to represent her. So Gray was arrested and charged with "unlawfully appearing as an attorney for a person without being employed by that person." These ridiculous charges, however, were quickly dropped. In another attempt to remove Attorney Gray from the scene, his draft board decided to change his draft status to 1-A, even though he was an active ordained minister, preaching at the Holt Street Church of Christ. That effort, too, was soon squelched. As a follow-up, however, Gray was accused by many in the white community as being "draft-dodger." A flyer was circulated in black neighborhoods, purportedly from an African American, with Fred's picture.

DRAFT DODGER
NAACP TROUBLEMAKER

This is the disgrace to our people. Such a person in the white race is an outcast, as you well know. Many complaints are now being heard, we are losing jobs, relief is limited.

The White man celebrates July 4th as Independence Day. Some Negroes have been discharged for minor offenses and Whites hired. By July 4th we are told there will be no jobs left for Negroes.

Many believe it's a Communist inspired plot being led by

King, Abernathy, Graetz, Nixon and Gray. They ride high, eat good, stay warm and pilfer the funds. We walk and suffer in many ways.

Let's run these five out of the state before we all have to leave.

Since Attorney Gray's suit challenged a state law, it was necessary to assemble a three-judge panel to hear the arguments. Judges chosen were Richard T. Rives, Seybourn Lynne, and the newest member of the bench, Frank M. Johnson, Jr., who had been appointed as a United States District Judge for the Middle District of Alabama only a few weeks before, on November 7, 1955! In the months and years ahead, Judge Johnson would become one of the great heroes of the civil rights movement, with his many courageous decisions in support of justice for oppressed people.

Attorney Fred Gray himself, who celebrated his twenty-fifth birthday just two weeks after Mrs. Parks's arrest, had opened his law practice only a year before, in September 1954. His opposition to racial discrimination and segregation developed when he was quite young. Though he trained to be a minister in the Church of Christ, and was ordained into that denomination, Gray was determined to become a lawyer.

As Fred expresses it, his goal was to "destroy everything segregated I could find." He also benefited from Alabama's "separate but equal" policy. Since there was no law school in the state that was open to Negroes, the state sent him to school at Case Western Reserve in Cleveland, Ohio.

Attorney Gray's practice was slow for the first year. But after December 1 he had plenty to keep him busy, since he became the primary attorney for the Montgomery Improvement Association. We saw each other frequently, since we attended most of the same meetings; and Fred and I soon became close friends, as we

The "movement" wedding of Fred and Bernice Gray, 1956. Bob Graetz, second from left, was a groomsman.

are today. The following June 17 I was one of Fred's groomsmen when he married Bernice Hill. Forty years after Mrs. Parks's arrest, Fred gave us a copy of his autobiography, *Bus Ride to Justice,* in which he inscribed a warm personal note referring to the work we did together during the boycott. His book describes not only the boycott, but also his many other civil rights cases over the years, his election to the Alabama legislature, and more.

Attorney Fred Gray's pledge to "destroy everything segregated I could find" continued to define his practice over many years. He was involved in numerous cases that dealt with racial discrimination and segregation, most of which he won. He has received many honors and is often called upon to address groups in this country and overseas.

We also formed a close and lasting relationship with Fred's older brother Thomas, who was a member of the Board of Trustees of the Montgomery Improvement Association, along with me. Frye Gaillard describes our friend in his book, *Cradle of Freedom: Alabama and the Movement that Changed America.*

> One man who took his measure of King was Thomas Gray. Thomas was a businessman, tough and unsentimental. He had served in the navy during World War II, where he saw combat in the Marshall Islands, and even before the bus boycott he had led a civil rights demonstration at the courthouse. He first met the Kings when Coretta bought a washing machine from his store [Dozier's Radio Service]. He thought of Martin as a nice young man, though not necessarily as a leader for the movement. Gray preferred the toughness of E. D. Nixon, and yet there was something about King from the start, a political shrewdness with all his talk about nonviolence and meeting hatred with love—those phrases that played so well in the press. Gray once complimented King for being clever.
>
> "I said, 'Martin, that's a nice ploy,'" Gray remembered. "He said, 'No, Tom, that is not a ploy.' I was surprised at first, and then said to myself, 'This man really means it.'"

In 1959, Thomas followed his younger brother into law, studying at the same school, Case Western Reserve in Cleveland, Ohio. When he was ready to take his state bar exams, he drove down to Columbus, staying with us during the ordeal. As he prepared to "hit the books" for some last minute cramming, Jeannie gave Thomas some good advice. "If you don't already know it, you can't learn it in a few hours tonight. You'll do better if you just relax." Deciding she was right, Thomas put the books away, played cards with us, got a good night's sleep, and aced the tests the next day. After practicing more than thirty years in Cleveland, attorney Thomas Gray was appointed as a federal administrative law judge, stationed in Montgomery, Alabama! When Jeannie and I travel to

Old friends reunited: from left, Bob Graetz, Fred Gray, Jeannie Graetz, and Juanita and Thomas Gray. Fred's wife, Bernice, had passed away when this photo was made in 2004.

Montgomery on our own these days, we call Thomas and Juanita to ask if "our room is ready." It always is.

Attorney Fred Gray did not have to wait long for a response to his federal lawsuit. On February 13 the Montgomery County Grand Jury was charged with the responsibility of determining whether Montgomery's black citizens had violated Alabama's anti-boycott law. I still remember with dread my own appearance before the grand jury on February 21, as one of its last witnesses. The lone African American member of the jury sat silently in a corner. Clearly I was not among friends that day. My impression was that the jurors didn't believe a word I said to them. That same afternoon the grand jury brought down one hundred and fifteen indictments, leading to the arrest of eighty-nine boycott leaders.

But once again the tactics of our opponents turned against them. Less than three months into the movement, the experience of being arrested and going to jail had become a badge of honor! Boycott leaders put on their best clothes and drove themselves to the county courthouse to be arrested. Some of the key participants, however, such as Mr. Rufus Lewis, had been inadvertently left off of the list. Coach Lewis had been the organizer of the very effective car pool. Some whose names were not on the list of those to be indicted argued with the clerks that they knew they were supposed to be arrested. "Please check the list again," they demanded. One of the most famous pictures from the Montgomery movement was of the group of arrestees, many of whom were ministers, posed on the steps of the county courthouse.

Friday, February 24, was the day set for the arraignment of the boycotters. The African American community celebrated by calling it a "Prayer and Pilgrimage Day." Everyone would walk wherever they went, as a demonstration of support for our leaders. Jeannie had a doctor's appointment that afternoon, for our month-old daughter Dianne, who had been born on January 24. With Dianne in a buggy, Jeannie walked across town to keep her appointment.

From these arrests, the prosecutors picked Dr. Martin Luther King, Jr., to be the first put on trial, and he would eventually prove to be the only one of the group actually tried in court. His trial began on March 19. Because we were now attacking segregation directly, through our federal suit, the NAACP had sent an attorney from New York to assist with the defense. I sat in the witness room for three days, nervously waiting to be called as a witness for the prosecution. Amazingly, the group of witnesses, which included both black and white, were all kept in the same room! A white reporter for the *Alabama Journal* was limited to writing about the dismal state of the chamber in which we were trapped. He was also glad to have me as part of the group, as he wrote:

Minister Brings Laugh

Rev. Graetz breaks the silence again. 'The most they (the boycott defendants) can get is six months. We're liable to get longer—just staying in here.'

Everyone laughs. Both Revs. Graetz and [white Episcopal rector Tom] Thrasher along with Negro Rev. A. W. Wilson [the pastor of Holt Street Baptist Church] keep spirits up with their humorous quips from time to time.

At an MIA board meeting before the trial began, I had suggested that we all attend the trial wearing white crosses with the message "Father, forgive them." During the trial the *Montgomery Advertiser* ran a photo of me standing beside Dr. King outside the Montgomery County courthouse. The cross is visible on my lapel.

On the last day of the trial, I was finally called to the witness stand, by the defense. Our lawyers had waived their right to a jury trial, though attorney Fred Gray had laughingly said to me, "It would be interesting to see if Montgomery County could produce 89 juries from their jury pool!" Soon after my testimony ended, both sides gave their closing arguments, and then the trial was over. Judge Eugene Carter surprised everyone by announcing his verdict immediately. Dr. King was guilty of conspiring to boycott the Montgomery city bus company. He was fined $500 plus $500 costs, or more than one year in prison at hard labor.

The local officials had certainly miscalculated if they thought the arrests would bring an end to the protest. Dr. King rose from being a local hero to being canonized worldwide. Montgomery's black citizens were more determined than ever to continue walking until they had won their victory. On the night of his conviction, mass meetings were held in several churches rather than the usual single gathering. No single sanctuary was large enough to hold the

Judges Frank M. Johnson, Jr., left, and Richard T. Rives.

excited crowds that gathered to cheer "the King."

On May 11 the federal district court heard the MIA's suit, *Browder v. Gayle,* in a courtroom in Montgomery's majestic federal building at the corner of Court and Church streets. Because of the constitutional issues involved, the case was heard not by one judge but by a three-judge panel, in keeping with federal court rules of procedure. And on June 5 the three judges issued their ruling. By a vote of two to one, the court declared, "There is now no rational basis upon which the separate but equal doctrine can be validly applied to public carrier transportation in Montgomery or in Alabama." (U.S. District Judge M. Frank Johnson, Jr., and U.S. Circuit Judge Richard T. Rives ruled in our favor; U.S. District Judge Seybourn Lynne of Birmingham ruled against us.)

Victory was ours, though we would not share its fruits for six more months!

After another two weeks of negotiating with the plaintiffs and the defendants, the district court issued an injunction to end segregation on Montgomery's city buses, due to go into effect in ten days.

But on the tenth day the defendants appealed the court's decision to the United States Supreme Court. And that was not all that the opposition had in mind for us. On June 1, circuit court judge Walter B. Jones had already added to our harassment by enjoining the NAACP from operating in Alabama.

It should be noted that Judges Johnson and Rives were far from the only white people in Montgomery who were supportive of our cause. Among those who were the most heroic were members of the Montgomery Council on Human Relations. The director of the Alabama Council on Human Relations, who was also staff for the Montgomery chapter, was a Methodist minister named Bob Hughes. A young man, quiet and small of stature, he more than made up for his lack of an imposing presence by his boldness and tenacity.

No sooner had the boycott begun than Bob Hughes and Rev. Tom Thrasher, the rector of a prestigious Episcopal Church in Montgomery and a leader of the Montgomery Council, approached the mayor to offer their services to bring people together from both communities. We thought at first that some kind of compromise could be worked out. But the city and bus company officials would no consider no option but a surrender by the African American community. And that was certainly not going to happen. Bob and Tom remained close to us during our entire stay in Montgomery. Tom and his wife even put us up overnight after the second bombing of our house in 1957. The FBI had been sure the bombers would come back, since they had not succeeded in killing us. And they had insisted that we not stay in our home overnight.

One of my greatest disappointments was that more white clergy were not openly supportive. But I learned soon enough that taking such a public position often meant the end of their ministry in that community. On May 31, 1956, a group of six Methodist ministers risked losing their pulpits by attending a mass meeting at Hall

Street Baptist Church. They were part of a much larger group of white pastors of many denominations who had joined a statewide, biracial organization to work behind the scenes to provide support for their black brothers and sisters. When the mass meeting ended, the police commissioner and several officers were waiting outside to get the ministers' license numbers. We were told that some of the ministers were later threatened and intimidated, and some did lose their pulpits.

We also held biracial meetings all over Alabama, always on black college campuses or at the black YMCA campground. Among those white pastors who attended was my good friend Russell Boggs, who had the audacity to invite me to speak and preach at his white Lutheran Church, even though he was aware that his members knew who I was.

Strange as it may seem today, there was danger involved in attending gatherings which brought black and white people together. On many occasions police would stand outside, writing down license numbers of white attendees. The object was to frighten people away and to punish those who would not be frightened. The White Citizens Council tried to bring economic pressure on any whites known to associate with blacks. People could lose their jobs, lose customers in their businesses, have their loans called at the banks, and more. There was one well-known case where a white Montgomery businessman took out a newspaper ad denouncing his wife's involvement in the interracial group, Church Women United. One wonders what it was like around the dinner table in that household. In another case, a prominent white architect who was sympathetic to the boycott was asked by his partners to leave his firm; he and his family had to relocate to Atlanta.

The Jewish community was disproportionately represented among our supporters. I have often attributed this phenomenon to the fact that Jews understood oppression better than Gentiles.

Their entire history was filled with long periods of oppression. Some of our closest Jewish friends had lost family members in the Holocaust during the Second World War. We remember especially Victor and Ann Kerns and Warren and Jane Katz. (Warren is the only one of that foursome still living.) We all had children about the same ages. The Kerns and Katz homes were oases for us, where we could escape from the pressures related to the boycott. We had to guard those friendships, however. During one gathering at the Katz home, I got into an argument on racial matters with another guest. Warren, who was a local businessman, and therefore in a vulnerable position, had to remind me that not all of their other friends agreed with us on everything. We have been in contact with the Kerns and Katz children in recent years, celebrating the Pesach (Passover) with them as often as possible.

Though we have praised our Jewish friends for years, our statements have been challenged on occasion. In March 2005 we led a group of high school students from the Miami Valley School in Kettering, Ohio, on a civil rights pilgrimage. Our first event in Montgomery was a Friday evening Sabbath worship at Temple Beth Or. After the service, several older members came to us individually to tell us how sorry they were that they had not been more supportive of Montgomery's black citizens during the boycott, because of their fear of reprisal.

We also had many white Christian friends and some whose undisclosed faith was totally personal. Foremost on that list would be Clifford and Virginia Durr. Clifford, born into a prominent family in Montgomery in 1899, practiced law in Montgomery, Milwaukee, and Birmingham. In 1926 he married Virginia Foster, whose brother-in-law was U.S. Senator-elect and future Supreme Court Justice Hugo Black. Black persuaded him to join Franklin Roosevelt's New Deal administration in 1933, first with the Reconstruction Finance Corporation, then the Federal Communications

Commission. After years of struggling against the anti-communist "witch hunts" of J. Edgar Hoover and the House of Un-American Activities Committee, he finally gave up and moved back to his hometown of Montgomery in 1951. Because of his support for black people and other oppressed groups, his legal practice never fully recovered. He was a strong supporter and mentor for attorney Fred Gray, MIA's chief counsel.

Virginia was born in Birmingham in 1903, in a Presbyterian manse. At least from the time she went away to college, she did not agree with the way black people or poor people were treated. From that time on, she lived her life "outside the magic circle," as her autobiography was titled. A personal friend of Eleanor Roosevelt and a strong opponent of segregation, Virginia has been called the "white matron of the civil rights movement." Clifford and Virginia were close friends of Mrs. Rosa Parks and Mr. E. D. Nixon and went with Mr. Nixon to get Mrs. Parks out of jail on December 1, 1955. The annual Clifford and Virginia Durr Memorial Lecture Series, established in their honor in the 1990s, has become one of our regular activities in Montgomery.

Another older couple who took us under their wings soon after we arrived in Montgomery in 1955 was Mr. and Mrs. I. B. Rutledge. Clara Rutledge was a proper lady, yet a stern foe of oppression in any form. She was active in the Women's International League for Peace and Freedom, a pacifist and integrationist group. Jeannie says Mrs. Rutledge "mothered" her. She was a "Lady Liberty" welcoming, gathering, and nurturing strangers to the "shores" of Alabama.

Aubrey and Anita Williams and their large extended family were also our strong supporters. Aubrey was the editor of the *Southern Farmer,* a magazine with a decidedly liberal slant. Their son Morrison and his wife Vivian had a farm outside of Montgomery, where all in our little "fraternity" loved to visit. It was a wonderful escape.

By August 1956, the summer's heat made it difficult for those walking to work. But they knew the end was in sight, so they continued on. Our family left for a trip to the Highlander Folk School, in Monteagle, Tennessee, bringing Mrs. Rosa Parks along with us. Just one year before, at a similar workshop at Highlander, Mrs. Parks had made her commitment never again to give up her seat on a bus. At the 1956 conference, I was to be a consultant for a workshop on public school integration. It was at that Highlander workshop that we first met Dr. Benjamin Mays, president of Morehouse College in Atlanta, and an important mentor of Dr. King. One of the few rigid rules at Highlander—and still is today—was that all participants shared equally in taking care of the household chores. One evening after dinner, Jeannie and I were honored to find ourselves in the kitchen with Dr. Mays, washing the dishes together!

Early in the morning on Saturday, August 25, our workshop experience came to an abrupt end. I was awakened to take an emergency phone call. *New York Post* reporter Ted Poston phoned to let us know that our house had been bombed. As our three-year-old Margee explained it, "Our house got broke!" By the time we had packed to leave, the entire workshop group was awake. They gathered around us and sang:

> We shall not, we shall not be moved;
> We shall not, we shall not be moved;
> Just like a tree that's planted by the water,
> We shall not be moved.

We got home to Montgomery just in time for Mayor W. A. (Tacky) Gayle to accuse us of leaving town just long enough for the MIA to plant the bomb as a publicity stunt. He and I carried on a running debate in the newspapers for a few days. On August 26 the paper ran a picture of me, with Margee and Bobby, measuring the bomb crater. It was fifteen inches deep and twenty-one inches across.

The children had obviously picked up from us a sense of what was going on in Montgomery. While the policemen were still guarding the house and keeping our neighbors and friends from coming to see us, Margee, age three, and Bobby, age two, went out to the front porch and shouted angrily to them, "Get away, old bad policemen!"

We tried to protect our children without smothering them. So we made up a game for them to play. Whenever we heard strange sounds outside, we would say, "Go hide!" They had to crawl behind our living room couch as fast as possible. They didn't know that our "game" was designed to protect them from flying glass, in case of another bombing.

I wrote in my log:

> Aug. 25—House bombed at approximately 3:00 AM. Front door and numerous windows damaged in addition to windows and doors of houses next door and across street. Bomb landed 43 feet in front of porch; police estimate 2 or 3 sticks of dynamite. No injuries; entire family in Tennessee at the time. God is still Lord in Montgomery, Alabama. Thank God we can put our trust in Him. Psalm 27.

The following month our opponents tried yet another new tactic. We began hearing from auto insurance companies that they could no longer continue to cover the station wagons that were the heart of the MIA's car pool. The MIA had received many thousands of dollars in donations from all over the world, much of which had been spent in buying and running the station wagons. Each vehicle had been titled in the name of one of our larger church congregations. After exhausting all possibilities through African

American insurance agents, we eventually got coverage through Lloyd's of London!

Those who worked against us never gave up. On November 13, the circuit court in Montgomery issued an injunction against the very operation of our car pool! But while the court was in session, word reached Montgomery that the U. S. Supreme Court had just affirmed the three-judge panel's June decision in *Browder v. Gayle*. This time we had truly won, but the victory would not be realized for more than a month, while the city filed one last desperation appeal, and the proper court orders were issued and received. For another five and a half weeks, the black people of Montgomery walked and shared rides everywhere they went—happily!

On Wednesday, November 14, mass meetings were held at two African American churches—7 PM at Hutchinson Street Baptist, and 8 PM at Holt Street Baptist (the site of the first mass meeting on December 5, 1955). The combined attendance at the two sites was estimated at eight thousand people. I'll never forget that night. Rev. Ralph Abernathy asked me to read the scripture passage—1 Corinthians 13, the love passage. When Ralph introduced me there was thunderous applause. A reporter sitting near the front asked him, "Isn't that peculiar, applauding the scriptures?" "We are a peculiar people," responded Ralph. In the middle of my reading, applause broke out again. I realized I had just spoken the words, "When I became a man, I put away childish things." The black people of Montgomery had become men and women in the truest sense of the word.

December 21, the first day back on the buses, was almost an anticlimax. For the next few weeks there were isolated instances of violence against black passengers riding in the front. But we had trained our people well to demonstrate love and nonviolence in all of their interactions with white people. Over a period of several weeks, we had conducted role-playing sessions at our mass meetings.

We told our people that no one would be allowed to return to the buses without being trained and without signing a pledge to remain totally nonviolent, no matter what violent acts were perpetrated against them. The MIA had circulated a pamphlet of instructions, concluding with "If another person is being molested, do not rise to go to his defense, but pray for the oppressor and use moral and spiritual force to carry on the struggle for justice. According to your own ability and personality, do not be afraid to experiment with new and creative techniques for achieving reconciliation and social change." Most of the bus riders remained faithful to their pledges.

Within three weeks, however, that resolve would be sorely tested. Early in the morning of January 10, 1957, our house and that of Rev. Abernathy, as well as First Baptist, Bell Street Baptist, Hutchinson Street Baptist, and Mount Olive Baptist churches were bombed within a period of a few hours. My journal reads:

> Jan. 10, 2:00 AM—Parsonage bombed for the second time. Much more damage than first one. Larger bomb, made up of eleven sticks of dynamite and one piece of TNT found in driveway, failed to explode. Fuse had been lit, had gone out. 'The hand of the Lord is not shortened.' Four Negro churches and the parsonage of Rev. Ralph Abernathy were also bombed.

If that larger bomb had exploded, as we were later informed, our whole neighborhood could have been leveled. Many people would have died, including our newborn son and the rest of our family. David Ellis Graetz had made his appearance on New Year's Day, the last of five babies born in Montgomery that day. One of the other fathers who shared the waiting room with me that day happened to be the law clerk of Judge Frank Johnson! After David's birth, my mother came down from Charleston, West Virginia, to

The Trinity parsonage after the first bombing. Fortunately no one was hurt and the house was not badly damaged, though the windows were blown out and household items were broken.

help us with child care. She later enjoyed sharing her "war" stories with her friends.

Montgomery detectives pieced together the events of that night. The bombers had called in false alarms to the police department to lure patrolmen away from the planned locations of the bombings. Our large bomb had been the first one to be thrown. When that one failed to detonate, our attackers circled back and used a second bomb, which had been meant for someone else. Detectives found a list of the planned bombing sites, which included Father Robert Dubose, a black Episcopal priest. We had gotten his bomb! As I stood outside with the crowd that had gathered in front of our house that early morning, we heard the sounds of other bombs exploding all around the city.

My sermon theme for the following Sunday, January 13, 1957, was "How Often Shall We Forgive," based on Matthew 18:21-35. It was my understanding that every Negro pastor in Montgomery had a similar message on that day.

We had an unexpected "problem" at our house after each of the bombings. Both black and white friends began bringing us food and offering to help us in other ways. Jeannie and I had always been pretty self-sufficient; we had a hard time accepting all these gifts, especially Jeannie. Mrs. Clara Rutledge helped us to get things into perspective. When she brought us a pot roast, Jeannie objected, explaining that others had already brought food, so we didn't need any more. Mrs. Rutledge's words of wisdom were "Jeannie, a lot of us feel really bad about what has happened to you. We need to do something to help. Some of us are ashamed to be white right now. It is important that you let us do what we can. You just put that roast in your freezer and eat it later."

Within weeks, several other explosions rocked Montgomery and an unexploded bomb containing twelve sticks of dynamite was found on Dr. King's porch. After some exceptional detective work, seven white men were arrested on February 1 for various bombings. All the suspects had ties to the Ku Klux Klan. Only four of the men were indicted by the Montgomery County Grand Jury. And only two of those, Raymond C. Britt, Jr., twenty-seven, and Sonny Kyle Livingston, Jr., nineteen, were put on trial on May 27, 1957. Though the evidence was overwhelming against the defendants, the jury of twelve white men took only a little over an hour and a half to find Britt and Livingston not guilty! James D. York, fifty-two, and Henry Alexander, twenty-seven, had both been indicted along with Britt and Livingston; but neither they, nor the other three men who had been arrested, were ever tried for the bombings.

In fact, to our knowledge, no white person was ever convicted of any violence or intimidation aimed at blacks or the black community during the bus boycott period. And in what has to be one of the supreme ironies of history, in 2006 Sonny Kyle Livingston, Jr., is a bail bondsman in Montgomery with his name prominently displayed on his office building located adjacent to the First Baptist

Church which was bombed on January 10, 1957.

In the bombings and subsequent acquittals of the suspects, we had lost one battle, but the real victory was already ours. Never again would the relationship between the black and white people of Montgomery, or of the nation, be the same. The "Movement" which began on December 1, 1955, would not be stopped. Indeed, it continues to this day. There is a telling line from "The Ballad of Harry Moore," sung by the a cappella singing group, Sweet Honey in the Rock: "No bomb can kill the dreams I hold, for freedom never dies."

There was one very moving moment for Jeannie and me relating to the bombings. Mrs. Gertrude Harris, a domestic worker with a limited income who lived not far from us, gathered contributions from her friends and neighbors for a special gift. On April 29, 1957, at a mass meeting at the Maggie Street Baptist Church, Mrs. Harris presented Jeannie with a set of new dishes and glasses, to replace the ones broken on January 10. Her message: "When they bombed the Graetzes, they bombed us." With those simple words, we knew that we had been officially accepted as bona fide members of the African American community.

Chapter 5

The World Will Beat a Path to Your Door

"If you build a better mousetrap, the world will beat a path to your door." So goes the old saying. We in Montgomery were certainly not in the business of building mousetraps; but the world did find its way to our doors. My wife Jeannie is convinced that the level of violence in Montgomery was decreased significantly by the presence of the watchful eyes of the many television cameras, reporters, and both national and international visitors. It seemed to us that most of them literally found their way to our front door at 1110 Cleveland Avenue, a street which has since been renamed "Rosa Parks Avenue."

The first reporter who talked with me was a local man, Bill McDonald, a part-time correspondent for *Time* magazine. He stayed in touch with us on a regular basis throughout our time in Montgomery. But Tom Johnson, writing for the *Montgomery Advertiser*, was the reporter who "introduced" us to the Montgomery community with two special reports in early January 1956. During the months that followed, reporters and others came to our city from all over the world.

Very early during the boycott, I had a surprise visitor. A white man walked into my office and introduced himself. "My name is Woody Draut," he told me. "I'm with the Federal Bureau of Investigation. And I'll be your primary contact with the Bureau." More than shocked, I was astounded. Woody explained to me that the FBI had investigated both Jeannie and me, as well as our families. (One day he said to me, "Your father-in-law has a great reputation back in Pennsylvania.") They wanted us to help them quietly by watching out for representatives of subversive organizations who might be trying to infiltrate the Montgomery movement. They, in turn, would appraise us of information they might have about such people.

We were instructed to keep our relationship with the agency completely confidential. And we were assigned pseudonyms to use when we submitted written reports. To hide our relationship with the bureau, we were given a secret phone number for the local FBI office, which would be answered with "Hello," rather than "FBI." (They were concerned about possible wiretaps by the local police.) During our years in Montgomery, we passed very little information along to Woody; but he was very helpful to us on several occasions. The FBI reports that we shared with the MIA were always from an "anonymous source." (Soon after we moved back to Columbus, Ohio, in September 1958, another stranger walked into my office. "I'm Bob Mahler," he said. I'll be taking Woody Draut's place.")

It was not until well after we had left Montgomery that we learned of the FBI's efforts to undercut the ministry and work of Dr. Martin Luther King, Jr. We don't know just when Director Hoover and his Bureau turned against the civil rights movement. But we do know that the assistance of FBI agents in Montgomery was invaluable to us during the bus boycott. On at least one occasion they enabled us to prevent the incursion of an organization that might have scuttled our entire effort simply by their presence. It was a group on the U.S. Attorney General's list of subversive organizations, which was attempting to get public credit for assisting us.

Among the first of our visitors from out of town was reporter

Dick Cleeman, from the *Minneapolis Tribune*, who came to see us on January 6, a month after the boycott began. Cleeman, who was white, had teamed up with black reporter Carl Rowan to tour the South in the aftermath of the U. S. Supreme Court's *Brown v. Board of Education* decision in 1954. That ruling had undermined the South's entire system of segregation by declaring that segregated schools were inherently unequal. Their highly successful series ran in the *Trib* under the title "Dixie Divided." Cleeman interviewed whites, while Rowan made contact with African Americans. Carl Rowan was one of our speakers the following December in the Montgomery Improvement Association's first annual "Institute on Non-Violence and Social Change." He later became a quite famous reporter and successful author.

A few days later, Dr. Preston Valien sent his own biracial group to Montgomery to study the phenomenon of the bus boycott. Valien was chairman of the Social Sciences Department of Fisk University in Nashville, Tennessee. (He too was a speaker at our Institute in December 1956.) Once again the group's white and black members interviewed only members of their own cultures. This created problems for those who came looking for us, since we lived in a black neighborhood. Anna Holden made an appointment to talk with me at 2 PM on Tuesday, January 24. She was scheduled to come to our house.

In one of her regular reports to Dr. Valien, she told of her appointment, saying, "He has been very much in the public eye for his work in the boycott, newspapers have done features, his name is on the lips of many who are disturbed about the boycott, etc." She then told of her difficulties finding us. Fearful of using a white taxi or the city bus, she decided to walk—it would have been illegal for her to use a black cab. Holden was more than a little uneasy about the police patrol cars that passed her on the way to and from the parsonage.

Unfortunately I was not home to receive our interviewer. As she reported to Dr. Valien, "Rev. Graetz was not home as his wife had delivered their third child in the hospital that day and I decided perhaps I had better not interview him and would turn him over to Ferron." My log indicates that Fisk student Donald Ferron interviewed me the following day. The day after that, it was a reporter from *Life* magazine who came to see us.

The Fisk interviewers discovered that many white people in Montgomery were not very happy with me, assuming incorrectly that I had played a major role in organizing the bus boycott. "That ole Rev. King and ole Graetz should be run out of town. They keep this mess going. You know I heard that Rev. King is going to take all your money and go buy a Cadillac with it. He's going from door to door asking for $2.00. Beatrice, don't you give him $2.00." This was the report of a black domestic worker, quoting her employer.

"There's a white-nigra preacher in on it too . . . He's down in a Lutheran Church on their part of town, I want you to know . . . He's been there two years now but they kept it mighty quiet . . . Nobody had no idea *that* was going on in Montgomery, but it was, his church sent him here and he lives right down there by the church and has his wife and kids down there . . ." (This white woman also blamed communists and the "NCCPA," surely meaning the NAACP.)

"The preachers started it . . . the Nigga preachers and that white preacher that has a Nigga church and lives down there with them . . . I had no idea *that* was going on in Montgomery . . ."

Anna Holden rode in a taxi one day, driven by a former bus driver who had lost his job because of the boycott, whose feelings were considerably stronger:

Driver: "They haven't handled this thing right. I sure wish

I could run the show."

Holden: "What would you do?"

Driver: "I'll tell you what I'd do. I'd get a posse and I'd hunt out that nigger preacher King and that white-nigger preacher and that man Gray and I'd shoot 'em down. That's what I'd do."

Montgomery's white residents had to blame the boycott on people like me. They had assumed for years that black people liked things the way they were. We heard over and over again, "Our Nigras wouldn't do something like this."

Even our friends passed along rumors to the Fisk team. Clara Rutledge had heard on the morning of her first interview that "Pastor Graetz had been run out of town without his clothes." Librarian Juliette Morgan told Anna Holden, "I heard that Rev. Graetz had left town with $2,000. A friend of mine checked with him right away, and of course he had done no such thing."

Holden also talked with Joe Azbell, city editor of the *Montgomery Advertiser*. "The only white person in Montgomery supporting this thing is Graetz, that Lutheran preacher," Joe told her. "Outside of Graetz, there is no white support for the boycott. And Graetz is a missionary worker], put here by the Lutheran Church to do missionary work among the 'Nigras'—he is a missionary, just like the missionaries sent the darkest Africa and he has something to gain by sticking with his flock. In fact, he has no alternative." (Azbell had told Holden earlier he believed there was little support among the common black people for the boycott.) During our time in Montgomery, I had believed that Azbell was a true friend who was trying behind the scenes to be helpful to us. Years later, when I read the complete text of his interview with Holden, I came to the conclusion that I had been wrong. His words were as negative as many others who were working against us. He was just a good reporter, who knew how to get people to talk.

THE MOST CELEBRATED and most remarkable aspect of the Montgomery Bus Boycott was its emphasis on love and nonviolence, in the spirit of India's Mohandas Gandhi. Dr. King had read about Gandhi and his teachings and was very much impressed by the Indian leader's powerful, though nonviolent, opposition to racism and oppression.

But the African American people of Montgomery, at the beginning of the movement, were not ready for Dr. King's message of love and nonviolence. In fact, he himself did not move automatically into that stance. Immediately after his house was bombed on January 30, 1956, both Dr. King and Rev. Abernathy applied for pistol permits. Dr. King said he wanted his watchmen to be armed. The permits were denied. And the two leaders also dropped that idea rather quickly. But I am sure there were many guns and other weapons in the hands of Montgomery's African Americans, who were ready to use them if they had to, even though they knew they could never win that battle. But it was clear in the black community that whatever the cost to themselves, they would no longer assent to the brutal treatment that had afflicted their people since the beginning of slavery. Stephen Foster's "Old Black Joe," whose head was "hanging low," had disappeared from Montgomery, Alabama, and would soon become an outdated image all across this nation.

It was vital to the success of the bus boycott that Dr. King carefully formulate his themes of love and nonviolence and inculcate them into the lives and thinking of his compatriots. Fortunately he had help in that regard. Not only did he study the life and teaching of Mohandas Gandhi for himself, but within days after the January 30, 1956, bombing of the Dexter parsonage, two dedicated disciples of Gandhi arrived in Montgomery with the stated purpose of introducing King to the heart of Gandhi's teachings. Both men were members of the Fellowship of Reconciliation, a long-standing pacifist organization. The first of them, an African American named Bayard Rustin, reached Montgomery on February 21. Rustin had proved his dedication to the principles of nonviolence by spending time in jail for his opposition to the draft during the Second World War.

Boycott leaders in Montgomery and civil rights leaders in the North had misgivings about Rustin's identification with the Montgomery movement, however, because he had once been a member of the Young Communist League. And just a few years before he showed up in Montgomery he had been arrested for homosexual activity. It was not only Rustin, however, who made us uneasy. All of our leaders, including me, were leery of any outsiders who came to us with offers of help. We dared not allow our movement to become anything but a homegrown protest by the black people of Montgomery.

Bayard was not with us for long. Not only did leaders from the North urge him to come home. I was told that Mr. Emory O. Jackson, editor of the *Birmingham World*, warned him, "If you don't leave immediately, I am going to expose you." I never saw Rustin in Montgomery after that, but he did remain active in civil rights work and later was one of the prime architects of the immensely successful 1963 March on Washington for Jobs and Freedom.

The second FOR member, a white man named Glenn Smiley, arrived in Montgomery on February 27, just six days after Rustin. His presence in town was almost secretive, though he did speak briefly at our mass meeting on March 1, the first after his arrival. As the boycott neared its end, Glenn also helped to train our people in nonviolence, preparing them to re-board the city buses. Whereas Bayard Rustin had visions of assisting the Montgomery leadership in broadening our movement into a regional, or even national protest, Glenn Smiley's primary agenda was to assist Dr. King in gaining a broader understanding of the moral stance of Mohandas Gandhi and in committing himself to lead the Montgomery protest in adopting that same stance—to resist evil and oppression in all its forms, but to do it totally with love and nonviolence. Smiley also became a presenter at our December 1956 "Institute on Non-Violence and Social Change," speaking at several sessions. Our friendship with Glenn continued until his death in the 1990s.

It did not take long for that message to become the core of Martin Luther King's teaching. We heard it every time he spoke. The movement in Montgomery, which had begun in anger, was little by little transformed into a Gandhian-style march of oppressed people, who looked their oppressors in the eyes and said, "You may abuse us; you may throw us into jail; you may even beat us and kill us; but you cannot stop us from insisting that you treat us with dignity and respect; and you cannot stop us from loving you and praying for you!" The white leaders knew how to deal with angry Negroes, but they were confounded by the presence of these new Negroes they had never seen before. Many times we heard Dr. King say in mass meetings, "Don't ever let them bring you down so low that you hate them."

OVER THE PAST FIFTY YEARS the question I have been asked most frequently is "What was Dr. King like?" And the answer is usually an extended speech since there are so many facets of his life and his personality that I want to talk about. Just about everyone is aware that Martin was a spellbinding orator, as well as a dreamer and a philosopher. He was one who could always be counted on to focus on "the big picture." Consider how many school children have recited Dr. King's famous 1963 "I Have a Dream" speech. Tapes and books of his sermons and speeches are still big sellers.

Martin Luther King, Jr., was the most intelligent, most articulate, most well-read person I ever met. He knew details of the philosophies of people whose names I could not even spell. I was in awe of him, as were most of his other co-workers. I have often

Two young Montgomery, Alabama, pastors in 1956. This photo was made at the time when Dr. King was being tried and convicted in a local court for violating an obscure Alabama anti-boycotting law. The cross on Graetz's lapel was worn—at Graetz's suggestion—by King's supporters during the trial. Graetz testified in the trial.

said that if someone were to rank all of the civil rights leaders in the modern movement, Martin would be at the top, all by himself. There would then be a substantial gap, and the rest of us would be bunched together, rising and falling in our rank orders from time to time.

It was also clear from the very first gathering at the Holt Street Baptist Church on December 5, 1955, that Dr. King understood the historical significance of our actions. And he communicated that awareness to the common people who were our "foot soldiers." He was able to speak to the largely uneducated masses, who swarmed into our meetings, in a way that lifted them to higher levels of self-awareness and self-dignity, and at the same time to communicate with them so clearly that they understood everything he said.

And Martin was consistent. When he uttered his oft-spoken truism, "Injustice anywhere is a threat to justice everywhere," we knew that he meant it. He was not so narrow-minded that he focused only on the rights of African Americans. I often heard him express his conviction that in the process of freeing America's black people we would free her white people as well. And when America mistakenly got involved in the war in Vietnam in the 1960s, he had the courage of his convictions, calling that action another expression of America's racism, even when many of his fellow civil rights leaders could not agree with him. I was among those who were afraid he was making a tactical error.

There is one more aspect of Dr. King's thinking that must be included, his sense of "Call." Momentarily reluctant to accept the position of president of the Montgomery Improvement Association, he very quickly came to the realization that God had selected him for that task. And for his thirteen years as the preeminent leader of the modern civil rights movement, he felt God's hand on his shoulder, leading him from one action site to another. Early on he was aware that following God's call surely meant he would be sacrificing his own earthly life; but Martin was determined that that was a price he was willing to pay.

Another question I am frequently asked is, "Did you really march with Dr. King?" Somehow the image of masses of people marching in protest is the primary picture that has remained from those historic days. Anyone who participated in the movement must have "marched." My usual response is, "I worked closely with

Dr. King. I was in many meetings with Dr. King. We were in each other's homes. But in those days we were much too busy running the bus boycott to do any marching."

In mid-March 1956, Dr. King was on trial, after eighty-nine of Montgomery's black citizens had been indicted by the Montgomery County Grand Jury on charges of violating the state's anti-boycott law. All of us supporters who attended the trial wore small crosses on our lapels reading, "Father, forgive them!" (I was proud to have been the author of that suggestion.) Joe Azbell, city editor of the *Montgomery Advertiser*, told me, "They can't figure you out, Bob, because you're a Christian."

By that time Jeannie and I had been totally accepted as part of the movement. I had served on a special committee dealing with protest activities. And in April I was made a member of the Board of Trustees of the Montgomery Improvement Association. In early 1958 I was elected secretary of the MIA board. (Many years later, my good friend and editor Randall Williams became only the second white person ever to serve on that board.)

We were impressed with the parade of church officials who came to Montgomery during our time there. The first I noted in my church log was Harold Fey, editor of *The Christian Century*, who arrived in February 1956. A year later Ted Gill, also from *The Christian Century*, was a visitor.

In April 1956, Alf Kraabel came to see us. He was in charge of intercultural outreach for the National Lutheran Council. And the following August, one of our house guests was Kai Eric Lindqvist, from Copenhagen, secretary of the Danish Inter-Church Aid Committee. He got special treatment. We invited Rosa and Raymond Parks to join us for dinner that evening. Lindqvist promised me he would send us a copy of what he wrote about Montgomery, as had many others. He was the only one, however, who kept that promise.

Our only problem was that it was written in Danish!

One of the two highest-ranking church officials who visited in our home was Oberkirchenrat Dr. Friedrich Hübner, Hanover-Herrenhausen, Germany, who was executive secretary for theological and ecumenical affairs for the Lutheran Church in his part of Germany. We gave him special treatment also. Jeannie prepared dinner for him and guests we invited on two successive evenings, first for four Lutheran pastors and their wives, and then for Mr. and Mrs. E. D. Nixon. Of equal rank with Hübner, another important guest in our home was an African bishop, whose name, unfortunately, I did not record.

Another visitor, a devout churchman though not a church official, was a newspaper editor from southern Illinois, by the name of Paul Simon. He came to Montgomery in the summer of 1956, wanting to find out firsthand what was happening in our city. Paul, a fellow Lutheran, agreed to speak with our youth group at Trinity. "Remember the name Paul Simon," I told them. "Someday you'll be saying 'President Paul Simon.'"

Paul later gave up his newspaper work to go into politics, serving as Illinois legislator and lieutenant governor, as well as U.S. congressman and senator from Illinois. He ran unsuccessfully for the offices of Illinois governor and U.S. president. I saw Paul frequently in Washington when I served as lobbyist for the Ohio Council of Churches in the 1970s and early 1980s. And Jeannie and I visited Paul and his wife Jean in their Illinois home from time to time. Sen. Simon died in 2003 after a long and distinguished career. Jean had preceded him in death.

Another churchman we saw from time to time was a white Southern preacher named Will Campbell, who seemed to show up here and there when civil rights activities were going on. With his unmistakable drawl, his guitar, and his country-style singing voice, he could be quite disarming. Though he appeared to be one

MIA station wagons lined up for a Life magazine shoot. This particular photo, however, was snapped by Jeannie Graetz.

of the "good old boys," his was a powerful voice for drastic change in the South. Will has written several fine books and is still on the speaking circuit, although in 2006 he is in failing health.

Among the secular reporters who came to see us was Lee Griggs, a photographer for *Life* magazine. His visit led to a couple of busy days for me. I helped him locate a tall ladder, so he could install brighter light bulbs in the church that was hosting the mass meeting in the evening. At mid-day I also arranged for twelve of the station wagons in the MIA's carpool to be brought to the field behind our house and church. Griggs barked orders from the top of that same ladder, having us arrange the vehicles in a line, a circle, etc. Soon the drivers had to leave for their afternoon shifts. But Lee had his pictures. The following week we were delighted to see one of those pictures covering a full page in *Life*. But we were even more delighted to see our two older children, Margee and Bobby, standing behind the house, watching the whole operation. Years later, when we were in Washington, D.C., our copy of that picture was stolen from us. But we have seen it again. The same picture is a part of one of the displays at the National Civil Rights Museum in Memphis, Tennessee!

My church log also lists a news conference that was held at Trinity Lutheran Church for African American reporters to interview Dr. King, Rev. Abernathy, Rev. Bob Hughes (director of the Alabama Council on Human Relations), and me.

Two of the special guests in our home came from India. They were eager to see and experience an American movement based on the principles of Gandhi. The first to come to our house was Mr. H. C. Heda, a member of Parliament from the state of Hyderabad, representing the Congress Party. I received a phone call from my friend Bob Hughes one afternoon. Mr. Heda was in his office and wanted to meet me. I told Bob that the next mass meeting would be held that very evening at the Holt Street Baptist Church, not far from us.

Jeannie gave me permission to invite them to dinner, if I would make a quick trip to the grocery store. Mr. Heda was Hindu, therefore a vegetarian. And Bob had stomach ulcers and was on a restricted diet. Miraculously she was able to prepare a dinner in quick order that satisfied everyone's tastes and needs. Mr. Heda was so impressed that he presented Jeannie with a carved ivory necklace with matching earrings! Reflecting on the caste system in India, he was amazed that we, who were members of a higher "caste," from the Indian perspective, would relate so totally with Negroes, America's equivalent of the "untouchables" of India.

On our way to the mass meeting, Mr. Heda explained that he would be unable to speak publicly, since he was officially representing his government. But he did agree to bring greetings. To his surprise, and ours, he was so overcome by what he saw and heard, his "greetings" turned into a stirring proclamation of support for our movement.

Our second Indian visitor was Mr. T. J. S. George, a newspaper editor from Bombay. He was a member of the Church of St. Thomas, which traces its history to the Apostle Thomas.

My log lists a few other significant visitors from out of town. Among the thousands who came to Montgomery were movie director Jeff Hayden and author John Killens, who spent time with Dr. King and me and a few others to talk about the possibility of producing a movie portraying the Montgomery Bus Boycott. Many years later there was such a movie, *The Long Walk Home*, though Hayden and Killens were not involved.

One of our most intriguing visitors was a young man named Allard K. Lowenstein, a political activist and "liberal," who arrived in Montgomery just after David was born in January 1957. The first time he came to our house, we were still recuperating from our second bombing. Newborn David had not received the attention he deserved, with everything else going on. So Al took the first photo of our baby. We were grateful that he later sent us a copy. Lowenstein also became our first visitor when we moved to Columbus, Ohio, in 1958. And we were with him from time to time when we later moved to Washington, D.C. (It was at a party in his home that we first experienced the delightful sound of steel drums.) Al was actively involved in liberal political causes for his entire life, serving as a U.S. Congressman from New York and as U.S. Ambassador to the United Nations. We were living in Washington, D.C., when he was elected to Congress in 1968. So we wrote to him, inviting him to stay with us while he looked for a home in the District. Tragically, Al Lowenstein was murdered in New York in March 1980.

Just weeks before we moved away from Montgomery in 1958, NAACP national leaders Roy Wilkins and Bob Carter paid an extended visit to our city. The MIA board set up a dinner meeting to honor these two, who had given our movement their enthusiastic support. It was one of the few times that Jeannie was able to go with me to such a special gathering.

Just a few weeks after the beginning of the boycott the editor of the *Montgomery Advertiser*, Grover Hall, had told his reporter Tom Johnson to ask me what it was like to be part of the pariah—that is, to be a social outcast. My response was that we had never experienced that feeling. We had many friends, white and black. It is difficult to remember how we managed time to get together with them. I was a full-time pastor, doing all the things required of me, with a growing and thriving church. I was putting in many hours on behalf of the Montgomery Improvement Association, driving in the car pool, going to meetings, serving on the board of trustees, speaking, raising money, hosting out-of-town visitors, etc. And Jeannie was as busy as she could be, serving as hostess par excellence while she took care of five small children, including Kathryn, who was born just a month before we left Montgomery.

The members of Trinity Lutheran Church were most gracious, given my extensive time commitment to the movement. Trinity's all-Negro congregation (except for our family) had been organized in 1915 by German Lutheran pastors who had come south from Columbus, Ohio. They had also set up a day school across the street from the church building, which continued to serve the community until just before we arrived in the summer of 1955.

Forty years later these black Lutherans were still in a distinct minority. The majority of African Americans belonged to Baptist churches, with the various types of Methodists bringing up a distant second place. But the members of Trinity were proud to be Lutherans, and their children tended to follow in their footsteps. The people at Trinity not only tolerated my investment of time in the movement, they too were actively involved. And they were ready and willing to volunteer their time to make sure the work of the church was done properly. We always had excellent leadership.

Many of our members were well-educated, some serving as school principals, teachers, and in other important positions.

Among our best friends in the black community were Lutheran Pastor Bill Griffen and his wife Ella Mae, Tom and Juanita Gray, and his brother attorney Fred Gray and his new wife Bernice. We raised our children together, except for Fred and Bernice, whose children came along later. We were back and forth in each other's homes. I was also close to Father Robert Dubose, an Episcopal priest. We shared the distinction of leading congregations of less common denominations in Montgomery's black community. On January 10, 1957, the second bomb that was thrown at our house was actually intended for Bob, according to investigators. Another family whose company we enjoyed was Dr. James Caple, his wife Yvonne, and their beautiful daughters. Jim was a local dentist.

We had plenty of local visitors who were not so welcome, in addition to the criminals who bombed our houses and churches and vandalized our cars. I think of the older white man from Montgomery who came to our door one day to report the decision that had been reached by him and his neighbors. They had held a meeting and voted that we should leave town! Or there was the police lieutenant who arrived at our home wanting to talk with us. When we learned that he was a transplant from the North, we expected some words of moderation from him. Instead what we heard was racist, mean, and even vicious, among the worst that had ever reached our ears. Jeannie was so angry and upset she left the room, not returning until our visitor had left.

We had another visitor whose intentions were good. A Catholic priest came by to meet us and to warn us about the terrible things the white people of Montgomery were likely to do to us. His words were not very comforting to Jeannie. (I happened to be out of town that day.) After the priest left, Jeannie called our friend Bob Hughes, who came to our house to talk with her. Bob told me later that he couldn't think of anything helpful to say. So he told Jeannie, "Just remember that God is in charge here, just as he is all over the world." After Jeannie heard these words, she said it was as if the weight of the entire world had been lifted from her shoulders. She knew that God was not only in charge, He had surrounded us with what she called a "Circle of Love" to protect us from danger, and to keep the hate from harming us.

And we cannot forget the Ku Klux Klan. Someone came to our house one day to report that a friend had overheard some Klan members talking about coming to our house to scare us. While we talked I glanced out the picture window in our living room. Indeed there was a long line of cars, filled with white men, parked in front of our house and church. I said to Jeannie, "If they came to see us, we ought to let them see us." We walked out onto our front porch and stood, looking at our threatening visitors. Finally they gave up and drove away. Just a few years ago we learned that our oldest daughter, Margee, then age four, had different memories of that day. She had run into the bathroom and climbed onto the toilet seat to look out the window at the Klansmen in their cars. But in her mind she must have gotten that image mixed up with an incident in the movie *To Kill a Mockingbird*, which she saw years later. There is a frightening scene where Scout is looking at a rabid dog. When Jeannie and I were sharing memories of our days in Montgomery with Margee (now called Meta), she talked about seeing the rabid dog in our front yard. The visit of the KKK must have been even more frightening to our children than we had realized.

I, too, did not comprehend for many years what an emotional impact the Klan had had on me. While researching and writing the portions of this volume that relate to Klan activity, I began having a series of dreams, which bordered on nightmares. In those dreams I was always struggling against wild animals that were attacking me.

Several times I nearly pushed Jeannie out of bed. Our son David, who is an army chaplain with many overseas deployments, said to me, "Dad, you are probably suffering from PTSD, post-traumatic stress disorder." We realized then that we had had to suppress our fears during the dangerous times merely to survive. Now they were coming to the surface. Sure enough, when I got to the less violent portions of the book, the dreams pretty well vanished.

The Klan had a difficult time frightening black people in those days. One Saturday during the year of the boycott, they decided to put on a show of force in Montgomery, inviting Klansmen from the entire region to gather in the downtown area dressed in their robes. Their ploy failed miserably. African Americans who happened to be shopping that day merely ignored them. We have a copy of an award-winning photo of a young black boy perched on a fire hydrant, calmly watching some robed Klansmen walk by. The fear was gone! And the downtown merchants shooed them away from their doorways, realizing that the KKK was bad for business.

They tried again on November 13, 1956, when the U. S. Supreme Court affirmed its decision outlawing bus segregation. Forty carloads of KKK members drove through black neighborhoods all over town, honking their horns. But our MIA leaders had been warned about their plans and word had gone out to Montgomery's black residents. When the Klan arrived, African Americans were there to greet them, sitting quietly on their porches in full view, with their porch lights on, waving to their "visitors!"

Somewhere around 1980, the KKK decided to hold their own "March from Selma to Montgomery," to protest America's affirmative action programs. The handful of Klan activists who made it all the way to the Montgomery city limits were met by policemen, who arrested a number of the Klansmen on weapons charges. But we dare not dismiss the Klan as no longer a threat. Though KKK numbers overall are miniscule today and the group has no popular or institutional support, there remain in our nation some Klan chapters and other hate groups which are committed to the principle of white supremacy. The Montgomery-based Southern Poverty Law Center tracks the activities of such organizations.

NOT ONLY DID WE RECEIVE many visitors in Montgomery. All of us who were in positions of leadership made regular trips out of town, mostly to raise money for the movement and to share our story with groups who wanted to know what was really going on. Since I was the one totally visible white person involved in the movement, I was regularly invited to preach or speak for African American groups all over Alabama.

The most impressive groups I addressed were at Ohio fund-raising rallies in Columbus in February 1956, and Toledo in March 1956. Many of the key people I met in Columbus became some of my closest associates when we moved back to that city in September 1958. I also spoke to several theological seminaries in different parts of the country, as well as church and secular groups in many locations. I had no way of knowing that this pattern would continue throughout my entire ministry.

As we moved closer to the time of our departure from Montgomery, we did not realize that our successful campaign there was not the conclusion, but only the first skirmish in the half-century-long series of activities which would come to be known as the modern civil rights movement.

Chapter 6

Farewell, Montgomery!—Hello, Columbus!

Jeannie and I thought we were likely to stay in Montgomery for many years. The level of violence had subsided considerably. The city's white population appeared to have accepted the reality of integration on the buses, even if that was not their choice. The "closet liberals," a small minority in this Southern metropolis, were openly relieved. Among many people in our city there appeared to be a grudging acceptance of the likelihood that further changes would be taking place as well. And we had counted on being part of that process.

But God seemed to have other plans for us. St. Philip Lutheran Church in Columbus, Ohio, issued a Call to me on January 25, 1958, to become their pastor. After flying to Columbus and meeting with the people there, I was convinced that we were supposed to stay in Montgomery. So I returned the Call. Then on May 28, when our bishop was visiting with us in Alabama, he hand-delivered a second Call from the same congregation. I was ready to send it back immediately, but the bishop urged me to pray about it and let the Lord decide what our future was to be. Jeannie and I were both shocked and disappointed when it became clear rather quickly that we were supposed to leave Montgomery. Jeannie told me, "You have to do what the Lord tells you to do, but I don't want to leave here!" On June 15, 1958, I accepted the Call to serve St. Philip, in spite of her pleadings. We did not leave, however, until more than two months later, since our fifth child was due to be born in July. Jeannie and I prepared to leave Montgomery unenthusiastically, "dragging our feet," but looking forward to whatever new adventures God had in store for us.

One reason we were reluctant to leave just then was that our church body, the American Lutheran Church, was in negotiations with the Lutheran Church/Missouri Synod. There was the possibility of a transfer of several of our congregations, including Trinity, from the ALC to the Missouri Synod. We wanted to stay, to help them through that process. Not long after our departure, Trinity did become part of the LC/MS.

Our final months in Montgomery seemed to be just as busy as the thirteen months of the bus boycott. In March 1957 I had been named as one of fifteen members of the Committee on the Overall Future Program of the Montgomery Improvement Association. Meeting often and for long hours, we tried to determine what should be the highest priorities for the African American community in Montgomery during the next decade. One year later, in March 1958, we presented a ten-point program, including voter registration, desegregation of public schools, access to libraries and parks, etc.

In mid-1957 I had also been asked to chair the planning committee for the MIA's second annual Institute on Nonviolence and Social Change, to be held in December on the second anniversary of the bus boycott. One of the speakers I invited was my friend Paul Simon.

Early in January 1958 I was notified that I was the recipient of the Russworm Award of the National Newspaper Publishers

Association, an African American organization. Mr. Emory O. Jackson, editor of the *Birmingham World*, drove to Montgomery and presented the certificate to me during our Sunday morning worship service at Trinity Lutheran. I still count that as one of the highest awards I have ever been given.

After my acceptance of the Call to St. Philip, Mr. Clifford Tyree, president of the congregation, took the train from Columbus to Montgomery to consult with me about matters I would need to deal with when we got back to Ohio. Jeannie and I learned quickly what a wonderful sense of humor he had. When Cliff first arrived at our home, he wanted to call his wife, Gertrude. Jokingly he told her I had led him through the white waiting room at the railway terminal, and that we had both been arrested! While he was in Montgomery, Clifford had an opportunity to attend at least one mass meeting. It helped to ease the strain of our leaving when our black friends and co-workers were able to see for themselves that we would be serving another African American congregation.

There was a minor setback in our plans to move to Ohio. The congregation had signed a contract to purchase a house not far from St. Philip, located in the Shepard Community. This area had been all white, but now had a few African American residents. The remaining white homeowners apparently panicked at the thought that another house might be "lost" to black people. The family from whom the church was buying the house told St. Philip they would not honor the contract. We assumed that their neighbors had put pressure on them not to sell. I had to rush to Columbus to find a rental house for us to move into. This time I was a guest of the Tyrees. Clifford and I soon found an acceptable house; and I went back to Montgomery to finish our preparations for moving. (A few months after our arrival in Columbus, the church bought a different house in Shepard, the same community we had tried to enter before, but which was now mostly black due to white flight.)

On Thursday, July 24, at 12:31 AM, our new daughter arrived—Kathryn Eileen Graetz. Since we already had two girls and two boys, we couldn't think of anything people should be giving us as baby gifts. So we put a note in the birth announcements, "Baby doesn't need a thing." Just a week later we received a check from Dr. Dale Lechleitner, our church body's American Missions director, enclosed with a poem:

To the Proud Parents:
"Baby doesn't need a thing."
True, indeed, but not for long.
Soon she'll learn with zest to sing
The common mortal 'Give me' song.
Give me milk and give me bread.
Give me play and restful bed.
Give me understanding love.
Give me manna from above.
Give me childhood free from care.
Give me youth that I may share,
Joy—sorrow, hope—concern,
Rich experience—to learn!
Through all these days of good or ill
The parents always foot the bill.
The children grow by leaps and bounds,
But mounting costs, the parent hounds.
So now—we send a little gift
Congratulations to convey;
If Katy is contented thrift,
We're sure her dad has bills to pay.
                    —Wanda & Dale Lechleitner

Before long we were engrossed in a round of farewells. Early in

Bob and Jeannie Graetz with the four children who lived in Montgomery. From left, Bobby, Dianne, Margee, and David. Kathryn, not pictured, was born two months before the move.

July, the Montgomery Council on Human Relations honored us at our last meeting with them, presenting us with a beautiful serving tray, which we still proudly use when we have company. Martin and Coretta King, with their two children, came by to see us before we left, bringing us a farewell gift of a silver serving tray. That gift hangs in an honored place on our dining room wall.

On August 4 the MIA had a special luncheon in our honor. When asked to speak, I told the gathering, "We feel free to leave now, since it has been rather peaceful. The only thing that would really keep us here for sure would be another bombing." My good friend Fred Gray was sitting beside me. With a smile, he responded, "We could arrange that!"

At the Monday evening, August 18, mass meeting, we were recognized once again and thanked for our participation in the movement. The MIA presented us with a check for $500. In those days that was a huge sum! Since I had been actively involved in a fund-raising campaign to build our "colored" YMCA a new building, we turned over $125 of the amount to that effort.

On Friday, August 22, Trinity Lutheran held a special dinner to celebrate our ministry with them. And the following Sunday I preached my farewell sermon. The single entry in my pocket calendar for the rest of that week is recorded on Tuesday—"Movers load up!"

It goes without saying that we, and those closest to us, had mixed feelings about our move to Columbus. But many of the reasons for our sadness were not immediately apparent. We knew that Raymond and Rosa Parks had moved to Detroit, Michigan, where Mrs. Parks's brother Sylvester lived. But we did not realize at that time that they had few options besides leaving Montgomery; since neither of them could find employment. Both had lost their jobs because of the boycott.

During our first months and years in Columbus, we had frequent visitors from Montgomery, who shared their own conclusions about our move. "We were sorry to see you go," they would tell us, "but we knew you had to leave. If you had stayed, the Klan would have killed you eventually."

There were other "unintended consequences" of our movement. The boycott had been so successful that the bus company went out of business soon afterward; they simply could not recover from the financial losses they had experienced. In fact, there then followed a long period of decline for public transportation in Montgomery due to demographic changes and official indifference or even hostility. Only now, a half-century after the boycott, is the municipal bus system slowly getting back close to adequately serving the community.

The very process of desegregation in our city had a negative impact on the black business community as well. As formerly all-white restaurants, theaters, and other establishments opened their doors to African Americans, their black-owned counterparts began to suffer. With fewer resources available than their white competitors, they had a difficult time staying in business. Many closed their doors, leading to the near collapse of the black business district in Montgomery.

When we bring groups to visit civil rights sites in that city, we always take them to the parsonage at 409 South Jackson Street that was home to the King family. But we are filled with sadness as we look to the next corner south, at High and Jackson streets, to see the nearly abandoned Ben Moore Hotel. That building had been the site of many dinners, meetings and frantic office activities during the boycott and the months following. It is our fervent hope that someone will see fit to restore that precious landmark.

In spite of the negative fallout from our movement, we still believe (and share with groups all across America) that Montgomery has made more progress in racial reconciliation than most cities in this country. Political, business, education, and religious leaders are celebrating their civil rights history as a positive force that helped to bring this metropolis to where it is today. And there are active organizations in Montgomery whose sole purpose is to work toward ever better ethnic relationships in their city. They include two biracial groups that have been in existence for more than two decades—"The Friendly Supper Club," meeting once a month for dinner; and "One Montgomery," which gathers every Tuesday morning to eat breakfast together, listen to guest speakers, and strategize about improving Montgomery.

Our longtime friend, Mrs. Johnnie Carr, in a photo made within the past few years when she was in her early nineties.

AS WE WERE MAKING OUR FINAL preparations for moving, Jeannie's older sister, Ruth Warner, had come from northwestern Pennsylvania to Montgomery to help us with our move. Before we loaded up, she took our three older children back to Pennsylvania with her, keeping them for a few days while we moved and got settled in.

St. Philip had rented half of a duplex for us at 1477 Bryden Road, not far from the church, as a temporary home. The fact that it was a duplex became a major problem for our young children. An older couple lived in the other half, separated from us by what was obviously a very thin dividing wall. From either side of the double, it was easy to hear everything that was happening on the other side. It was not unusual for us to hear a disembodied voice shouting, "Make those children be quiet!" As any parent knows, it was not possible to keep five active children still for long. To make matters worse, our stairway was next to the dividing wall. Every time the children went up or down the bare wooden stairs, the neighbors complained.

Jeannie listened carefully for the rare times when both of the neighbors left their house at the same time. As soon as they were gone, the games began. Jeannie and the children tramped up and down the stairway, shouting and singing. We were all glad when we moved into the Shepard Community. That was to be our home for the next nine years.

We had a surprise visitor the day after we moved into our temporary home. Because of our involvement in the Montgomery Bus Boycott, one of the local papers sent a reporter to record our arrival in Columbus. The next morning the paper carried its story on the front page, along with a picture of me carrying some children's toys into the house. It just happened that our friend Allard K. Lowenstein was sitting at the airport in Columbus, waiting for a flight. He picked up a paper and saw my picture. The next thing we knew, Al was getting out of a cab at our front door. He had a way of popping in and out of our lives from time to time.

MY CIVIL RIGHTS ACTIVITIES continued without interruption when we moved back to Ohio. Soon after I was installed as pastor of St. Philip on September 14, 1958, I was once again active in the Columbus chapter of the NAACP. And my calendar became filled more and more with notations of meetings of the Urban League, Near East Side Area Council, Columbus Council on Human Relations, Greater Columbus Committee for Fair Housing, Citizens Advisory Committee, and the Columbus Leadership Conference, all working to improve race relations in Columbus. The last organization was especially busy. A group of African American business and professional people, they met downtown for breakfast every Thursday morning. For years I was the only white member, not unusual for me. When another white pastor who served a black congregation applied for membership, the question was introduced and discussed over breakfast. As the debate got more heated, one man said, in exasperation, "Well, Bob Graetz is already a member!" The im-

Bob and Jeannie Graetz, outside St. Philip.

mediate response: "That's Graetz. The question we're debating is, 'Shall we admit white members into our group?'"

My calendar of speaking engagements (and Jeannie's as well) filled up rapidly, for a variety of groups in Columbus and elsewhere. On at least one occasion, I wasn't even aware that I was to be a guest speaker. Mrs. Hannah Barnett, one of our oldest members at St. Philip, issued an invitation to me and Jeannie to come to a program at her Lucy Dean Play School. We already had a conflict on that date, however. Several other times over the following months, we had to beg off for the same reason. Finally she asked us in plenty of time to come to a Christmas event. Shortly after the program began, Mrs. Barnett introduced her special guests, skipping over me by saying, "You'll hear from my pastor later on."

Jeannie turned to me with surprise on her face. "I think you are supposed to be the speaker," she whispered.

"I think you're right," I whispered back. And she was.

Fortunately for me, there were plenty of presentations by her students before she introduced me as the speaker. And since it was Christmas time, it was easy to think of something to say.

Mrs. Coretta King was invited to speak at the Mount Olivet Baptist Church in Columbus. The minister of the church capitalized on our presence in town by inviting Jeannie to introduce her. As the pastor was presenting Jeannie, he said some flattering things about my ministry in the civil rights movement, closing with the declaration, "Though his life was in constant danger, he was never afraid!" Then he asked me to say a few words. My comment to the congregation was, "I can't speak for the rest of those people in Montgomery, but there were times when I was scared to death!" I have always contended that the absence of fear is not the point. What you do when you are afraid is what makes the difference. We often had good reason to be afraid.

The "race relations climate" in Columbus was not nearly as

negative as it had been in Montgomery. The patterns of segregation and discrimination in Ohio, however, were based on custom, rather than law, which made them even more difficult to deal with. Largely because of a practice called "red-lining," Columbus was reputed to be the second most residentially segregated city in the nation, behind only Chicago. Realtors, bankers, and political leaders would determine which neighborhoods would be open for purchase or rent by African Americans. If there was a need for more housing for black residents, that same group of local leaders would decide which areas would be allowed to "turn colored." The newly opened neighborhoods would be marked on the city map with a red pencil.

What usually followed was a common practice, though mostly in the North. Realtors would find one or two homeowners in the target community who wanted to sell their homes, and who were willing to sell to African Americans. Once the new residents had moved in, those same realtors would go door to door, pointing out to other homeowners that the neighborhood was "turning colored." People were warned that they should sell their homes quickly, before the property values dropped. For those homeowners who sold their homes in a panic, the warning became a self-fulfilling prophecy. The purchase amounts they were offered were less than their houses were worth. Because these community changes usually took place at a time when the need for black housing was greatest, the new residents often paid inflated prices to get into their new homes. Unhappy white people blamed Negroes for devaluing their property. And the incoming black homeowners grumbled over the system that forced them to pay the realtors more than their homes were worth. After we arrived in Columbus, I worked with several groups attempting to deal with the evils of racial segregation in housing policies.

In his outstanding book, *Arc of Justice,* Kevin Boyle described the situation in the North during the 1920s, which continued into the 1960s and '70s:

> [M]any employers decided that all but the most menial and dangerous work should be reserved for whites. More and more white shopkeepers banned black customers from their stores and restaurants. And, most ominously, whites decided that blacks couldn't live wherever they wanted. They were to be hidden away in a handful of neighborhoods, walled into ghettos. Businessmen infused the real estate market with racist rules and regulations. White landlords wouldn't show black tenants apartments outside the ghetto. White real estate agents wouldn't show them houses in white neighborhoods. Bankers wouldn't offer them mortgages. Insurance agents wouldn't provide them with coverage. Developers wrote legal restrictions into their deeds, barring blacks from new housing tracts. (Page 9)
>
> "Lynching has been the peculiar institution of the south," declared a colored newspaper in an editorial circulated through NAACP headquarters. "Forceful residential segregation has taken root and is spreading so fast till if it's not soon checked it will become the peculiar institution of the North." (Page 201)

Those "racist rules and regulations" and "legal restrictions" also included a device known as a "restrictive covenant." Clauses would be inserted in property deeds that prohibited owners from ever selling the property to Negroes, and sometimes Jews or other groups. Some homeowners resisted inserting those clauses. They wanted to be able to sell their homes to African Americans quickly, in case the neighborhood began to turn black.

By the late 1950s, black communities all across the country had been energized by the Montgomery Bus Boycott. They were protesting loudly against a wide variety of forms of racial discrimination. As we moved into the 1960s, the "protest march" became an often-used tactic to allow communities to express their concerns. Our church was located about three miles from the center of Columbus, only one block away from a major east-west artery running through the city. So St. Philip Lutheran Church became a usual starting point for marches on city hall or the board of education.

Recently a member of St. Philip reminded me of a time when I had led some teenagers in picketing a Woolworth's store in Columbus. I had not realized how traumatic the experience had been for the young people. She remembered they were all so frightened that they stayed as close to me as possible. "If you had stopped suddenly," she told me, "we would all have landed on top of you."

Though I worked with groups that were attacking a wide variety of forms of racial segregation and discrimination, my major efforts were focused on what was referred to as "de facto segregation" in education. In Southern states, laws required black and white students to attend separate schools. In the North, virtually the same result was achieved by drawing school district lines in such a way that most schools were totally or nearly one-race facilities.

I spent a great deal of my available time getting acquainted with members of the Columbus Board of Education and their top administrators, making myself an unofficial advisor to them on desegregation issues. The white officials were more comfortable talking with me than with the large groups of angry black citizens who staged frequent protests at board meetings. What they did not know was that I was involved in regular, though secret, conversations with the leaders of the protest groups. My primary contact person was Mr. Waldo Tyler, an African American pharmacist, whose drug store was just a few yards from our church. Waldo and I conversed—some would say conspired—frequently. Knowing in advance what the protesters were going to demand, I could advise the education officials about their most appropriate responses.

When they followed my advice, the officials were often surprised and pleased that their attempts to move in a positive direction were well received.

We were not, of course, always successful. And our greatest failure started off looking like our greatest triumph. The Columbus Board of Education created a well-integrated and inclusive Council on Inter-Cultural Education, of which I was a member. We were given a budget and staff and charged with the responsibility of determining what steps the Columbus community desired, or would accept, in the process of desegregating Columbus's public schools.

We sent teams to study such programs in other urban centers. We brought in experts to talk with us and bought reference materials for council members to study. Most importantly, we held hearings in schools all over Columbus, to give parents and students an opportunity to share their feelings with us. It didn't take long for us to realize that we had become a buffer between the board and the public. In those hearings, we were very exposed targets for parents in both the black and white communities.

And we produced results. At the end of our studies and hearings, we drew up a long list of very specific steps the board of education could take to begin the process of desegregating Columbus's schools. Most of our recommendations for immediate action involved minor changes that would have been minimally disruptive, easy to implement, and likely to be readily accepted by the community. We wanted to help the board take immediate, positive steps toward breaking down the patterns of separation on the basis of race, without creating a massive program that would have surely created equally massive resistance from the community.

The board of education received our report, with its recommendations, at a public meeting. They thanked us for the contributions we had made, and then dissolved the council. Since Jeannie and I left Columbus within two months, moving to Washington, D.C.,

I was not aware at the time that our report was put on the shelf and almost totally ignored. A few years later a lawsuit was filed against the board. I was told that our report was a central piece in the plaintiffs' case. When it was determined that members of the board had not responded to the recommendations of the very council they themselves had established, it was obvious that they would be found at fault. The time had passed, however, when the easy steps we had suggested could be put into play. In order to correct the long-standing imbalance, it was necessary for our friend, U. S. District Judge Robert Duncan, to impose a massive, and disruptive, program of mandated busing that left no one really happy.

He said in his opinion:

> [T]hose public officials charged by law with the administration of the Columbus Public Schools have for the most part ignored repeated requests and demands for an integrated educational system. They have engaged in overt actions which readily permit an inference of segregative intent. They have repeatedly failed to seize opportunities, large and small, which would have promoted racial balance in the Columbus Public Schools."

As I look over my calendars for those tumultuous years in Columbus, I have a hard time remembering how I was able to serve as pastor at the same time. Every year, at our annual congregational meeting, I reported to the members of St. Philip about my commitment of time to the civil rights movement, asking them if that is what they wanted me to be doing. And each year, when they assented, I reminded them that they would have to volunteer to take care of many tasks at the church that I did not have time for. To this day, I am convinced that the level of lay involvement in the work of the congregation was a key ingredient in their strong growth. During the nine-plus years that we served at St. Philip, the congregation grew from about one hundred seventy to more than seven hundred members. And those members became active evangelists. By the time I had finished instructing each group of adults in preparation for membership, there was another group ready to begin.

There is another aspect of ministry that certainly contributed to our success as well. For the entire time that I have served as a pastor, I have concentrated much of my time on home visits to members and others who related to the congregations I have served. When I was a student pastor, my advisor had said to me, "Don't spend too much time on your sermons. Spend time with your people, and the sermons will write themselves." I have followed that good

Groundbreaking for addition to St. Philip, about 1965.

advice throughout my ministry and have encouraged younger colleagues to do the same.

Another big boost to our ministry at St. Philip was our series of
"interns," seminary students who would each spend a year working
with me full-time, learning how to be pastors and how to serve in
a multicultural setting. (Because of our very open and accepting
stance, St. Philip attracted many interracial couples who did not
feel welcome in other places. That openness is characteristic of St.
Philip to this day.) Many other students helped us out with their
volunteer time. The experience of being involved with St. Philip
was much valued.

We also carried on a major building program during our decade
at St. Philip, tripling the amount of space we had available. Even
with the extra room, the congregation was large enough that we
needed to have two worship services each Sunday morning.

Those were the busiest years of our lives. Several mornings
each week I had to leave the house early, before the children left
for school. I tried hard to get home for dinner each evening, usually jumping up from the table to race off to another meeting.
One evening during dinner, I stood up to get something from the
refrigerator. Our children, in chorus, said, "Bye, Daddy." But we
also worked hard to find times to do exciting things with the children, especially on camping trips. And we did not hesitate to take
them out of school if there was an opportunity to expose them to
alternative educational activities.

Jeannie and I were always active in our children's PTA groups as
well. The first Thanksgiving after we arrived in Columbus, I went to
a "Father and Child" PTA meeting with our first-grader Margee. As
a fun exercise, each of us fathers was given a square of construction
paper. We were to hold the papers behind our backs and tear out
the shape of a turkey, without looking! Knowing that my artistic
abilities were limited at best, I decided I should just make the best

of it. I rounded off three corners and made something like a head and neck on the fourth. To my surprise, when I brought the paper out, it looked like a turkey. Poor Margee was stunned. "Daddy," she asked, "did you cheat?" It didn't take long to convince her that I had not peeked. By the way, I won first prize for my turkey!

We also added to our family while in Columbus. Jonathan William was born on November 15, 1959; and Carolyn Jeanne joined us on May 1, 1963. She was the seventh, and the last! But we had successfully kept to our pattern—girl, boy, girl, boy, girl, boy, girl! Jeannie really had her hands full with seven children, the oldest just over ten years old.

Our oldest daughter turned six shortly after we arrived in Columbus. We had made plans for her to attend school at the Holt Street Baptist Church in Montgomery, the same church that had hosted the first mass meeting during the Montgomery Bus Boycott. We learned only after we had moved that she would not have been allowed to attend. The church had been informed that if they allowed our daughter to go to school there, the state's subsidy would have been cut off, because they would have been in violation of Alabama's school segregation laws. Margee would surely have been persecuted in the public school she would have attended. The white children in that school already knew who we were. As their buses passed by our house, they would shout "Nigger-lover!" if they saw us outside.

Instead, Margee and her brothers and sisters all had the opportunity to attend largely African American schools in Columbus. In a manner of speaking, they "grew up black." All of those experiences helped to prepare them for the far different set of relationships they would find in Washington, D.C., the site of our next ministry.

Chapter 7

ON THE ROAD
FOR CIVIL RIGHTS

During the time we served at St. Philip Lutheran Church, 1958–67, I tried hard to be the full-time pastor they had called me to be. The growth of the congregation, the enthusiasm of its members, and its lasting vitality would seem to indicate that I succeeded. But there were only a handful of people like me in our whole Lutheran church body at that time who dedicated any significant amount of time to civil rights activities. So I was constantly being called on for service outside of my own church.

Soon after we arrived in Columbus, I realized that my pattern of traveling all over the country would continue without interruption. I made a major time commitment to the Lutheran Human Relations Association. In July 1956, a month before our house in Montgomery was bombed for the first time, I had gone to Valparaiso, Indiana, to deliver a speech at LHRA's annual Institute on "The Montgomery Bus Boycott—My Part in It." After we moved north, I was elected to LHRA's national board. Several times a year we met in different parts of the country, always over the weekend. There we accepted invitations to preach or teach in local Lutheran congregations, where we could say the bold things about human relations that could have gotten their pastors into trouble.

I still remember the highest compliment I received after one of those presentations. A stern-faced man shook my hand warmly and held on. Finally he spoke. "You are most disturbing!" he told me, and walked away.

Later on I represented the LHRA at meetings of the Leadership Council on Human Rights, a Washington-based coalition of national civil rights groups. There were active chapters of the LHRA in many cities, including Columbus.

In August 1961 Jeannie and I took Bill Green and Reynelda Ware, two teenagers from St. Philip, to Miami Beach, Florida, for a Lutheran youth gathering of more than fourteen thousand people. (Reynelda later became a TV news anchor in Denver, Colorado. Bill Green's mother is still an active member of St. Philip.) We headed south, driving our Ford van, which we laughingly referred to as our "bus."

This was the year of the Freedom Rides, during which exceptionally brave biracial groups of activists rode buses through the South to test the compliance with federal regulations prohibiting segregation of facilities for interstate passengers. I recently read John Lewis's chilling personal account of his involvement in the Freedom Rides in his memoir, *Walking with the Wind.* In incidents in three Alabama cities—Anniston, Birmingham, and Montgomery—the riders were savagely attacked, some coming close to losing their lives.

We ourselves were nervous in our little interracial group of four, traveling through the same states as the Freedom Riders. We left our children with their two sets of grandparents and headed south with our African American teenagers. All of the parents involved, including our own, were worried about our safety. They sent us on our way with enough food for at least a week on the road. We all knew that our real problems would come when we got into the Deep South, where we would have to depend on black-owned restaurants and sleeping places. We were also aware that such a simple thing as finding available restrooms would be difficult. The lack of public facilities was a constant challenge for African American travelers in those days and we realized it could be even more challenging for our mixed-race party. As we journeyed, we found ourselves alternately in hilarious and frightening situations. We had occasional confrontations along the way with angry white men.

Dr. Martin Luther King, Jr., was one of the major speakers at the gathering in Miami Beach. He and I also shared in a panel presentation for a special interest group at the assembly. It was one of the few times Jeannie and I were together with Dr. King between our departure from Montgomery in 1958 and his death in Memphis ten years later.

In November 1962 I represented the American Lutheran Church at a conference in Chicago sponsored by the National Lutheran Council. The theme was "The Church's Concern for a Diverse

In 1961, I met again with Dr. King at a conference in Miami Beach. We are seated on either side of the man standing.

Society." Since the NLC planned to publish the proceedings of the conference in book form, I was asked to do a chapter summarizing the reports of study groups that met throughout the three-day gathering. Their oral reports to the conference were most interesting. But the recorders' notes passed along to me were not very helpful. So I constructed the chapter based on my own memories of what had been reported—I wonder how many "verbatim" accounts are put together in the same way.

The year 1963 was busier than most. In January I was back in Chicago representing the American Lutheran Church, this time for the "National Conference on Religion and Race." This four-day gathering brought together an array of top leaders of virtually every religious group in the United States, as well as activists like me from the same groups. This was the first time any such assemblage had ever been convened in this country.

I remember first the many addresses delivered by high-level ecclesiastics, who were deemed to be so important that their introductions were often nearly as long as their speeches. (I've never been that impressed with such descriptions of "pedigrees," even when they are about me.)

For dinner together one evening, our ALC contingent chose a Japanese restaurant near the conference hotel. At the urging of David Preus, who had spent time in Japan after World War II, we ate our dinner sitting on the floor on a raised platform. As one of our group lowered himself into place, he lost his balance, rolling through a bamboo curtain and sprawling on his back between two tables of very surprised diners. Apologizing profusely, he crawled back into his place. But the two young Japanese servers who took care of us were quite unsuccessful in suppressing their giggles each time they came to our table.

One day during a break in the schedule, I wandered through the elegant hotel where we had gathered, admiring the beautiful antique furniture in some of the sitting rooms. In one of those rooms I came across a woman leaning back in an overstuffed chair, with her shoes off. It was world-renowned gospel singer Mahalia Jackson, one of the celebrities who had been brought to Chicago to entertain us. Since no one else walked through while we chatted, I had a delightful one-on-one conversation with this lady, who impressed me as a beautiful, humble, ordinary person. I was reminded of an NAACP gathering in Columbus almost two years before. One of our special guests was Ralph Bunche, U.S. Ambassador to the United Nations. There, too, I wanted to have a look around the gorgeous mansion where we were meeting. And I happened upon Ambassador Bunche, leaning back with his shoes off. He said to me, "Yes, even Ralph Bunche gets sore feet sometimes."

A Jewish rabbi chaired the discussion group to which I was assigned in Chicago. We met several times during the conference. One morning our gathering was the first item on the agenda, right after breakfast. As I walked in, I saw that the rabbi was at the other end of the room looking out of the window. He had been the first to arrive. I called out to him, "Shalom alechem," an ancient Hebrew greeting, meaning "Peace be with you." He turned to me with a beatific smile on his face. "What a wonderful way to begin the day," he said.

My final memory is of a Catholic layman, William Stringfellow, who had been one of the organizers of the convocation. In one of its final sessions, he shocked us all with his analysis of this historic gathering. It was a wonderful thing we had done, he told us, except that it was "too little, too late, and too lily-white!" The stunned participants went back to their comfortable homes across the country, trying to figure out what they could do that would really make a difference.

Back in Columbus, we knew what we had to do. Most of those from our city who had represented various faith groups in Chicago met after our return to start planning for what we would later call a "Columbus Conference *of* Religion *on* Race."

IN AUGUST 1963, the American Lutheran Church again asked me to represent them at two back-to-back gatherings. The first was a quadrennial conference on human relations sponsored by the United Methodist Church, set for August 26-30 in Chicago. The second was a "March on Washington for Jobs and Freedom," sponsored by just about all of the major civil rights organizations in the country. Reluctantly I decided I could not attend both events; so I chose the church conference, since it was my church body that was sponsoring me.

In the meantime almost everyone I knew was urging me to go to Washington, D.C. Dr. King, who was a speaker at the Methodist convocation, finally convinced me that I would never forgive myself if I missed the big March on Washington. On Tuesday, August 27, I borrowed $100 from the petty cash fund in the office of the National Lutheran Council in Chicago, excused myself to my Methodist hosts, and took a limo to the airport. Martin King had left earlier on the flight he had reserved. I found myself on standby for one flight after another through the evening, finally succeeding in getting to Washington National Airport after midnight. Making my way to the hotel that was the resting place of most of the Columbus, Ohio, participants, I spent the night alternately napping in the lobby's overstuffed chairs and strolling through the streets of downtown Washington.

Martin was right. I never would have forgiven myself if I had stayed away from that spectacular event. Most people remember the March on Washington as the setting of Dr. King's "I Have a Dream" speech. But my sharpest memories are of the people. Throughout the morning hours, hundreds of buses rolled in from all parts of the country. In the scorching summer heat, the enormous crowd moved like an unstoppable flow of lava along the sides of the reflecting pool, from the Washington Monument to the Lincoln Memorial. I was disappointed to find myself pressed by the crowd to one side of the Lincoln Memorial, where I could not see the speakers. But the sound system carried their triumphant voices to every part of the gathering.

As we marched past a news camera, I gave a "V-for-Victory" sign with my fingers. A few weeks later, I got a letter from my old Montgomery friend, Rev. Bob Hughes, who was by that time a missionary in Southern Rhodesia. He had seen me in a newsreel. (More recently, PBS has produced a delightful documentary on the musical group Peter, Paul, and Mary, who sang at the March on Washington. Sure enough, PBS included the same news clip! We received dozens of phone calls and e-mails from friends who saw the television special.)

I shared my observations of the March on Washington in a letter I wrote to Lew Holm, at the *Lutheran Standard*, our church magazine:

Dear Lew:

It is difficult to express in words what it feels like to be a part of a peaceful demonstration by more than 200,000 people. I suppose the most striking thing of all is the fact that it was peaceful . . .

Perhaps the secret to this lies in the spirit of those who marched. They were jovial and happy. There was almost a festive mood . . . They were bidding welcome to a new day for the American Negro, and indeed for the whole American society. The spirit of victory filled their hearts—not that this demonstration marked the end of the struggle—on the contrary, there was a realization that this was the beginning of a massive campaign to eradicate the evil of racism from American life once and for all.

Those who gathered before the Lincoln Memorial on that day gave expression to their determination to keep pressing forward until the final victory is won. Their very presence there was evidence enough. (One man had even roller skated to Washington from Chicago, Illinois.) When one of the speakers [John Lewis] said to the crowd, "Before this is over we may have to march on Albany, Georgia, and Cambridge, Maryland, too," I heard people behind me saying, "Let's go!" And I believe they would have gone, too. They were ready. One marcher was overheard saying, "I'm dog tired, I'm dead tired, but I'd march again tomorrow."

What kind of people were these who marched on Washington? They seemed to come from all walks of life, from all economic levels. They were generally rather well dressed. One person said to me, "The ladies look like they got dressed up to go to church." This was not far from the truth. For the thing that struck me about them was that they seemed to be largely church people. It was not only the Negro church that was represented there. Ministers, officials and lay people were there from dozens of Protestant, Catholic and Jewish groups. It was as if the religious community of America was presenting itself in the Nation's capitol.

There are many who question the propriety of our being there at all. Some who are "on our side" have even expressed doubts about the strategy of the March. But consider this. We have long urged our people to write to their congressmen to register their opinions and to state their grievances. We who marched on Washington were writing to our congressmen also—not with pen and paper, but with our very bodies. We said to them in effect, "What we have to say to you is too important and too critical to entrust to a piece of paper that you may or may not pay attention to. What we have to say we must say in person."

. . . Words will no longer suffice. We must have action, and we must have it now . . .

[R]egardless of what some may think about the strategy of the March, its basic underlying principles of justice and equality of opportunity for all, its basic purpose of eliminating hatred and prejudice based on race and class, are biblical concepts themselves. Too often we give them merely lip service and not life service. By its presence, our church was taking its stand on the side of righteousness and justice, of freedom for all people . . . Negro comedian Dick Gregory was speaking to a Methodist Human Relations Conference in Chicago, Illinois, the day after the March. He said to them, "You had better come along with us, if for no other reason than this, that we are going to win, and it will be a lot better for you if you are with us."

We do not know at this point whether the Washington March will make any lasting impression on the members of the U.S. Congress. Only time will tell. But the impression is registered indelibly on the hearts of the 200,000 people who marched. They will not, they cannot ever be the same. Perhaps this is the most important gain after all. To have these thousands of people, dedicated and determined, return to their own communities, to carry on to victory in this revolution whose goal is simply the realization of the great American dream."

Yours in his service,

Robert Graetz

We could not know that just eighteen days later the civil rights movement would fall from its euphoric high to an abysmal low. On Sunday morning, September 15, 1963, during the Sunday School hour, a powerful bomb exploded in an outside stairwell at the Sixteenth Street Baptist Church in Birmingham, Alabama. The bodies of three fourteen-year-old girls, Cynthia Wesley, Addie Mae

Collins, and Carole Robertson, as well as eleven-year-old Denise McNair, were pulled from the rubble. Addie Mae's little sister Sarah survived the blast though she was partially blinded. It would be more than forty years before the last of the four men accused of this atrocity was brought to justice.

While I was at church getting ready for Sunday School, one of the teenagers from St. Philip came in and gave me the news. All we could do was stand and cry. A pall of gloom was suddenly cast over the entire African American community in this country, as well as over those white citizens who were sympathetic to our cause, or at least were not supportive of terrorist violence. How could anyone comprehend the nature of the hatred that was willing to destroy the lives of black children in order to preserve a "way of life" as the white supremacists claimed they were doing. Cynthia, Addie Mae, Carole, and Denise were not the only martyrs of the civil rights movement, nor were they the last. But their deaths were among the most painful to accept and to understand.

The bombing in Birmingham was a personal tragedy for us. We had known Denise's father, Chris McNair, who was an active member of St. Paul Lutheran Church in Birmingham. In the midst of his own personal grief after the bombing, Mr. McNair said, "We must not let this change us into something different than who we are. We must be human." The McNairs later set up a memorial room dedicated to Denise in their photo studio. We visit them frequently with our civil rights pilgrimage groups.

The civil rights movement was not halted by this tragedy, of course. Indeed the Birmingham movement continued to press ahead in its drive to achieve equal rights for all of its citizens. Their persistence, and the willingness of both adults and children to put their lives at risk, helped to move the Congress to pass the Civil Rights Act of 1964.

Columbus was one of many cities which staged protest actions to demonstrate our sympathy for the loss of the children in Birmingham. I took part in a march down Mount Vernon Avenue, the heart of the African American business section of Columbus. The event was sponsored by the Congress on Racial Equality (CORE).

BUT THERE WAS NO TIME to rest. Two weeks later I was back in Washington, D.C., for another conference on social action. At the same time I was writing a booklet for the American Lutheran Church, A Congregational Guide for Human Relations, to be published the following March. In the Introduction I said,

> Perhaps the most tragic aspect of this whole picture is that the Christian Church, which should have been leading the way in a demonstration of true love and brotherhood, has largely been bringing up the rear, and often fighting a desperate rearguard action to preserve racial segregation within its walls. As Dr. Martin Luther King, Jr., has put it, "The Church has too often been the taillight, when she should have been the headlight." Thank God this situation is changing rapidly today.

In late November 1964 I was in Washington, D.C., once more, this time as one of two delegates from the American Lutheran Church to a White House Interreligious Conference on Equal Opportunity. Two hundred Protestant, Catholic, and Jewish religious leaders, along with government officials, were brought together at Airlie House, an elegant conference center near Warrenton, Virginia.

My family was used to my being gone out of town frequently. When Jeannie looked at the name of this meeting, she wondered when I was going to give her an "equal opportunity" to go along on one of these trips. (That finally happened less than five years later, when I took Jeannie along to a conference in Austria!) We explained to our children that I was going to a White House conference. I said I might even meet the president. Our seven-year-old son David looked up wide-eyed and said, "You might get to be the President?!!"

My memories of Airlie House reflect the reality that I had never experienced such elegance in my life. When our chartered bus arrived from Washington, each of us had a servant to carry our bags and to make sure that all of our needs were met as we checked in. The meals were superb, with an almost limitless selection of foods, served buffet style. One evening, as I approached the meat-serving area, I beheld the largest roast turkey I had ever seen. Passing up all the other carvers, I headed straight for the big bird. My response to the question, "White or dark?" was an emphatic "Dark!" The chef severed an entire leg and laid it across my plate. It extended well beyond both sides of the large dinner plate. As I walked to my seat, in the spotlight of the stares of almost everyone in the room, I felt like Fred Flintstone.

At the Airlie House we heard presentations on poverty and racism, as well as federal laws and programs designed to ameliorate these societal problems. One of our presenters was John Doar, from the Civil Rights Division of the Department of Justice.

About four months later, in late March 1965, I was back in Montgomery for the last day of the Selma-to-Montgomery march. I walked around the grounds of the City of St. Jude, the site of the last evening's gathering and encampment before the final leg of the march to the state capitol building, occasionally finding someone I knew. Suddenly I saw John Doar, but not dressed in the suit and tie he had worn at the Airlie House. He was clad in jeans and very casual attire. "Hello, Mr. Doar," I said. "It's good to see you again." I reminded him that we had met at the White House conference.

By this time I realized from the shocked looks on Doar's face, and those of his companions, that they had intended to remain incognito. I quickly excused myself and didn't reveal his presence until after the event was over.

The background of the Selma March is complicated but significant. The Civil Rights Act of 1964, which grew largely out of the Birmingham campaign in 1963 and 1964, had not guaranteed the right to vote for all citizens. President Johnson had shared with civil rights leaders his concern that the country was not ready for further legislation at that time. But African American leaders were determined to get the ballot into the hands of their people. Groups based both in the North and the South were sending teams of activists into the Deep South to encourage black residents to attempt to register to vote. There was little progress, however, because white political leaders were just as determined not to give up power to people whom they considered to be inferior and unfit to participate in their own government.

Among the groups targeting Selma and Dallas County, Alabama, in 1963 and 1964 was the Student Nonviolent Coordinating Committee (SNCC, pronounced "Snick"), one of whose leaders was John Lewis (later, Congressman John Lewis of Georgia). But SNCC's efforts were becoming less productive. In December 1964 several members of the Dallas County Voters League traveled to Atlanta to the offices of the Southern Christian Leadership Conference. They were there to ask Dr. King to bring his organization to Selma, to get the campaign moving again. Among the group were Amelia Boynton and the Rev. Fred Reese, local leaders in Selma.

Many SNCC activists were unhappy that SCLC was moving into "their territory." But they wisely followed the local leaders, who had initiated the invitation to Dr. King. On January 18, King led his first march in Selma, with several hundred people, in a fruitless attempt to get prospective voters into the courthouse. The following month a peaceful protest march in Marion (coincidentally the hometown of the wives of Martin Luther King, Jr., Andrew Young, and Ralph Abernathy), in neighboring Perry County, was met with massive violence. During the ensuing melee, twenty-six-year-old Jimmy Lee Jackson was shot and later died.

In early March 1965, I had been as shocked as anyone else by the television pictures of what came to be known as "Bloody Sunday." The Selma marchers had first announced their intention to carry Jackson's body to the state capitol in Montgomery to lay it symbolically at the feet of Governor George C. Wallace, whom they blamed for the climate of violent resistance that had led to Jackson's death. That did not happen, of course, but after Jackson's funeral, the idea of a protest march from Selma to Montgomery grew among the activists working in Selma and Marion.

Thus, on Sunday, March 7, SNCC leader John Lewis and SCLC leader Hosea Williams led a column of marchers toward Montgomery. The march departed from the Brown Chapel A.M.E. Church and proceeded through downtown Selma and then onto Highway 80 and across the Edmund Pettus Bridge. When the marchers reached the Montgomery side of the bridge, they were attacked by a waiting group of state troopers and an unofficial "posse" of Dallas County deputies, using clubs, tear gas, and horses. The bloodied marchers were driven back to Brown Chapel.

This time there was ample evidence that the church was trying to be the "headlight" rather than the "taillight" in the civil rights movement. After the shocking scenes of Bloody Sunday were broadcast on network television, hundreds of clergy and lay people from many religious groups poured into Selma from all over the country. After two weeks of legal wrangling, the federal government intervened and prepared the way for a contingent to "march" from Selma to Montgomery beginning on Sunday, March 21.

A group of us in Columbus resolved to join them for the last day's walk, from the outskirts of Montgomery to the state capitol building. Five African American leaders and I began searching for space on any flight that would get us to Montgomery in time to join the march. There were plenty of seats to Atlanta, but none from there to Montgomery. There were also no direct flights to Montgomery; nor could we find a way to get there through any other city. Our only option was to charter a small plane, which would be expensive, but worth it.

When we arrived at the Columbus airport, a representative of the charter company met us at their gate. "I have bad news for you," he said. "There are thunderstorms to the south; so we have to take on a co-pilot." We had not realized that one of us had been scheduled to fly in the cockpit! Faced with a terrible dilemma, we had no choice but to draw straws to see who would be left behind. The "poor soul" who drew the short straw could get a seat on a regular airline to Atlanta, and then go on standby for a flight to Montgomery. But we all "knew" he wouldn't make it. The next day, however, when we were in Montgomery, we discovered that our friend found the flight he needed as soon as he arrived in Atlanta, and that the total combined cost of his flights was less than half of what the rest of us paid for our shares of the charter cost.

At plane-side our pilot checked us over, inquiring about our individual weights and lifting our bags one at a time, comparing their relative weights. Finally he placed us in the five passenger seats and arranged our bags in such a way that the plane was balanced from front to back and side to side.

Off we went, on a wild and exciting ride! It was a thrilling experience to fly in that small plane, watching the towns and roads and hills pass by underneath us—except for one thing. Our plane, of course, was too small to be pressurized. And even at the relatively low altitude this plane was flying, the atmospheric pressure was so diminished that our ears felt like they were exploding. After a while the pilot opened the cockpit door and told us, "We're going to stop in Louisville to get some fuel." "At last," I thought, "relief for our ears." But it didn't help. The descent merely reversed the pressure in our inner ears that had by then partially adjusted to the altitude of the flight. The painful agony on the ground was every bit as bad as it had been in the air.

I knew what was in store. Soon we heard, "We're dropping down to Nashville for fuel." And then, "We'll be fueling up in Birmingham." And we did encounter those storms we had been warned about. A couple of times we had to fly around and around masses of clouds, until they moved away from the airfields where we wanted to land. Finally we reached Montgomery. As the small plane touched down on the landing strip, we couldn't believe our eyes. It appeared that all available spaces at the airport, except for the landing strip that we were rolling along, were filled up with airplanes. They ranged from single-passenger propeller planes to full-sized jetliners. Now we understood better our difficulty in getting reservations on regular flights to Montgomery.

Our pilot was directed to one of the few remaining spaces at the airfield, several hundred yards from the terminal. Exiting from our plane, we took our suitcases and started the long hike. Halfway along, we came upon a group of African American men walking in the opposite direction. One of the men stuck out his hand to us. "I'm Nipsy Russell," he said. "And I'm Bob Graetz, from Columbus, Ohio," I replied, stunned to meet the famous comedian. The others were all equally famous actors and singers. Apparently they were on their way to get some things from their chartered plane.

As we drew closer to the terminal, we heard a booming voice on the loudspeaker. "Will those persons walking on the tarmac leave immediately. Otherwise you will be placed under arrest!" All these years after leaving Montgomery, on my first trip back, I was facing the threat that I had most feared during the days of the bus boycott, that of getting arrested and being placed in the white section of a jail. We quickened our pace. But the voice came again, with the same message. All of us were happy when we finally got safely inside the terminal. The others had been fearful, since they were in "foreign" territory. And I was fearful, since I knew what could happen in that Southern town.

We made our way to the boarding house where our group had made reservations, and later found transportation to the City of St. Jude, a Catholic complex which included a school, a hospital, and a church, all serving black residents of Montgomery. There the walkers who had come all the way from Selma had been joined by many thousands of people like us, who wanted to be part of the climactic walk to the state capitol the next day. It was there also that several nationally known singers and others entertained us.

Later that evening I led my Columbus friends on a walking tour of the community around Trinity Lutheran Church, where I had served from 1955–58. I wanted them to see that even in 1965 there were black neighborhoods in Montgomery that were unpaved, with few street lights, where people still lived in truly undesirable conditions. It was after dark, and we saw no one outside of the houses we were passing. My companions were growing uneasy. They didn't know these streets; nor were they that sure that I did. "There is no reason to be afraid," I assured my friends. "You don't see anyone in these houses. But someone is watching out for us from each one of them. We are as safe as we could possibly be."

Soon we arrived at the Trinity Lutheran Church building. We couldn't get inside; but I led them around the church and the parsonage next door, pointing out the places where bombs had landed. Then we crossed the street and went into a bar and sandwich shop on the corner. Knowing that eating together as a mixed racial group was still illegal in Montgomery, we threw caution to the wind and ordered snacks. It wasn't long before a young man walked up to our table and asked, "You're Rev. Graetz, aren't you?" When I confirmed his suspicions, he said, "We thought so." Apparently most of the patrons still recognized me after I had been gone for nearly seven years.

The next day felt to me, in some ways, like a reenactment of the March on Washington in 1963. The crowd at the City of St. Jude had swelled to several times the number who had gathered the evening before. The presence of the military units guarding us was much more obvious as well. As we moved slowly down the back streets toward Montgomery's "West Side" black community, soldiers lined the edges of the pavement. Behind them, before we got into an all-black neighborhood, stood mobs of white people, shouting their obscenities and threats, especially vicious when white marchers passed by. Some of these white hecklers acted as if they were ready to force their way past the bayonets of the soldiers.

As we headed north on Oak Street, I saw Mrs. Rose Dandridge, one of the older members of Trinity Lutheran Church, sitting on her porch, watching the "parade." Her husband Robert had been one of my strongest supporters when we had served the congregation in Montgomery. I broke loose from the marchers and raced across the lawn to give Mrs. Dandridge a hug and a brief greeting, then got back into line to continue the march. If Mr. Dandridge were still alive, he surely would have loved this day!

It wasn't long before we reached our goal, the Alabama State Capitol. But the closest the group could get was the sidewalk at the bottom of the long stairway leading up to the capitol's main door. Governor George Wallace had ordered Alabama state troopers into place, to keep us from getting too close to the building. We were told that the governor was in his office that day, peeking at the crowd between the drawn curtains. Dr. Martin Luther King, Jr., was standing with other civil rights leaders on a platform that been constructed on the street in front of the capitol building.

Dr. King reminded us that just the Sunday before, eight thousand people had started the march from Selma, most of them dropping out quickly to comply with the federal court's limit of three hundred marchers who would make the entire trip, guarded by a large number of well-armed federal troops. "They told us we wouldn't get here," he said. "And there were those who said that we would get here only over their dead bodies, but all the world knows that we are here." The crowd roared its approval. We had successfully confronted the highest power of the state of Alabama. And the President of the United States, Lyndon B. Johnson, had seen fit to support our campaign, calling upon Congress to pass a voting rights act, and closing his speech by announcing, "We shall overcome!" No one could miss the symbolism of his quoting from the "anthem" of the civil rights movement.

Soon the speeches were over and the crowd was told to disperse. We were warned to be especially careful as we made our way back to our homes. The significance of that warning became clear later that night, when Mrs. Viola Liuzzo, a white housewife from Detroit, Michigan, was murdered while driving marchers back to Selma. My companions and I were nervous as we made our way out of town. The soldiers had left their protective posts; but the angry white protestors were still hanging around.

THE CIVIL RIGHTS CAMPAIGN CONTINUED, with actions being carried out in various cities. But I stayed mostly in Columbus over the next two years, focusing on church work and local civil rights activities. I didn't realize that my time at St. Philip Lutheran was drawing to a close. By the end of 1967, I had been called to lead an experimental ministry in Washington, D.C. On November 12, as I preached my last sermon at the church and conducted my last worship service, I was surprised to see how many visitors were present, including several from other churches and synagogues. They

The Graetz family, about 1964. The children are, from left, Robert III, Carolyn, David, Kathryn, Dianne, Jonathan, and Margaret.

were all people with whom I had worked in various civil rights activities in Columbus. Soon I found out why they were there. After church, I was escorted back to the front of the sanctuary for a special program, whose speakers were those visitors.

Mr. Clifford Tyree, the president of the congregation, brought our family to the front to give us a parting gift from St. Philip, a color television set. Cliff said, "We want to make sure they always have some 'color' in their lives." (We assured them that the community we would serve in Washington would also be primarily African American.) The classic photo of that event is a picture of Jeannie and me standing at the front of the church with our seven children, all nine of us in tears. The day closed with a march to East High School across the street, for a special farewell dinner they had arranged.

A few days later the movers had loaded up our furniture and headed east. We worked into the night to finish clearing out the house and loading our car. It was about 4 AM when we finally finished. Our wonderful neighbors, including the Grays on one side and the Harrises on the other, who had already helped us in every way they could, came out in the early morning darkness to pray us on our way to a whole series of new adventures.

Chapter 8

OFF TO WASHINGTON!

This was not our first trip to Washington, D.C. A few years earlier, Jeannie and I had packed our van, loaded up our small utility trailer with a tent and other camping gear, and climbed aboard with our seven children for an excursion to the nation's capitol. Having located a camping ground with reasonable rates in northern Virginia, we reserved a spot for two weeks. Because we were a family of nine, they assigned us to the group camping area, next door to a girl scout troop.

That location was a mixed blessing. One evening when we drove back to camp in a heavy rain, we were grateful to find that the girls had closed the windows and door of our tent and covered up other exposed gear. On the other hand, our children loved learning the girl scouts' camping songs, with lyrics that included such delightful images as "greasy, grimy gopher guts."

Each morning for two weeks, we piled into the van, with lunches packed, and headed to downtown D.C. Several days, of course, were spent exploring the Smithsonian buildings. At noon the first day, we looked in vain for a marked picnic area on the vast expanse of the Washington Mall. So I inquired from a guard at one of the buildings as to whether we were allowed to eat lunch on the grassy field. He assured us it would be fine. We still felt a little uneasy, since we were the only ones eating there. But the next day two or three other families joined us. Each day the number increased! We concluded that everyone was waiting to see if someone else would try it.

But now we were coming as residents, not visitors. For the entire time we lived in the Washington area, we had little time to be tourists, though we hosted many friends and family members. Usually we gave them directions and maps and told them where to catch the right buses. Before our move into the District, we had a temporary home in the Wheaton area of Silver Spring, Maryland, just north of Washington, while the committee in charge of our ministry looked for a house in the target area of Washington that would be large enough for our family, with additional space that could be used for meetings and even a small worship group.

The plan for our experimental ministry was to bring a pastor, a social worker, and a community organizer into a largely African American neighborhood in the northern part of the Northeast quadrant of Washington (the District of Columbia was originally intended to be a square, with its addresses arranged into four quadrants). The pastor would be first on the scene. My brother-in-law, Bill Deutschmann, had initiated the proposal. He was our American Missions Regional Director, whose territory included the Washington area. Since I had had a variety of experiences living and working in black communities in several parts of the country, I was chosen to begin the experiment. We adopted the mission department's assigned number and called ourselves "Lutheran Mission 373."

The temporary housing arrangements turned out to be some-what traumatic. Our children had been accustomed to attending schools with a largely black student population. Now they were surprised to find themselves in classes that were just the opposite. Also, we arrived in November 1967, in the middle of the school year, so they were "new kids" to the children already there. That was certainly the experience of our youngest son, eight-year-old Jonathan. One day he came home from school with a sad look on his face. "I don't like white people!" he declared to his mom. Jonathan was unhappy that the white students were disrespectful toward the black janitor and the one black teacher in the school, in addition to using racially derisive language.

When the Flynn Wells family moved in a few houses from us, we were delighted. This African American family, whose children were the same ages as ours, made us feel more at home. They seemed to be just as happy to meet us. Our families were constantly together. Even so, we were all happy when a large, lovely house was purchased for us in the District at 700 Oglethorpe, NW. We had to wait several months, however, for the house to be renovated before we could move to our new location. It was a few blocks from our target area, but close enough to be acceptable. That would be the first time in years that we had enough space so that no more than two children had to occupy any one bedroom.

In the meantime I organized a Board of Advisors for Lutheran Mission 373, composed mostly of local clergy, including my brother-in-law, with whom I worked very closely. In March 1968 I was sent to the Urban Training Center in Chicago for an intensive one-month course in inner-city ministry. Included was a four-day "plunge." All of us in the class were told ahead of time not to wash, shampoo, or brush our teeth for a few days, wear old worn-out clothing, and hit the streets as if we were homeless. We were each given $6, just $1.50 per day, for emergency needs. March was particularly cold that year in Chicago. My first night on the street I spent eighty cents for a "room" in a flophouse. It was a six-foot cubicle with nothing but a bed. I didn't even get the whole night I paid for. About 2 am I was scared out by a very large rat! My most negative impressions of the experience, however, came from the so-called Christian missions.

They fed us, but only after they preached "at" us and condemned us all to hell. All of the students who participated came back with a new appreciation for the plight of the truly homeless. We also shared stories about the incredible generosity of the people we had met on the street, who in some cases shared the small bottles of wine they had begged money to purchase.

I had been aware that Dr. King and the leaders of the Southern Christian Leadership Conference had been working on plans for a "Poor People's Campaign," scheduled to take place in Washington, D.C., in the summer of 1968. So before I left for Chicago, I had written to Martin, offering my services. I had no way of knowing that within weeks after I wrote, the following April 4, his life would be snuffed out by an assassin's bullet, and Washington would go up in flames in the midst of a riot, as would many other cities across the country. And it happened on Good Friday!

We were still living in Wheaton at that time, since we had not yet moved into our new house in the District. Each morning during the rioting I put on my clerical garb, including my white collar, and drove south on Georgia Avenue into Washington. Every place I went, I saw rifle-bearing soldiers with fixed bayonets, machine guns on the roofs of buildings, and military vehicles cruising the streets. No civilian traffic was allowed, except for people like me, who could demonstrate that we had legitimate business there. I would liked to have attended Dr. King's funeral, but we were all much too busy to consider leaving town at that point. Those of us who served as bridges between the white and black communities needed to stay on the scene, to do whatever we could.

Much of my time during the riots was spent in the simple task of handing out food at a Lutheran church in downtown Washington. Truckloads of provisions were hauled into the church, where we sorted it out and gave sacks of groceries to people living in the nearby area. A well-dressed man walked into the church one day and said to me, "I'm embarrassed to be here. I have a check in my pocket for several hundred dollars. But my bank is closed, so I can't cash it. And even if I could, all the grocery stores have been burned." I simply told him, "That's why we're here."

We tried to establish good relationships with the people who came in for food. At one point when we ran out of supplies, I took advantage of the break in the action to walk around outside the church and talk with some teenagers who were hanging around. Judging by the large number that gathered around me, it was apparent that they needed someone who was ready to listen to what they were thinking and feeling. We weren't talking for long before a military personnel carrier came screeching up to the curb beside us, loaded with well-armed troops. A sergeant forced his way through the crowd to my side. "Are you all right?" he asked. "Sure," I said. "I'm just standing here talking with some of my friends." "Well," he told me, "we got a report that a mob of black kids had a white preacher cornered." As they drove away listening to our hilarious laughter, I realized that nothing could have helped more to cement my relationship with these young people.

The process of mourning the death of our great leader had been disrupted for us by the riots. It would even be appropriate to say that the riots were part of that mourning process. Hundreds of thousands of people whose hopes had been raised by the charismatic leadership of this new Moses now found those hopes dashed. "Whitey" had once more robbed them of any hope for changes in their miserable existence as second-class citizens within the wealthiest, most powerful nation in the world, whose majority population still did not understand their needs and their dreams. Now, in their abject misery, all they could think of was to lash out at somebody, at anybody. Someone had to pay for this dreadful deed.

The nation should have anticipated such a response. Even the titles of books written by protesting authors should have alerted us. There was James Baldwin's *The Fire Next Time,* published in 1963, and *Burn, Baby, Burn, the Watts Riot,* by Jerry Cohen and William S. Murphy, 1966, analyzing the outburst in Watts in 1965. The message of the rioters seemed to be, "If we can't be part of this society, then nobody can. We'll burn it down!"

OUR OWN RESPONSE to the murder of our dear friend and co-worker was a strange mixture. First, we had anticipated Dr. King's death for years. (I myself had not expected to survive Montgomery.) So none of us should have been surprised when the end came. Martin himself had often proclaimed his willingness to sacrifice his life for his cause.

On the other hand, most of us had inappropriately built our hopes and dreams on the one who had articulated those hopes and dreams. The well-being of the movement rose and fell on the fortunes of the leader of the movement. In retrospect, we now realize that was an unfortunate error. It was also unfair to Dr. King. But in the minds of many people across the country, Martin Luther King, Jr., was the movement! And when he fell, the movement came to a halt.

There is another factor that also needs to be explored. The rage that swelled to the surface after Dr. King's murder did not suddenly appear out of nothing. Even though the U.S. Congress had passed the Civil Rights Act in 1964 and the Voting Rights Act in 1965, African Americans had yet to be convinced that these measures would make a difference. Laws, regulations, and court decisions that had been on the books for years were yet to be enforced (for example, *Brown v. Board of Education*, handed down in 1954 and still largely unimplemented in many parts of the South by 1968). Black U.S. citizens were still beaten up, deprived of their rights and their livelihoods, even murdered, with impunity. Many black people were giving up hope that Dr. King's peaceful protests would ever win over the hearts and minds of white Americans. "Black Power" was more than a slogan. It was becoming a way of life. In that context, there was a real danger that Dr. King's influence over the movement was eroding. If he had lived longer, he might not have been venerated as he is today.

To us, Dr King's death was a personal loss. It was a reminder of our human frailty. There have been other civil rights leaders who have completed their missions and gone to their rest, whom we considered to be friends and co-workers. But there is none for whom we had higher respect. Dr. King was one of those unique individuals who enter history from time to time. Those of us who knew him were truly blessed. More than that, Martin's death inspired us to dedicate the remaining portion of our lives to the cause for which he died. And how fitting it was that Dr. King died while he was working to improve the lives of poor people!

THE ORIGINAL PLANS FOR THE Poor People's Campaign, before Dr. King was killed, called for masses of poor people, gathered from all over the country, to demand action by the federal government to deal with the problems of poverty. The campaign's objectives included improvements in jobs, income support, housing, and minimum wage. The stated aim was to "raise to a level of visibility the problem of poverty in this country." If federal officials refused to work for improvements, then first Martin, and ultimately thousands of people, would protest and be arrested, adhering to the same tactics of nonviolent civil disobedience that had been used so successfully in Montgomery more than a decade earlier.

On April 29, less than a month after King's murder, Rev. Ralph Abernathy and about one hundred other leaders met with government officials to explain their objectives. On May 7 a wagon train began making its way to Washington from the South, to be joined by eight other groups coming from all parts of the country. Thousands of poor people from virtually every ethnic group in the land gathered on the Washington Mall, setting up an encampment of plywood and canvas huts which they called "Resurrection City."

The religious community in and around Washington responded very positively. I was a member of the Lutheran Planning Council of Metropolitan Washington, which supported the objectives of the campaign, and also provided for the physical needs of the campers, such as food and sanitation supplies. We were part of a larger grouping of Protestants, Catholics, and Jews, called the Interreligious Legislative Task Force, that organized a massive campaign of support. During July 1968, the Task Force led the effort to pack the gallery of the U.S. House of Representatives every day with church leaders in clerical garb, to put more pressure on Congress to pass legislation concerning jobs, housing, and hunger. Lutherans were assigned to be present on Tuesdays.

Though the acknowledged moral leader of the civil rights movement was no longer with us, the movement had to go on. The Poor People's Campaign was put into action as planned. On the one hand, that effort was an incredible success. Every day, newspapers and television stations across the country carried the story. Some of us who lived in Washington set up an organization we called the "Legislative Task Force," a lobbying group whose sole purpose was to support the goals of the Poor People's Campaign. I was chosen chairman of that group. (This was a different group from the Interreligious Legislative Task Force noted above.) Soon we were mailing as many as six thousand newsletters to activists all over the country, who were in turn writing to their members of Congress. Much of the work of writing, assembling, and stuffing those newsletters took place in our home, around the dining room table. Jeannie and the children and the families of other task force members were pressed into action.

There is no question that issues of poverty in the U.S. received more attention that summer than they had for a long time.

Rev. Abernathy and other campaign leaders and participants took part in congressional hearings and met with federal officials. Some members of Congress and executives even came to visit the encampment, to hear for themselves the appeals of the poor people who had come to the nation's capital to plead their case.

On the other hand, the campaign made only limited gains in achieving its stated purposes. Few significant actions dealing with the problems of poverty were taken by either the legislative or the executive branch of the federal government. And the stance of peace and nonviolence, which had been observed for a month by most of the participants, finally came to an end. A group of some fifty thousand people, mostly from outside of Resurrection City, rallied on June 19 in a "Solidarity Day" in support of the poor people. When a small group of youths from the camp turned to violence after the rally, police drove them back to their "huts." A few days earlier another group of people had resorted to minor violence as they stormed the Supreme Court Building. Earlier in June, Bayard Rustin, our friend from Montgomery days, had been brought in to rescue the floundering movement that was threatening to get out of control. But even he had given up and left; the campaign never recovered.

Even the weather was against us. Rain poured down for most of the time of the encampment. Boardwalks criss-crossed the soggy mall. At one point flooding forced the evacuation of nearly one thousand campers to emergency shelters.

A political cartoonist for the *Washington Post* expressed our frustration the best. The cartoon showed an office worker reporting to a man behind the "Weather Bureau" desk. "There's a Rev. Abernathy who wishes to speak to you, sir." Another cartoon in the *Washington Star* pictured Abernathy in rain gear studying plans for building an ark! The legendary cartoonist Herblock showed another side of our frustration with a sketch of a camper standing beside a tent labeled "Jobs for the poor." In his hand was a newspaper that read, "Congressional committee votes for increases in pensions for congressmen," as a member of Congress walked by, saying, "We can't look out for everybody!"

Less than a year later, in March 1969, we observed another sign of this chasm between the haves and the have-nots. I was a participant in a Palm Sunday memorial service for Dr. King, sponsored by the Southern Christian Leadership Conference, Dr. King's organization. It was held at the Washington Cathedral. I reported to my Lutheran Mission 373 board,

> "It was interesting to see the largely white group leaving the Cathedral after Gen. Eisenhower's funeral while the largely black group was coming to pay their respects to the memory of Dr. King; one could scarcely avoid reflecting on the conclusions of the Kerner Report and its follow-up: 'two societies, separate and unequal.'"

Within a few short months of the assassination of the universally recognized leader of the civil rights movement, the Poor People's Campaign came to an ignominious end as police drove the remaining campers from the site. Unfortunately this was to have been Dr. King's legacy.

In Washington, D.C., it was back to business as usual. For me this meant shifting my time and energy to other aspects of the work of Lutheran Mission 373. By that time I had discovered that the residents of our target area in Northeast Washington had their community organized rather well. They appreciated my offers to do volunteer work for them, but they really didn't need me.

On the other hand, there were almost no significant community organizations in the adjacent Northwest quadrant of Washington, into which we had moved. Because the residents in that area were significantly higher on the economic scale, our church officials had assumed that they would "have it together" better than their poorer neighbors in the Northeast. Though I continued working with organizations in the original target community, my major efforts shifted rather quickly to the neighborhood where we lived. Before long we had brought together an ecumenical ministerial association, as well as several other community groups. Residents in that area were evidently just waiting for someone to light the fire.

Even before the Poor People's Campaign ended, however, I had acquired another new responsibility. Our church's Department of Metropolitan Ministry had organized a Conference of Inner City Clergy and Laity, calling together a group of about one hundred participants from around the country to meet in the Minneapolis/ St. Paul area, near our church headquarters. I was informed that I would be invited to that meeting. But my "activist" past must have caught up with me. A church official took it upon himself to remove my name from the list, apparently deciding that my presence would be too threatening. His veto was soon overturned and I was reinvited. At the gathering were representatives of a wide variety of ethnic groups—African American, Native American, Hispanic, etc. We organized ourselves as the Conference on Inner City Ministries, or CICM. For the time being we pronounced our name "sic 'em." If our church body were to make significant progress in human relations, we would change that to "kiss 'em;" if not, to "kick 'em!"

Elected as secretary of CICM's eleven-member national committee, I spent significant time and energy working with this group over the next few years. The following October, I was a delegate to the national convention of our American Lutheran Church in Omaha, Nebraska. CICM had organized a lobbying effort there which resulted in our church's setting aside $1 million of our national budget to fund local multi-cultural community organizations across the country! One of our top officials was dismayed by the action, angrily telling me that we had been "careless and wasteful" with the church's resources. A few years later, when our national convention was held in San Antonio, Texas, CICM organized itself again to lobby successfully for the ordination of women in the ALC.

When we moved in 1968 from the suburbs to our house at 7th and Oglethorpe, NW, our children experienced major trauma. They had lived nearly their entire lives in largely black communities and had attended mostly black schools and they were looking forward to returning to that familiar setting. None of us had taken into account the impact of the Black Power movement on the students in the schools they would attend. Suddenly our children were outsiders. Worse, at a time when their fellow students were entranced with the new slogan, "Black is beautiful," they were white! The elementary and high schools each had about three thousand students. The only other white children in the elementary school were part of a Mennonite family living near us. There were about two dozen white young people in the high school.

Our children ultimately made many friends, but first they had to overcome their schoolmates' built-in prejudice against white people. Most of our children remember some bad experiences while they were earning the respect of their classmates. Our youngsters learned about discrimination the hard way—by experiencing it, just as African American children had learned for many generations where the shoe had been on the other foot. In later years the children told us their acceptance was speeded up when they told their classmates that their parents had worked with Martin Luther King, Jr.!

Our middle son David had always been strong-willed and assertive. He made his adjustment differently. When he returned from school one day, Jeannie could see that he had been fighting. "What happened?" she asked. "I got into a fight," answered David. "Why?" "Some boy called me a nigger." David said. "And what did you do?" "I called him one right back." Our younger children did not even know what that word meant.

Even school administrators had to deal with the impact of black power on their schools. On one occasion, I helped the students at our nearby Paul Junior High School negotiate with their principal for permission to stage a demonstration for world peace. We resolved that conflict amicably, with the students parading with signs around the school.

Our oldest daughter, Margee, graduated from Coolidge High School in June 1970. The ceremony was held in the prestigious Washington Cathedral. Since my daughter was among the graduating students, I was asked to offer a prayer during the ceremony. Female students were sitting in a group at the front of the auditorium, with the male students behind them. The girls were first to receive their diplomas. I was thrilled when Margee stepped out of line to give me a hug as she passed across the chancel. When the girls had all been reseated, the principal announced, "The boys will please stand." No one moved. Again he spoke. "The boys will please stand." A voice from the male section sounded. "Ain't no boys here," he said. "We're men!" "Will the men please stand," said the principal. Applauding their own newfound respect, which they had demanded and received, the "men" stood and received their diplomas.

Margee had a part-time job at the Jr. Hot Shoppes restaurant near us on Eastern Avenue, the street that marked the border between Washington, D.C., and Maryland. One evening she called me from work. "Daddy, you've got to come here right now," she told me. "Rev. Abernathy is across the street in a park, preaching to a crowd of people." I hurried to the restaurant as quickly as I could and walked across the street. Ralph was certainly surprised to see me. We had not been together for about ten years. The next time we saw each other, several years later, he was speaking at Capital University in Columbus, Ohio, and I was giving a presentation at the Lutheran seminary across the street.

Margee, our oldest, was one of our more adventuresome children. The late 1960s was a time of many marches and demonstrations against racism and other forms of oppression, and for world peace. Margee took part in her share of them. On one occasion, she and I were involved in the same peace march, taking part with two different groups. The Washington police eventually dispersed the crowd with tear gas. I was north of the target area, and was able to make my way home fairly soon. But Margee was to the south. It was many hours before we saw our daughter.

On another occasion, when I was out of town, Margee was with a group of young people who were all arrested in a peace demonstration. At one o'clock in the morning, Jeannie had to drive downtown to the police station to bail our daughter out of jail, as did the other parents. One boy's parents could not be reached, so Jeannie bailed him out as well and brought him home.

Margee helped a number of groups to become more multicultural by her very presence, including the Washington, D.C., Junior Orchestra and a local drama group. We are proud to say that our children are still taking public stands against injustice wherever they see it.

THE YEAR 1969 BROUGHT US one of our most exciting adventures. I was named as one of seven delegates from our church body to a conference in Austria. It was the third of four regional gatherings sponsored by the Lutheran World Federation dealing with "Christian Social Responsibility." Some ninety delegates attended from North America, Africa, and both western and eastern Europe. Our good friend Walter Tarpley, a member of St. Philip Lutheran Church in Columbus, Ohio, was also a delegate.

For many years I had been reporting to Jeannie about all the interesting places I had traveled and promising that some day I would take her with me on one of these trips. By arranging for less expensive air transportation, housing, and meals, I was able to take Jeannie along to Austria. In fact our Sabena Airline tickets brought with them the free use of a Volkswagen automobile for three weeks. Even then it would not have been possible for us to travel together if it had not been for a dear friend, Dutch Grohs, the wife of another Lutheran pastor in the area. Dutch moved herself and her two children into our house for the three weeks that we would be gone. We filled the freezer and the pantry and left some cash with Dutch for other needs. When we returned, the freezer and the pantry were both bare, and the money was gone. But it was worth every penny.

The conference was held in Baden-bei-Wien, which means "The Baden that is close to Vienna." Since the meetings lasted only seven days, we still had two full weeks to travel around in Austria, with minor excursions into southern Germany and northern Italy. Our fluency in German was not great but we got along, staying mostly in farmhouses and in rooms over taverns. We just looked for signs saying "Zimmer frei," which means "room available." We'll never forget watching television pictures of our astronauts walking on the moon that summer, as we sat with a farm family in western Austria.

At the Baden conference I was part of the working group dealing with the relationship between the social ministry of the church and the social policies of governments. At first, most of us Westerners tried to speak cautiously. We were aware that our fellow Lutherans from eastern Europe would be returning to Soviet-dominated nations, where they would be held accountable for anything that came out of our deliberations. But it was they who led the way. They urged us to speak boldly to governments in the east and the west, without fear of the consequences. In our report to the conference, we reminded the group that it is still appropriate for Christians to engage in civil disobedience to influence their governments, as we had done in Montgomery and in many other cities during the civil rights movement. (Years later, when Jeannie and I were traveling in East Germany, we discovered that oppressed people in the entire eastern block followed our civil rights movement with great interest, even borrowing some of our tactics. Dr. King was a great hero to them.) Our working group also reminded the church that she has a special responsibility to minister to the disadvantaged, including members of minority races, the poor, and others who are exploited.

BY 1970 THE BOARD of Lutheran Mission 373 felt that we had learned as much as we could about our experimental ministry. There would always be opportunities for the church to provide specialized workers to assist local communities. In some situations, that effort might result in active, self-supporting congregations. But not where we were. There were already more churches than the community could support. My board advised me to begin looking for another position. Lutheran Mission 373 was officially closed at the end of May.

Meanwhile, the pastor of St. James Lutheran Church had accepted another call and had left in January. I served as interim pastor there until the end of 1970. When we had arrived in Washington in 1967, I had been asked to join St. James to give them some assistance. The congregation was mostly white though they had been trying diligently to add African American members. We brought in Mike Hickman, a black Howard University theological student, on a part-time basis to give St. James a better image. We also started having children's movie nights at church. Cruising the neighborhood streets in our Ford van, we gathered up the children. Our son Jon recently reminded us that the most we ever squeezed into the van was twenty-seven. That was obviously before the era of seat-belt laws.

In March 1970 we heard that a local theater was showing a documentary about Dr. King. Gathering together our seven children and many of their neighborhood friends, we headed for the movie house, filling a large portion of the central section of seats. The producers had put together news footage from the Montgomery Bus Boycott and the entire civil rights movement, including Dr. King's murder and its aftermath. Our biggest surprise was that my face appeared from time to time during the film. Theatergoers who were not part of our group probably never did figure out what was going on, as our children and their friends would call out occasionally, "There's Daddy!" "There's Mr. Graetz!" (We wish we had written down the name of the documentary, so we could locate a copy of it. We'd love to see it again.)

As hard as we tried at St. James, nothing worked. And the congregation's membership dwindled. When our organist retired to Florida, she offered to teach our son Bobby how to play that instrument, so he could take over for her. He had studied piano, but never organ. Yet this brave sixteen-year-old stepped in and played for worship services the rest of the year, and played well! The members of St. James did not give up entirely. Before the congregation ceased its operations, they donated their building and equipment to an African American congregation that was looking for a larger worship facility. Unfortunately the new congregation had the same problem in that neighborhood. Bringing in their members from another part of the city, they too were unsuccessful in winning their new neighbors.

By October 1970 I had accepted the position of legislative

representative (lobbyist) for the Ohio Council of Churches. And for the last three months of the year I was commuting between Washington and Columbus, Ohio. A new set of adventures was about to begin.

Chapter 9

THE 'GOOD GUY' LOBBYIST

As my ministry in Washington, D.C., drew to an end, members of the board of advisors grew more anxious for my family's financial well-being. They were afraid my salary would run out and we would have nowhere to go. But Jeannie and I were certain that God had another special ministry for us. We just didn't know what it was. I was interviewed for staff positions in different parts of the country. The agency where I most wanted to work turned me down, because, they said, I was "over-qualified."

In the meantime, my friend Jim Nichols, a Lutheran pastor in Columbus, was chairing a group charged with filling a staff position at the Columbus-based Ohio Council of Churches. They needed a director for their Ecumenical Commission on Church and Government (ECOCG) who would also serve as lobbyist for the Council. The interviews had been completed but the committee was not totally satisfied with its available choices.

As Jim was traveling to a meeting with his bishop, he shared his concern for finding a good director. He told the bishop, "Bob Graetz would be perfect for this position, but he is tied up in Washington." "Oh, no," said the bishop, "his ministry there is coming to an end." I got an emergency phone call that evening from Jim. Could I fly to Columbus and meet with the committee? Over the next few days I was interviewed individually by most members of Jim's group, and by Carlton Weber, the director of the Ohio Council of Churches.

Within days I was offered the position, which carried a salary of $12,800 a year, including a housing allowance. The challenges of this new opportunity thrilled me, but Jeannie and I had a problem. For my entire ministry we had lived in parsonages. Having never owned a house, we had no equity and precious little money in our bank account—families with seven children tend to be a little slow at building up savings.

First we had to find an available house that was large enough and in our price range. We wanted to live in a racially integrated neighborhood or one that was totally African American. But we dared not locate too close to St. Philip Lutheran Church as we did want to be perceived as getting in the way of the new pastor there. Before long we found a suitable house with an asking price of a little more than $26,000. Furthermore, we could buy the house on a 6 percent loan assumption, much lower than the going rate at that time. But the address was 100 Electric Avenue, in Westerville, Ohio. For years, this Columbus suburb had had the reputation of being a racist white enclave. We had a difficult time believing that God would bring us to a community like that. All the other doors, however, seemed to be closed, so we signed the contract. Later we realized that God was dealing with our own prejudices: We had to learn that not all white people were "bad!"

Now our only problem was paying for our new home. Since we were assuming the loan, we had to pay off the equity which the previous owner had accumulated. We emptied our bank account, borrowed our children's savings (promising to repay them with interest), and got an advance on my first month's salary. But we were still short. Fortunately for us, one of the members of the Council's board of directors was a banker from a small town northeast of Columbus. She made a personal loan to us off the books.

By early 1971, we were Ohioans once again. Since Jeannie and I married in 1951, no matter where we have moved, we have always come back to Ohio.

It did not take me long to find out that my new position was much more than a full-time job. My calendar for January 1970 lists meetings of a "Public Assistance Task Force" and a "Tax Reform Task Force," as well as the names of local councils of churches all over Ohio, denominational bodies, and meetings of several legislative committees at the Statehouse in Columbus. I began to meet lobbyists who worked for the League of Women Voters, Catholic Charities, and other non-profit organizations with whom I would be working closely for all the years I was with the Council. We called ourselves the "Good Guy Lobbyists."

I had been told that my responsibilities would fall into four main categories: 1) Become informed about legislative and congressional actions regarding the public policy issues of concern to the Ohio Council of Churches; 2) Provide information and guidance to church leaders about those public policy issues; 3) Develop personal relationships with members of the Ohio Legislature, state administrators, and our Ohio congressional delegation; and 4) Recruit, train, inform, and motivate a cadre of activists who would agree to lobby their legislators and members of Congress.

None of us had anticipated the impact of the November 1970 election of John Gilligan as Ohio governor. He wasted little time in offering a proposal to implement the major plank in his platform: making Ohio's tax structure more progressive by adding a state income tax to the mix of property and sales taxes. This change would provide additional funds for public services, including education and public welfare. The Ohio Council of Churches joined a large coalition of organizations supporting the governor's tax proposals. I found myself in an endless string of meetings, strategizing and maneuvering over every aspect of the budget bill. Our communications with church leaders and constituents at that time were heavily loaded with tax matters.

The massive changes in tax policy would not be put into action without extensive legislative deliberation. The state's budget was technically required to be adopted by June 30, the end of the fiscal year. But final action did not come until the end of September, after a series of interim resolutions to keep the state afloat. All of the compromises were finally worked out and both houses of the legislature and the governor were ready to sign off on the measure. The House adopted the bill. Action in the Senate was the only remaining step before it would be sent to the governor for his promised signature. All of us lobbyists, who had spent most of our waking hours on this measure since early in the year, were gathered in the Senate chamber. In accordance with their regular procedure, the chaplain of the Senate was called upon to open the session with a prayer. "Dear Lord," he began, "we have been laboring for these nine months. We pray that today we may be delivered!" The chamber exploded into laughter. The bill was passed and was soon signed into law.

Governor Gilligan turned out to be a courageous and positive leader on many issues, with the OCC supporting many of his initiatives. Tax reform was only one of the major issues of concern to the Ohio Council. Also on that list were many proposals to enhance the lives of those living in poverty; concerns for alleviating the oppression of racial minorities, migrant farm workers, women, the aging, the handicapped, and other groups; and proposals to reform the structures of government and make it more responsive to its citizens, including measures to achieve world peace.

I found myself devoting a major portion of my schedule to writing and speaking. In addition to preparing testimony for legislative committees on behalf of the Council, I wrote a monthly column

The man on the left is U.S. Senator Mark Hatfield, and the one on the right is a bearded Bob Graetz, as a Washington lobbyist.

on issues for the *Ohio Christian News,* periodic analyses of specific measures, weekly updates for the church leadership in Ohio while the Legislature was in session, and action alerts when we needed our constituents to write or call their law-makers.

I particularly enjoyed one writing assignment. From July 1973 through November 1987—several years after I left the Council of Churches—I wrote a monthly "Point of View" column for the *Catholic Times* of the Columbus Diocese. The column offered non-Catholics an opportunity to share our thoughts. Over the years I got more responses to those essays than from most things I have written.

I gave speeches to audiences ranging from annual denominational gatherings to small groups in individual congregations. I was the OCC staff member who had the major responsibility of speaking to news media on behalf of the Council. And I had the task of producing and hosting several radio and television programs each week, mostly interviewing legislators, public officials, and other community leaders on current issues.

To maximize the influence of church members on public officials, we organized legislative seminars, where we recruited, informed, and motivated our activists who then became members of a group we called Ohio Impact. Many state councils of churches had similar groups. Once a year we would gather our activists in Washington to lobby their members of Congress in person. State impact leaders met in Washington even more frequently.

I particularly appreciated those visits in Washington. Not only did I establish long-lasting relationships with the lawmakers and their staffs, but there were two other sites on Capitol Hill which I always included in my schedule. One was the office of my long-time friend Paul Simon, who was first elected to the House of Representatives from Illinois while I served at the Council. He made the resources of his office available to me in case I needed special help or information. The second was the office of U.S. Rep. John Conyers, from Detroit. After Mrs. Rosa Parks had moved north from Montgomery in the late 1950s, she became a member of Conyers's office staff in Detroit. Every time I talked with him, Rep. Conyers enjoyed telling me that he was the only member of Congress who had a staff person who got more requests to speak than the member did!

I have fond memories of one presentation I made to a Methodist Church in Arcadia, Ohio. They wrote to the Council complaining that "of the eight issues on which you pronounced decisions and lobbied, before the last Ohio Legislature, our group only agreed with two. It is rather disturbing to note that either grass roots opinions are grossly ignored or there is a serious communication gap."

When I met with this group, I explained that it was their own denominational representatives, along with those of the other faith groups, who determined the public stances of the Council. I also told them how to have a more effective impact on their own church leaders. Before I left that evening, several people from the church had become members of the Ohio Impact network!

To maximize the impact of the Council's lobbying efforts, we published an annual *Voting Record* for the Legislature, listing the issues on which the Council had positions and the votes of the members. Our first issue, after the 1971 legislative session, created quite a furor. We had weighted the votes according to the priorities of the OCC and given the members plus or minus scores, according to whether they voted with or against our positions. The result was that several members of the House ended up with negative totals. In the following years we gave the results on a range of 0-100 percent of support for the Council, but we certainly got their attention. And every year after that the members eagerly awaited our report. Jeannie, our children, and some of their friends volunteered many hours of their time folding and assembling copies of the *Voting Record*.

As if I did not have enough to do already, for a period I became a part-time staffer for the national lobbying group, Common Cause. And I was also asked to be a member of a task force on racism for my national church body, the American Lutheran Church. More in line with the expectations of my primary position, I became an unofficial chaplain to members of the Legislature and their staffs. Often I was asked to give counseling to or to pray with people at the Statehouse. And I was part of a weekly Legislative Prayer Breakfast.

There was one additional responsibility which I declined to accept. When Jimmy Carter was running for president in 1976, U.S. Senator Howard Metzenbaum was up for reelection. For several years some of my associates had encouraged me to run for the legislature or for congress. That year they urged me even more strongly to run for a seat in the U.S. House. Jimmy Carter was sometimes referred to as "Grits." His running mate was Fritz Mondale. "We have the perfect ticket," my friends told me. "We can campaign for Grits and Fritz, and Metz and Graetz!" Every time we think of this episode, Jeannie expresses her profound thanks to me that I didn't try it. She was afraid I might have won!

As MIGHT HAVE BEEN EXPECTED, I was particularly interested in legislation that dealt with race relations. I grew close to the African American members of the Legislature. Some of those relationships remain strong to this day. The one piece of legislation that was a priority in my mind, though it was largely symbolic, was the measure that made Martin Luther King Day a holiday in Ohio. It was sponsored by William Bowen, an African American senator from Cincinnati. I had the privilege of serving as secretary of the coalition that supported and successfully lobbied for the bill.

My first opportunity to speak to a group on King Day came on January 16, 1978, when I made a presentation at the Defense Construction Supply Corporation in Columbus. Nowadays my schedule for King Day presentations stays booked up for several years ahead. In 1973 I began another pattern that has continued to this day. I made my first speech on Dr. King and the Montgomery Bus Boycott to a school class. Before long our friend David Keck, then a teacher at Westerville High School, which our children attended, had me speaking to his history classes every year. Now Jeannie and I speak to many school groups, from pre-school to graduate classes, all over the country.

I was also instrumental in bringing African American leaders to programs of the Ohio Council of Churches. Our 1976 Ohio Pastors' Convocation featured a major address by then-Congressman Andrew Young from Atlanta. His speech followed a choral presentation by the Wilberforce University Choir and Singers, whose final selection was a partly spoken and partly sung rendition of "Battle

Hymn of the Republic." In my column in the *Catholic Times,* I told how much we had all been moved, then added:

> Andy Young said it for all of us. He talked about his friend Martin King and the total sacrifice he had made. He talked about the black experience, the readiness to make unbelievable sacrifices because one has seen "the glory of the coming of the Lord." The black person could complain that "I been 'buked and I been scorned"; but he survived, because his gaze was fixed on the other side of the Jordan . . .
>
> The young singers were the beneficiaries, Young explained, of the sacrifices of Martin Luther King and the others who walked the streets of Montgomery.
>
> I remembered an old woman in Montgomery who walked to work rather than ride the bus during the boycott. "I'm not doing this for myself," she said. "I've got a little grandson at home. I want him to be able to get on that bus and pay his money and take his seat." With that she walked off into the pouring rain.
>
> It is remotely possible that her grandson had grown up, moved to Ohio and gone to Wilberforce University. And that on a Tuesday night in January he stood on a stage at Vets' Memorial Auditorium in Columbus. And that he spoke the words of Dr. Martin Luther King, Jr., while an old freedom fighter sat in the audience and cried.

We were not so successful on another issue relating to oppression—the adoption of an Equal Rights Amendment to the U.S. Constitution that would have guaranteed equal rights and equal protection for women. Though the Council strongly supported the measure, working closely with the League of Women Voters, our lobbying efforts fell far short of those of our opponents. Phyllis Schaffley and a large group of women stormed the Statehouse when the proposal was being debated, encouraging our lawmakers to vote No. Ironically, they faced a practical problem that they had not counted on. The Ohio Statehouse was constructed when there were only a handful of women moving through its halls. And the women's restrooms were scattered and hidden; the secretarial staff could find them, but not public visitors. I found myself spending my precious time leading groups of women to their hidden restrooms.

I invested considerably more time and energy, but also without success, on a good-government proposal. For at least ten years I worked with my friend and dedicated volunteer David Horn on the issue of gerrymandering—the drawing of legislative and congressional district lines so as to favor one party or the other.

Both major parties have been guilty. The result often is weird district lines that group together large numbers of voters who support the minority party, so that that party ends up with safer districts but fewer of them. Voters are effectively disenfranchised. David and I worked together, each time with a different coalition of organizations, on a series of proposed constitutional amendments to address this problem. Our proposal required setting up a competition in the drawing of the lines, with the proposal having the most compact districts being accepted, thus taking the "politics" out of the process.

I still believe it was a great idea, but we never got very far with it. It was always the party out of power that supported our efforts—in other words, the party that didn't have the votes to enact the proposal.

In another type of gerrymandering, which is all too common, Democrats and Republicans have colluded to draw "safe districts" for both major political parties. Studies have shown that once a member of Congress gets past the first reelection, the member is virtually guaranteed to be able to serve as long as he or she wants to.

That kind of arrogant manipulation of the political system carries with it several tragic consequences.

The first, and most obvious, is that voters are effectively locked out of the process. A handful of professional politicians are allowed to determine who our elected representatives will be. That is quite the opposite of what a democracy is supposed to be. And with every decennial redistricting, the number of truly competitive congressional districts grows smaller. As a result, the parties are able to shift massive amounts of campaign finances into those few districts, further distorting the process.

A second consequence is that, since the contests in noncompetitive districts are basically internecine, the winners tend to come from the most conservative wing of the Republican Party and the most liberal wing of the Democratic Party. We have witnessed the impact of that shift in the bitter partisan battles that have become more common in the last decade or so in Congress.

And a third effect of gerrymandering, less obvious than the others, is that some minority groups tend to be underrepresented in Congress and in state houses. There are examples in a number of states of districts that are represented by African Americans who regularly win their races by huge margins. On the surface that would seem to favor the African American community. In reality, however, the impact is just the opposite. Many of those districts could be redrawn so that there is a realistic possibility of electing two black representatives where there is now one. The current system favors the incumbent officeholders, but not the larger community.

WE WEREN'T ALWAYS OPERATING under "full speed ahead" pressure. When the legislators went home for vacation or for some other reason, the lobbyists and the legislative staffers all breathed a sigh of relief. Secretaries and aides would say to me, "Now we can finally get something done!"

My work at the Statehouse became a family affair for a time. When I learned that aides working in some Statehouse agencies were appointed by legislators, I asked our son Jon if he was interested. He jumped at the chance. I put in a good word for him with a friend who worked for the Senate leadership, and Jon was soon on the job. A few months later I began to get requests for a campaign contribution for someone who was running for reelection. I explained that I could not make such contributions because of my position with the Council of Churches. When the requests kept coming, I realized what was happening, so I alerted Jon that he should not count on working in that job much longer. We realized we were both too naïve about the political "game." Sure enough, Jon was soon notified that his services were no longer needed.

I wore a full beard much of the time I served as a lobbyist. Late one spring, I decided to celebrate the approaching end of the legislative session by shaving it off. By that time, both legislators and their staff people knew me well enough that they didn't mind expressing their feelings, which ranged from "Good grief!" to "I don't know who you are, but up until last week I used to see your bearded father around here quite a bit."

As busy as my Council of Churches job was during normal legislative sessions, my survival abilities were tested in 1972 when the position of one of our program directors was eliminated due to budget cuts. Many of his responsibilities were shifted to other organizations, but those that remained were added to my list of obligations. And about that same time Henry Gerner, our Director of Poverty and Economic Justice, was out of action for months after a heart attack and quadruple bypass. Since the issues he worked on were a major focus of our legislative concerns, I was the only one on our staff who could fill in for him during those months. Jeannie and I were relieved and grateful when Henry returned to his job.

By the end of 1973, I had accepted a Call to serve as associate pastor of Christ the King Lutheran Church in the Columbus area, where we had become members. The Ohio Council of Churches started finding a replacement for me. A few months later, when a candidate had been chosen, he decided at the last minute that the job was not for him. So the process was started all over again. Once again the selection committee come down to the final interviews. I received a phone call from Carlton. "You know this job better than anybody. Would you do us a favor and take part in the last round of interviews of our final candidates?" Carlton took me to lunch between the morning and afternoon sessions. It was then that he asked me, "Would you be interested in coming back to your old job?" That very thought had been going through my own mind. Before long I had indeed gone back from the church to the Council.

Also in 1973, we took another significant step in our lives. Bob Swanger, the senior pastor at Christ the King Lutheran Church, liked to camp as much as we did. He and his family owned some acreage in Vinton County in southeastern Ohio. They invited us to go camping with them, and we fell in love with the area. It was much like my home in West Virginia. We began looking for land to buy not far from the Swangers. It just happened that in the summer of 1973 the Sheriff was auctioning off some parcels of land to pay for back taxes owed. We bought township maps and began to explore the sites that were going to be sold. Twice Jeannie went to Saturday auctions, when I was not available. At the second sale, taking our youngest son Jon with her, she bid successfully for a forty-acre plot of wilderness land. (Jon actually made the final bid.)

Our family decided to call the tract "The Promised Land," the name our daughter Dianne came up with. That land became our refuge. We traveled to Vinton County as often as we could, preparing the place for that time in the future when we could build a house and retire there. It would be six years before things began to develop in earnest. And then they developed in a way that we could not have imagined. God was at work again, leading us through another new adventure.

As I reported in my *Catholic Times* column, "Six years ago we purchased forty acres of wilderness land in Vinton County, in southeastern Ohio, which we call the Promised Land. As soon as we had carved a lane back through the woods, we built an outhouse (first things first!), then started on a pole barn, using trees from our woods, scavenged boards and rough-cut lumber from local sawmills."

I went on to tell the miraculous story about a friend, Gary Claar, who had quit his job in Columbus to build us a house on our wilderness land, and how we had gotten moved that summer to our rustic quarters, with neither electricity nor running water. I had combined vacation, study leave, and sabbatical to give me five months to work on the project. When the weather was bad, I worked on my study and writing projects; when it was good, I was a builder. Our house was years in building, as we slowly added amenities, little by little. It is still not complete. We even had a wind generator for a while, though we found out that wind energy is most unreliable in our part of the country.

I concluded my column with, "We have no idea where we are going from here. But we know that our future, just like our present and past, is in God's hands. There can't be a better way to live!"

Carlton Weber, OCC's director and my boss, was not pleased by what he had read in the *Catholic Times*. He asked me to appear before the Council's personnel committee to explain how I intended to fulfill my responsibilities to the Council of Churches while I was living seventy miles away. Though they accepted my explanation then, there were probably some misgivings a few years

The Graetz home at the Promised Land.

later when I was flooded in at home, unable to cross the creek at the bottom of our hill for four days after we received more than three inches of rain!

Our first winter at the Promised Land was the most difficult. We had spent all of our free time getting the house ready to move into, and almost none on accumulating a supply of firewood. Beginning in September 1979, I was back on the job in Columbus full-time. Each weekend I raced home to cut and split enough wood to carry Jeannie and our youngest daughter Carolyn through the following week. Somehow we survived, even when the snows came. Our land was at the top of a steep hill that was difficult to climb without a four-wheel-drive vehicle. Each Friday I parked our pickup truck at the bottom of the hill and walked the mile to our house, usually in the dark, and usually carrying groceries and clothes in both arms. I was never in better physical condition. (Our county and township later worked together to build a less-steep road for us on the other side of our hill.)

Carolyn lived with us at the Promised Land during her last two years of high school. Her school bus picked her up on the other side of the hill, one and a half miles from our house. For the first few weeks in the fall of 1979, Carolyn had to take off her shoes and wade across the creek at the bottom of the hill. Then one of our neighbors, Edsel Minton, made an announcement one Sunday in the little Methodist Church we attended in Vinton County. "Whoever's available tomorrow morning, we're going to meet on Sowers Road and build a foot-bridge for Carolyn." On Monday morning about a dozen men showed up with donated logs, lumber, tractor, nails, generator, circular saw, and hammers. By mid-afternoon, Carolyn had her bridge! If we didn't know it before, we learned that day how important it is to have and to be good neighbors.

Less than three years later, in 1982, I convinced the personnel committee that it was better for me to be reduced to three-quarter time and to hire an Impact Network Developer during the legislative session. A friend of mine named Bob Erickson, who had been doing similar work, stepped into that new position. And by the beginning of 1983 the finances of the Council had been reduced so much that several of us on the staff were reduced to half-time. I was even happier with that arrangement. Our personal financial needs had been lessened because we no longer had a mortgage to pay. We had borrowed money from Jeannie's parents for the construction materials used in our home. And our house in Westerville had appreciated sufficiently that the sale price covered the remaining balance on the mortgage, the amount we had borrowed from my in-laws, and the cost of a tractor, chain saw, and other equipment we had to have to live in the Promised Land. God was good!

I explained to the personnel committee that it was not possible to do my job on a half-time basis, but that I would do what I could. I was glad for the extra time to cut wood and do other jobs at home, as well as to get involved in what was going on in our new county. Many Sundays I was preaching at one of the churches in Vinton County or in one of our Lutheran Churches in the area that did not have a pastor. On June 26 of that year I preached for the first time at St. John Lutheran Church, outside of Logan. It was love at first sight. We really liked the people there. It was a small enough congregation they could afford to pay a pastor on only a third-time basis, or two days a week. I served as interim pastor on that basis for the rest of the year. As 1983 drew to an end, the congregation voted to call me as their pastor, still for two days a week.

The OCC's personnel committee, in the meantime, had concluded that they needed a full-time legislative agent. When Carlton asked me if I was ready to go back to full-time, I replied instead that I was ready to leave. At age fifty-five, I wasn't really retiring. As a matter of fact, I continued at St. John for thirteen more years before my official retirement. Even then my so-called "retirement" was simply a shift to a different set of activities every bit as busy as before, maybe more so.

We have mementoes given to us at the time of my retirement from the Council. And I also treasure the letters we received from members of the Congress and the Legislature. One state senator introduced a resolution honoring me for my service. Another one sent a note that said simply, "Dear Bob, No one ever retires!" One of the members of Congress I admired the most, U.S. Rep. Don Pease, wrote that he knew where Logan is, because he went to school at Ohio University, not far away. And my friend U.S. Senator Paul Simon, himself a Lutheran, wrote, "I don't know where Logan, Ohio, is, but tell the parishioners of St. John Lutheran Church that they are fortunate."

My best reflection on my years at the Council of Churches may be what I wrote in a December 1986 column for the *Catholic Times*.

Some years ago I served as resource to a class at Trinity Lutheran Seminary. A group of Lutheran pastors from several states had come together to learn how to deal more effectively with social issues. My role was to help them to understand the workings of government and the techniques of citizen lobbying. I was working as lobbyist for the Ohio Council of Churches at the time.

At the end of my last session with the group, the instructor asked, "Who would like to express our appreciation to Bob for what he's done with us?" One young man rose and walked to the front. Removing a crucifix from his own lapel, he placed it on mine, saying, "When you go back down to the Legislature, I want them to know for whom you are really working." Many times after that I was stopped in the halls of the Statehouse and asked, "What's that on your lapel?" I would tell the story of how I was given my crucifix. And I would remind the questioners and myself that it was Jesus Christ for whom I was really working.

Jeannie and I did not forget for whom we were working when I left the Council. Nor did we stop working to alleviate the oppression of those whom we often think of as "the least" of Jesus's brothers and sisters. But I did not, and could not, know at the time that there would be another oppressed group, to whom I had paid little attention, that would become increasingly important in my ministry and my life. And it was represented in our own family!

Chapter 10

A New Battleground

Slowly over time, the focus of our civil rights involvement broadened. When I was in high school, my concern was limited to a troubling inconvenience experienced by Jewish friends. Halfway through my undergraduate studies in college, that concern expanded to include a class of people with whom I had so far had no meaningful contact—American Negroes. Jeannie had similar limitations. Our ignorance of this new cultural group dissipated rapidly over the next few years, however, through direct personal contact with the Columbus chapter of the NAACP, St. Philip Lutheran Church, our African American fellow students on campus at Capital University, and later the members of Community Lutheran Church and our other neighbors in Los Angeles.

Our "crash course" in African American history and culture during those years could not totally prepare us for what we were to experience in segregated Alabama during the Montgomery Bus Boycott, or even in Columbus, Ohio, during the continuation of the civil rights movement. And unfortunately our single-minded focus during that time gave us the false impression that African Americans were the only group whose oppression warranted our concern. I felt like a slow learner when it came to matters dealing with discrimination against women, Native Americans, people with disabilities, the aged, poor people, etc. But my eyes were gradually opened, thanks in large measure to the ministry of members of those very groups, who played a major role in my education.

I came to understand that it is totally inappropriate to discriminate against anyone on the basis of something over which they had no control, such as race, gender, language, and culture. Over the years that list expanded regularly. But I also realized that all of us had to make personal choices, and some of us did not choose wisely. Those who took up drug habits could not blame society for the consequences. Lazy people who lost their jobs could not claim they had been unfairly treated (though many tried). And, in my mind, a person who "chose" the homosexual lifestyle could not expect to receive the approval of the society in which I lived and worked. That final assumption by me would soon be put to the test, within our own family.

Jeannie and I have warned other parents for years, "No two children are alike. Don't expect any of your children to fit a particular mold." That certainly was true in our family. We are extremely proud of all of our children, but they are as different as they could possibly be.

Margaret Ellen, or Margee, our first-born, arriving in November 1952, was a caregiver from the time she was small. We were delighted to have such an efficient "built-in" baby-sitter. (She later changed her name to Meta Ellis and now works off and on as a hospice nurse, one of the most demanding care-giving roles I can imagine.)

Diann Elaine, our second daughter, was born in January 1956, just after the bus boycott began! We couldn't imagine a sweeter, calmer child. What a gift from God in those strained times. We called her our "Little Sunshine Girl." Diann now works as a rural mail carrier, and is a delight to all her customers. She and Meta are both living in the High Desert in southern California.

David Ellis, who was next, epitomized the "strong-willed child."

The seven Graetz children, arranged here in birth order at a 1988 family picnic: from left, Margaret, Robert III, Diann, David, Kathryn, Jonathan, and Carolyn.

Jeannie remembers how angry he became when she would say to him, "If you can't discipline yourself, then we'll do it for you." He and I tangled often, but he is now the only member of our family in the military, an Army lieutenant colonel who is chief of chaplains at the Louisville, Kentucky, Veterans' Medical Facility. And he is the only one of our children who entered the full-time ministry. David was born January 1, 1957, only nine days before the second bombing of our house.

Kathryn Eileen was born in July 1958, just before we returned to Ohio. Though not the only one of our children with wanderlust, she exemplifies that spirit. More than twenty-five years ago, Kathryn traveled to Paris, France, where she met and fell in love with a Muslim man from Morocco. Living now with her own six children in a suburb of Paris, she has no desire to return to the USA. "It's too dangerous there," she tells us. (More than half of our twenty-six wonderful grandchildren are racially and culturally mixed.)

Jonathan William, or Jon, born in November 1959, is our preeminent scholar, now a math teacher in a private high school in Dayton, Ohio. (As might have been expected, he was bored to death in elementary school.) The Miami Valley School, where he teaches, is the most multicultural educational institution we have ever seen. Jon is deeply involved in civil rights studies and activities. He will surely be the one to whom our "civil rights mantle" passes when we are too old to continue our work.

And Carolyn Jeanne, the youngest, arrived in May 1963. She is probably our fiercest "mother-tiger." She has a daughter who was born with such severe disabilities that her very survival can be attributed to Carolyn's demands for proper medical treatment, as well as her own full-time "tender loving care." Nurses told us that without Carolyn's devotion, Elizabeth would surely have died within days of her birth. Carolyn, who lives in Pittsburgh, now has a stepson who also has severe disabilities, and a "yours, mine, and ours" family that includes ten mostly multiracial children.

Then there is Robert Sylvester Graetz, III, our second child and my namesake, who was born in March 1954. How I treasured those times when my father and my son and I, the three Roberts, were together. Bobby, who later called himself Ray, was a sweet and easygoing child, well-liked by members of our extended family. He was self-assured and "comfortable in his own skin," as some might say. But there was a feature of his personality that he would never deny and that he would never allow me to ignore. He was gay.

I HAD BEEN TAUGHT IN SEMINARY that homosexuality was sinful. In those days we didn't discuss the psychology or the genetic implications. We learned that the Bible called homosexuality a sin. A sin it was. End of argument.

Bobby realized at a fairly early age that he was different. But he refused to deny the reality of his own being. Our son never had the difficult task of "coming out" to his parents. He was never in "the closet." He would say to me, "Daddy, what does the Bible say about homosexuality?" Or "What does the Church teach about homosexuality?" And I would be forced to tell him what I had been taught. I had a much more difficult time answering his question, "What do *you* believe about homosexuality?" I loved my son. But that love and my understanding of scripture were irreconcilable. It took me years to resolve the dilemma.

When Bobby was a young boy he always told people that when he grew up he wanted to be "a pastor, just like my Daddy." But after he reached his teen years, and realized that my church had no place for him, he stopped saying it. I was just as pained as he was by the change in his dreams for his future.

After a brief stint in college, Bobby moved to San Francisco, known to be a much more friendly environment for a gay man. There he studied in an international school of fashion and design, becoming a highly skilled fashion designer. (For years he had been designing and making some of his own clothing at home.) On visits to California, we saw examples and pictures of some of the beautiful wedding dresses and other garments Bobby had created. But as proud as we were of what he had accomplished, the divide was still there. We loved and respected our son, but the best we could do was to try to ignore the question of his homosexuality as much as possible.

The first step in the process of my transforming and healing came at the hands of a retired seminary professor who presented a

Bible study on those passages that had seemed the most damning in regard to homosexuality. Hearing him, I realized for the first time that the New Testament does not condemn those whom we would classify today as having a "homosexual orientation." In fact the Bible writers were totally ignorant of the concept of sexual orientation. I remembered another seminary professor, under whom I had studied New Testament many years before, who had said to my class at one point, "This Greek word does not mean 'homosexuality,' but that's the way we translate it." I was puzzled at the time, but let the comment pass.

It dawned on me that Bible translators and commentators had interpreted biblical passages to fit their own understandings Now I needed to find out for myself if there were other ways of looking at those same passages. I began to do my own intensive study of the Bible verses involved. And I read everything I could get my hands on. But I had to proceed with caution and to be certain I was not just searching for an interpretation that would justify my son. I discovered that the patterns of sexuality condemned by the Bible are those in which a person has chosen an activity or a relationship that is harmful to someone else. One example of this pattern was a situation in which a heterosexual adult man made use of a young male apprentice for his sexual gratification. That had been a common practice in Roman society, The technical term for such a relationship is "pederasty." The Bible also condemns pedophilia, regardless of orientation.

Another good example is the story of Sodom and Gomorrah. Quite frequently, when people are challenging my position on this issue, the destruction of these two cities is cited as proof that God condemned homosexuality. I have two responses. First, the practice of raping males was common in history. A defeated army could be humiliated in this manner. Strangers and other men who were not wanted would learn quickly enough that they were not welcome. The message to the victims was simple: "We're going to show you that you have no value, by treating you like women." In a male-dominated society, everyone understood.

My second answer is to ask my challengers what the Bible itself says about the sin of Sodom. For most people the answer is simply, "Homosexuality." The real answer is quite different. "This was the guilt of your sister Sodom: she and her daughters had pride, excess of food, and prosperous ease, but did not aid the poor and needy." (Ezekiel 16:49, NRSV) According to the Bible, the real sin of Sodom was her inhospitality.

Nowhere does the New Testament label as sin the reality we understand today as homosexual orientation, the fact that someone might have a natural sexual or romantic attraction for persons of the same sex, rather than the opposite sex.

I discovered that there are prohibitions against homosexual actions in a few Old Testament law passages. In the book of Leviticus we read, "You shall not lie with a male as with a woman; it is an abomination." (Lev. 18:22, NRSV) But that same body of laws includes many regulations that are almost universally ignored today, such as the commandments which prohibit interbreeding of cattle, or the mixing of fabrics in garments, or the eating of pork and a wide variety of other meats, or the requirement that a disrespectful child should be stoned to death. And the New Testament passages that have been used to condemn homosexuality, when read in the original Greek language, are far from clear as to their correct translation or interpretation. Added to all of this is the fact that Jesus said not a single word on the subject of homosexuality.

In intellectual terms, I had bridged the gap between my son and me. But I was still haunted by the thought that Bobby and others had "chosen" a homosexual lifestyle. I had known women who, when they were younger, had come to believe that they were lesbians, but had later realized they were naturally heterosexual. I had to know. And once again, I was to be taught by members of an oppressed group, just as I had earlier been sensitized by women and by people with disabilities.

As Jeannie and I traveled to California to visit with Bobby, who now went by the name Ray, we met dozens of his gay and lesbian friends. These were down-to-earth, decent, "normal" people, many of them deeply committed Christians. When we would bring up the question of their "lifestyle choice," we always got the same response. "No one would choose this kind of life. We are condemned by society. We are fired from our jobs if we come out or are inadvertently discovered. We are rejected by our families. No one would choose this." Over the years, we have heard the same message from hundreds of gay and lesbian people.

Another question that surfaces regularly in conversations with straight people is the issue of promiscuity. There is a perception among many heterosexuals that promiscuous behavior is the norm among homosexuals. Our observations and conversations over the last two decades would indicate just the opposite. Certainly there are gays and lesbians whose sex lives would have to be described as "casual" at best. But we are convinced that their numbers, as a percentage of the total homosexual population, are no more than among heterosexuals, and probably less. We have met hundreds of gay and lesbian couples who have lived in faithful, committed, same-sex relationships for twenty, thirty, forty years and more.

On one trip to California, we worshiped with Ray and his partner at the Metropolitan Community Church of San Francisco. This congregation belongs to a denomination developed by and for members of the homosexual community, who either were no longer accepted or no longer felt comfortable in their home churches. Arriving during the hymn sing that opened the service, we took our seats, noting that there were no women present except

Jeannie. They told us later the women were holding a retreat. (We were pleased to note that the liturgy they had chosen to use that day was Lutheran!)

At the time for the introduction of visitors, the four of us stood. The worshippers applauded for five minutes, each one making eye contact with us! During the reception after the service, they all came to greet us. "We knew you were a gay man with his partner and his parents," they told us. "Most of us have been kicked out of our families and are no longer welcome in our homes. We were delighted to see a mom and dad who accepted their gay son. You just gained 127 new sons today!" Jeannie and I have heard many versions of that same sad story all across the country.

We had come full circle. No longer suspicious, no longer judging, no longer doubting, we could love our son unconditionally and affirm who and what he was. And we were ready to be his supporters and advocates.

BY THIS TIME ANOTHER cloud hung over our relationship with Ray, the threat of a new virus called HIV/AIDS. We didn't know much about it, except that it was deadly and was striking down gay men in huge numbers. There was no cure for this horrible scourge. We heard terrible stories about the cancers and other debilitating side effects of the infection. And we feared for our son's well-being. Ray assured us that he would be all right, but we prayed constantly for his health and safety.

St. John Lutheran Church, outside of Logan, Ohio, where I was the part-time pastor, was very supportive of us in our prayers for Ray. They shared our pain, even though they did not agree with our support for gays and lesbians. I did not want to turn them off totally by being too brash about our beliefs regarding homosexuality. From time to time, however, I would put in a few words which indicated what we believed. One Sunday morning a leading member walked out of the service in the middle of my sermon. Jeannie and I paid the member a visit immediately after church, saying, "We need to talk." "You may be right in what you believe," our member said, "but I was not brought up to believe that."

In 1994 our church body asked all of its congregations to hold group discussions on the subject of homosexuality. At the gathering at St. John, one of our members came with a list of questions she wanted me to answer. Among other things, she asked if I would conduct a wedding ceremony for two people of the same sex. I said I would not, because it was not only against the law in Ohio, but also in opposition to the policies of our congregation. "But what if it was not against the law," she wanted to know. I told her it would still be contrary to the wishes of our congregation. Still she persisted. "What if our congregation were not opposed?" I could have responded evasively, "Ask me again when that happens." Instead I gave her an honest and direct answer. "Certainly," I said. Two families left St. John soon afterward.

Not all prayers are answered in the way we would like them to be. Eventually Ray contracted HIV/AIDS. As his disease progressed, we made more frequent trips to the San Francisco area. In the last few months of his life, his sister Diann and her fiancé David Findlay took him into their home in a nearby community to help care for him. Jeannie and I took turns assisting with the nursing chores. She would fly out for two weeks, and I would go for one. My dad had died in November 1990. With our portion of the money left in his bank account, we were able to fly not only ourselves but most of Ray's siblings to see him before he died. Only his sister Kathryn, living in Paris, was unable to go.

Jon was the last of Ray's siblings to make the trip. When I discussed this chapter of the book with Jon, he wanted to tell his own story about their last time together:

I visited Ray just one week before he died, and my brief stay there changed my outlook on what it means to be a child of God. One of the afflictions Ray had to deal with in his advanced stages of AIDS was Kaposi's Sarcoma, a cancer usually reserved for very old men. Ray's lower legs were covered with the purple lesions that were associated with KS, and in his weakened state, he could not clean himself, and left alone, these lesions could become quite painful. One day while I was there, a gay friend of Ray's came to visit, bringing food, encouragement, and one more thing: humility. As I watched, he led Ray to a daybed near a large window that overlooked the hillside above the Pacific Ocean, sat him down and removed his pajama bottoms. While Ray reclined, he fetched a bowl of warm water and a soft washcloth. Then he knelt down and began to wash his legs. As simple an act as that was, I realized even then the enormity of that moment. This man was carrying out Christ's example he set when he washed the feet of his disciples. This man, shunned by society, was shaming the current church for their insensitivity to the needs of others. I thought to myself, *"Oh my God! Jesus has returned and we missed him because he's gay!"* I realized how much more closely the gay community was keeping to God's expectations for us, in the ways they cared for one another. My theology had met reality, and it had to evolve. I am eternally thankful to that man for opening my heart to this new reality.

On Friday, June 21, 1991, the day of the summer solstice, Ray's earthly life came to an end. He was just over thirty-seven years old. Jeannie was with him, and I flew out immediately to join her so we could mourn together. After two memorial services with family and friends in California, we flew back to Ohio. There we held another service for Ray on Sunday, June 30, at St. Philip Lutheran Church in Columbus, where he had grown up. That was the congregation

Robert Sylvester "Ray" Graetz III, 1954–1991.

where he had felt most totally accepted. A year before his death, Ray had made an extended visit back east. While in the Columbus area, he had attended church at St. Philip and visited the Clifford Tyree family at their home, as well as other close friends.

Since Ray's death, all of our activities in the Gay Rights Campaign have been done in memory of our son, who taught us so much about what it means to love unconditionally. We found kindred souls, including two families in our very rural county, who had lost

Panels in the AIDS Names Quilt Project sewn by Jeannie Graetz, in honor of her late son, Robert S. (Ray) Graetz III.

sons to AIDS. One of our first actions was to organize the Vinton County AIDS Task Force, to provide information and support to others who were dealing with this scourge. We also became active in other AIDS groups in central and southeastern Ohio, as well as a parents support group.

FOR THE FIRST FEW MONTHS after Ray died, we thought we could handle our grief on our own. But after a time we gave up and joined a grief recovery program in Athens, Ohio. They helped us enormously in working through some issues that we had not yet resolved.

Jeannie sewed a memorial panel for Ray that would become part of the AIDS Names Quilt Project. It is filled with reminders of his life and his contributions. His sisters and a cousin in California made a panel also, which is sewed next to Jeannie's in the quilt. During the next few years Jeannie and I made several trips to Washington, D.C., and elsewhere to be volunteers when the entire quilt or portions of it were displayed for public viewing.

But we wanted to transform our mourning into action. Opportunities would come soon enough, perhaps too soon. Our friend Leland Elhard, a professor at Trinity Lutheran Seminary in Columbus, was teaching a special interim class in December 1991. He asked if we would feel comfortable sharing the story with his class so soon after our tragedy. I agreed to speak. With Jeannie at my side, I shared our story, crying without shame through the entire presentation.

In the spring of 1992 I got a call from Pastor Laura Shreffler, who was on the planning committee for the annual meeting of our Southern Ohio Synod of the Evangelical Lutheran Church in America. That year our nation was marking the 500th anniversary of the arrival of Christopher Columbus on the shores of our continent. Some were celebrating that event; others, mourning it. Our church body wanted to use the occasion to shore up our concern for better human relations among all people. Most of our sixty-five synods were using the theme "Remembrance, Repentance, and Renewal."

"We don't have any Native American pastors in our synod," Laura said. "You are the closest we can come to it. Would you be willing to preach at our closing worship service?" I agreed immediately, determining that my sermon would cover more than our relationship with Native Americans. So on May 30, 1992, I spoke to the assembled delegates about our church's inconsistent record as we tried to reach out to oppressed groups, including Native Americans and African Americans. I talked about the many people we had left standing, unwelcome, outside of our church doors.

Then I said that our son would have liked to be there to speak with them, except that a few months earlier he had died with AIDS. I talked about our need to reach out to our sisters and brothers in the homosexual community, a group which the church had not yet deemed to be worthy of our love and concern, or that of Jesus.

After the worship service, as people milled around and scurried out of the session, a young man approached me, one whom I had never met. "I am a gay pastor," he confessed to me. "I am still in the closet, and I must remain that way. But thank you for what you said today." A woman stepped up to my side, telling me, "I just buried my husband a few months ago. For most of our married life, I kept his secret. And I am keeping it still. Thank you for your words."

Since Ray's death, and our "coming out," we have heard dozens, perhaps hundreds, of such tragic stories, of people who feel that they dare not reveal who God created them to be, because of the powerful prejudice against the gay community, a prejudice that seems to be stronger in the church than in any other segment of our society. And we reflect on the reality that Jesus never said one word about homosexuality, but that he constantly focused on our requirement to love all people, even our enemies and those who are unloving to us. Where is the love in the hearts of so-called churchmen who have nothing to say to gay people than to label them "fags" and "queers" and appeal to them to repent and change their "wicked" ways? Jesus reached out with love to touch the lepers of his day, who were as poorly received by the good people at that time as are today's victims of HIV/AIDS.

Jeannie and I speak out about our convictions at every opportunity, to encourage those who will listen to us to be more accepting and more inclusive of people from all cultures. And we have put those words into action as well. We joined several groups in our church body which are working on the same issues, and we give our financial support to others. The first was an organization simply called "The Network." Its sole purpose at the beginning was to find at least one thousand pastors and leaders in our church body who would publicly declare their support for greater inclusivity of gays and lesbians. By 1993 we had reached our goal. We had our own "coming out" at the churchwide assembly of our ELCA, in Kansas City. Holding a news conference with our presiding bishop, we proudly displayed banners with our names on them for all the world to see. Jeannie and I served as volunteers for that entire week. Later we joined another group called "Lutherans Concerned/North America," whose membership is mostly gay. (The Network is largely a heterosexual group.)

EARLY IN 1999, OUR DAUGHTER Carolyn called us from Pittsburgh. "Mom and Dad," she said, "I've met someone that you have to meet. His name is Mel White." She proceeded to tell us about this man who had been a ghostwriter for many of the nation's most prestigious radio and television evangelists. He had struggled valiantly against his own homosexual tendencies for many years, but he had finally come to realize that this was how God had made him. At that point in his life he decided he should celebrate, rather than change, his reality. He came out to Jerry Falwell, for whom he was then working, and openly declared his sexual orientation. He had since written a book, *Stranger at the Gate: To Be Gay and Christian in America*. We had to meet him; and we had to read his book.

On Saturday, March 11, 2000, after a lunch with our AIDS Parents Support Group, we drove to Dayton, Ohio. The next morning we finally met Mel face-to-face over breakfast, went to church with him, and attended a workshop of Soulforce, a group that had been formed by Mel and his partner, Gary Nixon. Following the teachings of Mohandas Gandhi and Martin Luther King, Jr., they had organized this group to confront the anti-gay teachings and practices of the major religious bodies in our country. Mel empha-

Bob and Jeannie Graetz (near top of photo) marching in a protest in Cleveland in 2000.

sizes that we must scrupulously observe nonviolence of the heart, the tongue, and the fist. No violent thoughts, words, or actions must ever be used as we boldly confront our oppressors.

Just two months after meeting Mel White, in May 2000, Jeannie and I found ourselves in Cleveland taking part in our first Soulforce action. What a surprise it was to see several very special people there, from out of our past—Yolanda King, the daughter of Martin Luther King; Arun Gandhi, the grandson of Mohandas Gandhi; and Jim and Phil Lawson, Methodist ministers who were longtime civil rights activists. We were confronting the United Methodist Church, which was holding its quadrennial conference. When the Methodists refused to change their policies, we carried out an act of civil disobedience which had been carefully choreographed with the Cleveland police department. We blocked the exit to the parking garage used by delegates, which was very visible from the building where the church body was holding its sessions. And we carried signs reading "No Exit without Justice!" and wore T-shirts proclaiming "Stop Spiritual Violence!"

Nearly two hundred of us were arrested. After we paid our fines of $155 each, out of our own pockets, the city had been enriched by more than $30,000 by our presence. Most of our group was processed rather quickly. But the main holding facility had been too crowded to keep all of us there. So ten men, including me, were transported by "paddy wagon" to another jail, miles away. Some of the African American prisoners there complained that they were not being cared for properly, because they had heard there had been a major disturbance downtown. One member of our group confessed that we were responsible for the disturbance, and he apologized. But he added, "We have someone in our group who used to work with Dr. Martin Luther King, Jr." That clearly piqued the curiosity of the prisoners, and we had some great conversations. On the way out, I was the last to be loaded into the paddy wagon

Bob Graetz, right rear, in the paddy wagon on the way to jail after being arrested for civil disobedience in May 2000.

for our return trip. All the prisoners wanted to shake my hand as I walked out of the jail.

Jeannie and I have taken part in several actions of Soulforce around the country, being arrested two more times, as we challenged the Roman Catholic bishops in Washington, D.C., and our own church body, the Evangelical Lutheran Church in America, in Indianapolis, Indiana. We also learned to broaden our vocabulary. We no longer refer only to gays and lesbians. Now we say "gay, lesbian, bisexual, and transgender persons." (GLBT) And sometimes we add "allies." (GLBTA)

Jeannie and I have made a complete transformation. We now believe that our individual sexual orientation is part of our "God-given-ness," whether or not the scientists ultimately discover that sexual orientation is part of our genetic inheritance. And we are comfortable with our new understandings of the pertinent scripture passages. But we continue to be perplexed by the fact that many religious groups seem to believe that homosexuality is the most important "sin" facing the church today, and surely a major threat to our society, our families, and our faith. Our own careful study of the Gospels has led us instead to the conclusion that, in Jesus's mind, the lack of love for our fellow human beings far outweighs all other sins and offers the greatest threat to our church and our world.

There is another reality that is even more perplexing to us. The Christian Church from the very beginning of its history has been faced from time to time with the need to reinterpret its beliefs and understandings. The early Christians had to deal with the issue of whether circumcision and other requirements of the Old Testament Law should be required of gentile converts. Thankfully the church decided we are basically free from that burden. Yet in almost every debate about homosexuality, someone will quote passages from Leviticus, totally a book of laws. Even now there are groups who insist on following certain portions of the Law. But they tend to select carefully those portions they believe still apply to us. With the exception of the Seventh Day Adventists, that doesn't usually include the requirements related to the Sabbath Day, the seventh day of the week—according to biblical terms, the period from sundown on Friday to sundown on Saturday. Outside of the passages dealing with the sacrifices required of the ancient Hebrews, there are more references to the Sabbath than any other portion of the Law. But how many of us today refrain from working or traveling or even walking on Saturday? Or on Sunday for that matter, for those who look upon that day as their Sabbath?

And what about those sacrifices? How many Christians today give even passing thought to the requirements in the Law for regular offerings of animals, grains, and other gifts to God? Or to our regular celebration of the Passover, including the killing, cooking, and eating of a young lamb? Or to the firm requirement that we give a tithe (one tenth) of our income to God?

When it comes to the Old Testament Law, we become very selective.

There are other issues on which church bodies have "changed their minds." I think of the question of women's ordination. St. Paul clearly says, "As in all the churches of the saints, women should be silent in the churches. For they are not permitted to speak, but should be subordinate, as the law also says. If there is anything they desire to know, let them ask their husbands at home. For it is shameful for a woman to speak in church." (1 Corinthians 14:33b-35, NRSV) Yet many Christian groups have decided that, though this restriction applied to Paul's time, it does not apply to ours. (In 1970 I had the privilege of traveling to San Antonio to our national church gathering, as part of a group that went to the meeting for the sole purpose of persuading our church body to change church policy by voting to ordain women. We succeeded.)

Another debate within the church has been over divorce. In our denomination, as in many others, there was a time when a divorced pastor would not be allowed to serve a congregation. Jesus had spoken out very clearly against divorce. But divorce, unfortunately, has become commonplace in our modern society. And the rate of divorce among church people is almost as high as among non-church people. Even worse, the rate among clergy has also grown alarmingly. Some denominations might find themselves with a severe leadership shortage if they suddenly de-frocked all their divorced pastors. Yet we have somehow found a way to forgive and overlook the divorces in our midst, in spite of Jesus's strong prohibition.

Or I think of the angry debates that raged for decades in the churches over the question of slavery. Though it seems far-fetched to Christians today, in an earlier time there were many who believed that Noah's condemnation of his grandson Canaan meant that all Africans were to be bound in slavery. "He said, 'Cursed be Canaan;

lowest of slaves shall he be to his brothers'" (Genesis 9:25, NRSV). This outburst from a drunken Noah followed an inappropriate action by Canaan's father Ham, not by Canaan himself.

The New Testament is much more compelling. We turn to St. Paul again: "Slaves, obey your earthly masters with fear and trembling" (Ephesians 6:5a, NRSV). "Slaves, obey your earthly masters in everything, not only while being watched and in order to please them, but wholeheartedly, fearing the Lord" (Colossians 3:22, NRSV). "Masters, treat your slaves justly and fairly, for you know that you also have a Master in heaven" (Colossians 4:1, NRSV). Paul also made it clear that he was not referring only to relationships with "kind" masters. "Slaves, accept the authority of your masters with all deference, not only those who are kind and gentle but also those who are harsh. For it is a credit to you if, being aware of God, you endure pain while suffering unjustly" (1 Peter 3:18-19, NRSV). And when Paul wrote to his friend Philemon regarding his runaway slave Onesimus, he asked Philemon to receive him as more than a slave, since Onesimus was now a Christian brother. But Paul never asked Philemon to free the slave. So the Bible clearly condones slavery, but I know of no religious community today that would be supportive of people owning slaves in this day and age.

I pray that someday the church also will look at homosexuality in a new light. Already there are youth groups in our own denomination and others which have expressed support for full acceptance of gays, lesbians, bisexuals, and transgendered people. The United Church of Christ, just days before these words were written, has boldly taken the public stance that its doors are open to people of all sexual orientations.

THERE IS ANOTHER ISSUE that I must address. Several people have shared with me their conviction that there is greater fear of homosexuality among African Americans than European Americans.

Whether that is the case, I cannot say. But if it is so, there are good reasons for this fear to have developed. In the first place, it has been my impression that black pastors on average are Biblically more conservative than white pastors. The reason could be simply that Baptist churches, a generally conservative denomination, tend to be dominant in African American communities. The historical basis for this reality is simply that white Southern Baptist slave-owners are the ones who passed along their beliefs to their slaves. One of the greatest miracles of all time, in my mind, is that there are any Christians at all among the African American population of this country, given the treatment that was accorded to them by their "Christian" masters.

A second reason has to do with the image of the black male in our society. During the entire period of slavery, and to a large extent also during the decades of extreme racial segregation, African American men have been put in the position where they were deprived of the opportunity to play the traditional role of the adult male in the family, that of protecting and providing for their families. Slave families for the most part were not allowed to remain intact and even the procreation role between male and female slaves was controlled for the economic benefit of the slaveowner. Even today, especially in economically deprived communities, where the unemployment rate tends to be consistently much higher than the rate in predominantly white areas, black men face even further obstacles to playing that traditional male role. So they must seek other means of creating "macho" male images for themselves. Since the image of the gay man does not fit that pattern, he becomes a threat to the masculinity of heterosexual men.

In the light of these realities, I find it difficult to understand another phenomenon that in recent years has been a subject of debate in the African American community. Groups of heterosexual men will gather together by themselves for the purpose of sharing homosexual activities. The practice is called "down-low." It is hard to reconcile a condemnation of those with a true homosexual orientation with an apparent acceptance of homosexual activities of heterosexual men.

I am happy to report that many recognized leaders of the civil rights movement now champion the concept of "gay rights" as part of that movement. Some of those leaders are loath to refer to gay rights as "civil rights," not wanting to diminish the image of the historical movement for African American civil rights. Several leaders spoke out on this question in the July 2004 issue of *Ebony* magazine. The challenge posed by *Ebony's* editors was, "Is gay rights a civil rights issue?"

Julian Bond responded, "Are gay rights civil rights? Of course they are. 'Civil rights' are positive legal prerogatives—the right to equal treatment before the law. These are rights shared by all—there is no one in the United States who does not—or should not—share in these rights."

Both Rev. Fred Shuttlesworth and Rev. Walter Fauntroy expressed reservations about homosexuality, while they supported the rights of gay people. Shuttlesworth said, "I will simply state that I believe all human beings should have their basic rights protected under the law." Fauntroy said, "I do not believe anyone should be discriminated against on the basis of their behavior as long as that behavior is not prohibited by law. That's why I have always been a defender of gay rights and their access to the essentials for life, liberty and the pursuit of happiness."

Congressman John Lewis, one of my all-time heroes, has been fearless on behalf of gay and lesbian people. As was Coretta Scott King, the late widow of Dr. King, as well as some of her children. Most members of Dr. King's family believe that he would surely be speaking out against homophobia if he were alive today. When the debate about our involvement in the Vietnam War was heating up in this country, many civil rights leaders urged Martin not to speak out against it. They were afraid of losing support for "their" movement. But in April 1967, Dr. King spoke at a rally in New York at Manhattan's Riverside Church sponsored by the group Clergy and Laymen Concerned about Vietnam. He told the gathering of more than three thousand people that he felt it was time to "break the betrayals of my own silences and to speak from the burnings of my own heart." Calling America "the greatest purveyor of violence in the world," he urged the young men of our country to offer themselves for alternative service as conscientious objectors, rather than to go to war.

As Dr. King was consistent with his principles when he risked his own standing in the civil rights movement by opposing the war in Vietnam, so we believe we must be consistent by opposing any form of oppression, discrimination, and intolerance, no matter what group is targeted. As Dr. King used to say, "Injustice anywhere is a threat to justice everywhere." We must be open to using new ideas and new tactics, as we deal with problems both new and old.

Chapter 11

'White Privilege'

A group in Birmingham, Alabama, invited me to be the keynote speaker for the Martin Luther King Day celebration in January 1998. It was their thirteenth annual Unity Breakfast. Jeannie and I had not been in this north Alabama city since 1957, when we had visited with our friends Jim and Jean Darnell. Jim and I, both white pastors, had been called to serve black Lutheran congregations in Alabama in 1955—Jim to St. Paul in Birmingham; I, to Trinity in Montgomery. Both cities were totally segregated. We would soon learn that the black citizens of both cities were also poised to challenge that system of segregation and the second-class citizenship that resulted from its rigid enforcement. Montgomery would be transformed by the now-famous bus boycott of 1955–56. In Birmingham the key event would be the so-called "Children's March" in 1963.

As I arrived to speak at the Unity Dinner, it had been thirty-five years since the African American children of this city had challenged the forces of Police Commissioner Bull Connor, demanding full first-class citizenship for themselves, for their parents, and for the generations to come. They had faced fire hoses, police dogs, and even jail, in their determination. And by their faithfulness and their persistence, they had created a city that was far different from the one into which they had been born.

Birmingham's mayor in 1998 was Richard Arrington, a black

man. Black and white citizens worked side-by-side in municipal offices and businesses virtually everywhere in this renewed city. The Birmingham-Jefferson Civic Center, in which we gathered that morning, was not far from the downtown stores that were the targets of the black marchers in the 1960s as they protested the lack of jobs for African Americans and the lack of access to lunch counters for black shoppers.

The plan was that after breakfast and a program, including my speech, the gathering would march from the City Hall, moving west six blocks to Kelly Ingram Park and the Sixteenth Street Baptist Church, It was to be a reversal of the route which the children had tried unsuccessfully to walk. As the huge crowd filled the street from curb to curb on our march, with the side streets carefully blocked off by white and black male and female police officers, I could not help but reflect on the reality that it was the black children of Birmingham who had turned their city around. Some of them, now adults, were marching with us that day! Those four girls who died in the bombing of the Sixteenth Street Baptist Church, and the two boys who were killed on the streets later that same day, had paid a terrible price for being participants in this campaign; but their sacrificial deaths helped to move the city into its rebirth.

Who could forget that horrible scene on Sunday morning, September 15, 1963, just over two weeks after the euphoria of the famous March on Washington and Dr. King's "I Have a Dream" speech. Children preparing for a Youth Sunday program at their church were unaware that a large bomb had been planted in the stairwell of the back entry to the building on Sixteenth Street, just outside the women's restroom. The four girls were innocently primping before their program. The two black boys had been killed in seemingly random shootings following the bombing.

But that was 1963. This was 1998. It was a new day, and a time to look forward, not backward. (All four of the white men who were implicated in the bombing are now either dead or in prison.) Since I had been part of the Alabama campaign, and a close co-worker of Dr. King, I was asked to come and to help celebrate the new Birmingham.

After breakfast I was introduced by Rev. Abraham Lincoln Woods, pastor of St. Joseph Baptist Church and cochair of the King Day celebration, along with Rob Langford, a retired FBI special agent. Rev. Woods is respected and revered in the city, well remembered for his courage as a civil rights leader. He had invited me to preach in his church the day before, on Sunday morning. St. Joseph was one of the larger African American congregations in Birmingham, and had been involved in the Birmingham campaign.

After I had been introduced on Sunday morning, I stepped into the pulpit and announced to the congregation, "Jeannie and I very much appreciate the opportunity to be here with you this morning. But I need to warn you that I am a Lutheran, and I'm not going to sound like a Baptist preacher." The congregation laughed, knowing exactly what I meant. After the service ended, one of the sisters came up to me. "You sounded like a Baptist preacher," she said. "You just didn't whoop!"

I didn't whoop at the breakfast gathering the next morning either, having a very serious message to bring to this assemblage. I began by telling my own story. I was born and grew up in West Virginia, a state that should have rejected racial segregation. It had, after all, split off from the state of Virginia at the time of the Civil War, when Virginia seceded from the Union. But in the 1930s and 1940s the public schools I attended were totally segregated. I explained to the crowd that I had grown up not really knowing any Negroes. For all I knew they could have been citizens of a foreign nation. Then I told them the story of my "race relations awakening" in college. I related my headlong plunge into the black community and my subsequent total involvement in the civil rights movement, sharing details about the Montgomery Bus Boycott of more than forty years before. I admitted that I was proud of the contributions which I had made to the movement.

Then I shifted to a new series of thoughts that had only recently been going through my mind. Reflecting on the plight of America's black people during slavery and the years of rigid segregation which followed, I told my listeners, "I never enslaved anyone. I never enforced segregation laws. I never required any black people to work long hours for half of the money they should have been paid. So I am not guilty of committing any of those offenses. I can't be blamed for those things.

"But," I continued, "black people, as a people, were enslaved; they were segregated; they were deprived of the wages they should have been paid for the work they did. And white people, as a people, enslaved, segregated, and deprived them. The resources of this nation's black people were systematically removed from them and transferred to the nation's white people. But all of that happened generations ago. So I am still not responsible for the transfer of resources.

"On the other hand, because of that transfer of resources, the white people who lived those many generations ago were financially better off than they should have been; and the black people who lived those many generations ago were worse off than they should have been. The extra resources of those white people were passed along from generation to generation. And the deprivations of those black people were also passed along from generation to generation.

"I am not responsible for this," I declared, "but I am wealthier today than I should have been; I have had a better education than I should have had; I have had greater opportunities in life than should have been mine; all because of that transfer of resources. And you who are African Americans are worse off than you should have been, because of that same transfer of resources.

"I used to take great pride in what I have accomplished in my life and the contributions I have made to the movement. 'After all, I'm white,' I said to myself, 'and I don't have to get involved unless I choose to.' But now I realize that the very fact of my being white means that I am automatically part of the problem, rather than part of the solution. And I, as a white man, must begin by telling you, 'I'm sorry.' I am sorry for what my people have done to your people. And I need to ask for your forgiveness. I cannot continue speaking to you this morning until I know that you have forgiven me."

At first the room was completely silent. Then I saw people leaping to their feet, shouting, "Somebody tell him!" Rev. Woods stood up beside me. "I forgive you," he assured me, as he gave me the warmest hug I had ever received. And from all over the room I heard the same words, "I forgive you!" before those words were drowned out in the thunderous applause that filled the hall. The standing ovation affirmed the forgiveness they had just granted. And we had liberated one another!

But I need to give credit where credit is due. Some months before my invitation to appear in Birmingham, I had been asked to speak to a group of people in the county seat of our very rural, very white, Vinton County, Ohio. My hosts were a group of home-schoolers at Calvary Assembly of God congregation in McArthur. I talked with them about the evils of racism, and about the need for Christians to repent of that evil and find ways to make amends to the people we have offended and wronged. The group was quite responsive and engaged in a lively discussion. As we were leaving, Steve and Lisa Young, members of the congregation, told me about a book, which they sent me afterwards. "You need to read this," they told me. The book was *Healing America's Wounds,* by John Dawson. And that book transformed my message and my life.

Dawson is a New Zealander with a white European heritage. But he has also lived in and has had extensive involvement in both African American and Native American communities in this country. Some ten years before my presentation, Dawson had spoken to a group of pastors in Birmingham, Alabama, dealing with some of the same issues that I spoke about. John Dawson and some of his colleagues had organized a group called the "International Reconciliation Coalition," with chapters around the world. Their focus is "dealing with conflict in a Christian way," centering on four steps:

> **Confession:** Stating the truth; acknowledgment of the unjust or hurtful actions of myself or my people group toward other persons or categories of persons . . .
>
> **Repentance:** Turning from unloving to loving actions.
>
> **Reconciliation:** Expressing and receiving forgiveness, and pursuing intimate fellowship with previous enemies.
>
> **Restitution:** Attempting to restore that which has been damaged or destroyed, and seeking justice wherever we have power to act or to influence those in authority to act. (*Healing America's Wounds*, pages 135-136)

In Dawson's book, he tells the story of a gathering of Christians of all races near the town of Chivington, Colorado, on January 14, 1993. This had been the site of the Sand Creek Massacre in the 1860s. Most Americans have never heard of this place. Members of the southern Cheyenne and Arapaho tribes had been assured that their relationship with white settlers was peaceful, and that their braves could go hunting for food without fear. While the men were gone, a cavalry unit of seven hundred troops under the command of Col. John Chivington attacked the village, slaughtering hundreds of people and mutilating their bodies.

(Chivington also happened to be a Methodist minister.)

One of the Native American pastors at the 1993 gathering told the group, "You white people need to realize that you are direct beneficiaries of this massacre." (Page 142) Author Dawson said the setting was especially personal for him. The white man who now owned the land was also named Dawson, and was a fellow Baptist. In a moving ceremony that lasted for hours, the European Americans who were present made personal confessions and asked forgiveness from their non-white sisters and brothers. Then they shared the Lord's Supper together.

Dawson also tells the story of a march of three thousand Christians in Springfield, Missouri, in 1992. Gathering in the town square, they stopped for prayer. "We ask for forgiveness," intoned one of the white pastors, "for the unjust lynching of Horace B. Duncan, Fred Coker, and Will Allen. We, as Your Church, repent of the mob violence . . . that took place on the Easter weekend of 1906 . . . We repent of our perpetuation—by sins of commission and omission—of the evils of racism, bigotry and prejudice, and ask for God to help us to heal the deep divisions which exist in our city." (Page 213)

There were more black people than white among the 2,300 who gathered in the civic center in Birmingham that morning in 1998. But both groups were well enough represented that I could say something to each of them. So I continued with a message that I have revised and expanded over the years since that presentation, but which remains the essence of my theme as I speak to groups all over America today.

We who are white can no longer evade our responsibility for the inequities and dysfunctions in our society by simply saying "I didn't do it." It is obvious that not one of us was present two hundred years ago or more; so we could not have been the ones who generated the evils of slavery or continued its existence. But the irrefutable fact is that every white person in this country has benefited from the shift of resources produced by slavery, which continued beyond slavery on a lesser scale into the period of rigid segregation and discrimination that followed. It is a phenomenon I have come to refer to as "white privilege."

And what, precisely, do I mean by "white privilege?" It would be quite difficult to claim that no black people were harmed economically by the practice of slavery, though some might still want to try. Just the Sunday before these words are written, Jeannie and I heard an ordained minister attempt to justify our history of slavery. He reminded us that slavery was common around the world at that time. Jeannie leaned over to me and whispered, "And that makes it right?" By the very nature of slavery, there was no regular remuneration for the work performed for the masters, beyond the provision of food, clothing, and housing, often minimal. The result of the slaves' work in the cotton fields was that cotton was produced and sold. And the payments for that cotton were deposited totally into the accounts of the slaveowners, not the slaves. It could easily be argued that each hour's wages not paid to a slave were actually stolen from the slave, and that the thief was the slaveowner himself!

With those stolen wages, slaveowners paid for the basic needs of their families, bought land, and sometimes amassed significant cash savings. Whatever they accumulated over their lifetimes, they passed along to their heirs, down through the generations, and ultimately to the white people who are living today. On the other hand, if those wages had been paid, the slaves who received them could have bought their own freedom, and that of their families. They could have acquired their own personal belongings, perhaps even land. And they too might have amassed significant cash savings to pass along to their heirs, down through the generations, and ultimately to the black people who are living today. It is clear, then, that the institution of slavery in this country resulted in a massive transfer of material resources from slaves to their masters, without the consent of those from whom the resources were taken.

Acknowledgment in principle that white privilege exists, however, is not sufficient. All of us who are white need to recognize that we have personally benefited from that phenomenon, just because we are white. The life that each one of us enjoys today has been enriched by the toil of slaves. We cannot quantify the amount of the benefits we have received. But we can surely accept the reality that we are better off today because of those benefits. Even white immigrants, who arrived in this country after slavery was abolished, have greater opportunities than black immigrants, or even our own native African Americans. Mr. Clifford Tyree, from St. Philip Lutheran Church in Columbus, once said to a group of white Lutheran seminarians, "When you wake up in the morning, you have a leg up on me—just because you are white and I'm black."

And the step which must follow, for each of us who have become aware of that reality, is to make a full, and public, confession. Even though it may have been unintentional, we have been guilty of racism, and we must admit it. That is what I did that morning in Birmingham for the very first time. It was also what had taken place at Sand Creek, Colorado, and in Springfield, Missouri. It was a very emotional experience for me, and certainly therapeutic, as I am sure it has been wherever people have made such a public confession.

I was reminded of something that had happened years before. A church official had asked me to write a booklet for white pastors who were considering service in African American communities. I readily agreed, realizing that the numbers of our black pastors were increasing too slowly to meet our needs. But first I turned to the real experts—my fellow pastors who were black themselves. I asked them all the same question: "What shall I say to white pastors who want to serve in African American communities?" And, with few exceptions, I got the same answer from them all. "Go home, white man. The problems are not here, but on your side of town. If you want to help us, do it where you are." The booklet was never written.

In 1998 I admitted publicly to those twenty-three hundred people that I was a recipient of white privilege. I confessed that I was part of the problem. I acknowledged that I realized that the major problems in race relations were on "my side of town." Now the way had been cleared to do something about the problems we could all identify. And that next step had to be taken, to find a way to make amends. Dawson's four steps were confession, repentance, reconciliation, and restitution.

At this point in my presentations, I can always see some faces glazing over. "Oh, no!" I can hear them thinking. "We're not going to talk about reparations." So I never use the word. Instead I begin with a "what if."

"What if my great-great-grandfather had borrowed $1,000 from your great-great-grandfather many years ago and never paid it back. And to this day nothing had been done about it. Would it be fair to forget about that debt and to go on as if nothing had happened? Can't we agree that everyone from my great-great grand-father down to me has benefited from his failure to pay his debt, and that everyone in your family has suffered? So what should we do—ignore the debt, or repay it?"

If the setting is one in which responses are allowed, this is when the questions come flying. "Who is supposed to pay the debt? And to whom? And how much are we supposed to pay?" This is also the point at which many white people take onto themselves the same defensive posture I had assumed earlier in my speech in Birmingham. "I never enslaved anyone. . . . I am not responsible."

But I persist: "We are talking about a debt that can be identified and even partially quantified, though with great difficulty. We are considering a debt that is owed by one group of people to another group of people. We cannot deny that the debt is owed. We can only search for a way to rectify the evil that it has caused in our nation."

I AM THE FIRST TO ADMIT that I do not know precisely how that debt is to be paid. It will have to be left to minds that are wiser than mine to find a reasonable solution, to find a way to repay the racial debt that keeps this nation's books permanently out of balance. I consider that my task is primarily to trouble the consciences of those who are willing to listen to me. I will return to reconciliation and restitution later in this chapter and in the last chapter of this book.

When Jeannie and I speak to younger school groups, we focus on the concept of fairness. Children can understand whether they are being treated fairly or not. We describe the realities black children faced in segregation—not being able to eat in "white" restaurants, drink from "white" fountains, play in "white" parks, swim in "white" pools, or relieve themselves in "white" restrooms. Then we ask the question, "Does that sound fair?" A chorus of "No's!" always follows.

We talk about the kinds of schools black children used to attend in our country (perhaps some still do); how they walked to school while white children rode past them in buses; how they sat in buildings that were poorly maintained, worked from textbooks discarded by the white schools, and learned from teachers whose own education had been inferior to that of their white counterparts. And again we ask, "Does that sound fair?"

Then we describe contemporary experiences, such as that of a child who appears to be from a Muslim country and who is ill-treated or put down by fellow students, and we ask the same question. Children always catch on. They want to be treated fairly and to be fair themselves.

Another concept we introduce to children of all ages is "respect," which we define as the acknowledgment that the person who is the object of the respect has value. "Respect," we tell our youthful listeners, "is a two-way street. You must recognize that you have value in yourself, and that the people around you also have value, even if they are different from you." We assure them that they are created by God and therefore must be really special. But people of a different color, or religion, or nationality, or level of ability, or sexuality, have also been created by God. So they too must be really special. We always close our presentations by showing the groups a new way to look at "race," which we write on the chalk board:

Respect
All
Cultures
Equally

A few years ago, we had the privilege of speaking at Pittsburgh's Pioneer School, a wonderful institution especially for children with a wide variety of disabilities. Two of our grandchildren attended the school. The students listened raptly as I talked about racism and how it had affected children.

After I finished speaking, including the new look at race, I asked if there were any questions. The bodies of these young people may have been crippled; but their minds were agile. And the questions flowed. One of the last to "speak" was a boy who could not talk. I had noticed his specially built wheelchair, loaded with electronic devices. When I pointed to his raised hand, his smile could not have been broader. Then he pressed a button on his console, and we all heard a mechanical voice speak the lesson of the day: "Respect all cultures equally." That lesson had been received.

Through the years that I worked with my friend M. L. King, I don't remember ever hearing him talk specifically about reparations for black people. Instead he frequently presented an image of two runners ready to begin a race. The finish line is the same for both; but one runner is fifty yards down the track when the race begins. No matter how hard he sprints, the second runner will never catch up with the one who had the head start. With the abolition of legal segregation, Dr. King would say, black runners were now on the same track as others. But their fellow runners had advantages that kept them in front: better education, favorable economic conditions, parents and family structures that were already geared to being supportive. Black people needed an extra boost to move them down the track to compete on an equal basis.

Randall Robinson expressed it differently in his book, *The Debt: What America Owes to Blacks:*

> No nation can enslave a race of people for hundreds of years, set them free bedraggled and penniless, pit them, without assistance in a hostile environment, against privileged victimizers, and then reasonably expect the gap between the heirs of the two groups to narrow. Lines, begun parallel and left alone, can never touch.

The theory behind the wide range of "affirmative action" programs that were developed in this country some years ago was that these programs would close the gap and bring the once-parallel lines together. A larger than normal percentage of black applicants would be selected for a police force, an entering college class, as newly hired employees in a private firm, etc. The governmental and private sectors engaged in a variety of forms of deliberate affirmative action calculated to redress the prior imbalances. There are African

Americans in prominent positions in government, in business, in academia, in every part of our society, who have excelled because of their talents and their own hard work, but also because affirmative action programs gave them an initial chance.

However, the seeds of self-destruction were built into these programs. It was anticipated that many participants in the programs might be less prepared to serve in their positions than some white applicants. After all, affirmative action was specifically designed to deal with the problem of the inferior educational experiences afforded to too many black Americans. Of course they were not as well prepared. How could they be?

The programs worked well for a while. But white America ultimately decided that black Americans had had enough time to catch up. Now they would have to make it on their own. To use Dr. King's metaphor, the advantaged runner might now be only twenty-five or even ten yards ahead at the start of the race. But the gap was still there. To this day, African Americans as a statistical group have an uphill battle to achieve at the same level as their white counterparts.

Some affirmative action efforts still exist, but sometimes in curious guise. At some historically black colleges and universities (HBCUs), tuition is now subsidized for white students. This practice does foster desegregation and may be justifiable given that large numbers of black students now choose to attend previously segregated white schools, while very few whites have voluntarily chosen to attend previously segregated black schools. (Why would they, given the decades of neglect and underfunding of the black institutions during segregation?) But how can we justify those situations where black students, who might have been enrolled under now-defunct affirmative action programs, are turned away but the no-better-qualified white sons and daughters of leading citizens, university trustees, and major donors are accepted?

Furthermore, we must recognize that to a large group of people the concept of "affirmative action" is merely a meaningless phrase. I am speaking about that vast underclass in our country, mostly black and Hispanic, the "permanently poor," who inhabit our inner cities (and increasingly the deteriorating suburbs), who depend largely on governmental programs to sustain their lives, who are without hope for the future and without a sense of their own personal value. Those are the ones for whom the impact of "the debt" owed to black America falls hardest. Until we find a way to balance the books in regard to that population, our nation will never be at peace with itself. Nor will we be able to claim the role of moral leadership in our world. I will return to this concern in the last chapter.

However, redressing America's past sins is not a one-way street. Whites are not the only ones with responsibilities to shoulder in today's society.

In Birmingham in 1998, I also had words which I directed to my African American sisters and brothers. "If we who are white confess our guilt that is associated with that whiteness, then it is incumbent upon you who are black to forgive us and to accept us as part of your family. We need you to recognize that not all white people are alike. Some of us are truly your allies. But we cannot work with you in a productive way until you have accepted us as your sisters and brothers, as we must also reach out to you as our sisters and brothers. Together we can solve the problems of our cities and our nation and our world. But if we remain separated, the gap will also remain forever unclosed, and our racial problems unresolved."

There is a great deal more that I could have shared with black listeners on that day, much of which has been articulated ever more boldly by African American leaders in recent years. It is obvious to us all that most of the problems that bedevil the black community today are rooted in their history of being victims of racism and discrimination. But these societal ills cannot be dealt with solely by trying to place the blame. Those in positions of leadership in the African American community must now take responsibility, not only for identifying the challenges that face us in our present-day world, but also for proposing action steps that all of us in our multicultural society can take together to meet those challenges.

We can no longer ignore the realities of the increase of violence, especially among young black males; or the drug culture that has destroyed so many thousands of lives; or the phenomenon of so many of our babies being born out of wedlock, and being raised without a significant father figure; or the problems of black entrepreneurs who struggle because they do not have the support of their own communities; or the put-down of hard-working students, who are charged by their classmates with trying to "act white." And the list goes on. We European Americans have to recognize that our role in dealing with these problems must be that of "supporting actors," whose presence is vital, but secondary. In the final chapter I want to make some suggestions as to how we may begin to deal with these pressing challenges.

Something new was introduced after my presentation in 1998, a statement called the "Birmingham Pledge." As he presented it on behalf of Operation New Birmingham, James Rotch said, "If this project were a new shopping center, today would be the grand opening. Today instead marks a campaign to eliminate racial prejudice for all times." The group in the civic center stood and read the statement together:

THE BIRMINGHAM PLEDGE

I believe that every person has worth as an individual.

I believe that every person is entitled to dignity and respect, regardless of race or color.

I believe that every thought and every act of racial prejudice is harmful; if it is my thought or act, then it is harmful to me as well as to others.

Therefore, from this day forward I will strive daily to eliminate racial prejudice from my thoughts and actions.

I will discourage racial prejudice by others at every opportunity.

I will treat all people with dignity and respect; and I will strive daily to honor this pledge, knowing that the world will be a better place because of my effort.

Participants were asked to sign the pledges, then to turn them over to the Birmingham Civil Rights Institute, an outstanding museum which opened in 1992 across the street from both the Sixteenth Street Baptist Church to the north and the Kelly Ingram Park, site of many confrontations during the Birmingham campaign, to the east. The Institute would serve as the repository of what was hoped would become many thousands of such pledges signed by people all over the country. That same pledge is now part of a large mural painted on the outside wall of a police station in Birmingham, at the corner of 1st Avenue and 18th Street, North. In recent years, we have brought hundreds of people to Birmingham and to the Civil Rights Institute. We hope that their lives have been changed to conform to the Birmingham Pledge, which they signed, and that the world has indeed become a better place because of their efforts.

I can think of no generation that has had a greater opportunity and also a greater obligation to work for racial reconciliation than those of us who stand at the cusp of the Jubilee Year of the modern civil rights movement. We must declare together: "Fifty years is long enough! It is time the balance the books!"

Chapter 12

A Look Back—
A Look Forward

As I began this volume, I asked "Why am I (still) here?" The question meant, "How is it that I physically survived a series of threats to my life over a period of years?" Asked a different way, the same question could mean instead, "What use does God still have for Jeannie and me, now that we are in our middle seventies, well beyond the usual retirement age?" Our immediate answer to that question is, "Plenty!" There are times when we dream about a day when we can feel bored, even for a brief time. We are on the road so much that our children have a joke about it. Arriving home from a trip, it is not unusual to check our telephone answering machine and find a message from one of the children, "It's 10:00 PM. Do you know where your parents are?"

We wouldn't have it any other way. God has been in charge of our lives, even when we tried to force our way into the driver's seat. We have friends who tell us they love getting our Christmas letters and sharing our experiences for the previous year, but that they get tired just reading them. We get tired, too, but we are rejuvenated by the memories of the adventures God has led us through and also by all the challenges that still lie ahead of us.

In 1996, Jon, our youngest son, enticed us into a new journey that would let us maintain our connection with the memories, scenes, and people from our past. At the same time it would help us build positive relationships among the cultural groups with whom we work, on into the future. Jon teaches high school math at the Miami Valley School, an extraordinary multicultural private school near Dayton, Ohio. Each spring their ninth- through twelfth-graders experience a month-long "immersion." All classes are suspended while the freshmen come together in retreat settings to explore who they are and how they relate to other people. Seniors, juniors, and sophomores are given choices among a dozen or more single-subject immersions offered by the school's faculty.

When Jeannie and I spoke at the Miami Valley School in 1995, the fortieth anniversary of the bus boycott, history teacher Bill Glisson told his students, with tears in his eyes, "Listen carefully to these voices. You are listening to history!" Lights flashed in Jon's mind. By the following year he had obtained our agreement to staff a "civil rights immersion" for the school. Nine students (five black and four white) signed up for the course. They were accompanied by us and Jon, as well as Peter Camm, foreign language chairman at the school. In six days we visited Birmingham, Atlanta, Montgomery, and Selma. The students documented their experiences with videotaped interviews of the people they met, developing those tapes into a video program which they shared with the entire school.

Among the most moving interviews were those with the Rev. John Cross and his daughter Barbara. Rev. Cross was pastor of Birmingham's Sixteenth Street Baptist Church at the time of the 1963 bombing. Barbara herself had been with the four girls who were killed, just before the bomb exploded. She told our students that the Sunday School lesson that day had dealt with forgiveness. Jon reported in an article that appeared in the MVS *Bulletin:* "The repeated acts of violence which were recounted to the MVS students were 'numbing' . . . since bombings were such regular accompaniments to the movement to assure civil rights for Southern blacks."

The *Dayton Daily News* carried an article about the school's immersion and our trip into the South. Not long afterward, I received a call from Larry Hoffsis, a friend of mine who was serving as pastor of Epiphany Lutheran Church, also in the Dayton area. "Can you do the same thing for us?" he wanted to know. Epiphany, a large, mostly white Lutheran church, had been linked for two years with Mt. Enon, a large, mostly black Baptist church. They had participated in a wide variety of activities together, under the auspices of a gathering of churches called "The Vineyard." The sole function of the organization was to bring churches together across cultural lines. The Mt. Enon/Epiphany link-up had worked exceptionally well. And they were looking for new things to do.

Beginning in 1997, and each year for the next few years, we spent an extended weekend in the South with a bus load of Baptists and Lutherans, visiting Birmingham, Montgomery, and Selma. And so began a new avocation for Jeannie and me. Since that time we have accompanied groups from many Northern cities on what we now call "civil rights pilgrimages." We spend from four to fourteen days on the road, visiting many more than the original four locations in the South. Usually traveling by bus, we show videos and teach our "classes" as we go. We take the groups to the sites where civil rights activities took place. We also bring them into contact with people who were there when the events happened and who can tell their own stories.

"A life-changing experience!" is a common response we hear from our participants. A German visitor, Ute Loheit, who was then serving a church in Dayton, took part in one of our pilgrimages for the Dayton churches. On her return to what used to be communist East Germany, she told her colleagues at home, "We visit the U.S. as tourists, and we go to the fun places and beautiful places. But we really need to go and learn about their civil rights history." Since then we have had the privilege of leading pilgrimages for several groups of Germans, along with their American hosts.

Jeannie and I have also traveled to Germany many times. Our church body in southern Ohio has established a relationship with the Lutheran Church in the state of Mecklenburg, the northernmost part of what used to be communist East Germany. We were amazed to discover how closely those living behind the Iron Curtain followed our American civil rights movement. On anniversaries of significant dates in Lutheran history, we have seen signs announcing programs dealing with Martin Luther and Martin Luther King. It amuses us that we were called "communists" during the movement. That label was automatically applied to anyone who was working for the rights of Negroes. In the minds of many segregationists, "communist" was a synonym for "liberal."

In June 1997, we led another tour group to Germany. One of our first activities was the biennial Kirchentag, an international gathering of church folk, mostly Protestant, from all over the world. There was a great variety of programs, displays, and worship experiences. The year before I had been asked by German church officials to offer a presentation on the American civil rights movement at the 1997 Kirchentag, to be held in Leipzig, in what was formerly East Germany. We brought with us Mrs. Johnnie Carr and her husband Arlam. Mrs. Carr, then in her eighties, was a leader in the African American community of Montgomery, even before the bus boycott began. (In 2006, Mrs. Carr is still going strong as the president of the Montgomery Improvement Association. Mr. Carr passed in 2005. And in 2005, Mrs. Carr also lost her childhood friend, Mrs. Rosa Parks. But she is undaunted and serves as an inspiration to all who meet her. She is now recognized as the senior stateswoman of the civil rights movement.) We can never forget the image of this little black lady, constantly surrounded by German students hanging onto her every word as she told her story. The young people were also fascinated by our own story, especially the fact that we served a number of black churches.

The purpose of our civil rights pilgrimages is not to "do the tourist thing" or merely to teach American history, civil rights or otherwise. Our real purpose is to create "life-changing experiences." We hope participants will return to their homes determined to relate more positively to members of other cultures and to work toward that "Beloved Community" that was at the heart of Dr. King's dream, that totally inclusive community in which people love, accept, and respect one another without reservation.

As we visit these cities several times a year, it occurs to us that each has at least one historically significant reality that can inspire life-changing experiences in its visitors.

Many of our tour groups begin with Atlanta, the birthplace of Martin Luther King, Jr. More than just a "birthing-place," Atlanta became an "inspiring-place" for young Martin. His parents and his grandparents encouraged this future reformer to challenge inequities and oppression and also never to forget that he himself was a beautiful and valued creation of almighty God. (Those who want to know more about the setting in which King was born should read *Daddy King*, by M. L. King, Sr., with Clayton Riley. Interestingly, Martin's closest friends often called him Mike, because he was actually named Michael when he was born. M. L. King, Sr., had his and his son's names changed to Martin, to reflect their identification with the spirit of the church reformer.) Atlanta now boasts a very fine visitors' center staffed by the National Park Service, just across the street from the historic Ebenezer Baptist Church, which helped to mold young Martin. Next door to the church is the tomb which holds Dr. King's remains.

The message of Atlanta has to be that parents and other adult mentors still play an enormously important role in filling the hearts of our young people with the dreams that will inspire them to become the best that God has created them to be. Martin always held onto the memory of his grandmother telling him, over and over, "Don't ever forget that you are somebody!" It is not only our words that will inspire the young people who look to us for guidance in their lives. The lives we live will mean more than anything we can say to them. It is incumbent upon us not only to bring into being the "Beloved Community," but also to stand up against oppression and bigotry wherever we find it. If we can be the inspiration to our children that Martin's family was to him, who knows what new reformers we will introduce into the world!

Our usual next stop is Montgomery, home of many civil rights sites. We like to take our groups up the length of Dexter Avenue in downtown Montgomery, beginning with the fountain that marks the former location of a slave auction block, then passing the building from which the order was sent to fire on Fort Sumter, thus starting the Civil War. We see the church which was served by Dr. King—a church whose congregation first held services in a former slave holding pen—and finally come to the state capitol building perched on a hill at the top of Dexter Avenue.

A block and a half from the lower end of Dexter is the point at which Mrs. Rosa Parks refused to give up her seat on a bus, leading to her arrest and the beginning of the Montgomery Bus Boycott. The site is now occupied by the Rosa Parks Library and Museum, part of the Montgomery campus of Troy University. The museum was dedicated in 2000 on the forty-fifth anniversary of the beginning of the boycott. It contains an actual bus from 1955 and a station wagon that had been part of the boycott's carpool, as well as many interactive exhibits. A children's annex has also been added.

On the campus of Alabama State University, south of the downtown area, is the National Center for the Study of Civil Rights and African American Culture, located in the Levi Watkins Library. This

Bob Graetz with staff members of the National Center for the Study of Civil Rights and African American Culture at Alabama State University. From left, historian Dorothy Autrey, director Janice Franklin, and historian Joseph Caver.

center houses a vast archive of historically important civil rights materials, including the papers of the Montgomery Improvement Association, E. D. Nixon, and Jo Ann Robinson. Jeannie and I have placed our papers there, too.

Montgomery is significant as the site of the beginning of the modern civil rights movement. More important than its timing, however, was the nature of that movement in this city. Far different from the planned events in many cities in the years following, the Montgomery action was an almost spontaneous uprising by ordinary people who were hungry for an opportunity to take a stand against the oppression they experienced. The leadership was assembled only after the action had begun. That has to be the message of Montgomery: People, common ordinary people, can make a difference!

As our "pilgrims" return to their homes, we hope they are more sensitive to the inequities in their own communities. And we hope they are committed to taking part in protests and other citizen actions to confront the evils that are present where they live, perhaps even organizing those protests themselves.

We also trust that as they take their own stands for justice they will be properly inspired by the courage of the people of Montgomery. But they must be aware that change never comes without some pain. The black people of Montgomery walked, they faced arrest and violence, some lost their jobs or their homes, a few lost their lives. Those forms of suffering would be unusual today. But we hope that our people have advanced to the point where they are convinced that whatever pain they may have to bear, it is worth it to achieve a just, equitable, and loving society.

Since there is so much to see and do in Montgomery, we usually make that our base for several days. A one-day visit to Selma is always on the agenda. Selma and Dallas County were the nexus of the voting rights campaign in 1965. It is hard for us today to fathom that black people could have been so systematically deprived of the simple right to vote. But that was indeed the reality, as it was for women prior to 1920. By keeping the vote out of the hands of their black citizens, white people all across the South could control all the facets of government, and of the entire society. Black people knew that as long as they could not vote, they would always remain second-class citizens.

They paid a high price to achieve full citizenship. People were jailed for simply protesting, they were trampled and clubbed on "Bloody Sunday" on the Edmund Pettus Bridge, and several people were murdered, all because they wanted to secure the right to vote for all people. And it was only with the passage of the Voting Rights

Act in 1965 that the structures of society really began to change. As more black people became voters, those holding the reigns of power began to listen and to change the way they governed.

The message of Selma is certainly obvious. People not only risked their lives, some died to secure the right to vote. And not only for themselves, but also, as Mr. E. D. Nixon used to say, "for the children coming on." One of the tragedies of the civil rights movement is that the American people and the national government did not really give their strong support to that movement until some white protesters lost their lives. Black people had had their lives snuffed out for years with no one being punished.

How well have we exercised the right to vote in our nation in recent years? I know many otherwise intelligent people who have told me that they have given up on our political systems. They no longer even vote. It is certainly easy to become cynical about politics these days. I know from the personal experience of working within the system just how much damage can be done by conniving, unprincipled officials. But I also know how much more damage can be done if we abdicate our role as active participants. When I was a lobbyist for the Ohio Council of Churches, I knew that I had no money to make campaign contributions, therefore no economic power. I also knew that when our people got excited about an issue and spoke up to their elected officials *and voted*, we got some things accomplished.

I remember the radio interview of a labor leader many years ago. Negotiations with management had ground to a halt and the union negotiators had walked out. During the interview, the labor leader kept using the imagery of a football game. "We have to get on the field and fight!" he would say. At the end of the time, the interviewer asked quietly, "How can you get in there and fight, if you've already walked off the field?" If people are to make a difference today, they must be citizens in the fullest sense of the word. We can no longer afford to have any of our people walk off the field.

Birmingham is another important stop for us. Birmingham is sometimes called "the City of Churches," since it has so many of them. During the height of the civil rights activities in the 1960s, it was also dubbed "Bombingham," because so many black homes and businesses were bombed. A black neighborhood which became a frequent target soon earned the nickname "Dynamite Hill." The worst of all the bombings, of course, was that of the Sixteenth Street Baptist Church in 1963, which killed the four girls.

It was morbidly appropriate that the lives sacrificed in this city would be those of children. There were, after all, many thousands of children, including some still in elementary school, who played an active role in the Birmingham campaign. They called it "the Children's March." If not for the involvement of the children in this campaign, it is unlikely that Birmingham's civil rights leaders would have been successful. These were not "the children coming on." They were the children already there who were ready to take on whatever adult roles might be necessary, and to do it in the face of great danger. These boys and girls were their own role models.

The displays in the Birmingham Civil Rights Institute tell the stories of both the children and the adults who took part in the Birmingham campaign. It is well worth the two or three hours it takes to see everything. Across the street to its north, visitors can watch a video and hear a presentation about the history of the Sixteenth Street Baptist Church. The stairwell in which the bomb was placed is no longer visible. The memory was so painful that church members had it walled off and a new entrance created. Two stained-glass windows must also be viewed. In the balcony is a modernistic Christ, opposing bigotry with one hand while he welcomes all people with the other. It was a gift to the church from the people of Wales, after the bombing. On the Sixteenth Street side of the building, not far from the point of the blast, is another portrait of Christ. Only his face and a portion of one arm were blown out by the bomb. It was as if even Jesus could not stand to watch such carnage.

Across the street to the east is Kelly Ingram Park, the scene of many confrontations between the children and Bull Connor's police and firemen during the campaign. The park is now filled with statues honoring the children—statues depicting police dogs, fire hoses, and children in jail; four truncated pillars memorialize the four girls who were killed.

And what is the message of Birmingham? It is that age is no determinant when it comes to taking part in an effort to secure freedom and justice. During my lifetime there have been active wars in which children have been kidnapped and forced to bear arms for their kidnappers. And we still honor the memory of the child soldiers of our own American Civil War. If they are qualified to take part in the destruction of wars, our children must also be given opportunities, and be encouraged, to take part in positive efforts to transform our society and our world. We have observed that this generation of young people is more open-minded than our own generation was, and more accepting of people who are different from themselves. There is hope!

Some of our groups spend additional time to traveling to Memphis, Tennessee, the city in which Dr. King was murdered. The Lorraine Motel, where King and his entourage were staying when he died, has been transformed into the National Civil Rights Museum, one of the finest we visit. It takes a good four hours to view its exhibits adequately. It is a sad place to visit, however, because of the displays relating to Dr. King's death and the search for his assassin. There is no way to turn a violent death into a glamorous presentation. Nor should there be.

The message of Memphis is obvious. The question each of us must answer is not, "How long am I going to live?" but "How am

I going to live the length of time that God gives me?" Our friend Martin was with us for only a little longer than thirty-nine years. Our son Ray lived a shorter time, being taken from us at the age of thirty-seven. Yet each made a contribution that cannot be measured in years. Martin led a worldwide campaign that influenced many nations and peoples to take charge of their own futures. As Jeannie and I can testify, Ray's primary influence was on his extended family, and on his hundreds of friends whose lives were enriched by his pleasant and accepting personality. He was well-liked even by those who were disturbed by the fact that he was homosexual. And we are convinced that through his influence many lives have been transformed. Members of our extended family are active in the gay rights movement today because they were inspired by Ray.

The journey from Atlanta to Memphis was a lifetime for Martin King; it is a life-changing time for pilgrims who are looking for meaning in their lives, while they study the lives of those who have gone on before them.

There is another important city that we visit, which has little to do with the life and death of Dr. King. It is Tuskegee, the home of what used to be Tuskegee Institute, now Tuskegee University. Booker T. Washington was the first president of this school for the education and training of former slaves. He arrived in 1881, just a few years after the end of the Civil War and the Reconstruction. After Union troops were withdrawn from the South, all hope of "colored people" being allowed to play any significant role in political or economic life was quashed. The last part of the nineteenth century was not a time to talk about "rights" or about "combatting oppression." The best that former slaves could hope for was survival.

It was in this setting that Booker T. Washington proclaimed his philosophy that African Americans should acquire as much education and skill-training as they possibly could, to improve their own situation and to make themselves more acceptable to the dominant white population. After all, in many parts of the South it was dangerous to support any education of Negroes. When we first came to Montgomery in 1955, we had heard horror stories about the white Lutheran teachers who had come south and who lived under constant threat to their lives.

Washington's approach was thought by some to be cowardly and accommodating. At the beginning of the twentieth century, Washington stood on one side of a philosophical debate opposite the great W. E. B. DuBois, who argued forcefully that blacks should be satisfied with nothing less than full equal rights immediately. But Washington was a practical man who wanted to offer the greatest help to the largest number of his people. In today's different age, his advice to black people, "Cast down your bucket where you are" still seems to be an appropriate message. When we speak with groups, we tell them not to wait for some big civil rights campaign to come along. Instead they should watch for daily opportunities to become "civil rights activists."

There are two more important sites for visitors to see in and near Tuskegee. Moton Field, just a few miles east of the city, was the home of the famed Tuskegee Airmen. Now in the process of restoration, it has been made a National Historic Site of the National Park Service. Beginning in July 1941, thousands of young African American men trained at Moton Field to be pilots and other flight personnel. Because of racial prejudice, as well as fears that the black pilots could not perform well, their involvement in World War II was delayed until 1943. But once in combat they exceeded everyone's expectations. Flying to protect the allied bombers, the Tuskegee Airmen achieved a perfect record. Not a single bomber being escorted by the distinctive red-tailed fighter planes of the Tuskegee Airmen was lost to enemy attackers.

Also within the city of Tuskegee is the Tuskegee Human and Civil Rights Multicultural Center, housed in a former bank building.

Attorney Fred Gray, lead counsel for the Montgomery bus boycott, founded the center in memory of his wife Bernice. Its most moving exhibit deals with the Tuskegee Syphilis Study. Over a forty-year period, the U.S. Public Health Service had involved six hundred African American men in a study of the effects of untreated syphilis. The men were led to believe they were receiving medical care; but in fact it was being withheld from them. When the grotesque experiment finally came to light, attorney Gray represented the survivors in a federal lawsuit. In 1997, President Bill Clinton made a public apology to the participants and their families on behalf of our nation.

THERE IS A QUESTION that comes up with regularity as we travel. Why do we continue to talk about how bad things used to be, and about the people who were martyred during the civil rights movement? Why don't we just leave well enough alone and emphasize the positive things? We have heard it said that if we do not remember our history, we are doomed to repeat it. Voltaire once declared that history never repeats itself, but people often do. We remind our listeners of the battles of the past, so that we will not have to fight them all over again.

Jeannie and I have been given many opportunities to speak out, both in formal and informal settings. I remember especially a speaking opportunity that was most unusual. In February 1997 a prison chaplain named Sam Atchison contacted me. He wanted me to make a presentation on Dr. King in a maximum-security prison in New Jersey. My hosts for this occasion were to be the members of a Christian fellowship, all of whom were serving life sentences. I could not take them to the civil rights sites we visit with our groups, or introduce them to our special friends. But I could bring those sites and those people to them through my personal sharing. I was heartened by the realization that my presence there may have helped to strengthen the relationships among the black and white members of this group, and of the other prisoners who came to hear me speak. But I did not comprehend until after my visit had ended that I was the one who had been blessed. These men, who faced a seemingly hopeless future in this prison, were letting down their buckets where they were. They were dealing in the only way they could with one of the most intransigent problems of our society, and doing it boldly and forthrightly.

We have struggled against oppression in many forms over the last fifty years. Recently, as our attention has been focused on issues regarding sexual orientation, friends have said to me, "Well, Bob, once this issue is resolved, what will your next challenge be?" My answer to them is usually, "I don't know what the next one will be. But I can guarantee you there will be a next one. Sinful human beings seem to have a need to have someone they can consider to be beneath them, someone they can speak ill of with impunity. There will always be another challenge."

That is why we must all remain vigilant. And that is why Jeannie and I pledge to continue to share our message wherever we are invited, as long as the Lord gives us the strength. We are inspired by the words of an ancient Hebrew prophet, words which we sometimes use to close our presentations:

"He has told you, O mortal, what is good; and what does the Lord require of you but to do justice, and to love kindness, and to walk humbly with your God." (Micah 6:8, NRSV)

Chapter 13

THE BELOVED COMMUNITY

"I have a dream today!" Dr. Martin Luther King, Jr., stood before the Lincoln Memorial in Washington, D.C., on August 28, 1963. He spoke to an unprecedented gathering of a quarter of a million people, of all colors and faiths, who filled the long mall between that building and the Washington Monument, and flowed around both sides of the Memorial. Many of his listeners were cooling their weary feet on that very hot day, dangling them in the reflecting pool that lay between the two structures. Dr. King's words resounded throughout the country, and are repeated countless times every year, especially on Martin Luther King Day in January. He called upon our nation to satisfy an unfulfilled promise, that one day his children would be judged, "not by the color of their skin, but by the content of their character." And he went on to describe what he himself often called "the Beloved Community."

King's dream of a Beloved Community envisioned a society in which all people respect and accept each other with love, regardless of the differences which now divide us. One in which we recognize those differences, whatever they may be, as part of the given-ness of our common humanity, and evidence of God's desire for variety in his world. A society where we see value in ourselves and in all of our fellow human beings, where no one is deprecated for falling short of some artificial standard that others have imposed. His Beloved Community was a vision of heaven.

Dr. King's speech that day, and those given by the other civil rights leaders, were not intended merely to entertain or impress us. They were calls to action. "It is time," they were all saying to us, "to stop talking and to get busy and do something concrete about dealing with the evils of racism and bigotry and the second-class citizenship which holds in bondage a large percentage of our population. Many of us who had gathered that day already had been very busy in this campaign. But the nation as a whole was still dragging its feet, in spite of the gains we had achieved in the courts and in Congress.

And what has transpired during the more than four decades from that day to the present? How have we responded to those calls to action? An objective analysis will show that we indeed have accomplished a great deal during that time, but that we still have a long way to go. There have been many more important court decisions, as well as legislative actions by Congress, state legislatures, and local governing bodies. Discriminatory actions, once required or at least encouraged by law, are now officially prohibited. On the other hand, racially segregated communities, which used to be rigidly enforced by law in the South and by custom in the North, are still with us in many parts of our land, though many of those neighborhoods are now the result more of economics than simply of race.

More African Americans are in high positions in government, academia, business, and elsewhere, than ever before. It is no longer a novelty to see a person of color in a corporate board meeting, even in the seat of the CEO. On the other hand, millions of black, Hispanic, and other minority people are hopelessly locked into extreme poverty. More African American men are in prison today than in college. The litany of statistics goes on and on.

As we have come to the end of the first Jubilee Year (fiftieth anniversary) of the civil rights movement and have moved into whatever phase may be next, we must ask, "What now? How can we deal with the seemingly intractable problems facing our nation and our world? How can we move closer to the creation of Dr. King's Beloved Community?"

I have never been particularly interested in "how-to" books. To me they seem much too simplistic. Nor have I been a fan of those who write articles telling us to "follow these ten steps," and you will achieve whatever it is that the author is promoting. So it is with reservation that I propose nine action steps for the reader who wants to play a more active role in the civil rights movement of the twenty-first century.

1.   FIRM UP THE COURAGE OF YOUR CONVICTIONS

Our convictions are those realities of which we are certain, the truths that we can always count on, the firm bases of our faith. The problem is that convictions can be misleading. For hundreds of years, slaveowners had the conviction that the Bible not only allowed, but even encouraged, slavery. Our convictions need to be based on realities that go beyond our own biases.

I know there are those among us and even in high leadership positions who are so sure of their own personal beliefs that they think everyone else must be wrong. Such people are usually not open to having their assumptions challenged by those who believe differently. It may be more appropriate to refer to their having closed-minded-ness, rather than convictions. (In the seminary we used to laugh about the old German Lutherans who would claim, "Wir haben die reine Lehre!"—"We have the pure teachings!" They "knew" that they were the only ones who understood the Bible correctly.)

The overwhelming themes that flow through the Hebrew Scriptures are the concepts of *righteousness*, which means living in obedience to God's will, and *justice*, which means treating all people fairly and with respect. And there is no doubt but that the primary theme in the words of Jesus in the New Testament gospels is *love*. If we aspire to a strong foundation for our convictions, we can do no better than to adhere to the proposition that relationships in our society need to be based on righteousness, justice, and love.

I also still believe, as I have written earlier, that confession of our personal involvement in this nation's racism is an absolute prerequisite to our being able to take a strong stand on our convictions. By admitting our guilt, we are declaring that we realize we cannot accomplish this task on our own. We need God's help to clear away the impurities and then to refill us with the necessary strength of character to move ahead.

2. Speaking Up and Speaking Out

I remember a meeting of the all-white Montgomery Ministerial Association, many years ago. I and a few other pastors had arranged for this group to engage in a joint worship experience with the black Ministerial Alliance. Even that proposal must have constituted too much of a threat to many of the white pastors. The group was strangely silent. Finally one of our members spoke up. "They say that silence is golden," he said, "but sometimes it's just plain yellow!" None of the men present wanted to be thought of as cowardly. And the proposal was quickly adopted.

Sometimes all it takes is one brief statement to change the mood of a group. When I hear a racist or homophobic comment, I try to be alert enough to say, "That offends me." It generally doesn't take much more than that. And sometimes those words lead to very productive conversations. We need to remind ourselves that "queer jokes," "West Virginia jokes," and other stories that belittle various groups, are more than jokes. They are hurtful to someone. They are violence of the tongue. Those of us who care need to put our tongues into action to respond to them. And if we speak up once, we will be strengthened to do so again and we will give others the courage to do the same. Exercise builds strength.

3. FACE TO FACE

Early in my ministry at St. Philip Lutheran Church, I met a television personality with whom I formed a long-lasting relationship. A sensitive and caring man, he said to me one day, "What can I do to help improve race relations in the Columbus area?" I'm not sure what he was expecting me to say, but my answer caught him off guard. "You can move into the black neighborhood where I live," I told him. "That's not exactly what I had in mind," he responded.

I hadn't really intended to embarrass my friend. The point I was trying to make was that there is one very good way to work toward better race relations. And that is to establish close, personal, face-to-face contacts with people of other races or cultures. When personal friendships are established across cultural lines, then genuine communication can take place. That is precisely how Jeannie and I have functioned throughout our lives, as we have formed warm and lasting relationships with many people of cultures other than our own. African American professionals with whom we have become close friends have shared their agonizing tales of being stopped by the police because they were driving expensive cars, which the police thought they must have stolen. Others told of shopping in stores which had few black customers, and seeing clerks follow them around, obviously expecting them to steal something. Black men have noticed white women take a firmer grip on their purses and step to the side as they passed by. White Americans need to hear for themselves how we have treated our fellow citizens, just because their skins are dark. We fear them, because we don't know them.

With virtually every oppressed group with whom we have worked, it has been members of those groups who have sensitized us to what their lives are like. We did not really understand our gay son until we had learned to know and love his friends. They showed their love for us by exposing to us the realities of the lives they were forced to lead, and the indignities they had to deal with on a daily basis.

We recently heard of a reality television episode in which a man, who believed homosexuality was wrong, agreed to spend thirty days with a gay man, living in the gay man's neighborhood in San Francisco, walking his streets, meeting his friends. At month's end, his attitude toward gay and lesbian people had been completely reversed. He cried as he said farewell to his new, and true, friend.

In Jeannie's sophomore year at Capital University, she was asked to room with a blind student named Georgia Griffith, from Lancaster, Ohio. Jeannie seized the opportunity, learned to read and write in Braille, and immersed herself in the world of the blind. We remained good friends with Georgia and her family for the rest of her life.

There is an old Native American saying, "You cannot know a man until you walk a mile in his moccasins." How true it is!

4. ONLY ONE PERSON

When the Underground Railroad Freedom Center opened in Cincinnati, the center's leaders held a big inaugural ceremony. Included in the printed program for the celebration was a remarkable picture. At an earlier time, a KKK group had scheduled some kind of "kneel-in" at a location not identified in the program. The photo shows a scattering of Klansmen, all kneeling in prayer. In the middle of the group, however, is one young African American woman, standing silently but defiantly as a protest against this racist group. The accompanying article explains that just a few minutes later the KKK gave up and left. One woman had overpowered them.

When we were living in Montgomery, I remember hearing about

P. D. East, a courageous white man in Petal, Mississippi. He was the editor and publisher of the *Petal Paper,* whose circulation was almost totally outside of his state, because his articles regularly challenged the racism of Mississippi. He was all alone, but he wouldn't give up.

Jeannie and I are old enough to have vivid memories of the Second World War. There was much that went on in Germany during that time that we did not learn about until the war was ended. Most shocking and shameful to us was the near total capitulation of the Christian Church to the Nazi government. We recently watched a video about Pastor Dietrich Bonhoeffer, who was hanged for his opposition to Hitler. In the film we saw photos of a number of churches, with swastikas boldly covering the crosses, with the total concurrence of the church leadership.

But there were courageous individuals, including many hundreds of clergy, who stood boldly against the evil they witnessed. Many paid the price of their own lives. We have twice visited the German concentration camp at Dachau, not far from Munich. The highlight of our first visit was a display of lists of priests, ministers, and rabbis who had been executed within those walls. When our Lord lays a burden on our hearts, it is necessary that we heed God's call, even if we are all alone in doing it!

5. SAVE THE STARFISH; HEAL THE WORLD

The story is told of two men who were walking together on the beach. One of them leaned down occasionally to pick up a starfish, which he would throw into the ocean. The other man watched this for a while without commenting. Finally he could hold it in no longer. "What in the world are you doing?" he asked.

"Saving the starfish," his friend replied.

"Don't you realize what a hopeless job that is? There are probably thousands of starfish washed up on this beach alone. What difference will it make if you throw some of them back?"

"Well," his companion responded, as he threw another starfish into the water, "it made a difference to that one."

As we ponder the wide range of societal problems that we need to deal with, we can easily become discouraged over the enormity of those problems. And indeed most of them will require massive efforts on the part of governmental and/or corporate entities. But while we are importuning our public officials and other leaders to develop programs to serve the people in greatest need, we don't need to stand around wringing our hands. There is plenty that we can do.

Those neighborhoods that are at the lowest economic levels, where the residents are the poorest, tend to be also those in which there is the greatest incidence of violence and drug abuse and other social problems. The residents of those neighborhoods are often characterized by a lack of hope for the future. Some of them have lived on welfare for several generations, with little likelihood that their status will ever improve. Where there is no hope, there is no reason to try to make things better. And children grow up with no positive role models to emulate.

What can we do to break this cycle of poverty, hopelessness, and negative self-images? We can try to save "this one."

I am a member of the board of trustees of the E. D. Nixon Foundation, in Montgomery, Alabama. Our mission is to preserve the legacy of Mr. Nixon, especially focusing on those whom he called "the children coming on." The E. D. Nixon Elementary School is located in an economically depressed neighborhood in Montgomery, just a few blocks from Mr. Nixon's former home. Our board has "adopted" the school. We are committing our resources to supporting the efforts of the administration and faculty to make a difference in the lives of our students.

Through the imposition of strict standards of discipline, offering significant rewards for positive actions, a strong emphasis on making sure every student attends school every day, and close personal relationships between adults and children, the lives of those children are being transformed. You can see it in their mature politeness as they greet visitors to the school building. You can see it in the pride on the faces of choir members as they sing for adult audiences. You can see it in the satisfied countenances of teachers who know that they are finally making a difference in the lives of their students. Those children know they are valued and loved. They have hope for their future.

In March 2005 we brought a group of students from Miami Valley School, in the Dayton, Ohio, area, into the South on a civil rights immersion. We had stopped at the park at the end of the Edmund Pettus Bridge, where just a day earlier thousands of people had gathered to celebrate the reenactment of Bloody Sunday. While I was being interviewed by a television crew, our young people were examining the monuments and murals. Unknown to me one of our young people got some trash bags out of the van and began to pick up the debris from the day before. As the other students pitched in, one of them asked the first young man, "What are we doing?"

"Healing the world!" was his answer.

We can make a difference.

6. Cast Down Your Buckets Where You Are

When we moved from Washington to Columbus at the beginning of 1971, Jeannie and I were puzzled about why God would lead us to move into what we had thought of as a racist white suburb of that city. But we learned soon enough that there were many like-minded people there, with whom we worked to help to change the mindset of the neighborhood that was to be our home for more than eight years. God knew better than we did about where our ministry was supposed to take place.

Again in 1979, a miraculous way was opened up for us to build a house on our forty acres of wilderness land in Vinton County, Ohio, which we called "the Promised Land." Once more we wondered. Vinton County, in the heart of southeastern Ohio, was very Appalachian, very poor, and very white. Why would we want to live here? We found out rather quickly, as we became a part of our new community and got deeply involved in a wide variety of activities.

At one point Jeannie raised a question at a church meeting. "Why are there no Red Cross blood drives in Vinton County?" She was asked to find the answer to her own question and soon she was in charge of the county's bloodmobiles, a position she has filled for more than twenty years (I have served as her chief assistant). She has a large group of volunteers who have selflessly donated their time and service over those years.

A few years after we moved to the Promised Land, I was elected to the board of the Jackson-Vinton Community Action Agency, a government-funded program which provides a wide range of services to poor citizens in two counties. I served for two five-year terms, including several years as board chair. It was during one of those latter years that I had the unfortunate experience of becoming the volunteer full-time acting director of the agency for two months, during a time of crisis.

Most recently, Jeannie and I have been very much involved with a non-profit corporation called the Sojourners Care Network. Two brothers, Rich and Marcus Games, had such a deep concern for troubled youth who needed foster care that they pooled their own funds to set up the agency. Now they are the codirectors of what has become a multi-million dollar enterprise that still provides foster care. But we have added a long list of specialized training programs: mentoring, transitional housing, and more. One of the first to be added was Youthbuild, which trains high school dropouts in construction skills while it helps them to earn their high school diplomas. Incidentally we have also introduced several African American people to our county as staff, program participants, and foster children. Jeannie and I are both members of the Sojourners board.

Before we moved to Vinton County, we never thought much about the needs of Appalachians. Though I had lived much of my life in West Virginia, the only state that lies totally in Appalachia, I was not really part of that culture, nor did I understand the richness of its heritage. Now we realize that we are once again part of an oppressed group, which has been treated by many outside forces as a third-world country, where resources could be harvested cheaply, to the enrichment of those outside of our region. For generations, the coal, oil, gas, and timber have flowed unceasingly out of our counties; but those who produced these products have remained among the lowest on the economic ladder in our nation. It should come as no surprise that when Jesse Jackson comes to the hills of southeastern Ohio to speak about his Rainbow Coalition, he speaks to receptive mostly white audiences. They understand that poverty has no color, and has no accent.

And we learned a lesson once again—that wherever God places us, that is where we are to serve.

7. The "Least of These"

It may be that living in Appalachia has helped us to understand the concept of poverty even better than we had before. Even though I worked closely with the Poor People's Campaign in 1968, and Jeannie and I were intimately involved in the work of the Legislative Task Force at that time, our experience of poverty related primarily to the African American communities in which we had lived and worked. In Montgomery we had visited in the shacks of people who were just barely existing. Even in Columbus we knew people who survived only because of the special assistance they received.

In Vinton County, we have discovered a new aspect of poverty. We are involved with several church and private groups whose sole function is to provide food, clothing, and other material assistance to people who have almost nothing to live on. When there is a distribution of federal surplus food, the parking lot is jammed long before the giveaway starts. The face of poverty is not limited to one color, or one culture, or one nation. The same kind of hopelessness that we have observed in the black ghettos of our country can be seen in the faces of Appalachia. The difference here is that the people are more spread out than they are in the inner cities, and perhaps easier to overlook.

We remember also our visits to the Navajo Nation in Arizona. We heard many stories of this once-proud people, who had been deceived by the U.S. government, driven from their lands, hunted down, and slaughtered mercilessly, and many of whom now live on their reservation in abject poverty.

The reality is the same. Whether in the hills, or along the city streets, or on the reservations, or among the impoverished marginal farms of our nation, there is poverty. And we, as a nation, have an obligation to deal with it. In Matthew 25, Jesus shared with us an image of the final judgment of the nations. He made it clear that our eternal fate will depend on whether we have ministered to the hungry, the thirsty, the stranger, the naked, the sick, and the imprisoned. Jesus made it even more personal, telling us that when we minister to "the least of these," we minister to him.

Though the same criteria certainly apply to us as individuals, keep in mind that this passage relates specifically to the judgment of the *nations!* It will not be enough for each of us, or even each of our churches and agencies, to provide more support to those who live in poverty. Unless our political and business leaders learn how to deal with this issue, our nation is condemned. We are convinced that the most serious form of oppression that threatens our country today is not only racial, it is also economic.

How are we to deal with this issue? It is imperative that we persuade the leaders of our nation to make the elimination of poverty a major national priority. We know it can be accomplished if we set our minds to it. We have done it many times before.

President Franklin D. Roosevelt took office during the Great Depression. Hunger and unemployment plagued our entire nation. Several federal programs were put into place. The entire country pulled together to deal with our common problems. And we prospered. Every time our country has found itself going to war, our citizens have sacrificed to make certain our armed forces have had all the resources they needed to do their job.

The one glaring exception to this pattern is the so-called "Global War on Terror" growing out of the "9-11" attack on our country. There have been considerable sacrifices; but they have fallen disproportionately upon several vulnerable groups. At this count, more than 2,000 of our young people have been killed in the war in Iraq, and untold tens of thousands have been wounded, some maimed for life. The poorest of our citizens, those most dependent on governmental assistance, have been told that their programs must be drastically cut to pay for the war. And the wealthiest people in the land, whose enormous tax cuts have already created huge deficits in our national budget, have been promised by the current administration that those tax cuts should be made permanent, even at time when we are going farther into debt to pay for a war in which we should not have gotten involved in the first place.

When Lyndon B. Johnson was president of the United States, he proclaimed a "War on Poverty." Though it was certainly not a total success, many of the programs that were part of that effort raised the standard of living for millions of people in our country.

If we determine collectively that a real war on poverty is an appropriate goal for us to achieve, we, as a nation, can do it. The only thing lacking is the will. Unfortunately our present national government is not moving in that direction. So it is imperative that we lobby our Congress and our president to take positive steps to deal with the enormous problems of poverty.

Let them know of the critical need for the creation of new meaningful jobs, and the training necessary for those jobs to be filled. Help them to understand the necessity for the development of imaginative new educational programs that will give this generation of children, about to be lost forever, some hope for a positive future. Remind them that if we do not provide for broader health insurance coverage for all of our citizens, and better programs of preventive medicine, we will be "penny-wise, but pound-foolish." The cost of picking up the pieces later will be much greater than the cost of facing the challenge now.

And let us not forget that even many of those living in poverty in this country are wealthy compared with the desperately poor in many parts of the world, especially in third-world countries. In terms of the obligations laid upon us by Jesus, we are equally responsible for ministering to "the least of these" who live in other parts of our world.

It used to be that people would talk about "pie in the sky by and by," meaning that they could deal with the deprivations of this world, knowing that someday they would experience the abundance that God had waiting for them in heaven. But in today's world that is no longer enough. Our very affluence and the ever-present influences of mass culture have created a strong desire among poor people to share the worldly goods they see around them. They will no longer be satisfied with empty promises.

If we, in this generation, do not find the national will to expend the same level of resources and energy to fight the war on poverty as we have dedicated to fighting our historic wars against other nations and the current war against terrorism, we may one day discover that we have created an internal enemy, every bit as fearsome and every bit as destructive as any enemy we have ever faced. And those within our nation who call themselves Christian will have to recognize that Jesus Christ himself is standing in judgment over us!

8. FIND A WAY TO PAY THE DEBT

I will not restate in detail the argument I posed earlier in Chapter 10 that white Americans have accumulated a massive debt which they still owe to black Americans. Nor will I propose a formula by which that debt can be satisfied. But I will suggest a possible approach which may be helpful. It was from the very poorest of our population that the resources were stolen which constitute the debt that we now owe. Would it not be reasonable to direct any "payment" on that debt toward the uplifting of the very poorest people in our land today?

Let me remind our readers that the concept of repaying a debt owed by one population of people to another is not unknown in our world. When the full story was known about the horrible Nazi atrocities that constituted the Holocaust, enormous sums were paid by governmental and corporate entities to Jewish families and to the nation of Israel, And years after the internment of Japanese-American citizens by our federal government during the Second World War, payments were made to those surviving families.

In neither case was it possible to determine the precise amount of the debt that needed to be satisfied, nor to be certain that all of the appropriate people were compensated. But reparations were paid.

We might recall that President Abraham Lincoln promised to provide each freed slave with "40 acres and a mule." Not only was that promise not kept by those who followed him in the White House, but during the following generations much of the land owned and worked by African American farmers was systematically stripped from their possession. Our own government often was a partner to those transactions.

Would it not be appropriate now to suggest that our federal government could begin its repayment of our racial debt by engaging in the new war on poverty I have just advocated? Let me respond to two possible objections.

"We tried that, and it didn't work." To the contrary, much of what was tried was very helpful to those whom the programs assisted. We just didn't do it wisely enough or broadly enough. And just because an earlier program was faulty is no reason to stop trying.

"We don't know how much we owe, and to whom. And we'll never be able to sort it all out." This is certainly correct. But what I am proposing does not depend on answering those questions. It bypasses the dilemma by focusing only on the need.

Let us remind ourselves once again that none of us, as individuals or groups, can accomplish the massive task that I am proposing. We can only succeed if enough of us raise our voices to persuade our leaders in Washington and in our state capitals that this is a challenge that can no longer be ignored.

9. A LIFE COMMITTED TO NONVIOLENCE

It was not solely by happenstance that Dr. King espoused the principle of total nonviolence during the Montgomery Bus Boycott. He had studied the activities of Mohandas Gandhi in India, who had resolutely opposed the domination of Great Britain over his nation. Bayard Rustin and Glenn Smiley, who were committed disciples of the Indian leader, had come to Montgomery in early 1956 for the purpose of schooling King on Gandhi's teachings. Gandhi had taught his followers that they must boldly stand up against the oppression of their foreign rulers, yet without any violence on the part of the oppressed people. "Blood may flow in the streets of

India," Gandhi said, "but it must be our blood."

British troops knew how to put down violent uprisings. But they were dumbfounded by the ranks of Gandhi's followers, who stood boldly and quietly before them, in dignified opposition to the evils of a racist society. Ultimately it was the peaceful and nonviolent stance of Gandhi that defeated the armaments and might of the British Empire; and India was freed!

Martin knew that story. And he saw the parallels between the conditions of the Indians and of his people in the southland of America. Martin also recognized that the technique of nonviolence had a logical side. "If we rely on guns," he would say to the crowds at the weekly mass meetings, "we won't succeed, because our white oppressors have many more guns than we do. If we try to use the political process, that will not work. Very few Negroes are allowed to vote. White people control all the structures of government. If we try to exercise our economic muscles, we cannot prevail. There is too little economic wealth in our communities to effect significant change. All we have is our bodies. We do not have to buy a service from our white oppressors, when that service demeans and belittles us. Yet, as we walk together in opposition to the oppression, we must not hate our oppressors."

One of Dr. King's favorite lines was, "Don't let anyone bring you down so low that you hate him!" He reminded the people of Montgomery that we were the people of God. Jesus had commanded us to love our enemies and to do good to those who were doing bad things to us. Our protest was a movement of loving, yet resolute opposition to racism and bigotry.

When the boycott ended after more than a year of walking and sharing rides, and the buses were relatively peacefully desegregated, I am convinced that it was the loving, Christian, peaceful, nonviolent stance of Montgomery's black citizens that persuaded the majority of the city's white population to accept the inevitable societal changes that were coming. I have often said in speeches, "It was the black Christians of Montgomery who taught the white Christians of Montgomery what it means to be Christians."

One of the gay rights organizations in which Jeannie and I are active is called "Soulforce," a name which is borrowed directly from Gandhi, a translation of Gandhi's term "Satyagraha." When Soulforce stages a public demonstration against the anti-gay policies of religious bodies, no one is allowed to take part until he or she has been trained in nonviolence. We speak of nonviolence of the heart, the tongue, and the fist. Our followers are called upon to commit themselves to refraining from violent thoughts, words, and actions in all they do. We refer to those who stand against us as our "opponents," not "enemies." And we pledge ourselves to respect our opponents as well as their beliefs, recognizing that they are just as committed to their cause as we are to ours.

Adhering to the posture of nonviolent opposition to social evils is not the easy approach; nor is it cowardly. Mel White, the leader of Soulforce, refers to that stance as "voluntary redemptive suffering." As we devote our lives to the elimination of prejudice and discrimination, and the development of positive multicultural relationships, we know that our message will not always be appreciated. There will be times when we will face powerful, even violent responses from those who believe we are wrong. Before the battle is joined, we must determine whether we are ready to accept the suffering our position may bring to us. I am reminded of Martin Luther's response to the charges against him, which nearly led to his execution. "I am bound by my conscience," said Luther. "Here I stand. I can do no other."

Jeannie and I understand what it means to place our lives in jeopardy. Attempts were made on our lives in Montgomery. We have been the objects of scorn, abuse, and violent threats, because of our stance on a variety of issues over the years, even though we have attempted to register our protests in a dignified, loving, and not "in-your-face" manner. But we would not change a thing if we were given an opportunity to live our lives all over again. The privilege of standing up for righteousness and justice and love is greater than any other reward we might have received.

ONE MORE WORD must be added. The modern civil rights movement began in the church. It was conducted by people of faith attempting to live out their understanding of God's call to them, to live lives centered in righteousness, justice, and love. When the movement was at its zenith, it achieved its goals because of the involvement of large numbers of people of many faiths.

Our human history would seem to be a betrayal of that call from God, as we survey the wars and conflicts around the world that have grown out of conflicts between and among people of differing faiths. Our faith commitments, which at one point in time were drawing us closer together, now seem to be creating unbridgeable chasms between us. There was a time when church bodies were falling all over each other to identify those tenets which we shared, and could celebrate. Now there are extremist groups within virtually every faith who seem hellbent on identifying every possible difference that divides us.

We must focus our attention once more on Dr. King's dream of the Beloved Community. We must look beyond our differences and think of those factors that we share: our common humanity, our need to partake equitably of the resources God has given to us all, our vulnerability to the destruction that flows out of hatred and animosity, our increasing interdependence as we move into a totally global society and economy. It is God who created us. It is God who calls us to be one people. It is God to whom we are responsible for what we do with our lives and our world.

There is a verse of scripture that was quoted often by Dr. King and which now is engraved in the black marble backdrop to the Civil Rights Memorial in Montgomery, which is dedicated to the memory of Dr. Martin Luther King, Jr., and forty other martyrs who gave their lives for the cause of human rights: "But let justice roll down like waters, and righteousness like an everflowing stream." (Amos 5:24, NRSV)

May that be our dream as we move toward the Beloved Community!

Bob and Jeannie Graetz

Index

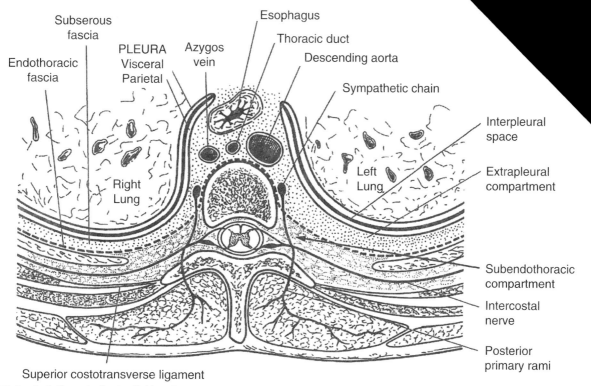

Figure 32-3   Endothoracic fascia divides the paravertebral space into subserous and extrapleural spaces. Note the attachment of endothoracic fascia to the vertebral body. (Reprinted with permission from Karmakar MK. Thoracic paravertebral block. Anesthesiology 2001;95:771–80. Copyright 2000–2003 Ovid Technologies, Inc.)

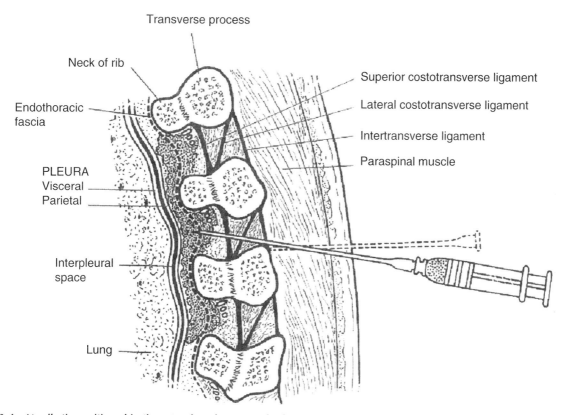

Figure 32-4   Needle tip positioned in the extrapleural paravertebral space. Note how the vertical spread of drugs can be inhibited by the necks of ribs dorsal to the endothoracic fascia. (Reprinted with permission from Karmakar MK. Thoracic paravertebral block. Anesthesiology 2001;95:771–80. Copyright 2000–2003 Ovid Technologies, Inc.)

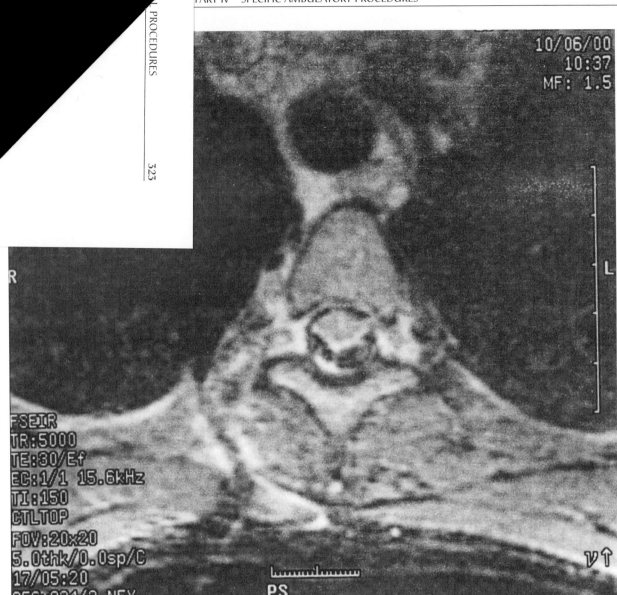

Figure 32-5   Magnetic resonance imaging of T3 paravertebral catheter on the left side. Note the catheter track and the position of the catheter tip closer to the side of the spine. This image is taken prior to injection of saline via the catheter. Note the proximity of pleura to the catheter.

extensive unilateral and contralateral blocks the drugs have to be delivered in the anterior extrapleural compartment. Although epidural spread was documented to account for contralateral spread by Purcell-Jones et al.,[11] a number of authors have documented prevertebral spread as the cause of contralateral analgesia.[10,12] It is likely that injections under pressure in the posterior subendothoracic compartment may follow the path of least resistance into the epidural space along the nerve roots to produce the epidural spread seen clinically with weakness in legs lasting several hours. Whether lower-limb weakness will occur as a consequence of prevertebral spread is currently unknown.

The second important fact is the communication between the thoracic and lumbar paravertebral spaces. Using cadavers, Saito et al.[13] have shown that injection into the lower thoracic paravertebral spaces "under" the endotho-racic fascia tracks to the retroperitoneal area via the medial and lateral arcuate ligaments behind the transversalis fascia where the spinal nerves lie. Although there is a lot of ambiguity with regard to terminology, clinical experience suggests that injections ventral to the endothoracic fascia result in extensive multisegment blocks with communications between the thoracic and lumbar areas[14] as well as limited contralateral spread. However, injections dorsal to the endothoracic fascia result in a much more restricted vertical spread of more or less three segments. Intuitively, advancement of the needle between pleura and the endothoracic fascia can risk pleural puncture and resultant pneumothorax. In the ambulatory setting avoiding pleural puncture is of paramount importance.

The third important anatomic detail is the level of the transverse process in relation to the palpable superior aspect of the spinous process. In the lumbar area the trans-

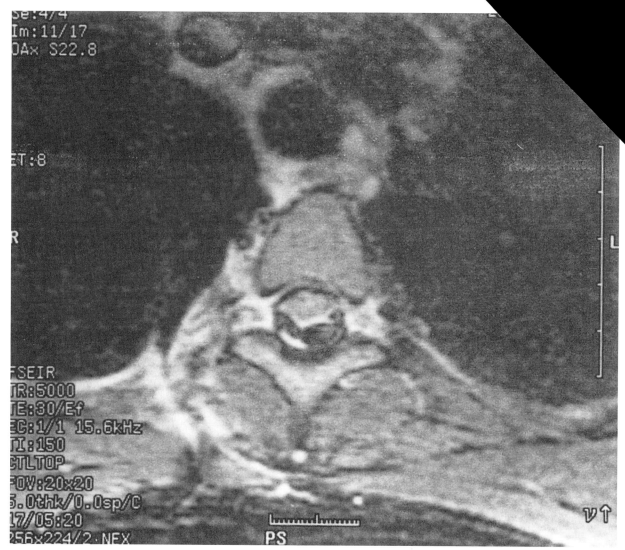

Figure 32-6 Magnetic resonance imaging of T3 paravertebral catheter after 20 mL of saline has been injected via the catheter. Note increased signal prevertebrally and on the contralateral side extrapleurally.

verse processes may be at the same horizontal level as the spinous process. However, in the thoracic area, the transverse process belongs to the vertebra one level below the level of the palpated spinous process owing to the oblique angle of the thoracic spinous process. For example, the superior aspect of T7 spinous process may be at the level of the transverse process of T8 vertebra. Similarly, the superior aspect of C7 vertebra corresponds to the transverse process of T1 vertebra and the T1 nerve root travels under the transverse process of T1 vertebra (Fig. 32-7). This is important to know when T1 block is planned to cover axillary node dissection during breast surgery.

Thus with drugs delivered in the paravertebral space, vertical, contralateral, and epidural spread can occur depending on the location of the needle tip in relation to endothoracic fascia and volume and force of injections. Further studies are needed to verify these observations.

A number of muscles covering the chest, such as the pectoral muscles, serratus anterior, and latissimus dorsi, are supplied by branches of brachial plexus and therefore are not anesthetized by PVBs. This is why patients feel discomfort with a functioning PVB when the pectoral muscles are dissected during mastectomy. Supraclavicular nerves that are branches of the cervical plexus are involved in cutaneous innervation down to the second intercostal space anteriorly as well as the anterior shoulder. This results in sparing of the upper chest with PVBs necessitating a superficial cervical plexus block for complete anesthesia of the anterior chest wall.

TECHNIQUE

A number of techniques have been used to initiate and maintain PVBs. In the original technique described by Eason and Wyatt,[2] the point of needle entry was 2–3 cm lateral to the superior aspect of the spinous process, perpendicular to the skin until the transverse process was contacted. The needle was walked superior to the transverse process to enter the paravertebral space. The supe-

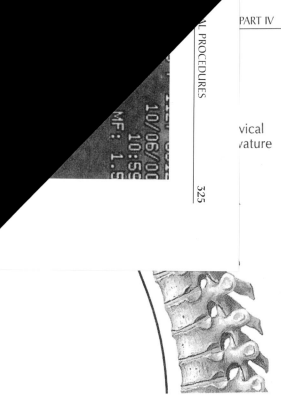

Figure 32-7 Lateral view of the spine. Note that the C7 spinous process top corresponds to the T1 vertebral transverse process. The angulations of mid to low thoracic spines make the spinous process correspond to the transverse processes of at least one vertebra lower. (From Netter FH [ed.], *Atlas of Human Anatomy*. King of Prussia, PA: Rittenhouse Book Distributors, 1997.)

rior angulation was suggested, as it was more likely to contact the intercostal nerves to elicit paresthesia. Later modifications included "walking" caudad to the transverse process for a fixed depth of 1–1.5 cm. A graduated 22 gauge Tuohy needle is used for this purpose. This modification probably is the reason behind reduced incidence of pneumothorax with the series from Greengrass et al.[8,15] and therefore is particularly useful in ambulatory surgical patients. It is likely that the posterior paravertebral space is broader inferiorly than closer to the lower border of the transverse process. The true incidence of pneumothorax is probably unknown, as none of the series reported so far have done prospective radiologic evaluations of patients to identify pneumothoraces not apparent on clinical examination. Loss-of-resistance to saline or local anesthetic is used additionally to confirm correct localization of the space.

Ultrasonography has been used to identify the depth of transverse process from the skin and estimate the safe depth that the needle can be inserted.[16] Richardson et al.[17] have described the use of pressure transducer to identify entry into the paravertebral space. The paraspinal muscles and the superior costotransverse ligament produce a positive-pressure wave during expiration and inspiration. Entry into the paravertebral space results in reduction in expiratory pressure. Entry into the pleural cavity produces negative pressures during inspiration and expiration. Tenicela and Pollan[18] have reported a more medial approach of walking laterally on the lamina until the needle

slips into the paravertebral space. Intuitively, the chances of puncture of dural sleeve, epidural spread, and pleural puncture should be higher with this technique, however there are no studies that have evaluated this technique comparatively to other techniques. In their series of 384 blocks in 130 patients they document one dural puncture and two intrathecal spreads. They also noted a 1.3% incidence of bilateral blocks and evidence of epidural spread in the form of motor sensory blocks of legs with thoracic paravertebral injections. This incidence is similar to the lateral approach described by Eason et al. modified by Naja and Lönnqvist[19] (1% intrathecal or epidural spread, 0.5% pneumothorax, and 0.8% pleural puncture).

Catheterization of the posterior paravertebral space is challenging and usually only 2–3 cm of the catheter can be advanced with difficulty. Buckenmaier et al.[20] have recently reported on the use of such a technique using a continuous catheter delivery system called Contiplex (B. Braun Medical Incorporated, Bethlehem, PA) to provide extended analgesia after breast surgery. The advantage of using this continuous catheter delivery system, according to these authors, is the potential to avoid entraining air should a pleural puncture occur.

Catheterization of the extrapleural paravertebral space is often done using loss of resistance to saline with the same landmarks. After the superior costotransverse ligament is punctured, the needle is advanced toward the vertebral body until loss of resistance to saline injection is felt. Often there is a subtle "pop" of entering the endothoracic fascia. In this location, inspiratory efforts by the patient do not suck in the fluid from the loss of resistance syringe, but there is loss of resistance to injection of saline. Often 5–6 cm of the catheter can be inserted in this location after initial distension of the area with local anesthetic. The use of peripheral nerve stimulators to identify needle location was initially reported by Bonica and Buckley[21] and has been used clinically by a few investigators.[22,23] Fine-tuning needle tip position with the nerve stimulator might also result in increased chances of pleural puncture compared to advancing the needle a fixed length after the transverse process is contacted. This is evident in the paper published by Naja and Lonnqvist.[19]

Sabanathan et al. created an extrapleural pocket paravertebrally and positioned a percutaneously inserted catheter in this pocket to provide continuous PVB after thoracotomies and esophagogastrectomies (Fig. 32-8). A similar technique is used in infants and children after thoracotomies. This technique will obviously not be applicable in the ambulatory setting.

In ambulatory surgical patients the technique that one should adopt must be easy and quick to perform with predictable success and lowest incidence of complications. The operative site should have uniform surgical anesthesia unless the technique is used for analgesic purposes. The multiple-injection technique popularized by Greengrass et al.[8,15] fulfills these criteria well. The patient is usually seated with the assistant providing the support to flex the thoracic and cervical spine. This assistant also helps with the injections and therefore it is important to train the supporting nursing staff with regard to the resistance of injection into the paravertebral space. Routine monitors are applied and the patient is sedated with intravenous (IV) fentanyl

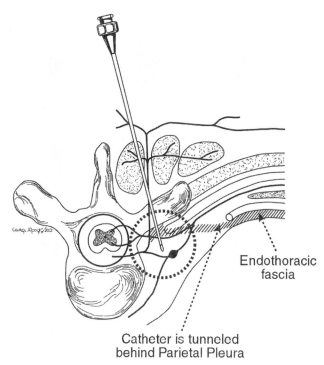

Endothoracic
fascia

Catheter is tunneled
behind Parietal Pleura

Figure 32-8 Position of the extrapleural catheter inserted by stripping the parietal pleura. The needle denotes the path taken by the percutaneous insertion of paravertebral block.

100–250 μg and IV midazolam 1–5 mg. The appropriate levels to be blocked are marked depending on the surgery planned. The vertebra prominence (the most prominent vertebra) is cervical 7 (C7) and usually has a notch in the middle of its superior border. The vertebrae are counted down from this point to identify the appropriate levels. For the lower thoracic segments, counting up from 4th lumbar vertebra is often easier as the spines are significantly angulated in the lower thoracic area (vide supra). The points of needle insertion are marked 2.5 cm lateral to the midpoint of the superior border of the spinous processes.[8]

After skin is prepared with antiseptic solution, local anesthetic infiltration is performed using a 25 gauge, 1.5-inch needle. In a thin patient, one often contacts the transverse process with this needle that provides an indication of the depth of transverse process during the insertion of the Tuohy needle. A 22 gauge, 3.5-inch Tuohy with etched centimeter graduations and wings connected to an extension tubing and a 20-mL syringe of local anesthetic is used for the actual block. The needle is inserted parasaggitally perpendicular to the skin with the aim of contacting the transverse process. If the transverse process is not contacted at about 3 cm depth, the needle is fanned superiorly and inferiorly to the same depth. The needle is advanced deeper only if the needle does not contact the transverse process with this initial fanning. A similar maneuver is made at depths 0.5 cm deeper incrementally until the transverse process is contacted. The needle is held between the two long fingers 1–1.5 cm proximal to the depth at which the transverse process is contacted. The needle is then pulled out subcutaneously and reinserted to walk off inferior to the transverse process. Often a "pop" is felt as

the superior costotransverse ligament is traversed and there is a loss of resistance to injection of local anesthetic. If the local anesthetic cannot be injected easily, the needle is advanced 1 mm at a time until the injection can be made easily after negative aspirations to rule out intravascular position of the needle tip. Usually 3–5 mL of the local anesthetic solution is injected at each site. Ropivacaine is commonly used because of its lower cardiovascular toxic potential. Ropivacaine 1% is often used at the segments covering the main surgical incision in breast surgery and 0.5% ropivacaine is used in the segments away from the surgical site. This possibly results in a denser surgical block at the incision site with faster onset in those segments although this fact has not been prospectively verified in any reported study. With such large doses there is a potential for local anesthetic toxicity. This is discussed further in the section on complications.

Table 32-1 lists the segments that need to be blocked and additional blocks required for various ambulatory chest, truncal, and abdominal procedures. Splanchnic nerves that are formed by T6–T12 spinal nerves supply the peritoneum. Therefore, bilateral T6–T12 blocks are required to accomplish complete peritoneal analgesia. Often with segmental analgesia and heavy sedation, surgeries such as ileostomy closure can be reasonably accomplished with less extensive blocks.

CLINICAL APPLICATIONS IN AMBULATORY SURGERY

Indications

PVBs can be used as a sole anesthetic technique or as an analgesic adjuvant for a variety of ambulatory surgical procedures on the chest and trunk. These include axillary lymph node biopsy/dissections, breast lumpectomies, simple and modified radical mastectomies, cosmetic procedures on the breast, inguinal, umbilical and ventral hernia repairs, thoracoscopic surgery, closure of ileostomy/colostomy, laparoscopic cholecystectomy, abdominal and chest wall procedures, and management of pain after fractured ribs.[24–26] These blocks can be used as adjuvants with interscalene blocks for shoulder surgery.

Breast Cancer Surgery and Axillary Dissections

Report of initial experience with PVBs for breast cancer surgery by Weltz et al.[4] and Greengrass et al.[27] generated a tremendous academic and public awareness of this technique for cancer surgery. They noted the average duration of sensory block was 23 hr and 9 of 15 patients required no opioids postoperatively for pain control. Over 93% of their patients reported that they were "very satisfied" with the technique. This not only resulted in cost savings but provided a different facet to breast cancer surgery, allowing the patient to recover in the comforts of home. Coveney et al.,[28] in a retrospective analysis, compared the anesthetic effectiveness, complications, patients' experience with pain, nausea, vomiting, and length of stay in 145 patients undergoing 156 breast cancer surgeries using PVB to a cohort

Table 32-1   Uses of Paravertebral Blocks

Surgical Procedure	Segments to Be Blocked	Unilateral/Bilateral	Additional Blocks Required
Breast lumpectomy (upper quadrants)	T1–T4	Unilateral	SCP block
Breast lumpectomy (lower quadrants)	T2–T6	Unilateral	None
Mastectomy	T1–T6	Unilateral	SCP block + local infiltration pectoral muscles or BP block
Bilateral gynecomastia excision	T2–T6	Bilateral	None
Breast implants	T2–T6	Bilateral	None
Thoracoscopy	T1–T7	Unilateral	SCP block, CT site
Axillary node dissection	T1–T3	Unilateral	None
Epigastric hernia	T6–T10	Bilateral	None
Umbilical hernia	T6–T11	Bilateral	None
Ileostomy/colostomy closure	T6–T11	Bilateral	None
Inguinal hernia	T11–L2	Unilateral	None
Femoral hernia	T11–L2	Unilateral	None
Multiple rib fractures	Congruent T spinal nerve roots	Unilateral	None
Chest wall surgery	Congruent T spinal nerve roots	Unilateral	None

Abbreviations: SCP, superficial cervical plexus; BP, brachial plexus; CT, chest tube.

of 100 matched patients undergoing the procedures under general anesthesia (GA). They noted that 90% of cases in the PVB group could be completed either with the block alone or the PVB with local anesthetic supplementation. The complication rate in this series was 2.6% with PVB. There was significant reduction in postoperative nausea and vomiting (PONV) in the PVB group (PVB 15.4% vs. GA 40%). Only 20% of patients in the PVB group required therapy for nausea compared to 39% in the GA group. The number of patients requiring opioid analgesia in the postoperative period was significantly lower in the PVB group (98% with GA vs. 25% with PVB). A significantly higher proportion of patients could be discharged home the same day with PVB (98% with PVB vs. 76% with GA). Duration of stay in the postanesthesia care unit (PACU) with PVB was shorter and patients experienced less painful movement with the shoulder. The authors have estimated cost savings to be about 22% with this intervention.

For radical mastectomy, analgesia of dissection of pectoral muscles may be provided with either local infiltration or heavier sedation combined with intermittent boluses of fentanyl and/or ketamine in small doses. Selective blockade of medial and lateral pectoral nerves could also be used to provide analgesia of pectoral dissection but has not been prospectively studied. As the incision often extends to the upper quadrants, superficial cervical plexus blocks will also be required to anesthetize the area covered by supraclavicular nerves.

Axillary node dissections for either radical mastectomy, sentinel node biopsy, excision of hydradenitis suppurativa, or accessory nipple could all be performed with unilateral or bilateral T1–3 PVBs.

Klein et al.[29] have reported on the use of multiple-injection technique for plastic reconstructive surgery of the breast. In their prospective trial comparing PVB to GA, they noted that 10% of patients in the PVB group required a reblock for failed segments and there was 1 failure out of 30 patients requiring conversion to GA. They also noted that patients with PVB had statistically significant lower pain scores only in the initial 24 hr postoperatively. Patients receiving PVB required fewer opioids during this period and experienced less pain during shoulder movement. Nausea scores were different only at the first 24 hr. They also pointed out that it took significantly longer time to initiate the block compared to induction of GA, which is common to most regional anesthesia techniques. Buckenmaier et al. have also described bilateral continuous PVB for reduction mammoplasty and noted that it significantly reduced pain scores and opioid use in a patient admitted to the ambulatory observation unit for 23 hr.[30] Recently,

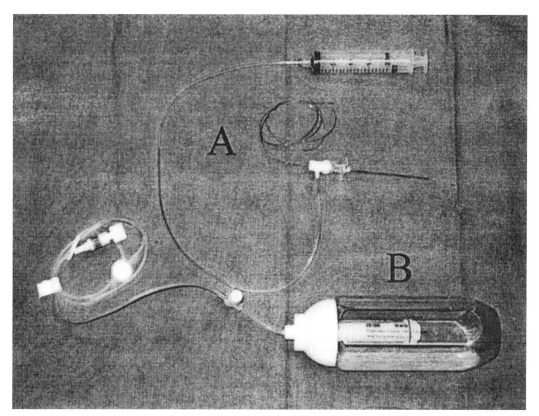

Figure 32-9 Catheter insertion assembly and the pump for ambulatory continuous paravertebral block. (Reproduced with permission from Buckenmaier CC III, Klein SM, Nielsen KC, et al. Continuous paravertebral catheter and outpatient infusion for breast surgery. Anesth Analg 2003;97:715–17. Copyright 2000–2003 Ovid Technologies, Inc.)

Buckenmaier et al. have extended this concept further by sending two patients home with PVB catheters at the T3 level (one bilateral and one unilateral).[20] The authors have inserted the catheters using a continous catheter delivery system and used an elastomeric infusion pump to deliver the local anesthetic at home (Fig. 32-9). They noted that in the patient with bilateral catheters, one of the pumps was not infusing overnight, which possibly could be due to resistance to infusion in the PVB or due to kinking of the catheter. Further studies are required to evaluate elastomeric devices for PVBs, as they may not perform predictably in the presence of additional resistance to delivery into a small confined space.

Terheggen et al.,[31] in a small group of patients, compared GA to PVB initiated with a single catheter inserted at T3–4 level for minor breast surgery. Although the pain scores in the PVB group were smaller in the early postoperative period with higher satisfaction scores, the incidence of nausea was similar between the two groups. The PVB group had 1/15 epidural spread and 1/15 pleural puncture. They have concluded that at present the risk-benefit ratio does not favor routine use of PVB for minor breast surgery. The number of patients in this study is small (total of 30 patients) and the authors have used a catheter technique with injection at a single level. An important factor noted by these authors is the comfort that PVB provided during needle localization of the breast lump. Pusch et al.,[32] in a randomized prospective study comparing single-injection PVB to GA for

breast surgery, noted that the time to perform the block could be significantly shortened to 4–9 min (compared to 24 min in the Klein et al.[29] study with multiple injections). They noted that the PVB was adequate in 93% of patients for surgery and resulted in lower pain scores and nausea postoperatively. They had a 1/42 incidence of epidural spread. Review of the large ambulatory anesthesia database at Duke University reveals the incidence of epidural spread to be 4/1155. Most anesthesiologists are familiar with dealing with hypotension associated with this complication. Usually, the epidural block resolves in 2–3 hr. Clinically it seems that only a portion of the drug enters the epidural space with restricted lower-limb block. To date, no evaluations have been made with regard to the role of speed and volume of injection in the incidence of this complication.

Herniorrhaphy

A variety of abdominal hernias can be corrected using PVB. The most common is inguinal hernia, which can be corrected using unilateral blockade of T11–L2.[33] Bilateral hernias will require bilateral blockade. It is easier to count the spinous processes from L4 upward. Because of the angulations of ribs in the T11 area, entering the space in this location can be challenging. A parasagittal insertion makes it easier than oblique walking of the needle under the transverse process. PVB has been compared to inguinal field blocks.[34,35] While patients achieved similar pain scores, the PVB group used less opioids, had less nausea, and had no urinary retention. Doing herniorrhaphy entirely under inguinal field block involves blocking the ilioinguinal nerve and the genital branch of the genitofemoral, overlapping branches from the adjacent nerves, and the neck of the peritoneal sac, thus necessitating multiple injections in sensitive areas of the body such as the pubic tubercle. Injection of local anesthetic in this area also obliterates surgical anatomy. PVBs are performed with three to four needle insertions in the back without obliterating the surgical anatomy in the operative area. This finding has been confirmed by Wassef et al.[33] in their study. Recently, Weltz et al.[36] reported that it takes only an average of 12.3 min to perform PVBs. In their series of 30 patients, the incidence of urinary retention was zero in the PVB group. The average PACU stay was only 2.5 hr and 20% of their patients required no postoperative opiates for analgesia. The average return to work or normal activities was only 5.5 days. They noted epidural spread in two patients resulting in slight delay in discharge from the PACU. Thus PVBs may have significant impact on the economics of performing inguinal herniorrhaphies as ambulatory surgical procedures.

Abdominal Procedures

A variety of abdominal procedures can be done as ambulatory surgeries with the use of PVB for analgesia. Naja and Lonnqvist[19] seem to have performed bilateral PVBs in 196 patients undergoing major abdominal procedures such as colectomy, gastrectomy, hysterectomy, laparoscopic cholecystectomy, and a variety of other procedures. They used a technique of neurostimulation and loss-of-resistance to initiate the blocks. They documented a 10-fold increase in the incidence of pleural punctures and fivefold increase in pneumothorax with bilateral PVBs compared to unilateral PVBs. For abdominal procedures, bilateral PVBs are required because of the peritoneal sensory supply. Thus the multiple-injection technique probably will be better in ambulatory surgical patients coming for closure of ileostomy/colostomy, laparoscopic cholecystectomy, and ventral hernia repair. For example, for umbilical hernia repair T9–T11 segments are blocked bilaterally. One has to pay attention to identifying the spinous process associated with the segments to be blocked as the lower thoracic spines have a significant downward angulation and may be at the level of transverse processes of 1–2 vertebrae below (vide supra). Often heavy sedation and/or light GA may be required should the peritoneum get stretched, or local infiltration of the peritoneal sac may be used. The greatest advantage of PVB in this setting is the reduction in opioid requirement postoperatively. There are no randomized trials evaluating PVB for abdominal procedures in the ambulatory setting to date.

Thoracoscopic Surgery

Currently thoracoscopic surgical patients are admitted to the hospital for at least 24–48 hr but many institutions are striving to send them home on the same day, particularly after thoracoscopic sympathectomy for hyperhydrosis. Richardson and Sabanathan[37] have used continuous PVBs for video-assisted thoracoscopic surgery (VATS) and document that it provides excellent analgesia. Ganapathy et al.[38] have reported on the use of continuous percutaneous PVB for minimally invasive cardiac surgery and document reduced opioid requirement, extubation at the end of surgery, and discharge at 48 hr. In a randomized trial, Dhole et al.[39] found PVB to be superior to thoracic epidural analgesia for minimally invasive cardiac surgery. Although there are no reports of prospective randomized trials on the use of PVB for ambulatory thoracoscopic surgery, it is not impossible that with the development of robotic surgery, improved thoracoscopic instrumentation, and ambulatory continuous regional analgesia at home, it will soon enter the realm of ambulatory surgery.

Trauma/Orthopedic Surgery

Rib fractures can be painful whether single or multiple. Often the patients are managed with either intercostal blocks or thoracic epidural analgesia, which necessitates admission to the hospital. Karmakar et al.[24–26] have used PVBs for acute pain management particularly in situations where insertion of epidural is contraindicated owing to spinal injury. The author has also used PVB to manage pleuritic chest pain associated with pneumonia.

Unilateral PVB of T11–L1 can facilitate bone harvesting from iliac crest. This is a useful adjunct in patients with rheumatoid arthritis with an unstable neck coming for fusion of wrist with harvesting of bone graft from iliac crest. Iliac crest bone donor site can be very painful and PVBs offer good analgesia following harvest. During shoulder arthroplasty under interscalene block, patients feel discomfort during reaming of the humerus as the inner aspect of the humerus is supplied by the T1 osteotomal segment. Addition of T1–T2 PVBs significantly improves analgesia. The author has on occasion encountered a patient following shoulder arthroplasty with functioning interscalene block complaining of pain on the inner aspect of the upper arm that improves with T1–2 PVBs initiated in the PACU.

Advantages

As a single-injection technique, PVBs provide the longest duration of postoperative analgesia[27] possibly because of drugs being confined to a small space. Unpublished data from Duke University Ambulatory Anesthesia database on over 2500 patients receiving PVBs for various breast surgeries reveals that pain measured by verbal analog scale (VAS) scores are less than 3/10 in 94.4% of patients 24 hr after surgery. More than 97% of patients have no PONV in the postoperative period. Opioid consumption is also significantly reduced starting from PACU to as late as a week later.

Paravertebral blocks eliminate the risk of hemodynamic changes associated with bilateral sympathetic block that occurs with epidural analgesia, allowing patients to ambulate faster. Inguinal herniorrhaphy performed under PVBs results in the lowest incidence of urinary retention.[35] Ho et al.[40] have documented resolution of ST-segment depression with high thoracic PVB under GA. Thus PVBs might be particularly useful in patients with ischemic heart disease undergoing chest wall or chest surgery, such as breast cancer surgery. Pulmonary function is better maintained with PVB,[41] compared to interpleural block,[42] and thus PVBs may be particularly useful in patients with respiratory compromise undergoing ambulatory surgical procedures. Paravertebral blocks are easy to perform. They produce complete sensory analgesia and abolish somatosensory-evoked potentials from the blocked segments,[43] resulting in reduction in stress response to surgery. Pulmonary function is preserved better with PVB.[42] PVBs are useful in the ambulatory setting in a medically/physiologically compromised patient. Buckenmaier et al.[44] have reported this fact on the use of PVB for ambulatory breast surgery in a patient with hypertrophic obstructive cardiomyopathy. D'Ercole et al.[45] have reported on a pregnant patient undergoing radical mastectomy with PVB.

Contraindications

In the ambulatory setting, scar in the thoracic segments to be blocked may potentially increase the complication rates of pleural puncture, pulmonary hemorrhage, and ineffective spread of the injected local anesthetic. Bilateral PVBs with a potential for bilateral Horner's syndrome could potentially affect cardiac conduction further in patients with bifascicular block and major conduction defects in the heart, but to date the role of PVB in the cardiac conducting system has not been evaluated. Local infection, allergy to local anesthetic, lack of patient consent, and vascular malformations at the puncture site could be considered legitimate contraindications. Although coagulopathy can lead to bleeding in the muscle resulting in a hematoma, this bleed is not in a confined space such as the central neuraxis and therefore is only a relative contraindication. The author has used PVBs for cardiac surgery with no problems associated with anticoagulation but this subset of patients have a chest tube inserted for surgical reasons. Thus in an ambulatory setting one needs to weigh the risk/benefit ratio of PVB for a surgical procedure in the presence of coagulopathy.

Complications and Side Effects

A number of complications have been described following PVBs but the incidence is low (2.6–5%).[5,28] Some complication rates may be higher depending on the technique used. These include pleural puncture (0.2–2%),[19] pneumothorax (0.2–1%),[19] pulmonary hemorrhage (rare), hypotension (3.9%),[19] epidural spread (1%), intrathecal spread (rare), local anesthetic toxicity, failed blocks (6–10%), pain at the site of injection (1–1.5%),[19] bruising, local hematoma (2–3%),[19] accidental intravascular injection, vascular puncture (5–8.7%),[19] postdural puncture

headache, nerve injury, myelopathy, and Brown-Séquard syndrome with alcohol injection.[1] Bilateral PVBs are associated with a tenfold increase in the chance of pleural puncture and fivefold increase in the chance of pneumothorax[19] with the technique used by Naja et al. with neurostimulation, whereas the experience at Duke University Ambulatory Surgery Center using the multiple-injection technique reveals the chances of pneumothorax to be less than 1 in 4000. Use of the hemostatic valve might reduce the chances of major pneumothorax but it may not prevent the incidence of pleural puncture. It is interesting to note that these complications are extremely low in children.[19]

It is common to have Horner's syndrome after high thoracic PVB. Similarly, numbness of C8 nerve distribution in the forearm can occur with high thoracic PVBs. Low-level local anesthetic toxicity can occur in a small number of patients. Plasma levels of local anesthetic measured during thoracic surgery using bupivacaine in adults[46] reveal that mean plasma levels can be as high as 4.9 μg/mL after 48 hr of infusion, and levels as high as 7.5 μg/mL have been reported with no clinical signs of toxicity. The same authors have reported on postoperative confusion in a few patients undergoing infusions via the PVB catheter, which resolved on cessation of infusion, signifying that prolonged infusion can lead to accumulation and result in low levels of local anesthetic toxicity. Use of drugs such as ropivacaine that have a lower cardiovascular toxic profile are highly recommended for this application. Cheung et al.[47] have reported on the serum levels of bupivacaine in 22 infants aged 1 day to 20 weeks after thoracotomies and direct insertion of extrapleural paravertebral catheters. After a bolus of 1.25 mg/kg, an infusion was continued for 48 hr with 0.125% bupivacaine at 0.2 mL/kg/hr. Mean bupivacaine levels were 1.6 ± 0.6 μg/mL. Three patients had levels greater than 3 μg/mL 30–48 hr later. Use of drugs like midazolam and propofol for sedation clinically counteracts the effects of low-level local anesthetic toxicity both on the cardiovascular system and on the central nervous system and they are highly recommended if relatively large doses are used in relation to the patient's weight.

FUTURE APPLICATIONS

With the evolution of minimally invasive surgery on the kidneys, lungs, and heart, PVB will be used to facilitate ambulatory surgeries in these areas. Use of PVB for refractory angina as an ambulatory procedure is potentially possible. The role of PVB in immunomodulation will be an interesting aspect to evaluate in the future.

SUMMARY

The PVB technique is versatile and it can be used for a variety of surgical procedures in the ambulatory setting. It is associated with a low incidence of complications and provides the longest duration of analgesia after a single injection. Currently the multiple-injection technique has the lowest complication rate. It can be used as a sole anesthetic technique or as an analgesic adjuvant combined with light GA. It provides excellent postoperative analgesia and reduces the incidence of PONV, and urinary retention.

REFERENCES

1. Karmakar MK. Thoracic paravertebral block. Anesthesiology 2001; 95:771–80.

2. Eason MJ, Wyatt R. Paravertebral thoracic block: a reappraisal. Anaesthesia 1979;34:638–42.

3. Wood GJ, Lloyd JW, Bullingham RE, Britton BJ, Finch DR. Postoperative analgesia for day-case herniorrhaphy patients: a comparison of cryoanalgesia, paravertebral blockade and oral analgesia. Anaesthesia 1981;36:603–10.

4. Weltz C, Greengrass R, Lyerly H. Ambulatory surgical management of breast carcinoma using paravertebral block. Ann Surg 1995;222:19–26.

5. Richardson J, Sabanathan S. Thoracic paravertebral analgesia. Acta Anaesthesiol Scand 1995;39:1005–15.

6. Vincent WS, Chan, Ferrante MF. Continuous thoracic paravertebral block. Chapter 17 in: Ferrante MF, VadeBoncouer TR (eds.), Postoperative Pain Management. New York: Churchill Livingstone, 1993.

7. Richardson J, Lonnqvist PA. Thoracic paravertebral block. Br J Anaesth 1998;81:230–38.

8. Greengrass R, Buckenmaier CC III. Paravertebral anaesthesia/analgesia for ambulatory surgery. Best Pract Res Clin Anaesthesiol 2002; 16:271–83.

9. Sabanathan S, Mearns AJ, Bickford Smith PJ, et al. Efficacy of extrapleural intercostals nerve block on post-thoracotomy pain and pulmonary mechanics. Br J Surg 1990;77:221–25.

10. Karmakar MK, Kwok WB, Kew J. Thoracic paravertebral block: radiological evidence of contralateral spread anterior to the vertebral bodies. Br J Anaesth 2000;84:263–65.

11. Purcell-Jones G, Pither CE, Justins DM. Paravertebral somatic nerve block: a clinical, radiographic and computed tomographic study in chronic pain patients. Anesth Analg 1989;68:32–39.

12. Lonnqvist PA, Hesser U. Radiological and clinical distribution of thoracic paravertebral blockade in infants and children. Paediatr Anaesth 1993;3:83–87.

13. Saito T, Den S, Tanuma K, et al. Anatomical bases for paravertebral anesthetic block: fluid communication between the thoracic and lumbar paravertebral regions. Surg Radiol Anat 1999;21: 359–63.

14. Saito T, Gallagher ET, Cutler S, et al. Extended unilateral anesthesia: new technique or paravertebral anesthesia? Reg Anesth 1996; 21:304–7.

15. Nielsen KC, Greengrass RA, Steele SS, et al. Unpublished data from Duke Ambulatory Anesthesia database.

16. Pusch F, Wilding E, Klimscha W, et al. Sonographic measurement of needle insertion depth in paravertebral blocks in women. Br J Anaesth 2000;85:841–43.

17. Richardson J, Cheema SP, Hawkins J, Sabanathan S. Thoracic paravertebral space location: a new method using pressure measurement. Anaesthesia 1996;51:137–39.

18. Tenicela R, Pollan SB. Paravertebral-peridural block technique: a unilateral thoracic block. Clin J Pain 1990;6:227–34.

19. Naja Z, Lonnqvist PA. Somatic paravertebral nerve blockade: incidence of failed block and complications. Anaesthesia 2001;56:1184–88.

20. Buckenmaier CC III, Klein S, Nielsen K, et al. Continuous paravertebral catheter and outpatient infusion for breast surgery. Anesth Analg 2003;97:715–17.

21. Bonica J, Buckley F. Regional analgesia with local anesthetics. In: Bonica JJ (ed.), The Management of Pain, 2nd ed. Malvern, PA: Lea & Febiger, 1990, vol 2, Chapter 94, p. 1913.

22. Wheeler LJ. Peripheral nerve stimulation end-point for thoracic paravertebral block. Br J Anaesth 2001;86:598–99.

23. Lang SA. The use of nerve stimulator for thoracic paravertebral block. Anesthesiology 2002;97:521.

24. Karmakar MK, Ho AM. Acute pain management of patients with multiple fractured ribs. J Trauma Injury Infect Crit Care 2003;54: 615–25.

25. Karmakar MK, Critchley LA, Ho AM, et al. Continuous thoracic paravertebral infusion of bupivacaine for pain management in patients with multiple fractured ribs. Chest 2003;123:424–31.

26. Karmakar MK, Chui PT, Joynt GM, Ho AM. Thoracic paravertebral block for management of pain associated with multiple fractured ribs in patients with concomitant lumbar spinal trauma. Reg Anesth Pain Med 2001;26:169–73.

27. Greengrass R, O'Brien F, Lyerly K, Hardman D, Gleason D, D'Ercole F, Steele S. Paravertebral block for breast cancer surgery. Can J Anaesth 1996;43:858–61.

28. Coveney E, Weltz CR, Greengrass R, Iglehart JD, Leight GS, Steele SM, Lyerly HK. Use of paravertebral block anesthesia in the surgical management of breast cancer: experience in 156 cases. Ann Surg 1998;227:496–501.

29. Klein SM, Bergh A, Steele SM, Georgiade GS, Greengrass RA. Thoracic paravertebral block for breast surgery. Anesth Analg 2000;90: 1402–5.

30. Buckenmaier CC III, Steele SM, Nielsen KC, Martin AH, Klein SM. Bilateral continuous paravertebral catheters for reduction mammoplasty. Acta Anaesthesiol Scand 2002;46:1042–45.

31. Terheggen MA, Willie F, Borel R, Inne H, Ionescu T, Knappe K. Paravertebral blockade for minor breast surgery. Anesth Analg 2002; 94:355–59.

32. Pusch F, Freitag H, Weinstabl C, Obwegeser R, Huber E, Wildling E. Single injection paravertebral block compared to general anesthesia in breast surgery. Acta Anaesthesiol Scand 1999;43: 770–74.

33. Wassef MR, Randazzo T, Ward W. The paravertebral nerve root block for inguinal herniorrhaphy: a comparison with field-block approach. Reg Anesth Pain Med 1998;23:451–56.

34. Klein SM, Greengrass RA, Weltz C, Warner DS. Paravertebral somatic nerve block for outpatient inguinal herniorrhaphy: an expanded case report of 22 patients. Reg Anesth Pain Med 1998;23: 306–10.

35. Klein SM, Pietrobon R, Nielsen KC, Steele SM, Warner DS, Moylan JA, Eubanks WS, Greengrass RA. Paravertebral somatic nerve block compared with peripheral nerve block for outpatient inguinal herniorrhaphy. Reg Anesth Pain Med 2002;27:476–80.

36. Weltz CR, Klein SM, Arbo JE, Greengrass RA. Paravertebral block anesthesia for inguinal hernia repair. World J Surg 2003;27: 425–29.

37. Richardson J, Sabanathan S. Pain management in video assisted thoracic surgery. Evaluation of localized rib resection: a new technique. J Cardiovasc Surg (Torino) 1995;36:505–9.

38. Ganapathy S, Murkin JM, Boyd DW, Dobkowski W, Morgan J. Continuous percutaneous paravertebral block for minimally invasive cardiac surgery. J Cardiothorac Vasc Anesth 1999;13:594–96.

39. Dhole S, Mehta Y, Saxena H, Juneja R, Trehan N. Comparison of continuous thoracic epidural and paravertebral blocks for postoperative analgesia after minimally invasive direct coronary artery bypass surgery. J Cardiothorac Vasc Anesth 2001;15:288–92.

40. Ho AM, Lim HS, Yim AP, Karmakar MK, Lee TW. The resolution of ST segment depression after high thoracic paravertebral block during general anesthesia. Anesth Analg 2002;95:227–28.

41. Richardson J, Sabanathan S, Mearns AJ, Shah RD, Goulden C. A prospective randomized comparison of interpleural and paravertebral analgesia in thoracic surgery. Br J Anaesth 1995;75:405–8.

42. Richardson J, Sabanathan S, Jones J, Shah RD, Cheema S, Mearns AJ. A prospective randomized comparison of preoperative and continuous balanced epidural or paravertebral bupivacaine on post

thoracotomy pain, pulmonary function and stress responses. Br J Anaesth 1999;83:387–92.

43. Richardson J, Jones J, Atkinson R. The effect of thoracic paravertebral blockade on intercostals somatosensory evoked potentials. Anesth Analg 1998;87:373–76.

44. Buckenmaier CC III, Steele SM, Nielsen KC, Klein SM. Paravertebral somatic nerve blocks for breast surgery in a patient with hypertrophic obstructive cardiomyopathy. Can J Anaesth 2002;49:571–74.

45. D'Ercole FJ, Scott D, Bell E, Klein SM, Greengrass RA. Paraverte-
bral blockade for modified radical mastectomy in a pregnant patient. Anesth Analg 1999;88:1351–53.

46. Berrisford RG, Sabanathan S, Mearns AJ, Clarke BJ, Hamdi A. Plasma concentrations of bupivacaine and its enantiomers during continuous extrapleural intercostal nerve block. Br J Anaesth 1993; 70:201–4.

47. Cheung SL, Booker PD, Franks R, Pozzi M. Serum concentrations of bupivacaine during prolonged continuous paravertebral infusion in young infants. Br J Anaesth 1997;79:9–13.

Centroneuraxial Blockade for Ambulatory Surgery

LILA ANN A. SUEDA   •   SPENCER S. LIU

INTRODUCTION

Spinal anesthesia has enjoyed a long history of enthusiasm and success. Spinal anesthesia remains a popular choice among anesthesiologists for its elegant simplicity, safety, and high success rate. It is well suited for a wide range of ambulatory surgical procedures, including lower-extremity orthopedic, gynecologic, urologic, and selected lower-abdominal operations. New innovations in technology (needles, catheters, and local anesthetics) have been responsible for the continued safety and efficacy of spinal/epidural anesthesia. This chapter will review patient selection for spinal anesthesia, pharmacologic choices of spinal anesthesia, and controversies of spinal anesthesia.

SPINAL ANESTHESIA FOR AMBULATORY SURGERY

Spinal anesthesia brings unique advantages and disadvantages to the ambulatory setting. It is associated with rapid onset, reliability, prompt achievement of discharge criteria, minimal side effects, and improved analgesia.[1] However, there are several potential factors limiting its popularity in this patient population. The first is the potential for postdural puncture headache (PDPH).[2,3] Nevertheless, the introduction of small-gauge, pencil-point spinal needles has decreased the incidence of PDPH to approximately 1%, thereby increasing its acceptance. Second, the use of spinal lidocaine has been associated with transient neurologic symptoms (TNS). This has sparked interest in the use of spinal adjuncts to decrease the overall dose of local anesthetic, the use of different local anesthetics to mimic the short duration of spinal lidocaine, as well as the use of smaller doses of lidocaine. Finally, spinal anesthesia can potentially delay discharge if micturition is used as a criterion for discharge.[4] While this remains controversial, recent evidence suggests that low-risk patients do not have to void prior to discharge.[5]

Knee Arthroscopy

Various types of anesthesia for outpatient knee arthroscopy, including local infiltration, epidural, spinal, or general anesthesia, have been utilized successfully. Factors such as patient preference (i.e., desire to be awake and watch or desire to be asleep), surgical operative conditions (i.e., need for muscle relaxation), operating room efficiency, side effects, and time to discharge need to be considered when planning anesthesia for this common ambulatory orthopedic procedure. The ideal anesthetic should meet patient satisfaction criteria, provide excellent operating condition, be quick and reliable, provide for rapid discharge, and be devoid of side effects. A recent review of evidence-based medicine regarding the optimal anesthetic technique suggests that many factors, including patient expectations, comorbidities, and the skill of the surgeon and anesthesiologist, may preclude the establishment of an "optimal" anesthetic technique.[6]

Spinal anesthesia can be advantageous as it is quick and easy to perform and highly reliable. Spinal anesthesia avoids the physiologic trespasses associated with general anesthesia and produces less postoperative neurocognitive changes. Furthermore, it is ideal in patients who prefer to observe the procedure on the monitor.

A prospective, randomized, double-blind study of 100 outpatients undergoing knee arthroscopy showed that 4 mg of bupivacaine compared to 3 mg of bupivacaine plus 10 μg of fentanyl produced reliable spinal anesthesia for outpatient knee arthroscopy with a shorter discharge time in the bupivacaine-fentanyl group—however, with a 1% block failure rate.[7] Postanesthesia care unit (PACU) stay was shorter in the bupivacaine-fentanyl group compared to the bupivacaine group (36, range of 10–103, vs. 55, range of 10–140 min). However comparing the bupivacaine-fentanyl with bupivacaine-only groups, the time to void (171 vs. 182 min), ambulate (158 vs. 166 min), and home-readiness (171 vs. 183 min) were not statistically significant. The incidence of TNS was 3%.

Another randomized, prospective, double-blind study comparing the use of low-dose lidocaine-fentanyl spinal anesthesia with conventional-dose lidocaine spinal anesthesia showed that spinal anesthesia with low-dose lidocaine and fentanyl provided adequate anesthesia with greater hemodynamic stability and faster recovery than spinal anesthesia with the conventional dose of lidocaine.[8] The times to full sensory regression (80 ± 21 vs. 110 ± 25 min), voiding (130 ± 34 vs. 162 ± 35 min), and discharge (145 ± 38 vs. 180 ± 31 min) were significantly shorter in the low-dose group compared to the conventional-dose group. Interestingly, the authors also noted a decreased incidence of TNS with the low-dose lidocaine compared with conventional-dose (3.6 vs. 32.7%).

In a randomized, prospective, double-blind study comparing 3% 2-chloroprocaine epidural anesthesia to 25 mg hyperbaric lidocaine plus 20 μg fentanyl spinal anesthesia for outpatients undergoing knee arthroscopy, no significant difference was found in operative conditions, discharge times, and recovery profiles.[9]

Laparoscopy

Selective spinal anesthesia, a technique that uses minimal doses of intrathecal agents, so that only the nerve roots supplying a specific area and only the modalities that are required to be anesthetized are affected, has been used for short-duration outpatient gynecologic laparoscopy.[10] It is an effective, acceptable alternative to general anesthesia.

A recent prospective, randomized, controlled trial that compared recovery profiles of patients undergoing selective spinal anesthesia using a hypobaric solution of lidocaine 10 mg and sufentanil 10 μg versus general anesthesia with propofol and nitrous oxide demonstrated shorter recovery characteristics with the use of low-dose local anesthetic and intrathecal opioid.[11] The times to exit operating room (6.0 vs. 11.9 min), straight leg raise (3.8 vs. 32.4 min), deep knee bend (3.8 vs. 76.1 min), Aldrete score > 9 (6.7 vs. 51.0 min), total phase I and II PACU stay (96.2 vs. 109 min) were significantly shorter in the spinal group compared to the general anesthesia group. A similar prospective, randomized, controlled trial compared the recovery profiles of patients undergoing selective spinal anesthesia and general anesthesia with desflurane and nitrous oxide.[12] Surgical conditions were rated good or excellent in 9 of 10 cases in the spinal group and excellent in 10 of 10 cases in the general anesthesia group. Shoulder discomfort occurred in 3 of 10 patients in the spinal group, which required treatment with supplemental intravenous (IV) fentanyl. Three of ten patients in the spinal group also reported mild or moderate postoperative nausea and 4 of 10 patients reported pruritus. While Aldrete scores were significantly better in the selective spinal anesthesia group, there was no significant difference in the duration of stay in the PACU between the two groups. Thus, spinal anesthesia can be a reasonable alternative to general anesthesia in selected patients in terms of recovery profile and operating conditions.

Extracorporeal Shock Wave Lithotripsy

Extracorporeal shock wave lithotripsy (ESWL) is a technique used to break up calculi in the kidneys or the upper ureters. High-energy shock waves are directed at the renal calculus, using high-energy or low-energy units. As the shock waves enter the body through the skin, dissipation of a small amount of energy occurs, resulting in pain during lithotripsy. The degree of pain varies depending on the type of lithotripsy unit used. For example, lithotripsy units employing a water bath, such as the Dornier HM3, require relatively high-intensity shock waves and anesthesia, whereas units that are coupled directly to the skin require lower-intensity shock waves and may require only light sedation.[13]

Currently, many anesthetic techniques are successfully used for ESWL, including general anesthesia, epidural anesthesia, spinal anesthesia, flank infiltration, and analgesia-sedation.[14] In a randomized, prospective, double-blind study comparing intrathecal sufentanil versus intrathecal 5% lidocaine, intrathecal sufentanil was shown to improve recovery profile. The times to ambulation (79 ± 16 vs. 146 ± 57 min), voiding (80 ± 18 vs. 152 ± 54 min), and home discharge (98 ± 17 vs. 166 ± 50 min) were faster in the intrathecal sufentanil group compared with the intrathecal 5% lidocaine group.[14]

A prospective, randomized study comparing general anesthesia with propofol and nitrous oxide to epidural anesthesia with 1.5% lidocaine demonstrated rapid recovery with minimal side effects with general anesthesia. The PACU recovery time (88 ± 39 vs. 51 ± 22 min) and total recovery time (178 ± 49 vs. 127 ± 59 min) were significantly longer in the epidural anesthesia group compared with general anesthesia group.[15]

Inguinal Herniorrhaphy

Inguinal herniorrhaphy is a common outpatient procedure that can be performed using either general anesthesia, regional anesthesia, or local anesthesia. Spinal anesthesia has the advantages of a more awake and alert patient and increased operating room efficiency. While low-dose bupivacaine with or without the addition of an opioid has been used in patients undergoing knee arthroscopy, it is uncertain whether low-dose bupivacaine would be effective in patients undergoing inguinal herniorrhaphy owing to the longer nature of the procedure and the need for a higher level of sensory blockade (i.e., thoracic nerve roots). A recent prospective, randomized, double-blind study that compared 6 mg 0.5% bupivacaine with 8% glucose + 25 μg fentanyl with 7.5 mg 0.5% bupivacaine with 8% glucose + 25 μg fentanyl showed that all parameters, including time to first urination (268 vs. 335 min) and time to home discharge (350 vs. 417 min) were longer in the higher-dose bupivacaine group.[16] A total of 17.5% of patients required catherization because of inability to void. The lower dose of bupivacaine resulted in a 5% failed spinal rate and an increased intraoperative fentanyl requirement (30% vs. 5%). The incidence of TNS was 2.5%. This suggests that spinal anesthesia may not be the preferred anesthetic technique in this patient population. Other regional anesthetic techniques, such as the use of an ilioinguinal-hypogastric nerve block (IHNB) as part of a monitored anesthesia care (MAC), should be considered. IHNB-MAC has been associated with a rapid recovery profile for outpatients undergoing inguinal herniorrhaphy.[17] The time to home readiness (133 ± 68 vs. 171 ± 40 and 280 ± 83 min) was significantly shorter in the IHNB-MAC group compared with general and spinal anesthesia (Table 33-1).

EPIDURAL ANESTHESIA FOR AMBULATORY SURGERY

For ambulatory surgical procedures, most anesthesiologists prefer the simplicity and rapid onset of reliable anesthesia achieved by spinal anesthesia. The onset of surgical anesthesia requires more time than with spinal anesthesia and sometimes can be technically challenging to perform than spinal anesthesia. However, continuous epidural anesthesia offers the advantage of administering additional local anesthetic should the surgical procedure last longer than anticipated and more precise titration of centroneuraxial anesthesia.

COMBINED SPINAL EPIDURAL ANESTHESIA FOR AMBULATORY SURGERY

As with epidural anesthesia, the performance of combined spinal epidural anesthesia (CSE) may require more time to perform, but offers the advantage of rapid onset of anesthesia with the ability to initiate epidural anesthesia if necessary. Unfortunately, there have been no controlled, randomized, prospective trials comparing CSE to other anesthetic techniques for ambulatory surgical procedures.

LOCAL ANESTHETICS

Procaine

Procaine is the oldest member of the ester group of local anesthetics and has a long history of intrathecal use. It is a water-soluble agent with poor lipid solubility and a short duration of action, making it potentially useful in the ambulatory surgical setting.[18] A prospective, randomized, double-blind study to compare the incidence of TNS with spinal procaine or lidocaine in ambulatory knee arthroscopy patients showed that the incidence of TNS was lower with procaine. However, procaine resulted in a lower quality of anesthesia (17% vs. 3%), a higher incidence of intraoperative nausea (17% vs. 3%), and a prolonged average discharge time (242 ± 47 vs. 213 ± 34 min) compared with lidocaine.[19] Furthermore, the frequency and intensity of pruritus with procaine was higher than with lidocaine (55% vs. 21%).[20] Thus, while its short duration of action and low incidence of TNS make procaine an attractive choice in ambulatory anesthesia, this needs to be balanced with its higher incidence of block failure, higher incidence of nausea, and longer discharge times.

Lidocaine

The amino amide local anesthetic lidocaine, discovered in 1948, is one of the most widely used local anesthetics because of its clinical efficacy and reasonable clinical toxicity.[18] Its rapid onset of dense anesthesia, complete motor block, and short to intermediate duration of action has made it the preferred spinal agent in outpatient surgery. However, the use of spinal lidocaine has come into scrutiny

Table 33-1 Recommended Spinal Anesthetics for Various Outpatient Procedures

Procedure	Spinal Anesthetic	Anesthetic Success	Mean Time from Injection Until Recovery (min)
Knee arthroscopy	Bupivacaine 3 mg Fentanyl 10 µg	99%	171
	Lidocaine 20 mg Fentanyl 25 µg	100%	145
	Ropivacaine 8 mg Clonidine 15–45 µg	100%	215
Laparoscopy	Lidocaine 10 mg Sufentanil 10 µg	90%	96
Extracorporeal shock wave lithotripsy	Sufentanil 15 µg	100%	98
Inguinal herniorrhaphy	Bupivacaine spinal not recommended Peripheral nerve block + MAC may be best technique		268–420

SOURCES: See references 7–8, 10, 13, 14, 16, and 30.

lately because of its association with TNS. Prospective, randomized, controlled trials have shown an increased incidence of TNS with spinal lidocaine compared to other agents, thus, decreasing the popularity of spinal lidocaine in ambulatory surgery.[21] While the etiology and significance of this problem remains controversial, the search for an "ideal" spinal agent continues.

Mepivacaine

Mepivacaine, also an amino amide local anesthetic, has the same pharmacologic properties and wide-spectrum clinical characteristics as lidocaine. Since its introduction for spinal anesthesia in the 1960s, its use has not been widespread, in part because of the popularity of lidocaine.[18] The increasing incidence of TNS with spinal lidocaine has prompted its reevaluation for outpatient surgery. Prospective, randomized clinical trials, however, have demonstrated a similar incidence of TNS with hyperbaric mepivacaine (30–37%) as with hyberbaric lidocaine.[22,23] In a recent prospective, randomized clinical trial comparing the incidence of TNS using isobaric 2% mepivacaine with isobaric 2% lidocaine, mepivacaine was associated with a higher incidence of TNS (7.5% vs. 2.5%), although this was not statistically significant.[24] The small sample size precludes conclusions with respect to the difference of TNS incidence between mepivacaine and lidocaine. Hence, more studies are needed to determine whether isobaric mepivacaine prevents TNS.

Prilocaine

Prilocaine was the second amino amide to be used clinically after lidocaine. Because of its structural similarity and potency, the clinical activity of prilocaine is very similar to that of lidocaine with respect to onset, degree of sensory and motor block, and duration of action. However, its use is associated with higher anesthetic failure rates as well as methemoglobinemia, thereby limiting its clinical use and availability in the United States.[18] However, the quest for a short-acting local anesthetic to replace lidocaine in ambulatory surgical procedures remains an important objective.

A randomized, controlled trial comparing the relative risk of TNS after spinal anesthesia with prilocaine, high-dose lidocaine, and low-dose bupivacaine demonstrated a lower incidence of TNS with prilocaine compared to lidocaine (3% vs. 30%).[25] While this study suggests that the characteristics of the spinal block with prilocaine were comparable to those of lidocaine, additional studies are required before concluding that the incidence of TNS with prilocaine is low enough to make it a useful alternative to lidocaine. In a rat model, the intrathecal administration of prilocaine and lidocaine induced comparable functional impairment and morphologic damage to nervous tissue, perhaps suggesting, in this model, that substitution for lidocaine is unlikely to reduce the risk of TNS.[26]

Ropivacaine

Ropivacaine, a long-acting amino amide local anesthetic, is chemically very similar to both bupivacaine and mepivacaine. It was developed with the objective of replacing bupivacaine because of its cardiac toxicity. It was originally not marketed for intrathecal use and hence it has been studied little.[18] The onset and duration of sensory and motor block are comparable with bupivacaine. Earlier studies suggested that, compared with bupivacaine, ropivacaine has a lower potency[27–29] and shorter duration of motor block.[30,31] A double-blind, randomized, crossover study in human volunteers showed that both ropivacaine and bupivacaine produced dose-dependent prolongation of sensory and motor block, with ropivacaine being half as potent as bupivacaine with a similar profile to bupivacaine in equipotent doses.[29]

To find a suitable alternative to lidocaine in ambulatory surgical procedures, studies using ropivacaine in low doses have been undertaken in patients undergoing anorectal surgery and knee arthroscopy. Previous studies evaluating ropivacaine for ambulatory surgery found that lower doses (8–10 mg) produced higher rates of block failures (lower-quality intraoperative analgesia and muscle relaxation) while higher doses (12–14 mg) produced no advantages over bupivacaine with respect to meeting discharge criteria. However, no cases of TNS were reported.[32] In a more recent study, the addition of small-dose intrathecal clonidine (15 μg) to low-dose ropivacaine (8 mg) resulted in adequate and short-lasting anesthesia for patients undergoing knee arthroscopy without TNS.[33] A recent randomized, controlled trial comparing small-dose intrathecal lidocaine versus ropivacaine for anorectal surgery in ambulatory surgery concluded that hyperbaric small-dose ropivacaine with fentanyl (4 mg ropivacaine with 20 μg fentanyl) is an acceptable anesthetic for anorectal surgery.[34] Time to sensory block regression to S2 (118 vs. 106 min), time to first void (187 vs. 180 min), time to reach discharge criteria (200 vs. 194 min), and incidence of TNS (0%) were comparable in the patients receiving lidocaine versus ropivacaine. Adequate intraoperative anesthesia was obtained in both groups.

While intrathecal ropivacaine may be considered a possible alternative, definitive conclusions can only be drawn after prospective studies with large number of patients, the use of concentrated solutions, and perhaps histologic or electrophysiologic studies are available.

Bupivacaine

Bupivacaine was created with the intent to create a more potent and longer-duration local anesthetic. Its duration of action is two to three times that of lidocaine.[18] The cardiac toxicity of bupivacaine is well known. A typical dose of hyperbaric bupivacaine (10–15 mg) produces spinal anesthesia for approximately 150–180 min. However, its long duration of action is considered to be a major disadvantage for its use in outpatient ambulatory surgery. While reduced doses of bupivacaine may decrease the duration of motor and sensory block, surgical anesthesia may be inadequate.

It has been shown in human volunteers that hyperbaric spinal bupivacaine produces dose-dependent sensory and motor block, with increased doses producing more cephalad spread and increased duration of action.[35] The incidence of TNS with bupivacaine is low (0–1%).[21,25]

Levobupivacaine

Levobupivacaine, the S-enantiomer of bupivacaine, is a new long-acting amino amide local anesthetic that was developed to decrease the cardiotoxicity associated with bupivacaine. Because of its close chemical relationship to bupivacaine, its potency, onset time, duration of sensory and motor block, peak block height, and hemodynamics are similar.[36]

In a study of elective orthopedic hip replacement using intrathecal 0.5% isobaric levobupivacaine and 0.5% isobaric bupivacaine, levobupivacaine and bupivacaine had a similar onset time (11 ± 6 vs. 13 ± 8 min), duration of sensory block (228 ± 77 vs. 237 ± 88 min), and duration of motor block (280 ± 84 vs. 284 ± 80 min).[37] This study also demonstrated that levobupivacaine was equally potent to bupivacaine for spinal anesthesia. While levobupivacaine is an alternative to bupivacaine, it does not offer any special advantages over bupivacaine. Because of its long duration of action, its role in ambulatory surgical procedures is limited.

ADJUVANTS

Adjuncts, such as vasoconstrictors, opioids, and alpha 2-adrenergic agonists, have been used in addition to local anesthetics in the intrathecal space for a variety of reasons. Vasoconstrictors, including epinephrine, phenylephrine, norepinephrine, and ephedrine, have all been added to the intrathecal space to prolong the duration of spinal anesthesia. Opioids and alpha-2 adrenergic agonists have been added to a smaller dose of local anesthetic to enhance its use for ambulatory surgery.

Opioids

The addition of lipophilic opioids in the intrathecal space has become a popular anesthetic technique. Intrathecal opioids selectively decrease nociceptive afferent input from Aδ and C fibers.[38] The addition of an opioid to a local anesthetic solution improves the quality of spinal anesthesia through a synergistic effect. The most commonly used opioids in the intrathecal space for ambulatory surgery are the highly lipophilic opioids (fentanyl, sufentanil) because of their quick onset, short duration of action, enhanced intraoperative analgesia, safe side-effect profile (minimal risk of respiratory depression) without prolonging time to discharge. The poorly lipid-soluble opioid morphine results in a slower onset of analgesia and a longer duration of action. Many investigators have evaluated intrathecal fentanyl with smaller doses of intrathecal local anesthetic in an attempt to modify anesthesia for ambulatory surgery.[39–41] The usual dose of intrathecal fentanyl ranged from 10 μg to 25 μg. Intrathecal fentanyl with a subtherapeutic dose of intrathecal lidocaine has been shown to enhance analgesia and improve the duration of sensory block without prolonging recovery of motor block or micturation.[42]

However, the use of intrathecal opioids can be associated with dose-related side effects, such as pruritus, urinary retention, and respiratory depression. The most frequent side effect occurring with the use of intrathecal opioids is pruritus, which is often mild in nature and easily treated.[42] Respiratory depression is rare with the usual clinical dose (i.e., fentanyl ≤ 25 μg or sufentanil ≤ 20 μg)[43,44] but may be observed with higher doses or in the parturient.[45,46] While intrathecal opioids may result in urinary retention, particularly with the hydrophilic ones, it has been shown that the lipophilic opioids have a more favorable profile.[42]

Alpha-2 Adrenergic Agonists

Alpha-2 adrenergic agonists, such as clonidine, can be a useful alternative analgesic adjuvant. While a primary spinal site is the main site of action, peripheral and brain stem sites may also be important.[47] Administered alone, intrathecal clonidine fails to produce reliable surgical anesthesia.[48] However, in conjunction with intrathecal local anesthetics, it prolongs both sensory and motor block by blocking the conduction of C and Aδ fibers.[38,49–51] Previous studies have demonstrated that intrathecal clonidine clearly increases the quality and duration of anesthesia when combined with local anesthetics.[52–54]

A recent randomized, prospective, blinded dose-response study observed that small-dose intrathecal clonidine (15μg) plus 8 mg intrathecal ropivacaine produced adequate and short-duration anesthesia for knee arthroscopy without compromising the benefits of low-dose ropivacaine.[33] While the time to void was shorter in the group receiving 8 mg plain ropivacaine (170 ± 52 vs. 189 ± 43 min), the quality of intraoperative analgesia and muscle relaxation was lower. The addition of 75 μg clonidine, while subjectively improving the quality of anesthesia, prolonged discharge time to 219 ± 36 min because of delayed postoperative micturation. This study also demonstrated that low dose of clonidine was not associated with side effects such as bradycardia, hypotension, or sedation.

The administration of intrathecal clonidine is associated with dose-related (i.e., > 1 or 2 μg/kg) hemodynamic effects (i.e., bradycardia, hypotension), sedation, and urinary retention. However, intrathecal clonidine has not been associated with respiratory depression.[38]

Cholinergics

Neostigmine is a novel adjuvant that has been used in the intrathecal space. It provides analgesia by a spinal action, preventing the breakdown of synaptically released acetylcholine.[38] It has been shown in both animal and human studies to produce analgesia without neurotoxicity. However, a dose-response study of the effects of intrathecal neostigmine added to bupivacaine in human volunteers showed a prolongation of the duration of sensory and motor block with 50 μg intrathecal neostigmine. This dose was also associated with a high incidence of nausea and vomiting and a prolonged time to discharge. While the smaller doses of neostigmine (6.25 and 12.5 μg) did not significantly prolong sensory and motor block, the high incidence of nausea and vomiting prevented the early accomplishment of discharge criteria.[55] Furthermore, clinical trials have found the use of intrathecal neostigmine unsatisfactory because of its prolonged motor block and high incidence of nausea and vomiting, thus decreasing the attractiveness of intrathecal neostigmine in ambulatory surgery.[56–58]

Epinephrine

Vasoconstrictors, such as epinephrine, have been utilized in the intrathecal space to prolong the duration of spinal anesthesia. This is thought to be the result of vasoconstriction of vessels supplying the dura mater and spinal cord leading to slower systemic vascular absorption.[47] However, this effect is not seen equally with all local anesthetics.

The adjuvant use of epinephrine (0.2 mg) with local anesthetic (i.e., low-dose bupivacaine and lidocaine) has been shown to prolong surgical anesthesia, motor block, and time to discharge, making it a poor alternative in the ambulatory surgery setting.[59,60]

CONTROVERSIAL ISSUES

Transient Neurologic Symptoms

TNS have been defined as pain or dysesthesia or both occurring in the legs or buttocks that appear from within a few hours until 24 hr after a full recovery from spinal anesthesia.[61] In 1993, Schneider et al.[62] were the first to publish a case report of four patients with transient neurologic impairment (radicular pain without neurologic deficits) after the injection of hyperbaric 5% lidocaine in the subarachnoid space for surgery in the lithotomy position. Since then, several prospective, randomized, controlled studies[63–66] have examined this phenomenon.

The risk of developing TNS after spinal anesthesia with lidocaine is significantly higher than with other local anesthetics. The incidence of TNS after lidocaine spinal anesthesia has ranged from 4 to 36%. However, it has been shown that changing the concentration of lidocaine from 5% to 0.5% does not decrease the incidence of TNS.[67] Furthermore, other risk factors for the development of TNS include ambulatory surgery as well as the type of surgery and positioning.[68] For example, surgery in the lithotomy position has an incidence of TNS of 30–36%, knee arthroscopy an incidence of 18–22%, and surgery in the supine position an incidence of 4–8%.[69]

The etiology of TNS remains largely unknown; however, several different etiologic mechanisms have been described, including direct neurotoxicity of local anesthetics, needle trauma, patient positioning, pooling of local anesthetic, and neural ischemia secondary to stretching of the sciatic nerve.[69] However, there has been no connection to neurologic pathology in the literature. Electromyography, nerve conduction studies, and somatosensory-evoked potential testing revealed no abnormalities in human volunteers with TNS after lidocaine spinal anesthesia.[70]

Despite the transient nature of this syndrome, patients experience a significant amount of discomfort. Treatment usually consists of nonsteroidal anti-inflammatory drugs (NSAIDs), muscle relaxants, and symptomatic therapy to increase comfort.[69]

Anticoagulation

The use of anticoagulants in the surgical population for the prevention of perioperative deep vein thrombosis is a common practice. This practice reduces the morbidity and mortality associated with thromboembolic complications related to surgery. However, this creates challenges for the anesthesiologist in the management of patients undergoing centroneuraxial blocks, as concern exists for the potential of spinal bleeding. It is generally agreed that regional anesthesia is contraindicated in the anticoagulated patient, and recent Consensus Recommendations for spinal anesthesia and anticoagulants can be found at the American Society of Regional Anesthesia website (www.ASRA.com). Nevertheless, the actual incidence of neurologic dysfunction from spinal hematomas associated with centroneuraxial blocks is unknown. The incidence of spinal hematoma following spinal anesthesia is cited to be less than 1 in 220,000 spinal anesthetics.[71]

Spinal hematoma, defined as symptomatic bleeding within the spinal neuraxis, is a potentially catastrophic complication of centroneuraxial blocks.[72] It is a medical emergency and if unrecognized can lead to spinal cord compression with permanent neurologic sequelae. In a literature review, Vandermeulen et al.[73] reported 61 cases of spinal hematoma between 1906 and 1994. These cases of spinal hematoma were associated with centroneuraxial blocks, and in 68% of the patients the spinal hematomas were associated with a hemostatic abnormality (i.e., heparin use, coagulopathy, thrombocytopenia, antiplatelet use, oral anticoagulants, thrombolytics, and dextran). In 87% of the patients, either a clotting abnormality or difficulty with needle placement was present. Neurologic compromise presented as progression of sensory or motor block in 68% of the patients and bowel/bladder dysfunction in 8% of the patients. Prognosis was good if patients underwent laminectomy within 8 hr of the onset of neurologic symptoms. However, only 38% of patients had partial or good neurologic recovery.

Table 33-2   Recommended Guidelines for Voiding as a Discharge Criterion for Ambulatory Spinal Anesthesia

Voiding prior to discharge not required:

1. Patients who receive spinal bupivacaine, levobupivacaine, or ropivacaine < 7.5 mg, spinal lidocaine, mepivacaine, or procaine.

Voiding may be required:

1. Patients who receive spinal bupivacaine, levobupivacaine, or ropivacaine > 7.5 mg.
2. Patients who have a history of urinary retention.
3. Patients whose surgeon requests that he/she void prior to discharge.

Guidelines:

• Fluids will not be restricted. Doing so may result in insufficient bladder volumes and/or postural hypotension. Suggested minimum total fluids prior to block wearing off (IV + PO, intraoperative + postoperative) around 1500 mL.

• Wait an interval of 30 min after block has resolved or when patient's block has resolved and feels the urge to urinate, whichever comes first.

• If patient does not void spontaneously, immediate use of bladder ultrasound to determine bladder volume.

• If bladder volume is > 600 mL, patient will have an in-and-out straight catheterization to relieve the bladder distention and be discharged home with instructions to return to the emergency department (ED) for further evaluation if unable to void within 8 hr of discharge.

• If bladder volume is < 400 mL, patient will be discharged home with instructions to return to the ED for further evaluation if they were unable to void within 8 hr.

• If bladder volume is 400–600 mL, then patient may be hydrated to bladder volume of 600 mL or spontaneous void, whichever comes first, based on judgment of the anesthesiologist.

• If patients live in an area where return to the ED would be inconvenient, patient may be allowed to wait until he/she spontaneously voids.

DISCHARGE CRITERIA

Recent evidence suggests patients considered at low risk for postoperative urinary retention can be safely discharged prior to voiding (Table 33-2).[74] Spinal anesthesia with epinephrine as an intrathecal adjunct[75] or with conventional-dose bupivacaine, levobupivacaine, or ropivacaine[76] may place patients at higher risk for postoperative urinary retention. In a cystometric evaluation of the recovery of bladder function after spinal anesthesia, all patients were able to void at cystometric capacity when seg-

mental anesthesia had reached the third sacral segment.[76] The length of detrusor block (defined as duration of time from spinal injection to return of urge at cystometric capacity together with the ability to completely empty the bladder without straining) was increased nearly 100% in patients receiving 10 mg bupivacaine compared to those patients receiving 100 mg lidocaine.

The addition of intrathecal lipophilic opioids to improve the anesthetic quality of low-dose lidocaine spinal anesthesia has not been found to increase the time to void or reach discharge criteria.[8,77–79] Removing the requirement to void after low-dose lidocaine spinal anesthesia may significantly decrease the time to discharge without increasing the risk of postoperative urinary retention.[4,5] Recent clinical trials utilizing low-dose lidocaine, bupivacaine, and ropivacaine spinal anesthesia have been associated with rapid times to full sacral regression and subsequent discharge. In these trials, patients were discharged home with voiding and none required treatment for postoperative urinary retention.[10,11,80] Ultrasound evaluation of bladder volume in patients who have not voided has been advocated as a useful tool to identify high-risk patients who should not be discharged prior to either voiding or bladder catheterization.[5] However, in those patients discharged prior to voiding, thorough education regarding the potential for postoperative urinary retention should be provided at the time of discharge. In addition, patients should be advised to seek medical intervention if they are unable to void within 6–8 hr after discharge.[4]

SUMMARY

As the number of patients having outpatient ambulatory surgery continues to increase, operating rooms and patients may benefit from prompt recovery profiles. Thus, spinal anesthesia is an excellent choice for outpatient ambulatory surgery because of its ease of performance, quick onset of anesthesia, and early discharge times while avoiding the physiologic trespasses associated with general anesthesia. While lidocaine remains a popular choice for ambulatory surgery, concerns with TNS have sparked interest in alternative local anesthetics or the use of intrathecal adjuvants to decrease the total dose of local anesthetic. Another concern for anesthesiologists is the growing use of anticoagulants to decrease the thromboembolic complications associated with surgery. This has led to the development of guidelines to manage patients undergoing centroneuraxial blockade in the presence of anticoagulation. Finally, there appears to be a growing consensus that ambulatory patients do not need to void prior to discharge after appropriate use of spinal anesthesia.

REFERENCES

1. Standl T, Eckert S, Schulteam EJ. Postoperative complaints after spinal and thiopentone-isoflurane anaesthesia in patients undergoing orthopaedic surgery: spinal versus general anaesthesia. Acta Anaesthesiol Scand 1996;40:222–26.

2. Pittoni G, Toffoletto F, Calcarella G, et al. Spinal anesthesia in outpatient knee surgery: 22-gauge versus 25-gauge Sprotte needle. Anesth Analg 1995;84:73–79.

3. Kang SB, Goodnough DE, Lee YK, et al. Comparison of 26- and 27-G needles for spinal anesthesia for ambulatory surgical patients. Anesthesiology 1992;76:734–39.

4. Marshall SI, Chung F. Discharge criteria and complications after ambulatory surgery. Anesth Analg 1999;88:508–17.

5. Mulroy MF, Salinas FV, Larkin KL, et al. Ambulatory surgery patients may be discharged before voiding after short-acting spinal and epidural anesthesia. Anesthesiology 2002;97:315–19.

6. Horlocker TT, Hebl JR. Anesthesia for outpatient knee arthroscopy: is there an optimal technique. Reg Anesth Pain Med 2003;28: 58–63.

7. Korhonen AM, Valanne JV, Jokela RM, et al. Intrathecal hyperbaric bupivacaine 3 mg + fentanyl 10 μg for outpatient knee arthroscopy with tourniquet. Acta Anaesthesiol Scand 2003;47:342–46.

8. Ben-David B, Maryanovsky M, Gurevitch A, et al. A comparison of minidose lidocaine-fentanyl and conventional-dose lidocaine spinal anesthesia. Anesth Analg 2000;91:865–70.

9. Pollock JE, Mulroy MF, Bent E, et al. A comparison of two regional anesthetic techniques for outpatient knee arthroscopy. Anesth Analg 2003;97:397–401.

10. Vaghadia H. Spinal anesthesia for outpatients: controversies and new techniques. Can J Anaesth 1998;45:64–70.

11. Stewart AVG, Vaghadia H, Collins L, et al. Small-dose selective spinal anesthesia for short-duration outpatient gynaecological laparoscopy: recovery characteristics compared with propofol anaesthesia. Br J Anaesth 2001;86:570–72.

12. Lennox PH, Vaghadia H, Henderson C, et al. Small-dose selective spinal anesthesia for short-duration outpatient laparoscopy: recovery characteristics compared with desflurane anesthesia. Anesth Analg 2002;94:346–50.

13. Salinas FV, Liu SS. Spinal anesthesia: local anaesthetics and adjuncts in the ambulatory setting. Best Pract Res Clin Anaesthesiol 2002; 16:195–210.

14. Lau WC, Green CR, Faerber GJ, et al. Intrathecal sufentanil for extracorporeal shock wave lithotripsy provides earlier discharge of the outpatient than intrathecal lidocaine. Anesth Analg 1997;84: 1227–31.

15. Richardson MG, Dooley JW. The effects of general versus epidural anesthesia for outpatient extracorporeal shock wave lithotripsy. Anesth Analg 1998;86:1214–18.

16. Gupta A, Axelsson K, Thorn S, et al. Low-dose bupivacaine plus fentanyl for spinal anesthesia during ambulatory inguinal herniorrhaphy: a comparison between 6 mg and 7.5 mg bupivacaine. Acta Anaesthesiol Scand 2003;47:13–19.

17. Song D, Greilich NB, White PF, et al. Recovery profiles and costs of anesthesia for outpatient unilateral inguinal herniorrhaphy. Anesth Analg 2000;91:876–81.

18. Tetzlaff JE. Clinical Pharmacology of Local Anesthetics. Boston: Butterworth-Heinemann, 2000.

19. Hodgson PS, Liu SS, Batra MS, et al. Procaine compared with lidocaine for the incidence of transient neurologic symptoms. Reg Anesth Pain Med 2000;25:218–22.

20. Mulroy MF, Larkin KL, Siddiqui A. Intrathecal fentanyl-induced pruritus is more severe in combination with procaine than with lidocaine or bupivacaine. Reg Anesth Pain Med 2001;26:252–56.

21. Pollock JE, Neal JM, Stephenson CA, et al. Prospective study of the incidence of transient radicular irritation in patients undergoing spinal anesthesia. Anesthesiology 1996;84:1361–67.

22. Salmela L, Aromaa U. Transient radicular irritation after spinal anesthesia induced with hyperbaric solutions of cerebrospinal fluid-diluted lidocaine 50 mg/mL or mepivacaine 40 mg/mL or bupivacaine 5 mg/mL. Acta Anaesthesiol Scand 1998;42:765–69.

23. Hiller A, Rosenberg PH. Transient neurologic symptoms after spinal anesthesia with 4% mepivacaine and 0.5% bupivacaine. Br J Anaesth 1997;79:301–5.

24. Salazar F, Bogdanovich A, Adalia R, et al. Transient neurologic symptoms after spinal anesthesia using isobaric 2% mepivacaine and isobaric 2% lidocaine. Acta Anaesthesiol Scand 2001;45:240–45.

25. Hampl KF, Heinzmann-Wiedmer S, Luginbuehl I, et al. Transient neurologic symptoms after spinal anesthesia: a lower incidence with prilocaine and bupivacaine than with lidocaine. Anesthesiology 1998;88:629–33.

26. Kishimoto T, Bollen AW, Drasner K. Comparative spinal neurotoxicity of prilocaine and lidocaine. Anesthesiology 2002;97:1250–53.

27. Polley LS, Columb MO, Naughton NN. Relative analgesic potencies of ropivacaine and bupivacaine for epidural analgesia in labor: implications for therapeutic indexes. Anesthesiology 1999;90:944–50.

28. Columb MO, Lyons G. Determination of the minimum local analgesic concentrations of epidural bupivacaine and lidocaine in labor. Anesth Analg 1995;8:833–37.

29. McDonald SB, Liu SS, Kopacz DJ, et al. Hyperbaric spinal ropivacaine: a comparison to bupivacaine in volunteers. Anesthesiology 1999;90:971–77.

30. Ackerman B, Hellenberg I, Trossvik C. Primary evaluation of the local anesthetic properties of the amino amide agent ropivacaine. Acta Anaesthesiol Scand 1998;32:571–78.

31. Feldman HS, Covino BG. Comparative motor-blocking effects of bupivacaine and ropivacaine, a new amino amide local anesthetic in the rat and dog. Anesth Analg 1988;67:1047–52.

32. Gautier PE, De Kock M, Steenberge AV. Intrathecal ropivacaine for ambulatory surgery. Anesthesiology 1999;91:1239–45.

33. De Kock M, Gautier P, Fanard L, et al. Intrathecal ropivacaine and clonidine for ambulatory knee arthroscopy: a dose-response study. Anesthesiology 2001;94:574–78.

34. Buckenmaier CC, Nielsen KC, Pietrobon R, et al. Small-dose intrathecal lidocaine versus ropivacaine for anorectal surgery in an ambulatory setting. Anesth Analg 2002;95:1253–57.

35. Liu SS, Ware PD, Allen HW, et al. Dose-response characteristics of spinal bupivacaine in volunteers. Anesthesiology 1996;85:729–36.

36. Alley EA, Kopacz DJ, Mcdonald SB, et al. Hyperbaric spinal levobupivacaine: a comparison to racemic bupivacaine in volunteers. Anesth Analg 2002;94:188–93.

37. Glaser C, Marhofer P, Zimpfer G, et al. Levobupivacaine versus racemic bupivacaine for spinal anesthesia. Anesth Analg 2002;94: 194–98.

38. Chiari A, Eisenach JC. Spinal anesthesia: mechanisms, agents, methods, and safety. Reg Anesth Pain Med 1998;23:357–62.

39. Hamber EA, Viscomi CM. Intrathecal lipophilic opioids as adjuts to surgical spinal anesthesia. Reg Anesth Pain Med 1999;24: 255–63.

40. Chilvers C, Vaghadia H, Mitchell G, et al. Small-dose hypobaric lidocaine-fentanyl spinal anesthesia for short duration outpatient laparoscopy. II. Optimal fentanyl dose. Anesth Analg 1997;84: 65–70.

41. Goel S, Bhardwaj N, Grover VK. Intrathecal fentanyl added to intrathecal bupivacaine for day case surgery: a randomized study. Eur J Anaesthesiol 2003;20:294–97.

42. Liu S, Chiu AA, Carpenter RL, et al. Fentanyl prolongs lidocaine spinal anesthesia without prolonging recovery. Anesth Analg 1995; 80:730–34.

43. Varrassi G, Celleno D, Capogna P, et al. Ventilatory effects of subarachnoid fentanyl in the elderly. Anaesthesia 1992;47:558–63.

44. Lu JK, Schafer PG, Gardner TL, et al. The dose-response pharmacology of intrathecal sufentanil in female volunteers. Anesth Analg 1997;85:372–79.

45. Ferouz F, Norris MC, Leighton BL. Risk of respiratory arrest after intrathecal sufentanil. Anesth Analg 1997;85:1088–90.

46. Lu JK, Manullang TR, Staples MH, et al. Maternal respiratory arrest, severe hypotension, and fetal distress after administration of

intrathecal sufentanil and bupivacaine after intravenous fentanyl. Anesthesiology 1997;87:170–72.

47. Veering BT, Stienstra R. Duration of block: drug, dose, and additives. Reg Anesth Pain Med 1998;23:352–56.

48. Malinovsky JM, Bernard JM. Spinal clonidine fails to provide surgical anesthesia for transurethral resection of prostate: a dose-finding pilot study. Reg Anesth 1996;21:419–23.

49. Klimscha W, Chiari A, Krafft P, et al. Hemodynamic and analgesic effects of clonidine added repetitively to continuous epidural and spinal blocks. Anesth Analg 1995;80:322–27.

50. Racle JP, Benkhadra A, Poy JY, et al. Prolongation of isobaric bupivacaine spinal anesthesia with epinephrine and clonidine for hip surgery in the elderly. Anesth Analg 1987;66:442–46.

51. Eisenach JC, De Kock M, Klimscha W. Alpha 2 adrenergic agonists for regional anesthesia: a clinical review of clonidine. Anesthesiology 1996;85:655–74.

52. Acalovschi I, Bodolea C, Manoiu C. Spinal anesthesia with meperidine: effects of added alpha-adrenergic agonists: epinephrine versus clonidine. Anesth Analg 1997;84:1333–39.

53. Dobrydnjov I, Samarutel J. Enhancement of intrathecal lidocaine by addition of local and systemic clonidine. Acta Anaesthesiol Scand 1999;43:556–62.

54. Niemi L. Effects of intrathecal clonidine on duration of bupivacaine spinal anaesthesia, haemodynamics, and postoperative analgesia in patients undergoing knee arthroscopy. Acta Anaesthesiol Scand 1994; 38:724–28.

55. Liu SS, Hodgson PS, Moore LM, et al. Dose-response effects of spinal neostigmine added to bupivacaine spinal anesthesia in volunteers. Anesthesiology 1999;90:710–17.

56. Yegin A, Yilmaz M, Karsli B, et al. Analgesic effects of intrathecal neostigmine in perianal surgery. Eur J Anaesthesiol 2003;20:404–8.

57. Tan PH, Kuo JH, Liu KH, et al. Efficacy of intrathecal neostigmine for the relief of postinguinal herniorrhaphy pain. Acta Anaesthesiol Scand 2000;44:1056–60.

58. Pan PM, Huang CT, Wei TT, et al. Enhancement of analgesic effect of intrathecal neostigmine and clonidine on bupivacaine spinal anesthesia. Reg Anesth Pain Med 1998;23:49–56.

59. Moore JM, Liu SL, Pollock JE, et al. The effect of epinephrine on small-dose hyperbaric bupivacaine spinal anesthesia: clinical implications for ambulatory surgery. Anesth Analg 1998;86:973–77.

60. Chiu AA, Liu SS, Carpenter RL, et al. The effects of epinephrine on lidocaine spinal anesthesia: a cross-over study. Anesth Analg 1995; 80:735–39.

61. Hampl K, Schneider M, Pargger H, et al. A similar incidence of transient neurologic symptoms after spinal anesthesia with 2% and 5% lidocaine. Anesth Analg 1996;83:1051–54.

62. Schneider M, Ettlin T, Kaufmann M, et al. Transient neurologic toxicity after hyperbaric subarachnoid anesthesia with 5% lidocaine. Anesth Analg 1993;76:1154–57.

63. de Weert T, Traksel M, Gielen M, et al. The incidence of transient neurological symptoms after spinal anesthesia with lidocaine compared with prilocaine. Anaesthesia 2000;55:1020–24.

64. Hampl KF, Heinzmann-Wiedmer S, Luginbuehl MC, et al. Transient neurologic symptoms after spinal anesthesia. Anesthesiology 1998; 88:629–33.

65. Hodgson PS, Liu SS, Batra MS, et al. Procaine compared with lidocaine for incidence of transient neurologic symptoms. Reg Anesth Pain Med 2000;25:218–22.

66. Liguori GA, Zayas VM, Chisholm MF. Transient neurologic symptoms after spinal anesthesia with mepivacaine and lidocaine. Anesthesiology 1998;88:619–23.

67. Pollock JE, Liu SS, Neal JM, et al. Dilution of spinal lidocaine does not alter the incidence of transient neurologic symptoms. Anesthesiology 1999;90:445–50.

68. Freedman JM, Li D, Drasner K, et al. Transient neurologic symptoms after spinal anesthesia: an epidemiologic study of 1,863 patients. Anesthesiology 1998;89:633–41.

69. Pollock JE. Transient neurologic symptoms: etiology, risk factors, and management. Reg Anesth Pain Med 2002;27:581–86.

70. Pollock JE, Burkhead D, Neal JM, et al. Spinal nerve function in five volunteers experiencing transient neurologic symptoms after lidocaine subarachnoid anesthesia. Anesth Analg 2000;90:658–65.

71. Horlocker TT, Wedel DJ. Neurologic complications of spinal and epidural anesthesia. Reg Anesth Pain Med 2000;25:83–98.

72. Horlocker TT, Wedel DJ, Benzon H, et al. Regional anesthesia in the anticoagulated patient: defining the risks (the second ASRA consensus conference on neuraxial anesthesia and anticoagulation). Reg Anesth Pain Med 2003;28:172–97.

73. Vandermeulen EP, Van Aken H, Vermylen J, et al. Anticoagulants and spinal-epidural anesthesia. Anesth Analg 1994;79:1165–77.

74. Pavlin DJ, Pavlin EG, Fitzgibbon DR, et al. Management of bladder function after outpatient surgery. Anesthesiology 1999;91:42–50.

75. Pavlin DJ, Pavlin EG, Gunn HC, et al. Voiding in patients managed with or without ultrasound monitoring of bladder volume after outpatient surgery. Anesth Analg 1999;89:90–97.

76. Kamphuis ET, Ionescu TI, Kuipers PWG, et al. Recovery of storage and emptying functions of the urinary bladder after spinal anesthesia with lidocaine and with bupivacaine in men. Anesthesiology 1998;88:310–16.

77. Ben-David B, Solomon E, Levin H, et al. Intrathecal fentanyl with small-dose dilute bupivacaine: better anesthesia without prolonging recovery. Anesth Analg 1997;85:560–65.

78. Vaghadia H, McLeod DH, Mitchell GWE, et al. Small-dose hypobaric lidocaine-fentanyl spinal anesthesia for short duration outpatient laparoscopy. I. A randomized comparison with conventional dose hyperbaric lidocaine. Anesth Analg 1997;84:59–64.

79. Martin R, Tsen LC, Tzeng G, et al. Anesthesia for in vitro fertilization: the addition of fentanyl to 1.5% lidocaine. Anesth Analg 1999; 88:523–26.

80. Ben-David B, DeMeo P, Lucyk C, Solosko D. A comparison of minidose lidocaine-fentanyl spinal anesthesia and local anesthesia/propofol infusion for outpatient knee arthroscopy. Anesth Analg 2001;93:319–25.

Office-Based Anesthesia: Techniques and Procedures

MEENA S. DESAI

ASPECTS OF CLINICAL CARE

As we foray into the ever-growing world of office-based anesthesia it becomes imperative that we are judicious in the selection of procedure, as well as in patient and practice selection. The proper selection and execution of all these factors will ensure the proper management of an office-based anesthesia practice.

Selection of Practices and Selection of Procedures

Procedure selection and practice selection go hand in hand and are guided by good judgment and the incorporation of certain principles. Our practice utilizes information incorporated in the American Society of Anesthesiologists (ASA) Guidelines for Office-Based Anesthesia, approved by the House of Delegates in 1999.[1] Consider the skill of the practitioner as the involvement of anesthesia allows the given surgeon or procedurist to extend his/her ability and realm as the anesthesiologist provides the benefit of a cooperative and compliant patient and a controlled operating situation. You must individually assess the skill of the given practitioner and the ability of the given office and its ancillary personnel. The principal factors used in this judgment involve the following:

- Consider excessive blood loss. The office-based ambulatory practice has no ability for transfusion.
- Postoperative pain control must be adequate with oral analgesics at home.
- The surgeon must be able to complete all procedures safely within a given period of time. The author's practice is comfortable with a 4-hr length limit in a given stretch for any given patient.
- Compliance with various state regulations as they are enacted (e.g., Pennsylvania has a 4-hr limit for ambulatory procedures; Florida has regulations concerning the amount of liposuction with other procedures, etc.).

The author's group, with a great deal of consideration, has made the controversial choice to limit our practice to professionals who have clinical privileges in hospitals to perform the same procedures. This rule does not apply to dental clients, as they do not traditionally have such admission privileges. The author's practice currently has limited dermatologic office-based practice as these practitioners often do not have admitting privileges and many dermatologists have begun to carry out more invasive procedures. It is the responsibility of the practitioner to not only do the procedure, but also take care of complications resulting from the procedure in a safe and timely manner.

PREOPERATIVE PATIENT SELECTION AND PREPARATION

Appropriate Patient Selection

Early on in the practice we understood the value of educating fellow specialists in proper patient selection. The surgeon or procedurist and his/her office medical staff are the first line in patient selection and we have developed guidelines that help them correctly identify appropriate office and ambulatory patients versus hospital candidates. The ASA physical status classification and specific comorbidities are key to appropriate patient selection. It is important to track all patient cancellations and categorize these monthly to review trends if further education is required to avoid delays and patient and practitioner inconvenience. The author has provided a suggested patient selection list that her practice currently uses. This list is revised and updated frequently (Fig. 34-1). These guidelines are derived from various sources and take many factors into account. The evaluation of the patient's current medical status and the stability of his/her medical status are paramount for appropriate patient selection. One must also consider "social" factors such as the psychologic status and the support system at home (help at home, ability

Criteria that suggest a patient may be *unsuitable* for a procedure in your office setting:

1. Unstable angina
2. Fresh myocardial infarct (MI):
   a. 0–3 months not done in office
   b. 3–6 months requires cardiologist/internist clearance
3. Severe cardiomyopathy
4. Uncontrolled hypertension (HTN)
5. Patients with internal defibrillator
6. End stage renal disease (on dialysis)
7. Sickle cell anemia (trait OK)
8. Patient on transplant list (major organ):
   a. heart
   b. lung
   c. kidney
   d. liver
9. Uncontrolled diabetes mellitus
10. Active multiple sclerosis
11. Severe chronic obstructive pulmonary disease (COPD)
12. Abnormal airway/difficult intubation
13. Malignant hyperthermia by history
14. Acute illegal substance abusers
15. Morbid obesity
16. Dementia—patient is not oriented
17. Psychologically unstable: rage/anger problems
18. Myasthenia gravis
19. Recent cerebral vascular accident (CVA) within 3 months
20. Obstructive sleep apnea

Figure 34-1 Nova Anesthesia Professionals patient selection criteria for selecting appropriate office-based patients.

to get to the hospital if a complication occurs at home, distance from the hospital, etc.).

Anesthetic Evaluation of the Patient

The cornerstone of the author's practice philosophy is to provide safety coupled with service. Traditional ideas of data acquisition have been changed to add an element of control that allows us to practice anesthesia knowing that the patients have undergone appropriate screening preoperatively. The author's practice supervises or performs the history and preoperative evaluations of every patient. This evaluation is usually done via telephone. A set of algorithms, specific to anesthesia, has been developed for the phone interview that efficiently obtains data. With appropriate training registered nurses (RNs) can perform these phone interviews in an average of 7–10 min/patient. Preprocedure verification and preoperative anesthesia consultation are performed in every case.

Collection of Pertinent Medical History and Data

The author's practice collects any pertinent historical data to determine the patient's current stability and medical maximization. Any complex patients are reviewed by an anesthesiologist. We also determine whether any addi-

tional testing will be beneficial for the procedure. As has been recommended by many[2–5] in the field, the author does utilize testing on an as-needed basis. Preoperative testing is not approached as a general medical screening but as a highly procedure-selective testing process. Noninvasive procedures or minimally invasive procedures require no preprocedure testing if the patient is reliably followed by a medical care team and there is no change in the patient's current medical status. Data of interest may be obtained from given specialists who are involved in the patient's care on an as-needed basis (e.g., remote electrocardiograms [ECGs], cardiac notes, etc.). Moderately invasive procedures such as face lifts, abdominoplasties, breast augmentation, and liposuction may involve additional testing. Figure 34-2 shows a testing table that is used at the author's practice. It behooves you to formulate a mechanism whereby your practices can initiate the ordering of any appropriate laboratory testing as soon as the patient is booked. If the front desk of the practice can apply the modified testing algorithms, this timely intervention is helpful in getting the process started.

Patient Instructions and Information

Along with testing and patient selection, practices should be involved in distributing various anesthesia-related instructions and literature at the time of the patient's office visit. At the time of scheduling, be sure to have the patient consent to obtain data from their health care specialists. The author's practice currently participates jointly with practices as per Health Insurance Portability and Accountability Act (HIPAA) of 1996 guidelines.[6] The author's practice has prepared a preoperative patient questionnaire that outlines the preoperative anesthesia interview (Fig. 34-3). This questionnaire can be faxed into the office and allows the patient to be prepared for the telephone anesthesia interview. The patient should also receive a written set of anesthesia preprocedure (Fig. 34-4) and postprocedure (Fig. 34-5) instructions. These instructions need to address fasting (NPO) guidelines, postoperative expectations, what to do if acute illness results, and so on. Postoperative procedure guidelines need to outline any restrictions and the need for availability of an escort. Most important, include clear instructions on how the patient can deal with an emergency. It is important to make sure that pre- and postprocedure anesthesia instructions and office instructions concur. The author's practice has combined instructions with many offices to minimize the paperwork a patient has to handle. Be sure to have the anesthesia HIPAA component included with the practices' HIPAA statements. Any patient should be allowed to request an anesthesiologist interview prior to the day of the procedure but the author and others[7] have found that most patients are satisfied with the thorough conversation trained nurses provide.

The anesthesiologist updates the history, performs a physical examination, and discusses and answers all questions prior to formulating an anesthetic plan with the patient's consent.

TESTING FOR MINIMALLY INVASIVE SURGERY (cataracts, gastrointestinal, dental, diagnostic imaging, minor gynecologic and urologic procedures)

For healthy individuals under the age of 50, with *no* comorbid conditions: no specific preoperative tests are indicated.

For patients over the age of 50 and for patients *with* comorbid conditions (e.g., HTN, CAD, DM): a history and physical examination within the past 6 months by a primary care physician is recommended. This history and physical examination is to establish that the patient's comorbid conditions are at their maximal medical management for undergoing an elective procedure with anesthesia.

TESTING FOR ASYMPTOMATIC PATIENTS FOR MODERATELY INVASIVE SURGERY (liposuction, facelifts, breast augmentations, other plastic and cosmetic procedures, laparoscopies, arthroscopies)

Test	Male	Female
Hgb/Hct	40 and older	12 and older
ECG (within 1 yr)	50 and older	50 and older
Beta HCG	N/A	Child-bearing age

Patients *with* comorbid conditions (HTN, CAD, DM, pulmonary disease) may require additional testing, and it will need to be *disease specific.*

Test	Disease
ECG	HTN, CAD, DM, pacemaker, MVP, arrhythmias within one year
Glucose	DM—serum or glucometer reading
Electrolytes	Patients on diuretics—within 1 month
BUN/Cr	Chronic renal disease
CXR	Advanced pulmonary/cardiac disease—if felt necessary by primary care physician

Significantly abnormal test results will need a statement addressing the patient's eligibility to undergo an elective procedure with anesthesia. This statement will be from a Medical Director or referred to the primary care physician if that is determined more appropriate.

Figure 34-2 Anesthesia preprocedure testing recommendations.

INTRAOPERATIVE CARE

Setup and Delivery of Care in Four Practice Categories

Induction and maintenance of office anesthesia can include intravenous (IV) and inhalation techniques. Short-acting agents are most appropriate and have great versatility of application. More important than agents or techniques is to provide an anesthetic that will give the patient a rapid recovery to normal function, with minimal

postoperative pain, nausea, or other side effects. The practice and site dictate the setup at each location. Many busy plastic surgeons have built one-room operating suites. The sporadic surgeon may be using a room that is outfitted as needed for procedures with IV sedation. The dental patient will also be outfitted in a room that can be used for IV sedation. Each location and procedure may require unique titration of anesthesia for successful results.

Make sure the operative suite is prepared for adjunctive care for selected procedures as needed (e.g., warming devices, eye protection for laser surgery, Foley catheter as needed, and antiembolism stockings).

The intraoperative anesthetic record should conform to established ASA standards. Tailor your records to conform to established Joint Commission on Accreditation of Healthcare Organizations (JCAHO), state, and ASA guidelines and standards.

The author's practice anesthetizing locations are outfitted as the site warrants and space allows. These locations fall into four main categories:

1. The one-room plastic surgical suite equipped to provide general anesthesia.
2. The sporadic surgeon who equips a large room for IV sedation on an as-needed basis.
3. The dental specialty that sporadically provides IV sedation for dental phobics.
4. The rapid-turnover gastrointestinal (GI) or ophthalmologic suite that provides IV sedation.

Many places have documented the standards and guidelines for monitoring and recommended equipment in the delivery of anesthesia care. The setup at each location encompasses the standards and guidelines set forth by the regulations for office-based anesthesia; however, the format is altered for portability. There are specific guidelines for the Office-Based Setting and the author's group follows the recommendations set forth in 1986 by the ASA House of Delegates.[1] We have modified our "anesthesia red cart" into a portable tackle box. There is a "bag" that holds all disposable items.

Portable monitors equipped with automatic external defibrillators (AEDs) are used for infrequent office locations. At the stationary suites with very frequent use the anesthesia cart and monitors are stationary and dedicated to the location.

Every site has available a source for positive-pressure delivery of oxygen. The dental suites' oxygen delivery systems are modified to have a positive-pressure oxygen delivery capability. A portable emergency tank of oxygen must be full and available should the occasion arise and standard delivery systems fail. Suction must be available at every site. The recovery area must also be equipped with monitors, oxygen, and suction. The author's group surveys and documents the layout of each facility prior to starting cases. It is important to do a site survey and document exits, plans for patient flow, locations of phones, bathrooms, emergency lighting, backup generators, and so on. These surveys should be updated as changes occur or at least on an annual basis. One must verify that the facility is in compliance with all local and state regulations. Along with the

Name:_____

Age: _____ Weight: _____ Height: _____

Date/Time: _____ Procedure: _____ Surgeon: _____

Person to drive you home: _____ Telephone#: _____

1. Please complete this form and have it available for your anesthesia telephone interview; if possible, please fax this form to 610-527-2775.
2. If you should have any questions or do not understand some of the items, we will clarify them at the time of your interview.
3. Please use the comment space to explain any "YES" answers and please provide dates if possible.

List all Medications/Herbals you currently take:

_____

_____

_____

List all previous operations:

_____

_____

_____

Any drug allergies:	N Y _____	Have you ever had a problem with anesthesia or with malignant hyperthermia?	N Y _____
Any latex allergies:	N Y _____	Has anyone in your family ever had a problem with anesthesia or malignant hyperthermia?	N Y _____
Do you smoke:	N Y _____	Could you be pregnant?	N Y _____
How many packs a day? _____		Date of last menstrual period	N Y _____
Do you drink alcohol?	N Y _____	*Do you have a history of:*	
How much? _____		Irregular heartbeat or arrhythmia? N	Y _____
Do you use recreational drugs?	N Y _____	Heart murmur/chest pain?	N Y _____
Do you have any of the following:		Mitral valve prolapse?	N Y _____
Asthma or bronchitis?	N Y _____	High blood pressure?	N Y _____
Emphysema?	N Y _____	Heart attack/angina?	N Y _____
Difficulty breathing?	N Y _____	Peptic ulcer disease?	N Y _____
Sleep apnea?	N Y _____	Hiatal hernia?	N Y _____
Diabetes?	N Y _____	Gastric ulcer/acid reflux?	N Y _____
Kidney problems?	N Y _____	Hepatitis/liver disease?	N Y _____
Bladder problems?	N Y _____	Stroke?	N Y _____
Thyroid disease?	N Y _____	Epilepsy?	N Y _____
Sickle cell disease?	N Y _____	Seizure?	N Y _____
Bleeding problems?	N Y _____	Migraines or headaches?	N Y _____
Anemia?	N Y _____	Do you wear contacts or glasses?	N Y _____
Blood transfusion?	N Y _____	Do you have a hearing aid?	N Y _____
Neck pain?	N Y _____	Do you have any loose/chipped teeth?	N Y _____
Back pain?	N Y _____	Do you have dentures, caps, bridgework, or braces?	N Y _____
Arthritis?	N Y _____		
Muscle weakness?	N Y _____		

Any additional comments or concerns not mentioned above?

_____

_____

_____

_____

Signature: _____   Date/Time _____

Figure 34–3   Nova Anesthesia Professionals patient preanesthesia questionnaire.

In preparation for your procedure with the comfort of intravenous sedation or general anesthesia please follow these instructions:

- **Do not eat anything solid after midnight** the night before your surgery. You may continue to have clear liquids up until four hours before your scheduled time of surgery. Clear liquids include only: water, clear juices (apple, cranberry, or other juices without pulp), clear tea or black coffee (no milk or creamer). **Do not have anything orally within four hours of your procedure** (no gum or hard candy), except specifically prescribed medications. Your cooperation is important in preventing vomiting during your procedure that could have serious consequences for you.
- You may take some heart and blood pressure medications as directed by the anesthesiologist with a very small sip of water one hour prior to the surgery, or the morning of the surgery. You may also be asked to take anti-nausea medications, antibiotics or stomach acidity medications with a small sip of water prior to your procedure.
- **You must have an adult to drive you home.**
- **You should have a responsible person with you for the rest of the day and evening.**
- **You should not drive for the remainder of the day and evening following your procedure.**
- Do not drink any alcoholic beverages for 24 hours before and after your surgery.
- You should wear loose comfortable clothes with short sleeves. Do not wear excessive make-up on the day of your surgery. You should wear your glasses instead of contact lenses. Do not wear jewelry.
- A nurse from Nova Anesthesia will contact you by telephone, prior to your procedure. They will evaluate your general health, discuss anesthetic issues and answer any questions you may have. Please keep your anesthesia questionnaire nearby to discuss your anesthesia concerns. Please leave day and evening phone numbers where you may be reached.
- If you develop a cold, flu, sore throat, or other illness, please notify your surgeon for further evaluation.
- If you do not follow the instructions or if your physical condition changes, your surgery may be canceled for your safety. Should you have any questions regarding these instructions please contact us at 610-527-1400.

Figure 34-4   Nova Anesthesia Professionals preprocedure information and instructions.

- **Since sedation and/or anesthesia have been used for your procedure, you must have an adult accompany you home. For your own safety and protection you must have a responsible individual with you at home for the remainder of the day and night.**
- Begin your diet with light foods (jello, soups, etc.) and advance to a more substantial diet as tolerated and instructed by your doctor. You are encouraged to drink as much liquid as you wish, unless you have a medical condition that limits your oral intake.

For the next 24 hours:

- You should rest and limit your activity for the remainder of the day.
- **Do not consume alcohol** for at least 24 hours, and longer if you are taking narcotics for pain control.
- **Do not drive** or operate machinery for the remainder of the day.
- Do **not** make important business or personal decisions for the remainder of the day.
- You will be contacted by a nurse from Nova Anesthesia regarding any problems or comments about your anesthesia.
- **If you have an emergency please contact your surgeon for further instructions.**

Figure 34-5   Nova Anesthesia Professionals postprocedure information and instructions.

site survey, collection and verification of the practitioner's state license, board specialty status, Drug Enforcement Administration (DEA) license, and hospital privileges is needed.

The Plastic Surgical Suite

Our general anesthesia operating suites give us the greatest flexibility in the numbers and types of plastic and cosmetic procedures performed.[8] The greatest challenge is in the appropriate dosing of medication in the operating room so as to avoid redosing pain medication in the recovery room, as this does delay discharge. The one-room general suite is outfitted much the same way an operating room is. The anesthesia machine, monitors, and end-tidal carbon dioxide and gas analysis monitoring systems are dedicated to the site and location. One must arrange for the recommended calibration of the general anesthesia machine by authorized personnel. The suites are equipped with all necessary materials for advanced cardiac life support (ACLS) protocols of resuscitation as well as with the suggested amount of dantrolene for the treatment of malignant hyperthermia. As the suites are designed for maximum efficiency, there is a separate recovery room with the recommended monitors, oxygen, and suction systems. Postanesthesia care unit (PACU) care is delivered by a RN with ACLS training. The greatest challenge in this area is posed by postprocedure pain and postoperative nausea and vomiting (PONV) management. The author's practice has found that the incidence of PONV is reduced by the elimination of nitrous oxide (N_2O) from the gas mixture. Patients with history of PONV are instructed to take histamine H_2 antagonists at bedtime and on the morning of the procedure. In addition, they are prescribed ondansetron (Zofran ODT—orally disintegrating tablets) to take in the pre- and postoperative periods as needed. The author's group found that rescue efforts for PONV are much more difficult than prophylaxis. Recently the author has begun to study whether prophylaxis with 12.5 mg of prometazine IV provides an equal alternative to the 5-hydroxytryptamine 3 (5-HT_3) antagonists. Postprocedure pain is managed with adequate intraoperative opioids and preoperative discussion regarding postprocedure sensations to anticipate. The author has found that the redosing of pain medication in the PACU does lead to a delay in discharge and it is important to give an adequate amount of analgesia intraoperatively. In the recovery area, the author's group utilizes nalbuphine in 5-mg increments with one repeat dose if needed. We have found that this provides comfort without respiratory depression and does not delay discharge.

Mobile Surgical Suite for IV Sedation

Intravenous sedation or total intravenous anesthesia (TIVA) techniques are employed when the patient and surgeon request this and when there is no availability for the use of inhalational agents for a general anesthetic. The sporadic surgeon in the author's practice requires all the same elements of care; however, the setup is for IV sedation and the monitors and equipment are portable. Our group utilizes a system that is portable in three components:

1. The monitor bag, which carries a lightweight monitor for ECG, noninvasive blood pressure (NIBP), pulse oximetry, and an AED.
2. The disposables bag, which carries fluids, nasal cannula, IV sets, laryngeal mask airway (LMA), Yankauer, and additional items (Fig. 34-6).
3. Medications including resuscitative drugs and controlled substances are in an organized setup within a tackle box. The opioids are double-locked with the tackle box and assigned to each particular physician as needed (Fig. 34-7).

TIVA techniques are utilized for moderate to deep sedation and the level is varied as the procedure dictates.[9,10] The author utilizes midazolam and fentanyl in bolus increments. We are careful to discontinue its use in the last 90 min of the procedure as its residual effects may affect the alertness of the patient. The author also utilizes ketamine judiciously because of its dissociative and analgesic properties at the beginning of the case, limiting its dose to no more than 25 mg to avoid dysphoric effects. Ketamine is especially useful during laser procedures, where the use of supplemental oxygen is limited. Additionally, the author titrates propofol or a mixture of methohexital and propofol (in equal concentrations) infusions to achieve an appropriate level of sedation. These drugs may be titrated with an infusion pump or a basic microdrip. Generally the titration level varies between 25 and 150 µg/kg/min. The author's group finds that the addition of methohexital adds a component of sedation that complements propofol, as clinically it provides a deeper sedation with less respiratory depression. The maximum dose of methohexital used is not to exceed 8 mg/kg, as this will bring undesirable side effects of shivering and masseter muscle spasm movements into play. Methohexital may also be used in bolus increments of 10–20 mg to augment levels of sedation or cover breakthrough alertness during the procedure. As with all sedation techniques, the liberal and appropriate use of lo-

Bags: Disposable Items	Quantity
Endotracheal tubes (6.0, 7.0, 8.0)	One of each
Yankauer suction	Two
Suction hose	One per patient
Nasal cannulas	3–4 (+ 1 for each additional patient)
Lactated ringers or normal saline	3–4 (+ 1 for each additional patient)
Ambu bag	One
Laryngeal mask airway (LMA)	One
IV tubing	3 each (minidrip and macrodrip)
Extension IV tubing	3–4 (+1 for each additional patient)
Extension tubing (infusion pump)	3–4 (+1 for each additional patient)
Rubber glove	2 (optional)
Stylettes	2 per bag
Manual sphygmomanometer	1
Stethoscope	1
Oxygen tank with wrench	1 each
Flashlight	1
Scissors	1

Figure 34-6   Nova Anesthesia Professionals anesthesiologist bag inventory.

cal anesthetics is invaluable to a successful anesthetic technique.

The universality of the use of midazolam, fentanyl, ketamine, methohexital, and propofol can be translated through all the surgical specialties. Procedures of 30 min or less duration are well managed with bolus techniques without the use of continuous infusions. In today's cost-conscious environment, indicated medications that offer real advantages should be used, and we are judicious in the addition of "newer" medications if no real benefit is quantified.

Dental Suite

Our most frequent dental specialties that require sedation are oral surgery, periodontics, prosthodontics, and pedodontics. Each specialty has different needs as the procedures that each specialty performs are quite varied. The author's group deals mostly with those dental specialists who have had some training and exposure in working with the anesthesia provider and the "sedated" patient. Education and training is required so they acquire an appreciation of the acuteness of an unprotected airway and its limitations. Everyone must have the same expectations, and patient safety must be the most important factor. Remember that expertise in providing sedation allows the practitioner to

Tackle Box	Quantity	Tackle Box	Quantity
Top Drawer Items		**2nd Drawer (continued)**	
Gauze		3 mL syringes	6–8 syringes
Stopcocks	2–3	5 mL syringes	5–6 syringes
Oral airways (6.0, 7.0, 8.0)	1 each	10 mL syringes	5–6 syringes
Nasal airways (20, 24, 28, 32)	1 each	Needles (18, 22 gauge)	8 each
ECG leads	1 bag	50% Dextrose	1 (50 mL vial)
Alcohol wipes		Ammonia inhalants	2–4
Bandaids			
Tape	1–2 rolls	**3rd Drawer**	
Laryngoscope (with batteries)	1	Thiopental (if available)	1 kit
C Batteries	1 extra set	Methohexital (if available)	1 (2.5 g vial)
Mac Blade # 3 (laryngoscope)	1	Dolasetron	2–4 (1 mL amp)
Miller Blade # 3 (laryngoscope)	1	Metoclopamide	2–4 (1 mL amp)
50% Dextrose (injection w/needle)	1	Glycopyrrolate	1 (20 mL vial)
Ketamine	1–2 **THESE DRUGS**	Atropine	1 (20 mL vial)
Midazolam	1–2 **IN DOUBLE**	Cefazolin	2 (1 g vial)
Fentanyl	1–2 **LOCK**	Ampicillin	2 (500 mg vial)
Meperidine	1 **BOX**	Clindamycin	2 (600 mg vial)
Labels (fentanyl, midazolam, methohexital)	1 roll each	Gentamycin	2 (2 mL vial)
Metaproterenol inhaler	1	Dexamethasone	1 (30 mL vial)
Propofol	10	Hydrocortisone	1 (2 mL act-o-vial)
		Furosemide	4 (4 mL vial)
1st Drawer			
Sodium bicarbonate (1 mEq/mL)	1	**4th Drawer**	
Epinephrine Inj (w/needle) (1 mg)	1	Succinylcholine	1 (10 mL vial)
1% or 2% Lidocaine (w/needle) (100 mg/mL)	1	Dopamine	1 (5 mL vial)
		Propanolol	1–2 (1 mL amps)
Amiodarone	3	Adenosine	4 (2 mL amps)
Calcium Chloride 10% (100 mg/mL)	2	Diphenhydramine	2–3 (1 mL amps)
Procainamide (1g/10mL)	2	Digoxin	2–3 (2 mL amps)
Surgilube	1 tube	Verapamil	2 (2 mL vial)
Tongue blades	10	Nitroglycerin tablets/ paste	1 (25 sublingual tab vial)
2nd Drawer		Hydralazine	2 (1 mL vial)
IV catheters (18, 20, 22 gauge)	10 each	Labetolol	2 (20 mL vial)
Temperature strips	12	Esmolol	2 (10 mL vial)
1% Lidocaine (10 mg/mL)	1 (50 mL vial)	Phenylephrine	2–4 (1 mL amps)
1 mL syringes	8–10 syringes	Ephedrine	2–4 (1 mL amps)
		Epinephrine	2–4 (1 mL amps)
		Flumazenil	1 (5 mL vial)
		Naloxone	2–3 (1 mL amps)

Figure 34-7 Nova Anesthesia Professionals anesthesiologist tackle box inventory.

accomplish a greater range of procedures and the training of the specialist is key.

Oral surgeons, in the office setting, most commonly require anesthesia for the extraction of impacted molars. These cases last typically 30–35 min and require a deep level of sedation. Intravenous sedation is titrated with bolus administration of midazolam 2–3 mg and fentanyl 50–100 μg at the start. Ketamine may be given up to 25 mg as one wishes. A propofol and methohexital infusion is titrated to 50–150 μg/kg/min. Infusion is stopped as the last molars are sutured, and the patient is typically able to walk to recovery within 7–10 min.

Periodontists often require anesthesia services for their phobic patients. They utilize anesthesia for gum surgery, dental implants, and planing and scaling of all mouth quadrants. Close communication with the practitioner, the patient, and the anesthesiologist regarding the details of the patient's phobia and the changing level of anesthesia from lighter to deeper levels is key. The need for patient cooperation during the procedure will necessitate changing levels of anesthesia as the procedure is performed. Continuous-infusion techniques provide the greatest flexibility with varying levels of anesthesia. Have the dentist select the lowest setting of water spray required with drilling, cleaning, and so on as the airway has decreased protective reflexes and the risk of aspiration increases. Alternatively, the anesthesiologist may lighten the anesthetic level so the patient may cooperate with swallowing to avoid aspiration. The use of a mouth prop is invaluable in keeping the mouth open in a sedated patient so that accessibility to the field is ensured. These must be placed before patient cooperation is lost as mouth opening can be an issue in the sedated patient.

Prosthodontists are the plastic surgeons of dentistry and the gamut of procedures includes dentures, partial plates, and crowns with post-and-core preparations. The prosthodontist needs to have many periods of patient cooperation that may involve making of molds, molding articular surfaces, and fitting prosthesis. The technique of continuous infusion of propofol at varying rates and increments of midazolam will provide satisfactory working conditions with effective patient comfort.

Special Considerations for Handicapped and Pediatric Patients

There are many perioperative issues to clarify in this challenging subset of patients. They require a thorough investigation of any other associated morbidity with their condition. In the dental office, especially with airway concerns, the author's group has elected not to deal with airway aberrancies, such as with Trisomy 21, and others that would compromise the patient's safety. The author's group notifies the pediatrician or local doctor that his/her patient is undergoing a procedure in the office with IV sedation. This allows the anesthesiologist a valuable resource in the event of postprocedure problems. One needs to communicate all pre- and postoperative instructions with the patient's guardian or caretaker. The legal guardian must accompany the patient to the procedure or consent must be obtained prior to the procedure.

The degree of disability (e.g., mental retardation) may dictate a certain depth of anesthesia. Make sure this can be safely accomplished in the office or dental chair setting. These patients often have an encumbrance with secretions and routine use of glycopyrrolate in this population is beneficial. Communication with the patient may be an issue. Will the anesthesiologist require the aid of translators or caretakers? These concerns must be recognized and ad-

dressed prior to the procedure date. Care of the handicapped and pediatric population may require a larger number of personnel, and the office facility must have dedicated manpower to handle their needs. Difficulty with communication also affects a timely discharge, and evaluation of mental status and return to baseline is more difficult to assess.

Special situations may exist in dentistry, and anesthesiologists need to be especially careful with the use of water and irrigation in the mouth as these patients have a deeper anesthetic and secretions may easily lead to aspiration and laryngospasm if the situation is not correctly managed. Children in an office-based environment have failure-to-rescue rate of 93%, attributable mainly to lack of preparedness.[11] To enter in the pediatric arena, in the office-based setting, the author feels that at minimum, an anesthesia extender who has a skill level of an RN with a pediatric background and pediatric advanced life support (PALS) certification is necessary to ensure a higher level of preparedness. The office staff may have very limited expertise in the area and a skilled person is invaluable.

Induction and preprocedure anxiolysis need to be addressed on an individual basis. Can an IV be started? Handicapped or needle phobics may need oral sedation prior to the venipuncture. Consider the situation with adequate manpower and skilled hands, as the anesthesiologist may have to attend to an IV and an airway at the same time. The author's group has chosen not to do cases that do not allow IV start in the office with ample help. Intramuscular anxiolytic/sedative drugs do introduce an additional risk that may be difficult to manage well in the office setting.

Remember to consider an increased time of at least 30 min for oral sedation to take effect and also an increased time of delayed awakening for discharge. Some oral sedatives used by the author's group include 0.3–0.5 mg/kg of midazolam alone or with the addition of oral ketamine 2 mg/kg. The addition of ketamine allows a faster separation from the caretaker (approximately 15–20 min vs. 30 min) and it offers some analgesia for the venipuncture.[12]

Special needs and arrangements must be accommodated with discharge and follow up care. Social issues must be considered, as these patients may need a greater degree of supervision at home or in their facility postprocedure. These discussions and arrangements should be made in advance of the procedure date.

Fast-Turnover Volume Practices

This type of practice (e.g., gastroenterology) has monitors and anesthesia materials housed in each procedure room. The emergency medications and "code cart" are present with an attached oxygen tank and suction machine at a close central location. The greatest challenge is posed by coupling the logistics of volume with the goal of efficiency. Patients are scheduled every 30 min and the process in place must ensure safety and speed. The average time from admission to discharge is usually 90 min. Anesthetic screening and data collection must be done well in advance of patient arrival. The goal is to keep the pace rapid while still making the patient care personal and friendly. Everyone involved in these settings is key in the success of each patient's procedure, anesthetic, and experience.

POSTPROCEDURE CARE

Care should be handed over in a predetermined and coordinated fashion to the PACU personnel. Immediate postoperative care may be in the same procedure room and then turned over to recovery personnel, or may be in an adjacent designated PACU. The facilities may have great variability; however, the standards for postanesthesia care as approved by the ASA House of Delegates must be followed.[13] Care for level 1 postprocedure patients should be with RNs with ACLS training. Fast tracking can be utilized if applicable.

Standards dictate the following criteria are met: all patients who receive general anesthesia, regional anesthesia, or monitored anesthesia care shall receive appropriate postanesthesia management. Patients transported to the PACU should be accompanied by a member of the anesthesia care team who is knowledgeable about the patient's condition and the patient shall be continually evaluated and treated during transport as needed. Upon arrival in the PACU the patient shall be reevaluated and a verbal report provided to the responsible PACU nurse by a member of the anesthesia care team who accompanies the patient. Discharge must be an objective and planned process. Several scoring data sheets for objective discharge are available.[14–17]

Fast tracking is the most efficient method of turnover in the office. The anesthetic technique aims to have a postprocedure patient who is awake, alert, and moves from the operating room bed to the PACU bed without assistance. Most general anesthetic discharges should occur within 60 min of awakening. The anesthesiologist typically turns the room over in 10 min and starts the next anesthetic; therefore, airway intervention should never be an issue in the previous patient.

The anesthesia practitioner can only leave patients in the care of the PACU nurses when postprocedure concerns are stable and he/she is not needed to be physically present to address them. The operating and recovery rooms are usually very close, and communication is key if any additional instructions are required in the PACU. To ensure efficient turnover and care, be sure that the caregiver is present in the PACU so that instructions can be discussed and follow-up appointments made. All patients should be followed with postprocedure calls, and responses should be documented and evaluated. The author's group uses a postprocedure satisfaction survey.

ANESTHESIA STAFFING FOR THE OFFICE-BASED PRACTICE

Clinical Training of Anesthesia Staff

Clinical training of staff in the office setting is crucial. The learning curve of the anesthesiologist is to become comfortable with the resources available. One requires experience and training to be comfortable with the allowances and the limitations of these resources. The author's practice dedicates a "one-on-one" clinical orientation to each of the sites for 1–2 days or as needed so that the anesthesiologist is comfortable with the setting and the practice and is aware of all emergency procedures. It is for these training reasons that "locum" staff has less utility in specialized offices in the office-based setting, as the "learning curve" cannot be adequately and comfortably addressed.

Clinical Training of Nursing Staff

Within the author's practice a set of specific anesthesia algorithms was designed to be easily administered in question format for the preanesthesia evaluation. Responses are noted and any aberrancies are flagged. The "flagged" patients are reviewed by an anesthesiologist and their status is resolved prior to the date of surgery or procedure. Many steps may be involved in data collection and acquisition that enable a judicious medical decision to be made. The author's group clinical nurse manager teaches any new nurse the standard process of this evaluation so that a consistent patient evaluation format is achieved and thereby ensures anesthesiologists that each patient has been properly evaluated. The reliability of this process allows anesthesiologists to maintain procedure efficiency and patient safety.

EMERGENCIES IN THE OFFICE-BASED SETTING

The key to dealing with emergencies in the office-based setting is to be prepared with emergency medications, supplies, and training. All resuscitation medications should be labeled and organized within a tackle box. Appoint an individual within the practice to check and update all emergency supplies as ACLS algorithms change. Keep emergency airway management equipment in the disposables bag. Make sure all anesthesia providers have updated ACLS training and maintain current credentials.

Preparedness for Dealing with Intraoperative and Postanesthesia Care Unit Emergencies

Intraoperative and PACU emergencies need to be dealt with immediately. Understand the limitations of the office and appropriately choose more acute avenues of care as necessary. Have 911 emergency plans and policies in place and do not hesitate to activate them, as the appropriate and timely dispensation of the patient can be lifesaving. Until 911 ambulance help arrives, administer the appropriate ACLS algorithms. Training for emergencies should be rehearsed well in advance through role-play.

It is very important to conduct emergency drills every 6 months with different scenarios so that role-playing prepares everyone for his/her role in the event of an emergency. All office personnel, both medical and administrative, should have a clear assigned role.

Emergency Cases in the Office-Based Setting

The author's group is generally not involved in postdischarge emergencies, such as bleeding after face lifts or breast implants. These procedures and patients are now in a higher risk category and may have hemodynamic instability. The anesthesia group may not be able to address this instability with blood and invasive monitoring, in the office-based setting, should that be required. Anesthesiologists may not have a policy regarding this, but each group may elect to evaluate each patient on a case-by-case basis.

Add-on Cases in the Office Setting

Add-on cases to the day's schedule are not considered emergencies and they are done after they have undergone the same rigorous medical evaluation and satisfy NPO and other guidelines. All the same policies and procedures should be carefully applied to these patients to ensure judicious medical practice.

Transfer Agreements

Transfer agreements must be in place (Fig. 34-8) in the event of an admission. Make sure the practitioner or surgeon has a signed transfer agreement to a nearby institution for the admission of patients. If the practitioner is a dentist, make sure he/she has a physician contact who will admit the patient and take care of all necessary measures at a nearby hospital. Children and handicapped patients are best handled by having their local primary care physician notified that their patient is to undergo a procedure with sedation in the office setting. This communication is useful in the event that the patient needs follow-up care.

SUMMARY

The surgical office-based practice has witnessed unprecedented growth.[18] This growth has also incurred issues of appropriate standards of medical care and liability. Anesthesiologists can offer much to advance safety, efficiency,

---

To facilitate the continuity of care and timely transfer of patients and records between _____ (Facility) and _____ (Hospital or Medical Center) the parties named above agree as follows:

1. When a patient's need for transfer from one of the above institutions to the other has been determined and substantiated by the patient's physician, the institution to which transfer is to be made agrees to admit the patient as promptly as possible, provided admission requirements in accordance with Federal and State laws and regulations are met.

2. The transferring institution will send with each patient at the time of transfer, or in the case of emergency, as promptly as possible, the completed transfer and referral forms mutually agreed upon to provide the medical and administrative information necessary to determine the appropriateness of the placement and to enable continuing care to the patient. The transfer and referral form will include such information as current medical findings, diagnosis, a brief summary of the course of treatment followed in the transferring institution, nursing information, ambulation status, and pertinent administrative and social information as available.

3. The transferring institution will be responsible for the transfer or other appropriate disposition of personal effects, particularly money and valuable, and information related to these items.

4. The transferring institution will be responsible for effecting the transfer of the patient , including arranging for appropriate and safe transportation and care of the patient during the transfer in accordance with applicable Federal and State law regulations.

5. Charges for services performed by either facility shall be collected by the institution rendering such services directly from the patient, third-party payor or other sources normally billed by the institution. Neither facility shall have any liability to the other for the charges.

6. The Governing Body of each facility shall have exclusive control of the policies, management, assets, and affairs of its respective institutions. Neither institution shall assume any liability by virtue of the agreement for any debts nor other obligations incurred by the other party to this agreement.

7. Nothing in this agreement shall be construed as limiting the rights of either institution to contract with any other facility on a limited or general basis.

8. The effective date of the agreement shall be _____ and performance shall continue until termination by either _____ or _____ by written notice as provided below.

9. Either party may terminate the agreement without cause for any reason upon thirty (30) days prior written notice to the other party.

_____   _____
Date   Date

_____   _____
Medical Director   Administrator

Figure 34-8 Nova Anesthesia Professionals transfer agreement.

and sound medical practice in this area.[18-21] There is a need to address issues and to develop procedures that "raise the bar" in this new and less-regulated environment. We must ensure that these processes are applied and followed consistently as the office-based practice evolves. Training and expertise should be applied toward making the office-based environment at least as safe as, if not safer than, the freestanding ambulatory surgery center for patients.

REFERENCES

1. ASA Guidelines for Office-Based Anesthesia (Approved by the House of Delegates on October 13, 1999). Practice Guidelines. www.ashq.org.

2. Macpherson DS, Snow R, Lonfgren R. Preoperative screening: value of previous tests. Ann Intern Med 1990;113:969–73.

3. Narr B, Hansen T, Warner M. Preoperative laboratory screening in healthy Mayo patients: cost effective elimination of tests and unchanged outcomes. Mayo Clin Proc 1991;66:155–59.

4. Roizen M, Cohn S. *Preoperative Evaluation for Surgery—What Laboratory Tests Are Needed?* St. Louis: Mosby-Year Book, 1993.

5. Fleisher L, Barash P. Preoperative cardiac evaluation for noncardiac surgery: a functional approach. Anesth Analg 1992;74:586–98.

6. *ASA Practice Management: The HIPPA Privacy Rule in Anesthesia and Pain Medicine Practices*, 2003.

7. Twersky R, Lebovits A, Lewis M, et al. Early anesthesia evaluation of the ambulatory surgical patient: does it really help? J Clin Anesth 1992;4:204–7.

8. Hoefflin S, Bornstein J, Gordon M. General anesthesia in an office based plastic surgical facility: a report on more than 23,000 consecutive office based procedures under general anesthesia with no significant anesthetic complications. Plast Reconstr Surg 2001;107: 243–51.

9. Ganzberg S, Weaver J. Anesthesia for office-based oral and maxillofacial surgery. Dent Clin North Am 1999;43:547–62.

10. Trytko R, Werschler WP. Total intravenous anesthesia for office-based laser facial resurfacing. Lasers Surg Med 1999;25:126–30.

11. Ross AK, Eck JB. Office based anesthesia for children. Anesthesiol Clin North Am 2002 Mar;20:195–210.

12. Report of Educational Meeting, The Society for Office-Based Anesthesia. J Clin Anesth 1998;10:445–48.

13. ASA Practice Guidelines for Postanesthetic Care. Anesthesiology 2002, Mar;96:742–52.

14. Aldrete JA, Kroulik D. A postanesthetic recovery score. Anesth Analg 1970;49:924–34.

15. Chung F, Chan VW, Ong D. A post-anesthetic discharge scoring system for home readiness after ambulatory surgery. J Clin Anesth 1995;7:500–506.

16. Marshall S, Chung F. Discharge criteria and complications after ambulatory surgery. Anesth Analg 1999;88:508–17.

17. Marshall S, Chung F. Assessment of "home readiness": discharge criteria and post discharge complications. Curr Opin Anaesthesiol 1997;10:445–50.

18. APSF Newsletter special section on office based anesthesia. APSF Newslett 2000;15(1).

19. Posner K. Liability profile of ambulatory anesthesia. Am Soc Anesthesiol Newslett 2000;64(6).

20. Domino KB. Office based anesthesia: lessons learned from the closed claims project. Am Soc Anesthesiol Newslett 2001;65(6).

21. Morello DC, Colon GA, Fredricks S, et al. Patient safety in accredited office surgical facilities. Plast Reconstr Surg 1997;99:1496.

Austere Environment Anesthesia

CHESTER C. BUCKENMAIER III

Anesthesiology as practiced in the developed world relies heavily on technology to allow ever more complex surgery to be performed with remarkable safety. A myriad of gadgets and monitors aiding in the practice of anesthesia by constantly confirming patient well-being surround the modern anesthesiologist. Occasionally, anesthesiologists find themselves in clinical situations where technology is lacking and resources severely constrained. This is particularly true for physicians who practice anesthesia for the military, disaster medicine, or humanitarian missions. The safe practice of anesthesia in these austere environments requires skills and preparation that are very different from the preparation most residents receive in modern anesthesiology training programs. Anesthesiologists who endeavor to perform anesthesia in difficult conditions often find that these conditions require an adjustment in thinking from what is the best anesthetic for the patient to what is the most practical anesthetic for the patient based on the environment. Anesthesia in austere environments is always challenging, yet extremely rewarding when one can provide a safe anesthetic under harsh conditions to those who often have the greatest need. This chapter will explore the issues and challenges anesthesiologists face when operating in austere conditions. How modern anesthesia technologies and techniques can be applied to overcome the challenges of austere-environment anesthesia (AEA) will also be discussed. The chapter is intended to provide a framework to assist in the planning and preparation for AEA.

THE PROBLEM

The advantages afforded the anesthesiologist in the modern world are considerable. Figure 35-1, graphically illustrates the basic problem of AEA, patient need versus available resources. The United States (US), for example, has a developed infrastructure of roads, vehicles, utilities, hospitals, and sophisticated medical technology that enables a tremendous resource base to be focused on relatively few

patients at any one time. The anesthesiologist performing AEA in less developed countries, during natural disasters, or on the battlefield will often find the reverse situation: little or no infrastructure, a limited resource base, and large numbers of patients requiring care in a compressed time frame. AEA presents the anesthesiologist with the daunting task of providing quality anesthesia with limited logistical support in a hostile environment. Quality care for patients under these circumstances requires the anesthesiologist to develop an anesthetic plan that goes well beyond taking a history and selecting an appropriate anesthetic.

Anesthetic plans for AEA must include factors that most anesthesiologists in the developed world would not consider. Local infrastructure, for example, can have a tremendous impact on anesthetic choice. The available roads,

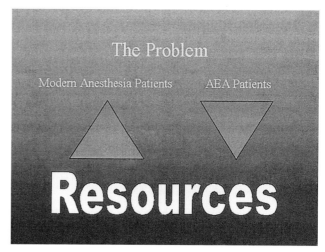

Figure 35-1 Comparing modern anesthesia patients with austere environment anesthesia (AEA) patients. In developed countries with modern medical services, the available resource base is broad and focused on relatively few patients. The triangle is flipped with AEA patients where the available resource base is narrow while the demand for service is great.

electrical services, sanitation services, and operating room facilities in a particular area will often impact on the type of anesthesia and surgical cases that can safely be performed. Limitations of local infrastructure can be overcome if sufficient resources are available to transport modern anesthesia infrastructure to the location where AEA is needed. This approach was exemplified by the U.S. Army in Operation Iraqi Freedom with the deployment of the 28th Combat Support Hospital (CSH) outside of Baghdad, Iraq (Fig. 35-2). While this concept addresses many of the issues involved with AEA, few organizations outside of the military have the resources to emulate this solution. In most cases, AEA practitioners will be forced to tailor their anesthetic to the environment they find themselves in and the equipment they can transport.

Local environmental and weather conditions will also greatly impact the performance of AEA. This is particularly true for missions following natural disasters. Extremes in temperature and terrain along with local dangerous faunae and diseases must be considered when planning for AEA. The anesthesiologist in modern society has little concern for personal safety while at work. This is not the case in austere environments where constant attention to personal and group safety is vital. Extremes in temperature can directly impact on patient health and indirectly impact patient care by degrading equipment, medications, and anesthesiologist performance. Terrain extremes can adversely impact practitioner and patient travel, impede communi-

cation, and limit resupply of consumable medical supplies. Environmental conditions and dangers encountered on the modern battlefield represent an extreme example of the impact environment can have on the performance of anesthesia. Although military anesthesia provides a useful example for operating in austere conditions, the influence of the modern battlefield environment and combat on anesthetic care is beyond the scope of this chapter.

The success or failure of any medical mission in an austere environment rests on a successful logistics plan. A successful plan must provide for medical equipment and supplies and material support for mission team members. The housing, feeding, and medical care of team members must take paramount importance in any medical mission to austere environments. Providing adequate shelter and supplies of safe food and drinking water can be extremely difficult in remote locations. Inconsistent or poor management of this vital issue can result in attrition of medical team members and degradation of overall mission performance. A member of the mission team should serve as the group health monitor and logistics officer. This individual is responsible for monitoring the health state of all mission participants, providing for field sanitation, obtaining potable water, ensuring sanitary food preparation, arranging for vector control, and coordinating medical services for team members when required. High-quality medical surveillance during the mission will enable mission planners to effectively intervene preemptively when team health care issues

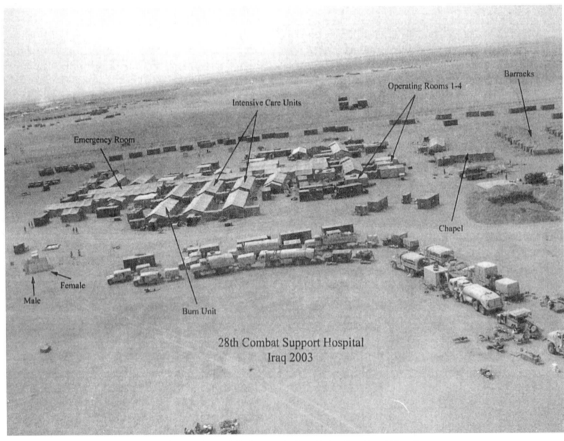

Figure 35-2   28th Combat Support Hospital outside Baghdad, Iraq during Operation Iraqi Freedom.

are present.[1] The individual performing this role should not be overly burdened with clinical responsibilities and should not serve as the mission leader.

The team logistician will also be responsible for medical resupply if required. Every effort should be made to bring all required medical supplies that will be needed during the mission. This is not always possible with controlled drugs or anesthetic gases. If the medical mission is of sufficient length or size that resupply of medical material will be needed, agreements between the supplier and the team must be established well in advance of mission execution. A plan and appropriate security equipment should be available to secure valuable medical machines and controlled substances from theft or unauthorized use.

The host nation's need for medical services can often be underestimated by local officials, particularly in developing nations. A recent medical mission by the author to Diébougou, Burkina Faso (formerly Upper Volta) is illustrative.[2] During initial consultation for the medical mission with Burkina Faso embassy officials in Washington, DC, concern was expressed that the city of Diébougou was too remote with too few patients to keep the mission team of 22 members fully occupied. These fears were unfounded with over 3000 patients presenting for evaluation during the 2-week mission, many trucked in from distant villages as word spread of the mission (Fig. 35-3).

Every effort should be made to obtain as much medical intelligence about a mission location early in the planning process. Discussions with local and state government and health officials should clearly define the scope of the proposed mission, the types of patients who will be managed, and the approximate number of patients who can be safely cared for during the mission. The paucity of medical services in some areas of the world can result in desperation of the local population and lead to possible confrontation (sometimes violent) between patients and mission participants. To reduce this possibility, the mission objectives should be clearly defined for the population through local leaders, and every effort should be made to avoid the appearance of inequality in the distribution of medical services to the population. Additionally, team medical professionals should endeavor to include local medical professionals in the medical project for educational exchange and training. This can greatly enhance local health care long after mission completion, reduce professional animosity, and enhance cultural understanding. These local providers familiar with regional health issues can become valuable allies and can serve as liaisons with the population.

Considerable time should be invested prior to the beginning of any AEA mission in learning about the host country's culture. Failure to understand local customs and behavior standards can result in significant personal embarrassment and possibly even physical harm in extreme circumstances. Detailed basic information on any country can be obtained via *The World Fact Book* (www.cia.gov/cia/publications/factbook) published annually by the Central

Figure 35-3 Patients presenting for medical service in Diébougou, Burkina Faso, November 2002.

Intelligence Agency (CIA). More important cultural information must come from mission supporters who are native to the host country and region where the mission will take place. The most critical component needed for successful cultural interaction is adequate interpreter support. The value of proficient and numerous interpreters supporting the mission cannot be overemphasized. Mission success can often hinge on the ability to effectively communicate with local officials and patients.

The preceding discussion outlines the major problems anesthesia practitioners will encounter when managing patients in austere environments. The remainder of the chapter will focus on techniques and equipment that can facilitate the practice of AEA.

GENERAL ANESTHESIA IN AEA

The ability to perform a general anesthetic must be a part of every AEA plan. Even if the AEA mission will be limited to surgical procedures that usually do not require general anesthesia (GA), this capability must be available for emergencies. GA is the standard anesthetic to which all other techniques are compared. In the developed world sufficient resources are available (electricity, compressed gas, modern anesthesia machines, operating rooms, etc.) for the safe and effective use of GA for any surgical case. Unfortunately, the availability of equipment and resources to perform a modern GA is often limited or nonexistent for AEA. Ventilation of the GA patient can always be accomplished with a bag-valve-mask device and oxygen. Though simple to perform, this approach is labor-intensive, results in greater fluctuation of ventilatory parameters, and can inhibit the performance of other patient monitoring and anesthetic care tasks.[3] The U.S. military has invested considerable resources in the development of an effective field anesthesia machine and this effort provides valuable insight into the use of GA in AEA. Petty,[4] in his historical perspective on the evolution of the military field anesthesia machine, listed the U.S. Army's design requirements for a new field anesthesia machine following World War II. These requirements included:

- Lightweight (less than 95 lb)
- Compact
- Have a two-canister carbon dioxide absorber
- Be able to accommodate large and small medical gas cylinders
- Have pressure regulators for oxygen and nitrous oxide
- Have a breathing circuit pressure gauge
- Be capable of delivering anesthetic mixtures over a temperature range of 4°–38°C

These initial design requirements resulted in the Ohio Model 785 Army Field Anesthesia Machine in 1967, but combat conditions in Vietnam and the end of the use of explosive anesthetic gases led to further development requirements. In 1977 the Ohmeda Model 885A incorporated a number of improvements over previous machines to include a universal vaporizer, gas-scavenging capabilities, and a pressure sensor nitrous oxide shutoff valve, to

Table 35-1   Forward Surgical Team Field Anesthesia Machine Requirements

- Has a functional ventilator
- Does not rely on compressed gases for operation
- Compatible with low-flow/low-pressure oxygen from a concentrator
- Electrical operation (for electronic pumps)
- Operation for 3 hr on battery backup
- Compact
- Digital ventilator display
- Food and Drug Administration approval
- Multiagent capable
- Inspired and expired gas monitoring capabilities

list a few.[4] The Ohmeda 885A remained the standard military field anesthetic machine until recently. It was replaced by the Dräger Narkomed M, which has most of the features found on anesthesia machines in any modern operating room. Unfortunately, the field anesthesia machines mentioned rely on a source of compressed gas and electricity to function properly, which may not be readily available in many AEA situations. As the U.S. military has deployed medical assets further forward on the modern battlefield, new requirements have been established to provide GA with limited resources. Table 35-1 outlines the requirements established by the U.S. Army Medical Materiel Development Activity (USAMMDA) for a draw-over vaporizer to support forward-deployed medical units.[5] Recently Reynolds et al.[6] proposed the combination of the Ohmeda Portable Anesthesia Complete draw-over vaporizer with an Impact 754 Eagle ventilator, which addresses many of the requirements outlined by USAMMDA (Fig. 35-4). The Impact 754 has an integrated compressor to provide positive-pressure ventilation when compressed gases are not available. Additionally, low-pressure oxygen from a cylinder or oxygen concentrator can be used with the ventilator. Continued research and technologic developments will improve the anesthesiologist's ability to provide GA in the most remote locations. Regardless of the field anesthesia machine technology chosen, extensive training on the equipment is required for its successful utilization in AEA.

Practitioners of AEA should endeavor to adhere to American Society of Anesthesiologists' standards for patient monitoring.[7] These standards include the presence of qualified anesthesia personnel in the operating room during any anesthetic procedure and the ability to continually monitor the patient's oxygenation, ventilation, circulation, and temperature. Capnography is a highly advantageous function of any monitoring plan and should be available if possible. Desirable characteristics of a field monitor include compact design, long battery life, ease of screen navigation and viewing, patient alarms, motion tolerance, invasive blood pressure capable, and a rugged case.

The Welch Allyn Propaq Encore is an example of a good monitor for AEA. Recent anecdotal reports from Operation Iraq Freedom have suggested that multifunction monitors are complicated, heavy, and require significant battery

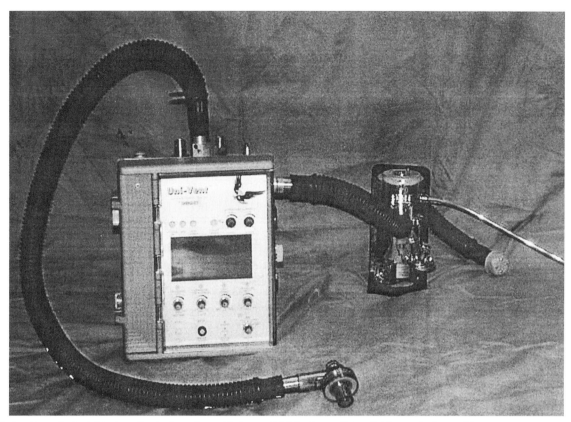

Figure 35-4   Ohmeda Portable Anesthesia Complete with Impact 754 Eagle ventilator field anesthesia machine.

power. Some military anesthesiologist's prefer separate electronic devices for monitoring blood pressure, pulse, and pulse oximeter, claiming greater simplicity and less battery power use. In addition, all monitoring capability is not lost if one device malfunctions. Equipment for obtaining manual vital signs should be readily available and providers should reinforce their skills at employing this equipment for dependable backup of electronic devices. Other technology, such as the compact Nonin Onyx 9500 pulse oximeter (Nonin Medical Inc., Plymouth, MN), can be extremely useful for checking patient pulse rates and oxygen saturation throughout the perioperative period.

Logistical support for GA in AEA can prove extremely difficult. Mechanical ventilation driven from an E-cylinder oxygen source can result in rapid depletion of this vital medical gas and degrade patient safety.[8] Triage of mission cases and anesthetic selection must be based on the availability of sufficient quantities of oxygen. The use of spontaneous ventilation during GA cases, whenever possible, will greatly reduce the amount of oxygen used when compared to positive-pressure ventilation. Oxygen concentrators when coupled with a ventilator such as the Impact 754 offer a viable alternative when oxygen sources are unavailable.[9]

During the planning stages of any AEA mission, the availability of electrical power must be assessed. Many areas in developing nations have no electrical service, or if electricity is available it may not be consistently accessible. In areas with electrical capability, the local plug pin configuration must be determined so appropriate plug adapters can be obtained for mission equipment. Also, information on the type of electricity used is needed. Most countries use either 110 Volts (V) (110–120 V) as in the United States or 220 V (220–240 V) and some countries use both. Information on the cycles per second, or Hertz (Hz), is also needed. In the United States 60 Hz is used while other countries use 50 Hz. Although most equipment is not affected by changes in Hz, some electronic appliances may run faster or slower (analog clocks for example).

Differences in voltage require converters or transformers to convert the electrical source to a power source appropriate for the electrical device. Do not confuse electrical adapters with converters and transformers; the former merely provide the correct pin configuration for the wall outlet and do not modify the electricity. As a general rule, electrical appliances (hairdryer, coffeemaker, etc.) can use a converter or transformer. Electronic devices (appliances with electronic motors, circuits, or chips) require a transformer. For most medical equipment, or if there is any doubt, take a transformer that is designed for long-term use. For a more detailed discussion on world electricity issues, the following Internet sites are recommended:

- www.walkabouttravelgear.com/wwelect.htm
- www.kropla.com/electric.htm

Electricity issues can also be addressed with portable generators, of which there are many sizes and capacities. However, the use of portable generators results in further logistical issues of transportation, fuel, and maintenance. In addition, the generating capability (watts = V × amps) brought on a mission must exceed the combined watts used by the connected equipment. For example, a medical device that uses 3 amps at 120 V would require 360 watts (3 amps × 120 V = 360 watts) and the combined watts of all the devices attached to the generator should not exceed its electrical generating capability (1 kW = 1000 watts).

The volatile anesthetic to be used on the mission will need to be determined based on personal preference and vaporizer requirements. Sevoflurane is becoming the current volatile agent of choice for austere-environment missions.[10] Limiting the volatile anesthetic to one agent simplifies logistical issues and sevoflurane has a number of properties that make it attractive. It has cardiovascular effects similar to those of isoflurane and has a low solubility that allows for rapid adjustments in anesthetic depth. Sevoflurane can be used as an induction agent as it is nonpungent and not irritating to the airway. Use of sevoflurane in the Ohmeda Portable Anesthesia Complete drawover vaporizer delivers clinically useful amounts for GA.[11] Finally, the benefits of sevoflurane use in pediatric patients are well established.[12]

Total intravenous anesthesia (TIVA) is another useful method for establishing and maintaining GA. The use of TIVA further simplifies the equipment required for ventilation during GA. TIVA with propofol has characteristics that make it an attractive selection for AEA, such as reduced postoperative nausea and vomiting (PONV), more rapid recovery from anesthesia, and improved patient satisfaction.[13] Additionally, most anesthesiologists are comfortable providing sedation with propofol. Unfortunately, propofol has properties known to support bacterial growth and environmental extremes can make storage of the drug per manufacturer recommendations difficult.[14] Propofol also does not have analgesic properties that necessitate its use with other pain medications. Dexmedetomidine, an alpha 2 receptor agonist, has potent sedative properties but, unlike propofol, it has analgesic properties and is not associated with respiratory depression despite deep sedation.[15,16] As new anesthetics are evaluated and become available, the utility of TIVA in AEA should increase. TIVA can be particularly useful when used as an adjunct to regional anesthesia (RA).

GA for AEA has the advantages of being quick, easy to establish, familiar to anesthesiologists, and often the only choice in many clinical situations. As the preceding discussion has outlined, GA has the disadvantage of being resource- and technology-intensive. In addition, postoperative recovery from GA can make this anesthetic a less desirable choice in austere conditions. When GA is the primary anesthetic, the increased incidence of PONV, drowsiness, and pain is the most frequent cause of prolonged postoperative stay in the modern ambulatory surgery setting.[17,18] In the resource-limited environment of AEA, difficult recovery from anesthesia can have a negative impact on team function and mission success as more personnel and resources will be required for postoperative patient management. Postanesthesia recovery areas in less developed countries may lack oxygen, monitors, and nursing support, further complicating recovery from GA. Ow-

ing to the resource-intensive nature of GA, mission leaders must carefully triage cases that require GA and consider the impact these procedures may have on overall patient care and mission objectives.

REGIONAL ANESTHESIA IN AEA

The use of long-acting peripheral nerve block (PNB) and continuous peripheral nerve block (CPNB) in the ambulatory surgery setting has received increased attention recently because of the improved outpatient analgesia and safety associated with the techniques.[19,20] The use of RA in austere conditions has many potential advantages, as listed in Table 35-2. The rapid recovery and ability to protect the airway associated with RA compared to GA is one particularly important advantage for AEA. Quick recovery after surgery facilitates patient movement through the field medical system, consumes fewer resources, and reduces the burden on mission medical professionals. The profound analgesia associated with RA results in reduced opioid requirements after surgery.[21,22] Reduced monitoring capability and international regulations can complicate the use of opioids in AEA. CPNB can provide extended perioperative analgesia, further reducing opioid requirements.

Many anesthesiologists prefer using a peripheral nerve stimulator to provide objective evidence of nerve localization for PNB and CPNB.[23] Desirable characteristics for field peripheral nerve stimulators include a light, compact, battery-operated design, with adjustable current (0–5 mA in 0.01 increments), impulse frequency (1–2 Hz), and impulse period (0.1–1 msec). Both visual and audible cues for an open or closed circuit should be part of the design. Methods allowing single operator adjustment of current output while operating the needle, such as foot pedals or palm controls, improve device versatility and operator efficiency.

A variety of needles and needle systems for conducting nerve stimulation with a stimulator and establishing a PNB are available. Insulated needles should have only the needle tip exposed for nerve stimulation. The wire connection

Table 35-2   Advantages of Regional Anesthesia in Austere Environmental Conditions

- Excellent operating conditions
- Profound perioperative analgesia
- Stable hemodynamics
- Limb-specific anesthesia
- Reduced need for other anesthetics
- Improved postoperative alertness
- Minimal side effects
- Rapid recovery from anesthesia
- Simple, easily transported equipment needed

SOURCE: Buckenmaier CC III, Lee EH, Shields CH, et al. Regional anesthesia in austere environments. Reg Anesth Pain Med 2003;28:321–27. Reprinted with permission.

passing current from the stimulator to the needle should be soldered to the needle. Clear extension tubing should also be integral to the needle allowing operator observation for blood during aspiration. Unlike the 17° bevel found on most needles, stimulating needles tend toward a blunter bevel of 30°–45° to enhance the tactile sensation of passing through tissue plains.[24] The anesthesiologist is also confronted with a plethora of needle systems for establishing CPNB. Continuous catheters can be broken down into two categories, stimulating and nonstimulating catheters. Stimulating catheters allow stimulation of the nerve through the catheter providing an objective indication that the catheter is in proximity to the nerve being blocked. Both the surgical block and subsequent analgesic block is injected through the catheter after satisfactory placement. Nonstimulating catheter systems allow injection of local anesthetic through the insulated needle when satisfactory nerve stimulation is obtained and a catheter for analgesia is placed after the surgical bolus injection of local anesthetic. Though catheter placement tends to be simpler using this method, there is no practical way to confirm the catheter is close enough to the nerve to be clinically effective other then successful analgesia after the operation. Evidence is lacking when comparing the two catheter systems for success of surgical block, ease of placement, and quality of postoperative analgesia. Although authors have expressed opinions on the merits of both systems, significantly more data will be required before recommendations on either system can be made with authority.[25,26] Securing CPNB catheters to prevent accidental removal in rough environments can also be difficult. Some authors recommend subcutaneous skin tunneling of the catheter to prevent dislodgement with patient movement and possibly protect against infection.[27,28] The author prefers using 2-octyl cyanoacrylate glue to bond the catheter to the skin because it is less invasive, easy, and may also provide a barrier to infection.[29]

For CPNB to be a viable pain management tool in AEA, infusion pumps must be available that can function properly and consistently in harsh conditions. Characteristics of a good field infusion device are listed in Table 35-3. A variety of portable infusion devices are currently available for infusion outside of a modern hospital environment (Fig. 35-5). The viability of prolonged CPNB analgesia use outside of the hospital has been demonstrated by a number of authors.[30–32] The utility of CPNB in AEA seems intuitive though practical experience using the technology in austere environments is needed.

Monitoring requirements for the performance of RA in AEA are the same as for GA. Mission efficiency can be improved with the establishment of a RA area, with appropriate patient monitoring capability, outside of the operating rooms. This area serves a variety of functions that can improve anesthesiologist efficiency and enhance patient flow through the medical system. Initial patient evaluation, counseling (often through an interpreter), medical record establishment, intravenous (IV) access, and premedication can all be instituted while prior cases are ongoing in the operating rooms. When RA is planned as the primary anesthetic technique, PNB and CPNB can be established well in advance of patient transfer to the operating room. The

Table 35-3   Characteristics of a Good Austere-Environment Anesthesia Infusion Pump

- Inexpensive
- Patient tamper-proof
- Stable infusion rates in extremes of temperature and pressure
- Battery-operated (electronic pumps)
- Disposable
- Patient-controlled bolus capable
- Programmable for a variety of infusion rates and bolus profiles
- Light and compact with carrying case
- Intuitive patient controlled shut-off
- Minimum 400-mL reservoir
- Easy to operate and program

RA area also provides an excellent environment for medical education activities with residents and local medical professionals.

The equipment needed for performance of RA in the austere environment requires significantly less space and weight when compared to GA. The preferential use of RA whenever possible can positively impact the logistical problems encountered in AEA. Though oxygen remains a vital resource, its consumption should be reduced when RA with spontaneous ventilation is used. Many patients will not require supplemental oxygen with RA when sedation can be limited or avoided. Local anesthetics are easily transported and shipment across international borders is usually not met with the bureaucratic difficulties involved with opioid transport.

RA possesses many characteristics that make it a "field friendly" choice in harsh environments. While GA capability will always be required, the need for compressed gas resupply, ventilators, and dependable sources of electricity makes GA more difficult to support logistically. The excellent operating conditions, profound postoperative analgesia, and improved postoperative recovery associated with RA make it a powerful tool in AEA.

PREPARATION FOR MEDICAL MISSIONS IN AUSTERE ENVIRONMENTS

The performance of anesthesia in austere environments requires the anesthesiologist to obtain skills and understanding beyond the traditional anesthesia education provided by most modern anesthesiology programs. Although basic anesthesia care concepts remain the same despite the environment, the reliance on technology and the abundance of resources in modern anesthesiology training programs do not necessarily provide the anesthesiologist with the tools or experience needed to provide anesthesia safely in austere conditions. Since military anesthesiologists are required to effectively provide AEA, military anesthesiology programs actively train their residents in AEA. The

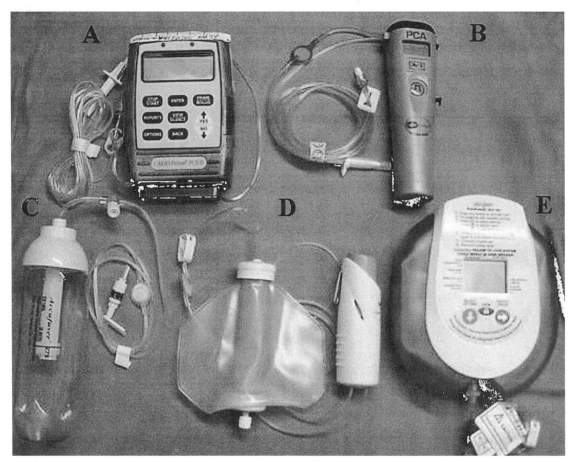

Figure 35-5   Portable infusion pumps. Electronic home infusion pumps: (A) (CADD-Prizm PCS II, Deltec Inc., St. Paul, MN); (B) (Palmpump, Sorenson Medical, Inc., West Jordan, UT). Disposable elastomeric infusion pumps: (C) (Accufuser, McKinley Medical LLLP., Wheat Ridge, CO); and (D) (On-Q C-bloc, I-Flow Co., Lake Forest, CA). Electronic disposable infusion pump: (E) (Painpump2, Stryker Instruments, Kalamazoo, MI).

Operational Anesthesia Rotation (OAR) at Walter Reed Army Medical Center, Washington, DC, provides an example of an AEA training program.[2] The OAR is a 1-month rotation that involves anesthesiology residents in the planning and execution of a 2- to 3-week medical mission in an austere environment, usually in cooperation with a civilian medical humanitarian mission. The program pairs a resident with an anesthesiologist experienced in AEA who mentors and supervises the resident during premission planning and during the field experience. Educational goals of this program are outlined in Table 35-4. Though the OAR is designed to help prepare military anesthesiologists for deployment during war, educational goals for any anesthesiologist involved in AEA are the same. Extensive familiarization with AEA equipment, to include its use in the modern hospital setting, is highly recommended prior to mission deployment.

Once anesthesia personnel are identified for an AEA mission, planning for the mission should begin months in advance. Appropriate military country clearances and passport documents can take considerable time to obtain. Particular attention should be given to individual medical screening for infectious disease prophylaxis. Health risk information and prophylaxis recommendations for the

mission host country can be obtained from the Centers for Disease Control and Prevention (www.cdc.gov). U.S. military planners can obtain medical threat information from the Armed Forces Medical Intelligence Center (www.mic.afmic.detrick.army.mil).

In the months prior to leaving, a series of informal meetings should be scheduled with all team members to disseminate information and outline mission objectives. These meetings provide a forum for discussing premission issues and allow inexperienced participants to learn from more AEA seasoned colleagues. Leadership roles should be clearly defined and established well before mission execution. A detailed logistics plan for medical supply and resupply should be a primary goal of the initial planning meetings. A site visit by the mission team leader and group health monitor/logistics officer should be accomplished with local officials well in advance of the mission. Many issues and problems will be resolved and other unforeseen issues will be identified by this visit that will allow preemptive solutions. The information obtained from the premission visit is vital for the anesthesia team to develop effective anesthetic equipment and supply lists. Although many anesthesia suppliers are willing to donate supplies for humanitarian missions, the cost of medical materials

Table 35-4 Operational Anesthesia Rotation Program Goals

- Preparations for working and living among patients and families with diverse cultural backgrounds while providing their health care
- Preparation for deployment to areas of high prevalence of endemic infectious diseases to include: medical threat estimation, medical intelligence information collection, medical operational plans development, and individual travel medicine consultation
- Public health aspects of humanitarian missions, such as relevant infectious diseases and risk/benefit issues of prophylaxis options
- Understanding basic food and water sanitation
- Effects of extreme environmental conditions on patients, staff, anesthetic equipment, and medications
- Universal precautions in austere environments
- Medical supply logistics with travel to and operations in harsh environments
- Fatigue and stress management
- Triage and medical resource allocation
- Spontaneous ventilation: its use in the field to avoid the need for ventilators, increase safety, and extend capabilities; its limitations in complex surgical procedures
- Total intravenous anesthesia: its use in austere conditions and the risks/benefits of this anesthetic
- Regional anesthesia: the appropriate use of regional anesthesia to extend capabilities in a mass-casualty situation, improve postoperative analgesia with limited patient monitoring, and minimize risk in austere environments

SOURCE: Buckenmaier CC III, Lee EH, Shields CH, et al. Regional anesthesia in austere environments. Reg Anesth Pain Med 2003;28:321–27. Reprinted with permission.

can strain even the most robust of budgets. Transport of these materials to the host country is also expensive. AEA anesthesiologists are forced to determine what is necessary for field anesthesia rather than what is desirable. Anesthesia equipment vendors are often eager to donate their devices to demonstrate equipments attributes in environmental extremes. The anesthesiologist will quickly learn the strengths and weaknesses of a particular device in these challenging conditions.

As the mission execution date approaches, efforts should be made to preship as much medical material to the mission site as funds will allow. Substantial stress is removed from team members if equipment and supplies can be prepositioned. Coordination with airline and customs officials well in advance of departure will greatly reduce the delay and frustration of transporting medical materials internationally. Finally, each anesthesia provider must pack for the mission. Since most international flights limit

baggage to two pieces per person, AEA participants will often use one bag for clothes and personal items and the second bag for medical supplies and equipment. To avoid excess weight charges, participants should meet prior to leaving to evenly distribute the weight among the travelers. A packing list for AEA missions is provided in Table 35-5. The list is intended to serve as a reference; modifications will be dictated by mission-specific needs as well as individual preferences.

Upon arrival in the host country, mission participants will frequently be asked to attend various cultural and educational activities. Enthusiastic participation in these important events should be a major goal of any AEA mission. The foundation for a successful mission is often established during these first interactions with host country officials. Mission participants should be thoroughly briefed ahead of time on local customs and standards of behavior. Regional environmental hazards and crime should also be discussed. It is a prudent policy for team members to travel in groups of two or more and to always inform the team leader of their destination.

Considerable time should be invested in mission site preparation before patients are accepted. Methods for evaluating and triaging patients for surgery must be clearly established among mission participants and local officials. Careful planning of the operating room schedule by surgeons and anesthesiologists can maximize mission efficiency and proficiently utilize limited resources. Complicated and resource intense operations should be accomplished early in the day. Procedures should also be established to handle medical emergencies and death.[33] Medical records should be produced and maintained to the same standards used in developed countries. A mission team member should be assigned to collect, secure, and maintain all medical records.

Sufficient nursing support is necessary to provide postoperative recovery services for the mission. Planners should not expect local nursing support from overburdened medical systems. A team member should be available 24 hr to intervene in the event of postoperative recovery difficulties. Mission leaders should establish firm daily start and end times for the operating room to avoid excessive fatigue and degradation of mission member performance. As the mission draws to a close, surgical cases should not be scheduled if sufficient time is not available for postsurgical follow-up.

The demand for care will often exceed the resources of any medical mission to an austere environment. The population seeking care should be kept informed of mission progress, particularly mission end points. Local officials should be used to assist in easing the disappointment of those who unfortunately do not receive the care they desire. Unless it is definite, any discussion of the team's return for another mission should not be made.

Anesthesia in harsh and underserved environments can provide the anesthesiologist with an intellectually stimulating and satisfying professional experience. For those anesthesiologists who practice disaster or military anesthesia, the training benefits of AEA missions are obvious. The benefits of improved understanding and interaction between cultures, though more subtle, are no less pro-

Table 35-5   Anesthesia in Austere Environments Checklist of Equipment

Monitors
- Portable monitors—battery-operated, three-lead and five-lead electrocardiograph, heart/pulse rate, pulse oximetry, impedance respiration, temperature, noninvasive blood pressure
- Electric converters
- Extension power cords
- Portable capnography* (Easy Cap II™, Nellcor Puritan Bennett Inc. Pleasanton, CA)
- Finger pulse oximeter
- Portable blood gas and electrolyte analyzer*
- Manual blood pressure cuff
- Stethoscope
- Precordial stethoscope, stickers, and earpiece
- Thermometer
- Portable ultrasound machine*

General anesthesia
- Portable ventilator*
- Oxygen concentrators*
- Portable generator*
- Infusion pumps
- Percutaneous tracheostomy/cricothyrotomy kits
- Retrograde intubation kit (long wire, tube exchanger, introducer needle)
- Draw-over anesthesia circuit
- Portable suction machine, tubing, and suction catheters
- Ambu bag
- Jackson-Rees circuits
- Anesthesia circuits
- Face masks (various sizes)
- Face mask strap
- Oxygen masks
- Laryngoscope handles, blades, spare bulbs
- Lighted stylette
- Magill forceps
- Endotracheal tubes with stylettes (various sizes)
- Laryngeal mask airways (various sizes)
- Oral and nasal airways (various sizes)
- Nasogastric tubes
- Lubrication jelly

Regional anesthesia
- Nerve stimulator
- Insulated nerve block needles (5, 10, 15 cm)
- Insulated continuous block needles with catheters (3.81, 5, 10, 15 cm)
- Topical skin adhesives, adhesive skin closure strips, clear adhesive dressings (for securing continuous catheters)
- Iodine spray 1%
- Tuohy needles 22 gauge, 10 cm
- Connecting tubing
- Spinal needles/kits
- Epidural needles/kits
- Disposable infusion pumps
- Sterile gloves (various sizes)

(Continued)

Table 35-5   Anesthesia in Austere Environments Checklist of Equipment (*Continued*)

Other supplies
- IV catheters (various sizes)
- IV tubing
- Central line kits
- Syringes (various sizes)
- Penrose drain tourniquets
- Alcohol swabs
- Bandage scissors/hemostats
- Plastic adhesive tape
- Plastic bags
- Gauze bandages
- Examination gloves (various sizes)
- Scavenger system tubing
- Medication labels for syringes
- Locking trunk to secure medications
- Tubing connectors
- Needles (various sizes)
- Intraosseous needles
- Batteries for all battery operated equipment
- Battery charger* (if needed)
- Record-keeping supplies (anesthesia preoperative forms, anesthesia intraoperative forms, progress notes)

Personal items
- Scrubs, hats, masks, and shoe covers
- Hip pack for drugs, personal equipment, passport, etc.*
- Utility knife
- Clothing appropriate for the environment and culture
- Insect repellant
- Prophylactic medication (malaria, HIV, etc.)
- Mosquito netting
- Sleeping bag
- Portable radio*
- Camera*
- Notebook, pen, and paper
- Personal lock for luggage
- Flashlight
- Sunscreen lotion
- Sunglasses
- Credit card
- Baby wipes (field bath)
- Medicated foot powder
- Personal hygiene items
- Plastic bags
- Laundry detergent
- Emergency contact information on card maintained on person
- Comfort food*

Medications
- Inhaled anesthetics
- Induction drugs—thiopental, propofol, ketamine

(Continued)

Table 35-5 Anesthesia in Austere Environments Checklist of Equipment (*Continued*)

- Neuromuscular blocking drugs—succinylcholine, nondepolarizing muscle relaxants
- Anticholinesterase drugs—neostigmine
- Anticholinergics—atropine, gycopyrrolate
- Sedatives—midazolam
- Benzodiazepine antagonist—flumazenil
- Nonsteroidal anti-inflammatory drugs—acetaminophen, ibuprofen, rofecoxib, etc.
- Opioids (oral/parenteral)—oxycodone, butorphanol, morphine, hydromorphone, fentanyl
- Opioid antagonist—naloxone
- Local anesthetics—lidocaine, mepivacaine, ropivacaine, bupivacaine, tetracaine
- Bronchodilators—albuterol, metaproterenol
- Antibiotics (oral/parenteral)
- Antiemetics—metoclopramide, ondansetron, promethazine
- Steroids—dexamethasone, methylprednisolone, hydrocortisone
- Nasal vasoconstrictors—oxymetazoline
- Dextrose 50%
- H_1 antagonists—diphenhydramine
- H_2 antagonists—cimetidine
- Sympathomimetics—epinephrine, phenylephrine, ephedrine
- Adrenergic receptor antagonists—esmolol, labetalol
- Other vasoactive drugs—hydralazine, verapamil
- Other desirable medications*—amiodarone, calcium chloride, dantrolene, furosemide, insulin, mannitol, sodium bicarbonate

*Desirable though not required.

Source: Modified from Fisher QA, Politis GD, Tobias JD, et al. Pediatric anesthesia for voluntary services abroad. Anesth Analg 2002;95:336–50, with permission.

found or important. Opportunities for AEA are abundant for those willing to accept the challenge.

REFERENCES

1. Gambel JM, Drabick JJ, Martinez-Lopez L. Medical surveillance of multinational peacekeepers deployed in support of the United Nations Mission in Haiti, June-October 1995. Int J Epidemiol 1999;28:312.
2. Buckenmaier CC III, Lee EH, Shields CH, et al. Regional anesthesia in austere environments. Reg Anesth Pain Med 2003;28:321.
3. Dockery WK, Futterman C, Keller SR, et al. A comparison of manual and mechanical ventilation during pediatric transport. Crit Care Med 1999;27:802.
4. Petty C. Historical perspective on the evolution of today's military field anesthesia machine. Milit Med 1990;155:66.
5. Reynolds PC. Personal communication, June 30, 2003.
6. Reynolds PC, Calkins M, Bentley T, Popa C. Improved anesthesia support of the forward surgical team: a proposed combination of drawover anesthesia and the life support for trauma and transport. Milit Med 2002;167:889.
7. American Society of Anesthesiologists. Standards for Basic Anesthetic Monitoring. Park Ridge, IL, American Society of Anesthesiologists, Conference Proceeding 1998.
8. Taenzer AH, Kovatsis PG, Raessler KL. E-cylinder-powered mechanical ventilation may adversely impact anesthetic management and efficiency. Anesth Analg 2002;95:148.
9. Reynolds PC. Oxygen supplementation of the Impact 754 ventilator. Milit Med 2002;167:196.
10. Affleck PJ, Needleman S. Sevoflurane and the 885A field anesthesia machine: clinical report. Milit Med 1997;162:762.
11. Reynolds PC, Furukawa KT. Letters to the Editor. Milit Med 2003; 168:ii–iii.
12. Russell SC, Doyle E. Paediatric anaesthesia. Br Med J 1997;314:201.
13. Visser K, Hassink EA, Bonsel GJ, et al. Randomized controlled trial of total intravenous anesthesia with propofol versus inhalation anesthesia with isoflurane–nitrous oxide: postoperative nausea with vomiting and economic analysis. Anesthesiology 2001;95:616.
14. Langevin PB, Gravenstein N, Doyle TJ, et al. Growth of *Staphylococcus aureus* in Diprivan and Intralipid: implications on the pathogenesis of infections. Anesthesiology 1999;91:1394.
15. Arain SR, Ebert TJ. The efficacy, side effects, and recovery characteristics of dexmedetomidine versus propofol when used for intraoperative sedation. Anesth Analg 2002;95:461.
16. Ebert TJ, Hall JE, Barney JA, et al. The effects of increasing plasma concentrations of dexmedetomidine in humans. Anesthesiology 2000;93:382.
17. Chung F, Mezei G. Factors contributing to a prolonged stay after ambulatory surgery. Anesth Analg 1999;89:1352.
18. Pavlin DJ, Rapp SE, Polissar NL, et al. Factors affecting discharge time in adult outpatients. Anesth Analg 1998;87:816.
19. Klein SM, Nielsen KC, Greengrass RA, et al. Ambulatory discharge after long-acting peripheral nerve blockade: 2382 blocks with ropivacaine. Anesth Analg 2002;94:65.
20. Klein SM, Buckenmaier CC III. Ambulatory surgery with long acting regional anesthesia. Minerva Anestesiol 2002;68:833.
21. Klein SM, Bergh A, Steele SM, et al. Thoracic paravertebral block for breast surgery. Anesth Analg 2000;90:1402.
22. Wang H, Boctor B, Verner J. The effect of single-injection femoral

nerve block on rehabilitation and length of hospital stay after total knee replacement. Reg Anesth Pain Med 2002;27:139.

23. De Andres J, Sala-Blanch X. Peripheral nerve stimulation in the practice of brachial plexus anesthesia: a review. Reg Anesth Pain Med 2001;26:478.

24. Buckenmaier CC III. Anaesthesia for outpatient knee surgery. Best Pract Res Clin Anaesthesiol 2002;16:255.

25. Copeland SJ, Laxton MA. A new stimulating catheter for continuous peripheral nerve blocks. Reg Anesth Pain Med 2001;26:589.

26. Ilfeld BM, Kayser Enneking F. Ambulatory perineural local anesthetic infusion. Tech Reg Anesth Pain Manag 2003;7:48.

27. Balamoutsos NG, Sfakiotaki TN, Antoniadou SP. A simple and reliable method of subcutaneous tunneling of epidural catheters. Anesth Analg 1996;82:1303.

28. Boezaart AP, Koorn R, Rosenquist RW. Paravertebral approach to the brachial plexus: an anatomic improvement in technique. Reg Anesth Pain Med 2003;28:241.

29. Klein SM, Nielsen KC, Buckenmaier CC III, et al. 2-Octyl cyanoacrylate glue for the fixation of continuous peripheral nerve catheters. Anesthesiology 2003;98:590.

30. Buckenmaier CC III, Klein SM, Nielsen KC, Steele SM. Continuous paravertebral catheter and outpatient infusion for breast surgery. Anesth Analg 2003;97:715–17.

31. Ilfeld BM, Morey TE, Wang RD, Enneking FK. Continuous popliteal sciatic nerve block for postoperative pain control at home: a randomized, double-blinded, placebo-controlled study. Anesthesiology 2002;97:959.

32. Rawal N, Allvin R, Axelsson K, et al. Patient-controlled regional analgesia (PCRA) at home: controlled comparison between bupivacaine and ropivacaine brachial plexus analgesia. Anesthesiology 2002;96:1290.

33. Fisher QA, Politis GD, Tobias JD, et al. Pediatric anesthesia for voluntary services abroad. Anesth Analg 2002;95:336.

Regional Anesthesia Techniques: Alternatives for Specific Procedures

CHESTER C. BUCKENMAIER III • SCOTT M. CROLL • YAIR RUBIN

PERIPHERAL NERVE BLOCK EQUIPMENT

Peripheral nerve stimulation, an alternative to paresthesia techniques, is a reliable, safe technique for the performance of most peripheral nerve blocks. However, the nerve stimulator is not a substitute for anatomic knowledge and the physician should never use the device to "hunt" for the nerve. Rather, since the motor nerve fibers are depolarized by lower current than the sensory nerves, the anesthesiologist can obtain objective evidence of successful nerve localization without eliciting a paresthesia. Paresthesias are often uncomfortable and anxiety-provoking for the patient. Since paresthesia techniques require greater patient participation, sedation for the block is more difficult, and patient acceptance of the block may decrease. Stimulation of the target nerve at a current of 0.5 mA or less suggests accurate needle placement for local anesthetic injection in most blocks when a nerve stimulator is used.

A variety of peripheral nerve stimulators and needle systems are being marketed today. Characteristics of a good peripheral nerve stimulator include light, compact, battery-operated design with adjustable current from 0 to 5 mA in 0.01-mA increments and 2-Hz impulse frequency. The digital display should be bright and easily read. The device should provide some visual or audible (or better both) signal of an open or closed circuit between the stimulator, the needle, and the patient. Stimulating needles should be insulated with only the very tip of the needle exposed for nerve stimulation. The wire connecting the needle to the stimulator should be attached to the needle (soldered). Clear extension tubing should also be integral to the needle to facilitate anesthetic injection and allow observation for blood during aspiration. Stimulating needles are typically beveled at 45° rather then 17° like more traditional needles to enhance the tactile sensation of the needle passing through tissue plains and reduce the possibility of neural trauma. Desirable characteristics of Tuohy continuous nerve block needles are similar to those of single-injection needles with the added ability to pass a peripheral nerve catheter without changing needle position (as often occurs in systems that require syringe removal for passage of the catheter). The Stimuplex (B. Braun, Bethlehem, PA) (Fig. 36-1) continuous nerve block sets are representative. Other continuous nerve block delivery systems are available.

Peripheral nerve blocks, perineural catheter technology, and the recent development of disposable infusion pumps (Fig. 36-2) may result in many conventionally inpatient procedures becoming appropriate for the ambulatory environment. The advantage of these systems for battlefield anesthesia, pain control in austere settings without the respiratory depression of opioids, is clear.

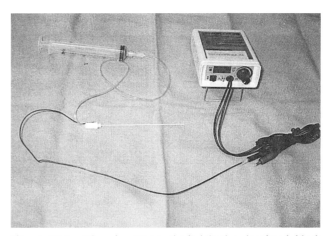

Figure 36-1 Stimuplex 10-cm single-injection insulated block needle with peripheral nerve stimulator (B. Braun, Bethlehem, PA).

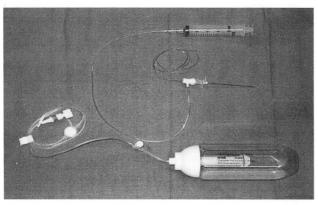

Figure 36-2   Paravertebral continuous catheter system with 18-gauge Tuohy needle and hemostasis valve/sideport (B. Braun, Bethlehem, PA). Accufuser disposable infusion pump also shown (McKinley Medical, Wheat Ridge, CO).

LOCAL ANESTHETICS

Local anesthetic selection for peripheral nerve block is based on onset of action, duration of action, and toxicity. The amide local anesthetics lidocaine, mepivacaine, bupivacaine, and ropivacaine predominate in peripheral nerve block anesthesia and though other local anesthetic options do exist, this discussion will be focused on these selections.

Lidocaine is an amide local anesthetic of rapid onset, short duration, and low toxicity. Lidocaine is valuable when rapid block onset is desirable though its short duration is a consequence. Lidocaine is particularly useful when combined with epinephrine 1:200,000 to test-dose perineural catheters. When catheters have been placed, lidocaine can be useful to speed block onset or evaluate catheter function.

Mepivacaine is an amide local anesthetic of rapid onset, intermediate duration, and intermediate toxicity. The onset time can be reduced by alkalinization with sodium bicarbonate. Mepivacaine is advantageous for procedures of short duration in which early return of motor function, ambulation, and patient discharge are desirable. Arthroscopic knee surgery is an example of a procedure of short duration that mepivacaine would be a suitable local anesthetic choice for peripheral nerve block. The predictable 4–6-hr motor and sensory block will provide excellent surgical conditions for this procedure and the patient can expect full function of the extremity for an expeditious recovery and discharge. Despite full motor and sensory function being regained within a few hours of surgery, the patient should always be cautioned by both the anesthesiologist and postanesthesia care unit (PACU) nurses to avoid full use of blocked extremities for 24 hr. Complete proprioceptive recovery can vary widely among patients because of the nerve block and other anesthetics used during the procedure. An ill-informed patient might prematurely trust that the limb will function normally, resulting in falls and further injury.

Bupivacaine is an amide local anesthetic of slow onset, long duration, and a high potential for toxicity. The molecule is highly lipophilic which facilitates nerve cell membrane penetration and explains the high potency of bupivacaine. Historically, bupivacaine has been the local anesthetic of choice when prolonged nerve blockade is desirable. Concerns over the significant cardiac toxicity associated with bupivacaine led to the development of ropivacaine, a chemical analog of bupivacaine. Ropivacaine is the first local anesthetic that is marketed as a levorotatory stereoisomer rather than a racemic mixture (combination of levo- and dextrorotatory molecules) like bupivacaine. Levorotatory enantiomers of local anesthetics are typically less toxic than dextrorotatory enantiomers. Multiple animal studies have found bupivacaine to be more cardiotoxic when compared to ropivacaine. This finding has been confirmed in human subjects. The advantage that reduced cardiac toxicity imparts to the use of ropivacaine in the clinical situation may be offset by concerns that it is less potent. Authors comparing the two local anesthetics for effectiveness at blocking the femoral nerve found bupivacaine and ropivacaine equally effective at similar volumes and concentrations. The two local anesthetics are equally effective at blocking the lumbar plexus and sciatic nerve, though duration of analgesia was longer with bupivacaine (ropivacaine 13 hr, bupivacaine 17 hr).

Levobupivacaine, a pure levorotatory enantiomer of bupivacaine, purportedly has similar potency but is less toxic than bupivacaine. Further study will determine the clinical advantage of this new local anesthetic preparation compared with ropivacaine.

All local anesthetics can result in acute central nervous system and cardiac toxicity if injected in sufficient amounts, usually after an unrecognized intravascular injection. Fastidious attention to detail during local anesthetic injection with slow incremental injection (3–5 mL) punctuated by frequent, gentle aspirations for blood will minimize but never eliminate the potential for intravascular injection. The increased margin of safety provided by the use of a less toxic but similarly effective long-acting local anesthetic like ropivacaine and possibly levobupivacaine (when compared to bupivacaine) is intuitive. Ropivacaine is used exclusively in the authors' practice as the long-acting local anesthetic of choice.

Considerable additional experience remains to be gained in the application of perineural catheter technology. Specifically, standard infusion concentrations and rates for effective analgesia required for the various blocks remain to be elucidated. The following is representative of the authors' experience in adults but is by no means the "final word" on perineural catheter infusion rates (Table 36-1). Plain 0.2% ropivacaine is used in the authors' practice (0.5 mg/kg/hr maximum infusion rate can be used to guide infusion therapy). Patient-controlled analgesia techniques are preferred when available as these systems usually result in a lower total dose of local anesthetic, increasing safety.

SITE-SPECIFIC ANESTHETIC OPTIONS

In an ambulatory setting there are numerous anesthetic plans that can be used either individually or in combination for a variety of procedures. These fall along a spectrum from the simple infiltration of local anesthetic (local/mon-

Table 36-1 Infusion Regimens for Continuous Peripheral Nerve Blocks

Catheter	Infusion Rate (mL/hr)		Patient-Controlled Infusion Rate
Interscalene		5–8	5 mL/hr with 2 mL bolus/20 min lockout
Supra/infraclavicular		5–10	5–8 mL/hr with 2 mL bolus/20 min lockout
Axillary		5–10	5–8 mL/hr with 2 mL bolus/20 min lockout
Paravertebral		5–10	5 mL/hr with 2 mL bolus/20 min lockout
Lumbar plexus		8–15	8–10 mL/hr with 2 mL bolus/20 min lockout
Sciatic nerve		5–10	5–8 mL/hr with 2 mL bolus/20 min lockout
Lumbar plexus and sciatic nerve	Lumbar plexus:	8–10	
	Sciatic nerve:	2–5	Usually avoided to prevent patient confusion

itored anesthesia care) to one or more peripheral nerve blocks to a general anesthetic. Surgery-specific factors requiring evaluation include whether or not a tourniquet will be used, anticipated length of surgery, innervation of the surgical site, expertise of the anesthesiologist, the surgeon's preference, and the need for muscle relaxation. Other important considerations include patient preferences and anxieties, prior history with general and regional anesthesia, nursing support, and availability of appropriate monitoring. Choosing a regional anesthetic may be advantageous in patients who have one or more of the following: a prior history of postoperative nausea and vomiting, a risk of aspiration, severe coronary artery disease, a known or potentially difficult airway, severe asthma, and a history of malignant hyperthermia. A final plan should be formulated by matching each patient's specific needs with an appropriate regional anesthetic. Examples of regional anesthetics that have successfully worked in the past for individual sites and procedures are listed in Tables 36-2 through 36-8.

UPPER-EXTREMITY BLOCKS

Cervical Plexus Block

The cervical plexus is formed from the anterior primary rami of C1–C4. The cervical plexus provides innervation to the muscles of the neck and the skin between the mandible (including behind the ear) and the clavicle. The cervical plexus block can be used to aid in anesthesia and analgesia for carotid endarterectomy, tracheostomy, and thyroid surgery. There are contributions to the phrenic nerve and therefore there is a significant incidence of ipsilateral phrenic nerve block with a deep cervical plexus block. With the deep cervical plexus block, the needle tip is in close proximity to the vertebral artery and to the vertebral foramen and there is a risk of intravascular or neuraxial injection of local anesthetic. If there is local anesthetic spread anterior to the prevertebral fascia, a Horner's syndrome will be seen and the possibility of a recurrent laryngeal nerve block may occur.

Table 36-2 Regional Anesthesia Techniques for General Surgery

Operative Site	Surgical Procedure	Regional Anesthesia Options
Breast and axilla	Breast lumpectomy	PVB at corresponding dermatomes on the ipsilateral side
	Mastectomy (simple, modified radical)	PVB T1–T6 ipsilateral side
	Sentinel node biopsy/axillary node dissection	PVB T1–T3 ipsilateral side
Abdomen and groin	Incisional/ventral hernia	PVB at corresponding dermatomes (bilateral if midline)
		Spinal/epidural
	Umbilical hernia	PVB T9–T11 bilateral
		Spinal
	Inguinal hernia	PVB T11–L2 ipsilateral side
		Ilioinguinal block
		Spinal
Genitalia	Circumcision	Penile nerve block
		Spinal
		Caudal (children)

Abbreviation: PVB, paravertebral block.

Table 36-3   Regional Anesthesia Techniques for Orthopedic Surgery

Operative Site	Surgical Procedure	Regional Anesthesia Options
Shoulder Clavicle Proximal humerus	Shoulder arthroscopy Shoulder hemiarthroplasty/total arthroplasty Rotator cuff repair Clavicle ORIF Proximal humerus ORIF	Interscalene block +/− intercostobrachial nerve block or paravertebral blocks T1–T2
Distal humerus Elbow	Distal humerus or elbow ORIF Olecranon fracture repair Elbow arthroscopy Ulnar nerve transposition	Supraclavicular block +/− intercosto-brachial nerve block (if tourniquet use)
Forearm Wrist	Fracture ORIF or closed reduction with percutaneous pinning Wrist arthroscopy Carpal tunnel surgery	Supraclavicular block Infraclavicular block Axillary block Individual nerve blocks at elbow Bier block
Hand and/or fingers	Carpal ORIF Digit ORIF	Supraclavicular block Infraclavicular block Axillary block Individual nerve blocks at level of wrist (for fingers) Digital block (for fingers) Bier block
Spine	Laminectomy	Spinal/epidural
Iliac Crest	Bone harvest	Paravertebral blocks T11–L2
Hip Femur	Total hip arthroplasty Hip arthroscopy Hip pinning Intramedullary nailing of the femur	Spinal Lumbar plexus + sciatic nerve blocks
Knee	Unicompartment/total knee arthroplasty Knee arthroscopy Uni- or multiligament knee reconstruction (e.g., anterior cruciate ligament)	Spinal/epidural Lumbar plexus/femoral nerve + sciatic nerve blocks
Tibia/fibula	Tibia/fibula fractures ORIF	Spinal Lumbar plexus/femoral nerve + sciatic nerve blocks
Ankle	Ankle fracture Ankle arthroscopy	Spinal Lumbar plexus/femoral nerve + sciatic nerve blocks (if thigh tourniquet use) Sciatic nerve block + saphenous nerve block (if tourniquet below knee or short tourniquet time) Bier block
Foot Toes	Bunionectomy Fracture ORIF	Spinal Sciatic nerve block (+ femoral nerve or saphenous nerve block if incision on medial side of ankle/foot) Ankle block Bier block Digital block (for toes)

Abbreviation: ORIF, open reduction and internal fixation.

Table 36-4 Regional Anesthesia Techniques for Plastic Surgery

Operative Site	Surgical Procedure	Regional Anesthesia Options
Breast	Breast reduction Breast augmentation (reconstruction)	Epidural Ipsilateral paravertebral block T2–T6
Fingers	Fracture ORIF Tendon repair Nerve repair	Supraclavicular block Infraclavicular block Axillary block Block of individual nerves at elbow or wrist Digital block (for fingers) Bier block (best suited for surgical times less than 90 min)

Abbreviation: ORIF, open reduction and internal fixation.

Table 36-5 Regional Anesthesia Techniques for Urology

Operative Site	Surgical Procedure	Regional Anesthesia Options
Kidney	Nephrectomy Lithotripsy for renal calculi	Epidural (combined with general anesthesia) Spinal
Ureter	Resection/reconstruction	Epidural (for postoperative analgesia)
Bladder	Calculi removal Stent placement Tumor resection	Spinal
Prostate	Transurethral resection of the prostate Prostatectomy	Spinal Spinal/epidural

Table 36-6 Regional Anesthesia Techniques for Vascular Surgery

Operative Site	Surgical Procedure	Regional Anesthesia Options
Carotid	Carotid endarterectomy	Superficial/deep cervical plexus block Cervical epidural

Upper extremity	Arteriovenous fistulas:
	  Proximal/upper arm
	  Distal/forearm
		Interscalene block
		Supraclavicular block
		Infraclavicular block
		Axillary block

Lower extremity	Varicose vein surgery	Lumbar plexus + sciatic nerve blocks Spinal

Table 36-7   Regional Anesthesia Techniques for Gynecology

Surgical Specifics	Surgical Procedure	Regional Anesthesia Options
No incision required	Diagnostic/operative hysteroscopy Dilatation and curretage Endometrial ablation	Spinal Paracervical blocks
Incision required	Vaginal hysterectomy Abdominal hysterectomy Suprapubic vaginal sling	Spinal/Epidural

Landmarks

Deep cervical plexus.   The patient is positioned supine with the head turned toward the nonoperative side. The transverse process of C6 (Chassaignac's tubercle) is palpated at the level of the cricoid cartilage. The mastoid process is palpated behind the ear. A line is drawn between the mastoid process and Chassaignac's tubercle. The transverse processes of the other cervical vertebrae will lie on or near this line. The first palpable transverse process below the mastoid process is C2. The transverse processes of C2–C4 are palpated and marked (the C4 transverse process lies approximately at the level of the mandible) (Fig. 36-3). The needle is inserted medially and caudally so that the tip of the needle is resting on the transverse process.

Superficial cervical plexus.   The posterior border of the sternocleidomastoid is identified and marked. The midpoint of the muscle is also identified and marked (Fig. 36-4).

Needle

22–25 gauge 3.7-cm/1.5-in. needle.

Local Anesthetic

Deep cervical plexus.   3–5 mL of local anesthetic at each level.

Superficial cervical plexus.   5–10 mL of local anesthetic.

The Block

Deep cervical plexus.   A 10-mL control syringe is attached to the needle. The needle is withdrawn 1–2 mm.

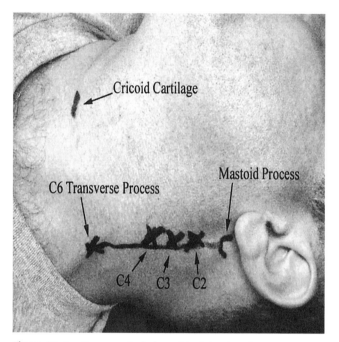

Figure 36-3   Deep cervical plexus block landmarks.

The local anesthetic is *slowly* injected with *frequent aspirations*. After the injection is completed, the needle is removed and the block is repeated at the next level.

Superficial cervical plexus.   The needle is inserted at the midpoint of the posterior border of the sternocleidomastoid muscle to approximately half the depth of the muscle, and 3–4 mL of local anesthetic is injected. A subcutaneous injection of local anesthetic is also made along the posterior border length of the sternocleidomastoid muscle.

Table 36-8   Regional Anesthesia Techniques for Thoracic Surgery

Operative Site	Surgical Procedure	Regional Anesthesia Options
Chest wall	Video-assisted thoracoscopy	Paravertebral blocks—ipsilateral corresponding levels (for postoperative analgesia)
	Rib fractures	Paravertebral blocks—ipsilateral corresponding levels (for postoperative analgesia)

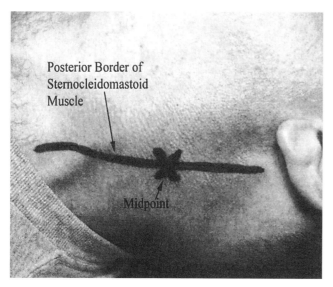

Figure 36-4   Superficial cervical plexus block landmarks.

Clinical Pearls

For carotid endarterectomies the surgeon needs to infiltrate the carotid body with local anesthetic as the cervical plexus does not innervate this structure. Many institutions perform only a superficial cervical plexus and have the surgeon infiltrate deeper structures as required.

Interscalene Brachial Plexus Block

The interscalene approach to the brachial plexus is particularly well suited for operations on the shoulder, clavicle, or upper arm. The approach preferentially blocks nerves of the cervical plexus (C3–4) and brachial plexus (C5–7). The ulnar nerve (C8–T1) is usually spared by this approach. The nerves of the brachial plexus emerge from their respective intervertebral foramina and course behind the vertebral artery. They then pass between the anterior and middle scalene muscles as the *trunks* (superior [C5–6], middle [C7], inferior [C8–T1]) of the brachial plexus are formed. The phrenic nerve (C3–5) lies anterior to the anterior scalene muscle and can be expected to be included in this block.

Landmarks

The patient is supine with his head turned toward the nonoperative side. The cricoid cartilage is identified, which indicates the C6 level. The lateral border of the sternocleidomastoid muscle is palpated and the fingers are moved laterally into the interscalene groove (between the anterior and middle scalene muscles). The internal jugular vein will often be noted to cross the border of the sternocleidomastoid muscle at this point. Initial needle insertion (at the level of C6) is indicated by an "X" in Fig. 36-5.

Needles

• 21-gauge, 5-cm insulated needle.
• 18-gauge, 5-cm insulated Tuohy needle for catheter placement. Catheters are introduced 3–5 cm.

Local Anesthetic

30–40 mL of local anesthetic will block the brachial plexus in most adults.

The Block

The nerve stimulator is initially set at 1.0–1.2 mA and muscle twitch in the shoulder (deltoid), biceps, forearm, or hand at 0.5 mA or less indicates adequate proximity to the brachial plexus for local anesthetic injection. The brachial plexus is rarely deeper then 1–2 cm from the skin (Fig. 36-6). Stimulation of the trapezius muscle suggests the needle tip is posterior to the plexus. Conversely, stimulation of the diaphragm indicates phrenic nerve stimulation and the needle tip is anterior to the plexus. Patients often develop a transient Horner's syndrome and hoarseness after this block. The patient should be warned of these side effects prior to the block. An intercostobrachial nerve block (subcutaneous injection of local from the axilla to the midpoint of the clavicle) should be performed for shoulder procedures. Paravertebral nerve blocks of T1–2 nerve roots can supplement this block for procedures with significant posterior dissections.

Clinical Pearls

As blockade of the phrenic nerve can be considered to occur 100% of the time with this block, other anesthetics may be warranted in patients with little or no respiratory reserve.

Supraclavicular Brachial Plexus Block

The brachial plexus is formed by the joining of the anterior primary divisions of C5 to T1, often with branches from C4 and T2 included as well. At the level of the trunks, the brachial plexus is at its most compact configuration. Therefore, blockade at this level has the greatest likelihood of blocking all the branches of the brachial plexus and has one of the most rapid onset times. The supraclavicular brachial plexus block is ideal for surgeries performed below the midhumeral level.

Landmarks

The patient is positioned supine with the head turned toward the nonoperative side. The posterior border of the sternocleidomastiod muscle is palpated at the C6 level and the fingers rolled laterally over the anterior scalene muscle until they lie in the interscalene groove (below the C6 level the groove may be harder to identify owing to the omohyoid muscle overlying the groove). The fingers are then moved inferiorly down the interscalene groove until they are approximately 1 cm from the clavicle (Fig. 36-7). This is the initial insertion site. The subclavian artery can be palpated at this point. The direction of initial needle insertion is lateral. The plane of the needle should be parallel to the bed (Fig. 36-8).

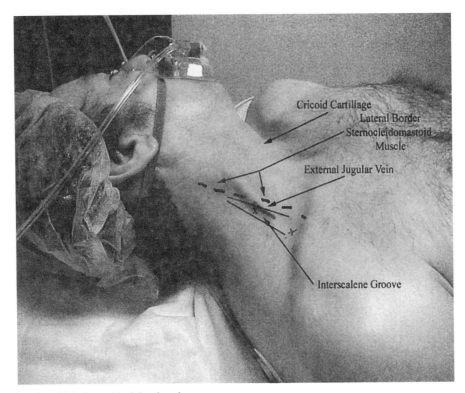

Figure 36-5   Interscalene brachial plexus block landmarks.

Needles

- 21-gauge, 5-cm insulated needle.
- 18-gauge, 5-cm insulated Tuohy needle for catheter placement. Catheters are inserted 3–5 cm.

Local Anesthetic

30–40 mL of local anesthetic will block the brachial plexus in most adults.

The Block

The nerve stimulator is initially set at 1.0–1.2 mA. Flexion of the thumb or fingers at 0.5 mA or less indicates proper needle placement. The brachial plexus can be quite deep at this location (may require longer needles in "thick-necked" individuals) but is often reached at 4–5 cm. Aspiration of bright-red blood suggests subclavian artery penetration, indicating the needle is too anterior. Stimulation of the musculocutaneous nerve (biceps contractions) usually indi-

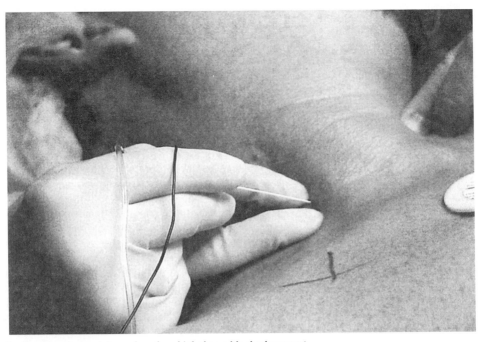

Figure 36-6   Needle direction during interscalene brachial plexus block placement.

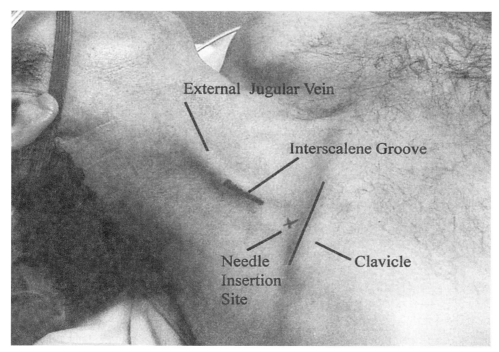

Figure 36-7   Supraclavicular brachial plexus block–subclavian perivascular technique landmarks.

cates the needle is too lateral. Pectoralis muscle contraction indicates too ventral needle insertion and latissimus dorsi contraction indicates too dorsal needle placement.

Clinical Pearls

Owing to the close proximity of the lung hilum, *the needle should never be directed medially.* If a tourniquet is used, blockade of the intercostobrachial nerve is required.

Intercostobrachial Nerve Block

The intercostobrachial nerve lies anterior and slightly superior to the axillary artery. It provides innervation to the skin along the upper medial border of the arm. A subcutaneous wheal of local anesthetic placed from the border of the pectoralis muscle insertion on the humerus to the inferior border of the axilla will usually block this nerve. The skin wheal should be placed as proximal as possible on the arm.

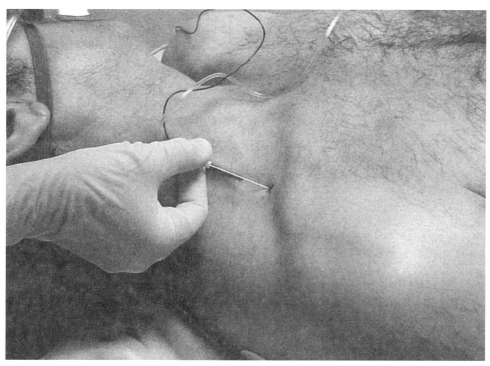

Figure 36-8   Needle direction during subclavian perivascular brachial plexus block placement.

Infraclavicular Brachial Plexus Block

As the nerves pass from underneath the clavicle and over the first rib they form the cords of the brachial plexus. The three cords, lateral, posterior and medial, are named for their position around the subclavian artery. Blockade at this level will normally block all major branches or the brachial plexus, as the musculocutaneous and axillary nerves have not usually separated yet. Also, the lung is more distant from the needle insertion site compared to the interscalene and supraclavicular approaches to the brachial plexus. However, owing to its intimate relationship with the artery, inadvertent arterial puncture is a risk, and at this location the ability to apply external pressure is difficult. This approach provides good anesthesia for forearm and hand surgeries.

Landmarks

The operative arm is externally rotated and abducted. The coracoid process is palpated. A mark is made 2 cm medial and 2 cm caudad from the coracoid process (Fig. 36-9). This is the site of needle insertion. The axillary artery is palpated as proximal as possible in the axilla; this is the direction of initial insertion. The needle is inserted at approximately 60-degree angle from the horizontal (Fig. 36-10).

The Block

The nerve stimulator is initially set between 1.0 to 1.2 mA. Finger and/or thumb flexion at 0.5 mA or less indicates adequate needle placement for local anesthetic injection. Stimulation of the musculocutaneous nerve indicates the needle is too lateral.

Local Anesthetic

30–40 mL of local anesthetic will block the brachial plexus in most adults.

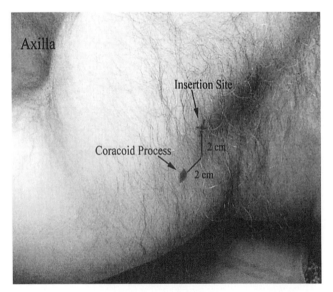

Figure 36-9   Infraclavicular brachial plexus block landmarks.

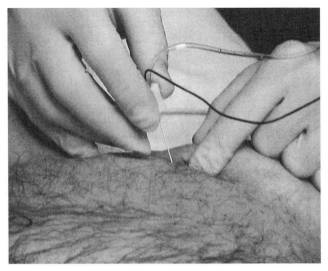

Figure 36-10   Needle direction during infraclavicular brachial plexus block placement.

Needles

- 21-gauge, 10-cm insulated needle.
- 18-gauge, 10-cm insulated Tuohy needle for catheter placement. Catheters are inserted 3–5 cm.

Clinical Pearls

Though some believe the intercostobrachial nerve is blocked with this approach, if an upper-arm tourniquet is to be used, the intercostobrachial nerve should be blocked separately. Perineural catheters that are placed with this approach are easier to maintain for prolonged periods when compared to blocks of the brachial plexus above the clavicle.

Axillary Brachial Plexus Block

At the level of the axilla, the brachial plexus has already divided into its branches. The four main nerves that innervate the forearm and hand are the ulnar, median, radial, and musculocutaneous nerves. In the axilla, the ulnar, median, and radial nerves travel adjacent to and within the same fascial compartment as the axillary artery. The musculocutaneous nerve travels separately, within the belly of the coracobrachialis muscle. Therefore, the axillary approach to the brachial plexus requires a minimum of two separate injections to provide adequate anesthesia for forearm and hand surgery. The distal location, compared to other brachial plexus approaches, results in the axillary block having negligible risks of respiratory compromise secondary to pneumothorax or phrenic nerve blockade. In addition, the peripheral location permits adequate tamponade to be applied to the artery with inadvertent puncture.

Landmarks

The patient is positioned supine with the operative arm abducted and externally rotated. The axillary artery is pal-

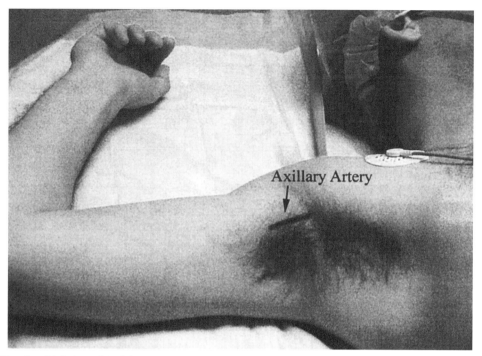

Figure 36-11   Axillary brachial plexus block landmarks.

pated as high up in the axilla as possible (Fig. 36-11). The needle is inserted superior to the axillary artery entering at a 45-degree angle (Fig. 36-12). To identify the coracobrachialis muscle, the biceps muscle is displaced laterally and the coracobrachialis muscle is palpated just medial to it. At the level of the upper half of the humerus, the needle is inserted into the coracobrachialis muscle to block the musculocutaneous nerve.

Needles

- 21-gauge, 5-cm insulated needle.
- 18-gauge, 5-cm insulated Tuohy needle for catheter placement. Catheters are inserted 3–5 cm.

Local Anesthetic

Median, ulnar and radial nerves.   30–40 mL of local anesthetic will block these nerves.

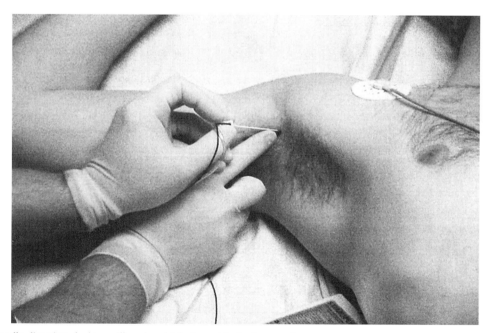

Figure 36-12   Needle direction during axillary brachial plexus block placement.

Musculocutaneous nerve. 10 mL of local anesthetic will block the nerve in most adults.

The Block

Median, ulnar, and radial nerves. The nerve stimulator is initially set between 1.0 to 1.2 mA. Finger flexion and/or thumb opposition at 0.5 mA or less indicates proper needle placement. Aspiration of bright-red blood means the needle has entered the axillary artery. The needle should then be advanced until the aspiration of blood stops (transarterial technique). Injection at this location will also provide blockade of the nerves.

Musculocutaneous nerve. The nerve stimulator is set to approximately 2.0 mA. The needle is fanned through the coracobrachialis muscle until vigorous biceps contraction is elicited (need to ensure that biceps contraction is not secondary to direct stimulation of the biceps muscle). There is no need to dial down the current.

Clinical Pearls

Application of distal pressure while injecting can help push the local anesthetic more proximally. Adducting the arm immediately postinjection can also help with proximal spread of local anesthetic. If a tourniquet is to be used, blockade of the intercostobrachial nerve is required (see "supraclavicular brachial plexus block").

PARAVERTEBRAL NERVE BLOCK _____

Paravertebral nerve blocks (PVBs) have been an established technique for providing analgesia to the chest and abdomen for many years. The current emphasis on health care cost containment has resulted in a rediscovery of anesthetic techniques, such as PVBs, that facilitate outpatient surgical management and promote early discharge. PVBs are highly versatile, serving as the primary anesthetic for breast surgery, herniorrhaphy, soft-tissue mass excisions, and bone harvesting from the iliac crest. PVBs are also a useful adjunct in laparoscopic surgery, cholecystectomy, nephrectomy, appendectomy, thoracotomy, thoracoscopy, obstetric analgesia, and minimally invasive cardiac surgery. In addition, PVBs are a valuable tool in treating chronic pain conditions of the chest and abdomen.

    The paravertebral space is a wedge-shaped anatomic compartment adjacent to the vertebral bodies. The space is defined anterolaterally by the parietal pleura, posteriorly by the superior costotransverse ligament (thoracic levels), medially by the vertebra, vertebral disk, and intervertebral foramina, and superiorly and inferiorly by the heads of the ribs. Within this space, the spinal root emerges from the intervertebral foramina and divides into dorsal and ventral rami. As the nerves pass through the paravertebral space, they are essentially "rootlets" and are not as tightly bundled with investing fascia as they are more distally. This anatomy likely enhances local anesthetic contact with the nerve roots, facilitating dense nerve blockade with small volumes

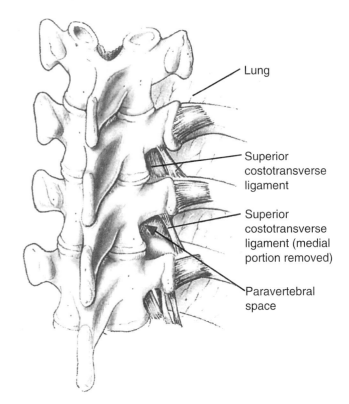

Figure 36-13 Paravertebral space boundaries. (Reprinted from Greengrass R, Steele S. Paravertebral blocks for breast surgery. Tech Reg Anesth Pain Manag 1998;2:8–12. With permission from Elsevier.)

of local anesthetic introduced into the space. In addition, sympathetic fibers of the ventral rami enter the sympathetic trunk via the preganglionic white rami communicantes and the postganglionic gray rami communicantes in this space. Because of the multiple neurologic structures confined within this compact space, local anesthetics introduced here can produce unilateral motor, sensory, and sympathetic blockade (Fig. 36-13).

Landmarks

The patient is placed upright with the neck and back flexed and the shoulders forward. The spinous process of each level planned for the block is palpated and marked at its superior aspect. From the midpoint of these marks a needle entry site is marked 2.5 cm laterally. In the thoracic area these marks should overlie the transverse process of the immediately caudal vertebra (because of the extreme angulation of the thoracic spinous processes). In the lumbar area the transverse process is at the same level as the spinous process or even one level above the spinous process.

    For mastectomy with axillary dissection, T1–6 are routinely blocked (Fig. 36-14). For sentinel node biopsy with possible axillary dissection, T1–3 blocks are sufficient. For breast biopsy, one injection is made at the dermatome corresponding to the needle localization plus additional injections one dermatome above and below this site. For inguinal herniorrhaphy, levels T11–L2 are blocked. For

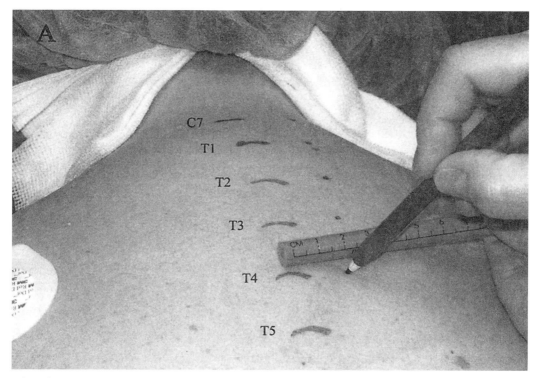

Figure 36-14   Thoracic paravertebral block landmarks for modified radical mastectomy. C7–T5 spinous processes are marked.

umbilical hernia, levels T9–11 are blocked bilaterally. Ventral hernia repair requires identification of the dermatomes involved and then blocking one additional level above and below.

Needles

- 22-gauge, Tuohy needle with extension tubing.
- 18-gauge, Tuohy needle with hemostasis valve/sideport assembly and 50 cm tubing. Catheters are placed 2–2.5 cm into paravertebral space.

Local Anesthetic

- 3–5 mL of local anesthetic at each space for multiple-injection techniques.
- 15–20 mL of local anesthetic for single-injection techniques.

The Block

Employing aseptic technique, a skin wheal is placed at each mark. The Tuohy epidural needle is attached via extension tubing to a syringe and the shaft of the needle is grasped by the dominant hand of the operator. The needle is inserted through the skin wheal and advanced anteriorly in the parasagittal plane (perpendicular to the back in all planes) until it contacts the transverse process (2–5 cm, depending on the body habitus of the patient) (Fig. 36-15). As a safety measure, to prevent unintended deep placement, the needle is grasped at a point from its tip that is equal to the estimated depth from the skin to the transverse process. Inserting the needle 1 cm past this predicted depth is allowed. If the trans-

verse process is not identified at an appropriate depth, it is assumed that the needle tip lies between adjacent transverse processes. The needle is then redirected cephalad and then caudad until the transverse process is successfully contacted. This depth is noted as the estimated distance to subsequent transverse processes. The needle is then withdrawn to the subcutaneous tissue and angled to walk off the caudad edge of the transverse process 1 cm. The author suggests the needle should be walked caudad. The reason for this is to minimize the possibility of a pneumothorax. If initial bony contact is made with the rib, walking caudally will invariably lead to contacting the transverse process at a more superficial point, thus minimizing inadvertent deep insertion. The rib, using the caudad technique, provides a "back stop" and an extra margin of safety in performing the block. Contrarily, walking cephalad (if one has inadvertently initially contacted rib) will lead to penetration of the pleura. This is clarified by Figure 36-16, where it was thought that walking cephalad gave a greater margin of safety. However, Fig. 36-16 clearly shows that walking caudad off the rib will invariably lead to contacting the transverse process (attached to the rib by the inferior costotransverse ligament). During continuous PVB placement, the catheter should be inserted only 2–2.5 cm into the paravertebral space (Fig. 36-17).

Clinical Pearls

At the thoracic levels it is common to appreciate a loss of resistance or a subtle "pop" as the needle passes through the superior costotransverse ligament. After aspiration of the syringe, 3–5 mL of local anesthetic is injected at each level. It is important to note that in the lumbar region, the transverse process is very thin. Hence the needle should

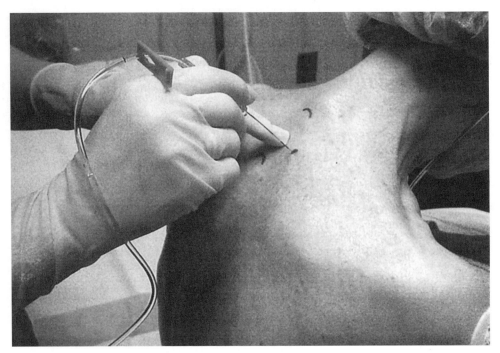

Figure 36-15   Needle direction during thoracic paravertebral block placement.

be inserted only 0.5 cm past the transverse process. In addition, there is no superior costotransverse ligament in this region. If a distinct "pop" is sensed here, then the needle has likely punctured the psoas fascia and should be withdrawn to a more shallow depth.

LOWER-EXTREMITY BLOCKS

Lumbar Plexus Block

The lumbar plexus is formed from the ventral rami of L1–4 with variable contributions from T12 and L5. The periph-

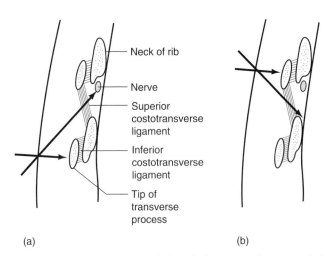

Neck of rib

Nerve

Superior costotransverse ligament

Inferior costotransverse ligament

Tip of transverse process

(a)   (b)

Figure 36-16   Paravertebral Block Technique. (a) Walking cephalad or (b) Walking caudad. (From Eason MJ, Wyatt R. Paravertebral thoracic block–a reappraisal. Anaesthesia 1979;34(7):638–42. Reproduced with permission from Blackwell Publishing.)

eral branches of the lumbar plexus include the iliohypogastric, ilioinguinal, genitofemoral, lateral femoral cutaneous, femoral, and obturator nerves. The plexus forms within the substance of the psoas major muscle and the peripheral branches continue toward the lower extremity between the psoas and the quadratus lumborum muscles. Of the multiple posterior approaches to the lumbar plexus, Winnie's technique offers the most consistent landmarks regardless of body habitus.

Landmarks

The patient is placed in Sims' position. The intersection of the intercristal line with a line drawn parallel to the spine from the posterior superior iliac spine (PSIS) determines the initial needle insertion point (usually 5 cm lateral from the midline in most patients) (Fig. 36-18).

Needles

- 21-gauge, 10-cm insulated needle. Consider 15-cm needle in patients with an increased body mass index (BMI).
- 18-gauge, 10-cm insulated Tuohy needle for catheter placement. Catheters routinely are inserted 5–10 cm.

Local Anesthetic

30–40 mL of local anesthetic will block the lumbar plexus in most adults.

The Block

The nerve stimulator is initially set at 1.0–1.5 mA and a quadriceps muscle twitch (femoral nerve) is sought as evidence of proximity to the lumbar plexus; this is usually

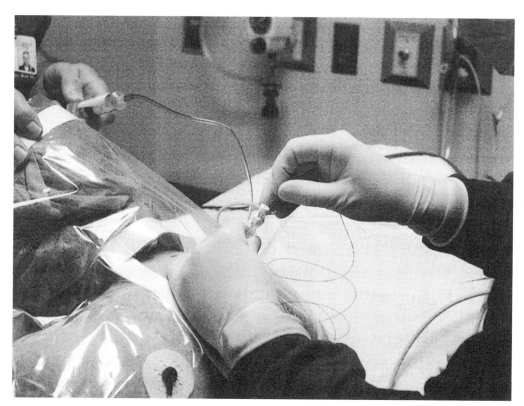

Figure 36-17 Continuous thoracic paravertebral block placement.

encountered at a depth of 5–8 cm from the skin. The needle is inserted perpendicular to all planes with slight adjustments of the needle tip caudad and cephalad if initial passes fail to stimulate the plexus (Fig. 36-19). If periosteum is contacted (usually the transverse process of L4), the needle should be directed more caudad. Occasionally, stimulation of the hamstring muscles of the posterior thigh will be noted while attempting to perform the lumbar

plexus block. This suggests sacral plexus stimulation (sciatic nerve) and indicates the needle tip is too caudal and medial. Injection here may lead to epidural spread or incomplete block of the plexus. Adjustment of the initial needle insertion point 1 cm cephalad and 1 cm lateral compensates for this error.

Clinical Pearls

This posterior approach will consistently block all the nerves of the lumbar plexus. When combined with a sciatic nerve block, complete anesthesia of the lower extremity can be achieved. This is an excellent approach for

Figure 36-18 Posterior approach to the lumbar plexus block—Winnie's technique.

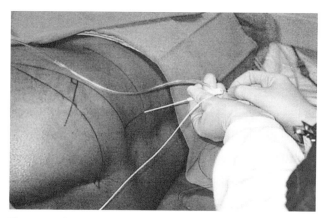

Figure 36-19 Needle direction during continuous posterior lumbar plexus block placement (Winnie's technique).

catheter placement and continuous infusions to the lumbar plexus.

Femoral Nerve Block

This block has been termed the "3-in-1 block," suggesting that the femoral, lateral femoral cutaneous, and obturator nerves could be blocked from a single perivascular injection just inferior to the inguinal ligament and lateral to the femoral artery. Since it was first described in 1973 by Winnie, the approach has been found to inconsistently block the obturator nerve. The approach will reliably block the femoral and lateral femoral cutaneous nerves and is valuable for surgical procedures of the knee and thigh.

Landmarks

With the patient supine, the femoral artery pulse is palpated and marked at the level of the inguinal ligament. The inguinal ligament is located between the anterior superior iliac spine and the pubic symphysis. Initial needle insertion for a femoral nerve block is 1–2 cm lateral to the femoral artery pulse (Fig. 36-20).

Needles

- 21-gauge, 5-cm insulated needle.
- 18-gauge, 10-cm insulated Tuohy needle for catheter placement. The catheter is inserted 5–10 cm for femoral nerve block, 15–20 cm for attempts at placing the catheter for lumbar plexus analgesia (success rate of approximately 40%).

Local Anesthetic

20–40 mL of local anesthetic will block these nerves in most adults.

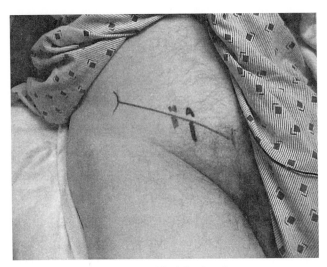

Figure 36-20   Femoral nerve block landmarks.

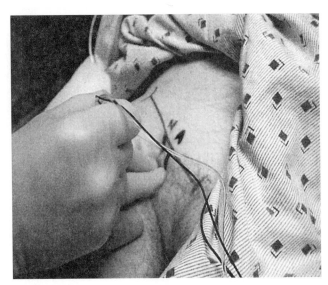

Figure 36-21   Needle direction during three-in-one block placement.

The Block

The nerve stimulator is initially set at 1.0–1.2 mA. The needle is directed slightly cephalad (Fig. 36-21). A brisk "snap" of the patella with current at 0.5 mA or less is indicative of successful stimulation of the femoral nerve. The nerve is often found to be superficial, rarely beyond 3 cm from the skin. Medial thigh twitching noted during performance of the block suggests the needle is too medial.

Clinical Pearls

The physician should resist the urge to use the patient's thigh as a hand rest. Stimulation of the femoral nerve can result in brisk vastus muscle twitching that can disrupt needle positioning. Combined with an obturator and sciatic nerve block, this block can provide complete anesthesia of the lower extremity.

Sciatic Nerve Block: Posterior Approach

The sciatic nerve, the largest nerve in the body, arises from the ventral rami of L4–S3 that form the sacral plexus. The sciatic nerve is actually two nerves in close apposition, the tibial and common fibular (peroneal) nerves. These nerves usually do not separate until the midthigh, though approximately 12% of the time the nerves can separate before leaving the pelvis. Of the various approaches to block the sciatic nerve, Labat's posterior technique (first described in 1924) has the advantage of also blocking the posterior femoral cutaneous nerve, which branches to the gluteus and uppermost medial and posterior thigh. This becomes important when thigh tourniquets are used for lower-extremity procedures.

Landmarks

The patient is placed in Sims' position. Labat's classic landmarks employ a line drawn between the greater trochanter

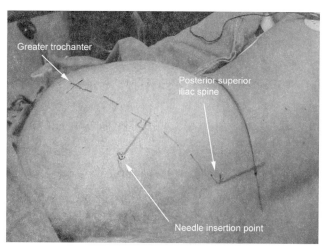

Figure 36-22 Posterior approach to the sciatic nerve block—classic Labat's technique.

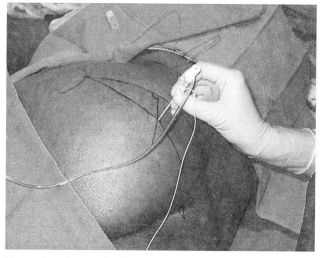

Figure 36-23 Needle direction during continuous sciatic nerve block placement (classic Labat's technique).

to the PSIS. A second line is drawn from the greater trochanter to the patient's sacral hiatus. The point of initial needle insertion is determined from a line drawn perpendicular from the midpoint of the first line to its intersection with the second line. A third line can be drawn along the "furrow" formed by the medial edge of the gluteus maximus muscle and the long head of the biceps femoris muscle. The furrow represents the course of the sciatic nerve toward the lower leg. The triangle formed by the three lines further defines initial needle placement, and subsequent adjustments of the needle within the triangle can improve success of sciatic nerve stimulation (Fig. 36-22).

Needles

- 21-gauge, 10-cm insulated needle for the majority of patients. 15-cm needles may be needed in the obese.
- 18-gauge, 10-cm insulated Tuohy needle for catheter placement. Catheters routinely are inserted 5–10 cm.

Local Anesthetic

20–30 mL of local anesthetic will block the plexus in most adults.

The Block

The nerve stimulator is initially set at 1.0–1.5 mA. The needle is inserted perpendicular to all planes (Fig. 36-23). Stimulation of the patient's gluteus maximus muscle is often encountered prior to sciatic nerve stimulation and the needle should be advanced through this. Successful needle placement in proximity to the sciatic nerve for local injection is observed with plantar flexion/inversion (tibial nerve) or dorsiflexion/eversion (common peroneal nerve) with 0.5 mA of current or less. Occasionally, hamstring muscle twitching will be noted, which suggests the needle tip has been placed too medial. Slight adjustment of the needle tip laterally will usually result in successful localization of the sciatic nerve.

Clinical Pearls

The posterior approach to the sciatic nerve combined with a lumbar plexus block will provide complete anesthesia of the lower extremity. Labat's approach is well suited for continuous catheter techniques. The addition of the "furrow" line can be especially useful in obese patients where palpation of traditional landmarks is difficult.

Sciatic Nerve Block: Raj Approach

Advantages of the Raj approach compared to other sciatic approaches are the shallow location of the nerve and its location between the semitendinosus and biceps femoris muscles in an easily palpated groove. Disadvantages of this technique are that it requires an assistant or device to support the leg, and that it can be awkward performing the block while still observing the toes. (See "Sciatic Nerve Block: Posterior Approach" for general information on the sacral plexus/sciatic nerve and surgical indications.)

Landmarks

The patient is positioned supine and the operative leg is raised to 90 degrees (Fig. 36-24). The greater trochanter and ischial tuberosity are identified. The midpoint between them is the insertion site (Fig. 36-25). The insertion site should lie in the groove formed by the biceps femoris and semitendinosus muscles. The needle is inserted perpendicular to all planes of the skin (Fig. 36-26).

Needles

- 21-gauge, 10-cm insulated needle.
- 18-gauge, 10-cm insulated Tuohy needle for catheter placement (bevel should be directed cephalad, catheters are inserted 3–5 cm beyond tip of needle).

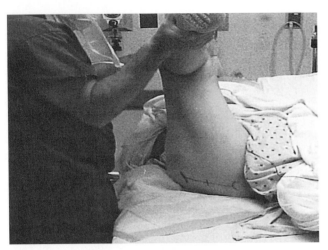

Figure 36-24   Patient positioning for sciatic nerve block (Raj's technique).

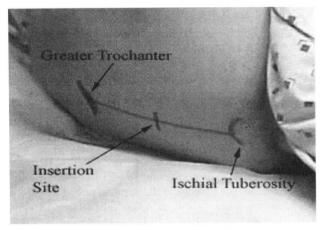

Figure 36-25   Sciatic nerve block landmarks (Raj's technique).

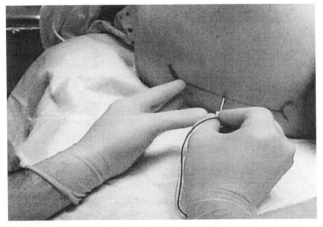

Figure 36-26   Needle direction during sciatic nerve block placement (Raj's technique).

Local Anesthetic

25–30 mL of local anesthetic will block the sciatic nerve in most adults.

The Block

The nerve stimulator is set initially between 1.0 and 1.2 mA. Toe flexion at 0.5 mA or less indicates adequate needle placement for local anesthetic injection. If dorsiflexion is elicited, the needle is too lateral. If there is direct stimulation of the adductor muscles, the needle is too medial.

Clinical Pearls

When other approaches to the sciatic prove difficult, this approach is often successful. Use of a table or Mayo stand to support the leg is an excellent substitute to having an assistant try to maintain the leg position and hold still.

Sciatic Nerve Block: Anterior and Lateral Approaches

The sciatic nerve provides the majority of the innervation to the leg. There are a number of approaches to sciatic nerve block in the upper thigh, each with advantages depending on the clinical situation. The anterior and lateral approaches allow blockade of the sciatic nerve with minimal manipulation of the lower extremity, which can be advantageous with traumatic injuries. The sciatic nerve passes inferolaterally under cover of the gluteus maximus, midway between the greater trochanter and ischial tuberosity. The nerve continues to the thigh passing posterior to the obturator internus, quadratus femoris, and adductor magnus muscles.

Landmarks

Anterior approach.   The patient is supine and a line is drawn from the anterior superior iliac spine to the pubic tubercle and divided into thirds. A second line is drawn medial from the cephalad aspect of the greater trochanter, parallel to the previous line. A line drawn perpendicular from the medial third of the first line will intersect the second line over the lesser trochanter of the femur. This represents the point of initial needle insertion (Fig. 36-27).

Lateral approach.   The sciatic nerve can be approached laterally in the thigh by palpating the groove between the biceps femoris and the vastus lateralis muscle. Initial needle insertion can be anywhere along this groove, realizing the more proximal blocks will enhance success (Fig. 36-28).

Needles

- 21-gauge, 15-cm insulated needle.
- 18-gauge, 15-cm insulated Tuohy needle for catheter placement. Catheters introduced 5–10 cm.

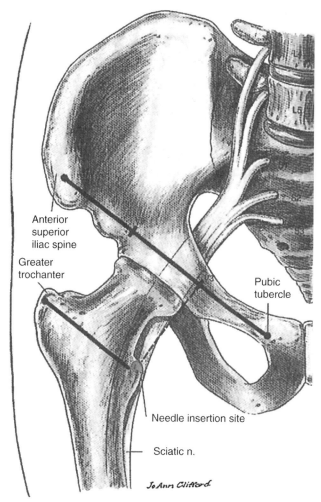

Figure 36-27   Anterior approach to the sciatic nerve block (Beck's technique) landmarks. (Reprinted with permission from Brown DL. *Atlas of Regional Anesthesia*. Philadelphia: WB Saunders, 1992.)

Local Anesthetic

30–40 mL of local anesthetic is utilized for both techniques.

The Block

Anterior approach.   The nerve stimulator is initially set at 1.5 mA and the needle is advanced to contact bone (Fig. 36-29). The needle is then directed past the medial edge of the femur 2–4 cm, and sciatic nerve stimulation (plantar flexion/inversion or dorsiflexion/eversion) is sought at a current of 0.5 mA or less. Stimulation of the hamstring muscle suggests the needle is deep to the nerve. If initial passes fail to stimulate the sciatic nerve, subsequent attempts are made more medial or lateral. Internal rotation of the leg can aid successful localization of the sciatic nerve using the anterior approach.

Lateral approach.   The nerve stimulator is set as above. The needle is advanced parallel to the bed to contact the femur. The needle is then withdrawn to skin and advanced

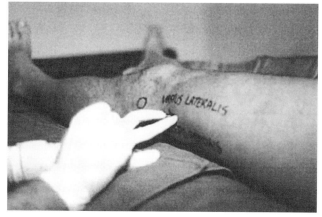

Figure 36-28   Lateral popliteal sciatic nerve block placement.

at a 30° angle posteriorly. Stimulation is sought as described above. If initial passes fail, subsequent attempts are made more anteriorly or posteriorly. Medial thigh (hamstring) twitch suggests the needle has passed too medial.

Clinical Pearls

These blocks depend on local anesthetic volume for success. Complete block of the leg will require a saphenous nerve block.

Popliteal Sciatic Nerve Block

The popliteal fossa is bordered laterally by the biceps femoris and medially by the semimembranosus muscles. The sciatic nerve usually divides into its two main components, the tibial and common peroneal nerves, as it passes through the popliteal fossa. The ability to easily define the borders of the popliteal fossa make this one of the easiest approaches to block the sciatic nerve's major branches (posterior tibial, superficial and deep peroneal, and sural nerves). These landmarks can even be identified in the morbidly obese. The disadvantage of this block lies

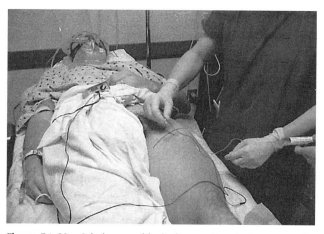

Figure 36-29   Sciatic nerve block placement—anterior approach.

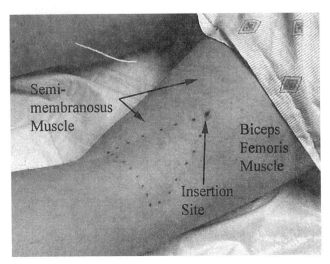

Figure 36-30 Popliteal sciatic nerve block landmarks.

in the fact that occasionally the sciatic nerve will divide prior to reaching the popliteal fossa, resulting in an incomplete block below the knee. (Note: the saphenous nerve, a branch of the femoral nerve, must be blocked separately to provide anesthesia to the medial calf and ankle)

Landmarks

The patient is positioned prone with the operative leg supported so that it remains slightly bent and the foot is free and not resting on the bed. The biceps femoris and semimembranosus muscles are identified (having the patient bend the knee against resistance will make these muscles more readily apparent and palpable). The apex of the popliteal fossa, where the two muscles meet, is located and marked; this is the initial insertion site (Fig. 36-30). The needle is inserted at a 45°–60° angle from the skin in a cephalad direction (Fig. 36-31). When a Tuohy needle is used, the bevel should be aimed cephalad.

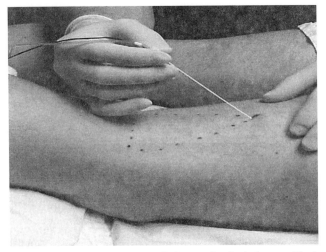

Figure 36-31 Needle direction during popliteal sciatic nerve block placement.

Needles

- 21-gauge, 10-cm insulated needle.
- 18-gauge, 10-cm insulated Tuohy needle for catheter placement. Catheters are inserted a minimum of 3–5 cm.

The Block

The nerve stimulator is initially set between 1.0 and 1.2 mA. Plantar flexion with inversion at 0.5 mA or less indicates adequate needle placement for local anesthetic injection. Dorsiflexion indicates too lateral needle placement. Aspiration of blood indicates too medial needle placement.

Local Anesthetic

30–40 mL of local anesthetic will block the sciatic nerve in most adults.

Clinical Pearls

If no motor response is obtained with initial stimulation, subsequent attempts should be made more lateral (rarely medial, where inadvertent vascular penetration is a risk). The more cephalad stimulation in the popliteal fossa can be obtained, the less likely the sciatic nerve will have divided, which vastly improves block success.

Ankle Block

The ankle contains five main peripheral nerves that innervate the foot. The tibial nerve provides innervation to the medial ankle and sole of the foot. The superficial peroneal nerve supplies sensation to the dorsum of the foot and toes. The deep peroneal nerve supplies sensation to the skin between the first and second toes. The sural nerve provides cutaneous innervation to the lateral side of the foot and fifth toe. The saphenous nerve, the only nerve that does not originate from the sciatic nerve, supplies the cutaneous sensation for the medial ankle but can also cover the medial foot up to the metatarsophalangeal joint. The ankle block works very well for foot-and-toe surgery, which facilitates early ambulation.

Landmarks and the Block

Tibial nerve.   The nerve is located behind the posterior tibial artery at the level of the medial malleolus. The artery is palpated and the needle inserted passing anterior to the artery. A nerve stimulator can be used to help localize the nerve. Local anesthetic is injected just deep to the artery.

Deep peroneal nerve.   The nerve runs lateral to the dorsalis pedis artery at the level of the foot. The artery is palpated and the needle is inserted lateral to the artery. If bone is contacted, the needle is withdrawn slightly before injecting.

Superficial peroneal nerve.   A subcutaneous wheal of local anesthetic is injected from the anterior border of the tibia to the lateral malleolus.

Sural nerve.   The needle is inserted lateral to the Achilles tendon and directed toward the lateral malleolus. Local anesthetic is infiltrated along this course.

Saphenous nerve.   A subcutaneous wheal of local anesthetic is directed anteriorly from the medial malleolus (Fig. 36-32).

Needles

- 22–25-gauge, 3.7-cm, 1.5-in. needle.
- 22-gauge, 5-cm insulated needle if using a nerve stimulator.

Local Anesthetic

Tibial, saphenous, and sural nerves.   3–5 mL each.

Deep peroneal nerve.   2–4 mL.

Superficial peroneal nerve.   5–10 mL.

Clinical Pearls

Many feel this is a volume block and some institutions will use up to 40 mL of local anesthetic for all five nerves. Some authors have raised concerns with regard to vascular occlusion when all five nerves are blocked with large volumes or solutions containing epinephrine. Injection around the ankle can be quite uncomfortable; preemptive analgesia can be very helpful.

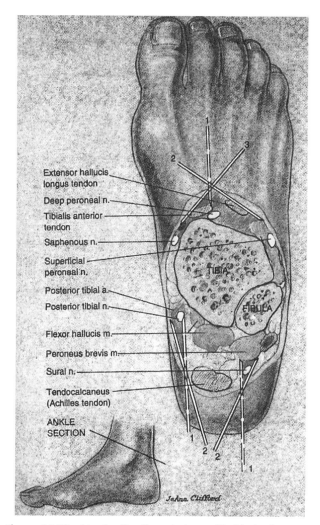

Figure 36-32   Needle directions during ankle block placement. (Reprinted with permission from Brown DL. *Atlas of Regional Anesthesia*. Philadelphia: WB Saunders, 1992.)

PATIENT SAFETY, SPECIAL SITUATIONS, AND CRISIS MANAGEMENT

The Adult Difficult Airway: Outpatient Implications

D. JOHN DOYLE

INTRODUCTION

Few areas in medicine have advanced as quickly and dramatically in the last few decades as clinical airway management. A mere three decades ago tracheal intubation by direct laryngoscopy, blind nasal intubation, and possibly surgical methods were the most one could reasonably expect from a clinician experienced in airway management (Table 37-1). Fiberoptic intubation, the laryngeal mask airway (LMA), the Bullard laryngoscope, and even the concept of airway management algorithms were all unavailable in those days. Indeed, a mere 70 years ago, around the time of the Great Depression, airway management during general anesthesia consisted primarily of maintaining spontaneous ventilation with the aid of careful head positioning and the use of oropharyngeal airways, although also available were tongue forceps designed to pull the tongue out of an obstructing position. Endotracheal intubation was rarely performed in those days, and positive-pressure ventilation was an exotic technology still in its early experimental phase. Clinical problem solving for the common airway problems, such as those shown in Table 37-2, was based almost entirely on ad hoc methods.

Now clinicians interested in airway management have an enormous selection of resources to choose from. Almost every imaginable form of laryngoscope is available to those with the funds to secure them. The LMA has practically revolutionized outpatient surgery. Countless books, CD-ROMs, videos, and Web pages are available to clinicians eager to learn more.

This chapter is concerned with clinical airway management in its many forms as it pertains to the ambulatory surgery environment. This includes classical topics such as laryngoscopy and intubation, prevention of aspiration, positive-pressure ventilation (PPV), as well as more recent developments such as the LMA and other supraglottic devices, and methods of awake intubation. Special emphasis is also placed on understanding the American Society of Anesthesiologists (ASA) airway management algorithm[1] and related algorithms[2,3] for the management of expected and unexpected airway difficulties.

CHAPTER OBJECTIVES

While the list of potential objectives for this chapter is quite large, the following are particularly important objectives for the reader to focus upon.

1. Identify the primary goals of clinical airway management.
2. Understand the functional anatomy of the airway, especially in relation to the innervation of the larynx and airway blocks.
3. Know the various methods to access the airway to predict whether or not intubation will be straightforward.
4. Understand the role of various laryngoscopes and equipment adjuncts in clinical airway management.
5. Understand the importance of a preestablished management plan (algorithm) in dealing with airway problems such as airway obstruction.

CLINICAL MOTIVATION

In the ASA Closed Claims study by Caplan et al.,[4] adverse clinical outcomes related to respiratory events constituted the single largest class of injury to anesthetized patients, with death or brain damage occurring in 85% of cases. Such events carry an enormous financial and emotional toll for all parties. Regrettably, most of these disasters could have been prevented by adequate monitoring or by better training.

Three injury mechanisms accounted for three-fourths of the adverse respiratory events: inadequate ventilation (38%), esophageal intubation (18%), and difficult tracheal intubation (17%). These results suggest that improvements in patient monitoring, in airway technology, and in

Table 37-1   A Brief History of Clinical Airway Management

Biblical Times	Death from airway obstruction recognized (trauma [strangulation], leprosy, abscess)
1700s	Metal and leather tubes inserted blindly into the trachea for treatment of drowning
c. 1700	Discovery of oxygen (Priestley and Lavoisier)
1842	Crawford Long discovers ether anesthesia
1854	Garcia, a professor of singing, develops indirect laryngoscopy
1878	Chloroform administered through tracheal tube (Macewen)
1885	O'Dwyer popularizes intubation for diphtheria
1895	Kirstein develops direct laryngoscopy
1900	Kuhn develops a flexometallic tracheal tube
WWI	Many casualties requiring head and neck surgery add impetus to widespread use of intubation in military hospitals; Magill introduces tracheal tube with inflatable cuff
1920	Chevalier Jackson designs improved laryngoscope allowing intubation under direct vision
1920s	Magill develops blind nasal intubation
1942	Griffiths introduces curare into clinical practice
1946	Mendelson describes aspiration pneumonitis
1950s	Popularization of the use of tracheal tubes for general anesthesia
1960s	Advent of electronic patient monitoring
1962	Sellick maneuver and rapid sequence induction developed
1940s–1970s	Continuing improvements in laryngoscope and tube designs; use of plastic
1970s	Development of implant-tested low-irritation, low-cuff-pressure disposable tracheal tubes
1980s	Popularization of fiberoptic intubation; introduction of pulse oximetry and capnography as noninvasive means of assessing oxygenation and ventilation
1990s	Popularization of laryngeal mask airway, rigid fiberoptic laryngoscopes (Bullard, Wu, etc.,), and ASA Practice Guidelines for Management of the Difficult Airway. Increased awareness of the special challenges of the "difficult extubation" patient
1995	Founding of the Society for Airway Management
2000s	Introduction of laryngeal mask airway ProSeal and other new airway devices

the clinical training of anesthesiologists may result in important safety advantages to patients undergoing general anesthesia.

GOALS OF CLINICAL AIRWAY MANAGEMENT

Clinical airway management has three goals:

1. Maintenance of adequate oxygenation (as measured by arterial oxygen tension [PaO_2] or arterial oxygen saturation [SaO_2])

2. Maintenance of adequate ventilation (as measured by end-tidal carbon dioxide tension [$ETCO_2$] or more ideally $PaCO_2$)

3. Protection of the airway from soiling (avoiding aspiration with its associated potential pulmonary complications)

Oxygenation

Oxygenation is controlled principally by adjusting the fraction of inspired oxygen (FIO_2) delivered to the patient, although positive end expiratory pressure (PEEP) adjustment is equally important to improve oxygenation in ventilated

Table 37-2   Airway Problems for Which Precompiled Solutions Must Be Learned to Handle Airway Emergencies with Grace

- Inadequate oxygenation
- Inadequate spontaneous ventilation
- Inadequate ventilation with positive-pressure ventilation
- Cannot ventilate when using face mask
- Cannot ventilate when using supraglottic airway device
- Cannot ventilate when using an endotracheal tube
- Low airway pressures
- High airway pressures
- Cannot intubate—elective case
- Cannot intubate—emergency case
- Cannot intubate or ventilate
- When to utilize an emergency surgical airway
- When to call for assistance

patients with acute lung injury (PEEP is the minimum lung-distending pressure over expiration; it is usually set between 2 and 5 cm H_2O in patients with normal lungs).

The minimum FIO_2 used in anesthesia is usually 0.25 (25%) and can be increased to 1.0 (100%), usually by decreasing the concentration of nitrous oxide (N_2O) or air administered to the patient. We usually adjust FIO_2 and PEEP to keep PaO_2 between 100 and 200 mmHg.

Ventilation

In spontaneous ventilation, negative pressure inside the lungs from diaphragmatic flattening draws in air. With PPV gas is forced into the lungs using a positive-pressure source such as a manual resuscitator or an automatic mechanical ventilator. PPV is often facilitated with muscle relaxation but it is not always necessary if the patient is well anesthetized.

Ventilation is determined by adjusting two ventilator parameters: tidal volume (TV) and respiratory rate (RR). Typically one starts with TV = 10 mL/kg and RR = 10/min and then adjusts according to $ETCO_2$ or arterial carbon dioxide tension ($PaCO_2$). On some older machines the TV delivered depends on the fresh gas flow (FGF), often set between 1 and 6 L/min (flows of 1–2 L/min are most economical).

Protection of the Airway from Soiling

Protection of the airway from soiling due to aspiration of gastric contents is achieved in unconscious patients (generally those under anesthesia or with head injury) by using a cuffed endotracheal tube (ETT). Unintubated patients may develop deadly aspiration pneumonitis if stomach contents spill into the lungs (especially if the pH

is < 2.5 or volume is > 25 mL).[5] Patients at risk of aspiration with the induction of general anesthesia are usually managed either with a rapid-sequence induction or with awake intubation.

MAJOR AIRWAY MANAGEMENT OPTIONS

As can be seen in Table 37-3, there are many airway management options for clinical anesthesia delivery, depending on clinical circumstances and equipment availability. The particular choice of technique will depend on clinical factors, clinician training, equipment preferences, equipment availability, the preferences of the patient (where appropriate), and other factors.

AIRWAY ASSESSMENT—HISTORY AND PHYSICAL EXAMINATION

In assessing any patient preoperatively, a history of difficult intubation or any clinical conditions known to be associated with a difficult airway should be sought. A review of previous anesthetic records, when available, can be especially helpful. In many cases patients are aware of past difficulties with intubation, such as when a tooth was damaged with intubation, and may even carry a letter describing the details (Fig. 37-1).

Table 37-3   Major Airway Management Options for Clinical Anesthesia Delivery

- Avoid general anesthesia—do case under local or regional anesthesia.
- General anesthesia with spontaneous breathing and an unprotected airway (e.g., using face mask, nasal cannulae, oral airway, nasopharyngeal airway, or nothing).
- General anesthesia with laryngeal mask airway (or other supraglottic airway device) and spontaneous breathing (airway still unprotected against aspiration).
- General anesthesia with spontaneous breathing and an airway protected using an endotracheal tube. An uncuffed tube is still popular with children, but provides less complete protection of the airway against aspiration of any regurgitated gastric contents.
- General anesthesia with positive-pressure ventilation and an endotracheal tube.
- General anesthesia with positive-pressure ventilation but using the laryngeal mask airway or other supraglottic airway device.
- Surgical airway (e.g., tracheostomy under local anesthesia, emergency cricothyroidotomy).

This is a model difficult airway form you can adapt for your clinical practice. It is suggested that you keep these forms readily available in the anesthesia lounge to report difficult airway information to the patient and to his or her physician. It is provided courtesy of John R. Davidson, MD, FRCPC.

IMPORTANT

To the physician:

This person was found to be a ***DIFFICULT INTUBATION***

on _____/_____/_____ at _____ (Hospital),

Tel: _____

Reasons for the difficulty included:

1) Poor neck mobility
2) Poor jaw mobility
3) Prominent teeth
4) Large/stiff tongue
5) Anterior larynx
6) Other (specify)

Ventilation with bag and mask was:

1) Easy
2) Difficult
3) Impossible

Ventilation adjuncts included:

1) Oropharyngeal airway
2) Nasopharyngeal airway
3) Other (specify)

Success was achieved: using (select from list):

1) Unconscious/paralyzed
2) Awake

1) Alternate blade (specify)
2) Light wand
3) Fiberoptic bronchoscope
4) Blind nasal
5) Retrograde
6) Other (specify)

For future anesthetics in fasted patients I would recommend:

1) Long preoxygenation, short-acting agents, early wake-up if success not forthcoming.
2) Awake intubation.

I hope this information is helpful to you.

IMPORTANT

To the Patient:

During general aesthesia (sleep for surgery) an oxygen tube is usually placed in the patient's throat. This assures an adequate supply of oxygen to the lungs, heart, brain, and other vital organs.

At the time of your recent anesthetic there was difficulty getting this tube into position. Such difficulties arise because of the relative position of a patient's mouth, teeth, and windpipe.

The attached form describes the problem in detail for the benefit of any anesthesiologist taking care of you in the future. Please keep this form and show it to your anesthesiologist if you ever have surgery in the future. It will warn the anesthesiologist and will enable him or her to take better care of you.

You should also get a MedicAlert bracelet to warn of this problem. The bracelet should say "DIFFICULT INTUBATION." The address information for the MedicAlert Foundation is as follows:

MedicAlert Foundation International
2323 Colorado Avenue
Turlock, California, USA 95382
http://www.medicalert.org

By phone, 24 hours a day:
888-633-4298
209-668-3333 from outside the U.S.

This is IMPORTANT! Knowing you are a "Difficult Intubation" could save your life in an emergency.

Figure 37-1   Model difficult airway form.

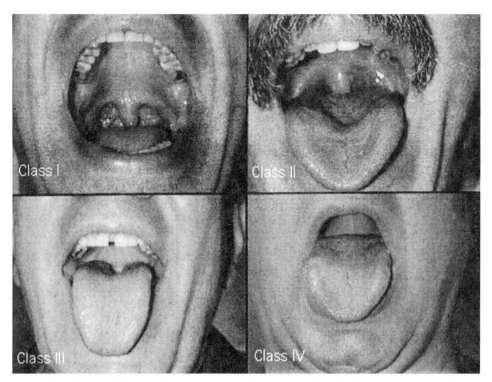

Figure 37-2   Mallampati classification of the oropharyngeal view. *Class I*: uvula, faucial pillars, soft palate visible; *Class II*: faucial pillars, soft palate visible; *Class III*: soft and hard palate visible; *Class IV*: hard palate visible only (added by Samsoon and Young). (Reprinted with permission from Figure 23-5. Barash PG, Cullen BF, Stoelting RK. *Clinical Anesthesia*. Copyright © 2001 Lippincott Williams & Wilkins. 0023 _0005_f.gif.)

General examination of the patient may reveal potential airway problems. Be especially wary of patients with a limited mouth opening, with limitations in neck flexion/extension, with large tongues, or with poor dentition. In particular, it has been suggested that the relative size of the base of the tongue is an important factor determining the degree of difficulty of direct laryngoscopy. A relatively simple grading system that involves preoperative ability to visualize the faucial pillars, soft palate, and base of the uvula was designed by Mallampati et al.[6] as a means of predicting the degree of difficulty in laryngeal exposure. This is illustrated in Figure 37-2.

Diseases associated with potential airway problems include congenital malformations, airway tumors and infections, maxillofacial or cervical spine trauma, morbid obesity, diabetes mellitus (DM), and rheumatoid arthritis (RA).[7] Table 37-4 lists some of the factors on general examination of the patient that may be indicative of possible problems. Some diseases and conditions associated with difficult airway management are listed in Table 37-5.

Numerous studies have examined predictors of difficult intubation.[8–12] For example, in a relatively recent study, Karkouti et al.[12] developed a model for predicting difficult laryngoscopic tracheal intubation in patients with seemingly normal airways using multivariable model development techniques. This analysis identified three simple factors that were "highly significant" for predicting difficult tracheal intubation: (1) limited mouth opening, (2) limited chin protrusion, and (3) limited atlanto-occipital extension.

PREDICTION OF DIFFICULT MASK VENTILATION

Ordinarily, should intubation be difficult, clinicians may provide ventilation and oxygenation via face mask ventilation. However, in some cases, mask ventilation can be difficult. Obviously, being able to accurately predict difficult mask ventilation may improve the safety of airway management. In a study of this matter by Langeron et al.,[13] difficult mask ventilation (DMV) was defined as the inability of an unassisted anesthesiologist to maintain the SaO_2 over 92% or to prevent or reverse signs of inadequate ventilation during positive-pressure mask ventilation under general anesthesia. With this definition, DMV was found in 75 of 1502 patients studied (5%), with one case of impossible ventilation. Of particular interest, DMV was anticipated by the anesthesiologist in only 13 patients, or 17% of the DMV cases. Using multivariate analysis, five criteria were identified as independent factors for DMV. These are listed in Table 37-6. The presence of two factors was found to indicate an especially high likelihood of DMV (sensitivity, 0.72; specificity, 0.73).

CLASSIFICATION OF DIFFICULT INTUBATION

Cormack and Lehane[14] have classified the view at laryngoscopy into four grades, as illustrated in Figure 37-3. Intubation in the presence of a Grade 1 view is almost always

Table 37-4   Some Clinical Factors in Airway Evaluation

Clinical history	Patient provides a "difficult intubation" letter (Fig. 37-1).
	Previous difficulty with intubation (review old anesthetic records).
	Patient reports that previous intubation was performed awake.
	Patient report of broken teeth at previous intubation.
Mouth opening	Should be adequate to easily allow laryngoscope plus endotracheal tube.
	Patients with temporomandibular joint disease may not be able to open widely.
Mallampati view of oropharynx	Rated from I to IV (see Fig. 37-2)
Thyromental distance	The thyromental distance is the distance of the lower mandible from the mentum to the thyroid. The neck should be fully extended during the measurement. If the thyromental distance is less than 6 cm (about three finger-breadths) there is less space for the tongue to be displaced during laryngoscopy.
Teeth	Edentulous patients are always easier to intubate. Patients with poor teeth or prominent teeth may be especially difficult to intubate.
Tongue	Tongue should not be large, immobile, or edematous.
Head mobility	Limited neck extension is associated with poor laryngeal view and difficult intubation. Almost all of the extension of the neck takes place at the atlanto-occipital joint. Patients with immobile heads (e.g., ankylosing spondylitis) may not be able to be positioned into the early-morning "sniffing position."

easy, while intubating with a Grade 4 view may be exceedingly difficult because the epiglottis is not visible. The view can often be improved using external laryngeal manipulation,[15] the "BURP" maneuver,[16] or a MacCoy laryngoscope blade.[17,18] Adjuncts such as a gum elastic bougie[19] can also be very helpful. Of course, documenting the view at each laryngoscopy with this system will assist other clinicians who may follow in your footsteps.

RAPID SEQUENCE INDUCTION

Sometimes informally known as a "crash induction," this is a method of inducing general anesthesia designed to reduce the risk of regurgitation and aspiration in individuals at risk [20] (Table 37-7). The technique is relatively contraindicated in patients suspected to have a difficult airway and in hemodynamically unstable patients. An assistant is needed to apply cricoid pressure (44 Newtons or approximately 10 lb) to compress the esophagus from the moment the drugs are given until the airway is protected with a correctly placed ETT with cuff inflated. The key steps to performing a rapid sequence induction are shown in Table 37-8.

CLINICAL PROBLEMS IN AIRWAY MANAGEMENT

Upper Airway Obstruction

Upper airway obstruction is common during general anesthesia. It results from loss of airway muscle tone, and usually occurs at the velopharynx, a particularly narrow segment of the upper airway.[21] Patients with a tendency to upper airway obstruction during ordinary sleep (obstructive sleep apnea[OSA]) are especially vulnerable to airway obstruction during general anesthesia or conscious sedation.[22] In addition, a variety of other clinical conditions may lead to upper airway obstruction (Table 37-9). Some techniques to relieve upper airway obstruction are listed in Table 37-10. In some of these cases supraglottic airway devices can be quite valuable (Table 37-11).

Laryngospasm

Laryngospasm is the protective reflex closure of the upper airway from spasm of the glottic musculature. This form of airway obstruction is especially common in children and is associated with light planes of anesthesia and the presence of foreign matter (e.g., blood or secretions) irritating the vocal cords. While laryngospasm can often be broken by deepening the depth of anesthesia with intravenous (IV) propofol or other IV agent, sometimes muscle relaxation (e.g., with succinylcholine 10–20 mg IV) is needed to allow the patient to be ventilated.[23] Failure to deal with laryngospasm can result in significant periods where the patient cannot be adequately ventilated, resulting in hypoxemia and hypercarbia. Some patients who are able to generate very large negative inspiratory pressures in attempting to breath against the obstruction may succumb to "negative-pressure pulmonary edema."[24] A proactive approach to preventing/terminating laryngospasm and pre-

Table 37-5   Some Diseases and Conditions Associated with Difficult Airway Management

Airway infections
- Abscess of upper airway
- Epiglottitis
- Ludwig's angina
- Quinsy
- Retropharyngeal abscess

Airway tumors
- Tumors of upper airway
- Oral malignancies
- Previous head and neck surgery
- Previous radiation treatment to head and neck

Trauma related
- Facial smash
- Fractured larynx
- Maxillofacial trauma
- Cervical spine trauma
- Trismus
- Temporomandibular joint injury

Other conditions
- Externally fixed head (e.g., halo traction)
- Wired jaws or teeth
- Congenital malformation
- Very anterior larynx
- Fused cervical spine (e.g., ankylosing spondylitis)
- Severe obesity
- Diabetes mellitus
- Rheumatoid arthritis
- Supraglottic or subglottic edema

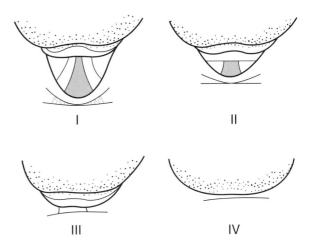

Classification of Laryngoscopy Views

Figure 37-3   Classification of the view at laryngoscopy, as proposed by Cormack and Lehane (1984). (http://www.nda.ox.ac.uk/wfsa/html/u09/u09d_t01.gif.)

venting hypoxemia and other complications is the mark of a seasoned anesthesiologist.

Stridor

Stridor, or noisy inspiration from turbulent gas flow in the upper airway, is often seen in airway obstruction, and al-

ways commands attention.[25] Whenever possible, attempts should be made to immediately establish the cause of the stridor (e.g., foreign body, vocal cord edema, tracheal compression by tumor, functional laryngeal dyskinesia, etc.).

The first issue of clinical concern in case of stridor is whether or not intubation is immediately necessary. If intubation can be delayed for a period, a number of potential options can be considered, depending on the severity of the situation and other clinical details. These include:

- Use of Heliox (70% helium, 30% oxygen);
- Expectant management with full monitoring, oxygen by face mask, and positioning the head of the bed for optimum conditions (e.g., 45–90 degrees);
- Use of nebulized racemic epinephrine or cocaine (but not both together) in cases where airway edema may be the cause of the stridor;
- Use of dexamethasone 4–8 mg IV every 8–12 hr in cases where airway edema may be the cause of the stridor.

Table 37-6   Predictors of Difficult Mask Ventilation

- Age over 55 years
- Body mass index exceeding 26 kg/m²
- Presence of a beard
- Lack of teeth
- History of snoring

SOURCE: Adapted from Langeron, Masso E, Huraux C, Guggiari M, Bianchi A, Coriat P, Riou B. Prediction of difficult mask ventilation. Anesthesiology 2000;92:1229–36.

Table 37-7   Clinical Factors Leading to Increased Risk of Pulmonary Aspiration with General Anesthesia

- Recent food or fluid ingestion
- Severe obesity
- Symptoms of gastroesophageal reflux
- Advanced pregnancy
- Severe ascites
- Opioid administration or other condition resulting in delayed gastric emptying
- History of gastroparesis or other motility disorder
- Bowel ileus or bowel obstruction

Table 37-8   Steps in a Rapid Sequence Induction

1. Ensure drugs, equipment, and assistants are ready and that all patient monitors are operational.
2. Remember that a rapid sequence induction is inappropriate in patients suspected to be difficult to intubate—awake intubation is preferable in these individuals.
3. Generously preoxygenate the patient.
4. Give induction drugs (e.g., propofol/succinylcholine) in predetermined doses (do not titrate to clinical effect by giving increments of drug). At the same time have your assistant apply cricoid pressure (44 Newtons of force, or about 10 lb).
5. Do not ventilate the patient while waiting for the drugs to take effect. (However, some authorities advocate gentle positive-pressure ventilation to reduce the chance of hypoxemia.)
6. Intubate when conditions are correct; inflate endotracheal tube cuff immediately.
7. Ensure endotracheal tube is in correct position (clinically and via capnography).
8. Have assistant relieve cricoid pressure.
9. Continue with the remainder of the anesthetic.

Difficult Extubation

Extubation is the process of removing an ETT from the patient's trachea. This should ordinarily only be done with the patient awake and obeying verbal commands. Even so, catastrophes following extubation can occur, such as total collapse of the airway in a patient with tracheomalacia. Sometimes it is wise to extubate over an ETT exchange catheter, such as in any patient who would be very difficult to reintubate. Such a device can be left in place and later used to facilitate reintubation should a trial of extubation end in failure. If reintubation becomes necessary, the exchange catheter can then be used as a guide to

Table 37-9   Factors That May Predispose to Upper Airway Obstruction

- History of obstructive sleep apnea syndrome
- Obesity
- Maxillary hypoplasia
- Mandibular retrusion
- Bulbar muscle weakness
- Nasal obstruction
- Adenotonsillar hypertrophy
- Upper airway foreign bodies
- Glottic/laryngeal edema
- Vocal cord pathology

SOURCE: Adapted from Hillman DR, Platt PR, Eastwood PR. The upper airway during anaesthesia. Br J Anaesth 2003;91:31–39.

Table 37-10   Some of the Techniques to Relieve Upper Airway Obstruction

- "Jaw thrust" maneuver
- Oropharyngeal airway
  - Guedel airway and variants
  - Cuffed oropharyngeal airway
- Nasopharyngeal airway
- Supraglottic airway (see also Table 37-11)
  - Laryngeal mask airway
  - Combitube
  - Laryngeal tube
- Intubation
- Surgical airway

direct the new ETT through the cords. Some exchange catheters can also be used to administer low-flow oxygen deep into the lungs (e.g., 2 L/min flow rate) as well as for capnography or even emergency jet ventilation in a manner similar to transtracheal jet ventilation (TTJV).[26–28]

THE ASA DIFFICULT AIRWAY ALGORITHM

The ASA has developed a useful algorithm for managing the patient with a difficult airway,[1] a summary of which is presented in Figure 37-4. The algorithm begins with the evaluation of the airway. Tables 37-4, 37-5, and 37-6 list some of the clinical factors to consider in this process. Upon completion of the evaluation, the clinician will have developed an impression as to the likelihood of difficulty with laryngoscopy and intubation, the potential need for awake intubation methods, the role of supraglottic devices like the LMA, and other related issues. If it is decided that the patient is likely going to be difficult to intubate by ordinary means, awake intubation is recommended. If, on the other hand, difficulty with intubation is not anticipated, anesthesia is induced in the usual manner, and should difficulties be encountered, one follows the "unanticipated difficult airway" arm of the algorithm, discussed later. A difficult airway cart should be readily available when any type of airway is being managed (Table 37-12).

Table 37-11   Popular Supraglottic Airway Devices

- Laryngeal mask airway (LMA Classic)
- Disposable LMA (LMA Unique)
- Flexible LMA (LMA Flexible)
- Intubating LMA (LMA FastTrack)
- LMA ProSeal
- Combitube
- Extraglottic airway devices—PAxpress (PAX)
- Laryngeal tube and variants
- Cuffed oropharyngeal airway

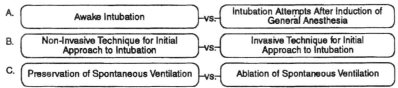

DIFFICULT AIRWAY ALGORITHM

1. Assess the likelihood and clinical impact of basic management problems:
   A. Difficult Ventilation
   B. Difficult Intubation
   C. Difficulty with Patient Cooperation or Consent
   D. Difficult Tracheostomy

2. Actively pursue opportunities to deliver supplemental oxygen throughout the process of difficult airway management

3. Consider the relative merits and feasibility of basic management choices:

4. Develop primary and alternative strategies:

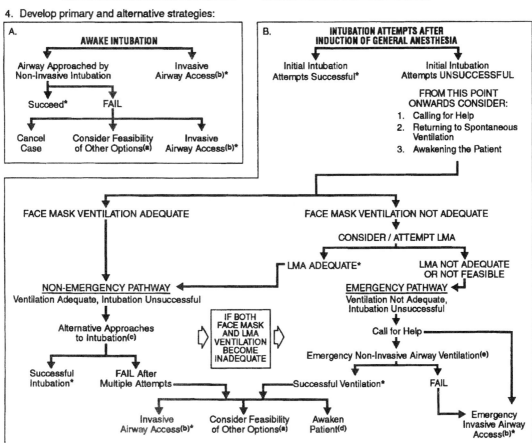

* Confirm ventilation, tracheal intubation, or LMA placement with exhaled CO₂

a. Other options include (but are not limited to): surgery utilizing face mask or LMA anesthesia, local anesthesia infiltration or regional nerve blockade. Pursuit of these options usually implies that mask ventilation will not be problematic. Therefore, these options may be of limited value if this step in the algorithm has been reached via the Emergency Pathway.

b. Invasive airway access includes surgical or percutaneous tracheostomy or cricothyrotomy.

c. Alternative non-invasive approaches to difficult intubation include (but are not limited to): use of different laryngoscope blades, LMA as an intubation conduit (with or without fiberoptic guidance), fiberoptic intubation, intubating stylet or tube changer, light wand, retrograde intubation, and blind oral or nasal intubation.

d. Consider re-preparation of the patient for awake intubation or canceling surgery.

e. Options for emergency non-invasive airway ventilation include (but are not limited to): rigid bronchoscope, esophageal-tracheal combitube ventilation, or transtracheal jet ventilation.

Figure 37-4   Algorithm for managing the patient with a difficult airway, developed by the American Society of Anesthesiologists. (Reprinted with permission from American Society of Anesthesiologists Task Force on Management of the Difficult Airway. Practice guidelines for management of the difficult airway: an updated report by the American Society of Anesthesiologists Task Force on Management of the Difficult Airway. Anesthesiology 2003;98(5):1269–77.)

Table 37-12   Inventory of a Difficult Airway Cart

Drawer One: Preps

Alcohol prep

Atomizer sprayer

Catheter, 22-gauge angio, 1 in.

Gauze, 3 in. by 3 in.

Glycopyrrolate, 0.2 mg/mL

Lidocaine, 1%, 50 mL

Lidocaine, 2%, 50 mL

Needle, 25-gauge, × 3.5 in. spinal

Needles, 19-gauge, 1.5 in.

Oxymetazoline hydrochloride spray (Afrin)

Silicone lubricant

Stopcocks, three-way

Syringes, 3 mL

Tetracaine, 0.45%, 49 mL

Tongue depressors

Xylocaine, 2%, jelly

Xylocaine, 5%, ointment

Xylocaine prep 4%, for topical spray

Drawer Two: Laryngeal mask airways, suction catheters, and Yankauer tip

No. 1 laryngeal mask (neonate/infants)

No. 2 laryngeal mask (babies/children)

No. 2.5 laryngeal mask (babies/children)

No. 3 laryngeal mask (children/small adults)

No. 4 laryngeal mask (normal/large adults)

Laryngeal mask tube extensions

Catheter, suction, 14 F, adult

Catheter, suction, 8 F, pediatric

Yankauer suction tips

Drawer Three: Blades, handles, and Combitube

Combitube

Laryngoscope handle (regular)

Laryngoscope handle (short)

Macintosh blade no. 2 (child)

Macintosh blade no. 3 (adult)

Macintosh blade no. 4 (adult, large)

Magill forceps (small)

Magill forceps (large)

Miller blade no. 1 (infant)

Miller blade no. 2 (child)

Miller blade no. 3 (adult, medium)

Drawer Four: Retrograde set and transtracheal jet ventilation (TTJV)

0.035 × 145-cm guidewire

Catheter, 14-gauge intravenous (IV) (TTJV)

Catheter, red rubber, Robinson urethral

Clamps, Kelly

Needle, 18-gauge thin-wall

Needle, epidural with catheter

Nerve hooks

Retrograde set (Cook)

Sutures, silk

Drawer Five: Airways and tube exchangers

Airway, Berman oral, 100 mm

Airway, Berman oral, 90 mm

Airway, Berman oral, 80 mm

Catheter, 14-gauge × 2 in.

Catheter, 16-gauge × 2 in.

Catheter, 18-gauge × 2 in.

Melker emergency cricothyrotomy kit (Cook)

Nasopharyngeal airway, 26 F

Nasopharyngeal airway, 28 F

Nasopharyngeal airway, 30 F

Nasopharyngeal airway, 32 F

Nasopharyngeal airway, 34 F

Needle, Benumof transtracheal (Cook)

Syringes, 20 mL

Tube exchanger, large with adapter (Sheridan)

Tube exchanger, medium with adapter (Sheridan)

Tube exchanger, small with adapter (Sheridan)

Drawer Six: Endotracheal tubes and lighted stylets

2.5 mm, uncuffed

3.0 mm, cuffed

3.0 mm, uncuffed

3.5 mm, uncuffed

4.0 mm, cuffed

4.0 mm, uncuffed

6.0 mm, cuffed

7.0 mm, cuffed

7.0 mm, armoured

8.0 mm, armoured

Stylet, adult

Stylet, pediatric

(Continued)

Table 37-12   Inventory of a Difficult Airway Cart (*Continued*)

Drawer Six: Endotracheal tubes and lighted stylets (*continued*)	
4.5 mm, cuffed	Lighted stylet, Anesthesia Medical Specialties
4.5 mm, uncuffed	Lighted stylet, Imagica
5.0 mm, cuffed	Lighted stylet, Imagica sheaths
5.0 mm, uncuffed	Lighted stylet, Laerdal, handle
5.5 mm, uncuffed	Lighted stylet, Laerdal, disposable stylets
5.5 mm, cuffed	
Drawer Seven: Masks, specialty blades, and miscellaneous	
No. 2 Patil-Syracuse mask for FOB	Bronch swivel elbow
No. 3 Patil-Syracuse mask for FOB	Bullard blade, adult
No. 4 Patil-Syracuse mask for FOB	Bullard blade, small
No. 5 Patil-Syracuse mask for FOB	Carbon dioxide analyzer, Easy Cap, disposable
No. 6 Patil-Syracuse mask for FOB	Scissors
Airway, Ovassapian	Tubing, oxygen supply
Airway, Williams, 10 cm	Tubing, suction connection
Airway, Williams, 9 cm	WuScope, adult
Augustine guide	WuScope, small
Belscope, adult	
Belscope, small	

In addition to the above items, from the original source, some clinicians may wish to include various other airway devices in their cart, such as a set of intubating laryngeal mask airways (FastTrack™), Parker Flextip® endotracheal tubes, an albuterol inhaler, Cetacaine® spray topical anesthesia, a gum elastic bougie, an endotracheal ventilation catheter, a surgical scalpel, epidural catheters (placed via the nose to deliver deep topical anesthesia), MADD® topical anesthesia sprayers, and preprinted difficult airway forms. It is also assumed that a fiberoptic bronchoscope and a bag/valve/mask resuscitator is available. Note also that the above selection of items may be beyond the resources of many departments and that many clinicians would prefer to use the more recent Glidescope video laryngoscope over a Belscope or a Wuscope, while others would be unhappy with any cart that did not include a Bullard laryngoscope.) Abbreviation: FOB, fibrotic bronchoscope.

Source: Reprinted with permission from Cooper SD, Benumof JL. Teaching management of the airway: the UCSD airway rotation. In: Benumof JL (ed.), *Airway Management: Principles and Practice*. St. Louis: Mosby, 1996.

In real life one frequently encounters the situation where one anticipates that there may be a slight increase in difficulty, but not to the extent that awake intubation would appear to be warranted. One approach in such a setting, at least in patients not at increased risk for aspiration, is to induce anesthesia with a view to promptly waking up the patient should intubation be unsuccessful. In such a setting one might employ propofol rather than thiopental and succinylcholine rather than, say, rocuronium for the induction sequence. One might also have immediately available a number of special airway devices, such as a gum elastic bougie,[18] an intubating LMA (ILMA),[29] a Trachlight stylette,[30] or one of several special laryngoscopes (Table 37-13). Note that if there is a high risk of aspiration, the patient judged to be difficult to intubate should ordinarily be managed by awake intubation in cases where regional anesthesia is impractical. Note also that while in many cases regional anesthesia can be useful to avoid the need for awake intubation, this approach can be particularly problematic should serious complications of regional anesthesia occur (seizures, cardiovascular collapse, and inadvertent total spinal) or should the procedure fail to provide adequate anesthesia.

AWAKE INTUBATION

Awake intubation involves ETT insertion in a conscious or lightly sedated patient and is usually performed because intubation under general anesthesia is judged to be too risky because of concerns about loss of the airway or con-

Table 37-13   Popular and Specialty Laryngoscopes

"Conventional" laryngoscopes
- Macintosh-type laryngoscopes
- Miller-type laryngoscopes and other straight-blade designs
- McCoy laryngoscope and variants

Rigid fiberoptic laryngoscopes
- Bullard laryngoscope
- Upsher laryngoscope
- Wu laryngoscope

Video laryngoscopes
- Glidescope Video Laryngoscope
- Storz Video Laryngoscope (Video Macintosh System)
- Weiss Video Laryngoscope

cerns about aspiration. While fiberoptic intubation under topical anesthesia is the most common means of carrying out awake intubation, other methods include awake blind nasal intubation using an Endotrol (or similar) tube, or using a Macintosh, Miller, or Bullard laryngoscope under topical anesthesia. A number of airway blocks can be used in addition to topical anesthesia (Table 37-14).

UNANTICIPATED DIFFICULT AIRWAY

The unanticipated difficult airway occurs more than occasionally in anesthesia practice (Fig. 37-5). Current techniques for predicting difficulty with laryngoscopy and intubation have a relatively low positive predictive value, suggesting that a precompiled plan for managing the unanticipated difficult airway is especially important. In such settings, experience shows that the LMA,[31-33] the Combitube,[34,35] and other supraglottic airway devices (Table 37-11) are often effective in establishing and maintaining a patent airway in "cannot intubate—cannot ventilate" situations. Of course, training programs should ensure that anesthesiologists are proficient in the use of a number of these airway devices, and are familiar with the conditions where their use is most advantageous.

In many cases the situation can be improved by repositioning the head to ensure that it is "early morning sniffing position" or by using a different laryngoscope (e.g., straight blade,[36] Bullard laryngoscope [37,38]). Also, if the larynx appears to be too anterior, it is often helpful to have an assistant push on the cricoid to displace the larynx to a more posterior position.[15,16] Finally, it should be mentioned that the author has had considerable success in intubating patients who would otherwise be difficult using a video laryngoscope known as the Glidescope (see Figs. 37-6 and 37-7); more information is available at www.glidescope.net.

The following algorithm is offered for situations where the view at laryngoscopy suggests that intubation may be difficult, but for which the patient can be ventilated by mask while under anesthesia following induction doses of anesthetic agents.

1. Ensure help is available and pulse oximeter is in place before starting. Preoxygenate generously.
2. Ensure head position is optimized (early-morning "sniffing position").
3. Note the "grade" of view at laryngoscopy (this will be needed when you write a note in the patient's chart about why the patient was difficult to intubate).
4. Decide how to approach your second attempt. Would a larger blade help? Would a straight blade help? Would a McCoy blade help lift the epiglottis out of the way? Would a gum elastic bougie help? Would external laryngeal manipulation help to move the larynx into a less anterior position?
5. You are allowed one final, third attempt at laryngoscopy and intubation. Wisdom may dictate that you give this chance to an experienced anesthesiologist should he or she drop by following your call for help. Alternately, you may choose to keep the patient asleep and use a special intubating technique (see 7 and 8).
6. If the patient cannot be intubated after three tries, allow him/her to awaken and proceed with awake intubation using a fiberoptic bronchoscope technique, a retrograde technique, or other method.
7. Alternately, insert intubating laryngeal mask airway (ILMA) and then an endotracheal tube via the ILMA (keeping the patient asleep).
8. Alternately, use Syracuse-Patil face mask to facilitate fiberoptic intubation (keeping the patient asleep).

REMEMBER TO CALL FOR HELP

Figure 37-5   Can Ventilate, Can't Intubate

Table 37-14   Popular Airway Blocks

- *Topical anesthesia of the airway.* Administer about 5 mL of aerosolized 4% lidocaine over 15 min. It is more effective after glycopyrrolate dries the airway mucosa. While it may provide anesthesia that is satisfactory for fiberoptic intubation, it is less effective with inflammation and secretions.
- *Superior laryngeal nerve (SLN) block.* The SLN block anesthetizes sensation from the superior larynx above the vocal cords. The block involves injecting 2 mL of 2% lidocaine just inferior to the greater cornu of the hyoid bone and superior to the thyroid cartilage.
- *Transtracheal topicalization.* Topical anesthesia of tracheal mucosa below the cords may be achieved with 4 mL of 2% lidocaine through the cricothyroid membrane and allowing the patient to cough. Use a 22-gauge angiocath, and aspirate air into a saline-filled syringe first to confirm placement.
- *Glossopharyngeal nerve (IX) block.* Blocks posterior third of tongue and tongue side of epiglottis. This intraoral block is best done after topical anesthesia of the tongue. The patient is asked to stick out the tongue and it is displaced laterally with a tongue blade. Place a 22-gauge, 9-cm (spinal) needle at the inferior portion of the posterior palatopharyngeal fold (tonsillar pillar) just deep to the mucosa. Aspirate prior to injection. Inject 2 mL of 2% lidocaine into the base of each anterior tonsillar pillar (palatoglossal arch).

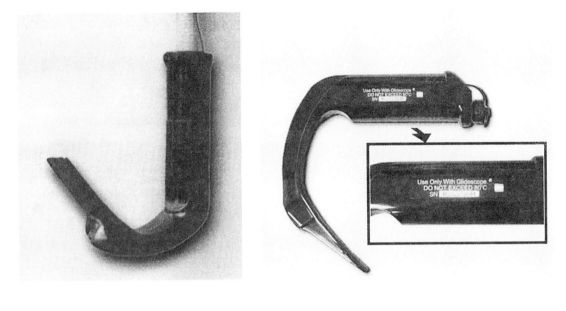

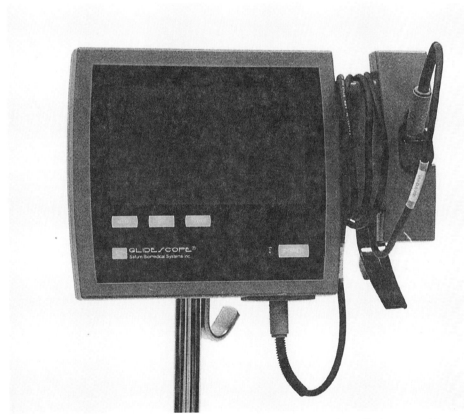

Figure 37-6   Top: Close-up views of the Glidescope handle. Courtesy Saturn Biomedical. Bottom: View of the monitor component of the Glidescope.

It is generally unwise to make more than three or four attempts at intubation in the setting of elective surgery; if the patient cannot be intubated in this number of attempts, the prudent course is generally to awaken the patient and develop a new plan based on awake intubation (Fig. 37-8). (This is why long-acting relaxants or high-dose fentanyl inductions are potentially problematic should intubation prove to be difficult.)

TRANSTRACHEAL JET VENTILATION

In desperate circumstances where neither intubation nor ventilation is possible, injection of oxygen under high-pressure directly into the trachea can be lifesaving. This is done by inserting a 14 gauge IV catheter or similar device through the cricothyroid membrane and applying intermittent bursts of high-pressure oxygen through this

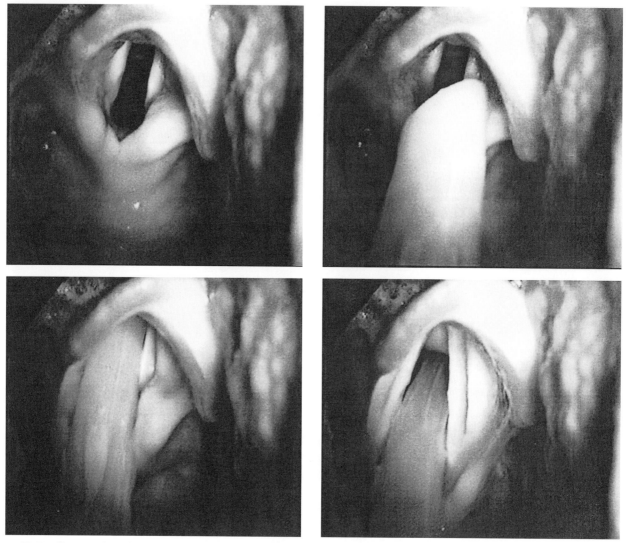

Figure 37-7   Close-up views from the Glidescope, as the endotracheal tube passes through the vocal cords. From case 112 of the author's unpublished series.

catheter (see Figs. 37-9 and 37-10). Experience shows that the catheter may kink, leading to problems. A special nonkinkable needle for TTJV is available from Cook (http://www.cookcriticalcare.com/discip/em_med/2_09/2_09_06.html).

The original description of this technique, known as TTJV, suggested using a 50-PSI pressure head, but clinical experience shows that barotrauma (e.g., pneumothorax) is common at this pressure. A more reasonable amount might be 10–20 PSI; no one knows what the "best" choice is yet. Complications of TTJV include pneumothorax, pneumomediastinum, pneumopericardium, subcutaneous emphysema, esophageal perforation, and infection.[39–41]

Because of these concerns, many experts advocate the use of an emergency cricothyroidotomy kit that uses ordinary ventilation pressures. One such kit is based on a design by Melker, and is available from Cook (http://www.cookcriticalcare.com/discip/anesthes/2_09/2_09_05.html).

MEDICAL CONDITIONS WITH AIRWAY IMPLICATIONS

Obesity[42,43]

Patients 20% over their ideal weight are obese. When they are 100% over this weight they are said to be "morbidly obese." The obese patient has a reduced functional residual capacity with reduced pulmonary oxygen stores, leading to rapid desaturation when apnea occurs. Obese patients with a short thick neck, a large tongue, and/or redundant folds of oropharyngeal tissue may be difficult to intubate and are at increased risk to develop airway obstruction. PPV may be more difficult in these patients because of decreased chest wall compliance (restrictive lung defect). The increased work of breathing associated with obesity leads patients to take smaller TVs and breathe at an increased RR, leading to atelectasis, ventilation/perfusion mismatching,

Use: To awaken patient after failed intubation, but in whom ventilation is difficult.

A strategy used when mask ventilation is becoming difficult after the induction of general anesthesia complicated by unsuccessful intubation. This is a setting where you want the patient to wake up and breathe spontaneously.

1. Ensure that the patient is not in laryngospasm and that the patient's head and jaw are positioned properly. Call for help.

2. Insert an airway of some kind:
   - Oral airway (or cuffed oropharyngeal airway)
   - Nasopharyngeal airway
   - Laryngeal mask airway (LMA)
   - Intubating LMA

WARNING: Airway insertion may lead to laryngospasm in lightly anesthetized patients.

3. Utilize a two-person technique whereby one person manages the mask and holds the jaw in position using both hands, while the other ventilates the patient by hand using the rebreathing bag.

4. As a last resort, a surgical airway (transtracheal jet ventilation, cricothyroidotomy) is sometimes needed.

Figure 37-8 "Bail-Out" Algorithm: CAN'T VENTILATE WELL, CAN'T INTUBATE (HAVE GIVEN UP ON INTUBATION)

and increased degrees of airway closure. Should a surgical airway become necessary, the situation is made much more difficult as the surgeon attempts to identify the trachea deep in a mound of adipose tissue. Finally, very obese patients are at increased risk of regurgitation/aspiration both be-

cause of increased intra-abdominal pressure and the high incidence of patients having large gastric fluid volumes.

Diabetes and the Airway[44,45]

The link between DM and difficult laryngoscopy has only been described in recent years. About one-third of long-term-type diabetics (juvenile onset) will present with laryngoscopic difficulties. This is due at least in part to diabetic "stiff joint syndrome" characterized by short stature, joint rigidity, and tight, waxy skin. The fourth and fifth proximal phalanx joints are most commonly involved. Patients with diabetic stiff joint syndrome have difficulty in approximating their palms and cannot bend their fingers backward ("prayer sign"). When the cervical spine is involved, limited atlanto-occipital joint motion may make laryngoscopy and intubation quite difficult. Glycosylation of tissue proteins from chronic hyperglycemia resulting in abnormal cross-linking of collagen is believed to be the cause.

Rheumatoid Arthritis[46,47]

Rheumatoid arthritis (RA) is a multisystem autoimmune disease with many anesthetic implications. Patients with RA may challenge the anesthesiologist at the time of tracheal intubation because of cervical spine instability. In addition, temporomandibular joint (TMJ) or cricoarytenoid joint immobility may limit safe access to the airway. The preoperative anesthetic assessment must focus on possible airway difficulties. Patients must be questioned and examined to elicit evidence of neck pain, limitation of cervi-

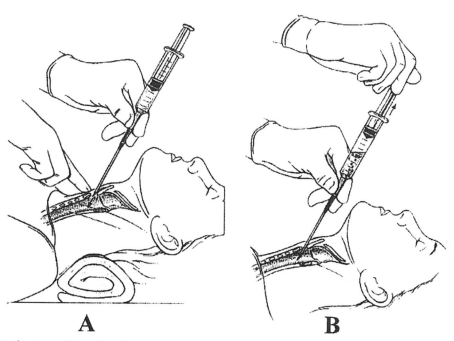

A   **B**

Figure 37-9   (A and B) The steps of insertion of a transtracheal jet ventilation catheter through the cricothyroid membrane into the trachea. (Reprinted with permission from Patel RG, Norman JR. The technique of transtracheal ventilation. J Crit Illness 1996;11:803–8.)

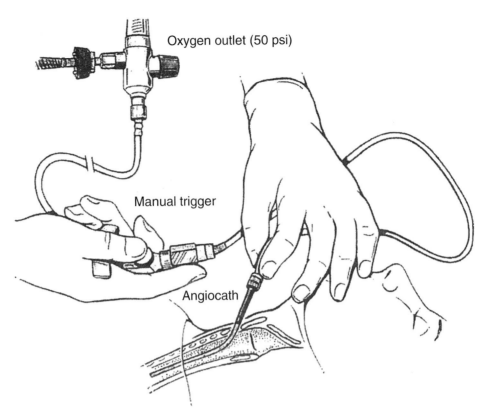

Oxygen outlet (50 psi)

Manual trigger

Angiocath

Figure 37-10   The application of transtracheal jet ventilation. Note that while the figure shows a 50-PSI pressure source in use, clinical experience suggests that lower amounts may be more appropriate. (Reprinted with permission from Patel RG, Norman JR. The technique of transtracheal ventilation. J Crit Illness 1996;11:803–8.)

cal spine movement, nerve root impingement, or spinal cord compression. Lateral cervical spine flexion-extension X-rays are potentially helpful in patients with cervical spine symptomatology to assess the possibility of cervical spine subluxation. The need for these X-rays in completely asymptomatic patients remains controversial; however, one should keep in mind case reports of neurologic damage after direct laryngoscopy and intubation in asymptomatic patients. Patients with cervical spine instability should generally be intubated and positioned awake before surgery to avoid neurologic injury. TMJs must be examined to ensure that mouth opening and anterior subluxation of the mandible will permit direct laryngoscopy. Patients demonstrating stridor or hoarseness require awake direct or indirect laryngoscopy to assess the possibility of arytenoid involvement and determine the size of the glottic opening. Finally, the larynx may be displaced and twisted from its usual location by erosion and generalized collapse of the cervical vertebrae.

other causes. The problem occurs more frequently in women. Pedunculated granulomas or polyps detected after the investigation of hoarseness are usually removed surgically as they can sometimes lead to airway obstruction. Remember also the potential exacerbation of bronchial asthma in patients with nasal polyps who receive aspirin, ketorolac, and other nonsteroidal anti-inflammatory drugs.

Thyroid Goiter[49]

Large thyroid goiters can lead to compression of the trachea and even tracheomalacia. This can worsen in the supine position and with the induction of general anesthesia. Retrosternal extensions of large goiters may act as mediastinal masses. Rarely, thyroid goiter may present as an oropharyngeal mass or cause bilateral recurrent nerve paralysis.

Airway Polyps[48]

Polyps may be found throughout the airway. Nasal polyps and polyps elsewhere in the airway can lead to partial or complete airway obstruction. Vocal cord granulomas and polyps may occur as a result of traumatic intubation, cord irritation from ETT movement or lubricant chemicals, and

Laryngeal Papillomatosis[50]

Patients with this condition may require frequent application of laser treatment for attempted eradication of the papillomas. Prior to treatment the airway may be close to obstruction from an overgrowth of lesions. During laser treatment, inspired oxygen concentration should be kept to the minimum practical amount, with the avoidance of N_2O, to reduce the chance of an airway fire. After treatment the airway will be raw and edematous. Laryngotracheomalacia may also be present, occasionally leading to complete upper airway collapse after extubation.

Tonsillitis and Other Tonsillar Disorders[51-53]

Tonsillectomy surgery may be required in adults and children either because tonsillar hypertrophy is causing partial airway obstruction or because of the nuisance of repeated tonsillar infections. Less commonly, tonsillar malignancy may require radical craniofacial surgery, while occult hypertrophic tonsillar masses in completely asymptomatic individuals may rarely lead to fatal airway obstruction with the routine induction of general anesthesia.

Airway considerations for general anesthesia for tonsillectomy include determining if the intubation will likely be easy and extubating the patient at the end of the procedure only when the patient is wide awake with a good cough reflex.

Bleeding after tonsillectomy may necessitate a return to the operating room. A number of important considerations apply in this setting. The stomach contains blood, so the patient is at risk of aspiration and a rapid sequence induction may be needed. The act of laryngoscopy may lead to torrential tonsillar bleeding. The patient may also be hypovolemic if the bleeding has been extensive. Finally, the possibility of a coagulopathy should also be entertained with unexpected bleeding.

REFERENCES

1. American Society of Anesthesiologists Task Force on Management of the Difficult Airway. Practice guidelines for management of the difficult airway: an updated report by the American Society of Anesthesiologists Task Force on Management of the Difficult Airway. Anesthesiology 2003;98:1269–77.

2. Crosby ET, Cooper RM, Douglas MJ, Doyle DJ, Hung OR, Labrecque P, Muir H, Murphy MF, Preston RP, Rose DK, Roy L. The unanticipated difficult airway with recommendations for management. Can J Anaesth 1998;45:757–76.

3. Deem S, Bishop MJ. Evaluation and management of the difficult airway. Crit Care Clin 1995;11:1–27.

4. Caplan RA, Posner KL, Ward RJ, Cheney FW. Adverse respiratory events in anesthesia: a closed claims analysis. Anesthesiology 1990;72:828–33.

5. Marik PE. Aspiration pneumonitis and aspiration pneumonia. N Engl J Med 2001;344:665–71.

6. Mallampati SR, Gatt SP, Gugino LD, Desai SP, Waraksa B, Freiberger D, Liu PL. A clinical sign to predict difficult tracheal intubation: a prospective study. Can Anaesth Soc J 1985;32:429–34.

7. Doyle DJ, Arellano R. Upper airway diseases and airway management: a synopsis. Anesthesiol Clin North Am 2002;20:767–87.

8. Wilson ME, Spiegelhalter D, Robertson JA, Lesser P. Predicting difficult intubation. Br J Anaesth 1988;61:211–16.

9. Frerk CM. Predicting difficult intubation. Anaesthesia 1991;46:1005–8.

10. Tse JC, Rimm EB, Hussain A. Predicting difficult endotracheal intubation in surgical patients scheduled for general anesthesia: a prospective blind study. Anesth Analg 1995;81:254–58.

11. Arne J, Descoins P, Fusciardi J, Ingrand P, Ferrier B, Boudigues D, Aries J. Preoperative assessment for difficult intubation in general and ENT surgery: predictive value of a clinical multivariate risk index. Br J Anaesth 1998;80:140–46.

12. Karkouti K, Rose DK, Wigglesworth D, Cohen MM. Predicting difficult intubation: a multivariable analysis. Can J Anaesth 2000;47:730–39.

13. Langeron O, Masso E, Huraux C, Guggiari M, Bianchi A, Coriat P, Riou B. Prediction of difficult mask ventilation. Anesthesiology 2000;92:1229–36.

14. Cormack RS, Lehane J. Difficult tracheal intubations in obstetrics. Anaesthesia 1984;39:1105–11.

15. Benumof JL, Cooper SD. Quantitative improvements in laryngoscopic view by optimal external laryngeal manipulation. J Clin Anesth 1996;8:136–40.

16. Takahata O, Kubota M, Mamiya K, Akama Y, Nozaka T, Matsumoto H, Ogawa H. The efficacy of the "BURP" maneuver during a difficult laryngoscopy. Anesth Analg 1997;84:419–21.

17. McCoy E. The McCoy laryngoscope. Anaesthesia 1998;53:202–3.

18. Aoyama K, Nagaoka E, Takenaka I, Kadoya T. The McCoy laryngoscope expands the laryngeal aperture in patients with difficult intubation. Anesthesiology 2000;92:1855–56.

19. Bahk JH, Ryu HG, Park C. Use of gum elastic bougie during difficult airway management. Anesth Analg 2003;96:1845.

20. Levitan RM. Patient safety in emergency airway management and rapid sequence intubation: metaphorical lessons from skydiving. Ann Emerg Med 2003;42:81–87.

21. Hillman DR, Platt PR, Eastwood PR. The upper airway during anaesthesia. Br J Anaesth 2003;91:31–39.

22. Benumof JL. Obstructive sleep apnea in the adult obese patient: implications for airway management. Anesthesiol Clin North Am 2002;20:789–811.

23. Chung DC, Rowbottom SJ. A very small dose of suxamethonium relieves laryngospasm. Anaesthesia 1993;48:229–30.

24. Herrick IA, Mahendran B, Penny FJ. Postobstructive pulmonary edema following anesthesia. J Clin Anesth 1990;2:116–20.

25. Noble VE, Bontempo LJ, Nadel ES, Brown DF. Stridor. J Emerg Med 2000;19:183–86.

26. Cooper RM. The use of an endotracheal ventilation catheter in the management of difficult extubations. Can J Anaesth 1996;43:90–93.

27. Cooper RM. Extubation of the difficult airway. Anesthesiology 1997;87:460.

28. Benumof JL. Airway exchange catheters for safe extubation: the clinical and scientific details that make the concept work. Chest 1997;111:1483–86.

29. Baskett PJF, Parr MJA, Nolan JP. The intubating laryngeal mask: results of a multicentre trial with experience of 500 cases. Anaesthesia 1998;53:1174–79.

30. Agro F, Hung OR. Cataldo R. Carassiti M. Gherardi S. Lightwand intubation using the Trachlight: a brief review of current knowledge. Can J Anaesth 2001;48:592–99.

31. Pennant JH, White PF. The laryngeal mask airway: its uses in anesthesiology. Anesthesiology 1993;79:144.

32. Benumof JL. Laryngeal mask airway and the ASA difficult airway algorithm. Anesthesiology 1996;84:686.

33. Brimacombe JR, Brain AIJ. The Laryngeal Mask Airway: A Review and Practical Guide. Philadelphia: WB Saunders, 1997.

34. Frass M, Frenzer R, Rauscha F, et al. Ventilation with the esophageal tracheal Combitube in cardiopulmonary resuscitation. Crit Care Med 1987;15:609–11.

35. Gaitini LA, Vaida SJ, Mostafa S, Yanovski B, Croitoru M, Capdevila MD, Sabo E, Ben-David B, Benumof J. The Combitube in elective surgery: a report of 200 cases. Anesthesiology 2001;94:79–82.

36. Miller RA. A new laryngoscope. Anesthesiology 1941;2:317.

37. Cohn AI, Zornow MH. Awake intubation in patients with cervical

spine disease: a comparison of the Bullard laryngoscope and the fiberoptic bronchoscope. Anesth Analg 1995;81:1283.

38. Watts DJ, Gelb AW, Bach DB, Pelz DM. Comparison of the Bullard and Macintosh laryngoscopes for endotracheal intubation in patients with a potential cervical spine injury. Anesthesiology 1997; 87:1335–42.

39. Benumof JL. The importance of transtracheal jet ventilation in the management of the difficult airway. Anesthesiology 1989;71: 769–78.

40. Metz S. Parmet JL. Levitt JD. Failed emergency transtracheal ventilation through a 14-gauge intravenous catheter. J Clin Anesth 1996; 8:58–62.

41. Patel RG. Percutaneous transtracheal jet ventilation: a safe, quick, and temporary way to provide oxygenation and ventilation when conventional methods are unsuccessful. Chest 1999;116:1689–94.

42. Dominguez-Cherit G, Gonzalez R, Borunda D, Pedroza J, Gonzalez-Barranco J, Herrera MF. Anesthesia for morbidly obese patients. World J Surg 1998;22:969–73.

43. Bond A. Obesity and difficult intubation. Anaesth Intens Care 1993; 21:828–30.

44. Salzarulo HH, Taylor LA. Diabetic "still joint syndrome" as a cause of difficult endotracheal intubation. Anesthesiology 1986;64: 366–68.

45. Reissell E, Orko R, Maunuksela EL, Lindgren L. Predictability of difficult laryngoscopy in patients with long-term diabetes mellitus. Anaesthesia 1990;45:1024–27.

46. Kolman J. Morris I. Cricoarytenoid arthritis: a cause of acute upper airway obstruction in rheumatoid arthritis. Can J Anaesth 2002;49: 729–32.

47. Vergnenegre A. Pugnere N. Antonini MT. Arnaud M. Melloni B. Treves R. Bonnaud F. Airway obstruction and rheumatoid arthritis. Eur Respir J 1997;10:1072–78.

48. Lund VJ. Diagnosis and treatment of nasal polyps. Br Med J 1995; 311:1411–14.

49. Abdel Rahim AA. Ahmed ME. Hassan MA. Respiratory complications after thyroidectomy and the need for tracheostomy in patients with a large goiter. Br J Surg 1999;86:88–90.

50. Restrepo S. Palacios E. Mastrogiovanni L. Kaplan J. Gordillo H. Recurrent respiratory papillomatosis. Ear Nose Throat J 2003;82:555–56.

51. Handler SD, Miller L, Richmond KH, Baranak CC. Posttonsillectomy hemorrhage: incidence, prevention and management. Laryngoscope 1986;96:1243–47.

52. Cohle SD. Jones DH. Puri S. Lingual tonsillar hypertrophy causing failed intubation and cerebral anoxia. Am J Forens Med Pathol 1993;14:158–61.

53. Tokumine J, Sugahara K, Ura M, Takara I, Oshiro M, Owa T. Lingual tonsil hypertrophy with difficult airway and uncontrollable bleeding. Anaesthesia 2003;58:390–91.

The Pediatric Difficult Airway: Outpatient Implications

STEVEN C. HALL

Pediatric patients increasingly come for surgical procedures on the day of surgery instead of being admitted to the hospital the night before. This practice is so pervasive that even children having high-risk procedures such as scoliosis repair, congenital heart surgery, and craniofacial reconstructions now routinely are admitted to the institution on the day of the procedure. This places several burdens on the anesthesiologist who will care for the child.

There is often a limited amount of time to evaluate the patient and ensure that he/she is a suitable candidate for anesthesia and surgery. In addition, important background information, such as previous hospital charts, must be readily available if it is to be of use in evaluation. If consultations have been obtained on the child, they must also be immediately available. Finally, there are often subtle, or not so subtle, pressures to proceed in spite of inadequate evaluation or preparation because the family has taken the time and effort to come today for the procedure, with strong expectations that the procedure will be performed that day without undue delay.

The effectiveness of evaluation and preparation of outpatients can be significantly enhanced by a variety of systems in the institution, such as extensive evaluations by the surgeon, preadmission screening by trained nursing staff, and preanesthetic clinics. These systems need to be coordinated to allow both the timely sharing of information and planning of appropriate anesthetic preparation and management.

Although these issues apply to all children having outpatient surgery, they are especially relevant for the child with an abnormal airway. Children scheduled for surgery with an abnormal airway come for one of three general reasons. They may be coming for a diagnostic procedure to identify the cause of the abnormality or to quantify the problem; they may be coming for a therapeutic procedure to improve the airway; they may be coming for a procedure unrelated to the abnormal airway. The fundamental issue in the reason for surgery is an estimate of whether the anesthesiologist will know more about the airway or the airway will be actually improved by the completion of the procedure. This dynamic is important in deciding how much evaluation and preparation is needed for the case.

PREANESTHETIC EVALUATION AND PREPARATION

The anesthesiologist should have a detailed understanding of the fundamental differences not only in the airway anatomy and function in children of different ages, but also the signs and symptoms of significant airway compromise, the radiologic features of various lesions, and the common airway abnormalities seen in childhood.[1,2] In addition, the anesthesiologist must have the variety of equipment and support needed to manage all eventualities in these situations. Finally, the anesthesiologist must have a clear set of plans and protocols for initial evaluation, preparation, and management that includes the treatment of potential complications, including precipitous complete loss of a patent airway.[3] Although most anesthesiologists feel confident in their airway skills, many clinicians do not have extensive experience with abnormal pediatric airways.

Causes of a difficult airway in children can be categorized into four general groups.[4,5] The first group contains children with congenital abnormalities who present with varying degrees of chronic obstruction. Examples include laryngomalacia, glottic webs, hemangiomas, vascular rings, and hypoplastic mandible. These conditions often present either shortly after birth or in infancy (Table 38-1). The second group includes infections of the airway, such as epiglottitis, croup, and diphtheria, or acquired abnormalities, such as foreign bodies, that present with progressive airway obstruction, often over a relatively short time frame. Because of the acute nature of presentation of these conditions, they are unlikely to be present in an outpatient scheduled for elective surgery. The exception to this is airway papilloma. Patients with this condition present with recurrent obstruction needing therapeutic intervention. The third group contains children without known

Table 38-1   Causes of Airway Obstruction in Childhood (Excluding Foreign Bodies)

Pharyngeal
   Tonsillar/adenoid hypertrophy
   Craniofacial abnormalities
   Micrognathia
   Tempomandibular joint ankylosis
   Macroglossia

Laryngeal
   Web
   Laryngomalacia
   Vocal cord paralysis
   Subglottic edema
   Subglottic stenosis
   Subglottic hemangioma
   Supraglottic or subglottic cyst
   Laryngeal papilloma

Tracheobronchial
   Hemangioma
   Tracheomalacia
   Tracheal compression by vascular structures
   Bronchospasm
   Bronchiolitis/pneumonia

congenital or acquired abnormalities, but who carry the diagnosis of stridor. There is a general misconception that stridor represents a specific diagnosis. It does not—stridor just means that there is an abnormal sound sometime during the ventilatory cycle. The timing and characteristics of this abnormality can give some indication of the underlying abnormality, but are rarely diagnostic. The fourth group is formed by children without known specific congenital or acquired abnormalities, but who are known to be difficult to visualize for intubation.

When a child with an at-risk airway is identified, the degree of obstruction and functional impairment must be assessed. The general appearance of the child is an important sign, since agitation, retractions, cyanosis, anxiety, weak or absent cry, and stridor can all be indications of significant obstruction.[6] Further examination includes evaluation of breath sounds, chest excursion, use of accessory muscles, ability to open the mouth, ability to take a deep breath, and mobility of the neck and mandible. A history from the parents or caregiver can give valuable information about any signs or symptoms related to the airway, such as wheezing, cyanosis, choking, or retractions. A history of either suspected or confirmed obstructive sleep apnea is useful in identifying patients who may have abnormal responses to general anesthesia, either with obstruction early in the course of induction or with prolonged periods of hypoventilation or obstruction during the recovery process.

If the examination of the child indicates signs of an abnormal upper or lower airway, further evaluation is needed. If there are signs of upper airway obstruction, radiologic studies to identify the exact site and degree of obstruction are indicated. If there are signs of lower airway obstruction, the exact cause needs to be identified. Wheezing, for instance, may be due to inadequately treated bronchospastic disease, such as asthma, or may be due to an active infection such as bronchiolitis. The approach is different. If the patient is asthmatic, aggressive treatment with beta agonists and a short course of steroids may be the best treatment to improve and stabilize the patient. However, if the patient has an active lower airway infection, the best treatment may involve delay of the case for several weeks until the infective process has resolved. If there is question about the severity and reversibility of the disease process, consultation with the child's pediatrician or allergist may be appropriate.

In addition to the evaluation directed toward the airway, there should also be an assessment of the overall health of the child. The presence of cardiac, neurologic, or pulmonary disorders is of special interest. Patients who were preterm at birth and had prolonged ventilatory or oxygen support have abnormal pulmonary mechanics that persist into childhood. Preterm patients may also be at risk for apneic spells during early infancy, especially under 6 months of age. Because these apneic spells can reappear in the postoperative period, there should be a clear institutional policy about which ex-preterm patients can be treated as outpatients and which must be admitted overnight for observation. There are a wide variety of opinions about which patients should be observed and for how long; in our institution, all preterm infants under 6 months of age must be observed for at least 12 hr before discharge.

Children with known syndromes may have airway obstruction as a part of the constellation of signs.[5,7–9] There is a wide spectrum of airway problems, ranging from the micrognathia seen with Pierre Robin syndrome to the hypoplastic mandible and retruded midface of the Treacher Collins syndrome. Down's syndrome patients have mild macroglossia, while children with Beckwith-Wiedemann syndrome may have such significant macroglossia that a tracheostomy may be required at an early age. Abnormalities of the midface can cause significant airway obstruction in children with Crouzon's and Apert's syndromes. Children with Klippel-Feil syndrome have fusion of the cervical spine, severely limiting flexion and extension. With these and countless other syndromes, there may be significant airway obstruction at the pharyngeal, laryngeal, and tracheal levels. Although the site of obstruction is usually consistent within each syndrome, each child must be evaluated to estimate the functional capacity of the child and effective degree of obstruction.

If other medical conditions are identified, such as cardiac disease or a seizure disorder, there should be a mechanism in the institution to allow evaluation before the day of surgery in order to avoid delay or possible cancellation. The department of anesthesiology should work with the local department of pediatrics and department of surgery to both develop policies and promote education of all practitioners involved in the child's care. By developing reasonable policies and consistent application of the policies, both the surgeon and the child's primary caregiver can efficiently and effectively prepare the child for elective pro-

Table 38-2   Medical Conditions Frequently Encountered in Children for Which Policies for Preanesthetic Preparation Are Useful

The child with:
Murmur of unknown etiology
Known cardiac disease
Insulin-dependent diabetes
Asthma
Ex-preterm
Bronchopulmonary dysplasia
Sickle cell anemia or other hemoglobinopathy
Seizures

cedures. Medical conditions that are suitable for prospective policy development are listed in Table 38-2.

Laboratory evaluation of patients with known or suspected abnormal airways is centered on radiologic studies.[5,10] Lateral and posteroanterior (PA) radiographs of the head and neck can be especially useful, with other examinations like computerized tomography (CT) scans occasionally offering useful information. However, normal radiographs do not guarantee an absence of functional obstruction. Flow-volume loops can occasionally be useful in cooperative children to demonstrate dynamic obstruction during the respiratory cycle.

Hematologic and chemical laboratory studies are obtained as a routine less frequently than in previous years. In most children's hospitals, it is common to not obtain any routine laboratory work on healthy children when they are undergoing procedures that are unlikely to require transfusion. Complete blood counts or a hemoglobin count is often obtained if transfusion is likely or, in some centers, if the child is under 1 year of age. If there are specific issues, such as a known hemoglobinopathy or coagulation disorder or recent changes in seizure medications, laboratory work is obtained before proceeding with elective procedures. In some institutions, coagulation studies are obtained on all patients undergoing tonsillectomy and adenoidectomy, though there is not universal consistency on this practice. Identifying patients who need laboratory work and obtaining the studies before the day of surgery will minimize delays on the day of the procedure. However, this works best only if abnormal laboratory results are reported to the anesthesia department when obtained so that a determination can be made before the day of surgery if additional studies or preparation are needed.

PREMEDICATION

The use of premedication is controversial, especially in children with an abnormal airway. Premedication has multiple roles, including secretion control, vagolysis, anxiolysis, and decreasing cardiovascular responsiveness to the induction period. One of the belladonna drugs such as atropine or glycopyrrolate is especially useful in children under 1 year because of its drying actions on secretions and its vagolytic activities. In infants, vagally-mediated reflex bradycardia can be precipitated by induction of anesthesia, laryngoscopy, or surgical pain. Many pediatric anesthesiologists will administer atropine or other belladonna drug intramuscularly preoperatively or intravenously at the time of induction to minimize these reflexes in infants.

Sedative or anxiolytic sedation in children over 1 year of age has both adherents and detractors.[11–13] The asymptomatic, but anxious, older child or adolescent may benefit from sedation for relief of anxiety and decreased hypertensive response to the perioperative experience. Many different types of drugs can be used, with no proven superiority of one agent over another. Benzodiazepines and, to a lesser extent, barbiturates and opioids are the most commonly used medications, with significant bias between institutions about which regimens are preferred. Because children, in general, hate injections, it is reasonable to consider alternative methods of administration, such as oral, nasal, or rectal administration, for premedication. An example of probably the most commonly used technique is oral midazolam, 0.5–0.7 mg/kg up to 20 mg/kg, in a flavored syrup.[14] The overall principle in choosing premedicants centers around the individual's needs and probable response to sedative agents. If the patient is particularly debilitated, has a tenuous airway, or has marginal ventilatory reserve, premedication may be poorly tolerated and precipitate hypoventilation, airway obstruction, oxygen desaturation, or hypotension. Although it is easy to take the position that all children with an abnormal airway should not receive premedication, there is actually no proof in the literature to support this far-reaching statement. Instead, the known potential adverse effects of premedication should be considered in the context of potential advantages in selected patients of less anxiety, better cooperation, and less psychologic trauma.

An alternative or adjunct to premedication that is considered by some is parental presence during induction of anesthesia.[15,16] There is certainly increased interest in the lay public in having a parent present during the induction of anesthesia in a child, even if the child's airway is at risk. However, parental presence may be an appropriate approach only if certain conditions are met. The involved surgical, anesthesia, and nursing staff must all be enthusiastic about its use and understand its limitations; the involved parent must be reasonable and understand what is expected of him/her in the operating theater; the child must be cognizant enough to benefit from parental presence; the child must be medically stable enough that a smooth induction is anticipated; and there must be clear protocols in place about informed consent, infection control, and personnel assigned to monitor and direct the parent. With these restrictions, some children may suffer less separation anxiety if a parent is present until the child loses consciousness. However, if the anesthesiologist anticipates difficulty during induction, the needs of both the child and the anesthesiologist dictate that parental presence should not be allowed.

Table 38-3   Recommended Fasting Requirements

1. No solids on the day of surgery (unless the surgery is *known* to be late in the day. Then, a light, nonfatty breakfast) is recommended
2. Clear liquids, ad lib, until 2–3 hr before surgery
3. Breast milk until 4 hr before surgery if the child is under 1 year old; otherwise, 6 hr
4. Milk and solids 6 hr before surgery
5. Fatty foods require at least 8 hr of fasting

FASTING

There is widespread recognition that fasting requirements have been too strict in the past and have potentially been a cause of complications.[17] Fasting guidelines were initially developed to minimize the volume of material in the stomach at the time of induction, minimizing the risk of aspiration. This was felt to be especially important for inhalation inductions, such as commonly used for children with at-risk airways. However, prolonged fasting can cause hypoglycemia, relative hypovolemia, and distress to the child and parent. Research into gastric emptying in children led to the recognition that clear liquids reliably leave the stomach within 2 hr of ingestion in nonstressed children of all ages. Ingestion of clear liquids within 2–3 hr preinduction also diminished thirst, hunger, and irritability in children.[18–22] Consequently, more liberal guidelines have been recommended and adopted widely.[23] In our institution, we use the guidelines in Table 38-3. It is useful to ensure that parents clearly understand these restrictions when their child is scheduled for elective outpatient surgery. A preoperative phone call stressing the time of fasting, as well as written materials given ahead of time to the parents, will minimize delays because of inadequate fasting time.

ROOM PREPARATION

Preparation of the anesthesia machine and associated equipment is similar to that for any pediatric anesthetic. In addition to standard equipment, it is useful to have immediately available several pieces of equipment that may be needed for establishment of the airway. These include endotracheal tubes (with stylet) a half size larger and smaller than expected; an assortment of laryngeal mask airways; oral and nasal mask airways; a Magill's forceps; a tube exchanger; a fiberoptic laryngoscope; a cricothyrotomy kit and jet injector; and a light wand. It is our practice to have three drugs drawn up or immediately available for cases in which the airway may be at risk, including atropine or glycopyrrolate, succinylcholine, and epinephrine. The epinephrine is available for all cases where there is a potential of sudden deterioration and arrest.

Rocuronium has become increasingly popular as a substitute for succinylcholine. It has the advantages of relatively rapid onset and lack of parasympathetic stimulation, but is not as rapid in onset as succinylcholine. Its use in emergent and urgent situations continues to evolve.

Probably the single most important and overlooked aspect of proper preparation is the status of qualified help. If an endoscopist is involved in the procedure, he/she should be available not only during induction, but in the operating suite. Airway equipment should be prepared and checked by the endoscopist before induction. An age-appropriate tracheostomy setup should always be available. The endoscopist will be of little help in an emergency if he/she and his/her equipment is not available on a moment's notice. In cases in which no endoscopist is involved, it is useful to ascertain whether skilled help is readily available during induction. This will often be in the person of another anesthesiologist or colleague skilled in airway management. If at all possible, patients with at-risk airways should be cared for only when optimal types of personnel and equipment are available.

MONITORING

Standard monitoring of electrocardiograph, stethoscope, pulse oximeter, blood pressure cuff, and capnograph are appropriate for induction and maintenance of most cases. Temperature monitoring should be added for all except the shortest cases. All these monitors are accurate and reliable, especially as trend monitors, in children of all ages and should be used for all patients. Technical difficulties may limit their use in the smallest preterm patients.

One of the monitors that is frequently underutilized is the stethoscope. The precordial stethoscope was, for years, the hallmark of the pediatric anesthesiologist. The monitor was used to continually evaluate both breath and heart sounds during the case, with an absence of breath sounds heralding airway obstruction and a softening of heart sounds indicating a significant drop in blood pressure and cardiac output. With the advent of the widespread use of pulse oximetry and capnography, the stethoscope is used less by many practitioners. However, direct observation of the patient and the precordial stethoscope can give immediate feedback about adequacy of the airway and ventilation before there are noticeable changes in electronic monitoring. Consequently, attention to direct observation and use of the stethoscope expand the capabilities of the anesthesiologist and increase patient safety.

ANESTHETIC TECHNIQUE

Although there may be a wide variety of potential causes of the airway obstruction, the anesthetic considerations fall into several consistent categories. The anesthetic technique chosen depends on several factors, including those related to age of the patient, underlying medical conditions, need for spontaneous ventilation, anticipated difficulty in maintaining the airway, and length of the procedure. Only after considering all these factors can the anesthesiologist make a definitive decision about proceeding.

The newborn presents a completely different set of challenges during induction compared to the infant, child, or adolescent. For instance, the newborn is less likely to maintain adequate blood pressure and cardiac output in response to standard induction regimens compared to older children. An example of this is the work of Friesen and Lichtor, which demonstrated that induction doses of halothane, isoflurane, fentanyl, and ketamine in preterm infants caused significant drops in blood pressure that were, in most cases, only partly reversed by surgical incision.[24] The immature cardiovascular system of the newborn, as well as the dependence on heart rate instead of increasing stroke volume to maintain cardiac output, underscores the need to carefully consider the cardiodepressant actions of an anesthetic in newborns and infants, independent of underlying cardiac disease.

There is a need for specific levels of anesthetic changes as the child matures.[25,26] Using minimum alveolar concentration (MAC) of inhalation agents as a proxy for all induction agents, the requirement for anesthetic necessary to prevent movement after surgical intervention climbs dramatically after birth, peaks in infancy, and then slowly declines over childhood, with a small rise in adolescence. This underlying increasing need for greater anesthetic depth must be balanced against other factors, such as underlying cardiac disease, that can produce a deterioration in physiologic status with increasing depth of anesthesia.

There are technical considerations related to age. Although intravenous inductions are routinely used in adolescents and adults, they are less common in infants and children. The ability to establish vascular access is more difficult in the newborn and, especially, the small infant. Finding and cannulating a vein with either a 22- or 24-gauge indwelling cannula is often easier in the newborn than in the 3–6-month-old infant because the newborn has very little subcutaneous fat to obscure direct visualization of the vein. Care must be taken in insertion of cannulas in the newborn because it is relatively easy to push a plastic cannula through the vein itself, even with the metal stylet removed.

AIRWAY MANAGEMENT

The anesthesiologist must make a fundamental decision about airway management before starting the induction. Does the airway need to be established before induction? This is extraordinarily rare in children, especially in children healthy enough to be outpatient candidates. Consequently, the second question that must be asked is whether a specific anesthetic technique is needed or optimal. Spontaneous ventilation provides the advantage of continuation of ventilation, but the disadvantage of potential hypoventilation at deeper levels of anesthesia that may be needed for rigid laryngoscopy and bronchoscopy. Controlled ventilation provides the advantage of a still field for bronchoscopy, but the disadvantage of dependence on the ability to maintain adequate ventilation with potential collapse of the airway and air trapping.

The decision about the suitability of either spontaneous or controlled ventilation should be made in conjunction with the endoscopist, if the procedure involves one. The potential change in airway tone and dynamics with either technique should be discussed. Traditionally, spontaneous ventilation has been used when there is some question about the nature of the airway obstruction because it has been felt that a spontaneously breathing patient has a greater degree of safety related to maintaining the dynamics of the airway most similar to the awake state, as well as allowing the endoscopist to examine these dynamics.

If controlled ventilation is chosen, a wide variety of agents can be used. The choice of volatile agent, fixed agent, and relaxant is made according to underlying medical conditions of the patient, anticipated length of the procedure, and personal preference. If the patient has a history of bronchospastic disease, addition of at least some volatile agent may decrease the tendency for intraoperative bronchospasm.

If spontaneous ventilation is chosen, there are several agents to choose from. Inhalation induction is usually accomplished with either halothane or sevoflurane, but there is increased interest in the use of propofol infusions with adjuncts as an alternative. The traditional inhalation induction has been with halothane, and many practitioners have used this technique for many years, sometimes switching to isoflurane for maintenance. The great advantages of halothane are its lack of expense, its profound depression of airway reflexes, and prolonged analgesia. However, it also can cause significant myocardial depression and dysrhythmias in the presence of hypercarbia.[27–29] Practitioners have used halothane for many years, learning to balance the advantages against its limitations. Sevoflurane does not produce the same degree of depression of airway reflexes as halothane,[30] but does have faster onset/emergence characteristics, as well as less myocardial depression and dysrhythmia production.[31–33] Sevoflurane is rapidly replacing halothane in the United States, despite its increased cost. Current trainees have limited exposure to halothane, making its use in only the most critical of situations—an at-risk airway—troublesome.[34] Of interest, because sevoflurane does not produce the same depression of airway reflexes, it is often useful to add small amounts of an opioid or propofol during airway endoscopy procedures to provide additional analgesia.

Propofol is also increasingly being used for patients undergoing procedures with spontaneous ventilation.[35] After an induction bolus, infusion in the range of 200–300 μg/kg/min is started and titrated to provide adequate anesthesia and ventilation. Judicious supplementation with fentanyl or lidocaine or additional propofol boluses are used during the most stimulating portions of the procedure. Although there is a lack of controlled trials comparing this technique with others, it is gaining increasing acceptance because of the lack of operating room pollution, rapid awakening, and ease of use.

Nitrous oxide is commonly used to speed induction and decrease the amount of other agents used in pediatrics. However, its use in patients with potential airway problems can be problematic. If the patient is hypoxemic at rest or if the anesthesiologist anticipates obstruction during induction, it is prudent to use 100% oxygen instead of an oxygen/nitrous oxide mixture. In patients with critical airway obstruction, some practitioners will use a mixture of helium and oxygen to increase the airflow characteristics. However, a relatively high concentration of helium is needed to get significant improvement in flow, ensuring that a relatively low level of oxygen will be used. During induction, it is not unusual for the child to develop some degree of upper airway obstruction. The degree of obstruction depends on underlying pathology. Patients with laryngomalacia, for instance, may worsen if the child struggles and increase their inspiratory force during induction. This will improve as the child is anesthetized and resumes quiet breathing. In many cases, gentle application of positive airway pressure will keep the airway patent.[36] If this pressure is ineffective, a chin lift and jaw thrust will often restore patency. Further measures include oral or nasal airways, a shoulder roll, or a blanket under the head. If none of these maneuvers is successful, consider the insertion of a laryngeal mask airway or a supraglottic airway.[37-42] It is unusual to have to give a muscle relaxant and insert an endotracheal tube, but it is a maneuver that should be considered.

After induction, establishment of the airway can be performed in a variety of methods. If the procedure is a diagnostic one, laryngoscopy and evaluation of the airway will be performed by the endoscopist. If rigid scopes are used, the anesthesiologist will share the airway and provide ongoing ventilation through a variety of methods. On the other hand, if the airway is to be examined through the use of a fiberoptic bronchoscope, the options include introduction directly, insertion through a laryngeal mask airway, or insertion through an endotracheal tube.[43] With any of these techniques, close communication between the anesthesiologist and endoscopist is needed to ensure adequate conditions, oxygenation, and ventilation. The anesthesiologist must readily communicate when the endoscopist needs to stop and allow reestablishment of adequate ventilation.

During diagnostic procedures and some therapeutic procedures, such as laser excision of papilloma, the endoscopist may require prolonged access to the airway.[44-46] Four techniques are commonly used. The first technique is endotracheal intubation, often with a small tube, with the endoscopist working around it. The second technique is apneic oxygenation, in which the anesthesiologist establishes an adequate level of anesthesia and then hyperventilates for a short time. The endoscopist is then given complete access to the airway, with ventilation being reestablished after about a minute or whenever the oxygen saturation starts to drop. A third technique is jet ventilation. These patients are given a relaxant to prevent respiratory movements, as well as provide a motionless field. A fourth technique is insufflation. After establishment of an adequate depth of anesthesia and spontaneous ventilation, a catheter attached to the fresh gas source of the anesthesia machine is inserted through the nares to the back of the nasopharynx. The patient may be maintained at an adequate depth of anesthesia with this method, but if oxygen and a volatile agent are the anesthetic used, there should be scavenging of exhaled gases to minimize exposure of operating room personnel.

If sources of ignition, such as a laser or electrocautery, are used during airway surgery, safety precautions must be taken to prevent accidental fires.[47] If an endotracheal tube is in the airway, it is a possible fuel for a fire. There are commercially available tubes made of metal or silastic that are resistant to ignition. It is also possible to cover a standard endotracheal tube with copper foil to reflect laser beams. Although this latter technique is inexpensive, it is not a guarantee against ignition if the same area is struck by the beam more than once. The single best preventive measure is vigilance. The endoscopist must make every effort to ensure that a laser or electrocautery is not used in a manner where there is uncertainty about the tissue or substance being contacted. Time and effort must be expended in ensuring that the operator is constantly aware of where flammable materials should be avoided. If an endotracheal tube does catch fire, it should be immediately removed. Turning off the oxygen alone allows the tube to continue burning in the airway until all oxygen is consumed. After the tube is removed, direct bronchoscopy should be performed to assess whether there has been significant damage to the airway.

Hypoventilation with subsequent dysrhythmias is probably the most common complication of airway surgery. Hypoxemia can occur because of hypoventilation based on the airway lesion, pulmonary disease, or insertion of a bronchoscope too distally to provide adequate ventilation. Hypercapnia and subsequent dysrhythmias are caused by the same conditions; although hypercapnia is often more a problem than hypoxemia because of the use of enriched oxygen mixtures. It is useful to be prepared for the possibility of sudden airway obstruction. The team of anesthesiologist and endoscopist must communicate easily and have a clear understanding of who will restore the airway if lost and whether this will be done by mask, endotracheal tube, or rigid bronchoscope.

POSTANESTHETIC CARE

Postanesthetic care is an extension of care in the operating room.[48] The postanesthetic care area should be equipped to care for all ages of children who receive care in the operating room, with proper-sized airway, monitoring, resuscitation, and vascular access equipment always available. Nursing should be trained in the unique aspects of pediatric care and be comfortable with children of the ages presenting to the unit. Pediatric advanced life support (PALS) training is strongly recommended, as is attention to age-specific policies and procedures. It is as important that postanesthetic nursing staff be as comfortable caring for these patients as operating room, anesthesia, and surgical personnel.

The anesthesiologist should stay with the child until the patient can consistently maintain an independent airway and is awakening as expected. Monitoring with pulse oximetry, electrocardiogram, and blood pressure should be done on all patients, as well as temperature. During the early stages of recovery, the patient may develop sudden airway obstruction related to the underlying lesion or laryngospasm if still partially anesthetized and subjected to a painful stimulus.

Postintubation croup is a potential airway complication postoperatively that is more common in children than in adult practice. In the preadolescent patient, the narrowest area of the airway is at the level of the cricoid. Pressure on this mucosa can result in significant swelling and relative obstruction of airflow. Factors that increase the likelihood of croup include traumatic or repeated intubations, coughing or "bucking" on the tube, intubation for over an hour, surgery in a position other than supine, and an endotracheal tube fit that prevents an air leak until pressures above 25 cm H_2O are used. Children with congenital narrowing of the larynx, such as those with Down's syndrome or congenital subglottic stenosis, are also at risk.

Postintubation croup usually becomes symptomatic within the first hour after extubation, but may develop later. The maximum edema usually occurs at 4 hr after extubation and resolves by 24 hr. It characteristically presents with a "barky" cough, retractions, and tachypnea. Cyanosis or duskiness, a soft voice, or patient distress is a sign of advanced airway obstruction. Although postintubation croup usually resolves without endangering the patient, the child is at risk for progressive airway obstruction and hypoxemia. For this reason, symptomatic therapy is usually given.

The initial therapy is humidified oxygen by face mask. Nebulized racemic epinephrine (0.5 mL of 2.25% epinephrine in 2.5 mL saline) is commonly administered by face mask to vasoconstrict the laryngeal mucosa. Racemic epinephrine has traditionally been used, even though only the l-isomer is active, because of supposed decreased cardioactive side effects, though the lesser side effects may be related more to dilution and poor absorption. After racemic administration, improvement is usually noticed immediately. Because of the limited length of action of the vasoconstriction, the patient must be reexamined after 1 hr to see whether there has been a "rebound" recurrence of the edema and obstruction. Although a single treatment is usually adequate, racemic administration can be repeated at hourly intervals, rarely limited by the development of tachycardia.

Another treatment commonly used is steroid administration. The efficacy of this modality is controversial. The bulk of research has been on viral laryngotracheobronchitis, not postintubation croup. However, most practitioners agree that a single dose of steroid, such as 1 mg/kg of dexamethasone, will reduce swelling over the next 4–6 hr.

Rarely, postintubation croup is severe enough to warrant prolonged observation in the hospital by personnel equipped to provide immediate airway support. Patients who continue to have a barky cough, but are without other signs of respiratory distress, may be difficult to judge. However, the new onset of this stridor is worrisome, and prolonged observation or indirect visualization of the glottis may be needed. If the patient is to be discharged home, parents should be instructed not only to observe the child frequently through the night, but also to bring the child immediately back to the hospital if there are any signs of respiratory distress. If there is any doubt by either the medical staff or parents about the advisability of discharge, the child should be admitted for observation overnight.

The same concept of prolonged observation and admission, if necessary, is used for all patients with continued partial obstruction of the airway. If the patient shows new signs of obstruction, evidence of tiring or loss of energy, or an inability to cry or speak with normal levels of volume, there should be a focused reevaluation of the child, including consultation with an endoscopist, to ensure that there is not an increase in the level of obstruction or functional impairment. If there is question about the status of the patient, the conservative approach is to admit the child for observation in a monitored setting overnight.

SUMMARY

The prospect of caring for a child with an abnormal airway frightens many clinicians, especially in an outpatient setting. Proper and extensive preanesthetic evaluation and preparation, coupled with a rational and calm approach to perioperative management, will minimize the difficulty in managing the patient. Flexibility in management and preparation for sudden deterioration of the airway are important principles in ensuring the best possible course for the patient.

REFERENCES

1. Litman RS, Weissend EE, Shibata D, Westesson PL. Developmental changes of laryngeal dimensions in unparalyzed, sedated children. Anesthesiology 2003 Jan;98(1):41–45.
2. Infosino A. Pediatric upper airway and congenital anomalies. Anesthesiol Clin North Am 2002;20:747–66.
3. Meursing AE. Anaesthesia for day care surgery, patient selection, evaluation, preoperative preparation and selection of drugs. Acta Anaesthesiol Belg 1999;50(1):29–34.
4. Hall SC. The difficult pediatric airway—recognition, evaluation, and management. Can J Anaesth 2001;48:R1–5.
5. Myer CM, Cotton RT, Shott SR. *The Pediatric Airway: An Interdisciplinary Approach.* Philadelphia: JB Lippincott, 1995.
6. Bordet F, Allaouchiche B, Lansiaux S, et al. Risk factors for airway complications during general anaesthesia in paediatric patients. Paediatr Anaesth 2002 Nov;12(9):762–69.
7. Jacobs IN, Gray RF, Todd NW. Upper airway obstruction in children with Down syndrome. Arch Otolaryngol Head Neck Surg 1996 Sep;122(9):945–50.
8. Mitchell RB, Call E, Kelly J. Ear, nose and throat disorders in children with Down syndrome. Laryngoscope 2003 Feb;113(2):259–63.
9. Nargozian C, Ririe DG, Bennun RD, Mulliken JB. Hemifacial microsomia: anatomical prediction of difficult intubation. Paediatr Anaesth 1999;9(5):393–98.
10. Rudman DT, Elmaraghy CA, Shiels WE, Wiet GJ. The role of airway fluoroscopy in the evaluation of stridor in children. Arch Otolaryngol Head Neck Surg 2003 Mar;129(3):305–9.
11. Litman RS, Kottra JA, Berkowitz RJ, Ward DS. Upper airway obstruction during midazolam/nitrous oxide sedation in children with enlarged tonsils. Pediatr Dent 1998 Sep–Oct;20(5):318–20.

12. McGraw T. Preparing children for the operating room: psychological issues. Can J Anaesth 1994;41:1094–103.

13. Schofield NM, White JB. Interrelations among children, parents, premedication, and anaesthetists in paediatric day stay surgery. Br Med J 1989;299:1371–75.

14. Brosius KK, Bannister CF. Midazolam premedication in children: a comparison of two oral dosage formulations on sedation score and plasma midazolam levels. Anesth Analg 2003 Feb;96(2):392–95.

15. Hannallah RS. Pediatric ambulatory anesthesia: role of parents. J Clin Anesth 1995 Nov;7(7):597–99.

16. Kam PC, Voss TJ, Gold PD, Pitkin J. Behaviour of children associated with parental participation during induction of general anaesthesia. J Paediatr Child Health 1998 Feb;34(1):29–31.

17. Friesen RH, Wurl JL, Friesen RM. Duration of preoperative fast affects blood pressure response to halothane in infants. Anesth Analg 2002;95:1572–76.

18. Schreiner MS, Triebwasser A, Keon TP. Ingestion of liquids compared with preoperative fasting in pediatric outpatients. Anesthesiology 1990;72:593–97.

19. Splinter WM, Stewart JA, Muir JG. The effect of preoperative apple juice on gastric contents, thirst, and hunger in children. Can J Anaesth 1989;36:55–58.

20. Welborn LG, Norden JM, Seiden N, et al. Effect of minimizing preoperative fasting on perioperative blood glucose homeostasis in children. Paediatr Anaesth 1993;3:167–71.

21. Cote CJ. NPO after midnight for children: a reappraisal. Anesthesiology 1990;72:589–92.

22. Ferrari LR, Rooney FM, Rockoff MA. Preoperative fasting practices in pediatrics. Anesthesiology 1999;90:978–80.

23. American Society of Anesthesiologists Task Force on Preoperative Fasting. Practice guidelines for preoperative fasting and the use of pharmacologic agents to reduce the risk of pulmonary aspiration: application to healthy patients undergoing elective procedures. Anesthesiology 1999;90:896–905.

24. Friesen RH, Lichtor JL. Cardiovascular depression during halothane anesthesia in infants: a study of three induction techniques. Anesth Analg 1982;61:42–45.

25. Gregory GA, Eger EI II, Munson ES. The relationship between age and halothane requirements in man. Anesthesiology 1969;30:488–91.

26. Lerman J, Robinson S, Willis MM, Gregory GA. Anesthetic requirements for halothane in young children 0–1 month and 1–6 months of age. Anesthesiology 1983;59:421–24.

27. Diaz JH. Halothane anesthesia in infancy: identification and correlation of preoperative risk factors with intraoperative arterial hypotension and postoperative recovery. J Pediatr Surg 1985;20:502–7.

28. Friesen RH, Wurl JL, Charlton GA. Haemodynamic depression by halothane is age-related in paediatric patients. Paediatr Anaesth 2000;10:267–72.

29. Barash PG, Glanz S, Katz JD, et al. Ventricular function in children during halothane anesthesia: an echocardiographic evaluation. Anesthesiology 1978;49:79–85.

30. Epstein RH, Stein AL, Marr AT, Lessin JB. High concentration versus incremental induction of anesthesia with sevoflurane in children: a comparison of induction times, vital signs, and complications. J Clin Anesth 1998 Feb;10(1):41–45.

31. Kandasamy R, Sivalingam P. Use of sevoflurane in difficult airways. Acta Anaesthesiol Scand 2000 May;44(5):627–29.

32. Meretoja OA, Taivainen T, Raiha L, et al. Sevoflurane-nitrous oxide or halothane-nitrous oxide for paediatric bronchoscopy and gastroscopy. Br J Anaesth 1996 Jun;76(6):767–71.

33. Morimoto Y, Mayhew JF, Knox SL, Zornow MH. Rapid induction of anesthesia with high concentrations of halothane or sevoflurane in children. J Clin Anesth 2000 May;12(3):184–88.

34. Splinter W. Halothane: the end of an era? Anesth Analg 2002;95(6):1471.

35. Choudhury M, Saxena N. Total intravenous anaesthesia for tracheobronchial stenting in children. Anaesth Intens Care 2002 Jun;30(3):376–79.

36. Reber A, Geiduschek JM, Bobbia SA, et al. Effect of continuous positive airway pressure on the measurement of thoracoabdominal asynchrony and minute ventilation in children anesthetized with sevoflurane and nitrous oxide. Chest 2002 Aug;122(2):473–78.

37. Ebata T, Nishiki S, Masuda A, Amaha K. Anaesthesia for Treacher Collins syndrome using a laryngeal mask airway. Can J Anaesth 1991 Nov;38(8):1043–45.

38. Ellis DS, Potluri PK, O'Flaherty JE, Baum VC. Difficult airway management in the neonate: a simple method of intubating through a laryngeal mask airway. Paediatr Anaesth 1999;9(5):460–62.

39. Harnett M, Kinirons B, Heffernan A, et al. Airway complications in infants: comparison of laryngeal mask airway and the face mask–oral airway. Can J Anaesth 2000;47:315–18.

40. Inada T, Fujise K, Tachibana K, Shingu K. Orotracheal intubation through the laryngeal mask airway in paediatric patients with Treacher-Collins syndrome. Paediatr Anaesth 1995;5(2):129–32.

41. Selim M, Mowafi H, Al-Ghamdi A, Adu-Gyamfi Y. Intubation via LMA in pediatric patients with difficult airways. Can J Anaesth 1999 Sep;46(9):891–93.

42. Thomas PB, Parry MG. The difficult paediatric airway: a new method of intubation using the laryngeal mask airway, Cook airway exchange catheter and tracheal intubation fibrescope. Paediatr Anaesth 2001;11(5):618–21.

43. Walker RW. The laryngeal mask airway in the difficult paediatric airway: an assessment of positioning and use in fibreoptic intubation. Paediatr Anaesth 2000;10(1):53–58.

44. Derkay CS. Recurrent respiratory papillomatosis. Laryngoscope 2001 Jan;111(1):57–69.

45. Borland LM. Airway management for CO_2 laser surgery on the airway: Venturi jet ventilation and alternatives. Int Anesthesiol Clin 1997;35:99–106.

46. Dalmeida RE, Mayhew JF, Driscoll B, McLaughlin R. Total airway obstruction by papillomas during induction of general anesthesia. Anesth Analg 1996;83:1332–34.

47. Mattucci KF, Militana CJ. The prevention of fire during oropharyngeal electrosurgery. Ear Nose Throat J 2003;82(2):107–9.

48. Hall SC. Pediatric postanesthesia recovery care. J Clin Anesth 1995;7:600–5.

PONV: Prevention and Treatment in the Ambulatory Setting

ASHRAF S. HABIB • TONG J. GAN

INTRODUCTION

In the United States, over 60% of surgical procedures performed each year occur in an ambulatory setting.[1] Adequate control of postoperative nausea and vomiting (PONV) is one of the major goals of ambulatory anesthesia. While the incidence of PONV has decreased from 75% to 80% when ether and cyclopropane were used, the overall incidence of PONV has remained remarkably constant in the 20–30% range over the past two decades.[2,3] In certain high-risk patients the incidence is still as high as 70%.[4,5] Furthermore, it is estimated that approximately 0.2% of all patients may experience intractable PONV, leading to a delay in recovery room discharge and/or unanticipated hospital admission, thereby increasing medical costs.[6] The estimated cost of PONV to a busy ambulatory surgical unit was estimated to range from $0.25 million to $1.5 million per year in lost surgical revenue.[7]

Nausea and vomiting are also among the most unpleasant experiences associated with surgery and one of the most common reasons for poor patient satisfaction rating in the postoperative period.[8] Philip reported that patients ranked the absence of PONV as being more important than an earlier discharge from an ambulatory surgical unit.[9] Macario et al. quantified patients' preferences for postoperative outcomes. Postoperative nausea and vomiting were among the 10 most undesirable outcomes after surgery. Indeed, patients allocated the highest amount (about $30) to avoid PONV out of a total of $100 they were allowed to spend to avoid all complications.[10] Gan and colleagues also reported that surgical patients were willing to pay up to $100, at their own expense, to avoid PONV.[11]

In addition to the unpleasant experience and cost implications, PONV may also be rarely associated with serious complications such as wound dehiscence, pulmonary aspiration of gastric contents, hematoma formation beneath skin flaps, dehydration, electrolyte disturbances, Mallory-Weiss tear, and esophageal rupture.[12–14]

PHYSIOLOGY

PONV encompasses a triad of symptoms and signs. Nausea is typically described as a subjectively unpleasant sensation associated with the awareness of the urge to vomit. Vomiting is the actual physical phenomenon of the forceful expulsion of gastric contents from the mouth. Retching is physiologically similar to vomiting and is defined as the labored, spasmodic, rhythmic contractions of the respiratory muscles without expulsion of gastric contents.

The complex act of vomiting involves coordination of the respiratory, gastrointestinal, and abdominal musculature. It is controlled by the vomiting center, which is located in the lateral reticular formation of the medulla oblongata in close proximity to the nucleus of the solitary tract in the brain stem and has access to the motor pathways that are responsible for the visceral and somatic output involved in vomiting.[15] The vomiting reflex has two main detectors of the need to vomit: the gastrointestinal tract (GIT) and the chemoreceptor trigger zone (CTZ) in the area postrema.[16] The vagus is the major nerve involved in the detection of emetic stimuli from the GIT and has two types of afferent fibers involved in the emetic response: mechanoreceptors, located in the muscular wall of the gut, that are activated by contraction and distension of the gut as well as chemoreceptors, located in the mucosa of the upper gut, that are sensitive to noxious chemicals.[17] Stimulation of the vagal afferents leads to activation of the CTZ in the area postrema. The latter is a U-shaped structure a few millimeters long located on the dorsal surface of the medulla oblongata at the caudal end of the fourth ventricle. It is one of the circumventricular organs of the brain and is outside the blood-brain barrier and the cerebrospinal fluid (CSF) barrier, and thus can be activated by chemical stimuli received through the blood as well as the cerebrospinal fluid.[18] Several other stimuli can affect the vomiting center, including afferents from the oropharynx,

Table 39-1   Risk Factors for Postoperative Nausea and Vomiting (PONV)

Anesthetic Factors	Patient Factors	Surgical Factors
1. Volatile agents 2. Nitrous oxide 3. Opioids 4. High doses of neostigmine	1. Female gender 2. History of PONV or motion sickness 3. Nonsmoking status 4. Pain 5. High levels of anxiety	1. Long surgical procedures 2. Certain types of surgery (e.g., intra-abdominal; major gynecologic; laparoscopic; breast; ear, nose, and throat; strabismus)

mediastinum, peritoneum, and genitalia as well as afferents from the central nervous system (CNS) (cerebral cortex, labyrinthine, visual, and vestibular apparatus).[15]

Different types of receptors are involved in the transmission of impulses to the vomiting center. Cholinergic receptors are found in the vomiting center and vestibular nuclei. The area postrema is rich in dopamine (D_2), opioid, and serotonin 5-hydroxytryptamine 3 ($5\text{-}HT_3$) receptors.[19,20] The nucleus tractus solitarius is rich in enkephalins and in histaminic (H_1), muscarinic cholinergic, and neurokinin-1 (NK-1) receptors; the latter are also found in the dorsal motor nucleus of the vagus nerve.[21,22]

RISK FACTORS FOR PONV

Identification of patients at high risk for PONV enables targeting prophylaxis to those who will benefit most from it. Universal PONV prophylaxis is not cost-effective, is unlikely to benefit patients at low risk for PONV, and would put them at risk from the potential side effects of antiemetic agents. Patient-, anesthesia-, and surgery-related risk factors have been identified (Table 39-1). Anesthesia-related risk factors include the use of volatile agents, which cause PONV during the early postoperative period (within 0–2 hr),[23] nitrous oxide, which increases the risk for postoperative vomiting,[24] opioids,[5,23] and high doses of neostigmine (> 2.5 mg) for the reversal of neuromuscular blockade.[25] Patient-related factors include female gender,[5,26] history of PONV or motion sickness,[5,26,27] and nonsmoking status.[5,26] High levels of anxiety and postoperative pain, especially of pelvic or visceral origin, may also be associated with a higher incidence of PONV.[28–30]

While some studies reported an increased susceptibility to PONV during the first 7 days of the menstrual cycle,[31,32] this was not confirmed in other studies.[33] Recently, a systematic review of the results of all available studies suggested that the phase of the menstrual cycle had no impact on the occurrence of PONV.[34] Another recent systematic review also reported that an increased body mass index (BMI) is not a risk factor for PONV.[35] Long surgical procedures (each 30 min increase in duration increases PONV risk by about 60%)[26] and certain types of surgery also carry a greater risk of PONV.[4,26,36] In adults, high incidences of PONV are found in intra-abdominal surgery, major gynecologic surgery, laparoscopic surgery, breast surgery, neurosurgery, eye, and ear, nose, and throat (ENT) surgery. Pediatric operations at high risk for PONV include strabismus, adenotonsillectomy, hernia repair, orchidopexy, penile surgery, and middle-ear procedures.[37–39] In a prospective study of 2722 patients, how-

ever, Apfel et al. could not demonstrate an association between type of surgery and the risk of PONV.[5] They suggested that the high incidence of PONV after certain operations might be caused by the involvement of high-risk patients. The incidence of PONV increases after the age of 3 years with a peak incidence of about 40% in the 11–14-year age group.[5,40,41] Prior to puberty, gender differences for postoperative vomiting have not been identified.[42] A number of PONV risk scores have been developed. These are summarized in Table 39-2.

CURRENTLY AVAILABLE OPTIONS FOR THE PROPHYLAXIS AND TREATMENT OF PONV

A number of strategies are available for the prophylaxis and treatment of PONV. In the ambulatory setting, the ideal antiemetic agent should be highly efficacious, free from

Table 39-2   PONV Risk Scores

Author [n patients]	Score	
Palazzo[146] [147]	Log_{it} postoperative sickness = $-5.03 + 2.24$ (postoperative opioids) $+ 3.97$ (previous sickness history) $+ 2.4$ (gender) $+ 0.78$ (history of motion sickness) $- 3.2$ (gender $\times$ previous sickness history)	
Koivuranta[27] [1107]	Score = 0.93 (if female) + 0.82 (if previous PONV) + 0.75 (if duration of surgery over 60 min) + 0.61 (if nonsmoker) + 0.59 (if history of motion sickness)	
Apfel[5] [2722]	Risk factors 1. Female gender 2. History of motion sickness or PONV 3. Nonsmoker 4. Use of postoperative opioids	Risk of PONV 1. 10% if 0 factors 2. 21% if 1 factor 3. 39% if 2 factors 4. 61% if 3 factors 5. 79% if 4 factors

Table 39-3   Options Available for the Management of PONV

A. Pharmacologic techniques
  a. Monotherapy
    i. Older-generation antiemetics:
      1. Phenothiazines: aliphatic (promethazine, chlorpromazine), heterocyclic (perphenazine, prochlorperazine)
      2. Butyrophenones: droperidol, haloperidol
      3. Benzamides: metoclopramide, domperidone
      4. Anticholinergics: scopolamine
      5. Antihistamines: ethanolamines (dimenhydrinate, diphenhydramine), piperazines (cyclizine, hydroxyzine, meclizine)
    ii. Newer-generation antiemetics
      1. Serotonin 5-hydroxytryptamine 3 (5-HT_3) receptor antagonists: ondansetron, granisetron, dolasetron, tropisetron
      2. Neurokinin-1 (NK-1) receptor antagonists
    iii. Nontraditional antiemetics: dexamethasone, propofol
  b. Combination of two or more of the above antiemetics
    i. 5-HT_3 receptor antagonists + droperidol
    ii. 5-HT_3 receptor antagonists + dexamethasone
    iii. Other combinations
B. Nonpharmacologic techniques: acupuncture, acupressure, laser stimulation of the P6 point, transcutaneous acupoint electrical stimulation, hypnosis
C. Additional measures with potential antiemetic effects
  c. Ephedrine
  d. Supplemental oxygen
  e. Benzodiazepines
  f. Adequate hydration
  g. Good pain relief
  h. Alpha-2 adrenergic agonists
D. Multimodal approach

SOURCE: Reproduced with permission from Habib AS, Gan TJ. Evidence-based management of postoperative nausea and vomiting: a review. Can J Anaesth 2004;51:326–41.

side effects notably sedation, have a long duration of action to cover the postdischarge period, and be cheap. Unfortunately, none of the currently available antiemetics possesses all of these characteristics. Table 39-3 lists the different options currently available for PONV management.

Serotonin Receptor Antagonists

The 5-HT_3 receptor antagonists are highly specific and selective for nausea and vomiting. Members of this group exert their effects by binding to the 5-HT_3 receptor in the CTZ and at vagal afferents in the gastrointestinal tract. Their favorable side effects profile, and in particular the lack of sedation, makes them particularly suitable for ambulatory surgery. However, these agents are still under patent and consequently more expensive compared with the older-generation traditional antiemetics.

Ondansetron was the first member of this group to be marketed in the United States and was the most widely studied. The antivomiting efficacy of ondansetron is better than its antinausea efficacy.[43] It is most effective when given at the end of surgery.[44,45] The recommended dose for prophylaxis is 4–8 mg intravenous (IV) in adults and

50–100 µg/kg in children.[43] The best number needed to treat (NNT) to prevent PONV with the best documented regimen for ondansetron was 5–6. This was achieved with a dose of 8 mg intravenously and 16 mg orally.[43] The side effects of ondansetron include headache (number needed to harm [NNH] = 36), dizziness, flushing, elevated liver enzymes (NNH = 31), and constipation (NNH = 23).[43]

Dolasetron is structurally related to tropisetron and granisetron. The recommended IV dose for the prophylaxis and treatment of PONV is 12.5 mg.[46] The timing of administration of dolasetron appears to have little effect on its efficacy when administered for the prophylaxis of PONV.[47] Dolasetron is a prodrug and has to be metabolized into hydrodolasetron, its active moiety, to exert its antiemetic effect.

Tropisetron has been studied in Europe and showed efficacy in the management of PONV. The recommended prophylactic dose is 2–5 mg.[48] The NNT (95% Confidence Interval [CI]) for the prevention of nausea, vomiting, and PONV combined at 24 hr postoperatively were 7 (5–11), 5 (4–8), and 5 (4–6), respectively.[48]

Granisetron has also been used for the management of PONV in a dose of 0.35–3 mg.[49,50] Although most studies have demonstrated efficacy at 1 mg for prophylaxis, a recent study suggested it might be efficacious at lower doses.[51] For the treatment of established PONV, a dose of 0.1 mg was found to be efficacious.[52]

Ramosetron is another 5-HT$_3$ receptor antagonist with general properties similar to those of ondansetron. It is used in the management of nausea and vomiting induced by cancer chemotherapy. It has also been shown to be effective for PONV prophylaxis in a dose of 0.3 mg given at the end of surgery.[53]

There is no evidence that there is any difference in efficacy between the various 5-HT$_3$ receptor antagonists when appropriate doses are used. Therefore, acquisition cost is the main factor that differentiates the 5-HT$_3$ compounds from one another.[42]

Steroids

The mechanism of the antiemetic action of corticosteroids is not well understood. An anti-inflammatory and/or membrane-stabilizing effect may play a role.[54] The release of endorphins resulting in mood elevation, a sense of well-being, and appetite stimulation may also underlie the antiemetic properties of corticosteroids.[55] A recent study suggests that betamethasone has no effect on ipecacuanha-induced vomiting, a serotonin-mediated pathway.[56]

After the successful use of dexamethasone in the prevention and treatment of chemotherapy-induced emesis; this agent has been evaluated and found to be effective for the management of PONV.[57,58] It has the advantages of being cheap, devoid of sedative adverse effects, and long-acting. The recommended dose is 5–10 mg in adults[59–61] and 150 μg/kg in children.[60] More recently, smaller doses (2.5–5 mg) have been found to be effective.[59,62] Dexamethasone appears to be most effective when administered prior to induction of anesthesia, rather than at the end, in preventing early PONV (0–2 hr).[62] There are no reports of dexamethasone-related adverse effects in the doses used for the management of PONV.[60] The long duration of action of dexamethasone makes it particularly effective for the control of late PONV. The NNT (95% CI) for the prevention of early (0–6 hr postoperatively) and late (0–24 hr postoperatively) nausea with 8 mg dexamethasone were 5 (2.2–21) and 4.3 (2.3–26), respectively. For early and late vomiting, the NNT (95% CI) for early and late vomiting were 3.6 (2.3–8) and 4.3 (2.6–12), respectively.[60]

Propofol

The mechanism of the antiemetic action of propofol is not known. It is not due to the intralipid emulsion in the formulation and propofol appears to have direct antiemetic property.[63] A recent study demonstrated that propofol infusion was associated with a reduction in the levels of serotonin and its metabolite, 5-hydroxy-indole acetic acid (5-HIAA), in the area postrema and CSF.[64]

Total intravenous anesthesia (TIVA) with propofol is associated with a lower incidence of PONV compared with inhalational agents.[65–67] In one study, this technique was equally efficacious to ondansetron 4 mg in the prevention of PONV.[4] The antiemetic effect of propofol is most pro-

nounced in the early postoperative period. It is not useful for PONV prophylaxis if given only as a bolus for induction of anesthesia.[68] Continuous subhypnotic propofol infusion and the use of patient-controlled antiemesis (PCAE) with propofol were also found to be effective in the treatment of PONV.[69,70] The effective plasma concentration of propofol for the 50% reduction in nausea scores has been found to be 343 ng/mL. This is much lower than the range required for sedation (900–1,300 ng/mL) and anesthesia (3000–10,000 ng/mL).[71]

Older-Generation Antiemetics

The use of some of the older-generation antiemetics is limited in the ambulatory setting owing to their side effects, notably sedation. Furthermore, there is a lack of recent well-designed trials investigating the use of low doses of these agents.

Butyrophenones

The neuroleptic drugs haloperidol and droperidol have significant antiemetic effects. They are strong D$_2$ receptor antagonists that act at the CTZ and area postrema. Droperidol acts centrally to modulate the actions of dopamine, norepinephrine, and serotonin. It has been suggested that droperidol may occupy gamma-aminobutyric acid (GABA) receptors postsynaptically, resulting in decreased neurotransmission with a buildup of dopamine in the intersynaptic cleft. This results in an imbalance of dopamine and acetylcholine, which alters the normal transmission of impulses in the CNS.[72,73] Since this can occur in the CTZ, it is thought that this may be the mechanism by which droperidol exerts its antiemetic effect.[74]

Droperidol has been extensively used in anesthesia. In a dose of 1.25 mg, it was more cost-effective than ondansetron 4 mg and was recommended as a first-line agent for PONV prophylaxis.[75] The NNT to prevent early nausea was 5. For both early and late vomiting, the best efficacy was with 1.5–2.5 mg (NNT = 7).[76] In children, the recommended dose is 50–75 μg/kg with a NNT of 4.[76] It has a long duration of action (as long as 24 hr following administration) probably owing to its strong binding affinity to the emetic receptors, even though its half-life is relatively short (3 hr).[77] Droperidol is most effective when given at the end of surgery.[76] It is also effective when given concomitantly with a patient-controlled analgesia (PCA) system using morphine with a NNT (95% CI) of 5.1 (3.1–15) and 3.1 (2.3–4.8) for the prevention of nausea and vomiting, respectively, over the first 24 hr postoperatively.[78] Sedation and drowsiness are important side effects of droperidol and are dose-dependent. Low doses of droperidol (0.625–1.25 mg) were not associated with any increased sedation or prolongation of PACU stay compared to ondansetron 4 mg.[79]

In December 2001, the Food and Drug Administration (FDA) issued a new 'black box' warning on droperidol, which is the most serious warning for a FDA-approved drug. The FDA noted that its use has been associated with QT-segment prolongation and/or torsades de pointes, and in some cases resulted in fatal cardiac arrhythmias. The incidence of cardiac adverse events after the administration of droperidol has been estimated at 74 in 11 million. Following the black box warning, there has been a 10-fold decrease in the use of droperidol in the United States.[80] The black box warning on droperidol was, however, challenged by a number of experts in the field.[81]

Benzamides

Metoclopramide is the most commonly used antiemetic in this group. It is a prokinetic agent that blocks D_2 receptors in the gastrointestinal tract and centrally at the CTZ and area postrema. It also increases lower esophageal sphincter tone and enhances gastric motility, which may prevent the delayed gastric emptying caused by opioids.[82] In addition, metoclopramide possesses parasympathomimetic activity. At high concentrations, it has been shown to have weak serotonin receptor antagonistic effect.[83] High-dose metoclopramide (1–2 mg/kg) has been used successfully in the management of chemotherapy-induced emesis. In order to reduce the side effects seen with these doses, notably sedation and dystonic reactions, lower doses (0.1–0.2 mg/kg) have been employed in the management of PONV. However, the efficacy of metoclopramide in preventing PONV at these doses is uncertain, with approximately 50% of studies showing it to be no more effective than placebo.[84] In a systematic review of randomized placebo-controlled studies involving metoclopramide, Henzi et al. reported that there was no significant antinausea effect. The NNT to prevent early (0–6 hr) and late (within 48 hr) vomiting were 9.1 and 10, respectively.[85] A recent study, however, suggested that 20 mg might be an efficacious dose.[86]

Anticholinergics and Antihistamines

Anticholinergics are one of the oldest classes of antiemetics. They block muscarinic cholinergic CNS emetic receptors in the cerebral cortex and pons.[40] Atropine and scopolamine are tertiary amines that cross the blood-brain barrier and have efficacy against motion sickness and PONV.[87] Scopolamine has the most potent antiemetic properties in this class of drugs with a NNT of 3.8 for the prevention of PONV.[88] The transdermal preparation should be applied the evening prior to or 4 hr before the end of surgery.[88] Its limitations include a 2–4 hr onset of effect, as well as its medical contraindications and age-related considerations.[89] The NNH for the most commonly reported side effects was 5.6, 12.5, 50, and 100 for dry mouth, visual disturbances, dizziness, and agitation, respectively.[88]

The antihistamines include the ethanolamines (dimenhydrinate, diphenhydramine) and the piperazines (cyclizine, hydroxyzine, meclizine). They act by blocking acetylcholine receptors in the vestibular apparatus and histamine H_1 receptors in the nucleus of the solitary tract. The NNT (95% CI) to stay completely free from nausea with dimenhydrinate was 8 (3–20) during the first 6 hr postoperatively and 6 (3–33) for the period from 0 to 48 hr. For vomiting, the NNT (95% CI) was 7 (4–50) and 5 (3–8) for the early and the 48-hr period, respectively.[90] Cyclizine 50 mg IV/intramuscular (IM) is used extensively for the

prophylaxis and treatment of PONV in the United Kingdom.[91] The parenteral formulation is not available, however, in the United States. The major disadvantages of the antihistamines include sedation, dry mouth, blurred vision, urinary retention, and delayed recovery room discharge.[92]

Phenothiazines

The antiemetic effects of phenothiazines have been attributed to blockade of D_2 receptors in the CTZ. They also have moderate antihistaminergic and anticholinergic actions. The phenothiazines have an aliphatic or heterocyclic ring attached to the tenth position of a tricyclic nucleus. The aliphatic phenothiazines (promethazine, chlorpromazine) have less antiemetic potency and more sedative effects than the heterocyclic phenothiazines (perphenazine, prochlorperazine).[22,93] Promethazine is an effective antiemetic with a long duration of action. In a dose of 12.5–25 mg given toward the end of surgery, it has been shown to be effective for PONV management.[94] Its use, however, is limited by sedation and prolonged recovery from anesthesia.[84] A recent study, however, did not show increased awakening time or duration of postanesthesia care unit (PACU) stay when promethazine 25 mg IV was compared to ondansetron 4 mg IV and placebo in patients undergoing middle-ear surgery.[94] The use of lower doses of promethazine (6.25 mg) has not been investigated in clinical trials. Similarly, chlorpromazine demonstrated efficacy in the prevention and treatment of PONV.[22,95] Its many side effects, particularly sedation and hypotension, limit its use as an antiemetic.

The heterocyclic phenothiazines (prochlorperazine and perphenazine) have been used extensively in the management of PONV. Both have similar antiemetic efficacy, but perphenazine causes more sedation.[22,93] These compounds have, however, a higher incidence of extrapyramidal side effects, including akathesia, acute dystonias, and tardive dyskinesia.[54] Other side effects of the phenothiazines include hypotension, restlessness, anticholinergic side effects, and the neuroleptic malignant syndrome.[84]

Nonpharmacologic Techniques

Several investigators have shown a useful effect of nonpharmacologic methods in the management of PONV. A few studies, however, failed to demonstrate a beneficial effect. Lee and Done performed a systematic review of 24 randomized trials of acupuncture, electroacupuncture, transcutaneous electrical nerve stimulation, acupoint stimulation, and acupressure. They found that there was a significant reduction in early PONV (0–6 hr) in adults treated with acupuncture compared with placebo and that antiemetics (metoclopramide, cyclizine, droperidol, prochlorperazine) versus acupuncture techniques were comparable in preventing early and late (0–48 hr) PONV in adults. These techniques were more effective for controlling nausea than vomiting. In children, however, no benefit was found.[96] More recently, however, the effectiveness of acupuncture for the prophylaxis of PONV in children has been demonstrated.[97–100] In a recent randomized, placebo-controlled study in patients undergoing breast surgery; Gan and colleagues reported similar efficacy of electroacupuncture at the P6 point and prophylactic ondansetron. Of interest, electroacupuncture patients reported less pain compared with the other groups.[101] The comparable efficacy of acupoint electrical stimulation to ondansetron for both the prophylaxis and treatment of PONV was also confirmed in two recent studies in ambulatory patients. When used for prophylaxis, the combination of ondansetron and acupoint electrical stimulation was associated with lower incidence of PONV, less need for rescue antiemetics, as well as improved quality of recovery and patient satisfaction, compared to ondansetron alone.[102,103] Hypnosis has also been found effective when compared with placebo.[104] Although some earlier reports suggested that ginger root might have a beneficial effect for PONV prophylaxis, this has not been confirmed in a recent meta-analysis.[105]

Other Interventions with Potential Antiemetic Effects

Benzodiazepines

Benzodiazepines were found to be effective for the prophylaxis of PONV.[106–108] The successful use of midazolam in cases of persistent PONV and after failure of other antiemetics has also been described.[109–111] The suggested mechanism of the antiemetic effect of midazolam is by decreasing dopamine input at the CTZ in addition to decreasing anxiety. It may also decrease adenosine reuptake leading to reduced synthesis, release, and postsynaptic action of dopamine at the CTZ.[110] Alternatively, midazolam may reduce serotonin release by binding to the GABA benzodiazepine complex.[112]

Ephedrine

Intramuscular ephedrine (0.5 mg/kg) has been shown to be effective for PONV prophylaxis, especially in the early postoperative period (0–3 hr).[113–115] It has also been suggested that ephedrine might have a specific antiemetic effect, as there was no difference in postoperative blood pressure between the ephedrine- and the placebo-treated patients.[115]

Alpha-2 Adrenergic Agonists

Alpha-2 adrenergic agonists significantly reduce the incidence of PONV in both children and adults.[116,117] It has been suggested that the antiemetic effect of clonidine might be secondary to a reduction in the use of volatile agents and opioids, or a reduction in sympathetic tone.[117]

Supplemental Oxygen

In two studies by one group, oxygen supplementation (80%) intraoperatively or both intraoperatively and for 2 hr postoperatively was effective in achieving a significant reduction in the incidence of PONV compared to patients receiving 30% oxygen.[118,119] The authors suggested that supplemental oxygen might reduce PONV by ameliorating subtle intestinal ischemia, thereby reducing release of serotonin and other emetogenic substances from compromised bowel.[119] A more recent study in women undergoing ambulatory gynecologic surgery did, however, call into question the efficacy of supplemental oxygen. In this study, there was no difference in the incidence of PONV between patients who received 80% and 30% oxygen given intraoperatively and for up to 1 hr postoperatively.[120] Similarly, in patients undergoing breast surgery the perioperative administration of 50% oxygen was not effective in reducing the incidence of PONV compared to 30% oxygen.[121]

Hydration

In patients undergoing ambulatory surgery, the administration of 20 mL/kg bolus of an isotonic solution preoperatively was associated with significantly less nausea on the first postoperative day, compared to patients who received a bolus of 2 mL/kg.[122] The precise mechanism is not known but may be related to a better perfusion of the gastrointestinal tract, thus reducing the release of peripheral serotonin from the gut.[123] In a more recent study, a combination of colloid and crystalloid fluid resuscitation was associated with less PONV and less use of rescue antiemetics, compared with the administration of crystalloids alone, in patients undergoing major abdominal procedures.[124]

Combination Antiemetic Therapy and the Multimodal Approach

Since none of the available antiemetics is entirely effective for preventing PONV, especially in high-risk patients, there has been a growing interest in investigating the efficacy of combining antiemetics from different classes. In addition to enhancing efficacy, a synergistic interaction between a combination of two or more antiemetics might also permit a reduction in total dose, thereby reducing side effects. The available literature clearly demonstrates improved PONV prophylaxis when using a combination of agents compared to monotherapy.[60,125] The most commonly studied combinations have included a 5-HT$_3$ receptor antagonist combined with either droperidol or dexamethasone. Both combination regimens are equally efficacious with a similar side effects profile.[126,127] The addition of TIVA with propofol to a combination of ondansetron and droperidol further improved antiemetic efficacy.[128] In patients undergoing office-based surgery the addition of ondansetron or dolasetron to a combination of dexamethasone and droperidol increased cost but did not result in a better PONV prophylaxis.[129]

As the etiology of PONV is multifactorial, a more improved prophylaxis might be achieved by the adoption of a multimodal approach to the management of PONV. This approach involves a combination of antiemetics that block different receptors in the CNS, use of less emetogenic anes-

Table 39-4   Strategies to Keep the Baseline Risk of PONV Low

A. Use of regional anesthesia
B. Avoid emetogenic stimuli
    Nitrous oxide
    Inhalational agents
    Etomidate and ketamine
C. Minimize the following:
    Intraoperative and postoperative opioids. Adequate analgesia should, however, be achieved by incorporating local anesthetics, nonsteroidal anti-inflammatory drugs (NSAIDs), and opioids as required.
    The dose of neostigmine. Consider limiting the dose to a maximum of 2.5 mg in adults.
D. Consider the following:
    Total intravenous anesthesia (TIVA) with propofol
    Adequate hydration, especially with colloids
    Use of intraoperative supplemental oxygen (Inspiratory oxygen fraction [FiO_2] = 0.8)
    Anxiolytics, e.g., benzodiazepines
    Nonpharmacologic techniques, e.g., acupuncture
    Alpha-2-adrenergic agonists, e.g., clonidine

SOURCE: Reproduced with permission from Habib AS, Gan TJ. Evidence-based management of postoperative nausea and vomiting: a review. Can J Anaesth 2004;51:326–41.

thesia techniques, adequate IV hydration, and effective pain control involving both opioid and nonopioid analgesics. Table 39-4 describes a number of strategies for keeping the baseline risk of PONV low.

Scuderi et al. tested a multimodal approach to the management of PONV in women undergoing outpatient laparoscopy. Their multimodal critical-care algorithm consisted of TIVA with propofol and remifentanil, no nitrous oxide, no neuromuscular blockade, aggressive IV hydration (25 mL/kg), triple prophylactic antiemetics (ondansetron 1 mg, droperidol 0.625 mg, and dexamethasone 10 mg), and ketorolac 30 mg. Control groups included standard balanced outpatient anesthetic with or without 4 mg ondansetron prophylaxis. Multimodal management resulted in a 98% complete response rate (no PONV and no antiemetic rescue) in the PACU. No patient in this group vomited before discharge, compared with 7% of patients in ondansetron group and 22% of patients in the placebo group.[130] Subsequently, more studies confirmed the efficacy of a multimodal approach, especially in high-risk patients.[131,132]

POSTDISCHARGE NAUSEA AND VOMITING

While the prophylaxis and management of PONV occurring in the PACU has significantly improved, nausea and vomiting occurring after discharge from PACU remains undertreated. Nausea and vomiting occurring in the PACU

may not accurately predict the incidence after discharge. Approximately 36% of patients who experience postdischarge nausea and vomiting do not experience any nausea or vomiting prior to discharge. In an analysis of all studies evaluating patient-reported symptoms after outpatient surgery, the overall incidence of nausea and vomiting occurring following discharge from hospital has been estimated to be 17% (range 0–55%) and 8% (range 0–16%) respectively.[133] This not only leads to a delay in resumption of daily activities, but also can be distressing to the patients in the absence of available treatment.[134] Most of the available antiemetics have short half-lives and may not be effective after discharge. In a recent meta-analysis, the NNT to prevent postdischarge nausea after ambulatory surgery was 12.9, 12.2, and 5.2 after the prophylactic administration of ondansetron 4 mg, dexamethasone, and a combination of two antiemetics, respectively. For postdischarge vomiting, the NNT was 13.8 for ondansetron 4 mg and 5 for combination treatment. In this analysis, droperidol was not effective for the prophylaxis against postdischarge nausea and vomiting. These results suggest that prophylaxis with a single agent should not be used routinely in low-risk ambulatory patients and that high-risk patients are best managed with a combination strategy.[135]

RECOMMENDED STRATEGY FOR PONV PROPHYLAXIS

The risk of PONV should be estimated for each patient. No prophylaxis is recommended for patients at low risk for PONV except if they are at risk for medical consequences from vomiting, e.g., patients with wired jaws. For patients at moderate to high risk for PONV, regional anesthesia should be considered as there is an 11-fold increased risk for PONV in patients receiving general anesthesia compared to those receiving a regional anesthetic.[26] If this is not possible or contraindicated and a general anesthetic is used, a multimodal approach to the management of PONV should be considered to keep the baseline risk of PONV low (Table 39-4).

Combination antiemetic therapy is superior to monotherapy for PONV prophylaxis.[60,136,137] The addition of TIVA to a combination of two antiemetics results in a further improved prophylaxis.[128] Figure 39-1 illustrates a suggested algorithm for PONV prophylaxis.

RECOMMENDATIONS FOR THE TREATMENT OF ESTABLISHED PONV

There is a paucity of data on the use of antiemetics for the treatment of PONV in patients who failed prophylaxis or did not receive prophylaxis.

The 5-HT_3 receptor antagonists were the most commonly tested drugs in rescue trials. Similar to their use in PONV prophylaxis, the antivomiting efficacy of the 5-HT_3 receptor antagonists is more pronounced than their antinausea efficacy. There is no evidence of dose-responsiveness for these agents when used for rescue. Therefore, small

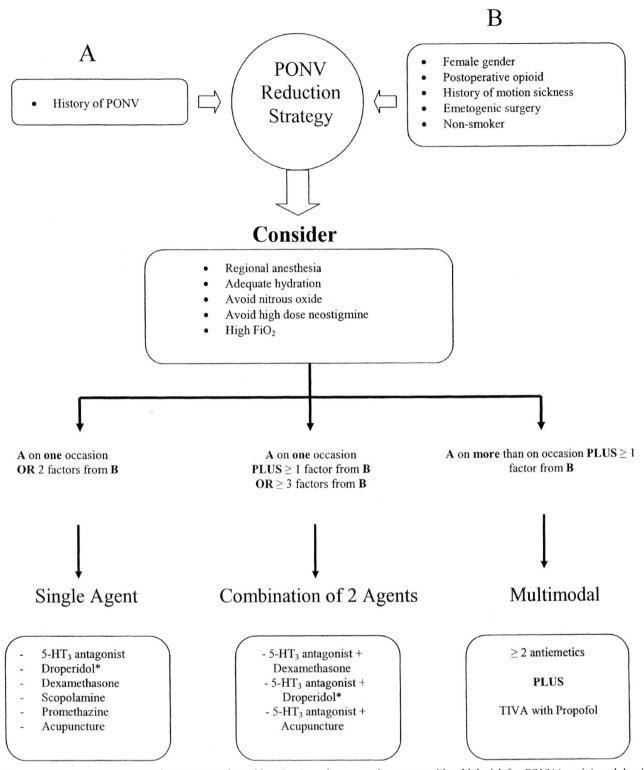

Figure 39-1   PONV: postoperative nausea and vomiting. Emetogenic surgery is surgery with a high risk for PONV (e.g., intra-abdominal surgery, gynecologic surgery, breast surgery, strabismus surgery, and ear, nose, and throat surgery). *Consider the FDA's "black box" warning on droperidol. (Reproduced with permission from Habib AS, Gan TJ. Evidence-based management of postoperative nausea and vomiting: a review. Can J Anaesth 2004;51:326–41.)

doses of these agents have been recommended for treatment: ondansetron 1 mg, dolasetron 12.5 mg, granisetron 0.1 mg, and tropisetron 0.5 mg.[138]

In patients who fail ondansetron prophylaxis, there is evidence to suggest that the use of ondansetron for rescue is no more effective than placebo.[139] A drug acting at a different receptor might be more effective in this case.[140] There are some data from chemotherapy-induced nausea and vomiting to suggest that granisetron might be efficacious for treating patients who fail ondansetron prophylaxis.[141,142] Such evidence is lacking in the PONV literature. There is also a striking lack of evidence on the therapeutic efficacy of older-generation antiemetics in the treatment of established PONV. Droperidol was not different from ondansetron when used for the treatment of established PONV.[143] On the other hand, ondansetron 4 mg was more effective than metoclopramide 10 mg in the treatment of established PONV.[144,145]

When evaluating PONV after surgery, the role of medication and mechanical factors should be considered first. Such contributing factors might include opiates, blood draining down the throat, or bowel obstruction. Then rescue therapy can be initiated. If PONV occurs within 6 hr postoperatively, patients should not receive a repeat dose of the prophylactic antiemetic; a drug from a different class should be used for rescue. Beyond 6 hr, PONV can be treated with any of the agents used for prophylaxis except dexamethasone and scopolamine, which are longer-acting.

SUMMARY

Ambulatory surgery is continuing to grow in the United States. PONV is a major problem in this setting as it prolongs the time to discharge and reduces patient satisfaction. The risk of PONV should be evaluated in every patient. No prophylaxis is warranted for patients at low risk for PONV unless there is risk of medical sequelae from vomiting. The first step in reducing PONV risk is to reduce baseline risk factors. For patients at moderate to high risk, antiemetics should be used either as monotherapy or in combination for PONV prophylaxis. There is increasing evidence that a better prophylaxis might be achieved by using a combination of agents acting at different receptors. The incidence of nausea and vomiting occurring after discharge from the ambulatory surgery center is also significantly decreased by using a combination regimen. The adoption of a multimodal approach to the management of PONV should be considered in patients at high risk for PONV. In patients who develop PONV despite receiving prophylaxis, an antiemetic acting at a different receptor should be used for rescue within the first 6 hr after surgery. After 6 hr, PONV can be treated with any of the drugs used for prophylaxis except dexamethasone and scopolamine.

REFERENCES

1. *Vital and Health Statistics: Ambulatory and Inpatient Procedures in the US.* Atlanta, GA: Centers for Disease Control, 1996.

2. Bonica J, Crepps W, Monk B, Bennett B. Post-anesthetic nausea, retching and vomiting. Anesthesiology 1958;19:532–40.

3. Cohen MM, Duncan PG, DeBoer DP, Tweed WA. The postoperative interview: assessing risk factors for nausea and vomiting. Anesth Analg 1994;78:7–16.

4. Gan TJ, Ginsberg B, Grant AP, Glass PS. Double-blind, randomized comparison of ondansetron and intraoperative propofol to prevent postoperative nausea and vomiting. Anesthesiology 1996;85: 1036–42.

5. Apfel CC, Laara E, Koivuranta M, Greim CA, Roewer N. A simplified risk score for predicting postoperative nausea and vomiting: conclusions from cross-validations between two centers. Anesthesiology 1999;91:693–700.

6. Gold BS, Kitz DS, Lecky JH, Neuhaus JM. Unanticipated admission to the hospital following ambulatory surgery. JAMA 1989;262: 3008–10.

7. Hirsch J. Impact of postoperative nausea and vomiting in the surgical setting. Anaesthesia 1994;49:30–33.

8. Myles PS, Williams DL, Hendrata M, Anderson H, Weeks AM. Patient satisfaction after anaesthesia and surgery: results of a prospective survey of 10,811 patients. Br J Anaesth 2000;84:6–10.

9. Philip BK. Patients' assessment of ambulatory anesthesia and surgery. J Clin Anesth 1992;4:355–58.

10. Macario A, Weinger M, Carney S, Kim A. Which clinical anesthesia outcomes are important to avoid? The perspective of patients. Anesth Analg 1999;89:652–58.

11. Gan T, Sloan F, Dear Gde L, El-Moalem HE, Lubarsky DA. How much are patients willing to pay to avoid postoperative nausea and vomiting? Anesth Analg 2001;92:393–400.

12. Watcha MF, White PF. Postoperative nausea and vomiting: its etiology, treatment, and prevention. Anesthesiology 1992;77:162–84.

13. Wilder-Smith OH, Martin NC, Morabia A. Postoperative nausea and vomiting: a comparative survey of the attitudes, perceptions, and practice of Swiss anesthesiologists and surgeons. Anesth Analg 1997;84:826–31.

14. Kapur PA. The big "little problem." Anesth Analg 1991;73: 243–45.

15. Wang SC, Borrison HL. A new concept in the organization of the central emetic mechanisms: recent studies on the site of action of apomorphine, copper sulphate and cardiac glycosides. Gastroenterology 1952;22:1–12.

16. Andrews PLR. Vagal afferent innervation of the gastrointestinal tract. In: Cevero F, Morrison JFB (eds.): *Progress in Brain Research*, Vol. 67. London: Elsevier Science Publishers, 1986, pp. 65–86.

17. Leslie RA. Comparative aspects of the area postrema: fine-structural considerations help to determine its function. Cell Mol Neurobiol 1986;6:95–120.

18. Stafanini E, Clement-Cormier Y. Detection of dopamine receptors in the area postrema. Eur J Pharmacol 1981;74:257–60.

19. Waeber C, Dixon K, Hoyer D, Palacios JM. Localisation by autoradiography of neuronal 5-HT$_3$ receptors in the mouse CNS. Eur J Pharmacol 1988;151:351–52.

20. Palacios JM, Wamsley JK, Kuhar MJ. The distribution of histamine H1-receptors in the rat brain: an autoradiographic study. Neuroscience 1981;6:15–37.

21. Wamsley JK, Lewis MS, Young WS III, Kuhar MJ. Autoradiographic localization of muscarinic cholinergic receptors in rat brainstem. J Neurosci 1981;1:176–91.

22. Howat DDC. Anti-emetic drugs in anaesthesia; a double blind trial of two phenothiazine derivatives. Anaesthesia 1960;15:289–97.

23. Apfel CC, Kranke P, Katz MH, Goepfert C, Papenfuss T, Rauch S, Heineck R, Greim CA, Roewer N. Volatile anaesthetics may be the main cause of early but not delayed postoperative vomiting: a randomized controlled trial of factorial design. Br J Anaesth 2002; 88:659–68.

24. Tramer M, Moore A, McQuay H. Omitting nitrous oxide in general anaesthesia: meta-analysis of intraoperative awareness and postop-

erative emesis in randomized controlled trials. Br J Anaesth 1996; 76:186–93.

25. Tramer MR, Fuchs-Buder T. Omitting antagonism of neuromuscular block: effect on postoperative nausea and vomiting and risk of residual paralysis: a systematic review. Br J Anaesth 1999;82: 379–86.

26. Sinclair DR, Chung F, Mezei G. Can postoperative nausea and vomiting be predicted? Anesthesiology 1999;91:109–18.

27. Koivuranta M, Laara E, Snare L, Alahuhta S. A survey of postoperative nausea and vomiting. Anaesthesia 1997;52:443–49.

28. Andersen R, Krohg K. Pain as a major cause of postoperative nausea. Can Anaesth Soc J 1976;23:366–69.

29. Jenkins LC, Lahay D. Central mechanisms of vomiting related to catecholamine response: anaesthetic implication. Can Anaesth Soc J 1971;18:434–41.

30. Rees MR, Clark RA, Holdsworth CD, Barber DC, Howlett PJ. The effect of beta-adrenoceptor agonists and antagonists on gastric emptying in man. Br J Clin Pharmacol 1980;10:551–54.

31. Beattie WS, Lindblad T, Buckley DN, Forrest JB. Menstruation increases the risk of nausea and vomiting after laparoscopy: a prospective randomized study. Anesthesiology 1993;78:272–76.

32. Honkavaara P, Lehtinen AM, Hovorka J, Korttila K. Nausea and vomiting after gynaecological laparoscopy depends upon the phase of the menstrual cycle. Can J Anaesth 1991;38:876–79.

33. Gratz I, Allen E, Afshar M, Joslyn AF, Buxbaum J, Prilliman B. The effects of the menstrual cycle on the incidence of emesis and efficacy of ondansetron. Anesth Analg 1996;83:565–69.

34. Eberhart LH, Morin AM, Georgieff M. [The menstruation cycle in the postoperative phase: its effect of the incidence of nausea and vomiting]. Anaesthesist 2000;49:532–35.

35. Kranke P, Apfel CC, Papenfuss T, Rauch S, Lobmann U, Rubsam B, Greim CA, Roewer N. An increased body mass index is no risk factor for postoperative nausea and vomiting: a systematic review and results of original data. Acta Anaesthesiol Scand 2001;45:160–66.

36. Fabling JM, Gan TJ, El-Moalem HE, Warner DS, Borel CO. A randomized, double-blinded comparison of ondansetron, droperidol, and placebo for prevention of postoperative nausea and vomiting after supratentorial craniotomy. Anesth Analg 2000;91:358–61.

37. Larsson S, Jonmarker C. Postoperative emesis after pediatric strabismus surgery: the effect of dixyrazine compared to droperidol. Acta Anaesthesiol Scand 1990;34:227–30.

38. Haigh CG, Kaplan LA, Durham JM, Dupeyron JP, Harmer M, Kenny GN. Nausea and vomiting after gynaecological surgery: a meta-analysis of factors affecting their incidence. Br J Anaesth 1993;71: 517–22.

39. Honkavaara P. Effect of transdermal hyoscine on nausea and vomiting during and after middle ear surgery under local anaesthesia. Br J Anaesth 1996;76:49–53.

40. Lerman J. Surgical and patient factors involved in postoperative nausea and vomiting. Br J Anaesth 1992;69:24S–32S.

41. Rowley MP, Brown TC. Postoperative vomiting in children. Anaesth Intens Care 1982;10:309–13.

42. Gan TJ, Meyer T, Apfel CC, Chung F, Davis PJ, Kovac A, Philip BK, Sessler DI, Temo J, Tramer MR, Watcha MF. Consensus guidelines for managing postoperative nausea and vomiting. Anesth Analg 2003;97:62–71.

43. Tramer MR, Reynolds DJ, Moore RA, McQuay HJ. Efficacy, dose-response, and safety of ondansetron in prevention of postoperative nausea and vomiting: a quantitative systematic review of randomized placebo-controlled trials. Anesthesiology 1997;87:1277–89.

44. Sun R, Klein KW, White PF. The effect of timing of ondansetron administration in outpatients undergoing otolaryngologic surgery. Anesth Analg 1997;84:331–36.

45. Tang J, Wang B, White PF, Watcha MF, Qi J, Wender RH. The effect of timing of ondansetron administration on its efficacy, cost-effectiveness, and cost-benefit as a prophylactic antiemetic in the ambulatory setting. Anesth Analg 1998;86:274–82.

46. Graczyk SG, McKenzie R, Kallar S, Hickok CB, Melson T, Morrill B, Hahne WF, Brown RA. Intravenous dolasetron for the prevention of postoperative nausea and vomiting after outpatient laparoscopic gynecologic surgery. Anesth Analg 1997;84:325–30.

47. Chen X, Tang J, White PF, Wender RH, Quon R, Sloninsky A, Naruse R, Kariger R, Webb T, Norel E. The effect of timing of dolasetron administration on its efficacy as a prophylactic antiemetic in the ambulatory setting. Anesth Analg 2001;93:906–11.

48. Kranke P, Eberhart LH, Apfel CC, Broscheit J, Geldner G, Roewer N. [Tropisetron for prevention of postoperative nausea and vomiting: a quantitative systematic review]. Anaesthesist 2002;51: 805–14.

49. Wilson AJ, Diemunsch P, Lindeque BG, Scheinin H, Helbo-Hansen HS, Kroeks MV, Kong KL. Single-dose i.v. granisetron in the prevention of postoperative nausea and vomiting. Br J Anaesth 1996; 76:515–18.

50. Mikawa K, Takao Y, Nishina K, Shiga M, Maekawa N, Obara H. Optimal dose of granisetron for prophylaxis against postoperative emesis after gynecological surgery. Anesth Analg 1997;85:652–56.

51. D'Angelo R, Minkowitz H, Dalby P, et al. A pilot, randomized, double-blind, dose-ranging study of intravenous granisetron in the prevention of postoperative nausea and vomiting (PONV) in subjects undergoing abdominal hysterectomy. New York Society of Anesthesiologists Postgraduate Assembly, 2002.

52. Taylor AM, Rosen M, Diemunsch PA, Thorin D, Houweling PL. A double-blind, parallel-group, placebo-controlled, dose-ranging, multicenter study of intravenous granisetron in the treatment of postoperative nausea and vomiting in patients undergoing surgery with general anesthesia. J Clin Anesth 1997;9:658–63.

53. Fujii Y, Saitoh Y, Tanaka H, Toyooka H. Ramosetron for preventing postoperative nausea and vomiting in women undergoing gynecological surgery. Anesth Analg 2000;90:472–75.

54. Kovac AL. Prevention and treatment of postoperative nausea and vomiting. Drugs 2000;59:213–43.

55. Harris AL. Cytotoxic-therapy-induced vomiting is mediated via enkephalin pathways. Lancet 1982;1:714–16.

56. Axelsson P, Thorn SE, Magnus W. Betamethasone does not prevent nausea and vomiting induced by ipecacuanha. Anesthesiology 2003;99:A500.

57. Fujii Y, Tanaka H, Toyooka H. The effects of dexamethasone on antiemetics in female patients undergoing gynecologic surgery. Anesth Analg 1997;85:913–17.

58. Liu K, Hsu CC, Chia YY. Effect of dexamethasone on postoperative emesis and pain. Br J Anaesth 1998;80:85–86.

59. Liu K, Hsu CC, Chia YY. The effect of dose of dexamethasone for antiemesis after major gynecological surgery. Anesth Analg 1999; 89:1316–18.

60. Henzi I, Walder B, Tramer MR. Dexamethasone for the prevention of postoperative nausea and vomiting: a quantitative systematic review. Anesth Analg 2000;90:186–94.

61. Wang JJ, Ho ST, Lee SC, Liu YC, Ho CM. The use of dexamethasone for preventing postoperative nausea and vomiting in females undergoing thyroidectomy: a dose-ranging study. Anesth Analg 2000;91:1404–7.

62. Wang JJ, Ho ST, Tzeng JI, Tang CS. The effect of timing of dexamethasone administration on its efficacy as a prophylactic antiemetic for postoperative nausea and vomiting. Anesth Analg 2000;91: 136–39.

63. Ostman PL, Faure E, Glosten B, Kemen M, Robert MK, Bedwell S. Is the antiemetic effect of the emulsion formulation of propofol due to the lipid emulsion? Anesth Analg 1990;71:536–40.

64. Cechetto DF, Diab T, Gibson CJ, Gelb AW. The effects of propofol in the area postrema of rats. Anesth Analg 2001;92:934–42.

65. Price ML, Walmsley A, Swaine C, Ponte J. Comparison of a total intravenous anaesthetic technique using a propofol infusion, with an inhalational technique using enflurane for day case surgery. Anaesthesia 1988;43:84–87.

66. Doze VA, Shafer A, White PF. Propofol-nitrous oxide versus thiopental-isoflurane-nitrous oxide for general anesthesia. Anesthesiology 1988;69:63–71.

67. Lebenbom-Mansour MH, Pandit SK, Kothary SP, Randel GI, Levy L. Desflurane versus propofol anesthesia: a comparative analysis in outpatients. Anesth Analg 1993;76:936–41.

68. Tramer M, Moore A, McQuay H. Propofol anaesthesia and postoperative nausea and vomiting: quantitative systematic review of randomized controlled studies. Br J Anaesth 1997;78:247–55.

69. Kim SI, Han TH, Kil HY, Lee JS, Kim SC. Prevention of postoperative nausea and vomiting by continuous infusion of subhypnotic propofol in female patients receiving intravenous patient-controlled analgesia. Br J Anaesth 2000;85:898–900.

70. Gan TJ, El-Molem H, Ray J, Glass PS. Patient-controlled antiemesis: a randomized, double-blind comparison of two doses of propofol versus placebo. Anesthesiology 1999;90:1564–70.

71. Gan TJ, Glass PS, Howell ST, Canada AT, Grant AP, Ginsberg B. Determination of plasma concentrations of propofol associated with 50% reduction in postoperative nausea. Anesthesiology 1997;87:779–84.

72. Corssen G, Reves JG, Stanley TH. Neuroleptanalgesia and neuroleptanesthesia. In: Intravenous Anesthesia and Analgesia. Philadelphia: Lea & Febiger, 1988, p. 175.

73. Janssen PA. The pharmacology of haloperidol. Int J Neuropsychiatry 1967;3 (Suppl):10–18.

74. Borison HL, Wang SC. Physiology and pharmacology of vomiting. Pharmacol Rev 1953;5:193–230.

75. Hill RP, Lubarsky DA, Phillips-Bute B, Fortney JT, Creed MR, Glass PS, Gan TJ. Cost-effectiveness of prophylactic antiemetic therapy with ondansetron, droperidol, or placebo. Anesthesiology 2000;92:958–67.

76. Henzi I, Sonderegger J, Tramer MR. Efficacy, dose-response, and adverse effects of droperidol for prevention of postoperative nausea and vomiting. Can J Anaesth 2000;47:537–51.

77. Fischler M, Bonnet F, Trang H, Jacob L, Levron JC, Flaisler B, Vourc'h G. The pharmacokinetics of droperidol in anesthetized patients. Anesthesiology 1986;64:486–89.

78. Tramer MR, Walder B. Efficacy and adverse effects of prophylactic antiemetics during patient-controlled analgesia therapy: a quantitative systematic review. Anesth Analg 1999;88:1354–61.

79. Fortney JT, Gan TJ, Graczyk S, Wetchler B, Melson T, Khalil S, McKenzie R, Parrillo S, Glass PS, Moote C, Wermeling D, Parasuraman TV, Duncan B, Creed MR. A comparison of the efficacy, safety, and patient satisfaction of ondansetron versus droperidol as antiemetics for elective outpatient surgical procedures. S3A-409 and S3A-410 Study Groups. Anesth Analg 1998;86:731–38.

80. Habib AS, Gan TJ. Food and Drug Administration black box warning on the perioperative use of droperidol: a review of the cases. Anesth Analg 2003;96:1377–79.

81. Gan TJ, White PF, Scuderi PE, Watcha MF, Kovac A. FDA "black box" warning regarding use of droperidol for postoperative nausea and vomiting: is it justified? Anesthesiology 2002;97:287.

82. Harrington RA, Hamilton CW, Brogden RN, Linkewich JA, Romankiewicz JA, Heel RC. Metoclopramide: an updated review of its pharmacological properties and clinical use. Drugs 1983;25:451–94.

83. Fozard JR. Neuronal 5-HT receptors in the periphery. Neuropharmacology 1984;23:1473–86.

84. Rowbotham DJ. Current management of postoperative nausea and vomiting. Br J Anaesth 1992;69:46S–59S.

85. Henzi I, Walder B, Tramer MR. Metoclopramide in the prevention of postoperative nausea and vomiting: a quantitative systematic review of randomized, placebo-controlled studies. Br J Anaesth 1999;83:761–71.

86. Quaynor H, Raeder JC. Incidence and severity of postoperative nausea and vomiting are similar after metoclopramide 20 mg and ondansetron 8 mg given by the end of laparoscopic cholecystectomies. Acta Anaesthesiol Scand 2002;46:109–13.

87. Golding JF, Stott JR. Comparison of the effects of a selective muscarinic receptor antagonist and hyoscine (scopolamine) on motion sickness, skin conductance and heart rate. Br J Clin Pharmacol 1997;43:633–37.

88. Kranke P, Morin AM, Roewer N, Wulf H, Eberhart LH. The efficacy and safety of transdermal scopolamine for the prevention of postoperative nausea and vomiting: a quantitative systematic review. Anesth Analg 2002;95:133–43.

89. Bailey PL, Streisand JB, Pace NL, Bubbers SJ, East KA, Mulder S, Stanley TH. Transdermal scopolamine reduces nausea and vomiting after outpatient laparoscopy. Anesthesiology 1990;72:977–80.

90. Kranke P, Morin AM, Roewer N, Eberhart LH. Dimenhydrinate for prophylaxis of postoperative nausea and vomiting: a meta-analysis of randomized controlled trials. Acta Anaesthesiol Scand 2002;46:238–44.

91. Ahmed AB, Hobbs GJ, Curran JP. Randomized, placebo-controlled trial of combination antiemetic prophylaxis for day-case gynaecological laparoscopic surgery. Br J Anaesth 2000;85:678–82.

92. Dundee JW, Loan WB, Morrison JD. A comparison of the efficacy of cyclizine and perhenazine in reducing the emetic effects of morphine and pethidine. Br J Clin Pharmacol 1975;2:81–85.

93. Dundee JW, Moore A, Love WJ, et al. Studies of drugs given before anaesthesia. VI. The phenothiazine derivatives. Br J Anaesth 1965;37:332–52.

94. Khalil S, Philbrook L, Rabb M, Wells L, Aves T, Villanueva G, Amhan M, Chuang AZ, Lemak NA. Ondansetron/promethazine combination or promethazine alone reduces nausea and vomiting after middle ear surgery. J Clin Anesth 1999;11:596–600.

95. Dryberg V, Johansen SH. Pre-anaesthetic medication with chlorpromazine. Acta Anaesthesiol Scand 1958;2:133–47.

96. Lee A, Done ML. The use of nonpharmacologic techniques to prevent postoperative nausea and vomiting: a meta-analysis. Anesth Analg 1999;88:1362–69.

97. Boehler MMD, Mitterschiffthaler GMD, Schlager AMD. Korean hand acupressure reduces postoperative nausea and vomiting after gynecological laparoscopic surgery. Anesth Analg 2002;94:872–75.

98. Schlager A, Offer T, Baldissera I. Laser stimulation of acupuncture point P6 reduces postoperative vomiting in children undergoing strabismus surgery. Br J Anaesth 1998;81:529–32.

99. Rusy LMMD, Hoffman GMMD, Weisman SJMD. Electroacupuncture prophylaxis of postoperative nausea and vomiting following pediatric tonsillectomy with or without adenoidectomy. Anesthesiology 2002;96:300–305.

100. Somri M, Vaida SJ, Sabo E, Yassain G, Gankin I, Gaitini LA. Acupuncture versus ondansetron in the prevention of postoperative vomiting: a study of children undergoing dental surgery. Anaesthesia 2001;56:927–32.

101. Gan TJ, Parrillo S, Fortney JT, Georgiade G. Comparison of electroacupuncture and ondansetron for the prevention of postoperative nausea and vomiting. Anesthesiology 2001;95:A22.

102. Coloma M, White PF, Ogunnaike BO, Markowitz SD, Brown PM, Lee AQ, Berrisford SB, Wakefield CA, Issioui T, Jones SB, Jones DB. Comparison of acustimulation and ondansetron for the treatment of established postoperative nausea and vomiting. Anesthesiology 2002;97:1387–92.

103. White PF, Issioui T, Hu J, Jones SB, Coleman JE, Waddle JP, Markowitz SD, Coloma M, Macaluso AR, Ing CH. Comparative efficacy of acustimulation (ReliefBand) versus ondansetron (Zofran) in combination with droperidol for preventing nausea and vomiting. Anesthesiology 2002;97:1075–81.

104. Enqvist B, Bjorklund C, Engman M, Jakobsson J. Preoperative hypnosis reduces postoperative vomiting after surgery of the breasts: a prospective, randomized and blinded study. Acta Anaesthesiol Scand 1997;41:1028–32.

105. Ernst E, Pittler MH. Efficacy of ginger for nausea and vomiting: a

systematic review of randomized clinical trials. Br J Anaesth 2000;84:367–71.

106. Splinter W, Noel LP, Roberts D, Rhine E, Bonn G, Clarke W. Antiemetic prophylaxis for strabismus surgery. Can J Ophthalmol 1994;29:224–26.

107. Splinter WM, MacNeill HB, Menard EA, Rhine EJ, Roberts DJ, Gould MH. Midazolam reduces vomiting after tonsillectomy in children. Can J Anaesth 1995;42:201–3.

108. Khalil SN, Berry JM, Howard G, Lawson K, Hanis C, Mazow ML, Stanley TH. The antiemetic effect of lorazepam after outpatient strabismus surgery in children. Anesthesiology 1992;77:915–19.

109. Prasad V, Till CB, Smith A. Midazolam—an anti-emetic? Anaesthesia 2002;57:415.

110. Di Florio T. The use of midazolam for persistent postoperative nausea and vomiting. Anaesth Intens Care 1992;20:383–86.

111. Di Florio T, Goucke CR. The effect of midazolam on persistent postoperative nausea and vomiting. Anaesth Intens Care 1999;27:38–40.

112. Racke K, Schwore H, Kilbinger H. The pharmacology of 5 HT release from enterochromaffin cells. In: Reynolds DJM, Andrews PLR, Davis PJ (eds.), Serotonin and the Scientific Basis of Antiemetic Therapy. Oxford: Oxford Clinical Communications, 1995, pp. 84–89.

113. Rothenberg DM, Parnass SM, Litwack K, McCarthy RJ, Newman LM. Efficacy of ephedrine in the prevention of postoperative nausea and vomiting. Anesth Analg 1991;72:58–61.

114. Naguib K, Osman HA, Al-Khayat HC, Zikri AM. Prevention of post-operative nausea and vomiting following laparoscopic surgery—ephedrine vs propofol. Mid East J Anesthesiol 1998;14:219–30.

115. Hagemann E, Halvorsen A, Holgersen O, Tveit T, Raeder JC. Intramuscular ephedrine reduces emesis during the first three hours after abdominal hysterectomy. Acta Anaesthesiol Scand 2000;44:107–11.

116. Mikawa K, Nishina K, Maekawa N, Asano M, Obara H. Oral clonidine premedication reduces vomiting in children after strabismus surgery. Can J Anaesth 1995;42:977–81.

117. Oddby-Muhrbeck E, Eksborg S, Bergendahl HT, Muhrbeck O, Lonnqvist PA. Effects of clonidine on postoperative nausea and vomiting in breast cancer surgery. Anesthesiology 2002;96:1109–14.

118. Goll V, Akca O, Greif R, Freitag H, Arkilic CF, Scheck T, Zoeggeler A, Kurz A, Krieger G, Lenhardt R, Sessler DI. Ondansetron is no more effective than supplemental intraoperative oxygen for prevention of postoperative nausea and vomiting. Anesth Analg 2001;92:112–17.

119. Greif R, Laciny S, Rapf B, Hickle RS, Sessler DI. Supplemental oxygen reduces the incidence of postoperative nausea and vomiting. Anesthesiology 1999;91:1246–52.

120. Purhonen S, Turunen M, Ruohoaho UM, Niskanen M, Hynynen M. Supplemental oxygen does not reduce the incidence of postoperative nausea and vomiting after ambulatory gynecologic laparoscopy. Anesth Analg 2003;96:91–96.

121. Purhonen S, Niskanen M, Wustefeld M, Mustonen P, Hynynen M. Supplemental oxygen for prevention of nausea and vomiting after breast surgery. Br J Anaesth 2003;91:284–87.

122. Yogendran S, Asokumar B, Cheng DC, Chung F. A prospective randomized double-blinded study of the effect of intravenous fluid therapy on adverse outcomes on outpatient surgery. Anesth Analg 1995;80:682–86.

123. Gan TJ, Mythen MG, Glass PS. Intraoperative gut hypoperfusion may be a risk factor for postoperative nausea and vomiting. Br J Anaesth 1997;78:476.

124. Moretti EW, Robertson KM, El-Moalem H, Gan TJ. Intraoperative colloid administration reduces postoperative nausea and vomiting and improves postoperative outcomes compared with crystalloid administration. Anesth Analg 2003;96:611–17.

125. Habib AS, Gan TJ. Combination antiemetics: what is the evidence? Int Anesthesiol Clin 2003;41:119–144.

126. Sanchez-Ledesma MJ, Lopez-Olaondo L, Pueyo FJ, Carrascosa F, Ortega A. A comparison of three antiemetic combinations for the prevention of postoperative nausea and vomiting. Anesth Analg 2002;95:1590–95.

127. Habib AS, El-Moalem HE, Gan TJ. The efficacy of the 5-HT$_3$ receptor antagonists combined with droperidol for PONV prophylaxis is similar to their combination with dexamethasone: a meta-analysis of randomized controlled trials. Can J Anaesth 2004;51(4):311–19.

128. Habib AS, White WD, Eubanks S, Pappas TN, Gan TJ. A randomized comparison of a multimodal management strategy versus combination antiemetics for the prevention of postoperative nausea and vomiting. Anesth Analg 2004;99:77–81.

129. Tang J, Chen X, White PF, Wender RH, Ma H, Sloninsky A, Naruse R, Kariger R, Webb T, Zaentz A. Antiemetic prophylaxis for office-based surgery: are the 5-HT$_3$ receptor antagonists beneficial? Anesthesiology 2003;98:293–98.

130. Scuderi PE, James RL, Harris L, Mims GR III. Multimodal antiemetic management prevents early postoperative vomiting after outpatient laparoscopy. Anesth Analg 2000;91:1408–14.

131. Hammas B, Thorn SE, Wattwil M. Superior prolonged antiemetic prophylaxis with a four-drug multimodal regimen—comparison with propofol or placebo. Acta Anaesthesiol Scand 2002;46:232–37.

132. Eberhart LH, Mauch M, Morin AM, Wulf H, Geldner G. Impact of a multimodal anti-emetic prophylaxis on patient satisfaction in high-risk patients for postoperative nausea and vomiting. Anaesthesia 2002;57:1022–27.

133. Wu CL, Berenholtz SM, Pronovost PJ, Fleisher LA. Systematic review and analysis of postdischarge symptoms after outpatient surgery. Anesthesiology 2002;96:994–1003.

134. Carroll NV, Miederhoff P, Cox FM, Hirsch JD. Postoperative nausea and vomiting after discharge from outpatient surgery centers. Anesth Analg 1995;80:903–9.

135. Gupta AM, Wu CL, Elkassabany N, Krug CE, Parker SD, Fleisher LA. Does the routine prophylactic use of antiemetics affect the incidence of postdischarge nausea and vomiting following ambulatory surgery? A systematic review of randomized controlled trials. Anesthesiology 2003;99:488–95.

136. Habib AS, El-Moalem HE, Gan TJ. Is the combination of 5-HT$_3$ receptor antagonists with droperidol or dexamethasone more effective than each agent alone for PONV prophylaxis? Anesthesiology 2001;95:A20.

137. Habib AS, Gan TJ. Combination therapy for postoperative nausea and vomiting—a more effective prophylaxis? Ambul Surg 2001;9:59–71.

138. Kazemi-Kjellberg F, Henzi I, Tramer MR. Treatment of established postoperative nausea and vomiting: a quantitative systematic review. BMC Anesthesiol 2001;1:2.

139. Kovac AL, O'Connor TA, Pearman MH, Kekoler LJ, Edmondson D, Baughman VL, Angel JJ, Campbell C, Jense HG, Mingus M, Shahvari MB, Creed MR. Efficacy of repeat intravenous dosing of ondansetron in controlling postoperative nausea and vomiting: a randomized, double-blind, placebo-controlled multicenter trial. J Clin Anesth 1999;11:453–59.

140. Habib AS, Gan TJ. The effectiveness of rescue antiemetics following failure of prophylaxis with ondansetron or droperidol. J Clin Anesth. In press.

141. Carmichael J, Keizer HJ, Cupissol D, Milliez J, Scheidel P, Schindler AE. Use of granisetron in patients refractory to previous treatment with antiemetics. Anti-Cancer Drugs 1998;9:381–85.

142. de Wit R, de Boer AC, vd Linden GH, Stoter G, Sparreboom A, Verweij J. Effective cross-over to granisetron after failure to ondansetron, a randomized double blind study in patients failing ondansetron plus dexamethasone during the first 24 hours following highly emetogenic chemotherapy. Br J Cancer 2001;85:1099–101.

143. Tramer MR, Moore RA, Reynolds DJ, McQuay HJ. A quantitative systematic review of ondansetron in treatment of established postoperative nausea and vomiting. Br Med J 1997;314: 1088–92.

144. Diemunsch P, Conseiller C, Clyti N, Mamet JP. Ondansetron compared with metoclopramide in the treatment of established postoperative nausea and vomiting. The French Ondansetron Study Group. Br J Anaesth 1997;79:322–26.

145. Polati E, Verlato G, Finco G, Mosaner W, Grosso S, Gottin L, Pinaroli AM, Ischia S. Ondansetron versus metoclopramide in the treatment of postoperative nausea and vomiting. Anesth Analg 1997;85:395–99.

146. Palazzo M, Evans R. Logistic regression analysis of fixed patient factors for postoperative sickness: a model for risk assessment. Br J Anaesth 1993;70:135–40.

Ambulatory Anesthetic Management of Common Diseases

SCOTT E. HELSLEY

INTRODUCTION

The current state of health care is one of continuous change and innovation. One new trend is a dramatic increase in surgical procedures that are being performed on an outpatient basis. For example, in 1999 it was reported that over 60% of all surgical procedures in North America were performed on outpatients.[1] Along with this comes a trend toward including more complex surgeries and sicker patients. It is the duty of the health care team to prevent these patients from becoming casualties in this health care revolution.

The combination of increasing case complexity in terms of both the patients and the procedures offers a unique opportunity. As members of the perioperative team, anesthesia providers play a pivotal role in the care of complex ambulatory patients. Overall reduction of ambulatory surgery risk in patients with preexisting disease centers on the optimization of the patient's condition prior to arrival in the operating room. In order to achieve this one must understand both the physiologic trespass of the procedure and the patient's underlying condition(s). An incomplete understanding of either of these issues may place the patient at risk and may result in avoidable suffering (both physical and financial).

This chapter was written to provide guidance in the anesthetic management of patients presenting for ambulatory surgery who have common underlying medical conditions. As this is not a basic medical primer, the author assumes the reader is familiar with the physiology and pathology of the disease processes that will be discussed. This review provides information from recent studies along with contemporary practices that have been safely implemented in many patients but have yet to undergo the scrutiny of double-blind, prospective evaluations. The rationale for much of what we do as anesthesia providers often comes from the collective experience of our specialty owing to the scarcity of well-designed clinical trials. However, the trend toward evidence-based medicine is a favorable one and one that most health care providers welcome.

When one speaks of ambulatory surgery it is perhaps important to distinguish day cases done at a tertiary medical center versus those done at a freestanding ambulatory surgery center or even office-based surgery. An increasing number of cases are being performed at ambulatory surgery centers. It stands to reason that providers should be slightly more conservative in their patient selection when doing cases at a freestanding ambulatory center. Often the decision to keep or discharge a patient hinges on how smoothly the procedure went in terms of both surgical issues and general stability of the patient during the intraoperative and immediate postoperative period. It is never convenient when an unplanned admission arises but it is easier to deal with when one is already at a center with overnight facilities. As discussed elsewhere in this book, many ambulatory facilities offer overnight care, albeit at a reduced care level compared to an inpatient floor. For purposes of this chapter the term "ambulatory surgery" refers to a patient at a freestanding ambulatory surgery center. Any place where surgery is performed and anesthesia is delivered should have such facilities and equipment available to handle any emergency that might arise. Emergency airway equipment, chest tubes, invasive monitoring devices, complete drug inventory including dantrolene, inotropes, as well as access to laboratory tests and blood products must be obtainable in a reasonable amount of time.

MANAGEMENT OF SPECIFIC CONDITIONS

Perioperative Management for the Diabetic Patient

For any disease one must understand not only the underlying disorder itself but also its effects on other organ systems. Diabetes is a case in point. The underlying disorder is a defect in glucose metabolism, the ramifications of which can affect every organ system. Because of this, the preoperative evaluation is very important. In addition to determining the nature of the patient's condition (i.e., type I vs. type II diabetes) and his/her medication regimen, a search for end-organ pathology is warranted. These patients are at risk for silent ischemia because of autonomic neuropathy. In this patient population the risk of ischemic heart disease is two to four times that of nondiabetics.[2] For this reason those with risk factors for coronary artery disease should undergo further testing. However, patients with good functional capacity (defined as ability to climb two flights of stairs or equivalent) undergoing ambulatory surgery are thought to be low risk and require no further testing.[3] Diabetics with known cardiac disease should be evaluated in accordance with the American Heart Association (AHA) guidelines for patients undergoing cardiac surgery.[4] In addition to cardiac pathology, these patients are at risk for neuropathy, nephropathy, and hypertension. One important consideration is that the incidence of difficult laryngoscopy is increased 10-fold in patients with diabetes.[5]

Perioperative glucose control may be an area where we can improve patient outcomes. Reports in the literature have associated hyperglycemia with increases in postoperative wound infections. Most of these reports focus on cardiac patients;[6,7] however similar results have been seen with diabetics in other surgical populations as well.[8] At the present time there are no studies of this phenomenon in day surgery patients. In spite of this, it seems logical that normoglycemia will be better for the patient than the alternative.

How then does one manage these patients when they present for ambulatory surgery? A reasonable place to begin is with the preoperative medication regimen. Figures 40-1 and 40-2 outline the current protocol for diabetic patients used at Duke University Medical Center preoperative screening clinic. This is what the author recommends to these patients. As the readers can imagine, patient compliance is variable, but overall it has worked well.[9]

Intraoperative management of diabetics is relatively straightforward. Most ambulatory cases are relatively short. For cases expected to last over 2 hr in type I diabetics a glucose check during the case with insulin supplementation for those patients with readings of over 200 mg/dL seems rational. Otherwise a check in the recovery area will suffice. The main concern regarding these patients is cardiovascular monitoring (i.e., five-lead electrocardiogram [ECG] to monitor for ischemia). If additional monitoring such as an arterial line or pulmonary artery catheter is felt necessary, this patient is not a candidate for ambulatory surgery at all. In addition, diabetics are likely at increased risk for perioperative nerve injuries, so meticulous attention during positioning is required. A detailed discussion of optimum patient positioning to avoid stretch-induced nerve injuries is provided in the recent literature.[10]

Postoperative management in these patients is relatively straightforward. A fingerstick glucose should be checked in the recovery room. A level of 200 mg/dL or greater probably needs to be covered with subcutaneous insulin; oth-

erwise patients should resume their normal regimen once they are able to eat and are free of nausea.

Perioperative Management for the Patient with Cardiovascular Disease

Hypertension

Hypertension has been shown to be strongly associated with intraoperative adverse cardiac events in ambulatory surgery.[1] As with diabetics, the main concern in hypertensive patients is end-organ pathology and associated disease. Therefore, the history and physical exam should focus on the cardiovascular and neurologic systems as these patients are at increased risk for heart disease and stroke. When is the blood pressure too high for ambulatory surgery? There really is no simple answer to this question. A survey of anesthesiologists in the United Kingdom revealed considerable variability regarding which patients they would or would not anesthetize based on presenting blood pressures and evidence of end-organ pathology.[11] The American College of Cardiology/AHA guidelines recommend postponing surgery if the diastolic pressure is greater than 110 mmHg.[4] Unfortunately this does not address systolic pressure, which is associated with increased risk of myocardial ischemia.[12] Although guidelines do not yet exist regarding isolated systolic hypertension, Prys-Roberts recommends that patients with systolic pressures of greater than 180 mmHg be medicated preoperatively with atenolol and then reassessed.[13] No prospective data exist regarding these recommendations but it is hoped that this will change in the future.

For ambulatory surgery it cannot be overemphasized that each patient should be considered on an individual basis. Absolute numerical cutoffs are not sufficient. One must look at the patient and consider both the patient's comorbidities and the nature of the surgical procedure. The patient's baseline blood pressure should also be considered. If a patient presents with a systolic pressure of 185 mmHg and that is his/her usual pressure, this is perhaps different than someone presenting with this elevated pressure who is usually normotensive. Postponement of the latter patient's procedure for a workup (assuming the hypertension was not attributed to preoperative anxiety) is indicated. Of course, this must be looked at in terms of the procedure. It would not be in a patient's best interest to postpone, for instance, the removal of a painful ganglion cyst just because his/her blood pressure was 185/90 mmHg. Delay would perhaps be more of a consideration in a patient with an identical blood pressure about to undergo a laparoscopic cholecystectomy.

Coronary Artery Disease

Patients with unstable coronary syndromes are not candidates for ambulatory surgery. Patients with stable coronary syndromes who are medically optimized can be considered candidates, especially for minimally invasive procedures. So, for instance, a patient with stable angina who is on medical management would be a candidate for cataract or

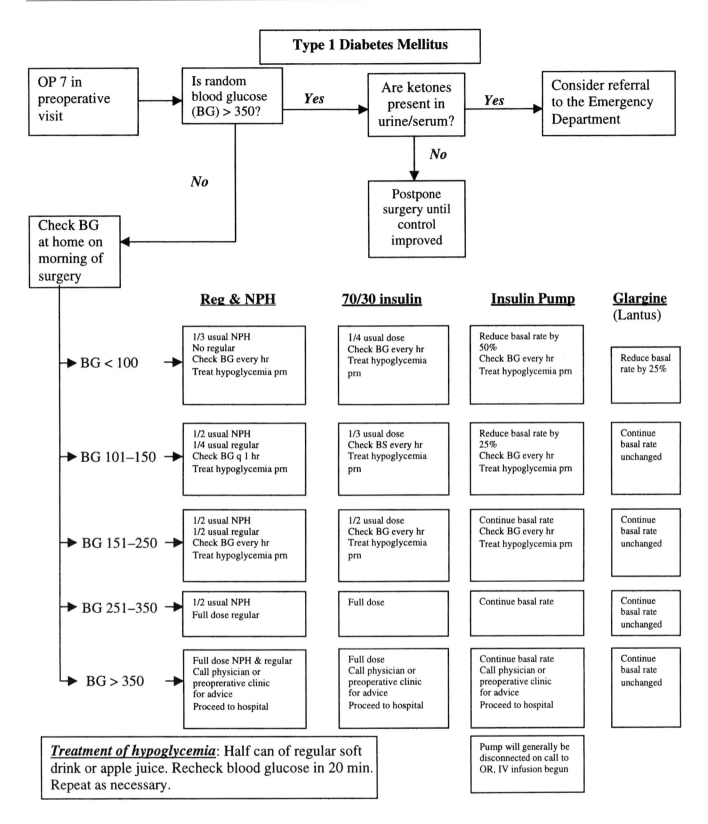

Figure 40-1   Type 1 Diabetes Mellitus preoperative management protocol. Abbreviations: Reg, regular insulin; NPH, NPH insulin; IV, intravenous. (Olson R, personal communication, 2002.)

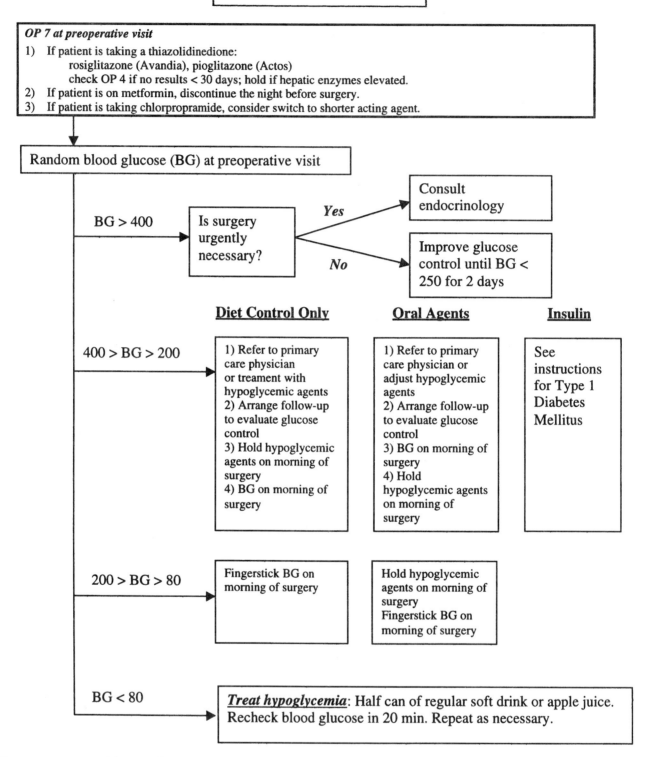

Figure 40-2   Type 2 Diabetes Mellitus preoperative management protocol. (Olson R, personal communication, 2002.)

carpal tunnel surgery but not laparoscopic cholecystectomy at an ambulatory surgery center. It would be prudent to do this at a hospital where the patient could be admitted overnight and monitored. General recommendations for perioperative evaluation of patients with coronary artery disease undergoing noncardiac surgical procedures exist.[4] The authors of those recommendations make a distinction between high-, intermediate-, and low-risk procedures. Most ambulatory procedures fall into the low-risk category. Although these guidelines do not include any specifications for ambulatory surgery, there is no obvious reason why they should not apply.

A detailed discussion of cardiac pathology and ways to maximize the myocardial oxygen supply-demand ratio is beyond the scope of this chapter; they are discussed elsewhere.[14] However, one topic pertinent to this subject is coronary stents. There are data showing catastrophic outcomes in patients who underwent noncardiac surgery within 2–4 weeks after coronary stent placement.[15] It appears that the risk is related to interruption of anticoagulation resulting in stent thrombosis. Thus these patients remain a high risk for at least 1 month after their intervention.

Common Rhythm Disturbances

Atrial fibrillation is present in about 0.4% of the American population.[16] Patients with long-standing atrial fibrillation who are otherwise hemodynamically stable are candidates for ambulatory surgery. Important considerations include comorbidities, which most commonly are ischemic heart disease and/or hypertension. Also, for the anticoagulated patient, the timing of the surgery and the suspension of the anticoagulation regimen must be coordinated, usually in consultation with the patient's cardiologist or primary care physician. Patients with new-onset or hemodynamically unstable atrial fibrillation should undergo a thorough cardiology evaluation before elective surgery.

Long QT syndrome is a relatively rare condition. It deserves mention though because it is becoming more frequently diagnosed and some drugs used in anesthesia may precipitate or exacerbate the condition. This disorder is characterized by impaired cardiac repolarization resulting in prolongation of the QT interval of the ECG, which can lead to torsade de pointes and sudden death. A current review of this syndrome has recently been published.[17] Congenital and acquired forms of the disorder exist. Often the presenting pattern is that of unexplained fainting or family history of sudden death with ECG findings of long QT interval. A partial list of agents commonly encountered in perioperative patient management that can produce QT interval prolongation is provided in Table 40-1. Patients with long QT syndrome as well as others with tachyarrhythmias such as Wolff-Parkinson-White syndrome should be referred to a cardiologist before undergoing any elective surgical procedures.

Valvular Heart Disease

Patients with valvular heart disease can be candidates for ambulatory surgery provided they are hemodynamically stable and symptom-free. The invasiveness of the procedure must be taken into consideration. Anticoagulated patients with artificial valves must have provisions made for possible suspension of their anticoagulant therapy in consultation with their hematologist or cardiologist. Also, it is worth keeping in mind the implications of anticoagulation on regional anesthesia. This topic is covered in another chapter of this text. Considerations must also be made regarding endocarditis prophylaxis. The key reference for this is Dajani et al.[18]

The most common cardiac valvular condition is mitral valve prolapse. This condition is especially common in women, with a reported incidence as high as 17%.[19] The keys to evaluating patients suspected of having this condition are detailed history (e.g., dyspnea on exertion, chest pain, palpitations) and echocardiography. Those patients with significant valvular pathology must be differentiated from those with "purely functional disease."[20] Patients without evidence of mitral regurgitation do not require antibiotic prophylaxis.[18,20] The reader is encouraged to consult the AHA antibiotic prophylaxis recommendations.[18]

Table 40-1 Drugs That May Prolong the QT Interval

Agent (class)	Use
Albuterol	Bronchodilator
Amiodarone	Antiarrhythmic
Chlorpromazine	Antipsychotic/tranquilizer
Dobutamine	Inotrope
Dolasetron	Antiemetic
Ephedrine	Inotrope
Epinephrine	Inotrope
Fosphenytoin	Anticonvulscent
Haloperidol	Antipsychotic/tranquilizer
Levofloxacin	Antimicrobial
Methadone	Opioid analgesic
Nicardipine	Calcium channel blocker
Octreotide	Somatostatin analogue
Ondansetron	Antiemetic
Phenylephrine	Vasopressor
Procainamide	Antiarrhythmic
Risperidone	Antipsychotic/tranquilizer
Ritodrine	Uterine tocolytic
Tacrolimus	Immunosuppressant
Terbutaline	Uterine tocolytic

Source: Adapted from www.qtdrugs.org.

The care of patients with other valvular abnormalities has been well summarized in textbooks.[21]

Perioperative Management for the Patient with Pulmonary Disease

Obstructive Airway Disease

Obstructive airway disease is classically divided into asthma and chronic obstructive pulmonary disease (COPD). The hallmark and main distinguishing feature of asthma is reversible airway obstruction with hyperresponsive airway tissue. Patients with COPD are thought to have more of a fixed obstructive pattern. As discussed by Stoelting and Dierdorf, this is not a perfectly clear distinction, as patients suffering from COPD also exhibit airway hyperreactivity.[22] Patients with these conditions are candidates for ambulatory surgery so long as their respiratory compromise is not severe and the proposed surgical procedure is not likely to lead to further respiratory embarrassment.

Asthma is a common condition affecting over 10 million patients in the United States.[23] The major perioperative concern with this patient population is bronchospasm and impairment of ventilation. The preoperative evaluation focuses on identifying agents that trigger the patient's asthma. Concern for the anesthesia providers might include avoidance of nonsteroidal anti-inflammatory drugs (NSAIDs) as well as noxious stimuli (consider deep extubation if patient is an acceptable candidate), and possibly intubation with ketamine for its bronchodilating properties. In addition, the perioperative use of inhaled steroids and albuterol is of potential benefit. Avoidance of airway instrumentation is also useful, especially if the surgery is amenable and the patient agreeable to a regional anesthetic. As discussed elsewhere in this text, regional anesthesia is extremely well suited to ambulatory surgery.

Perioperative bronchospasm is a serious concern. Data from the American Society of Anesthesiologists (ASA) closed claims analysis reported a high incidence of brain damage or death in cases of bronchospasm. Interestingly, only about half of those patients had a history of smoking or pulmonary disease.[24] Therefore, even when a patient gives no history of airway disease, bronchospasm is possible. Also, there are other causes of bronchospasm besides intrinsic pulmonary disease; aspiration and anaphylaxis come immediately to mind.

When should an asthmatic patient have elective ambulatory surgery postponed? Although there are no firm guidelines on this, the author's preference is to postpone surgery in asthmatics who are dealing with acute upper-respiratory infections even if they are not febrile. Also, if a patient is actively wheezing on exam preoperatively and does not clear with albuterol, postponing the procedure should be given strong consideration. A peak flow meter is a useful gauge of patient optimization, especially if a baseline number is available for reference. If a patient is at 80% or less of his/her usual level, he/she is not optimized on the therapy. In some patients a course of oral steroids preoperatively may be of benefit.[25]

For patients falling into the COPD category, the same concerns apply as mentioned for asthmatics. Patients with COPD tend to be older and have other associated comorbidities, particularly cardiovascular problems. For those patients having minimally invasive procedures, pulmonary function testing is not necessary; however, those patients who are worsening in their disease course or who are not on medications may benefit from pulmonary function testing to assess response to bronchodilator therapy.

Although regional anesthesia is of potential benefit in this patient population, caution is warranted. With central neuraxial block there is a potential with high block level for compromise of the accessory muscles of respiration. Patients with respiratory disease may be more dependent on these muscles. Also, regarding peripheral nerve blocks of the upper extremity and trunk, concerns exist with risk of pneumothorax (particularly in patients with hyperinflated lungs that are characteristic of COPD). In addition, the ipsilateral phrenic nerve paralysis that inevitably follows successful interscalene brachial plexus block may be problematic in patients with preexisting severe lung dysfunction. Controlling postoperative pain in patients with COPD is an issue. Respiratory depression with opioid medication is undesirable. Potential means to minimize opioid requirements include regional anesthesia/analgesia, NSAIDs (provided the patient can take them), wound infiltration with local anesthetic, and acetaminophen.

Obstructive Sleep Apnea

One of the most important conditions to identify preoperatively in the surgical patient is obstructive sleep apnea (OSA). This is a relatively common entity occurring in about 4% of men and 2% of women.[26] Unfortunately it is underdiagnosed and patients often come for their procedure with this condition unrecognized. Careful questioning during the preoperative interview can elucidate important information. Key questions include a history of snoring, daytime somnolence, decreased sleep latency, and observed apnea episodes during sleep by a partner.[27] Patients giving a positive history should be referred for polysomnography studies. Although most OSA patients are obese men, this is not always the case. It is worth keeping in mind that OSA can occur in patients with normal body habitus who have other airway abnormalities. It may also occur in children with tonsillar hypertrophy. Patients with OSA are at risk of difficult ventilation/intubation, so a careful airway evaluation is mandatory. Also, the cardiovascular system should be evaluated in these patients as they are at risk of right ventricular failure and pulmonary hypertension.

Patients who use continuous positive airway pressure (CPAP) machines should bring them to their surgery. These patients by definition have severe OSA and should be at the very least watched overnight and thus are not candidates for more invasive ambulatory procedures. It is imperative that these patients be monitored closely with pulse oximetry.

Perioperative care of the OSA patient presents several difficulties. As mentioned above, the airway can be a problem but also anesthetic agents can aggravate the situation by further reducing the respiratory drive. Postoperative opioid medications likewise will lead to respiratory depression. For these reasons, OSA patients represent a higher risk for ambulatory surgery. The recurrent theme throughout this chapter is that the patient, procedure, and anesthetic must be considered together. There are situations where these patients may be operated on as outpatients. Minimally invasive procedures where postoperative opioid medications will not be needed and long-acting sedatives are not administered are acceptable in these patients. Regional anesthesia is well suited to this patient population as it can reduce opioid and anesthetic requirements. A reasonable policy for these patients should be adopted. One reported by Daley and colleagues sounds reasonable. These authors observe all of their patients who have any degree of OSA in their postanesthesia care unit (PACU) stay for 12 hr after their last sedative or opioid dose.[28] For these reasons most surgical procedures are not suitable for these patients on an outpatient basis. A recent article provides a thorough review of the anesthetic implications of OSA.[29]

Perioperative Management for the Patient with End-Stage Renal Disease

Like most of the other conditions discussed in this chapter, end-stage renal disease (ESRD) has implications for other organ systems, making perioperative management more challenging. The first major concern is the etiology of the renal failure. Diabetes and hypertension are the usual causes. In such patients concomitant pathology in other organ systems (e.g., cardiovascular, central nervous) are common. A detailed history and physical examination with appropriate investigations targeting these other systems is warranted. Younger patients with primary renal etiologies such as polycystic kidney are potentially less complicated. Nonetheless, important concerns in these patients include fluid and electrolyte balance. Patients presenting for elective surgery should have had their last dialysis within the last 24 hr. Electrolytes, particularly potassium, are important. A reasonable cutoff for elective surgery is a potassium level of 6.0 or greater. For patients with an elevated potassium level an ECG should be obtained to evaluate for signs of hyperkalemia. Patients with renal failure are also at higher risk of bleeding from impaired platelet function. Many practitioners avoid central neuraxial blocks in these patients for this reason along with the fact that fluid management is made more difficult secondary to sympathectomy-induced reductions in preload and afterload. Anemia is common in this patient population and is usually well tolerated. These patients should be given blood during dialysis if necessary because banked blood may have a potassium concentration as high as 21 mEq/L.[30] Since a dialysis-dependent patient has no way of eliminating potassium or excess circulating volume on his/her own, fluid replacement should only replace losses and potassium-containing fluids should be avoided (e.g., lactated Ringer). These patients also should be treated as being at risk for aspiration, as gastric emptying can be impaired. Table 40-2 lists certain drugs that should

be avoided or used with extreme caution in patients with ESRD because of active or toxic metabolites that require renal excretion. Other drugs, like succinylcholine, can be used safely in these patients with modest hyperkalemia.[31]

The most commonly performed surgical procedure in patients with ESRD is hemodialysis vascular access. Estimates show that this accounts for 20% of ESRD hospitalizations, costing $675 million annually.[32] These costs can be significantly reduced by performing these access surgeries on an outpatient basis.[32] Data exist showing the outpatient setting to be safe for these types of procedures provided there is appropriate patient selection.[33] Concerns still exist for these patients. Up to a 2.1% incidence of fatal cardiac events within 7 days after surgery has been reported while no significant difference in outcome between patients who received general anesthesia, brachial plexus block, or local infiltration by the surgeon was observed.[34]

Brachial plexus blockade is an excellent anesthetic technique for the creation or repair of a dialysis arteriovenous fistula. Approaches to blocking the brachial plexus are described in detail elsewhere in this text. Advantages include improved blood flow through the fistula and excellent pain control.[35] Also, the potential hemodynamic stresses of induction of general anesthesia are avoided. Contrary to what many believe, the pharmacokinetics of bupivacaine[36] and mepivacaine[37] do not appear to be altered in ESRD patients.

SUMMARY

This chapter provides a brief overview of some common conditions that exist in patients presenting for ambulatory surgery. The main emphasis, however, is on the fact that

Table 40-2 Drugs Commonly Used in Anesthesia with Prolonged Deleterious Effects in Patients with End-Stage Renal Disease

Drug (metabolite)	Potential Effect
Morphine (morphine-6-glucuronide)	Analgesia, potential respiratory depression
Meperidine (normeperidine)	Seizures
Diazepam (oxazepam)	Excessive sedation
Midazolam (1-hydroxy-midazolam)	Excessive sedation
Nitroprusside (thiocyanate)	Neurotoxicity
Vecuronium (desacetyl-vecuronium)	Prolonged paralysis
Pancuronium (3-hydroxy-pancuronium)	Prolonged paralysis

SOURCE: Adapted from Sladen RN. Anesthetic considerations for the patient with renal failure. Anesth Clin North Am 2000;18:863–82.

Table 40-3   Internet Resources for Preoperative Anesthetic Management of Common Diseases

Website Address	Sponsor	Topics Covered
www.qtdrugs.org	University of Arizona Health Science Center	Drugs to avoid in long QT syndrome
www.americanheart.org	American Heart Association	Guidelines for bacterial endocarditis prophylaxis, preoperative evaluation algorithms
www.sleepapnea.org	American Sleep Apnea Association	Information about obstructive sleep apnea, including perioperative evaluation
www.gasnet.org	Multiple sponsors	Many valuable resources pertaining to all aspects of anesthesiology
www.theanswerpage.com/anesthesiology	Multiple sponsors	Broad anesthesiology information resource in a question-of-the-day format

any evaluations of the surgical candidate should take into consideration both the patient's condition and the surgery itself. Ambulatory surgery represents a challenge because preoperative evaluation and optimization takes on perhaps a greater significance. Unplanned hospital admissions, emergency room visits, and unforeseen complications take a heavy toll on both the patient and the health care system. The importance of the preoperative evaluation is perhaps best illustrated by the evolution of preoperative screening units. These clinics allow patients to be seen by clinicians familiar with perioperative implications of anesthesia, surgery, and coexisting medical conditions prior to the day of their surgery. Thus a window of time exists for therapeutic maneuvers to increase the patient's suitability for surgery or to allow for postponement of the procedure. It is never a good thing when a case must be canceled on the day of surgery. Preoperative screening clinics help reduce that.

Throughout this chapter references to the medical literature are provided. Many of these refer the reader to review articles or text materials. It is hoped that the reader will consult these from time to time as needed. Stoelting and Dierdorf's *Anesthesia and Co-existing Disease* is perhaps the most useful text on that subject in general.[38] It should be on every anesthesia provider's bookshelf. As an added resource, Table 40-3 provides useful Internet websites. These offer a quick and convenient reference.

The ambulatory management of surgical patients with significant comorbidities is only going to increase. Therefore, it is in the best interest of providers of anesthesia to continue research endeavors in this patient population. In the future, perhaps more evidence-based guidelines will exist for optimization of the perioperative management of patients presenting for ambulatory surgery.

REFERENCES

1. Chung F, Mezei G, Tong D. Pre-existing medical conditions as predictors of adverse events in day-case surgery. Br J Anaesth 1999;83: 262–70.

2. American Diabetes Association (ADA). Consensus development conference on the diagnosis of coronary heart disease in people with diabetes. Diabetes Care 1998;21:1551–59.

3. Chassot PG, Delabays A, Spahn DR. Preoperative evaluation of patients with, or at risk of, coronary artery disease undergoing noncardiac surgery. Br J Anaesth 2002;89:747–59.

4. Eagle KA, Berger PB, Calkins H, et al. ACC/AHA guideline update for perioperative cardiovascular evaluation for non-cardiac surgery-executive summary: a report of the American College of Cardiology/American Heart Association Task Force on Practice Guidelines. Circulation 2002;105:1257–67.

5. Hogan K, Rusy D, Springhan SR. Difficult laryngoscopy in diabetes mellitus. Anesth Analg 1988;67:1162–65.

6. Zerr KJ, Furnary AP, Grunkemeier GL, et al. Glucose control lowers the risk of wound infection in diabetics after open heart operations. Ann Thorac Surg 1997;63:356–61.

7. Golden SH, Peart-Vigilance C, Kao WHL, et al. Perioperative glycemic control and the risk of infectious complications in a cohort of adults with diabetes. Diabetes Care 1999;22:1408–14.

8. Yamashita S, Yamaguchi H, Sakaguchi M, et al. Longer-term diabetic patients have a more frequent incidence of nosocomial infections after elective gastrectomy. Anesth Analg 2000;91:1176–81.

9. Olson R. Personal communication, 2002.

10. Coppieters MW, Van De Velde M, Stappaerts KH. Positioning in anesthesiology. Anesthesiology 2002;97:75–81.

11. Dix P, Howell S. Survey of cancellation rate of hypertensive patients undergoing anaesthesia and elective surgery. Br J Anaesth 2001;86: 789–93.

12. Howell SJ, Hemming AE, Allman KG, et al. Predictors of postoperative myocardial ischemia: the role of intercurrent arterial hypertension and other cardiovascular risk factors. Anaesthesia 1997;52:107–11.

13. Prys-Roberts C. Isolated systolic hypertension. Anaesthesia 2002; 57:607.

14. Stoelting RK, Dierdorf SF. Ischemic heart disease. In: Stoelting RK, Dierdorf SF (eds.), Anesthesia and Co-existing Disease, 4th ed. New York: Churchill Livingstone, 2002, pp. 1–24.

15. Kaluza GL, Joseph J, Lee JR, et al. Catastrophic outcomes of noncardiac surgery soon after coronary stenting. J Am Coll Cardiol 2000;35:1288–94.

16. Stoelting RK, Dierdorf SF. Abnormalities of cardiac conduction and cardiac rhythm. In: Stoelting RK, Dierdorf SF (eds.), Anesthesia and Co-existing Disease, 4th ed. New York: Churchill Livingstone, 2002, pp. 67–92.

17. Khan IA. Long QT syndrome: diagnosis and management. Am Heart J 2002;143:7–14.

18. Dajani AS, Taubert KA, Wilson W, et al. Prevention of bacterial endocarditis: recommendations by the American Heart Association. Circulation 1997;96:358–66.

19. Savage DD, Garrison RJ, Devereux RB, et al. Mitral valve prolapse in the general population. 1. Epidemiological features: the Framingham Study. Am Heart J 1983;106:571–76.

20. Hanson EW, Neerhut RK, Lynch C. Mitral valve prolapse. Anesthesiology 1996;85:178–95.

21. Stoelting RK, Dierdorf SF. Valvular heart disease. In: Stoelting RK, Dierdorf SF (eds.), *Anesthesia and Co-existing Disease*, 4th ed. New York: Churchill Livingstone, 2002, pp. 25–44.

22. Stoelting RK, Dierdorf SF. Asthma. In: Stoelting RK, Dierdorf SF (eds.), *Anesthesia and Co-existing Disease*, 4th ed. New York: Churchill Livingstone, 2002, pp. 193–204.

23. Mannino DM, Homa DM, Akinbami LJ, et al. Surveilance for asthma—United States, 1980–1999. MMWR Surveil Summ 2002 Mar 29;51:1–13.

24. Cheney FW, Posner KL, Caplan RA. Adverse respiratory events infrequently leading to malpractice suits: a closed claims analysis. Anesthesiology 1991;75:932–39.

25. Kabalin CS, Yarnold PR, Grammer LC. Low complication rate of corticosteroid-treated asthmatics undergoing surgical procedures. Arch Intern Med 1995;155:1379–84.

26. Young T, Palta M, Dempsey J, et al. The occurrence of sleep-disordered breathing among middle-aged adults. N Engl J Med 1993;328:1230–35.

27. Ogan OU, Plevak DJ. Anesthesia safety always an issue with obstructive sleep apnea. APSF Newslett 1997;12:14–15.

28. Daley MD, Norman PH, Coveler LA. Additional safety issues cited for sleep apnea cases. J Clin Monitor Comput 1998;14:213.

29. Loadsman JA, Hillman DR. Anaesthesia and sleep apnoea. Br J Anaesth 2001;86:254–66.

30. Sladen RN. Anesthetic considerations for the patient with renal failure. Anesth Clin North Am 2000;18:863–82.

31. Schow AJ, Lubarsky DA, Olson RA, et al. Can succinylcholine be used safely in hyperkalemic patients? Anesth Analg 2002;95:119–22.

32. Becker BN, Breiterman-White R, Nylander W, et al. Care pathway reduces hospitalizations and cost for hemodialysis vascular access surgery. Am J Kidney Dis 1997;30:525–31.

33. Wilson SE, Connall TP, White R, et al. Vascular access as an outpatient procedure. Ann Vasc Surg 1993;7:325–29.

34. Solomonson MD, Johnson ME, Ilstrup D. Risk factors in patients having surgery to create an arteriovenous fistula. Anesth Analg 1994;79:694–700.

35. Mouquet C, Bitker MO, Bailliart O, et al. Anaesthesia for creation of a forearm fistula in patients with endstage renal failure. Anesthesiology 1989;70:909–14.

36. Rice ASC, Pither CE, Tucker GT. Plasma concentrations of bupivacaine after supraclavicular brachial plexus blockade in patients with chronic renal failure. Anaesthesia 1991;46:354–57.

37. Rodriguez J, Quintela O, Lopez-Rivadulla M, et al. High doses of mepivacaine for brachial plexus block in patients with end-stage chronic renal failure: a pilot study. Eur J Anaesth 2001;18:171–76.

38. Stoelting RK, Dierdorf SF. *Anesthesia and Co-existing Disease*, 4th ed. New York: Churchill Livingstone, 2002.

Ambulatory Regional Anesthesia and Anticoagulation

THOMAS F. SLAUGHTER

INTRODUCTION

Although regional anesthesia has long been within the purview of obstetrical and orthopedic anesthesia practitioners, few within our specialty recognized the momentum driving the current resurgence of regional anesthesia. Patient, and government-mandated, demand for improved pain management no doubt have contributed to this surging popularity of regional anesthesia. However, equally important are data demonstrating improved outcomes. In a recent review comprising 141 trials and 9559 patients, central neuraxial blockade (spinal and/or epidural) reduced overall mortality by 30%, deep venous thrombosis by 44%, pulmonary embolism by 55%, and respiratory depression by 59% as compared to patients receiving general anesthesia alone. Transfusion requirements were reduced by 50% and were accompanied by additional reductions in myocardial infarctions and perioperative renal failure.[1] Given results such as these, and the relative rarity of major complications, increasing popularity of regional anesthesia techniques is of little surprise.

Major neurologic complications after regional anesthesia are rare; however, the potential nonetheless exists and appears increased in patients with coagulopathies—whether due to underlying disease or secondary to drug administration. Perioperative anticoagulation, a mainstay therapy for prevention of postoperative venous thrombotic complications after orthopedic surgery, more recently has been employed after most major surgeries.[2] Furthermore, potent anticoagulants, specifically antiplatelet regimens, increasingly are prescribed to reduce risk for recurrent stroke, peripheral vascular thrombosis, and acute coronary syndromes.[3] In fact, given the improving efficacy of anticoagulant regimens and aging demographics of our population, it is possible to conceive of a time in the near future at which a majority of surgical patients will be exposed to some form of perioperative anticoagulation. Do we simply forgo regional anesthesia techniques in patients requiring perioperative anticoagulants? To do so will unnecessarily deprive many patients of adequate perioperative analgesia and potentially expose them to increased perioperative morbidity and mortality. How, then, do we determine which patients safely may undergo regional anesthesia and which must receive an alternative anesthetic? Unfortunately, there are no simple answers. Each patient must be carefully and independently evaluated to assess risk and benefit of regional anesthesia in a specific setting.

Fortunately, recommendations pertaining to administration of regional anesthesia in the anticoagulated patient are available as published proceedings of the Second American Society of Regional Anesthesia (ASRA) Consensus Conference on Neuraxial Anesthesia and Anticoagulation.[4] However, data supporting these recommendations are, in many cases, limited, with resulting guidelines based on "expert opinion" as opposed to empirical evidence. The ASRA guidelines, and this chapter, in large part focus specifically on risks associated with central neuraxial blockade in anticoagulated patients. Obviously, bleeding—and the concomitant potential for nerve compression—may occur with nonneuraxial regional anesthetic techniques; however, given the fact that spinal hematoma represents the most serious and potentially devastating complication of regional anesthesia, it seems reasonable that the ASRA Consensus Conference, and likewise this chapter, focus primarily on risks associated with central neuraxial blockade as opposed to plexus and peripheral nerve blocks. Without doubt, the ASRA Consensus Conference summary provides core knowledge with which all practitioners of regional anesthesia must be familiar; however, informed decision making in this setting further necessitates an understanding of normal hemostasis, preoperative evaluation of coagulation, the pharmacology of currently available anticoagulants, as well as familiarity with published literature on which the ASRA recommendations have been based. Throughout this chapter, all recommendations regarding management of regional anesthesia in the setting of anticoagulation are based on published proceedings of the Second ASRA Consensus Conference on Neuraxial Anesthesia and Anticoagulation (available at www.ASRA.com).[4]

PHYSIOLOGY OF HEMOSTASIS

Plasma–Mediated Hemostasis

Fundamentally, the coagulation cascade constitutes an amplification system to rapidly accelerate thrombin generation at sites of vascular injury. After vascular injury, inactive trace plasma proteins are activated enzymatically in a cascading series of reactions, resulting in exponential increases in the concentration of end product—thrombin—at the injury site. Thrombin is the key regulatory enzyme in the hemostatic process—responsible for converting soluble plasma fibrinogen to an insoluble fibrin clot.[5] Equally important, thrombin plays a critical role in platelet activation as well as affecting activity of the fibrinolytic system.

For ease of discussion, the coagulation cascade traditionally is split into extrinsic and intrinsic pathways (Fig. 41-1). The extrinsic pathway, commonly assessed using the prothrombin time (PT) assay, only recently has been recognized as most important for the *in vivo* response to vascular injury.[6] At the time of vascular injury, tissue factor present in vascular subendothelium is exposed to flowing blood. Factor VIIa, ubiquitous in plasma, binds exposed tissue factor to create an enzymatic complex capable of activating factor X of the common pathway to generate thrombin.

The intrinsic pathway, commonly assessed using the activated partial thromboplastin time (aPTT) or the activated clotting time (ACT), appears to act as an amplification system to enhance further thrombin generation in the wake of extrinsic pathway activation.[6] The intrinsic pathway is stimulated further when blood contacts negatively charged surfaces (i.e., glass) or under specific conditions of complement activation. However, relevance of these pathways to normal hemostatic responses appears limited. Both the extrinsic and intrinsic pathways culminate in the final common pathway in which thrombin converts fibrinogen into a stable cross-linked fibrin clot.[5]

Platelet Adhesion and Aggregation

Under normal conditions platelets do not adhere to vascular endothelium. However, vascular injury exposes subendothelial proteins (i.e., collagen, von Willebrand factor, fibronectin), inducing platelet adhesion. Platelet adhesion triggers platelet activation with release of storage granule contents (including prostanoid endoperoxides) and expression of active glycoprotein receptors on platelet surface membranes.[7,8] Of particular importance is the activation of platelet surface glycoprotein IIb/IIIa (GPIIb/IIIa) complexes, which bind fibrinogen to "bridge" adjacent platelets, thereby generating a hemostatic plug. Stimulation by thrombin provides a critical alternative pathway for platelet activation. In addition to forming an important "skeletal" component of the hemostatic plug and delivering hemostatically active proteins to sites of vascular injury, platelet activation modifies platelet membrane phospholipid composition to facilitate binding of coagulation activation complexes—a process essential to propagation of coagulation and thrombin generation.[5]

Fibrinolysis

The fibrinolytic system comprises a delicately balanced series of pro- and antifibrinolytic enzymes responsible for maintaining vascular patency by dissolving fibrin clot. The key mediator responsible for degradation of fibrin, and in some circumstances fibrinogen, is the enzyme plasmin.[9]

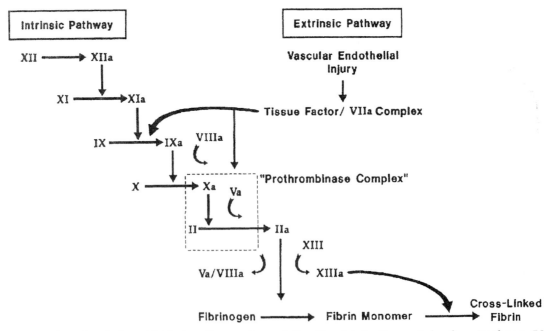

Figure 41-1   Summation of extrinsic and intrinsic pathways of coagulation. (Reprinted with permission from Estafanous FG, Barash PG, Reves JG [eds.], *Cardiac Anesthesia: Principles and Clinical Practice.* Philadelphia: JB Lippincott, 1994, p. 622.)

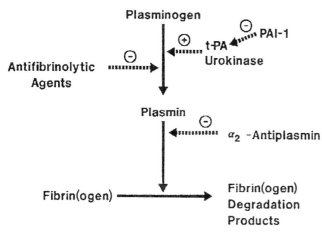

Figure 41-2 Principal mediators of fibrinolysis in vivo. Dashed lines demonstrate sites of action for promoters and inhibitors of fibrinolysis. (Reprinted with permission from Estafanous FG, Barash PG, Reves JG [eds.], *Cardiac Anesthesia: Principles and Clinical Practice.* Philadelphia: JB Lippincott, 1994, p. 623.)

Physiologically, plasmin is generated in tandem with clot formation—to downregulate the thrombotic process (Fig. 41-2). However, a number of pathophysiologic conditions as well as extrinsic administration of thrombolytic drugs (i.e., tissue plasminogen activator [t-PA], streptokinase, urokinase) are capable of activating the fibrinolytic system. In addition to degrading fibrin clot, plasmin is capable of cleaving platelet surface receptors to downregulate platelet activity. Furthermore, plasmin-mediated degradation of cofactors Va and VIIIa further limits thrombin generation by inhibiting the coagulation cascade.[5]

PREOPERATIVE EVALUATION OF HEMOSTASIS

Historically, preoperative assessment of hemostasis consisted of obtaining a standard panel of laboratory assays the evening prior to surgery—most commonly the platelet count, PT, aPTT, and in some cases the bleeding time. In today's cost-conscious medical environment, however, this practice has been seriously challenged. More important, the screening assays have proved of little value in identifying patients at increased risk for bleeding complications.[10] In fact, when applied nonselectively to preoperative populations, no laboratory-based assay of coagulation has proved more effective than a directed medical history.

If a significant preoperative bleeding disorder exists, a thorough and directed history and physical examination generally will lead to its identification. A patient's prior response to hemostatic challenges can prove extremely helpful in assessing current risk for perioperative bleeding. Hemostatic challenges are relatively common throughout life, and the preoperative history should be directed toward eliciting bleeding complications related to prior surgery such as tonsillectomy or circumcision. Oral surgery is a particularly good test of hemostasis owing to high concentrations of fibrinolytic enzymes in the oral cavity. Fur-

ther challenges to the hemostatic system include childbirth and menses.

Additional important considerations in the preoperative hemostatic history include determination of recent drug use (both prescription and nonprescription) as well as consideration of coexisting diseases that may affect hemostasis. In particular, hepatic and renal dysfunction should elicit further evaluation of the hemostatic system. Finally, family history must not be overlooked in the preoperative evaluation. A positive family history for a bleeding disorder should increase the clinician's suspicion for an inheritable bleeding disorder—although a negative history does not necessarily exclude this possibility. Variable penetrance and a high rate of spontaneous mutations, in the case of hemophilia, contribute to the limited value of a negative family history.

If the preoperative history proves suggestive of a bleeding disorder, further laboratory-based evaluations would be indicated and consultation with a hematologist may prove helpful. There are situations in which immediate laboratory screening for assessment of coagulation may be indicated, such as patients who are unable to provide a history or who have no prior exposure to a hemostatic challenge. In addition, surgeries known to affect the coagulation status or those for which bleeding could prove disastrous may necessitate further preoperative evaluation of coagulation. However, the fact remains that the most effective screening method to assess perioperative bleeding risk remains a directed medical history. In the absence of a preoperative history suggestive of bleeding, routine laboratory assessment of coagulation is rarely indicated.

SPINAL HEMATOMAS

Based on an exhaustive literature review compiling over 850,000 epidural and 650,000 spinal anesthetics, Tryba reported the incidence of spinal hematoma at less than 1 in 150,000 epidural anesthetics and less than 1 in 220,000 spinal anesthetics (95% confidence interval).[11] As further evidence of the rare occurrence of spinal hematomas, Vandermeulen and colleagues reviewed 18 clinical trials including over 200,000 patients receiving either epidural or spinal anesthesia for whom no cases of spinal hematoma were identified.[12] Regardless, the American Society of Anesthesiologists (ASA) analysis of closed claims reported that spinal cord injury resulting from spinal hematoma was one of the more common complications resulting in claims during the past decade.[13] Given the severity of the complication, underreporting seems likely, and the 'true' incidence of spinal hematoma after central neuraxial anesthesia remains unknown.

Despite the apparent rarity of spinal hematomas, considerable evidence suggests that patients with impaired hemostasis are at increased risk for this complication after central neuraxial blockade. In an extensive literature review, by Vandermeulen and colleagues, 61 cases of spinal hematoma (46 after epidural anesthesia; 15 after spinal anesthesia) reported between 1906 and 1994 were examined for possible predisposing factors.[12] In 42 of 61 cases, some form of coagulation disorder, either intrinsic or drug-induced, could be implicated as contributing to spinal hematoma formation. Furthermore, in nearly 90% of these episodes the resulting spinal hematoma was attributable to either a disorder of hemostasis or "difficulty with needle placement."[12]

Although bleeding and hematoma formation are not unique to central neuraxial anesthesia, the closed space of the spinal canal is particularly susceptible to vascular compromise in the setting of an enlarging hematoma. The diagnosis of spinal hematoma no doubt represents an extreme presentation of peridural hemorrhage—with the majority of vascular injuries thrombosing before symptomatic increases in spinal canal pressure. Most spinal hematomas are epidural in location and attributable to injury of Batson's venous plexus. Less common are subdural and subarachnoid hematomas, which have been attributed to disruption of radicular arteries and veins.[14] Subarachnoid hematomas are distinctly uncommon—presumably due to a limited subarachnoid vascular supply as well as dilution and clearance of blood by cerebrospinal fluid within the subarachnoid space.

Frequently attributable to vascular injury associated with central neuraxial blockade, spinal hematomas have been associated with vascular malformations as well as neoplastic disease. Indeed, the literature is replete with descriptions of spontaneous spinal hematomas identified in the absence of central neuraxial blockade; and in some cases, in the absence of concomitant anticoagulants and/or coagulopathies.[15] However, even in the case of spontaneous spinal hematoma, disorders of coagulation appear to be an important predisposing factor. Schmidt and Nolte[16] reviewed data surrounding 326 patients diagnosed with spontaneous spinal, subdural, or epidural hematomas and noted that most occurred in the setting of coagulation disorders. Groen and Ponssen further reported that some form of coagulopathy was present in 25% of 199 patients presenting with spontaneous spinal hematoma.[17] In the setting of neuraxial anesthesia, bleeding at the time of epidural placement (i.e., "bloody tap") has been reported in 1–10% of cases and as many as 18% of parturients.[18,19] Clearly, for the majority of patients bleeding resolves without clinical sequelae; however, any impairment of normal hemostasis would be expected to increase the potential for subsequent development of a spinal hematoma.

Regardless of the rarity with which symptomatic spinal hematomas occur, failure to appropriately diagnose and treat these patients results in devastating neurologic impairment with, not unexpectedly, dire medicolegal implications. Although the published literature generally cites severe back pain as an early sign of spinal cord compression, Vandermeulen's review of 61 cases of spinal hematoma associated with central neuraxial anesthesia cited progression of sensory or motor blockade as the presenting sign in two-thirds of patients.[12] Additional symptoms may include bowel or bladder dysfunction, meningismus, or local tenderness (Table 41-1). Suspicion of spinal hematoma necessitates immediate diagnostic imaging by magnetic resonance imaging (MRI), computerized tomography (CT), or myelography followed by emergent surgical decompression. In Vandermeulen's case series review, paraplegia occurred on average 14.5 ± 4 hr postoperatively.[12] Neurologic

Table 41-1   Signs and Symptoms Consistent with Spinal Hematoma

Impaired coagulation

Traumatic needle/catheter insertion

Muscle weakness

Back/lower-extremity pain

Urinary retention

Paraplegia

recovery is unlikely if surgical decompression is delayed longer than 12 hr—and the best chance for recovery occurs in patients undergoing surgery within 8 hr of symptom onset.[15] Vigilance remains the most effective means for limiting morbidity related to spinal hematoma. By carefully assessing preoperative risk for surgical bleeding and diligently monitoring neurologic recovery at frequent intervals postoperatively, the adverse consequences of spinal hematoma can be mitigated.

CENTRAL NEURAXIAL BLOCKADE IN THE ANTICOAGULATED PATIENT

Standard Intravenous Unfractionated Heparin

Standard unfractionated heparin is a heterogeneous mixture of glycosaminoglycans purified from animal tissues (most commonly porcine intestinal mucosa or bovine lung). Heparin produces anticoagulant activity by binding antithrombin in plasma and inducing a conformational change to augment antithrombin binding and subsequent inhibition of coagulation factors IIa (thrombin), IXa, Xa, and XIa.[20,21] Heparin's anticoagulant activity occurs immediately after intravenous (IV) injection. The biologic half-life of unfractionated heparin is roughly 30–60 min but is prolonged with higher doses. Heparin displays substantial pharmacokinetic and pharmacodynamic variability between patients, necessitating monitoring to achieve and maintain therapeutic targets. Heparin's anticoagulant effect is most commonly monitored with the aPTT with elevations of 1.5–2-fold baseline values considered adequate for management of venous thrombosis.[20] In emergent situations, the anticoagulant effect of heparin may be reversed by administration of protamine or fresh frozen plasma (FFP).

Few would dispute the risks associated with performing central neuraxial anesthesia in the setting of heparin-mediated anticoagulation. It is difficult to conceive of a clinical situation warranting neuraxial blockade in the presence of therapeutic heparin anticoagulation. However, a common clinical scenario is the patient for whom heparin anticoagulation is planned intra- or postoperatively. What is the risk for spinal hematoma in these settings? Fortunately, published literature provides a basis for assessing this risk.

The "landmark" study regarding central neuraxial anesthesia preceding intraoperative heparin administration is attributable to Rao and El-Etr.[22] After excluding patients with preoperative coagulopathies, continuous epidural or spinal anesthetics (3164 and 847 patients, respectively) were performed before vascular surgical procedures. At 50–60 min after neuraxial blockade, heparin was administered to maintain the ACT at twice the baseline value. Postoperatively, patients received intermittent low-dose injections of unfractionated heparin, and the catheters were removed 24 hr after surgery—60 min before a scheduled heparin injection. No cases of spinal hematoma were reported. In a similar trial, Odoom and Sih placed epidural catheters in 1000 patients preceding intraoperative heparin administration.[23] In contrast to the patients in Rao and El-Etr's study, these patients also were administered a coumarin oral anticoagulant preoperatively. Epidural catheters were removed 48 hr postoperatively after laboratory confirmation of "normal" coagulation. No spinal hematomas occurred.

Further investigations by Ellison et al.[24] and Baron et al.[25] reported heparin administration intraoperatively in a cumulative sample of nearly 2000 patients with no subsequent spinal hematomas. Important considerations common to these trials, however, were that heparin administration was delayed after central neuraxial blockade, adjuvant anticoagulants and patients with preexisting coagulopathies were excluded, and dosing/monitoring of anticoagulation was carefully regulated.

Delay between central neuraxial blockade and subsequent heparin administration provides an important safety measure, as evidenced by the work of Ruff and Dougherty.[26] In an observational investigation, Ruff and Dougherty reported the incidence of spinal hematoma after lumbar puncture in the setting of stroke.[26] Lumbar punctures were performed to exclude the diagnosis of intracerebral hemorrhage before heparin administration. Spinal hematomas reportedly occurred in 7 of 342 patients, with no spinal hematomas reported in patients not receiving heparin. Factors identified as contributing to development of spinal hematoma in this setting were heparin administration within 1 hr of lumbar puncture, concurrent aspirin administration, and traumatic punctures. No doubt one could argue that larger needle sizes and possibly less skilled expertise in needle placement contributed to the high incidence of spinal hematoma in this setting; however, these data argue for delaying heparin administration after central neuraxial blockade as well as minimizing the potential for vascular trauma at the time of needle and/or catheter insertion.

Central Neuraxial Blockade and Standard Intravenous Unfractionated Heparin

In the patient currently anticoagulated with heparin, neuraxial anesthesia should be avoided until heparin administration can be discontinued and normal hemostasis assured

by laboratory testing. Discontinue heparin at least 4–6 hr preceding the need for central neuraxial anesthesia and confirm normalization of the aPTT before proceeding. Should heparin administration be required intraoperatively, heparin administration must be delayed a minimum of 1 hr after central neuraxial blockade. Heparin administration should be directed by appropriate monitoring to ensure that excessive anticoagulation does not occur. Removal of indwelling neuraxial catheters must occur under the same precautions as needle insertion—delaying catheter removal until normalization of coagulation.

Low-Dose Subcutaneous Unfractionated Heparin

Low-dose subcutaneous heparin administration remains a common approach for prevention of postoperative thromboembolic disease. Typically administered as a subcutaneous injection of 5000 U every 12 hr, low-dose heparin has proved a highly efficacious antithrombotic.[27] A majority of patients demonstrate no measurable effects on common hemostasis assays such as the aPTT; however, a small fraction of patients, perhaps 2–4%, may achieve "therapeutic" anticoagulation despite this low-dose regimen. Onset of anticoagulation is delayed after subcutaneous injection, but peak plasma concentrations typically occur within 2 hr after administration. Monitoring of anticoagulation in this setting generally is not recommended as the degree of anticoagulation achieved is immeasurable with common laboratory testing. Older patients and those with severe coexisting disease appear at greater risk for an exaggerated anticoagulant response.

Risk of spinal hematoma after central neuraxial anesthesia in the setting of low-dose subcutaneous unfractionated heparin appears low. Although isolated case reports of this complication appear in the literature,[12,28,29] nine published case series comprising over 9000 patients reported no spinal hematomas in the setting of low-dose subcutaneous unfractionated heparin.[30]

Central Neuraxial Blockade and Low-Dose Subcutaneous Unfractionated Heparin

If possible, subcutaneous heparin administration should occur 1 or more hr after central neuraxial blockade. Similarly, withdrawal of an epidural catheter should occur 1–2 hr before subcutaneous heparin administration.[30] To minimize the potential for spinal hematoma, it is critically important that adjuvant anticoagulant drugs be avoided during the period of central neuraxial blockade and catheterization. Similarly, any underlying coagulopathy will increase substantially the risk for spinal hematoma after central neuraxial blockade. In the absence of debilitating disease or extremes of age, monitoring of the aPTT after subcutaneous heparin administration appears unnecessary. However, in patients receiving heparin for more than 5 days, performance of a platelet count may be prudent to exclude the possibility of thrombocytopenia secondary to heparin-associated thrombocytopenia (HAT).[31]

Low-Molecular-Weight Heparins

Low-molecular-weight heparins (LMWHs) comprise a class of drugs derived from chemical purification of standard unfractionated heparin. As the name implies, low-molecular-weight fractions are acquired after enzymatic and/or hydrolytic processing of unfractionated heparin. Low-molecular-weight heparin fragments express different biologic activities and characteristics than standard unfractionated heparin.[20] Specifically, LMWHs possess more predictable biologic availability after subcutaneous injection, have longer half-lives (approximating 4–6 hr, providing for once- or twice-daily dosing), and lack the need for laboratory monitoring. In contrast to the strong inhibitory activity against thrombin exhibited by standard unfractionated heparin, the LMWHs preferentially inhibit factor Xa of the common pathway. Although monitoring is not commonly performed, it is complicated by the need for specialized laboratory-based measurements of anti-Xa activity.[32] Furthermore, in an emergent situation the anticoagulant activity of LMWHs is only partly reversible by protamine.

Initial reports of LMWH administration in the setting of neuraxial anesthesia appeared quite favorable. European reviews by Bergqvist et al.[33] and Bachmann et al.[34] including nearly 20,000 patients identified only a single case of spinal hematoma after neuraxial anesthesia in patients receiving LMWHs. However, shortly after introduction of LMWHs into the United States it became evident that these drugs posed a different perioperative risk profile as compared to standard unfractionated heparin. As of 2002, over 60 cases of spinal hematoma in association with central neuraxial anesthesia and LMWH were identified in the United States.[4] The explanation for this increased incidence of spinal hematomas in the United States is subject to speculation; however, in the United States LMWHs are commonly administered at a higher and more frequent dose than that used in Europe. Furthermore, European practitioners were early to adopt practice guidelines regarding LMWH dosing and time of central neuraxial blockade and catheter removal.

Central Neuraxial Blockade and Low-Molecular-Weight Heparins

Minimizing the potential for development of spinal hematoma in the setting of LMWH therapy requires extreme vigilance with regard to timing of drug administration, central neuraxial blockade, and catheter removal. In addition, neuraxial anesthesia should be avoided in patients with preexisting coagulopathies or those receiving adjuvant anticoagulant drugs when perioperative LMWH therapy is planned. Should traumatic needle placement occur resulting in a "bloody tap," consideration should be given to delaying initiation of LMWH therapy for 24 hr.[4]

If LMWH is administered preoperatively, central neuraxial blockade should be delayed for a minimum of 10–12 hr. Higher-dose regimens of LMWH may necessitate delay of central neuraxial blockade for 24 hr. With single daily dosing of LMWH, the first dose of LMWH should be administered 4–8 hr after surgery. Indwelling neuraxial catheters may be retained postoperatively; however, catheter removal should occur a minimum of 10–12 hr after the last dose of LMWH, and subsequent dosing of LMWH should be delayed for a minimum of 2 hr after catheter removal. In the setting of twice-daily dosing of LMWH, the neuraxial catheter should be removed before initiation of LMWH therapy as the potential for bleeding and spinal hematoma formation is likely high.[4] However, central neuraxial anesthesia may be used in this setting if the first dose of LMWH is delayed until 24 hr after central neuraxial blockade. Neurologic deficits have been reported as long as 12 or more hr after removal of epidural catheters in the setting of anticoagulation with LMWHs; therefore, careful neurologic assessment at frequent intervals remains critical to minimizing the potential for neurologic injury associated with spinal hematoma after central neuraxial blockade.

Coumarin Oral Anticoagulants

Warfarin is a 4-hydroxycoumarin derivative that mediates antithrombotic activity by blocking regeneration of vitamin K from its epoxide. Vitamin K is an essential component for generation of clotting factors II (thrombin), VII, IX, and X. Vitamin K is needed to add γ-carboxyglutamic acid residues to these clotting factors—a component necessary for binding calcium and for allowing these factors to bind to platelet phospholipid surfaces during formation of coagulation activation complexes.

Warfarin is absorbed from the gastrointestinal tract in 1.5–2 hr and has a half-life of approximately 40 hr.[35] Effects of warfarin on the coagulation system are monitored with the PT assay and are dependent on the half-life of vitamin K–dependent clotting factors.[36] In particular, factor VII with a half-life of only 5 hr falls rapidly after initiating warfarin therapy to produce a prolongation of the PT assay. Similarly, on discontinuation of warfarin therapy, levels of factor VII are rapidly repleted with partial normalization of the PT assay; however, factors II, IX, and X with half-lives ranging between 24 and 48 hr require several days for repletion. The intensity of anticoagulation achieved with a given dose of warfarin is highly variable with numerous confounding effects posed by diet, adjuvant medications, and coexisting medical conditions. To account for assay variability between institutions, monitoring of coumarin-based anticoagulation is frequently reported as the International Normalized Ratio (INR). The INR is simply a description of the PT ratio (patient PT/control PT) modified by a factor termed the International Sensitivity Index (ISI), which reflects the sensitivity of a particular institution's test reagents as compared to international standards. Typically, low-intensity anticoagulation is reflected by INRs between 2 and 3, with higher INR values signifying greater degrees of anticoagulation.[32]

Central neuraxial anesthesia generally would be contraindicated in any patient with ongoing coumarin oral anticoagulant therapy. Several studies support the safety of performing central neuraxial anesthesia in patients who have recently discontinued oral anticoagulants. Odoom and Sih reported no neurologic complications in 950 patients undergoing vascular surgical procedures after preoperative oral anticoagulants.[23] Although the degree of anticoagulation in these patients is unclear, laboratory testing suggested some degree of anticoagulation existed preoperatively. Epidural catheters were retained for 48 hr postoperatively. A large case series published by Horlocker and colleagues similarly reported no spinal hematomas in 188 patients receiving epidural catheters in the setting of low-dose coumarin therapy.[37] These data suggest that with careful attention to assuring preoperative normalization of hemostasis, it is possible to safely perform central neuraxial anesthesia in patients recently initiating or discontinuing coumarin oral anticoagulants. Failure to ensure normalization of coagulation before central neuraxial blockade has been associated with the occurrence of spinal hematoma.[38,39]

Central Neuraxial Blockade and Coumarin Oral Anticoagulants

Coumarin oral anticoagulants should be discontinued a minimum of 4–5 days preceding the need for central neuraxial blockade. Furthermore, normalization of hemostasis should be ensured preoperatively by determination of the PT assay. In the presence of active anticoagulation, central neuraxial blockade would be contraindicated. Presence of any adjuvant anticoagulant medications will increase the potential for bleeding—possibly without affecting the laboratory assessment of anticoagulation as reflected by the PT assay.

If the postoperative management includes use of an indwelling neuraxial catheter, similar attention to ensuring normal hemostasis should occur before catheter removal.[40] Epidural catheters must not be removed in the presence of therapeutic anticoagulation.[4] In emergent situations, vitamin K and/or FFP may be administered to reverse rapidly the effect of coumarin oral anticoagulants.[41] In the setting of postoperative coumarin therapy, neuraxial catheters should be removed prior to elevations of the PT assay and INR. As with all forms of central neuraxial anesthesia, monitoring of neurologic status should be extended into the period after removal of the neuraxial catheter—as long as 24 hr after catheter removal. If the INR exceeds 1.5 at the time of catheter removal, neurologic monitoring should be extended beyond 24 hr.

Thrombolytics

Thrombolytic agents promote clot lysis by accelerating the enzymatic conversion of plasminogen to plasmin. Plasmin impairs the hemostatic process at multiple levels including fibrin degradation to disrupt the hemostatic plug, destruction of select plasma coagulation factors (i.e., fibrinogen, cofactors Va and VIIIa), and cleavage of platelet surface receptors to impair platelet adhesion and aggregation.[42] Thrombolytics are commonly employed to achieve revascularization in acute coronary syndromes, venous thromboembolism, and peripheral arterial occlusion.[43] Although the half-life of the most commonly employed

thrombolytics (i.e., tPA, streptokinase, urokinase) ranges from 5 to 30 min, the effects of these drugs on hemostasis are long-lived and generally require repletion of degraded plasma proteins for normalization of coagulation.[44] Several days may be required for resumption of normal hemostasis. In emergent situations, it may be possible to reduce thrombolytic activity by administration of an antifibrinolytic drug (i.e., aprotinin, epsilon aminocaproic acid, tranexamic acid) and then to replete degraded coagulation factors by administration of blood components including cryoprecipitate and platelets.[42]

While there are no prospective studies addressing the safety of central neuraxial anesthesia with thrombolytic therapy, the relatively common occurrence of hemorrhagic complications after thrombolytics dictates against central neuraxial blockade.[45,46] Several reports of spinal hematoma in the setting of central neuraxial anesthesia and thrombolytic therapy have appeared in the literature.[47–49] In some cases exposure to thrombolytics occurred after spinal or epidural blockade with thrombolytics having been administered to treat postoperative myocardial ischemia.

Central Neuraxial Blockade and Thrombolytics

Administration of thrombolytic drugs is associated with substantial risk for bleeding complications. Despite a lack of supporting evidence in the published literature, central neuraxial blockade should be avoided in patients who recently have received or are expected to receive thrombolytic therapy. There are no data to suggest a safe period after thrombolytic administration at which time central neuraxial blockade would no longer pose increased risk for spinal hematoma.[50] However, given surgeons' reluctance to pursue elective surgery in these patients, a minimum delay of 10 days–2 weeks between thrombolytic therapy and central neuraxial blockade may be prudent. A detailed laboratory-based assessment of coagulation to assure normalization of hemostasis before proceeding with central neuraxial blockade is justified.

Antiplatelet Agents

Aspirin and Nonsteroidal Anti-inflammatory Drugs

Given increasing therapeutic indications for aspirin and nonsteroidal anti-inflammatory drugs (NSAIDs), patient exposure to antiplatelet drugs preoperatively has become nearly ubiquitous. Aspirin and NSAIDs are rapidly absorbed after oral ingestion; however, their relatively short half-lives in plasma belie the duration of resulting platelet dysfunction.[51] Both aspirin and NSAIDs acetylate platelet cyclooxygenase to inhibit platelet aggregation.[52] In the case of aspirin, platelet inhibition is irreversible for the life of the platelet, whereas with other NSAIDs platelet aggregation generally returns to normal over 1–3 days.

Aspirin and other NSAIDs administered in isolation appear to pose minimal risk for spinal hematoma after central neuraxial anesthesia. Several relatively large trials have assessed the potential for spinal hematoma in this setting. In the Collaborative Low-Dose Aspirin Study in Pregnancy (CLASP) trial, 2783 parturients undergoing epidural anesthesia were randomized to receive aspirin 60 mg daily until delivery.[53] Of the 1422 subjects receiving aspirin, no spinal hematomas were identified. In another trial of 924 subjects, Horlocker and colleagues noted no increased bleeding at needle or catheter placement in the 39% of patients receiving antiplatelet drugs preoperatively; in addition, no spinal hematomas were reported.[54] Furthermore, case reports of spinal hematoma associated with central neuraxial anesthesia and NSAID therapy are distinctly unusual.[12,55]

Thienopyridine Derivatives

Ticlopidine and clopidogrel, antiplatelet drugs structurally related to thienopyridines, selectively inhibit adenosine diphosphate (ADP)-induced platelet aggregation. Rapidly absorbed after oral ingestion, the thienopyridines' short plasma half-lives again fail to reflect the prolonged duration of platelet dysfunction resulting from exposure to these drugs—typically 14 days for ticlopidine and 7 days for clopidogrel.[56]

With the exception of a few case reports describing spinal hematoma after central neuraxial blockade in the setting of either ticlopidine or clopidogrel, there is little empirical data with which to clarify risk associated with these drugs.[57–59] Given the general caution with which surgeons approach these patients and the consensus that therapy with thienopyridines poses increased risk for bleeding, pursuit of central neuraxial anesthetic techniques in patients exposed to these drugs merits extreme caution and might best be avoided until additional data assessing risk in this setting becomes available.

Glycoprotein IIb/IIIa Inhibitors

Recent recognition of the importance of platelet surface glycoprotein receptors to platelet adhesion and aggregation, regardless of the stimulatory pathway leading to platelet activation, has led to development of several novel inhibitory agents of platelet surface GPIIb/IIIa receptors. In contrast to aspirin and the thienopyridine derivatives, whose platelet inhibitory effects may be overridden under circumstances of strong platelet-stimulatory activity, the GPIIb/IIIa inhibitors have proved a potent selective means for disrupting the platelet contribution to hemostasis.[46] Platelet-inhibitory effects occur immediately after IV administration, and as with other platelet antagonists discussed thus far, platelet-inhibitory effects substantially exceed plasma half-lives of the respective GPIIb/IIIa inhibitors (platelet inhibition duration: eptifibatide and tirofiban, 8 hr; abciximab, 48 hr).[60,61]

As with the thienopyridine derivatives, few empirical data exist to clarify the risk of central neuraxial blockade in association with GPIIb/IIIa administration. Given preliminary data reporting excessive surgical hemorrhage, and frequent concomitant administration of adjuvant anticoagulants in these patients, central neuraxial blockade best

may be avoided in the presence of active anticoagulation with GPIIb/IIIa inhibitors pending availability of additional safety data.

Central Neuraxial Blockade and Antiplatelet Agents

In the case of aspirin and NSAIDs, a substantial literature supports the safety of performing central neuraxial blockade despite ongoing therapy with these drugs. In the case of isolated therapy with aspirin or NSAIDs, no alterations in approach to regional anesthetic technique appear warranted. However, administration of these antiplatelet drugs to patients with preexisting coagulopathies or to those receiving adjuvant anticoagulants will increase the risk for spinal hematoma after central neuraxial blockade.

In the case of thienopyridine derivatives and GPIIb/IIIa inhibitors, no prospective inquiries assessing risk of central neuraxial blockade in association with these drugs have been published. Surgical bleeding appears to be increased when performed during active anticoagulation with either drug class. A consensus of the surgical literature suggests that elective surgery be delayed a minimum of 8 hr after eptifibatide or tirofiban and 48 hr in the case of abciximab to minimize potential for excessive bleeding.[4] Manufacturers further recommend that epidural procedures be avoided during therapy with GPIIb/IIIa inhibitors. In addition, several case reports have been published describing spinal hematoma formation in association with central neuraxial blockade and thienopyridine administration. In the case of both thienopyridine derivatives and GPIIb/IIIa inhibitors, central neuraxial anesthetic techniques likely pose substantial risk for spinal hematoma and would best be avoided allowing time for discontinuation of the drug and normalization of platelet function.

Direct Thrombin Inhibitors

Given the importance of thrombin and the thrombotic process to many vascular diseases, it comes as little surprise that substantial pharmaceutical research efforts are focused on development of novel anticoagulants with greater specificity and potency than heparin and coumarin derivatives.[62] Several direct thrombin inhibitors derived from leech saliva (bivalirudin: The Medicines Company, Cambridge, MA; lepirudin and desirudin: Aventis Pharmaceuticals, Paris, France) have proved particularly efficacious as antithrombotics and are now in various phases of clinical testing and development. Argatroban, another novel direct thrombin inhibitor, has been employed as an alternative anticoagulant in the settings of HAT and cardiopulmonary bypass.[63] Monitoring modalities specific to these anticoagulants are not yet widely available. In fact, optimal dosing for these agents has yet to be determined. No "reversal agents" are available for any of these compounds, and severe bleeding has been associated with administration of each of the direct thrombin inhibitors.

Central Neuraxial Blockade and Direct Thrombin Inhibitors

Given limited availability of these drugs thus far, there are no empirical data to define their risk for spinal hematoma in the setting of central neuraxial blockade. Efficacy of these drugs to reduce morbidity and mortality associated with acute coronary syndromes and other vascular disease, however, suggests their use no doubt will increase the risk for spinal hematoma. Although there are no data to support specific recommendations regarding the use of central neuraxial anesthesia in association with direct thrombin inhibitors, a prudent course of action would appear to be avoidance of central neuraxial blockade pending availability of additional safety data.

Herbal Therapies

Self-administered herbal therapies increasingly have gained favor among patients as alternative therapy for a variety of illnesses. Although the efficacy of these herbal agents remains unclear, there is preliminary evidence to suggest that some of these compounds may affect hemostasis and thereby affect the potential for perioperative bleeding. Garlic, gingko biloba, and ginseng all have been reported to possess platelet-inhibitory activity.[64] In a few instances, herbal therapies have been implicated in spontaneous hemorrhagic complications.[65,66] No prospective randomized trials assessing the potential for herbal therapies to enhance perioperative hemorrhagic risk have been published.

Central Neuraxial Blockade and Herbal Therapies

The potential for any single herbal therapy to potentiate development of spinal hematoma after central neuraxial anesthesia appears remote. At present, ASRA guidelines do not recommend modification of regional anesthetic practice in the setting of herbal therapies.[4] However, potential for drug interactions with herbal therapies remains and administration of herbal therapy in conjunction with adjuvant anticoagulants may increase the risk for spinal hematoma in the setting of central neuraxial blockade.

PLEXUS AND PERIPHERAL NERVE BLOCKS IN THE ANTICOAGULATED PATIENT

Thus far, our discussions of regional anesthesia in the anticoagulated patient have related exclusively to central neuraxial blockade—and with good reason. Spinal hematoma represents one of the most feared complications of neuraxial anesthesia—frequently resulting in catastrophic outcomes for the patient. A considerable literature exists reporting this complication, providing, in some cases, evidence to support recommendations regarding central neuraxial blockade in the setting of anticoagulant therapy.

In contrast, there are no prospective randomized trials, or even substantial case series, examining the incidence of bleeding complications after plexus or peripheral nerve blockade. In fact, there are few reports of complications after performance of these blocks in anticoagulated patients. No doubt, this fortuitous finding is attributable in part to availability of space to allow enlargement of an expanding hematoma without compromising adjacent nerves. Published evidence from the cardiology and vascular radiology literature further supports this hypothesis—as the incidence of nerve injury after vascular access procedures to the groin using relatively large introducer catheters is rare.[67]

This is not to say, however, that vascular injury does not occur after plexus or peripheral nerve blockade. Significant bleeding, in some cases requiring transfusion, has been reported after nonneuraxial regional anesthetic blocks—most often in the case of lumbar plexus or psoas compartment blocks.[68–71] Specifically, large retroperitoneal hematomas have been reported in association with psoas compartment block performed in proximity to LMWH administration—as well as both ticlopidine and clopidogrel.[72–74] In most cases reported blood loss, as opposed to nerve injury, proved to be the most significant complication. Again, the lack of substantial published literature makes specific recommendations regarding nonneuraxial regional anesthesia in the setting of anticoagulation difficult. A conservative approach would be simply to apply the ASRA Consensus Conference recommendations for central neuraxial blockade to nonneuraxial regional anesthetic techniques. However, this is likely too restrictive an approach, which will unnecessarily exclude patients from receiving the benefits of perioperative regional anesthesia. No doubt, increasing perioperative anticoagulation and growing applications for regional anesthesia techniques will provide greater understanding of the risks and benefits specific to these approaches.

SUMMARY

Neurologic complications after regional anesthesia are rare. However, in the presence of impaired coagulation, risk for bleeding complications after regional anesthesia clearly is increased. At the very least, the potential for paraplegia in the setting of impaired hemostasis after central neuraxial blockade necessitates a detailed assessment of risks and benefits.

Therapeutic anticoagulation generally precludes central neuraxial blockade; however, plexus and peripheral nerve blockade may be reasonable if potential benefits outweigh the risk posed by subsequent bleeding and hematoma formation. Furthermore, these considerations should be discussed carefully with the patient preoperatively and documented during the preoperative consent process. Lesser degrees of anticoagulation may be compatible with neuraxial as well as other forms of regional anesthesia. In general, exposure to multiple anticoagulants or the presence of a preexisting coagulopathy in the setting of anticoagulant administration will increase the potential for bleeding after regional anesthesia. A careful medical history directed

Table 41-2   Steps to Minimize Risk for Spinal Hematoma after Central Neuraxial Blockade

Ensure normalization of coagulation before needle placement

Use midline approach for needle insertion

Avoid multiple attempts at needle insertion

Delay anticoagulant administration at least 1 hr after needle/catheter placement

Monitor and limit anticoagulation during presence of epidural catheter

Ensure normalization of coagulation before catheter removal

Assess for neurologic recovery after needle insertion or catheter removal

at assessment of bleeding risk must be incorporated into the preoperative evaluation. Evidence suggestive of increased bleeding risk may necessitate preoperative laboratory assessment of coagulation.

Several simple measures are available to reduce the potential for bleeding complications after regional anesthesia in the setting of anticoagulant drugs (Table 41-2). First, if possible, discontinue anticoagulant medications and delay the regional anesthetic until normalization of coagulation as documented by laboratory testing. Furthermore, resumption of the anticoagulant should be delayed as long as possible after needle placement (minimum of 1 hr). Second, catheter removal carries substantial risk for bleeding and hematoma formation; therefore, catheter removal should occur using the same precautions adhered to during needle placement. Finally, vigilant monitoring is needed postoperatively to verify recovery of neurologic function and to ensure that excessive degrees of anticoagulation do not occur after needle and/or catheter placement. More dilute concentrations of local anesthetic may be appropriate for continuous infusion so as not to mask neurologic deficits associated with spinal hematoma formation. Clinical applications for anticoagulants will no doubt continue to evolve, creating increased numbers of patients for whom preoperative anticoagulation is the norm. As such, careful preoperative assessment and communication between the surgical and anesthesia teams will be critical to enhance and to expand further the indications for regional anesthesia in the perioperative setting.

REFERENCES

1. Rodgers A, Walker N, Schug S, et al. Reduction of postoperative mortality and morbidity with epidural or spinal anaesthesia: results from overview of randomised trials. Br Med J 2000;321:1493.

2. Spandorfer J, Merli G. Anticoagulation and elective surgery. N Engl J Med 1997;337:938.

3. Anand SS, Yusuf S. Oral anticoagulants in patients with coronary artery disease. J Am Coll Cardiol 2003;41:62S.

4. Horlocker TT, Wedel DJ, Benzon H, et al. Regional anesthesia in the anticoagulated patient: defining the risks (the second ASRA Consensus Conference on Neuraxial Anesthesia and Anticoagulation). Reg Anesth Pain Med 2003;28:172.

5. Furie B, Furie BC. Molecular and cellular biology of blood coagulation. N Engl J Med 1992;326:800.

6. Gailani D, Broze GJ Jr. Factor XI activation in a revised model of blood coagulation. Science 1991;253:909.

7. Weiss HJ. Platelet physiology and abnormalities of platelet function (first of two parts). N Engl J Med 1975;293:531.

8. Weiss HJ. Platelet physiology and abnormalities of platelet function (second of two parts). N Engl J Med 1975;293:580.

9. Vassalli JD, Sappino AP, Belin D. The plasminogen activator/plasmin system. J Clin Invest 1991;88:1067.

10. Munro J, Booth A, Nicholl J. Routine preoperative testing: a systematic review of the evidence. Health Technol Assess 1997;1:i.

11. Tryba M. [Epidural regional anesthesia and low molecular heparin: Pro]. Anasthesiol Intensivmed Notfallmed Schmerzther 1993;28:179.

12. Vandermeulen EP, Van Aken H, Vermylen J. Anticoagulants and spinal-epidural anesthesia. Anesth Analg 1994;79:1165.

13. Cheney FW, Domino KB, Caplan RA, et al. Nerve injury associated with anesthesia: a closed claims analysis. Anesthesiology 1999;90:1062.

14. Masdeu JC, Breuer AC, Schoene WC. Spinal subarachnoid hematomas: clue to a source of bleeding in traumatic lumbar puncture. Neurology 1979;29:872.

15. Kreppel D, Antoniadis G, Seeling W. Spinal hematoma: a literature survey with meta-analysis of 613 patients. Neurosurg Rev 2003;26:1.

16. Schmidt A, Nolte H. [Subdural and epidural hematomas following epidural anesthesia: a literature review]. Anaesthesist 1992;41:276.

17. Groen RJ, Ponssen H. The spontaneous spinal epidural hematoma: a study of the etiology. J Neurol Sci 1990;98:121.

18. Ben-David B. Complications of regional anesthesia: an overview. Anesthesiol Clin North Am 2002;20:665.

19. Tryba M, Wedel DJ. Central neuraxial block and low molecular weight heparin (enoxaparine): lessons learned from different dosage regimes in two continents. Acta Anaesthesiol Scand 1997;Suppl 111:100.

20. Morris TA. Heparin and low molecular weight heparin: background and pharmacology. Clin Chest Med 2003;24:39.

21. Stow PJ, Burrows FA. Anticoagulants in anaesthesia. Can J Anaesth 1987;34:632.

22. Rao TL, El-Etr AA. Anticoagulation following placement of epidural and subarachnoid catheters: an evaluation of neurologic sequelae. Anesthesiology 1981;55:618.

23. Odoom JA, Sih IL. Epidural analgesia and anticoagulant therapy: experience with one thousand cases of continuous epidurals. Anaesthesia 1983;38:254.

24. Ellison N, Jobes DR, Schwartz AJ. Implications of anticoagulant therapy. Int Anesthesiol Clin 1982;20:121.

25. Baron HC, LaRaja RD, Rossi G, et al. Continuous epidural analgesia in the heparinized vascular surgical patient: a retrospective review of 912 patients. J Vasc Surg 1987;6:144.

26. Ruff RL, Dougherty JH Jr. Complications of lumbar puncture followed by anticoagulation. Stroke 1981;12:879.

27. Collins R, Scrimgeour A, Yusuf S, et al. Reduction in fatal pulmonary embolism and venous thrombosis by perioperative administration of subcutaneous heparin: overview of results of randomized trials in general, orthopedic, and urologic surgery. N Engl J Med 1988;318:1162.

28. Greaves JD. Serious spinal cord injury due to haematomyelia caused

by spinal anaesthesia in a patient treated with low-dose heparin. Anaesthesia 1997;52:150.

29. Sandhu H, Morley-Forster P, Spadafora S. Epidural hematoma following epidural analgesia in a patient receiving unfractionated heparin for thromboprophylaxis. Reg Anesth Pain Med 2000;25:72.

30. Liu SS, Mulroy MF. Neuraxial anesthesia and analgesia in the presence of standard heparin. Reg Anesth Pain Med 1998;23:157.

31. Slaughter TF, Greenberg CS. Heparin-associated thrombocytopenia and thrombosis: implications for perioperative management. Anesthesiology 1997;87:667.

32. Hirsh J, Dalen J, Guyatt G. The sixth (2000) ACCP guidelines for antithrombotic therapy for prevention and treatment of thrombosis. American College of Chest Physicians. Chest 2001;119:1S.

33. Bergqvist D, Lindblad B, Matzsch T. Risk of combining low molecular weight heparin for thromboprophylaxis and epidural or spinal anesthesia. Semin Thromb Hemost 1993;19 (Suppl 1):147.

34. Bachmann MB, Michaelis G, Biscoping J, et al. [Neurologic complication following spinal anesthesia for manual detachment of the placenta]. Geburtshilfe Frauenheilkd 1990;50:231.

35. Hirsh J, Dalen J, Anderson DR, et al. Oral anticoagulants: mechanism of action, clinical effectiveness, and optimal therapeutic range. Chest 2001;119:8S.

36. Hirsh J, Poller L, Deykin D, et al. Optimal therapeutic range for oral anticoagulants. Chest 1989;95:5S.

37. Horlocker TT, Wedel DJ, Schlichting JL. Postoperative epidural analgesia and oral anticoagulant therapy. Anesth Analg 1994;79:89.

38. Badenhorst CH. Epidural hematoma after epidural pain control and concomitant postoperative anticoagulation. Reg Anesth 1996;21:272.

39. Woolson ST, Robinson RK, Khan NQ, et al. Deep venous thrombosis prophylaxis for knee replacement: warfarin and pneumatic compression. Am J Orthop 1998;27:299.

40. Wu CL, Perkins FM. Oral anticoagulant prophylaxis and epidural catheter removal. Reg Anesth 1996;21:517.

41. Hirsh J. Reversal of the anticoagulant effects of warfarin by vitamin K1. Chest 1998;114:1505.

42. Slaughter TF, Greenberg CS. Antifibrinolytic drugs and perioperative hemostasis. Am J Hematol 1997;56:32.

43. Wright RS, Kopecky SL, Reeder GS. Update on intravenous fibrinolytic therapy for acute myocardial infarction. Mayo Clin Proc 2000;75:1185.

44. Rosenquist RW, Brown DL. Neuraxial bleeding: fibrinolytics/thrombolytics. Reg Anesth Pain Med 1998;23:152.

45. Fennerty AG, Levine MN, Hirsh J. Hemorrhagic complications of thrombolytic therapy in the treatment of myocardial infarction and venous thromboembolism. Chest 1989;95:88S.

46. Juran NB. Minimizing bleeding complications of percutaneous coronary intervention and glycoprotein IIb–IIIa antiplatelet therapy. Am Heart J 1999;138:297.

47. Baron EM, Burke JA, Akhtar N, et al. Spinal epidural hematoma associated with tissue plasminogen activator treatment of acute myocardial infarction. Catheter Cardiovasc Interv 1999;48:390.

48. Dickman CA, Shedd SA, Spetzler RF, et al. Spinal epidural hematoma associated with epidural anesthesia: complications of systemic heparinization in patients receiving peripheral vascular thrombolytic therapy. Anesthesiology 1990;72:947.

49. Rabito SF, Ahmed S, Feinstein L, et al. Intrathecal bleeding after the intraoperative use of heparin and urokinase during continuous spinal anesthesia. Anesth Analg 1996;82:409.

50. Da Silva MS, Sobel M. Anticoagulants: to bleed or not to bleed, that is the question. Semin Vasc Surg 2002;15:256.

51. Steinhubl SR. Antiplatelet therapy: aspirin. J Invasive Cardiol 2003; 15 (Suppl B):11B.

52. Schafer AI. Effects of nonsteroidal anti-inflammatory therapy on platelets. Am J Med 1999;106:25S.

53. CLASP: a randomised trial of low-dose aspirin for the prevention and treatment of pre-eclampsia among 9364 pregnant women. CLASP (Collaborative Low-dose Aspirin Study in Pregnancy) Collaborative Group. Lancet 1994;343:619.

54. Horlocker TT, Wedel DJ, Schroeder DR, et al. Preoperative antiplatelet therapy does not increase the risk of spinal hematoma associated with regional anesthesia. Anesth Analg 1995;80:303.

55. Gerancher JC, Waterer R, Middleton J. Transient paraparesis after postdural puncture spinal hematoma in a patient receiving ketorolac. Anesthesiology 1997;86:490.

56. Quinn MJ, Fitzgerald DJ. Ticlopidine and clopidogrel. Circulation 1999;100:1667.

57. Benzon HT, Wong HY, Siddiqui T, et al. Caution in performing epidural injections in patients on several antiplatelet drugs. Anesthesiology 1999;91:1558.

58. Kawaguchi S, Tokutomi S. [A case of epidural hematoma associated with epidural catheterization which occurred on 12th days after the last medication of ticlopidine hydrochloride]. Masui 2002;51:526.

59. Mayumi T, Dohi S. Spinal subarachnoid hematoma after lumbar puncture in a patient receiving antiplatelet therapy. Anesth Analg 1983;62:777.

60. Kleiman NS. Pharmacokinetics and pharmacodynamics of glycoprotein IIb–IIIa inhibitors. Am Heart J 1999;138:263.

61. Sreeram GM, Sharma AD, Slaughter TF. Platelet glycoprotein IIb/IIIa antagonists: perioperative implications. J Cardiothorac Vasc Anesth 2001;15:237.

62. Eikelboom J, White H, Yusuf S. The evolving role of direct thrombin inhibitors in acute coronary syndromes. J Am Coll Cardiol 2003;41:70S.

63. Chen JL. Argatroban: a direct thrombin inhibitor for heparin-induced thrombocytopenia and other clinical applications. Heart Dis 2001;3:189.

64. Abebe W. Herbal medication: potential for adverse interactions with analgesic drugs. J Clin Pharm Ther 2002;27:391.

65. Matthews MK Jr. Association of Ginkgo biloba with intracerebral hemorrhage. Neurology 1998;50:1933.

66. Vale S. Subarachnoid haemorrhage associated with Ginkgo biloba. Lancet 1998;352:36.

67. Fransson SG, Nylander E. Vascular injury following cardiac catheterization, coronary angiography, and coronary angioplasty. Eur Heart J 1994;15:232.

68. Ben-David B, Stahl S. Axillary block complicated by hematoma and radial nerve injury. Reg Anesth Pain Med 1999;24:264.

69. Ekatodramis G, Macaire P, Borgeat A. Prolonged Horner syndrome due to neck hematoma after continuous interscalene block. Anesthesiology 2001;95:801.

70. Johr M, Salathe M. [Paraplegia following pneumonectomy: an anesthesiological or a surgical complication?]. Schweiz Med Wochenschr 1988;118:1412.

71. Vaisman J. Pelvic hematoma after an ilioinguinal nerve block for orchialgia. Anesth Analg 2001;92:1048.

72. Klein SM, D'Ercole F, Greengrass RA, et al. Enoxaparin associated with psoas hematoma and lumbar plexopathy after lumbar plexus block. Anesthesiology 1997;87:1576.

73. Maier C, Gleim M, Weiss T, et al. Severe bleeding following lumbar sympathetic blockade in two patients under medication with irreversible platelet aggregation inhibitors. Anesthesiology 2002;97:740.

74. Weller RS, Gerancher JC, Crews JC, et al. Extensive retroperitoneal hematoma without neurologic deficit in two patients who underwent lumbar plexus block and were later anticoagulated. Anesthesiology 2003;98:581.

Ambulatory Anesthesia for Morbid Obesity

KAREN C. NIELSEN • SUSAN M. STEELE

INTRODUCTION

The word "obesity" comes from the Latin word "obesus," which means "fattened by eating."[1] Obesity is a chronic disorder that affects almost one-third of the U.S. population. Today 64.5% of the American adult population is overweight or obese (Fig. 42-1).[2] Every year, this epidemic causes at least 300,000 related deaths in the United States.[3] It has been estimated that approximately 9.4% of the total health care costs in the United States are attributed to obesity and physical inactivity.[4] In addition, obesity is a condition that is increasing in children and adolescents. Approximately 15% of American children and adolescents are victims of this epidemic.[5] Morbid or extreme obesity also is increasing significantly in the American population and is found today in approximately 4.7% of adults.[2]

ETIOLOGY

Obesity is a complex and multifactorial disease,[6] which occurs when energy intake is higher than energy expenditure over an extended period of time. Several causes have been related to this catastrophic disease, including nonbalanced diet (e.g., increased dietary fat content), sedentary lifestyle, socioeconomic factors, ethnic influences, and genetic predisposition.

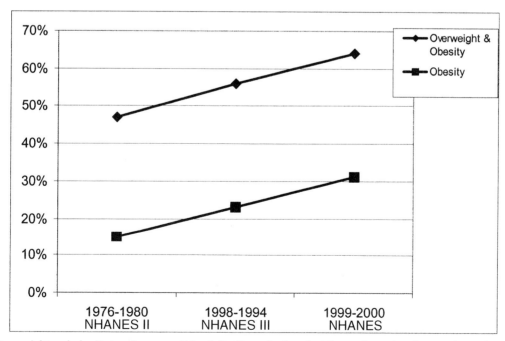

Figure 42-1 Overweight and obesity trends among U.S. adults. (From Centers for Disease Control and Prevention website, www.cdc.gov–National Health and Nutrition Examination Survey [NHANES] data.)

DIAGNOSIS OF OBESITY

Body mass index (BMI) is a measurement widely used to grade body weight. BMI is defined as a measurement of the relationship between height and weight:

$$BMI = body\ weight\ (kg)/height^2\ (m)$$

Two classifications have been used to grade overweight and obesity. The first one classifies BMI in five categories: $< 25\ kg/m^2$ = normal weight, $25–30\ kg/m^2$ = overweight, $> 30\ kg/m^2$ = obesity, $> 35\ kg/m^2$ = morbid obesity, $> 55\ kg/m^2$ = super morbid obesity.[7] The U.S. National Institute of Health (NIH)[8] and the World Health Organization (WHO)[9] standardized the classification based on the BMI categories (kg/m^2) as following: underweight (< 18.5), normal weight ($18.5–24.9$), overweight or preobesity ($15–29.9$), obesity class I ($30–34.9$), obesity class II ($35–39.9$), and obesity class III (≥ 40). The idea behind these guidelines is that increasing categories of BMI are related to increasing health risks associated with obesity and its comorbidities. This is exemplified by the work of Katzmarzyk and colleagues,[10] which demonstrated that when compared to normal-weight individuals, there is an increased risk of mortality in the underweight category in addition to increasing levels of risk across the overweight, obesity class I, and obesity class II and III.

PATHOPHYSIOLOGY OF OBESITY AND ANESTHETIC IMPLICATIONS

Avicena (A.D. 980–1037), a Persian physician and philosopher, wrote an entire chapter about obesity in one of his books stating:

> Severe obesity restricts the movements and maneuvers of the body . . . breathing passages are obstructed and the flow of air is hindered leading to nasty temperament . . . On the whole, these people are at risk of sudden death . . . because their veins are small and compressed. They are vulnerable to stroke, hemiplegia, palpitation, diarrhea, fainting, and high fever due to their cold temperament . . . men are infertile and produce little semen . . . similarly, very obese women do not become pregnant, and if they do, they abort, and their libido is weak.[11,12]

Obesity has been linked for centuries to increased perioperative morbidity[13] and mortality[14] resulting from its pathophysiologic modifications and association with chronic diseases (Table 42-1).[15] Various studies have reported that the mortality rate is significantly increased for morbidly obese patients during the perioperative period. Postlethwait and Johnson[16] demonstrated that the mortality rate in obese patients was 6.6% compared to 2.6% in nonobese patients undergoing gastrointestinal surgery. Furthermore, a BMI ≥ 40 is associated with a two-fold higher risk for all-cause mortality than a BMI of 30–31.9.[13] A review of the deleterious modifications caused by obesity will be presented as well as the need for a careful anesthetic preoperative evaluation and optimization, intraoperative management, and postoperative care.

Table 42-1 Medical Conditions Associated with Obesity

Organ or System	Comorbidities
Cardiovascular	Angina pectoris Coronary artery disease Obesity-induced cardiomyopathy Hypertension Congestive heart failure Sudden cardiac death
Endocrine	Non-insulin-dependent diabetes mellitus (type 2) Insulin resistance/hyperinsulinemia Glucose intolerance Dyslipidemia (hypercholesterolemia, hypertriglyceridemia) Menstrual irregularities Infertility
Respiratory	Obstructive sleep apnea Obesity hypoventilation syndrome Asthma Dyspnea
Gastrointestinal	Hiatal hernia Gastroesophageal reflux disease Gallbladder disease (gallstones, cholecystitis) Liver dysfunction
Musculoskeletal	Osteoarthritis (especially weight-bearing joints) Back pain
Neoplastic	Increased risk for cancer (uterine, endometrial, cervical, ovarian, postmenopausal breast, gallbladder, kidney, colorectal and prostate)
Wound	Impaired wound healing Increased risk of wound infection
Hematologic	Polycythemia High levels of fibrinogen

Cardiovascular System and Obesity

Cardiovascular disease is the leading factor for the increased morbidity and mortality associated with obesity.

Obesity produces an increase in total blood volume and cardiac output because of the high metabolic activity of excessive fat. Cardiac output proportionally increases with weight[17] in approximately 20–30 mL/kg of excess body fat. Circulating blood volume also rises to perfuse the fat tissue—0.1 L/min of blood is necessary for each kilogram of fat tissue. The increase in cardiac output results mainly from increased stroke volume and right and left ventricular dilatation. The left ventricular enlargement leads to increased left ventricular wall stress and compensatory eccentric hypertrophy[17] reducing compliance and left ventricular diastolic function. The ventricular dysfunction will lead to elevated left ventricular end-diastolic pressure and finally pulmonary edema.[18] Left ventricular dysfunction can occur if ventricular wall stress remains elevated because of inadequate capacity of hypertrophy. When these cardiac structural and hemodynamic changes result in congestive heart failure, the diagnosis of obesity cardiomyopathy is made. The major causes of death in patients with obesity cardiomyopathy are progressive congestive heart failure and sudden cardiac death.[19,20]

Heart rate is usually normal. Splanchnic blood flow is approximately 20% higher while cerebral and renal blood flows are normal.[21] Hypertension is common in obese patients.[22] The mechanism of this comorbidity in this particular patient population is not clear. Expansion of the circulating blood volume results in hypervolemia and increased cardiac output, which are characteristics of hypertension in obese patients. This condition also leads to ventricular hypertrophy and a progressively noncompliant left ventricle that, when combined with increased blood volume, raises the risk of cardiac failure.[23] Exercise tolerance in morbidly obese patients is very low,[24] as well as their cardiovascular response to stress during the perioperative period. These deleterious modifications can be reversible to some extent with weight loss.[25,26] Table 42-2 lists the cardiovascular changes related to obesity.

Preoperative cardiovascular evaluation is mandatory in morbidly obese patients.[27,28] Pharmacologic treatment of associated comorbidities must be optimized before anesthesia and surgery. Electrocardiogram alterations compatible with ischemia must be further evaluated by cardiology using a stress test or dipyridamole-thallium scintigraphy.

Respiratory System and Obesity

Morbid obesity itself can cause significant respiratory system alterations.[29] The metabolic activity of fat produces an increased basal metabolic rate due to an elevation of oxygen consumption and carbon dioxide production. However, normocapnia or even hypocapnia can be preserved by hyperventilation.[30] In addition, morbidly obese patients have markedly reduced functional residual capacity (FRC) caused by a decreased expiratory reserve volume and total lung capacity. FRC may fall within the range of the closing capacity during normal respiration in the supine position leading to ventilation-perfusion mismatch, right-to-left shunt, and arterial hypoxemia.[31,32] Interestingly, Eichenberger and colleagues[33] reported that morbidly obese pa-

Table 42-2   Cardiovascular System Changes in the Obese Patient

Cardiovascular Parameters	Obesity-Induced Changes
Heart rate	Normal
Blood pressure	↑
Cardiac output	↑
Blood and plasma volumes	↑
Stroke volume	↑
Preload	↑
Afterload	↑
Left ventricle	Hypertrophy
Left ventricle function	↓
Cardiac diameter	↑ 20–55%
Cerebral blood flow	Normal
Renal blood flow	Normal
Splanchnic blood flow	↑ 20%

tients present with atelectasis even before the use of any medication. Ultimately the reduction in FRC impairs the ability of obese patients to tolerate periods of apnea, resulting in rapid desaturation after induction of general anesthesia regardless of preoxygenation.

Respiratory system compliance is exponentially decreased as a function of increased BMI.[34] Compliance is mainly decreased owing to reduced chest wall compliance related to fat accumulation around the ribs, intra-abdominal cavity, and under the diaphragm. Lung compliance is also decreased as a consequence of increased pulmonary blood volume.[30] Table 42-3 lists the respiratory system changes related to obesity.

Obstructive Sleep Apnea

Obstructive sleep apnea (OSA) affects approximately 5% of morbidly obese patients and is defined as cessation of airflow for more than 10 sec despite continuing ventilatory effort, five or more times per hour of sleep. OSA is usually associated with a decrease in arterial oxygen saturation (SaO_2) of more than 4%. Sleep is disrupted when OSA is present owing to increased ventilatory effort-induced arousal, which causes daytime sleepiness and altered cardiopulmonary function such as hypoxia, hypercapnia, systemic and pulmonary hypertension, and cardiac arrhythmias (second-degree atrioventricular block and ventricular disrhythmias).[35] Repeated hypoxemia results in secondary polycythemia and increased risk of cerebrovascular disease and ischemic heart disease. In addition, recurrent hypoxemia leads to pulmonary vasoconstriction and right ventricular failure.[36]

Table 42-3   Respiratory System Changes in the Obese Patient

Respiratory Parameters	Obesity-Induced Changes
Functional residual capacity	↓
Expiratory reserve volume	↓
Total lung capacity	↓
Lung compliance	↓
Chest wall compliance	↓
Oxygen consumption	↑
Carbon dioxide production	↑
Arterial oxygenation	↓
Alveolar-arterial oxygenation gradient	↑
Intrapulmonary shunt during anesthesia	↑
Respiratory acidosis during sleep	May be present

Apnea occurs owing to collapse of pharyngeal airway during sleep. Obesity can cause OSA by two mechanisms: first, there is an inverse relationship between obesity and pharyngeal area,[37] and second, reduction of the patency of pharynx, which is determined by the transmural pressure across its wall, and the compliance of the wall. The deposition of fat in the pharyngeal structures (uvula, tonsils, tonsillar pillars, tongue, aryepiglottic folds, and lateral pharyngeal walls) results in decreased patency of the pharynx. The last will increase the probability that relaxation of the upper airway muscles will collapse the soft-walled pharynx between the uvula and the epiglottis.[38] In addition, the deposition of fat into the lateral pharyngeal walls not only narrows the airway but also changes the shape of the pharynx from a normal ellipse shape with a long transverse and a short anteroposterior axis to an ellipse with a short transverse and a long anteroposterior axis.[39] The patency of the pharynx is also decreased by the amount of anterior cervical neck fat.[40] Consequently, increased neck circumference is a better predictor of the incidence and severity of OSA than general obesity.[41]

OSA has important implications for perioperative management. Because most adults with OSA are undiagnosed, all obese patients should be routinely asked about nocturnal snoring, snorting, or apnea and diurnal somnolence.[42,43] Other signs and symptoms consistent with a clinical presumptive diagnosis of OSA are morning headaches, frequent nocturia, nocturnal diaphoresis and enuresis, decreased cognitive and intellectual function, and behavioral and personality changes.[35] Formal sleep study (polysomnography) is indicated to confirm the clinical diagnosis and quantify the severity of OSA.

Obesity Hypoventilation Syndrome

Obesity hypoventilation syndrome (OHS) results from the excessive weight of the chest wall impeding respirations, and it should be suspected in obese patients with a history of congestive heart failure, nocturnal asthma, or extreme shortness of breath. The diagnosis of OHS is confirmed by arterial blood gas that demonstrates an arterial oxygen tension (PaO_2) of < 55 mmHg or an arterial carbon dioxide tension ($PaCO_2$) of > 47 mmHg. Respiratory acidosis is initially limited to sleep of patients with OSA. Nevertheless, alteration in the control of breathing is a long-term consequence of OSA, which will lead to progressive desensitization of the respiratory centers to hypercapnia. Eventually, these changes may progress to type II respiratory failure and Pickwickian syndrome.[44]

Airway and Obesity

Morbidly obese patients usually present with several characteristics that may result in difficulties in airway management. These include a high and anterior larynx, restricted mouth opening, macroglossy, excessive palatal and pharyngeal soft tissue, short neck with large circumference, limited cervical spine and atlanto-occipital flexion and extension due to large cervical and thoracic fat pads.[45] In addition, large breasts may render difficult movement of the laryngoscope. Surprisingly, Ezri and colleagues[46] demonstrated that morbid obesity is a predictor of difficult intubation—not because of an increased BMI but due to other factors associated with obesity. These factors include history of OSA, abnormal upper teeth, Mallampati class III and IV, and the distribution pattern of body fat rather than the BMI.

Careful airway assessment is vital, including previous anesthetic history of difficult intubation and its management by evaluation of previous anesthetic records and patient questioning. Physical examination is also essential to identify abnormalities related to obesity and its severity that may interfere with airway patency maintenance, mask-ventilation, and endotracheal intubation. Mallampati class assessment can be useful, as previously described.

Gastrointestinal System and Obesity

Intra-abdominal pressure is markedly increased in morbidly obese patients leading to higher incidence of hiatal hernia. Gastric emptying is delayed in this patient population[47,48] with 90% presenting increased residual gastric volume (> 25 mL) with lower pH (< 2.5).[49] These changes would enhance the risk for aspiration of gastric contents followed by pulmonary complications (aspiration pneumonitis). Although the overall risks of aspiration are very small (1 in > 2000 cases), Olsson et al.[50] found that 83% of the aspiration cases involved patients with one or more risk factors for aspiration (e.g., delayed gastric emptying, obesity). Despite these commonsense beliefs, contradictory work has been published. Wisen and Hellstrom[51] reported that gastric emptying is actually faster in obese patients. These authors also demonstrated that the main difference is related to the larger gastric volume in obese patients, which is approximately 75% greater than in normal-weight individuals, then leading to larger residual volume. Despite these controversies, morbidly obese patients should always be considered as "full stomach."[52] Hepatic steatosis is common in morbidly obese patients and may lead to liver dysfunction with secondary modifications in biotransformation of drugs.[53]

Obesity-Induced Drug Pharmacokinetics and Pharmacodynamics Modifications

Obesity leads to alterations in drug distribution, binding, and elimination of many drugs.[54] Drug distribution to the various compartments of the body is modified because of the high proportion of body fat, reduced total body water, increased blood volume and cardiac output, altered protein binding, and drug lipophilicity.[55] Hydrophilic drugs have similar volumes of distribution, elimination half-life, and metabolic clearance when compared to lean patients. Lipid-soluble drugs (e.g., thiopental, benzodiazepines, propofol, inhalational anesthetic agents) have an increased volume of distribution with reduced half-life elimination. Their effect may persist for some time after discontinuation unless the clearance is increased. Protein binding can be decreased owing to increased levels of lipoproteins, cholesterol, triglycerides, and free fatty acids. The reduced binding will increase drug free plasma concentrations.[56] Protein binding can also be increased for other drugs. Local anesthetics have a higher protein binding when increased concentrations of alpha-1 glycoprotein are present and consequently reduced free plasma concentration occurs.

Muscle relaxants have to be carefully administered in morbidly obese patients. Overdose is not unusual because of surgeon's demand for additional relaxation or by reduced respiratory compliance.[57] Atracurium/cisatracurium seems to be the most appropriate nondepolarizing muscle relaxant to be used in morbidly obese patients owing to its non-organ-dependent elimination.[58] Furthermore, morbidly obese patients have a higher plasma cholinesterase activity than normal, and higher doses of succinylcholine (1.2–1.5 mg/kg) are recommended.[59]

Inhalational or volatile agents metabolism may be altered owing to liver dysfunction and possibly lead to nephrotoxicity. This was demonstrated by Bentley and colleagues[60,61] when they reported that obese patients metabolize halothane and enflurane in higher concentrations of inorganic fluoride than lean patients. Sevoflurane as well as isoflurane does not appear to have the previous pattern of metabolism in morbidly obese patients.[62,63]

Careful use of opioids should be applied for morbidly obese patients, especially in the postoperative period. Fentanyl appears to have similar pharmacokinetics in obese and nonobese patients, being a good option for morbid obesity management.[64] Longer elimination half-life is expected for sufentanil and alfentanil.[65,66]

GENERAL ANESTHESIA FOR MORBID OBESITY

Obesity is a predictor of severe negative perioperative outcomes related to general anesthesia.[67–69]

Premedication

Sedatives and opioids should be given orally or intravenously with concomitant patient monitoring. Intramuscular and subcutaneous administration routes should be avoided since absorption is unpredictable.[70] Morbidly obese patients should receive acid aspiration prophylaxis even if symptoms of gastroesophageal reflux disease are not present.[70] Histamine H_2 receptor antagonists, antiacids, and prokinetic agents can be used. Antisialagogue drugs must be used if awake fiberoptic intubation is indicated.

Induction, Intubation, Ventilation, Maintenance, and Extubation

Each patient should be carefully evaluated for selection between awake intubation or intubation under general anesthesia. Endotracheal intubation should be used in morbidly obese patients because of the existing high risk for regurgitation and aspiration of gastric contents. Considerations about potential difficulties with mask ventilation[71] and endotracheal intubation must be made. In fact, in two series of morbidly obese patients undergoing abdominal surgery, the incidence of difficult intubation was 13% and 24%, and the incidence of awake intubation was 8%.[72,73] Indeed, another large series of patients undergoing surgery for OSA demonstrated that the incidence of failed intubation was 5%. These findings reinforce the importance that all appropriate equipment for difficult airway management, including fiberoptic devices, laryngeal mask airway, gum elastic bougie, and special laryngoscopes (e.g., Bellhouse or Bullard), should readily available to anesthesiologists.

If endotracheal intubation under general anesthesia is selected, preoxygenation (3–5 min) is critical owing to rapid desaturation related to existing compromised FRC. Reverse Trendelenburg (30 degrees) is the recommended position for induction because it provides the longest safe apnea period when compared to the 30-degree backup Fowler and horizontal-supine positions.[74] A rapid-sequence induction with cricoid pressure (Sellick maneuver) is also indicated, especially for patients with predictable airway management difficulties. After intubation, spontaneous breathing should be avoided to prevent hypoxia and hypercarbia. Inspired oxygen fractions (FiO_2) of 0.5–1.0 should be used to help maintain adequate $PaCO_2$.[75] Mechanical ventilation is mandatory and should be adjusted according to the needs of each patient, including large tidal volumes with appropriate respiratory frequency. Positive end-expiratory pressure (PEEP) of 10–15 cm H_2O can be used to avoid reduction in lung volume by unopposed intra-abdominal pressure, increased FRC, open collapsed air passages, and consequently hypoxemia and other mechanical respiratory alterations.[34,75–76]

The choice of an anesthetic for general anesthesia maintenance in morbidly obese patients remains controversial.[77] Obese patients are at high risk for both aspiration and acute upper-airway obstruction after tracheal extubation.[78] Hence rapid recovery is desirable to guarantee early active airway control and to reduce postoperative respiratory complications. Juvin et al.[79] demonstrated that desflurane seems to be the most appropriate anesthetic for this patient population. Desflurane is related to faster and more predictable postoperative recovery when compared to propofol or isoflurane. Sevoflurane is also related to faster recovery, and extubation should only be performed with fully awake patients. After extubation, patients should be kept in a sitting position (45 degrees).[80]

Postoperative Considerations

Morbidly obese patients develop more atelectasis during general anesthesia than nonobese patients. This finding was demonstrated by Eichenberger and colleagues,[33] who reported that 24 hr after the end of surgery, atelectasis persisted in morbidly obese patients, whereas complete reabsorption occurred in nonobese patients. Morbidly obese patients generally remain longer and are more immobilized than lean patients. The absence of early mobilization contributes to the slower disappearance of atelectasis and high risk for thromboembolic complications.

Obese patients with OSA are at risk for apnea, which can be associated with death during the postoperative period. This patient population also has an increased risk of opioid-induced upper-airway obstruction, and the need for frequent monitoring is crucial.[81]

REGIONAL ANESTHESIA FOR MORBID OBESITY

Regional anesthesia (RA) is an attractive alternative for morbidly obese patients undergoing surgery. RA offers several advantages when treating this patient population, including minimal airway intervention, less cardiopulmonary depression, improved patient tolerance to surgical positioning and respiratory effects of the anesthetic, decreased intra- and postoperative opioid consumption as well as the risk for opioid-induced airway obstruction, and therefore superior postoperative analgesia.[27,82] Despite these advantages, RA in the obese can be technically challenging (Fig. 42-2). These challenges are related to difficulties on patient positioning, identifying the usual bony and muscular landmarks,[83] and the depth of needle penetration. The loss of anatomic landmarks also contributes to difficulty in positioning indwelling catheters for RA.[84]

It seems intuitive that obesity makes identification of important anatomic landmarks more difficult[83,85] when performing RA that could lead to increased block failure. Though previous studies[86,87] have been contradictory, some

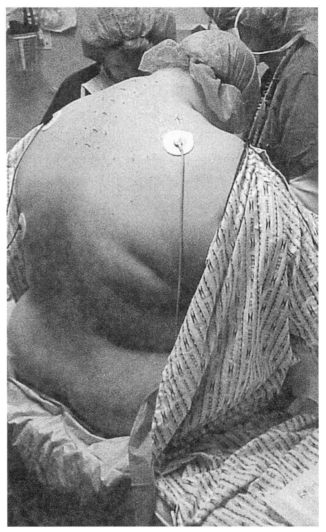

Figure 42-2   Preparation of morbidly obese patient (body mass index 55.1 kg/m²) to undergo ambulatory bilateral simple mastectomies under bilateral continuous paravertebral blocks.

authors reported a positive association between overweight and more frequent block failure in obese patients. For example, Carles et al.[86] performed 1468 brachial plexus blocks at the humeral canal using a nerve stimulator. The authors reported block failure in 4.9% of all cases. Unadjusted block failure rate was independent of weight, age, gender, experience of anesthesiologist, and type of surgery. Similarly, Conn et al.[87] found no association between interscalene block failure for shoulder surgery and patient weight and height. Conversely Gatra and colleagues,[88] evaluating the efficacy of supraclavicular brachial plexus block for anesthesia of the upper limb, found block failure to be more common in obese and noncooperative patients. The study, however, had a small sample size, and the authors provided neither a definition of "obesity" nor information about whether the association between obesity and block failure was statistically significant.

Some studies recommend the use of special techniques to facilitate RA in obese patients.[89] Pham-Dang and colleagues[90] found a significantly reduced failure rate of continuous axillary brachial plexus block using a new technique in which the approach to the neurovascular sheath was guided under fluoroscopy. Others have suggested the use of ultrasonography guidance to improve performance of regional anesthesia procedures in obese patients.[85]

Appropriate equipment is indispensable, particularly appropriate-length needles. Insulated needles used to perform single-injection peripheral nerve blocks (PNB) are available in different lengths varying from 2.54 to 15.24 cm. Insulated Tuohy needles used to perform continuous peripheral nerve blocks (CPNB) are available in similar lengths. Surprisingly, these lengths are not useful for the entire population of morbidly obese patients, in particular for lower-extremity blocks (e.g., lumbar plexus and sciatic nerve blocks). Based on a vast experience with RA in morbidly obese patients (13.5% of our patient population) in the ambulatory setting, the authors suspect that 20-cm-length needles may be necessary to offer these techniques to "super" morbidly obese patients. Spinal needles are available in longer lengths. Pencil point needle length ranges up to 12.7 cm and Quincke needles up to 17.78 cm. Ideally, pencil points needles should be preferred but longer needles are not commercially available at the moment.

Local anesthetic requirements are reduced in morbidly obese patients for spinal and epidural blocks. Some investigators demonstrated that the increased intra-abdominal pressure shifts blood from the inferior vena cava into the epidural space, thus decreasing the volume of the epidural and subarachnoid spaces. The volume is further decreased by fatty infiltration, and therefore, reduced doses of local anesthetics are suggested (75–80% of the usual doses).[91,92] These modifications can also lead to unpredictable local anesthetic spread and variability in block level.[93,94] If extension of centroneuraxial block reaches levels above T5, respiratory compromise may result, as well as cardiovascular collapse from autonomic blockade.[52] For these reasons, PNB should be preferred to centroneuraxial blocks when indicated (e.g., unilateral lower-extremity surgery).

Morbidly obese patients must position themselves according to the regional anesthesia technique chosen by the anesthesiologist before sedation. This will facilitate their care and decrease health care staff injuries.

PRACTICAL CONSIDERATIONS

Venous Access

Peripheral venous access can be difficult in morbidly obese patients because of the extensive amount of subcutaneous fat.[27,84] Central venous access is equally more difficult to establish[95] and associated with significant morbidity[96] when compared to normal-weight patients. Ultrasound guidance can improve success rates and decrease complications associated with central line placement,[97] potentially assisting anesthesiologists when caring for these patients. Another valuable option to facilitate central venous access was described by Johnson and Tobias.[98] These authors suggested the use of an 18-gauge, 15-cm spinal needle instead of the standard 6.25-cm introducer needle from central venous kits. The introducer needle can be too short or the entry angle may be too acute, making passage of the catheter impossible or leading to obstruction after placement.

Although it is recommended that a central venous line should be inserted routinely in obese patients, contradictory statements have been reported. Juvin and colleagues[99] demonstrated that successful peripheral line placement could always be obtained in obese patients overcoming the absolute need for a central line, which is ideal for the ambulatory setting.

Patient Positioning and Transfer

Most of the available beds, wheelchairs, operating tables, imaging equipment, and even scales are not designed to accommodate the alarming growth of morbidly obese patients in the United States. In addition, health care staff injuries related to the care of these patients is increasing. The weight limit of each table should be carefully checked for each patient to avoid putting the patient and the staff at risk.

Once anesthetized, morbidly obese patients are difficult to move to any position. For this reason, patients must position themselves when possible to decrease manpower and potential injuries to themselves and to the staff. Patients should be anesthetized on the operating table to avoid unnecessary transfer.

One of the most deleterious positions for morbidly obese patients is an improper prone position, which is associated with severe cardiopulmonary impairment. If the abdomen is compressed, the diaphragm will be displaced and chest wall movement will be restricted.[100] In addition, inferior vena cava compression will reduce venous return to the heart and lead to hypotension.[101] Increased intrathoracic pressures generated during mechanical ventilation can also contribute to hypotension.[102] Despite these possible adverse effects, morbidly obese patients can safely tolerate the prone position with the use of appropriate equipment.[103,104]

Monitoring

Morbidly obese patients undergoing selected ambulatory surgery should be optimized, thus not requiring invasive monitoring. Noninvasive monitoring, including blood pressure (with appropriated cuff size), electrocardiography, capnography, pulse oximetry, and neuromuscular blockade monitoring, should be used. Patients with severe cardiopulmonary disease requiring monitoring should not undergo surgery in the ambulatory setting but as inpatients.

IS THERE A BODY MASS INDEX LIMIT FOR PATIENTS UNDERGOING AMBULATORY ANESTHESIA?

The Royal College of Surgeons considered morbid obesity (BMI > 35 kg/m^2) a contraindication for day-case surgery in the United Kingdom.[105] However, Davies and colleagues[106] reported that there is no evidence that morbid obesity (BMI > 35 kg/m^2) solely is an exclusion criterion for outpatient surgery.

Morbidly obese patients should be optimized to undergo ambulatory anesthetic procedures. At the authors' institution, morbidly obese patients are individually evaluated according to their physical and medical conditions and the type of surgery being proposed. As a general rule, there is no BMI limit for surgical procedures that can be performed under RA techniques. When general anesthesia is mandatory, BMI should not exceed 55 kg/m^2.

SUMMARY

Obesity is a public health problem that causes severe pathophysiologic modifications increasing perioperative morbidity and mortality with a negative impact on patient outcomes.[107] Anesthetic management of morbid obesity represents a great challenge to anesthesiologists. Knowledge of pathophysiology is critical as well as the numerous concomitant diseases associated with this condition. Regional anesthesia techniques should be used whenever possible to decrease the deleterious effects of general anesthesia to this patient population.

REFERENCES

1. Fisher A, Waterhouse TD, Adams AP. Obesity: its relation to anaesthesia. Anaesthesia 1975;30(5):633–47.
2. Flegal KM, Carroll MD, Ogden CL, Johnson CL. Prevalence and trends in obesity among US adults, 1999–2000. JAMA 2002; 288(14):1723–27.
3. Allison DB, Fontaine KR, Manson JE, Stevens J, VanItallie TB. Annual deaths attributable to obesity in the United States. JAMA 1999; 282(16):1530–38.
4. Colditz GA. Economic costs of obesity and inactivity. Med Sci Sports Exerc 1999;31(11 Suppl):S663–67.
5. Ogden CL, Flegal KM, Carroll MD, Johnson CL. Prevalence and trends in overweight among US children and adolescents, 1999–2000. JAMA 2002;288(14):1728–32.
6. Hacker DC, Deitel M. The Etiology of Obesity. Obes Surg 1991; 1(1):21–27.
7. Bray G. Pathophysiology of obesity. Am J Clin Nutr 1992;55: 488S–494S.
8. National Institutes of Health. Clinical Guidelines on the Identification, Evaluation, and Treatment of Overweight and Obesity in Adults—The Evidence Report. National Institutes of Health. Obes Res 1998;6(Suppl 2):51S–209S.
9. World Health Organization. Obesity: preventing and managing the global epidemic. Report of a WHO consultation on obesity. Geneva, 1998 3–5 June, 1997.
10. Katzmarzyk PT, Craig CL, Bouchard C. Original article underweight, overweight and obesity: relationships with mortality in the 13-year follow-up of the Canada Fitness Survey. J Clin Epidemiol 2001;54(9):916–20.
11. Nathan B. A medieval view on obesity. Obesity Surgery 1992;2:217.
12. Alvarez-Cordero R. Treatment of clinically severe obesity, a public health problem: introduction. World J Surg 1998;22(9):905–6.
13. Sjostrom LV. Morbidity of severely obese subjects. Am J Clin Nutr 1992;55(2 Suppl):508S–515S.
14. Calle EE, Thun MJ, Petrelli JM, Rodriguez C, Heath CW Jr. Body-mass index and mortality in a prospective cohort of U.S. adults. N Engl J Med 1999;341(15):1097–105.
15. Pi-Sunyer FX. The obesity epidemic: pathophysiology and consequences of obesity. Obes Res 2002;10 Suppl 2:97S–104S.
16. Postlethwait RW, Johnson WD. Complications following surgery for duodenal ulcer in obese patients. Arch Surg 1972;105(3): 438–40.
17. Alpert MA, Hashimi MW. Obesity and the heart. Am J Med Sci 1993; 306(2):117–23.
18. Alpert MA, Lambert CR, Terry BE, Cohen MV, Mukerji V, Massey CV, et al. Interrelationship of left ventricular mass, systolic function and diastolic filling in normotensive morbidly obese patients. Int J Obes Relat Metab Disord 1995;19(8):550–57.
19. Alpert MA. Obesity cardiomyopathy: pathophysiology and evolution of the clinical syndrome. Am J Med Sci 2001;321(4):225–36.
20. Duflou J, Virmani R, Rabin I, Burke A, Farb A, Smialek J. Sudden death as a result of heart disease in morbid obesity. Am Heart J 1995; 130(2):306–13.
21. Alexander JK. Blood volume, cardiac output, and distribution of systemic blood flow in extreme obesity. Cardiovasc Res Center Bull 1962;1:39–44.
22. Alexander JK. Obesity and cardiac performance. Am J Cardiol 1964; 14:860–65.
23. Alpert MA, Lambert CR, Terry BE, Cohen MV, Mukerji V, Massey CV, et al. Influence of left ventricular mass on left ventricular diastolic filling in normotensive morbid obesity. Am Heart J 1995;130(5):1068–73.
24. Alpert MA, Singh A, Terry BE, Kelly DL, Villarreal D, Mukerji V. Effect of exercise on left ventricular systolic function and reserve in morbid obesity. Am J Cardiol 1989;63(20):1478–82.
25. Alpert MA. Management of obesity cardiomyopathy. Am J Med Sci 2001;321(4):237–41.
26. Benotti PN, Bistrain B, Benotti JR, Blackburn G, Forse RA. Heart disease and hypertension in severe obesity: the benefits of weight reduction. Am J Clin Nutr 1992;55(2 Suppl):586S–590S.
27. Shenkman Z, Shir Y, Brodsky JB. Perioperative management of the obese patient. Br J Anaesth 1993;70(3):349–59.
28. Kannel WB, D'Agostino RB, Cobb JL. Effect of weight on cardiovascular disease. Am J Clin Nutr 1996;63(3 Suppl):419S–422S.
29. McGinnis JM, Foege WH. Actual causes of death in the United States. JAMA 1993;270(18):2207–12.
30. Luce JM. Respiratory complications of obesity. Chest 1980;78(4): 626–31.
31. Ray CS, Sue DY, Bray G, Hansen JE, Wasserman K. Effects of obesity on respiratory function. Am Rev Respir Dis 1983;128(3):501–6.
32. Biring MS, Lewis MI, Liu JT, Mohsenifar Z. Pulmonary physiologic changes of morbid obesity. Am J Med Sci 1999;318(5):293–97.
33. Eichenberger A, Proietti S, Wicky S, Frascarolo P, Suter M, Spahn DR, et al. Morbid obesity and postoperative pulmonary atelectasis: an underestimated problem. Anesth Analg 2002;95(6):1788–92.
34. Pelosi P, Croci M, Ravagnan I, Tredici S, Pedoto A, Lissoni A, et al. The effects of body mass on lung volumes, respiratory mechanics, and gas exchange during general anesthesia. Anesth Analg 1998; 87(3):654–60.
35. Strollo PJ, Jr., Rogers RM. Obstructive sleep apnea. N Engl J Med 1996;334(2):99–104.
36. Kessler R, Chaouat A, Weitzenblum E, Oswald M, Ehrhart M, Apprill M, et al. Pulmonary hypertension in the obstructive sleep apnoea syndrome: prevalence, causes and therapeutic consequences. Eur Respir J 1996;9(4):787–94.
37. White RA, Verbin C, Kopchok G, Scoccianti M, de Virgilio C, Donayre C. The role of cinefluoroscopy and intravascular ultrasonography in evaluating the deployment of experimental endovascular prostheses. J Vasc Surg 1995;21(3):365–74.
38. Barsh LI. The origin of pharyngeal obstruction during sleep. Sleep Breath 1999;3(1):17–22.
39. Mayer P, Pepin JL, Bettega G, Veale D, Ferretti G, Deschaux C, et al. Relationship between body mass index, age and upper airway measurements in snorers and sleep apnoea patients. Eur Respir J 1996; 9(9):1801–9.
40. Koenig JS, Thach BT. Effects of mass loading on the upper airway. J Appl Physiol 1988;64(6):2294–99.

41. Davies RJ, Stradling JR. The relationship between neck circumference, radiographic pharyngeal anatomy, and the obstructive sleep apnoea syndrome. Eur Respir J 1990;3(5):509–14.

42. Gentil B, Lienhart A, Fleury B. Enhancement of postoperative desaturation in heavy snorers. Anesth Analg 1995;81(2):389–92.

43. Vidhani K, Langham BT. Obstructive sleep apnoea syndrome: is this an overlooked cause of desaturation in the immediate postoperative period? Br J Anaesth 1997;78(4):442–43.

44. Murphy PG. Obesity. In: Hopkins PM (ed.), Foundations of Anaesthesia. Basic and Clinical Sciences. London: Mosby, 2000, pp. 703–711.

45. Brodsky JB. Anesthetic management of the morbidly obese patient. Int Anesthesiol Clin 1986;24(1):93–103.

46. Ezri T, Gewurtz G, Sessler DI, Medalion B, Szmuk P, Hagberg C, et al. Prediction of difficult laryngoscopy in obese patients by ultrasound quantification of anterior neck soft tissue. Anaesthesia 2003; 58(11):1111–14.

47. Horowitz M, Collins PJ, Cook DJ, Harding PE, Shearman DJ. Abnormalities of gastric emptying in obese patients. Int J Obes 1983; 7(5):415–21.

48. Maddox A, Horowitz M, Wishart J, Collins P. Gastric and oesophageal emptying in obesity. Scand J Gastroenterol 1989;24(5): 593–98.

49. Vaughan RW, Bauer S, Wise L. Volume and pH of gastric juice in obese patients. Anesthesiology 1975;43(6):686–89.

50. Olsson GL, Hallen B, Hambraeus-Jonzon K. Aspiration during anaesthesia: a computer-aided study of 185,358 anaesthetics. Acta Anaesthesiol Scand 1986;30(1):84–92.

51. Wisen O, Hellstrom PM. Gastrointestinal motility in obesity. J Intern Med 1995;237(4):411–18.

52. Oberg B, Poulsen TD. Obesity: an anaesthetic challenge. Acta Anaesthesiol Scand 1996;40(2):191–200.

53. Cohen S, Gondret R, Mankikian B. [Massive obesity and anesthesia]. Rev Prat 1993;43(15):1950–55.

54. Abernethy DR, Greenblatt DJ. Pharmacokinetics of drugs in obesity. Clin Pharmacokinet 1982;7(2):108–24.

55. Blouin RA, Kolpek JH, Mann HJ. Influence of obesity on drug disposition. Clin Pharm 1987;6(9):706–14.

56. Wasan KM, Lopez-Berestein G. The influence of serum lipoproteins on the pharmacokinetics and pharmacodynamics of lipophilic drugs and drug carriers. Arch Med Res 1993;24(4):395–401.

57. Fox GS. Anaesthesia for intestinal short circuiting in the morbidly obese with reference to the pathophysiology of gross obesity. Can Anaesth Soc J 1975;22(3):307–15.

58. Weinstein JA, Matteo RS, Ornstein E, Schwartz AE, Goldstoff M, Thal G. Pharmacodynamics of vecuronium and atracurium in the obese surgical patient. Anesth Analg 1988;67(12):1149–53.

59. Bentley JB, Borel JD, Vaughan RW, Gandolfi AJ. Weight, pseudocholinesterase activity, and succinylcholine requirement. Anesthesiology 1982;57(1):48–49.

60. Bentley JB, Vaughan RW, Gandolfi AJ, Cork RC. Halothane biotransformation in obese and nonobese patients. Anesthesiology 1982;57(2):94–97.

61. Bentley JB, Vaughan RW, Miller MS, Calkins JM, Gandolfi AJ. Serum inorganic fluoride levels in obese patients during and after enflurane anesthesia. Anesth Analg 1979;58(5):409–12.

62. Frink EJ Jr, Malan TP Jr, Brown EA, Morgan S, Brown BR Jr. Plasma inorganic fluoride levels with sevoflurane anesthesia in morbidly obese and nonobese patients. Anesth Analg 1993;76(6):1333–37.

63. Strube PJ, Hulands GH, Halsey MJ. Serum fluoride levels in morbidly obese patients: enflurane compared with isoflurane anaesthesia. Anaesthesia 1987;42(7):685–89.

64. Bentley JB, Borel JD, Gillespie TS, Vaughan RW, Gandolfi AJ. Fentanyl pharmacokinetics in obese and non-obese patients. Anesthesiology 1981;55:A177.

65. Schwartz AE, Matteo RS, Ornstein E, Young WL, Myers KJ. Pharmacokinetics of sufentanil in obese patients. Anesth Analg 1991; 73(6):790–93.

66. Bentley JB, Finley JM, Humphrey LR, Gandolfi AJ, Brown BR. Obesity and alfentanil pharmacokinetics. Anesth Analg 1983;62:S251.

67. Forrest JB, Rehder K, Cahalan MK, Goldsmith CH. Multicenter study of general anesthesia. III. Predictors of severe perioperative adverse outcomes. Anesthesiology 1992;76(1):3–15.

68. Brooks-Brunn JA. Predictors of postoperative pulmonary complications following abdominal surgery. Chest 1997;111(3):564–71.

69. de Jong RH. Body mass index: risk predictor for cosmetic day surgery. Plast Reconstr Surg 2001;108(2):556–61.

70. Cooper JR, Brodsky JB. Anesthetic management of the morbidly obese patient. Semin Anesth 1987;6:260–70.

71. Langeron O, Masso E, Huraux C, Guggiari M, Bianchi A, Coriat P, et al. Prediction of difficult mask ventilation. Anesthesiology 2000; 92(5):1229–36.

72. Buckley FP, Robinson NB, Simonowitz DA, Dellinger EP. Anaesthesia in the morbidly obese: a comparison of anaesthetic and analgesic regimens for upper abdominal surgery. Anaesthesia 1983; 38(9):840–51.

73. Dominguez-Cherit G, Gonzalez R, Borunda D, Pedroza J, Gonzalez-Barranco J, Herrera MF. Anesthesia for morbidly obese patients. World J Surg 1998;22(9):969–73.

74. Boyce JR, Ness T, Castroman P, Gleysteen JJ. A preliminary study of the optimal anesthesia positioning for the morbidly obese patient. Obes Surg 2003;13(1):4–9.

75. Santesson J. Oxygen transport and venous admixture in the extremely obese. Influence of anaesthesia and artificial ventilation with and without positive end-expiratory pressure. Acta Anaesthesiol Scand 1976;20(4):387–94.

76. Pelosi P, Ravagnan I, Giurati G, Panigada M, Bottino N, Tredici S, et al. Positive end-expiratory pressure improves respiratory function in obese but not in normal subjects during anesthesia and paralysis. Anesthesiology 1999;91(5):1221–31.

77. Cork RC, Vaughan RW, Bentley JB. General anesthesia for morbidly obese patients—an examination of postoperative outcomes. Anesthesiology 1981;54(4):310–13.

78. Rose DK, Cohen MM, Wigglesworth DF, DeBoer DP. Critical respiratory events in the postanesthesia care unit. Patient, surgical, and anesthetic factors. Anesthesiology 1994;81(2):410–18.

79. Juvin P, Vadam C, Malek L, Dupont H, Marmuse JP, Desmonts JM. Postoperative recovery after desflurane, propofol, or isoflurane anesthesia among morbidly obese patients: a prospective, randomized study. Anesth Analg 2000;91(3):714–19.

80. Vaughan RW, Bauer S, Wise L. Effect of position (semirecumbent versus supine) on postoperative oxygenation in markedly obese subjects. Anesth Analg 1976;55(1):37–41.

81. Keamy MF, 3rd, Cadieux RJ, Kofke WA, Kales A. The occurrence of obstructive sleep apnea in a recovery room patient. Anesthesiology 1987;66(2):232–34.

82. Rawal N, Sjostrand U, Christoffersson E, Dahlstrom B, Arvill A, Rydman H. Comparison of intramuscular and epidural morphine for postoperative analgesia in the grossly obese: influence on postoperative ambulation and pulmonary function. Anesth Analg 1984; 63(6):583–92.

83. Adams JP, Murphy PG. Obesity in anaesthesia and intensive care. Br J Anaesth 2000;85(1):91–108.

84. Fox GS, Whalley DG, Bevan DR. Anaesthesia for the morbidly obese: experience with 110 patients. Br J Anaesth 1981;53(8):811–16.

85. Wallace DH, Currie JM, Gilstrap LC, Santos R. Indirect sonographic guidance for epidural anesthesia in obese pregnant patients. Reg Anesth 1992;17(4):233–36.

86. Carles M, Pulcini A, Macchi P, Duflos P, Raucoules-Aime M, Grimaud D. An evaluation of the brachial plexus block at the humeral canal using a neurostimulator (1417 patients): the efficacy, safety, and predictive criteria of failure. Anesth Analg 2001;92(1):194–98.

87. Conn RA, Cofield RH, Byer DE, Linstromberg JW. Interscalene block anesthesia for shoulder surgery. Clin Orthop 1987(216):94–98.

88. Gatra A, Barrou L, Mekki-Berrada R, Akallal L, Benaguida M,

Komiha A. [Brachial plexus block and locoregional anesthesia of the upper limb: apropos of 50 cases]. Acta Chir Belg 1986;86(6): 344–48.

89. Naja Z, Lonnqvist PA. Somatic paravertebral nerve blockade. Incidence of failed block and complications. Anaesthesia 2001;56(12): 1184–88.

90. Pham-Dang C, Meunier JF, Poirier P, Kick O, Bourreli B, Touchais S, et al. A new axillary approach for continuous brachial plexus block: a clinical and anatomic study. Anesth Analg 1995;81(4): 686–93.

91. Hodgkinson R, Husain FJ. Obesity and the cephalad spread of analgesia following epidural administration of bupivacaine for cesarean section. Anesth Analg 1980;59(2):89–92.

92. Taivainen T, Tuominen M, Rosenberg PH. Influence of obesity on the spread of spinal analgesia after injection of plain 0.5% bupivacaine at the L3-4 or L4-5 interspace. Br J Anaesth 1990;64(5): 542–46.

93. Pitkanen MT. Body mass and spread of spinal anesthesia with bupivacaine. Anesth Analg 1987;66(2):127–31.

94. Hogan QH, Prost R, Kulier A, Taylor ML, Liu S, Mark L. Magnetic resonance imaging of cerebrospinal fluid volume and the influence of body habitus and abdominal pressure. Anesthesiology 1996; 84(6):1341–49.

95. El-Solh A, Sikka P, Bozkanat E, Jaafar W, Davies J. Morbid obesity in the medical ICU. Chest 2001;120(6):1989–97.

96. Jefferson P, Ball DR. Central venous access in morbidly obese patients. Anesth Analg 2002;95(3):782.

97. Randolph AG, Cook DJ, Gonzales CA, Pribble CG. Ultrasound guidance for placement of central venous catheters: a meta-analysis of the literature. Crit Care Med 1996;24(12):2053–58.

98. Johnson G, Tobias JD. Central venous access in morbidly obese patients. Anesth Analg 2001;93(5):1363.

99. Juvin P, Blarel A, Bruno F, Desmonts JM. Is peripheral line placement more difficult in obese than in lean patients? Anesth Analg 2003;96(4):1218.

100. Palmon SC, Kirsch JR, Depper JA, Toung TJ. The effect of the prone position on pulmonary mechanics is frame-dependent. Anesth Analg 1998;87(5):1175–80.

101. Lee TC, Yang LC, Chen HJ. Effect of patient position and hypotensive anesthesia on inferior vena caval pressure. Spine 1998; 23(8):941–47.

102. Toyota S, Amaki Y. Hemodynamic evaluation of the prone position by transesophageal echocardiography. J Clin Anesth 1998; 10(1):32–35.

103. Brodsky JB, Oldroyd M, Winfield HN, Kozlowski PM. Morbid obesity and the prone position: a case report. J Clin Anesth 2001; 13(2):138–40.

104. Mahajan RP, Hennessy N, Aitkenhead AR, Jellinek D. Effect of three different surgical prone positions on lung volumes in healthy volunteers. Anaesthesia 1994;49(7):583–86.

105. Royal College of Surgeons of England. Guidelines for Day-Case Surgery. London: Royal College of Surgeons, March 1992.

106. Davies KE, Houghton K, Montgomery JE. Obesity and day-case surgery. Anaesthesia 2001;56(11):1112–15.

107. Choban PS, Flancbaum L. The impact of obesity on surgical outcomes: a review. J Am Coll Surg 1997;185(6):593–603.

Complications of Ambulatory Regional Anesthesia and Their Treatment

JEFFREY M. RICHMAN • CHRISTOPHER L. WU

INTRODUCTION

In the ambulatory surgical environment where speed of patient recovery is at a premium, regional anesthesia may be especially useful in facilitating patient convalescence and discharge. Peripheral and central neuraxial regional anesthetic techniques may confer several advantages, including a decreased cost utilization, favorable patient-oriented outcomes, superior analgesia, and decreased side effects such as postoperative nausea and vomiting (PONV), which may delay discharge and recovery of the ambulatory surgical patient. Thus, the use of regional anesthesia may be an especially important part of contemporary ambulatory anesthesia practice.

Despite the many advantages of regional anesthetic techniques for the ambulatory surgical patient, several complications may occur from the perioperative use of regional anesthesia. Complications from regional anesthesia can be generally grouped into either immediate (intraoperative) or delayed (postoperative before and after hospital discharge) complications. Many of these complications are not life-threatening but may be relatively common and delay patient convalescence. A few complications may be fatal without immediate treatment.

ADVANTAGES OF REGIONAL ANESTHESIA FOR AMBULATORY SURGERY

By providing superior postoperative analgesia, decreasing certain side effects, improving patient-oriented outcomes, and possibly decreasing costs, both peripheral and central neuraxial regional anesthetic techniques may be especially beneficial in the ambulatory surgical setting. As the number of outpatient surgical procedures continues to increase,[1] optimizing postoperative pain and nausea is important in ambulatory surgical patients as inadequate control of pain and side effects such as PONV are among the leading causes of prolonged stays or readmission following outpatient surgery.[2–6] Despite the advances in surgical techniques[7,8] that minimize surgical trauma, postop-

erative pain in ambulatory surgical patients is still a significant problem and our traditional reliance on opioids may not be optimal in ambulatory surgical patients owing to the opioid-related side effects that may delay hospital discharge after outpatient surgery. Use of peripheral and central neuraxial regional anesthetic techniques with local anesthetics has been shown to decrease postoperative pain in ambulatory surgical patients.[9–14] These techniques may be especially effective as part of a multimodal approach to postoperative pain control.[15]

Use of regional anesthetic techniques in the ambulatory setting may decrease the incidence of PONV.[16] For instance, the incidence of PONV for peripheral nerve blocks is reported to be 4.3–8.8% compared to 5–39% for surgeries performed under general anesthesia.[16] Control of PONV is important as it not only prolongs discharge time but also is one of the outcomes that patients would most like to avoid.[17,18] In addition, poorly controlled PONV may interfere with the intake of oral analgesics and control of postoperative pain. Finally, regional anesthetic techniques may be associated with an improvement in patient satisfaction and some measures of economic outcomes including recovery time and anesthesia-controlled operating room time.[19,20]

COMPLICATIONS

Immediate Complications

Hypotension

Hypotension is a common side effect of regional anesthesia that is seen primarily with central neuraxial blockade, but may occur with peripheral nerve blocks (PNBs) as well. Accidental neuraxial injection during paravertebral, interscalene brachial plexus, lumbar plexus, and deep cervical plexus blockade is uncommon but may result in hypotension. Vasovagal episodes, massive hemorrhage, intravascular injection of local anesthetics, and systemic absorption of adjuvant agents such as clonidine may all contribute to the development of hypotension from PNB.

While hypotension rarely occurs secondary to PNB, the incidence is so high with central neuraxial anesthesia that it is commonly considered a side effect rather than a complication, depending on the degree of hypotension and associated symptoms. Significant hypotension can lead to morbidity or even death, especially in high-risk patients, such as those with coronary artery disease, poorly controlled hypertension, cerebrovascular disease, and renal or hepatic impairment. Although the incidence of hypotension following spinal anesthesia is reported to be 10–40%,[21] the exact incidence of hypotension for central neuraxial block is difficult to elucidate as there is little agreement about a definition for hypotension in the medical literature. Comparisons of the incidence of hypotension between studies is therefore limited by the values defined as hypotension, along with variability in the pharmacologic agent and dose used, the combination of additives such as clonidine that may augment hypotension, and variations in the surgical population such as age differences or surgical procedure. Single injection spinal, which is the most commonly performed central neuraxial block for ambulatory surgery, appears to have a higher incidence of hypotension than a titrated continuous spinal or epidural anesthetic.[22] Low-dose spinals combined with lipophilic opioids provide surgical anesthesia with less hypotension than traditional doses of local anesthetic for the same procedure.[22] Parturients, the elderly, hypovolemic patients, and patients with chronic hypertension may be more likely to experience a larger drop in blood pressure with central neuraxial blockade.

Pathophysiology. Preganglionic sympathetic blockade with resultant arterial and arteriolar vasodilation usually results in about a 20% drop in blood pressure after central neuraxial anesthesia and is the primary mechanism for hypotension.[23] The degree to which systemic vascular resistance (SVR) is reduced is related in a nonlinear fashion to the number of spinal segments blocked, with more cephalad migration resulting in a greater degree of hypotension.[22] With a sympathetic block of the lumbar and sacral segments there is an increase in sympathetic tone in the unblocked thoracic segments to compensate and maintain total SVR near baseline.

A decline in blood pressure of > 30% is often associated with a drop in cardiac output,[23] which is primarily due to a decreased venous return to the heart.[22] Sympathetic blockade affects the intrinsic tone of the venous system, causing a reduction in the tone of venous capacitance vessels and decreased return of blood to the heart. The level of sympathetic block after spinal anesthesia is typically two spinal levels above the sensory level[24] but may extend as many as six dermatomal levels higher.[25] Cardiac output may be further reduced by bradycardia resulting from blockade of the cardiac-accelerator fibers, the Bezold-Jarisch reflex, and decreased venous return enhancing vagal tone. The mechanisms of bradycardia are addressed elsewhere in the chapter. The combined effects of decreased SVR and decreased cardiac output may result in significant hypotension and contribute to morbidity and mortality.

Treatment.   Maintenance of venous return, which can be accomplished by volume loading and positioning of the patient, is the primary treatment for mild hypotension resulting from central neural blockade (CNB). These measures are inadequate for larger drops in blood pressure. Elevation of the lower extremities (10°) and the head (5°) can maximize venous return.[23] Fluid loading, which may prevent a decrease in the central venous pressure (CVP) and cardiac index, has been shown to have little benefit when used without an adrenergic agonist.[26–29] Volume loading with 15 mL/kg within 15 min before spinal anesthesia reduced the incidence of hypotension compared to placebo, but was effective only during the first 15 min of anesthesia.[26] Fluid administration may be important in the prevention of bradycardia and asystolic arrest, but it does not prevent the decrease in SVR, the primary cause of hypotension in CNB. Judicious use of fluids is not recommended as excessive fluid loading may lead to additional complications in susceptible patients, including pulmonary edema, urinary retention, and peripheral edema.[22]

Symptomatic hypotension should be managed with vasoactive drugs, such as phenylephrine and ephedrine, that will increase SVR or cardiac output. Prophylactic administration of vasoactive drugs may be of benefit. Dihydroergotamine 10 μg/kg intramuscular (IM) 15 min before spinal anesthesia decreased the incidence of hypotension occurring beyond 15 min to a greater extent than a fluid bolus.[26] Prophylactic IM phenylephrine at doses of 1.5 and 3 mg has been shown to prevent a statistically significant decrease in hypotension compared to both hypertensive and normotensive controls.[30]

Nausea

Nausea is a minor side effect that may be seen in conjunction with regional anesthesia. In the ambulatory setting, nausea may delay or prevent discharge of patients. There is a paucity of information on nausea as a side effect of regional anesthesia in the medical literature. This is likely because nausea in this setting is almost always secondary to factors other than the regional anesthetic. Nausea is often an early indicator of hypotension from central neuraxial anesthesia, but typically resolves with the return of normotension. Anxiety and pain, due to inadequate analgesia, may also contribute to nausea both intraoperatively and postoperatively. Nausea may occur secondary to surgical stimulation, especially in upper-abdominal procedures, middle-ear surgery, and strabismus surgery; however, these procedures rarely have a regional component to the analgesia. Adjunctive agents including intrathecal opioids will increase the likelihood of nausea, although long-acting hydrophilic opioids such as morphine would not be used in ambulatory surgery patients. In general, regional anesthesia is more likely to decrease the incidence of nausea (as systemic use of opioids may be reduced and inhalation agents may be avoided or reduced) and has been recommended as a primary alternative to general anesthesia in decreasing the incidence of PONV.[31]

Bradycardia

Bradycardia from regional anesthetics occurs most frequently with CNB, but may also occur with PNB (e.g., interscalene brachial plexus block for shoulder surgery). Spinal anesthesia appears to have a higher incidence of bradycardia than epidural techniques. Risk factors for developing bradycardia during central neuraxial anesthesia include: male gender, baseline heart rate < 60 bpm, American Society of Anesthesiologists (ASA) physical status I, use of beta-blocking drugs, sensory level above T6, age < 50 years, and prolonged PR interval.[32–34] Peak block height has the weakest correlation with the severity of bradycardia, while baseline bradycardia, ASA physical status I, age < 50 years, and beta-blockade are the strongest predictors of bradycardia.[32,34] Age < 50 years may be the most common risk factor, possibly owing to the increased vagal tone found in younger patients.[32] Male patients may also be 10 times more likely than women to develop bradycardia during epidural anesthesia, although this figure may be high.[35] Bradycardia does not necessarily occur immediately after CNB but rather usually develops 15 min or longer from the time of anesthetic injection.[36] Bradycardia has been reported after spinal anesthesia as long as 320 min after admission to the postanesthesia care unit (PACU).[37]

Pathophysiology.   There are multiple effects of central neuraxial anesthesia that contribute toward the development of bradycardia. Most of these effects are related either directly or indirectly to the blockade of efferent sympathetic fibers. Sympathetic blockade may reach two to six spinal segments higher than sensory blockade; therefore, even a midthoracic sensory level may result in blockade of the cardiac accelerator fibers that originate from T1–4. This results in unopposed cardiac vagal input with negative inotropic and chronotopic effects. While blockade of the cardiac accelerators does play a role in the development of bradycardia, it does not appear to be the predominant mechanism involved as bradycardia is frequently noted even with lumbar or low thoracic levels of sensory blockade.

Decreased SVR with redistribution of blood to the lower extremities and splanchnic beds decreases venous return and appears to play a more significant role in the development of bradycardia after CNB. Reduced venous return has been demonstrated to result in vagal predominance with resultant bradycardia.[38,39] Baron et al. reported that using lumbar epidural dosed to T8–12 dermatomal sensory levels, there was an 82% decrease in CVP without volume preloading.[38] Three reflex responses can decrease preload that may account for the development of bradycardia. Decreased stretch of the pacemaker cells within the myocardium results in a slower heart rate.[32] Low-pressure baroreceptors located in the right atrium and vena cava may account for a second mechanism for bradycardia secondary to decreased venous return.[34] The third reflex is the Bezold-Jarisch reflex, where receptors located in the left ventricle may paradoxically cause vagal firing with a decrease in ventricular volume.[40] The sum of these three reflex responses allows the heart to slow its rate in response to decreased filling pressures to increase filling time and improve stroke volume. With severe hypovolemia, however, symptomatic bradycardia may ensue and possible progress to cardiac arrest.

Treatment and prevention.   Patient selection when choosing central neuraxial anesthesia may play a key role in the prevention of severe bradycardia. It may be wise to consider other modalities in patients with multiple risk factors for bradycardia if there is no clear benefit for CNB in these patients. Caution should also be applied when rapid blood loss or the use of vasodilators is expected. When central neuraxial blockade is indicated or desired for patients with multiple risk factors for bradycardia, interventions to decrease vagal tone should be considered.

Maintenance of adequate preload is the mainstay of prevention, as multiple studies have documented.[32] Prophylactic preloading is not universally practiced[36] but volume loading and prompt replacement of losses should be practiced in patients who have multiple risk factors and are not at risk for congestive heart failure. Fluid replacement should be closely monitored in patients with heart disease. In older patients, low vagal tone and relative sympathetic predominance have been documented during epidural anesthesia after administration of 20 mL/kg intravenous (IV) fluid bolus, which may increase the risk of ischemia in patients with underlying coronary artery disease.[32]

Fluid replacement alone may be inadequate in many cases to prevent or treat bradycardia after CNB, necessitating the use of pharmacologic agents. Mixed alpha- and beta-adrenergic agent drugs may be beneficial when hypotension and bradycardia are both present, but this may also be inadequate.[41] Early treatment with a vagolytic drug such as atropine may also be indicated, especially in high-risk patients. The early administration of epinephrine may be critical to maintaining coronary perfusion when bradycardia is profound or a full cardiac arrest occurs.[32]

Patient positioning must also be considered, as this may have significant effects on preload. Sudden changes in position, or maintenance of reverse Trendelenburg, a flex, or sitting position (e.g., shoulder surgery) may increase the risk of bradycardia by decreasing preload.[34,37] Patient positioning continues to be important even after the patient is in the PACU. Ponhold and Vicenzi demonstrated that the incidence of severe bradycardia (heart rate < 50 bpm) in the PACU was significantly higher in the Trendelenburg position (60%) than in the horizontal (20%) or hammock (head and legs elevated) (10%) position.[37]

Failure Rates of Regional Anesthesia

Regional anesthesia offers many benefits to patients but is not entirely without risks. Therefore, it is important to have an understanding of failure rates for different procedures so that an adequate risk-benefit analysis may occur. It is difficult to analyze failure rates for many regional anesthetic techniques owing to limited data for certain procedures. There also exists a great deal of variability in skill and experience among different practitioners that may skew the results of clinical trials designed to assess failure rates. The learning curves of students at training institutions may also affect results. Patient variability may also affect the success rate: a disproportionate number of young, thin, anatomically normal individuals may result in a higher success rate as opposed to a patient population of older, obese, or anatomically abnormal patients. Variations in technique, volume of local anesthetic injected, and the type and concentration of local anesthetic will have significant effects on failure rates. Finally, definitions as to what constitutes success or failure may differ among studies; i.e., partial blockade may be documented as a failure in one study and a success in another.

For spinal anesthesia, failure rates after successful dural puncture are very low, reported as 3.1% in one prospective study of 1891 patients[42] and 1% in a prospective study of 3230 orthopedic patients.[43] The most common reason for failure was an inadequate level of anesthesia for the surgical procedure.[42] A study comparing the effect of needle size (25-, 27-, and 29-gauge) in Quincke-type spinal needles showed no difference in success rate among the three needle sizes, although use of the 29-gauge spinal needle resulted in a slightly longer time to achieve dural puncture.[44] The inability to achieve dural puncture is not well reported; however, obesity, prior back surgery, anatomic abnormalities in the spine, lack of experience by the practitioner, and poor patient cooperation may be likely to increase failure rates. Rates for failed single injection caudal or epidural injection, which may be used in ambulatory surgery patients, are not well described, but are likely to be higher than for spinal anesthesia owing to anatomic variation within the epidural space.

For brachial plexus blocks, there is a great deal of variability among practitioners in success rates and significant differences in failure based on varying approaches. Supraclavicular and infraclavicular brachial plexus blockade have higher success rates than single injection axillary brachial plexus blockade.[12] Success rates of over 97% are reported with supraclavicular and infraclavicular brachial plexus blocks in several large prospective studies;[45,46] however, failure rates as high as 28% for supraclavicular and 47% for infraclavicular brachial plexus blocks are reported.[12] Axillary brachial plexus blockade has reported failure rates of 7–42%, with single injection techniques having a lower likelihood of success than multiple injection techniques.[12] No significant differences have been consistently identified for brachial plexus blocks using a paresthesia technique compared with the use of a nerve stimulator.[12]

Peripheral nerve blocks involving the lower extremity, abdomen, and thorax have not been studied to the same extent but are becoming increasingly utilized. Rates of successful lower extremity blocks appear to be generally lower than that of the brachial plexus. Success rates for complete block of the sciatic nerve distribution are reported as 66–97%,[47–49] 40–100% for lateral femoral cutaneous nerve blocks,[50] 73–95% for psoas compartment blocks,[51,52] 92–95% for femoral nerve blocks,[53,54] and 94% for paravertebral blocks.[55] Larger volumes of local anesthetic and multiple injection techniques may improve the success rates. Although potentially high failure rates are noted in multiple studies, success rates of greater than 90–95% appear to be possible with experienced practitioners, use of peripheral nerve stimulators, and adequate doses of local anesthetics.

Minor Side Effects of Brachial Plexus Blockade Above the Clavicle

Interscalene and supraclavicular brachial plexus blockade techniques are unique owing to the large number of addi-

tional nerves and vascular structures that run in close proximity to the brachial plexus in the neck. Several nerve structures in the neck are affected so frequently after injection of local anesthetic in the interscalene groove that these effects are considered to be side effects rather than complications. It is important to warn patients prior to performing these blocks of the likelihood of these side effects and their transient nature so that they are not perceived as complications. It is also crucial for the practitioner to recognize the patient population in which these side effects could become serious complications.

Recurrent laryngeal nerve blockade.   Hoarseness secondary to unilateral recurrent laryngeal nerve blockade occurs occasionally with interscalene brachial plexus block and occurs less frequently (1.3%) with supraclavicular block.[12,22] This is rarely serious, but could result in sudden obstruction of the airway in a patient who has a contralateral recurrent laryngeal nerve injury and may increase aspiration risk in susceptible individuals. Airway edema or hoarseness secondary to a compressive hematoma should always be considered as these complications are potentially life-threatening.

Phrenic nerve blockade.   Blockade of the ipsilateral phrenic nerve is reported to occur nearly 100% of the time with successful interscalene brachial plexus block and may occur with supraclavicular brachial plexus blocks and rarely with infraclavicular brachial plexus blocks.[12,22] Most patients remain asymptomatic from hemidiaphragmatic paralysis, but some will report symptoms of mild dyspnea or altered respiratory sensation secondary to a 20–40% reduction in forced vital capacity (FVC) and forced expiratory volume at 1 sec (FEV$_1$).[22] Interscalene brachial plexus block is contraindicated in patients with contralateral phrenic nerve paralysis and relatively contraindicated for individuals who have significantly diminished respiratory capacity who may not be able to tolerate a 20–40% reduction in FVC or FEV$_1$. Bilateral interscalene brachial plexus blockade is therefore contraindicated due to the certainty of complete paralysis of the diaphragm.

Horner's syndrome.   The combination of ipsilateral pupillary constriction, ptosis, enopthalmos, and loss of sweating commonly occurs following interscalene and supraclavicular approaches to the brachial plexus. Horner's syndrome occurs secondary to local anesthetic blockade of the cervical sympathetic chain, with a reported incidence of 20–90%.[12] There is no harm to the patients from this side effect; however, failure to warn them in advance may result in anxiety on their behalf of a serious complication.

Local Anesthetic Toxicity

Local anesthetic toxicity is a feared, but relatively uncommon complication of regional anesthetic techniques that may lead to seizures or even cardiac arrest and death. Systemic toxicity may result from accidental IV or intra-arterial injection or from vascular absorption of local anesthetic. Patients may experience dizziness or light-headedness, tinnitus, visual changes, and perioral tingling or numbness, which may be followed by tremors, muscle twitching, and eventually loss of consciousness and generalized tonic-clonic convulsions.[22] Further increases in local anesthetic concentration may lead to central nervous system (CNS) depression and cardiovascular disturbances, vasodilatation, hypotension, myocardial conduction abnormalities, arrhythmias, bradycardia, and cardiac arrest.[22] The incidence of toxicity is directly related to several factors: dose of local anesthetic, type of local anesthetic, and vascularity of site injected. Increasing the dose of a local anesthetic injected will raise the likelihood of toxic reactions. Maximum recommended doses of varying local anesthetics have been widely published for epidural and PNBs, although widely available data have demonstrated excellent safety profiles with higher doses for PNBs. Among the local anesthetics, bupivacaine and etidocaine have been demonstrated to have the worst safety profiles with regard to cardiac toxicity, while lidocaine and mepivacaine are among the safest.[56,57] Injection at highly vascular sites, such as intercostal, brachial plexus, and caudal analgesia, may result in a higher incidence of local anesthetic toxicity.[23] Bypass of the lungs (e.g., injection directly into the carotid or vertebral artery), which serve as a repository for local anesthetics, may result in toxicity at significantly lower doses.[23] Blockade of multiple nerves may result in higher plasma concentration of local anesthetics even when a lower total dose is utilized.[58]

Incidence of seizure and cardiac toxicity. The overall incidence of seizure from regional anesthetics is reported as 0.22–4/1000,[56,59] although the frequency varies considerably among different procedures. In a retrospective review of 26,450 patients, brachial plexus anesthesia resulted in an overall seizure rate of 2/1000 procedures, but the incidences for interscalene (7.6/1000) and supraclavicular (7.9/1000) approaches to the brachial plexus were among the highest of all regional anesthetic techniques.[56] Intercostal nerve blocks, which by far have the highest rate of local anesthetic absorption,[23] were not used in either of the large trials evaluating local anesthetic toxicity. Caudal epidural anesthesia was reported to have the second highest incidence of seizure at 6.9/1000. The most likely explanation for the increased incidence of seizure with caudal and supraclavicular brachial plexus blockade is that relatively large volumes of local anesthetic are used at these sites and the vascularity is significantly greater than at epidural or other peripheral locations. Additionally, fewer patients received an epinephrine-containing test dose during caudal anesthesia than those receiving epidural anesthesia, which might affect seizure rates.[56] Auroy et al. reported an incidence of 0.75/1000 patients for all peripheral nerve blocks, 0.13/1000 for epidural analgesia, and 0.27/1000 for intravenous regional anesthesia (IVRA) in a prospective study of 103,730 people.[59] Local anesthetic toxicity is not seen with spinal anesthesia owing to the low doses used and relative avascularity. Bupivacaine was associated with a statistically significant higher frequency of seizure compared with other local anesthetics.[56]

In the study by Auroy and colleagues, none of the patients who developed seizures progressed to cardiac arrest, and the overall incidence of cardiac arrest for epidural and PNBs was 0.1 and 0.14/1000, respectively (cardiac arrests did not appear to be related to local anesthetic toxicity).[59]

This mirrors the retrospective review in which no patient developed adverse cardiovascular changes.[56] Despite the extremely low incidence of cardiac arrest from local anesthetics, new long-acting amide local anesthetics (e.g., ropivacaine and levobupivacaine) with improved safety profiles have been introduced.[60–65] Although ropivacaine, levobupivacaine, and bupivacaine have a similar duration of action and onset time, bupivacaine has been demonstrated to cause seizure at lower plasma levels and cardiac toxicity at significantly lower plasma levels than the other two drugs.[60,63,64] Given the extremely low incidence of cardiac arrest from local anesthetics, routine replacement of bupivacaine with levobupivacaine or ropivacaine is probably unwarranted; however, when large total doses of local anesthetic will be used or impaired hepatic metabolism is present, the use of ropivacaine or levobupivacaine in place of bupivacaine may be prudent.

Pathophysiology. Toxicity of local anesthetics results primarily from binding of sodium channels in the CNS and cardiovascular system. The carbon dioxide (CO_2) tension and pH influence plasma concentrations of local anesthetics. An elevated arterial CO_2 will increase cerebral blood flow and delivery of local anesthetic to the brain, while an acidotic state will increase the amount of free drug available, resulting in a decrease in the seizure threshold.[23] CNS toxicity follows a two-stage process, with inhibitory neurons blocked at lower concentrations (resulting in generalized convulsions), and at higher concentrations, a global CNS depression is seen.[60] The amygdala and hippocampus are thought to be the site of action of local anesthetic drugs in the CNS.[22,23] Cardiotoxicity can also be divided into two components (indirect and direct). Indirect cardiotoxicity reveals an initial stimulating effect followed by a depressive component at higher concentrations.[60] Direct myocardial actions consist of negative inotropy, chronotropy, and dromotropy. Bupivacaine appears to be more cardiotoxic because it enters the sodium channel rapidly but leaves slowly, resulting in impairment of conduction and contractility and life-threatening reentrant arrhythmias that are often refractory to treatment.[23]

Management of local anesthetic toxicity. While prevention via careful technique, frequent aspiration, slow injection, minimizing doses, and the use of epinephrine as a marker of intravascular injection is the best management, intravascular injection or absorption will occasionally occur. Should signs of local anesthetic toxicity be present, injection should be immediately stopped and control and management of the airway should take priority. The development of respiratory acidosis will worsen the outcome, so assisted ventilation may be needed, although frequently it is not necessary. Anticonvulsant medications (benzodiazepines, barbiturates, and propofol) should be used early but care should be taken if evidence of cardiovascular collapse is occurring owing to the risk of hypotension with these agents. In the rare episodes that cardiac toxicity occurs, vasopressors and expansion of intravascular volume may be necessary along with cardiopulmonary resuscitation. Bretylium is recommended for recalcitrant arrhythmias, although atrioventricular pacing and cardiopulmonary bypass may be necessary in the case of bupivacaine toxicity.[23]

Allergic reaction to local anesthetic.   True allergic reactions to local anesthetics are very rare, with most reported reactions representing allergy to an additive or metabolite, a side effect of epinephrine, or local anesthetic toxicity. Between the two types of local anesthetics, ester agents are far more likely to produce true allergic reaction than amides. Procaine and tetracaine are hydrolyzed to para-aminobenzoic acid, a well-known allergen. Methylparaben and metabisulfite are preservatives that are added to some amide local anesthetics that may cause allergic reactions in susceptible individuals. The benefit of skin testing for local anesthetic allergy is questioned by some, but should probably be used when true allergy is suspected.[22]

Pneumothorax

Pneumothorax is a potential complication of any regional anesthetic technique performed in the thorax or lower neck. In many cases, a pneumothorax may be small and clinically insignificant, but a large pneumothorax (20–25%) or one in a patient with preexisting respiratory compromise may be life-threatening, especially if combined with positive-pressure ventilation. A chest tube will be necessary in some patients who develop clinically significant pneumothorax. Pneumothorax may go undetected for hours; therefore, ambulatory surgery patients should be warned before discharge to go to the emergency room if chest pain or breathing difficulty develops. The incidence is difficult to quantify owing to operator variability but is expected to be highest with intercostal nerve blocks and least likely with thoracic epidurals. The reported incidence of pneumothorax with intercostal nerve blocks ranges from 0.073 to 19%.[66] Brachial plexus anesthesia may result in pneumothorax, with the axillary approach having almost no risk and the supraclavicular approach having the highest reported risk (0–6.1%).[23] Modified supraclavicular and infraclavicular approaches to the brachial plexus have been described and performed with no incidence of pneumothorax, although these studies are relatively small.[67–69] In the hands of an experienced practitioner, the incidence of pneumothorax from supraclavicular or infraclavicular brachial plexus blockade is likely to be less than 1%. Paravertebral analgesia is another technique that carries risk of placing a needle through the pleura, although the reported incidence of pneumothorax with this technique is quite small (0.035–0.5%).[70] The incidence of pneumothorax from epidural anesthesia is not reported in studies but is likely to be extremely low as there are few case reports and needle entry into the chest wall would require significant error in placement.

Cardiac Arrest

Cardiac arrest secondary to a regional anesthetic is a rare but devastating complication, with an incidence that is much higher in spinal anesthetics (6.4/10,000 patients) than any other technique (1/10,000 patients).[59] Fatal outcomes from cardiac arrest were reported in 23% of these patients.[59] Cardiac arrest may be due to local anesthetic toxicity, ischemia, hypotension, respiratory arrest, or arrhythmias. Bradycardia with progression to cardiac arrest from spinal anesthesia occurs six times more frequently than from any other cause. The simplest way to decrease vagal predominance during spinal anesthesia may be to maintain adequate preload by volume loading and prompt replacement of fluid losses. As sudden decreases in preload can trigger cardiac arrest during central neuraxial anesthesia, it may be prudent to contemplate a different technique when the use of vasodilators or rapid blood loss is expected.[32] When severe bradycardia or cardiac arrest occurs, early use of epinephrine (0.01–0.1 mg/kg) is recommended to maintain coronary perfusion pressure,[71] although atropine and ephedrine have also been successfully used.[34] Although epinephrine is recommended as the primary treatment of severe bradycardia and cardiac arrest in this setting,[71] epinephrine alone occasionally may be ineffective as it is not a vagolytic drug and the increased contractility may contribute to reflex slowing attributed to the Bezold-Jarish reflex.[32] An animal study suggested that the use of vasopressin and atropine might be more effective than epinephrine alone when treating cardiac arrest during epidural anesthesia.[72] In the setting of severe bradycardia or cardiac arrest, it is important to institute cardiopulmonary resuscitation to ensure adequate circulation of drugs to the heart.

Total Spinal

High spinal or total spinal may occur by several mechanisms: the relative excessive dose of an intended spinal, cephalad spread with hypobaric or hyperbaric solutions, unintended intrathecal injection from epidural catheters, and unintended intrathecal injection from PNBs including brachial plexus blocks and retrobulbar blocks. With high spinal, the patient will typically report numbness or weakness in the hands and dyspnea. The anesthesiologist should always be prepared to provide airway support and breathing assistance and to intubate if necessary, although in many situations, supplemental oxygen and reassurance will be all that is required. Diaphragm function will often be retained with high spinal, but in patients with poor pulmonary function, ventilatory assistance may be necessary. Hypotension and anxiety will frequently accompany high spinal; therefore, the use of vasopressors and occasionally mild sedatives is likely required. Total spinal anesthesia, which would be expected after inadvertent intrathecal injection, presents often as apnea, loss of consciousness, and hypotension requiring immediate intervention.

The incidence of total spinal from central neuraxial blockade is thought to be less than 0.2%.[22] Numerous case reports of total spinal have been reported secondary to retrobulbar anesthesia, with a reported incidence of 1:350–1:15,000.[23,73–75] Symptoms first appear approximately 2 min after administration of the retrobulbar block, peak in 20 min, and resolve in 2–3 hr.[23,74] The symptoms from brain stem anesthesia may include confusion, shivering, convulsions, paralysis, loss of consciousness, apnea, hypotension, bradycardia, nausea, and vomiting.[23] Treatment should be based on the symptoms.

Delayed Complications

Pain at Injection Site

Localized tenderness, bruising, and small hematomas secondary to regional anesthetics are not uncommon, but are rarely of significance. Pain may be secondary to direct tissue trauma, inflammation, muscle spasm, hematoma, abscess, local anesthetic toxicity, or direct nerve injury. Local anesthetics can cause focal myonecrosis, the effect of which is enhanced by epinephrine.[22] Chloroprocaine, which contains the chelating agent ethylene diamine tetra-acetic acid (EDTA), is associated with an increased incidence of back pain after epidural administration compared with other local anesthetics, although even the elimination of EDTA or reduction of the solution's pH did not eliminate the high incidence of backache.[76–79] Total volume and concentration of chloroprocaine positively correlate with the incidence and severity of pain.[22] Back pain after epidural or spinal anesthesia is commonly reported but generally is of limited duration and not perceived as a major complication by patients. The possibility of epidural abscess, which may initially present as back pain, must be ruled out as permanent neurologic sequelae may result from a missed diagnosis. The incidence of localized soreness at the site of injection from central neuraxial anesthesia ranges from 10 to 25%, while the incidence of generalized backache is lower.[80,81] Disc injury after difficult lumbar puncture has been reported.[22] The factor most closely associated with back pain, however, is duration of surgery, regardless of the type of anesthetic, suggesting that most back pain is not related to central neuraxial anesthesia.[22] The incidence of back pain rises from 18% after 1 hr to as high as 50% in surgeries lasting more than 4 hr.[80] Preexisting back pain is not a contraindication to spinal anesthesia, but patients should be counseled that their pain might be worse after surgery regardless of anesthetic technique chosen.

Disturbance of Micturition

Disturbance of micturition is one of the most common adverse effects of central neuraxial anesthesia and may frequently prevent discharge of ambulatory surgical patients, yet is one of the least studied complications of regional anesthesia. It may take up to 8 hr to regain full function of the detrusor muscles and even one episode of excessive distension of the bladder may have long-term damaging effects on the ability to micturate in the future.[23] The incidence of urinary retention has been reported to be as low as 1% with epidural bupivacaine and fentanyl or as high as 90% when large doses of epidural morphine are used.[23] Avoidance of intrathecal opioids and long-acting local anesthetics may decrease the risk of urinary retention in ambulatory surgery patients. Some advocate routine bladder catheterization after neuraxial opioids, and evidence of the ability to void is recommended in patients receiving central neuraxial anesthesia before discharge in the ambulatory setting.

Postdural Puncture Headache

With the introduction of smaller spinal needles, the problem of postdural puncture headache (PDPH) in the ambulatory surgical patient is often not considered to be a significant complication. However, a systemic review of the literature suggests that the incidence (but not necessarily the severity) of PDPH may be higher than expected (up to approximately 9%) and may affect postdischarge recovery of the ambulatory surgical patient.[82]

Pathophysiology. The presumed etiology of PDPH is due to leakage of cerebrospinal fluid (CSF). In patients with PDPH, the loss of CSF (which may be as high as 11.9 mL/min[83]) is greater than the rate of replacement (approximately 0.35 mL/min),[84] which may result in low intracranial pressure causing traction on pain-sensitive cranial structures (e.g., blood vessels, meninges, and cranial nerves, especially V, IX, and X), especially when the patient assumes the upright position with an increased transdural lumbar CSF pressure.[85] Other mechanisms may contribute to the severity of PDPH. Compensatory cerebrovasodilatation secondary to CSF volume loss with an activation of adenosine receptors may result in a vascular component of PDPH in some patients.[86,87]

Experimental and clinical evidence suggests that CSF leakage results in the development of PDPH. Removal of CSF (approximately 20 mL) results in a PDPH while restoration of intracranial pressure with injection of intrathecal saline completely eliminates PDPH.[88] Magnetic resonance imaging (MRI) after dural puncture reveals intracranial reduction in CSF volume of up to 158.6 mL.[89,90] Leakage of CSF into the epidural space in patients with PDPH has also been shown by myeloscopy and myelography.[91] Finally, a decrease in intracranial pressure resulting from CSF leakage will affect cochlear function as a result of decrease in intralabyrinthine pressure. Disturbances in auditory function have been documented in patients with PDPH[92–94] with the severity of hearing loss correlating with severity of PDPH[93,95] and resolution of hearing loss after epidural blood patch treatment.[95,96]

Clinical presentation. The pathognomonic characteristic of PDPH is the postural nature of the headache, which is increased when the patient is upright and decreased when the patient is supine. The severity of PDPH varies and may be categorized as mild (little interference with daily activities, not confined to bed, no associated symptoms), moderate (some interference with daily activities, confined to bed for part of the day, associated symptoms may be present), or severe (bedridden, unable or unwilling to stand, associated symptoms always present).[92] Associated symptoms may include musculoskeletal (neck or back stiffness), vestibular (nausea, vomiting, dizziness, vertigo), cochlear (tinnitus, decreased hearing, hearing loss), or ocular (diplopia, photophobia, blurred vision) disturbances.[92] Auditory symptoms have been reported to occur in 3.5–12% of patients with PDPH.[93,94] In addition, ocular symptoms have been reported in 3.4–13% of patients with PDPH and may include visual field defects, transient visual obscurations, and nystagmus.[92,94] Dysfunction of cranial nerves III, IV, and VI due to decreased CSF pressure may result in diplopia and difficulty with accommodation. Although typically a nonfatal complication of central neuraxial anesthesia, PDPH may in extremely rare cases cause severe CSF leakage resulting in tearing of the cerebral bridging veins and subdural hematoma.

Approximately 70–90% of patients will develop symptoms within 48 hr of dural puncture (40–65% will have symptoms within the first 24 hr).[92,94] The median duration of PDPH in patients who experienced spontaneous recovery (no active treatment) is approximately 5 days[92] with approximately 70% of patients spontaneously recovering within 1 week; however, some patients may experience PDPH for several months.[94] Although diagnosis of PDPH is in most cases straightforward owing to the postural character of the headache after dural puncture, PDPH is a diagnosis of exclusion, and other etiologies of headache must be considered.

Risk factors for PDPH development.

There are several patient characteristics that may contribute to development of PDPH. There is a decrease in incidence of PDPH with an increase in age.[94–98] A multivariate analysis of 1021 spinal anesthetics showed a significant inverse correlation between frequency of PDPH and age.[94] Randomized data also suggest that elderly patients have a significantly lower incidence of PDPH when compared to younger patients.[97] Although the reason why elderly patients have a lower incidence of PDPH is not clear, elderly patients may have a diminished sensitivity to pain, decreased elasticity of dural fibers, diminished reactivity of cerebral vessels, or narrowed intervertebral foramina in the epidural space, thus preventing CSF leakage and maintaining higher epidural space pressures.[99] Traditionally, women were thought to have a higher incidence of PDPH;[95] however, more recent data suggest that there is no difference in the incidence of PDPH between men and women.[94]

There are also several spinal needle characteristics (e.g., size and shape) that may contribute to the development and severity of PDPH. When comparing needles of the same design, smaller-diameter needles are associated with a lower incidence of PDPH[100] as larger needles generally produce larger dural punctures and greater rates of transdural fluid leak.[101–103] Meta-analyses demonstrated that the incidence of PDPH was significantly less when a smaller needle was used compared to that with a larger needle of the same design with a significant reduction in incidence of severe PDPH with smaller needles.[100] Needle tip design is also an important determinant in the development of PDPH, with noncutting (blunt-tip, pencil point such as the Whitacre) needles being associated with a lower incidence of PDPH than cutting needles (e.g., Quincke).[100,104]

Although the exact arrangement of the dural fibers is still somewhat controversial, longitudinal bevel ("parallel") insertion of the Quincke needle may decrease the incidence of PDPH as dural fibers (which if uniformly arranged parallel to the long axis of the dura) would less likely be cut, thus diminishing CSF leakage and incidence of PDPH.[101,105,106] Several clinical studies have demonstrated a decreased incidence of PDPH with a "parallel" insertion of needles.[94,105–107] In addition, there is also some suggestion that a paramedian (versus midline) insertion of a spinal needle will result in a decrease in CSF leak and possibly lower incidence of PDPH.[101,108–110]

Treatment of PDPH.   Treatment of PDPH generally falls into two categories: conservative therapy (includes pharmacologic interventions), which alleviate the symptoms until the dural puncture heals, and invasive therapy (e.g., epidural blood patch [EBP]), which attempts to stop the leakage of CSF. Although there are no guidelines as to which option is preferred, the clinician should take the patient's preferences into consideration.

Patients with mild PDPH may require only nonsteroidal anti-inflammatory drugs (NSAIDs) for relief of PDPH; however, some patients may also need opioids (e.g., codeine with acetaminophen) to alleviate PDPH. Although supportive or conservative therapies such as maintenance of adequate hydration and bed rest as needed may be part of the treatment regimen, prospective studies have demonstrated that incidence of PDPH is not related to duration of recumbency[111,112] and increasing oral fluid intake per se has not been shown to decrease incidence of PDPH.[113] In addition, methylxanthines, such as caffeine and theophylline, may cause cerebral vasoconstriction and produce analgesia by blocking peripheral adenosine receptors and antinociception through central noradrenergic mechanisms.[114] Although the use of caffeine may have an efficacy of approximately 75%, the analgesic effects are generally only temporary.[115]

EBP is the definitive treatment for PDPH. Although the exact mechanism by which EBP exerts its action is not known, it is thought that relief of PDPH occurs immediately as a result of mass effect from epidural blood increasing intracranial pressure followed by a sealant effect of blood over the dural puncture allowing replenishment of lost CSF.[116] The combination of CSF and blood may facilitate onset of coagulation and stronger clot formation[117] with fibroblastic activity and collagen deposition seen over the dural puncture site at 48 hr and 2 weeks, respectively.[118] Although initial studies used lower volumes (< 10 mL) of blood and were associated with higher failure rates, more recent studies recommend use of approximately 15–20 ml of autologous blood,[116] which results in a primarily cephalad spread covering an average of 9–10 spinal segments with the majority of clot restricted to three to five segments around the injection site.[116,119] The efficacy of EBP is typically reported at approximately 90% after the first EBL and 97.5% after the second EBP;[120] however, more recent data suggest that complete relief may occur in only 75% of patients.[121] Common transient symptoms that may occur during injection of EBP include back pain (> 35%), lower extremity pain (12%), lower extremity sensory disturbances and weakness in the lower extremities (18%), neck discomfort, and radicular pain most likely secondary to nerve root compression (as demonstrated on MRI)[116,122] with most symptoms resolving within 3 days. Other rare complications of EBP include intraocular hemorrhage from rapid epidural injections, cranial nerve palsy, infectious meningitis, adhesive arachnoiditis, epidural abscess, and obliteration of the epidural space.[123,124]

Transient Neurologic Syndrome

Although lidocaine historically has been the local anesthetic of choice because of its faster onset and shorter duration of action compared to other local anesthetics (e.g., bupivacaine), cases of cauda equina syndrome[125] associated with the concurrent use of continuous intrathecal catheters and lidocaine raised concerns about the safety and neurotoxicity of intrathecal lidocaine. Subsequently, a case series of patients who postoperatively had symptoms of buttock and lower extremity pain and underwent spinal anesthesia with lidocaine was the first to acknowledge what is now *recognized* as "transient neurologic symptoms" (TNS).[126] Randomized and observational trials that have followed strongly suggest that TNS is predominately associated with the use of lidocaine spinal anesthesia.[127,128]

Although superficially, it may seem reasonable to attribute TNS to neurologic injury from intrathecal lidocaine since animal data suggest an increased neurotoxicity of lidocaine compared to other local anesthetics such as bupivacaine,[129] the exact etiology of TNS is not clear. Other possible causes include local anesthetic toxicity specific to lidocaine, neural injury or ischemia secondary to needle trauma, sciatic nerve stretching or positioning, and musculoskeletal dysfunction.[127] In fact, the etiology of TNS may not even be of neurologic origin per se. Electrophysiologic testing (electromyography, nerve conduction studies, somatosensory evoked potentials) performed prior to and after lidocaine spinal anesthesia in patients with TNS revealed no changes or evidence of a direct neurotoxic effect of intrathecal lidocaine.[130] Furthermore, factors that contribute to the development of the cauda equina syndrome (increased dose and concentration of lidocaine, addition of vasoconstrictors) do not appear to be associated with an increase in incidence of TNS.[127] Although intrathecal lidocaine is associated with an increase in incidence of TNS, decreasing the concentration of lidocaine (from 5% to 0.5%), changing the baricity or osmolarity, or adding glucose does not seem to influence the development of TNS.[127,131,132]

Risk factors for the development of TNS include lidocaine spinal anesthesia, outpatient surgical status, and the lithotomy position.[128] When compared to those receiving bupivacaine spinal anesthesia, the adjusted relative risk for development of TNS after lidocaine spinal anesthesia is approximately 5.[128] Randomized, controlled studies indicate that the incidence of TNS after lidocaine spinal anesthesia ranges from approximately 15 to 40% with other local anesthetics (e.g., mepivacaine, bupivacaine, procaine) having a TNS incidence of generally less than 5%.[131–138] Lithotomy position has been shown to be an independent risk factor for the development of TNS.[128,133] Although outpatient surgical status (possibly due to earlier ambulation) has also been shown to be associated with an increased incidence of TNS,[128] the reason for this is not clear and not all of the data available support this association.[139]

Patients with TNS typically describe a cramping or burning pain in their thighs with approximately half noting lower back pain and/or radiation of the pain to the lower extremities.[127] The severity of pain varies but a mean visual analog score averages to approximately 6 (on a scale of 1–10).[127,131,133] The onset of pain occurs generally within 12–24 hr after surgery and may last anywhere from a few hours to several days. There are no reports of long-term or persistent TNS. Treatment of TNS is supportive and includes opioids, NSAIDs, and muscle relaxants. NSAIDs

may be especially effective in treating TNS[127] and interventional therapy such as trigger point injections may also be an effective therapeutic option.[140]

Neuropathy

Neuropathy after regional anesthesia is not uncommon, although it will often be missed unless a careful physical examination and history is performed. Most cases are mild and resolve in days to months, but in rare instances, paresthesias and motor weakness may persist permanently. It is often difficult to determine whether nerve damage is secondary to a regional anesthetic, surgical injury, or positioning injury. Patients must be made aware of the possibility of transient neuropathy and the rare possibility of permanent nerve damage when a regional anesthetic is considered.

Incidence and risk factors. The incidence varies according to the type of regional anesthetic, with spinal anesthesia having the highest rate of neurologic injury lasting longer than 3 months (spinal 0.059%, epidural 0.02%, peripheral nerve block 0.019%).[21,59] Direct injury to the spinal cord is rare but has been reported both from thoracic penetration of the cord during epidural placement and spinal anesthesia with damage to the conus medularis.[141,142] In nearly all cases, a paresthesia on needle placement was in the same distribution as the subsequent injury. For peripheral nerve blocks, the incidence of dysesthesias lasting more than 1 week is probably between 1% and 5%, although the reported incidence varies between 0.04 and 32%.[22,143–145]

Severe pain on injection may correspond with intraneural injection and may increase the incidence of neuropathy, although the absence of pain does not guarantee that no nerve injury has occurred. There is still debate as to whether there is an increased incidence of nerve damage when regional anesthetics are performed under general anesthesia, as the patient's feedback of intense pain would be absent. Several trials on both adult and pediatric patients do not support this concern, but other studies have demonstrated an increased incidence of nerve injury when regional anesthesia is performed under general anesthesia.[22] Although the exact risk of performing regional anesthetics under heavy sedation or general anesthesia is unknown, it may be best to avoid this practice in most adults if possible.

Since the majority of persistent paresthesias postoperatively are associated with the elicitation of paresthesias during needle manipulation or pain on injection, some have argued that the use of a nerve stimulator may decrease the incidence of neuropathy. A comparison of the transarterial technique for axillary brachial plexus block to a paresthesia technique demonstrated a higher rate of nerve damage when paresthesias were sought (2.8% vs. 0.8%).[146] In all cases of neuropathy from the transarterial group, an unintentional paresthesia was elicited during needle placement.[146] The use of a nerve stimulator during brachial plexus blockade does not appear to reduce the risk of nerve damage when compared to a paresthesia technique in other studies.[145,147] There is a lack of adequate prospective trials at this time to support the safety of one technique over the other.

There may be added risk with the supplementation of incomplete blocks or repeated blocks on an extremity. The risk of persistent paresthesias is not increased with repeated blocks performed within a 1–8-week period.[145] Repeated blocks performed while the extremity is still partly anesthetized may increase the risk of neurologic sequelae if they prevent the ability to detect intraneural injection.[22] A study on axillary brachial plexus blocks showed a 23% incidence of persistent dysesthesias in patients who had a more distal reblock compared with an 11% incidence in those who did not receive supplementation.[148] Data on the risks of multiple injection techniques (where needle manipulation in a potentially numb plexus occurs) are still not available. Laboratory evidence suggests that preexisting neurologic dysfunction (diabetes, drug induced, idiopathic, traumatic) may increase the risk of local anesthetic-induced nerve injury.[22,149] It is believed that any injury that impairs axonal flow may predispose the nerve to denervation after an additional insult.[22] Regional anesthesia did not increase the risk of postoperative neuropathy in patients with existing ulnar neuropathy undergoing ulnar nerve transposition.[149]

The type of needle and orientation in relation to the nerve fibers used in block placement has been implicated in the incidence and persistence of neurologic deficit. Short beveled needles that are designed to allow the nerve to roll away from an advancing needle may be associated with a decreased incidence of nerve fascicle injury, but are reported to have increased severity (likely due to impalement of the nerve and crushing of the fibers) of nerve injury when it occurs.[22,151,152] Conversely, cutting needles may be more likely to cause transient neuropathies, but the likelihood of severe and permanent damage is reduced.

There are concerns that with continuous catheter techniques, an increase in complications would result owing to the larger-gauge needle size required and increased difficulty and manipulation required to place a catheter. Continuous-catheter techniques have not been shown to increase the risk of neuropathy in PNB.[144] These catheters have been used in ambulatory surgery to provide analgesia in the home environment and are demonstrated to be safe; however, they are not without complications (e.g., dislodgement, knotting, shearing, kinking, breakage, infection).

Pathophysiology.   Nerve damage may occur due to a wide variety of factors, many of which are not related to a regional anesthetic (direct damage to the nerve from surgical manipulation, transection, hematoma formation, entrapment, scarring, stretch, ischemia, and tourniquet use). The pathogenesis of neuropathy after nerve block includes direct transection of nerve fascicles, pressure-induced ischemia (pressures generated during intraneural injection can be as high as 700 mmHg),[23] compression by hematoma (intraneural or extraneural), direct toxicity of injected agents, vascular compromise, prolonged vasoconstriction, and herniation of nerve fibers through perineural gaps created by needle trauma.[22,153] Neurologic deficits related to regional anesthesia that arise within the first 24 hr are most likely second-

ary to intra- or extraneural hematoma, intraneural edema, or a lesion involving a sufficient number of nerve fibers to allow immediate diagnosis.[145] In many cases, the symptoms are not present immediately upon resolution of the block, but present days to weeks later. Delayed presentation may represent alternative etiologies such as tissue scar formation, herniation of nerve fibers through perineural gaps created by needle trauma, or delayed ischemic complications.[22,145] Local anesthetic toxicity clearly plays some role in the development of neuropathy in both PNBs and spinal anesthesia. High concentrations of local anesthetics are neurotoxic and clinically used concentrations of lidocaine and tetracaine have neurotoxic potential.[154,155] Bupivacaine has been identified as an independent risk factor for worsening of ulnar nerve function compared with other anesthetics[150] and high-concentration lidocaine may increase the risk of neuropraxia after spinal anesthesia.[59] Subclinical neuropathy is often present before and after clinical nerve deficits are noted.[145]

Meningitis

Aseptic meningitis is the most benign neurologic complication, with symptoms (fever, nuchal rigidity, photophobia) typically presenting within 24 hr of dural puncture and resolution within a few days.[21] Microscopic examination of CSF is characterized by polymorphonuclear leukocytosis; bacterial CSF cultures are negative.[21] It is possible that aseptic meningitis can result from introduction of skin disinfectants into the CSF.[23] Bacterial meningitis is a far more serious complication, but the incidence is rare with epidural anesthesia and 1:21,500–1:40,000 after spinal anesthesia.[156,157] Dural puncture in a patient with sepsis is considered a risk for meningitis (owing to the potential for introduction of contaminated blood into the cerebrospinal fluid and disruption of the blood-brain barrier), although there is conflicting evidence in the literature regarding this.[22] The potential risk of introducing bacteria into the CSF with dural puncture in a septic patient warrants careful consideration of the benefits and alternatives for the patient considered and should prompt the use of empiric antibiotic therapy prior to performing central neuraxial block.

Epidural Abscess

An epidural abscess is a devastating but fortunately rare complication of central neuraxial blockade that may result in complete paraplegia. Auroy et al. reported no cases in over 70,000 central neuraxial blocks,[59] nor were any cases reported in Kane's review of 115,000 neuraxial blocks[157] and only one case reported in 100,000 neuraxial anesthetics in the review by Moen et al.[156] Risk factors for epidural abscess may include immunosuppression, diabetes, steroid administration, sepsis, infection, faulty sterile technique, and extended duration of catheterization.[158] The presentation begins with localized back pain and tenderness with fever and leukocytosis, and may have variable neurologic signs and symptoms.[159] The median time of onset of symptoms is 8 days after catheterization.[160] Progressive neurologic deterioration may follow and is cause for immediate surgical decompression. MRI scanning is the diagnostic procedure of choice and should be conducted at the earliest suspicion, ideally prior to the onset of neurologic symptoms.[159] Persistent neurologic deficit appears to be more likely in patients with thoracic than with lumbar epidural abscess.[22] Skin flora (*Staphylococcus aureus*) is the most likely pathogen;[161] therefore, antimicrobial therapy should be instituted with coverage for gram-positive organisms. As with meningitis, sepsis and local skin infection (not at the site of needle placement) may be a contraindication to performing spinal or epidural owing to the possibility of introducing bacteria to the epidural space. An epidural catheter has the potential to serve as a focus for secondary infection and provide a pathway for bacteria to reach the epidural space. Prolonged duration of catheterization has been considered a risk factor for the development of an epidural abscess, although this is not a proven risk. Certainly, careful attention to sterile technique and maintenance of a sterile insertion site, along with careful observation of the patient at least daily for signs of local or systemic infection, is warranted.

Epidural Hematoma

Epidural hematoma is another rare, but catastrophic complication associated with central neuraxial anesthesia. The epidural space contains a large venous plexus that may be engorged in some states (obstetric patients, obesity) and can be easily punctured by spinal or epidural needles. The incidence of a traumatic occurrence to a blood vessel from epidural needle or catheter puncture is 1–10% with an incidence as high as 18% in obstetric patients.[22,162] The use of large-gauge needles and multiple attempts at cannulation will increase the risk of a bloody tap. In normal individuals, bleeding is self-limited and does not expand into a hematoma large enough to cause any neurologic symptoms; however, in patients with dysfunctional coagulation, bleeding may continue with an expansive hematoma formation that may begin to compress the spinal cord or its nerve roots. Reports of epidural hematoma in patients with normal coagulation status are indeed very rare, with most cases occurring in patients with coagulopathy (whether secondary to a disease process or the administration of an anticoagulant). The incidence of epidural hematoma remains low, with reports of 1 in 150,000 after epidural block and 1 in 220,000 after spinal block.[23] The recent introduction of low-molecular-weight heparins (LMWH) and new antiplatelet drugs was associated with a rise in the incidence of epidural hematoma, which has prompted the release of guidelines regarding the use of regional anesthesia (central neuraxial blocks) in anticoagulated patients.[163]

New pharmacologic agents that alter the coagulation cascade have been introduced over the last decade that have been demonstrated to reduce the incidence of deep venous thrombosis in surgical patients and reduce morbidity and mortality by up to 70%.[23] A series of consensus statements on the timing of neuraxial needle/catheter insertion or removal in the presence of various anticoagulants has been published.[163] One of the difficulties in detecting epidural hematoma in ambulatory patients is that the onset of symptoms may occur after the patient has been discharged home, a situation that may result in delayed diagnosis and treatment.[164] Thus, the ambulatory surgical patient may be at risk since epidural hematoma is a medical emergency that will lead to spinal cord compression with possible permanent paresis. Unlike epidural abscess, which frequently has pain, fever, and leukocytosis as a warning sign prior to the loss of neurologic function, epidural hematomas may present as painless, progressive neurologic deterioration. In any patient where hematoma is suspected, immediate diagnostic MRI and neurosurgical consultation should be performed. Failure to diagnose and treat in a timely manner will commonly result in permanent damage.

SUMMARY

The use of peripheral and central neuraxial regional anesthetic techniques provides many potential benefits for the ambulatory surgical patient, including superior analgesia, decreased PONV, and possibly improved patient satisfaction and decreased overall costs. Despite these advantages, there are risks and complications associated with the use of regional anesthesia in the ambulatory surgical patient. Many of these complications are transient and easily treated; however, a few complications may be life-threatening or cause permanent damage. Some complications may even occur after the patient has been discharged from the hospital. The clinician should take both the benefits and risks of regional anesthetic techniques into consideration in discussing the anesthetic options with the ambulatory surgical patient. If both agree on a regional anesthetic technique, the clinician should individualize and tailor the regional anesthetic technique to the ambulatory surgical setting.

REFERENCES

1. Duffy SQ, Farley DE. Patterns of decline among inpatient procedures. Public Health Reports 1995;110:674–81.

2. Fancourt-Smith PF, Hornstein J, Jenkins LC. Hospital admissions from the Surgical Day Care Centre of Vancouver General Hospital 1977–1987. Can J Anaesth 1990;37:699–704.

3. Fraser RA, Hotz SB, Hurtig JB, et al. The prevalence and impact of pain after day-care tubal ligation surgery. Pain 1989;39:189–201.

4. Alexander JI. Pain after laparoscopy. Br J Anaesth 1997;79:369–78.

5. Gold BS, Kitz DS, Lecky JH, et al. Unanticipated admission to the hospital following ambulatory surgery. JAMA 1989;262:3008–10.

6. Twersky R, Fishman D, Homel P. What happens after discharge? Return hospital visits after ambulatory surgery. Anesth Analg 1997; 84:319–24.

7. Hellberg A, Rudberg C, Kullman E, et al. Prospective randomized multicentre study of laparoscopic versus open appendectomy. Br J Surg 1999;86:48–53.

8. Hendolin HI, Paakonen ME, Alhava EM, et al. Laparoscopic or open cholecystectomy: a prospective randomised trial to compare postoperative pain, pulmonary function, and stress response. Eur J Surg 2000;166:394–99.

9. White PF. The role of non-opioid analgesic techniques in the management of pain after ambulatory surgery. Anesth Analg 2002;94: 577–85.

10. Mulroy MF, Larkin KL, Batra MS, et al. Femoral nerve block with

0.25% or 0.5% bupivacaine improves postoperative analgesia following outpatient arthroscopic anterior cruciate ligament repair. Reg Anesth Pain Med 2001;26:24–29.

11. Mulroy MF, Burgess FW, Emanuelsson BM. Ropivacaine 0.25% and 0.5%, but not 0.125%, provide effective wound infiltration analgesia after outpatient hernia repair, but with sustained plasma drug levels. Reg Anesth Pain Med 1999;24:136–41.

12. Neal JM, Hebl JR, Gerancher JC, et al. Brachial plexus anesthesia: essentials of our current understanding. Reg Anesth Pain Med 2002;27:402–28.

13. D'Alessio JG, Rosenblum M, Shea KP, et al. A retrospective comparison of interscalene block and general anesthesia for ambulatory surgery shoulder arthroscopy. Reg Anesth 1995;20:62–68.

14. Wu CL, Rouse LM, Chen JM, et al. Comparison of postoperative pain in patients receiving interscalene block or general anesthesia for shoulder surgery. Orthopedics 2002;25:45–48.

15. Crews JC. Multimodal pain management strategies for office-based and ambulatory procedures. JAMA 2002;288:629–32.

16. Borgeat A, Elkatodramis G, Schenker CA. Postoperative nausea and vomiting in regional anesthesia: a review. Anesthesiology 2003;98:530–37.

17. Sinclair DR, Chung F, Mezei G. Can postoperative nausea and vomiting be predicted? Anesthesiology 1999;91:109–18.

18. Macario A, Weinger M, Carney S, et al. Which clinical anesthesia outcomes are important to avoid? The perspective of patients. Anesth Analg 1999;89:652–58.

19. Chan VW, Peng PW, Kaszas Z, et al. A comparative study of general anesthesia, intravenous regional anesthesia, and axillary block for outpatient hand surgery: clinical outcomes and cost analysis. Anesth Analg 2001;93:1181–84.

20. Williams BA, Kentor ML, Williams JP, et al. Process analysis in outpatient knee surgery: effects of regional and general anesthesia on anesthesia-controlled time. Anesthesiology 2000;93:529–38.

21. Hyderally H. Complications of spinal anesthesia. Mt Sinai J Med 2002;69:55–56.

22. Ben-David B, Rawa R. Complications of neuraxial blockade. Anesthesiol Clin North Am 2002;20:431–55.

23. Faccenda KA, Finucane BT. Complications of regional anesthesia: incidence and prevention. Drug Safety 2001;24:413–42.

24. Brull SJ, Green NM. Time courses of zones of differential sensory blockade during spinal anesthesia with hyperbaric tetracaine or bupivacaine. Anesth Analg 1989;69:342–47.

25. Chamberlain DP, Chamberlain BD. Changes in the skin temperature of the trunk and their relationship to sympathetic blockade during spinal anesthesia. Anesthesiology 1986;65:139–43.

26. Arndt JO, Bomer W, Krauth J, et al. Incidence and time course of cardiovascular side effects during spinal anesthesia after prophylactic administration of intravenous fluids or vasoconstrictors. Anesth Analg 1998;87:347–54.

27. Coe AJ, Revanas B. Is crystalloid preloading useful in spinal anesthesia in the elderly? Anaesthesia 1990;45:785–86.

28. Critchley LA, Short TG, Gin T. Hypotension during subarachnoid anesthesia: haemodynamic analysis of three treatments. Br J Anaesth 1994;72:151–55.

29. Park GE, Hauch MA, Curlin F, et al. The effects of varying volumes of crystalloid administration before cesarean delivery on maternal hemodynamics and colloid osmotic pressure. Anesth Analg 1996;83:299–303.

30. Nishikawa K, Yamakage M, Omote K, Namiki A. Prophylactic IM small-dose phenylephrine blunts spinal anesthesia-induced hypotensive response during surgical repair of hip fracture in the elderly. Anesth Analg 2002;95:751–56.

31. Gan TJ, Meyer T, Apfel CC, et al. Consensus guidelines for managing postoperative nausea and vomiting. Anesth Analg 2003;97:62–71.

32. Pollard JB. Common mechanisms and strategies for prevention and treatment of cardiac arrest during epidural anesthesia. J Clin Anesth 2002;14:52–56.

33. Liu S, Paul GE, Carpenter RL, et al. Prolonged PR interval is a risk factor for bradycardia during spinal anesthesia. Reg Anesth 1995;20:11–14.

34. Lovstadt RZ, Granhus G, Hetland S. Bradycardia and asystolic cardiac arrest during spinal anaesthesia: a report of five cases. Acta Anaesthesiol Scand 2000;44:48–52.

35. Curatolo M, Scaramozzino P, Venuti FS, et al. Factors associated with hypotension and bradycardia after epidural blockade. Anesth Analg 1996;83:1033–40.

36. Geffin B, Shapiro L. Sinus bradycardia and asystole during spinal and epidural anesthesia: a report of 13 cases. J Clin Anesth 1998;10:278–85.

37. Ponhold H, Vicenzi MN. Incidence of bradycardia during recovery from spinal anaesthesia: influence of patient position. Br J Anaesth 1998;81:723–26.

38. Baron JF, Decaux-Jacolot A, Edouard A, et al. Influence of venous return on baroreflex control of heart rate during lumbar epidural anesthesia in humans. Anesthesiology 1986;64:188–93.

39. Jacobsen S, Sofelt S, Brocks V, et al. Reduced left ventricular diameters at onset of bradycardia during epidural anesthesia. Acta Anaesthesiol Scand 1992;36:831–36.

40. Mark AL. The Bezold-Jarish reflex revisited: clinical implications of inhibitory reflexes originated in the heart. J Am Coll Cardiol 1983;1:90–102.

41. Gratadour P, Viale JP, Parlow J, et al. Sympathovagal effects of spinal anesthesia assessed by the spontaneous cardiac baroreflex. Anesthesiology 1997;87:1359–67.

42. Tarkkila PJ. Incidence and causes of failed spinal anesthetics in a university hospital: a prospective study. Reg Anesth 1991;16:48–51.

43. Puolakka R, Haasio J, Pitkanen MT, et al. Technical aspects and postoperative sequelae of spinal and epidural anesthesia: a prospective study of 3,230 orthopedic patients. Reg Anesth Pain Med 2000;25:488–97.

44. Tarkkila PJ. Difficulties in spinal needle use: insertion characteristics and failure rates associated with 25-, 27- and 29-gauge Quincke-type spinal needles. Anaesthesia 1994;49:723–25.

45. Franco CD, Vieira ZE. 1,001 subclavian perivascular brachial plexus blocks: success with a nerve stimulator. Reg Anesth Pain Med 2000;25:41–46.

46. Borgeat A, Ekatodramis G, Dumont C. An evaluation of the infraclavicular block via a modified approach of the Raj technique. Anesth Analg 2001;93:436–41.

47. Cuvillon P, Jeannes P, Mahamat A, et al. Comparison of the parasacral approach and the posterior approach, with single- and double-injection techniques, to block the sciatic nerve. Anesthesiology 2003;98:1436–41.

48. Morris GF, Lang SA, Dust Wn, Van der Wal M. The parasacral sciatic nerve block. Reg Anesth 1997;22:223–28.

49. Chang PC, Lang SA, Yip RW. Reevaluation of the sciatic nerve block. Reg Anesth 1993;18:322–23.

50. Shannon J, Lang SA, Yip RW, Gerard M. Lateral femoral cutaneous nerve block revisited: a nerve stimulator technique. Reg Anesth 1995;20:100–4.

51. Tokat O, Turker YG, Uckunkaya N, Yilmazlar A. A clinical comparison of psoas compartment and inguinal paravascular blocks combined with sciatic nerve block. J Int Med Res 2002;30:161–67.

52. Capdevilla X, Macaire P, Dadure C, et al. Continuos psoas compartment block for postoperative analgesia after total hip arthroplasty: new landmarks, technical guidelines and clinical evaluation. Anesth Analg 2002;94:1606–13.

53. Seeberger MD, Urwyler A. Paravascular lumbar plexus block: block extension after femoral nerve stimulation and injection of 20 vs. 40 mL mepivacaine 10 mg/mL. Acta Anaesthesiol Scand 1995;39:769–73.

54. Casati A, Fanelli G, Beccaria P, et al. The effects of single or multiple injection on the volume of 0.5% ropivacaine required for femoral nerve blockade. Anesth Analg 2001;93:183–86.

55. Naja Z, Lonnqvist PA. Somatic paravertebral nerve blockade: incidence of failed block and complications. Anaesthesia 2001;56: 1184–88.

56. Brown DL, Ransom DM, Hall JA, et al. Regional anesthesia and local anesthetic-induced systemic toxicity: seizure frequency and accompanying cardiovascular changes. Anesth Analg 1995;81:321–28.

57. Naguib M, Magboul MM, Samarkandi AH, Attia M. Adverse effects and drug interaction associated with local and regional anesthesia. Drug Safety 1998;14:221–50.

58. Atanassoff PG, Weiss BM, Brull SJ. Lidocaine plasma levels following two techniques of obturator nerve block. J Clin Anesth 1996; 8:535–39.

59. Auroy Y, Narchi P, Messiah A, et al. Serious complications related to regional anesthesia: results of a prospective survey in France. Anesthesiology 1997;87:479–86.

60. Graf BM. The cardiotoxicity of local anesthetics: the place of ropivacaine. Curr Top Med Chem 2001;1:207–14.

61. Gunter JB. Benefit and risks of local anesthetics in infants and children. Paediatr Drugs 2002;4:649–72.

62. Ivani G, Borghi B, van Oven H. Levobupivacaine. Minerva Anesthesiol 2001;67:20–23.

63. Mather LE, Chang DH. Cardiotoxicity with modern local anaesthetics: is there a safe choice? Drugs 2001;61:333–42.

64. Foster RH, Markham A. Levobupivacaine: a review of its pharmacology and use as a local anesthetic. Drugs 2000;59:551–79.

65. Convery PN, Milligan KR, Quinn P, et al. Efficacy and uptake of ropivacaine and bupivacaine after single intra-articular injection in the knee joint. Br J Anaesth 2001;87:570–76.

66. Shanti CM, Carlin AM, Tyburski JG. Incidence of pneumothorax from intercostal nerve block for analgesia in rib fractures. J Trauma 2001;51:536–39.

67. Klaastad O, Lilleas FG, Rotnes JS, et al. A magnetic resonance imaging study of modifications to the infraclavicular brachial plexus block. Anesth Analg 2000;91:929–33.

68. Klaastad O, VadeBoncouer TR, Tillung T, Smedby O. An evaluation of the supraclavicular plumb-bob technique for brachial plexus block by magnetic resonance imaging. Anesth Analg 2003;96: 862–67.

69. Brown DL, Cahill DR, Bridenbaugh LD. Supraclavicular nerve block: anatomic analysis of a method to prevent pneumothorax. Anesth Analg 1993;76:530–34.

70. Greengrass R, Buckenmaier CC. Paravertebral anaesthesia/analgesia for ambulatory surgery. Best Pract Res Clin Anaesthesiol 2002; 16:271–83.

71. Caplan RA, Ward RJ, Posner K, Cheng FW. Unexpected cardiac arrest during spinal anesthesia: a closed claims analysis of predisposing factors. Anesthesiology 1988;68:5–11.

72. Krismer AC, Hogan QH, Wenzel V, et al. The efficacy of epinephrine or vasopressin for resuscitation during epidural anesthesia. Anesth Analg 2001;93:734–42.

73. Weidenthal DT, King JW. Cardiopulmonary arrest after retrobulbar anesthesia in a patient with an orbital roof defect. Am J Ophthalmol 1995;120:535–36.

74. Tatum PL, Defalque RJ. Subarachnoid injection during retrobulbar block: a case report. AANA J 1994;62:49–52.

75. Kobet KA. Cerebral spinal fluid recovery of lidocaine and bupivacaine following respiratory arrest subsequent to retrobulbar block. Ophthalmic Surg 1987;18:11–13.

76. Fibuch EE, Opper SE. Back Pain following epidurally administered MPF Nesacain. Anesth Analg 1989;69:113–15.

77. Stevens RA, Urmey WF, Urquhart BL, et al. Back pain after epidural anesthesia with chloroprocaine. Anesthesiology 1993;78:492–97.

78. Levy L, Randel GI, Pandit SK. Does chloroprocaine (Nesacaine MPF) for epidural anesthesia increase the incidence of backache? Anesthesiology 1989;71:476.

79. Drolet P, Veillette Y. Back pain following epidural anesthesia with 2-chloroprocaine (EDTA-free) or lidocaine. Reg Anesth 1997;22:303–7.

80. Brown EM, Elman DS. Postoperative backache. Anesth Analg 1961;40:683.

81. Ben David B, Maryanovsky M, Gurevitch A, et al. A comparison of minidose lidocaine-fentanyl versus conventional dose lidocaine spinal anesthesia. Anesth Analg 2000;91:865–70.

82. Wu CL, Berenholtz SM, Pronovost PJ, et al. Systematic review and analysis of postdischarge symptoms after outpatient surgery. Anesthesiology 2002;96:994.

83. Wang LP, Schmidt JF. Central nervous side effects after lumbar puncture. Dan Med Bull 1997;44:79–81.

84. Cutler RW, Page L, Galicich J, et al. Formation and absorption of cerebrospinal fluid in man. Brain 1968;91:707–20.

85. Khurana RK. Intracranial hypotension. Semin Neurol 1996;16:5–10.

86. Raskin NH. Lumbar puncture headache: a review. Headache 1990; 30:197–200.

87. Fernandez E. Headaches associated with low spinal fluid pressure. Headache 1990;30:122–28.

88. Kunkle EC, Ray BS, Wolff HG. Experimental studies on headache: analysis of the headache associated with changes in intracranial pressure. Arch Neurol Psych 1943;49:323–58.

89. Vakharia SB, Thomas PS, Rosenbaum AE, et al. Magnetic resonance imaging of cerebrospinal fluid leak and tamponade effect of blood patch in postdural puncture headache. Anesth Analg 1997;84:585–90.

90. Grant R, Condon B, Hart I, Teadale GM. Changes in intrathecal CSF volume after lumbar puncture and their relationship to post-LP headache. J Neurol Neurosurg Psych 1991;54:440–42.

91. Lieberman LM, Tourtellotte WW, Newkirk TA. Prolonged post-lumbar puncture cerebrospinal fluid leakage from lumbar subarachnoid space demonstrated by radioisotope myelography. Neurology 1971;21:925–29.

92. Lybecker H, Diernes M, Schmidt JF. Postdural puncture headache (PDPH): onset, severity, and associated symptoms: an analysis of 75 consecutive patients. Acta Anaesthesiol Scand 1995;39:605–12.

93. Fog J, Wang LP, Sundberg A, et al. Hearing loss after spinal anesthesia is related to needle size. Anesth Analg 1990;70:517–22.

94. Lybecker H, Moller JT, May O, et al. Incidence and prediction of postdural puncture headache: a prospective study of 1021 spinal anesthesias. Anesth Analg 1990;70:389–94.

95. Vandam LD, Dripps RD. Long-term follow-up of patients who received 10,098 spinal anesthetics. JAMA 1956;161:586–91.

96. Wang LP, Fog J, Bove M. Transient hearing loss after spinal anesthesia. Anaesthesia 1987;42:1258–63.

97. Sundberg A, Wang LP, Fog J. Influence on hearing of 22 G Whitacre and 22 G Quincke needles. Anaesthesia 1992;47:981–83.

98. Dittmann M, Schaeffer HG, Renke F, et al. Spinal anaesthesia with 29 gauge Quincke point needles and post dural puncture headache in 2,378 patients. Acta Anaesthesiol Scand 1994;38:691–93.

99. Gielen M. Post dural puncture headache (PDPH): a review. Reg Anesth 1989;14:101–6.

100. Halpern S, Preston R. Postdural puncture headache and spinal needle design: metaanalyses. Anesthesiology 1994;81:1376–83.

101. Ready LB, Cuplin S, Haschke RH, et al. Spinal needle determinants of rate of transdural fluid leak. Anesth Analg 1989;69:457–60.

102. Cruikshank RH, Hopkinson JM. Fluid flow through dural puncture sites. Anaesthesia 1989;44:415–18.

103. Dittmann M, Schafer HG, Ulrich J, et al. Anatomical re-evaluation of lumbar dura mater with regard to postspinal headache. Anaesthesia 1988;43:635–37.

104. Sprotte G, Schedel R, Pajunk H, et al. An "atraumatic" universal needle for single-shot regional anesthesia: clinical results and a 6 year trial in over 30,000 regional anesthesias (German). Reg Anaesth 1987;10:104–8.

105. Mihic DN. Post-spinal headache and relationship of needle level to longitudinal dural fibers. Reg Anesth 1985;10:76–81.

106. Norris MC, Leighton BL, DeSimone CA. Needle bevel direction and headache after inadvertent dural puncture. Anesthesiology 1989;70:729–31.

107. Takkila PJ, Heine H, Tervo RR. Comparison of Sprotte and Quincke needles with respect to postdural puncture headache and backache. Reg Anesth 1992;17:283–87.

108. Hatfalvi BI. The dynamics of post-spinal headache. Headache 1977;17:64–66.

109. Hatfalvi BI. Postulated mechanisms for postdural puncture headache and review of laboratory models. Reg Anesth 1995;20: 329–36.

110. Kempen PM, Mocek CK. Bevel direction, dura geometry, and hole size in membrane puncture. Reg Anesth 1997;22:267–72.

111. Cook PT, Davies MJ, Beavis RE. Bed rest and postlumbar puncture headache: the effectiveness of 24 hours' recumbency in reducing the incidence of postlumbar puncture headache. Anaesthesia 1989;44:389–91.

112. Thornberry EA, Thomas TA. Posture and post-spinal headache. Br J Anaesth 1988;60:195–97.

113. Dieterich M, Brandt T. Incidence of post-lumbar puncture headache is independent of daily fluid intake. Eur Arch Psychiatr Neurol Sci 1988;237:194–96.

114. Sawynok J. Pharmacological rationale for the clinical use of caffeine. Drugs 1995;49:37–50.

115. Choi A, Laurito CE, Cinningham FE. Pharmacologic management of postdural puncture headache. Ann Pharmacother 1996;30: 831–39.

116. Beards SC, Jackson A, Griffiths AG, et al. Magnetic resonance imaging of extradural blood patches: appearances from 30 min to 18 h. Br J Anaesth 1993;71:182–88.

117. Cook MA, Watkins-Pitchford JM. Epidural blood patch: a rapid coagulation response. Anesth Analg 1990;70:567–72.

118. DiGiovanni AJ, Galbert MW, Wahle WM. Epidural injection of autologous blood for postlumbar-puncture headache. Anesth Analg 1972;51:226–32.

119. Szeinfeld M, Ihmeidan IH, Moser MM, et al. Epidural blood patch: evaluation of the volume and spread of blood injected into the epidural space. Anesthesiology 1986;64:820–22.

120. Wu YW, Hui YL, Tan PP. Experience of epidural blood patch for post-dural puncture headache. Acta Anaesthesiol Scand 1994;32: 137–40.

121. Safa-Tisseront V, Thormann F, Malassine P, et al. Effectiveness of epidural blood patch in the management of post-dural puncture headache. Anesthesiology 2001;95:334–39.

122. Tarkkila PJ, Miralles JA, Palomaki EA. The subjective complications and efficiency of the epidural blood patch in the treatment of postdural puncture headache. Reg Anesth 1989;14:247–50.

123. Purdy EP, Ajimal GS. Vision loss after lumbar epidural steroid injection. Anesth Analg 1998;86:119–22.

124. Lowe DM, McCullough AM. 7th nerve palsy after extradural blood patch. Br J Anaesth 1990;65:721–22.

125. Rigler M, Drasner K, Krejcie T, et al. Cauda equina syndrome after continuous spinal anesthesia. Anesth Analg 1991;72:275–81.

126. Schneider M, Ettlin T, Kaufmann M, et al. Transient neurologic toxicity after hyperbaric subarachnoid anesthesia with 5% lidocaine. Anesth Analg 1993;76:1154–57.

127. Pollock JE. Management of the patient who develops transient neurologic symptoms after spinal anesthesia. Techn Reg Anesth Pain Manag 2000;4:155–60.

128. Freedman J, Li D, Drasner K, et al. Risk factors for transient neurologic symptoms after spinal anesthesia. Anesthesiology 1998;89: 633–41.

129. Ready L, Plumer M, Haschke R. Neurotoxicity of intrathecal local anesthetics in rabbits. Anesthesiology 1985;63:364–70.

130. Pollock J, Burkhead D, Neal J, et al. Spinal nerve function in five volunteers experiencing transient neurologic symptoms after lidocaine subarachnoid anesthesia. Anesth Analg 2000;90:658–65.

131. Pollock J, Liu S, Neal J, Stephenson C. Dilution of spinal lidocaine does not alter the incidence of transient neurologic symptoms. Anesthesiology 1999;90:445–49.

132. Hampl KF, Schneider MC, Thorin D, et al. Hyperosmolarity does not contribute to transient radicular irritation after spinal anesthesia with hyperbaric 5% lidocaine. Reg Anesth Pain Med 1995;20:363–68.

133. Pollock JE, Neal JM, Stephenson CA, et al. Prospective study of the incidence of transient radicular irritation in patients undergoing spinal anesthesia. Anesthesiology 1996;84:1361–67.

134. Hampl KF, Schneider MC, Pargger H, et al. A similar incidence of transient neurologic symptoms after spinal anesthesia with 2% and 5% lidocaine. Anesth Analg 1996;83:1051–54.

135. Liguori GA, Zayas VM, Chisholm M. Transient neurologic symptoms after spinal anesthesia with mepivacaine and lidocaine. Anesthesiology 1996;88:619–23.

136. Martiniez-Bourio R, Arzuaga M, Quintana JM, et al. Incidence of transient neurologic symptoms after hyperbaric subarachnoid anesthesia with 5% lidocaine and 5% prilocaine. Anesthesiology 1998;88:624–28.

137. Hampl KF, Heinzmann-Wiedmer S, Luginbuehol I, et al. Transient neurologic symptoms after spinal anesthesia. Anesthesiology 1998;88:629–33.

138. Hodgson P, Liu S, Batra M, et al. Procaine compared with lidocaine for incidence of transient neurologic symptoms. Reg Anesth Pain Med 2000;25:218–22.

139. Corbey MP, Bach AB. Transient radicular irritation (TRI) after spinal anaesthesia in day-care surgery. Acta Anaesthesiol Scand 1998;42:425–29.

140. Naveira FA, Copeland S, Anderson M, et al. Transient neurologic toxicity after spinal anesthesia, or is it myofascial pain? Two case reports. Anesthesiology 1998;88:268–70.

141. Mayall MF, Calder I. Spinal cord injury following an attempted thoracic epidural. Anaesthesia 1999;54:990–94.

142. Reynolds F. Damage to the conus medularis following spinal anesthesia. Anaesthesia 2001;56:238–47.

143. Ghani KR, McMillan R, Peterson-Brown S. Transient femoral nerve palsy following ilio-inguinal nerve blockade for day case inguinal hernia repair. J R Coll Surg Edinb 2002;47:626–29.

144. Bergman BD, Hebl JR, Kent J, Horlocker TT. Neurologic complications of 405 continuous axillary catheters. Anesth Analg 2003; 96:247–52.

145. Horlocker TT, Kufner RP, Bishop AT, et al. The risk of persistent paresthesias is not increased with repeated axillary block. Anesth Analg 1999;88:382–87.

146. Selander D, Edshage S, Wolff T. Paraesthesia or no paraesthesia? Nerve lesions after axillary blocks. Acta Anaesthesiol Scand 1979; 23:27–33.

147. Fanelli G, Casati A, Garancini P, Torri G. Nerve stimulator and multiple injection technique for upper and lower limb blockade: failure rate, patient acceptance, and neurologic complications. Anesth Analg 1999;88:847–52.

148. Weeks L, Barry A, Wolff T, et al. Regional anesthesia and subsequent long-term pain. J Hand Surg 1994;19:342–46.

149. Kalichman MW, Calcutt NA. Local anesthetic-induced conduction block and nerve fiber injury in streptozotocin-diabetic rats. Anesthesiology 1992;77:941–47.

150. Hebl JR, Horlocker TT, Sorenson EJ, Schroeder DR. Regional anesthesia does not increase the risk of postoperative neuropathy in patients undergoing ulnar nerve transposition. Anesth Analg 2001;93:1606–11.

151. Selander D, Dhuner K-G, Lundborg G. Peripheral nerve injury due to injection needles used for regional anesthesia. Acta Anaesthesiol Scand 1977;21:182–88.

152. Rice AS, McMahon SB. Peripheral nerve injury caused by injection needles used in regional anaesthesia: influence of bevel configuration, studied in a rat model. Br J Anaesth 1992;69:433–38.

153. Borgeat A, Ekatodramis G. Nerve injury associated with regional anesthesia. Curr Top Med Chem 2001;1:199–203.

154. Lambert LA, Lambert DH, Strichartz GR. Irreversible conduction

block in isolated nerve by high concentrations of local anesthetics. Anesthesiology 1994;80:1082–93.

155. Hodgson PS, Neal JM, Pollock JE, Liu SS. The neurotoxicity of drugs given intrathecally (spinal). Anesth Analg 1999;88:797–809.

156. Moen V, Irestedt L, Raf L. Review of claims from the patient insurance: spinal anesthesia is not completely without risks. Lakartidningen 2000;97:5769–74.

157. Kane RE. Neurologic deficits following epidural or spinal anesthesia. Anesth Analg 1981;60:150–61.

158. Kindler CH, Seeberger MD, Staender SE. Epidural abscess complicating epidural anesthesia and analgesia: an analysis of the literature. Acta Anaesthesiol Scand 1998;42:609–13.

159. Royakkers AA, Wiligers H, van der Ven AJ, et al. Catheter-related epidural abscesses-don't wait for neurologic deficits. Acta Anaesthesiol Scand 2002;46:611–15.

160. Okano K, Kondo H, Tsuchita R, et al. Spinal epidural abscess associated with epidural catheterization: report of a case and a review of the literature. Jpn J Clin Oncol 1999;29:49–52.

161. Sato S, Sakuragi T, Dan K. Human skin flora as a potential source of epidural abscess. Anesthesiology 1996;85:1276–82.

162. McNeill MJ, Thornburn J. Cannulation of the epidural space: a comparison of 18- and 16-gauge needles. Anaesthesia 1988;43: 154–55.

163. Horlocker TT, Wedel DJ, Benzon H, et al. Regional anesthesia in the anticoagulated patient: defining the risks (the second ASRA Consensus Conference on Neuraxial Anesthesia and Anticoagulation). Reg Anesth Pain Med 2003;28:172–97.

164. Porterfield WR, Wu CL. Epidural hematoma in an ambulatory surgical patient. J Clin Anesth 1997;9:74–77.

Postoperative Complications of Ambulatory Anesthesia

MICHAEL RONAYNE • FRANCES CHUNG

INTRODUCTION

Over the past two decades surgical patient care has undergone a major change. While in the past, most of the surgical procedures required inpatient admissions, now most of the performed operations, an estimated 65% of operations in North America, are completed in ambulatory settings.[1] While severe or life-threatening adverse events are extremely rare among ambulatory surgery patients, complications such as pain, nausea/vomiting, sore throat, myalgia, drowsiness, and urine retention are not infrequent. Ambulatory surgery may also be complicated by prolonged hospital stay, unanticipated admissions, and unscheduled return hospital visits, and their incidence conveys important information regarding the quality of care and excess burden for both health care providers and patients.[2]

MORTALITY/MAJOR MORBIDITY

Ambulatory surgery and anesthesia have been shown to be safe with a very low incidence of mortality or major morbidity. Warner et al. prospectively studied 38,598 patients and found 33 patients had experienced either major morbidity or died within 30 days of ambulatory surgery.[3] Four patients died (1:11,273), two of myocardial infarction and two in automobile accidents. The nonaccidental mortality rate was 1:22,545. Of the 31 patients who developed major morbidity, including 2 who subsequently died, 14 had a myocardial infarction, 7 had a central nervous system deficit, 5 had a pulmonary embolism, and 5 had respiratory failure. In only 4 of the 31 patients who developed major morbidity was there an apparent direct relationship to an intraoperative or immediate postoperative adverse event. No apparent direct relationship was seen in the other 27 patients. Indeed the incidence of myocardial infarction, central nervous system deficit, and pulmonary embolism in the study group was similar to the predicted incidence from population-based epidemiologic data. The question was asked if these morbidities were just untimely

events or was the ambulatory surgery and anesthesia contributory?

Natof reported that no death occurred and only 106 patients (0.8%) had mainly surgical complications within 2 weeks after ambulatory surgery among 13,433 patients.[4] Mezei and Chung also reported no death within 30 days of ambulatory surgery among 17,638 patients.[5] In the largest study to date, Fleisher et al. studied 564,267 ambulatory procedures and found a mortality rate of 2.4/100,000 cases on the day of surgery and a mortality rate of 41/100,000 within 7 days postoperatively.[6]

Ambulatory surgery has an excellent safety record. Mortality or major morbidity is rare and the incidence of such adverse events is similar to the predicted incidence from population-based epidemiologic data.

PROLONGED HOSPITAL STAY

Discharge time indicates the length of time elapsed from the end of surgery until a patient is discharged home. Discharge time has a direct bearing on cost of recovery after surgery. There is no universally agreed definition of appropriate length of stay after ambulatory surgery as studies differ in their criteria for defining delayed discharge from hospital.[7] Pavlin et al. defined delayed discharge as more than 50 min in the Phase 1 postanesthesia care unit (PACU) and more than 70 min in the Phase 2 PACU.[8] Junger et al. took a duration of 6 hr or more as a prolonged hospital stay.[9] Chung and Mezei used the mean discharge time of the largest surgical subspecialty as a reference.[10] Risk factors for prolonged hospital stay may be classified as preoperative, intraoperative, or postoperative (Table 44-1).

Preoperative Factors

Type of surgery has been shown to be a significant predictor of length of postoperative stay. A significantly longer stay is associated with procedures resulting in a high inci-

Table 44-1   Summary of Risk Factors for Prolonged Hospital Stay

Preoperative factors:	Type of surgery
	Strabismus surgery
	Urologic surgery
	Trauma surgery
	Maxillofacial surgery
	Increasing age
	Female gender
Intraoperative factors:	Duration of surgery
	Anesthesia technique (general vs. regional)
Postoperative factors:	Pain
	Nausea/vomiting
	Drowsiness/dizziness
	Cardiovascular events
	Unavailability of escort home

dence of excessive pain and postoperative nausea and vomiting (PONV). Among patients receiving general anesthesia, strabismus surgery and urologic procedures were associated with the longest length of stay.[10] Trauma and maxillofacial surgery are also associated with prolonged hospital stay.[9] Increasing age also predicts delayed discharge[8-10] with a 10-year difference in age being associated with a 2% change in length of stay.[10] Of preexisting medical conditions, only congestive heart failure showed an association with length of stay among patients receiving monitored anesthesia care.[10] Female gender has also been associated with prolonged stay.[9] Patients who were admitted early in the morning had the longest duration of postoperative stay, while patients admitted later in the day had an increasing rate of unanticipated admission.[9]

Intraoperative Factors

Intraoperative factors shown to be associated with prolonged postoperative stay include duration of surgery and anesthesia technique. Duration of surgery is associated with prolonged hospital stay[8-10] with each 30-min increase in the duration of surgery being associated with a 9% increase in the length of postoperative stay.[10] General anesthesia is also associated with prolonged stay.[8,9] Pavlin et al. found that patients who received a peripheral nerve block had a shorter length of postoperative stay than those who received a general anesthetic for plastic or upper extremity surgery.[8]

Postoperative Factors

Postoperative factors that prolong hospital stay include excessive pain, PONV, drowsiness, dizziness, cardiovascular events, and the unavailability of an escort home. Excessive pain and PONV are predictors of delayed discharge.[8-10] Time to home-readiness has been shown to be 2.5 times longer in patients with persistent symptoms in the PACU.[11] Dizziness, drowsiness, and cardiovascular events in the PACU are associated with prolonged stay.[10] The unavailability of an escort home and the inability to void after surgery are also associated with prolonged stay.[8] In addition, Pavlin et al. found that the length of postoperative stay varied depending on the nurse administrating Phase 2 care.[8]

Postoperative risk factors can be minimized with optimal management. A shorter hospital stay will result if the incidence of excessive pain, PONV, drowsiness, and dizziness is decreased. Multimodal analgesia for pain management and multimodal antiemetic therapy for PONV may achieve this. The prompt availability of escorts will also prevent delayed discharge.

UNANTICIPATED ADMISSION

Unanticipated hospital admission is the admission of patients booked for ambulatory surgery owing to unforeseen problems such as surgical or anesthetic complications. Unanticipated hospital admission after surgery has become an important measure of outcome in ambulatory surgical care. One method of assessing the success of an ambulatory unit is to evaluate the number of patients requiring admission to hospital as this represents failure of the system to fulfill the purpose for which it was created. Of seven studies in the literature addressing unanticipated admission, two were prospective and five were retrospective.[12-18] The unanticipated admission rate ranged from 0.28% to 2.5%. Individual procedures such as laparoscopic cholecystectomy[19] and microdiscectomy[20] may have higher unanticipated admission rates. The causes of unanticipated admission can be due to surgical, anesthesia, medical, or social reasons[21] (Table 44-2).

Surgical Factors

The highest percentage of admissions were related to surgical factors in all seven studies. The most common surgical causes of admission were pain, bleeding, the performance of more extensive surgery than had been planned, and surgical misadventure. Independent surgical predictors of admission were length of surgery,[12,14,15] type of surgery,[12,14] and surgery completed after 3 P.M.[12] Patients who have surgery that exceeds 1 hr are 7.5 times more likely to be admitted.[15] Ear, nose, and throat (ENT) and urologic surgery[8] and lower-abdominal/urologic and laparoscopic surgery[14] have also been shown to be associated with increased admission rates.

Anesthetic Factors

Anesthetic-related causes of unanticipated admission include PONV, drowsiness, and aspiration. PONV is a significant cause of unanticipated admissions. Gold et al.[14] found that 17% of unanticipated admissions were due to PONV, which was similar to the percentage found by Fortier and Chung[12] at 14.4%. Approximately 2% of unan-

Table 44-2   Causes of Unanticipated Hospital Admission (%)

Factor	Fortier[12]	Osborne[13]	Gold[14]	Biwas[18]	Greenburg[16]	Fancourt-Smith[17]
Bleeding	7.4	23.4	18	13.3	14.7	26
Pain	12.1	11.1	18	7.1	24.4	8.8
Other surgical complications	6	27	7	7.5	ND	17.6
More extensive surgery	3.3	18.6	6	21.5	13.9	9.6
Somnolence	2.3	4.9	3	3.5	ND	ND
Aspiration	1.9	1.2	3	0.4	ND	2.4
PONV	14.4	ND	17	2.6	11.6	0.08
Urinary retention	ND	ND	5	0.8	4.6	ND
Cardiorespiratory	6.5	ND	9	ND	20.9	21
Social admissions	19.5	8.6	ND	5.7	ND	4.8

Abbreviations: ND, no data; PONV, postoperative nausea and vomiting.

SOURCE: Adapted with permission from Imasogie N, Chung F. Effect of return hospital visits on economics of ambulatory surgery. Curr Opin Anesthesiol 2001;14:575.

ticipated admissions were due to excessive drowsiness postoperatively while 1.8% were due to suspected aspiration.[12]

Medical Factors

Medical factors accounted for 0–20.1% of unanticipated admissions.[12–18] Patients with multiple comorbid conditions are now undergoing ambulatory surgery and these preexisting conditions are predictive of perioperative adverse events.[22] While Gold et al.[14] found that preexisting medical conditions did not predict unanticipated admission, Fortier and Chung[12] found that preexisting heart disease, asthma, diabetes, hypertension, and thyroid disease were associated with unanticipated admission. American Society of Anesthesiologists (ASA) physical status II or III is predictive of unanticipated admission, but increasing age is not.[12]

Social Factors

Social reasons accounted for 0–19.5% of unanticipated admission.[12–18] A total of 19.5% of all unanticipated admissions were for social reasons, including patient request (6%), surgeon request (7%), and the unavailability of an escort (6.5%).[12]

The identification of patients at increased risk for unanticipated admission is essential. It is important to recognize the independent variables affecting admission rates in order to predict the type of surgery and patient with the greatest risk for admission. The recognition of these factors will help in the provision of appropriate quality care for the ambulatory surgery patient.

RETURN HOSPITAL VISITS

A return hospital visit may be defined as either any readmission to the hospital as an inpatient or to the ambulatory surgery unit, or to the emergency room with subsequent discharge within 30 days of the original surgery.[23]

Mezei and Chung studied 17,638 patients and found 1.1% of patients returned to the hospital within 30 days of ambulatory surgery,[5] while Twersky et al. studied 6243 patients and found a return hospital visitation rate of 3%.[23] However, in both studies, the majority of return hospital visits were not due to complications of the surgical procedure. Mezei and Chung found the return hospital visitation rate due to complications of surgery to be 0.15%, while Twersky et al. had a higher rate of 1.3%.

Complications of the surgical procedure may be surgical, medical, or anesthetic in nature. Surgical complications are the most common cause of a return hospital visit[5,23] (Table 44-3). These include bleeding, excessive pain, infection, and urinary retention. Bleeding was the most common reason for a return hospital visit due to surgical complications, with three-quarters of these patients being treated and discharged through the emergency room.[23] Urologic surgery was found to be an independent predictor of return hospital visits, which may be due to the increased risk of complications such as hematuria, urinary retention, and infection in these patients.[5,23] The majority of patients who return to hospital due to surgical complications do so within 7 days of the surgical procedure.[23]

No return hospital visits occurred due to anesthetic complications.[5,23] Anesthetic-related complications such as PONV usually occur immediately after surgery in the PACU and may lead to unanticipated admission, but once these patients are discharged home, anesthesia-related symptoms do not cause readmission. Only one readmission in 17,638 patients was due to a medical complication, a pulmonary embolism after knee arthroscopy.[5]

Table 44-3 Causes of Return Hospital Visits and Readmission (%)

Authors	Bleeding	Other Surgical Complications	Pain	Urinary Retention	Infection
Twersky[23]	41	14.6	9.7	6	15.8
Mezei[5]	11.5	57	3.8	7.6	3.8

SOURCE: Adapted with permission from Imasogie N, Chung F. Effect of return hospital visits on economics of ambulatory surgery. Curr Opin Anesthesiol 2001;14:576.

Return hospital visits are principally due to surgical complications such as bleeding, excessive pain, infection, and urinary retention. Anesthetic and medical complications rarely cause return hospital visits.

CARDIORESPIRATORY ADVERSE EVENTS

Ambulatory surgery is safe and the incidence of a major cardiorespiratory adverse event is extremely low. The incidence of myocardial infarction, pulmonary embolism, or respiratory failure within 30 days of ambulatory surgery has been shown to be 1:3220, 1:9018, and 1:9018, respectively.[3]

While cardiovascular adverse events such as hypertension, hypotension, myocardial ischemia, and arrhythmias are among the most common intraoperative adverse events in ambulatory surgery,[1,22,24] they may also occur in the immediate postoperative period but with much lower frequencies.[1,22,24,25] Perioperative cardiovascular events may result in prolonged hospital stay,[10] while cardiovascular events warranting unanticipated hospital admissions are infrequent. While preoperative cardiovascular disease may be predictive of intraoperative cardiovascular adverse events (Table 44-4), it is not predictive of postoperative cardiovascular events.[22,24] Thus cardiovascular complications experienced in the PACU were not predicted by the patient's preoperative medical history.[22,24] When compared with younger patients, the cardiovascular event rate among the elderly is fivefold higher intraoperatively and remains twofold higher in the PACU[25] (Fig. 44-1).

Respiratory events are the second most frequent intraoperative adverse events occurring, with a frequency of < 1%.[1] Although infrequent, respiratory events may result in unanticipated hospital admission.[12,14] Obese patients are at an increased risk of both intraoperative and postoperative respiratory adverse events.[22] Preoperative smoking and asthma have been shown to be independent risk factors for postoperative respiratory events[22] (Table 44-4). Smoking is associated with coughing, laryngospasm, bronchospasm, apnea, and breath-holding.[26]

The identification of those at risk for cardiorespiratory adverse events postoperatively will allow closer monitoring of these patients in the PACU. Preoperative cardiovascular disease has not been shown to predict postoperative cardiovascular adverse events.[22] However, smoking, asthma, and obesity are associated with postoperative respiratory events.[22]

POSTOPERATIVE PAIN

The presence of moderate to severe pain postoperatively remains a significant problem after ambulatory surgery. Not only does it cause considerable patient discomfort but it may also result in prolonged hospital stay,[8–10] unanticipated admission,[12–17] return hospital visits,[23] precipitation of PONV, and delay in the patient's return to his/her normal functional level.[27] Pain is the symptom that patients would like to avoid most postoperatively.[28]

The incidence of postoperative pain is related to the type, duration, and invasiveness of surgery. Thirty to forty percent of discharged patients have moderate to severe pain after ambulatory surgery.[29–33] Severe pain has been shown to be the most common adverse event in the PACU, with an incidence of 5.3%.[34,35] Long surgical procedures and certain types of operation (orthopedic surgery, urologic surgery, plastic surgery, hernia repair, and laparoscopic cholecystectomy) tend to be associated with severe

Table 44-4 Association between the Presence of Preexisting Medical Conditions and Adverse Outcomes

Medical condition	Associated adverse outcome
Congestive heart failure	12% prolongation of postoperative stay
Hypertension	2-fold increase in the risk of intraoperative cardiovascular events
Asthma	5-fold increase in the risk of postoperative respiratory events
Smoking	4-fold increase in the risk of postoperative respiratory events
Obesity	4-fold increase in risk of intraoperative and postoperative respiratory events
Gastroesophageal reflux	8-fold increase in the risk of intubation related adverse events

SOURCE: Reprinted with permission from Chung F, Mezei G. Adverse outcomes in ambulatory anesthesia. Can J Anaesth 1999;46:R21.

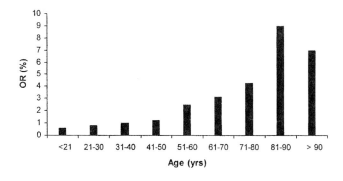

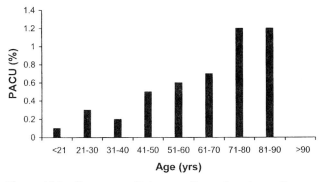

Figure 44-1 Frequency of intraoperative and postoperative cardiovascular adverse events by age group. (Reprinted with permission from Chung F, Mezei G, Tong D. Adverse events in ambulatory surgery: a comparison between elderly and younger patients. Can J Anaesth 1999;46:317.)

pain.[29,30,34,36] Excessive pain has been shown to be a significant independent predictor of total recovery duration.[37] Thus severe pain causes prolonged hospital stay,[8–10] which may disrupt patient flow and increase institutional costs. Severe pain also has been shown to be the primary reason for 2.3–24.8% of unanticipated admissions.[12–17,34] While Chung et al. found that no return hospital visits were due to excessive pain,[34] Twersky et al. found that 9.8% of return hospital visits were primarily due to pain.[23]

The success of ambulatory surgery depends to a large extent on the effective control of postoperative pain. Ambulatory surgery analgesia must allow the patient to be discharged safely and without delay. Multimodal analgesia gives more effective pain control[38,39] and facilitates discharge.[19] Optimizing postdischarge pain management is extremely important to maximize the benefits of ambulatory surgery. Moderate-to-severe postoperative pain decreases the patient's postoperative functional level to a considerable degree[27] and may also lead to sleep deprivation.[30] The ability to provide effective pain relief postdischarge remains a major challenge in ambulatory anesthesia. The analgesic technique should aim to lower the pain scores and facilitate earlier mobilization and rehabilitation.[40]

Dispensing appropriate analgesia with clear instructions for the patient is important. Fifty percent of patients have reported that instructions about pain control were either unclear or nonexistent.[29] The administration of prepacked analgesics for postoperative pain control with clear instructions has the potential for improving patient comfort at home.[31] Ambulatory surgery units should audit their analgesic treatment for mild, moderate, and severe pain by routinely calling every patient postdischarge to monitor analgesic effectiveness.

POSTOPERATIVE NAUSEA AND VOMITING

PONV is one of the most important and frequent complications of ambulatory surgery. It is a strong predictor of prolonged postoperative stay[8–10] and has been shown to account for 12–17% of unanticipated hospital admissions.[12,14,16] The true incidence of PONV may not be apparent in the PACU as it may not begin until patients are discharged and become more mobile at home.[36] Up to 35% of patients experience PONV at home postdischarge, many of whom did not experience emetic symptoms in the PACU.[41] The incidence of PONV at 24 hr postsurgery has been shown to be twice that in the PACU.[42] PONV can also affect the postoperative functional level of the patient and his/her satisfaction with ambulatory surgery and anesthesia.[1,27,43] It not only causes significant patient discomfort, it may also cause dehydration, place tension on suture lines, and increase the risk of pulmonary aspiration.[44]

PONV is a multifactorial entity, comprising patient, surgical, and anesthetic risk factors.[45] Apfel et al. concluded that female gender, a history of PONV or motion sickness, nonsmoking status, and use of opioids were most predictive.[46] The incidence of PONV with the presence of none, one, two, three, or all four of these risk factors was about 10%, 20%, 40%, 60%, and 80%, respectively. This simplified risk score has been shown to be better than more complex risk scores.[47] A prophylactic antiemetic strategy should be considered for patients with at least two of these four identified predictors.[46]

Surgical Factors

Apfel et al. found that when other risk factors such as anesthesia technique and duration of operation were considered, type of surgery was not an independent risk factor for PONV.[46] However, a large study of 17,638 ambulatory patients showed an increased risk for PONV among patients undergoing breast augmentation, strabismus repair, shoulder surgery, ENT/dental surgery, and laparoscopic sterilization.[42] This study also found that the risk of PONV increases with increasing duration of surgery.[42]

Anesthetic Factors

General anesthesia has been shown to significantly increase the risk of PONV when compared with regional anesthesia or monitored anesthesia care.[42] Volatile anesthetics[48] and nitrous oxide are risk factors for PONV.[45] PONV is strongly associated with pain and its management. Pain precipitates PONV and opioids are potent emetics.

Patient Factors

The risk of PONV for men is one-third that of women, while smokers have two-thirds of the risk compared with that of nonsmokers.[42] Patients with a previous history of PONV have a threefold increased risk of similar postoperative symptoms,[42] while patients with motion sickness are also at increased risk.[46]

A reduction in baseline risk factors can lower the incidence of PONV.[45] The avoidance of general anesthesia where possible is recommended.[45] When general anesthesia is used, the avoidance of volatile anesthetics and nitrous oxide with minimal use of neostigmine and opioids is beneficial.[45] Optimal balanced analgesia should be the goal as pain also precipitates PONV.

To maintain the efficiency and cost-saving benefit of ambulatory surgery, effective antiemetic administration and prophylaxis for certain patients is desirable. Routine antiemetic prophylaxis is not recommended.[44,45,49] Prophylactic antiemetics benefit select patients, and their routine use in all patients is not justified on the basis of available evidence.[45,49] The high-risk patient should be identified and prophylactic antiemetic medication administered accordingly. Combination therapy is superior to monotherapy for prophylaxis.[45,50] Drugs with different mechanisms of action should be used to optimize efficacy.[45,50]

SORE THROAT

Symptoms of postoperative throat discomfort such as sore throat, hoarseness, and dysphagia are common after ambulatory surgery and are associated with trauma to the pharynx and larynx. In a prospective study of 5264 ambulatory surgical patients, the overall incidence of sore throat was 12.1% at 24 hr postsurgery.[51] Intraoperative airway management was the most significant factor in the causation of sore throat. Patients with an endotracheal tube had the greatest incidence (45.4%), followed by patients with a laryngeal mask airway (LMA—17.5%), while patients with a face mask had the lowest incidence (3.3%). The ease or difficulty of intubation was not associated with postoperative sore throat in this study. The avoidance of an endotracheal tube will decrease the risk of a postoperative sore throat. When a tracheal tube is essential, the use of smaller tracheal tubes with cuffs that have a small area of contact with the tracheal mucosa and careful control of the intracuff pressure with a careful determination of the cuff-seal point may be beneficial.[52] Consideration should be given to using the anesthetic gas mixture or saline to inflate the cuff. Lubricants containing local anesthetic agents are not useful and may actually increase the incidence of sore throat.[52]

The reported incidence of sore throat after use of the LMA varies widely, which may be due to differences in insertion skills and techniques, lubricants, and cuff pressure that may or may not be controlled.[52] The occurrence of pharyngeal trauma and thus the incidence of postoperative sore throat can be reduced by inflation of the LMA cuff before insertion.[53] There is conflicting evidence as to whether limitation of pressure exerted on the pharyngeal mucosa by the LMA cuff reduces postoperative sore throat.[52] Rieger et al. found that LMA cuff pressure was not a factor in the causation of sore throat,[54] while Burgard et al. found minimizing cuff pressure reduced the incidence of this complication.[55] Lubrication of the LMA with a local anesthetic gel does not decrease the incidence of sore throat.[56] The use of a water-soluble lubricant or saline is preferred. The use of a larger-size LMA is associated with an increased incidence of sore throat, i.e., size 5 LMA as opposed to a size 4 in men and size 4 LMA as opposed to size 3 in women.[57] An increased incidence of sore throat was associated with an increased number of insertion attempts and a longer duration of the surgical procedure.[57] The use of the oropharyngeal airway does not appear to increase the incidence of sore throat.[58] Blind suctioning of the oropharynx may cause tissue trauma and postoperative discomfort. The use of soft suction catheters under direct vision may be beneficial.

The technique of airway management is the most important factor in the causation of postoperative sore throat in ambulatory surgery. Awareness of the factors that cause pharyngeal trauma and the use of simple preventive measures perioperatively can reduce the incidence of sore throat and increase patient satisfaction with ambulatory surgery.

MYALGIA

The reported incidence of succinylcholine-induced myalgia ranges from 1.5% to 89% with a commonly quoted figure of around 50%.[59] It usually lasts 2 or 3 days but may persist for up to 1 week. Patients who undergo minor operations are most likely to suffer as early ambulation increases both incidence of pain and its severity. Patients undergoing ambulatory surgery are therefore particularly at risk. Iatrogenic postoperative myalgia is unacceptable in modern anesthetic practice, and the most effective way to prevent succinylcholine-induced myalgia is to avoid the use of succinylcholine itself. If succinylcholine is used in ambulatory anesthesia, the incidence and severity of postoperative myalgia may be decreased by pretreatment with a small dose of a nondepolarizing neuromuscular blocker[60,61] or intravenous lidocaine.[60] Collins et al. found the incidence and severity of succinylcholine-induced myalgia was decreased significantly by 3 mg of d-tubocurarine to a level similar to that in patients who did not receive succinylcholine.[61] There is evidence that combining precurarization with intravenous lidocaine may be more effective in decreasing myalgia than either agent alone.[60] Mikat-Stevens et al. showed no difference in the incidence of postoperative myalgia in ambulatory patients who received mivacurium or succinylcholine pretreated with 3 mg of d-tubocurarine and lidocaine 1 mg/kg.[62] The incidence of postoperative myalgia in both groups was approximately 20%. There seems to be a baseline incidence of myalgia in ambulatory patients that is unrelated to the choice of muscle relaxant. The position of the patient during surgery (especially the position of the head, neck, back, and upper and lower limbs) while lying on the operating table for prolonged periods may also contribute to postoperative myalgia.

DROWSINESS/DIZZINESS

Postoperative drowsiness or dizziness may complicate ambulatory surgery and persist for up to 24 hr in approximately 10% of patients.[63] The incidence of drowsiness and dizziness was found to be highest in patients undergoing laparoscopy or general surgery.[63] Drowsiness may also cause prolonged postoperative hospital stay.[8] Adequate hydration perioperatively has been shown to significantly decrease the incidence of both drowsiness and dizziness.[64]

URINARY RETENTION

Voiding has traditionally been considered a requirement to discharge a patient after ambulatory surgery. There is a concern that patients may develop urinary retention after discharge. However, the value of requiring all patients to void has been questioned.[65] Inability to void has been reported to delay discharge in 5–19% of patients after ambulatory surgery.[8] Pavlin et al. found that patients with a low risk of urinary retention undergoing nonpelvic surgery or gynecologic surgery with intraoperative catheterization could be safely discharged home without voiding as the incidence of urinary retention is less than 1%.[66] Patients with a history of urinary retention or those undergoing hernia or anal surgery were found to have a higher risk of urinary retention. These patients had a 5% incidence for urinary retention with a recurrence rate of 25% postdischarge.[66] Patients who have undergone spinal or epidural anesthesia are also at a higher risk, with an incidence for urinary retention of 13%.[67] However, ambulatory patients may still be discharged before voiding after short-acting spinal and epidural anesthesia.[68]

A patient at high risk of urinary retention should have the bladder emptied by catheterization if unable to void when otherwise ready for discharge. The patient may then be discharged if he/she is reliable and has ready access to a medical facility but cautioned to return if unable to void within 8 hr.[66] The use of ultrasound monitoring of bladder volume in the PACU facilities the determination of when to catheterize patients at high risk of urinary retention.[67]

BLEEDING

Excessive bleeding postoperatively is an uncommon complication after ambulatory surgery. When it does occur, it may give rise to both unanticipated admission and a return hospital visit with or without readmission. Bleeding has been shown to account for 7.4–26% of all unanticipated admissions.[12–14,16–18] Twersky et al. found that bleeding was the primary reason for 41.5% of hospital return visits and 76% of these patients were treated and discharged through the emergency room.[23] Vaghadia et al. retrospectively studied 172,710 outpatient procedures and found that 64 patients (0.04%) experienced unanticipated admission or readmission to hospi-

tal within 48 hr due to bleeding.[69] Gynecologic surgery and urologic surgery accounted for 51% and 36% of bleeders, respectively.[69] Therapeutic abortion and transurethral prostatectomy were the two procedures most likely to result in this complication. While 55% of bleeders were noted to have excessive bleeding in the operating room or in the PACU, 45% bled primarily at home.[69] Most bleeders could be identified within 30–45 min of arrival in the PACU.

POSTOPERATIVE FUNCTIONAL LEVEL

Complete return of patients to their preoperative functional level represents the ultimate success of ambulatory surgery and anesthesia. However, postoperative symptoms such as pain, nausea/vomiting, malaise, sore throat, and myalgia are associated with a decrease in postoperative functional level and interfere with the activities of daily living.[27] Swan et al. showed that ambulatory surgery patients experienced decreased functional status during the first 7 postoperative days and only 22% of patients had returned to work 1 week after surgery.[70] These findings suggest that although the provider "cost" may have been reduced with the transition to ambulatory surgery, a significant portion of the cost and impact of their care may have been merely shifted to the patient and their family.

SUMMARY

Ambulatory surgery has an excellent safety record. Major morbidity is rare but less serious non-life-threatening events occur with a higher incidence and may result in prolonged hospital stay, unanticipated admission, or hospital readmission. These symptoms persist postdischarge[71] and may cause significant patient discomfort and decrease both patient satisfaction and postoperative functional level[27,43] (Figs. 44-2, 44-3). The occurrence of these adverse events is now a major area of quality assessment and an area where improvement should be targeted. Continual audit of

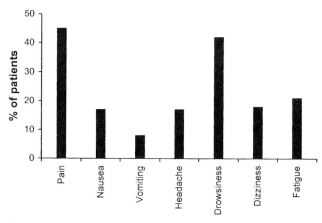

Figure 44-2   Incidence of postdischarge symptoms. (Data from Wu CL, Berenholtz SM, Pronovost PJ, et al. Systemic review and analysis of postdischarge symptoms after outpatient surgery. Anesthesiology 2002;96:994–1003.)

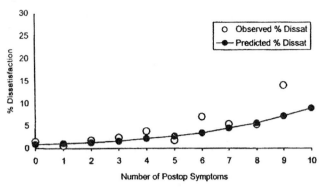

Figure 44-3   Predicted (solid circles) and observed (open circles) dissatisfaction with anesthesia based on number of postoperative symptoms. (Reprinted with permission from Tong D, Chung F, Wong D. Predictive factors in global and anesthesia satisfaction in ambulatory surgical patients. Anesthesiology 1997;87:862.)

adverse events should be performed in each ambulatory surgery center to ensure that a high quality of care is maintained and to recognize potential areas of improvement within each center in order to minimize the incidence of adverse events postoperatively.[72]

REFERENCES

1.   Chung F, Mezei G. Adverse outcomes in ambulatory anesthesia. Can J Anaesth 1999;46:R18–26.

2.   Armanious S, Chung F. Quality management in ambulatory surgery. Probl Anesth 2001;13:458–67.

3.   Warner MA, Shields SE, Chute CG. Major morbidity and mortality within 1 month of ambulatory surgery and anesthesia. JAMA 1993; 270:1437–41.

4.   Natof EN. Complications associated with ambulatory surgery. JAMA 1980;244:1116–18.

5.   Mezei G, Chung F. Return hospital visits and hospital readmissions after ambulatory surgery Ann Surg 1999;230:721–27.

6.   Fleisher LA, Pasternak LR, Herbert R, Anderson GF. Inpatient hospital admission and death after outpatient surgery in elderly patients: importance of patient and system characteristics and location of care. Arch Surg 2004;139(1):67–72.

7.   Imasogie N, Chung F. Risk factors for prolonged stay after ambulatory surgery: economic considerations. Curr Opin Anaesthiol 2002;15:245–49.

8.   Pavlin DJ, Rapp SE, Polissar NL, et al. Factors affecting discharge time in adult outpatients. Anesth Analg 1998;87:816–26.

9.   Junger A, Klasen J, Benson M, et al. Factors determining length of stay of surgical day-case patients. Eur J Anaesthiol 2001;18:314–21.

10.   Chung F, Mezei G. Factors contributing to a prolonged stay after ambulatory surgery. Anesth Analg 1999;89:1352–59.

11.   Chung F. Recovery pattern and home readiness after ambulatory surgery. Anesth Analg 1995;80:896–902.

12.   Fortier J, Chung F. Unanticipated admission after ambulatory surgery: a prospective study. Can J Anaesth 1998;45:612–19.

13.   Osborne GA, Rudkin GE. Outcome after day-care surgery in a major teaching hospital. Anaesth Intens Care 1993;21:822–27.

14.   Gold BS, Kitz DS, Lecky JH, et al. Unanticipated admission to the hospital following ambulatory surgery. JAMA 1989;262:3008–10.

15.   Mingus ML, Bodian CA, Bradford CN, et al. Prolonged surgery increases the likelihood of admission of scheduled ambulatory surgery patients. J Clin Anesth 1997;9:446–50.

16.   Greenburg AG, Greenburg JP, Tewel A, et al. Hospital admission following ambulatory surgery. Am J Surg 1996;172:21–23.

17.   Fancourt-Smith PF, Hornstein J, Jenkins LC. Hospital admissions from the surgical day care center of Vancouver General Hospital 1977–1987. Can J Anaesth 1990;37:699–704.

18.   Biwas TK, Leary C. Postoperative hospital admission from a day surgery unit: a seven year retrospective survey. Anaesth Intens Care 1992;20:147–50.

19.   Michaloliakou C, Chung F, Sharma S. Preoperative multimodal analgesia facilitates recovery after ambulatory laparoscopic cholecystectomy. Anesth Analg 1996;82:44–51.

20.   Shaikh S, Chung F. Pain, nausea, vomiting and ocular complications delay discharge following ambulatory microdiscectomy. Can J Anaesth 2003;50:514–18.

21.   Imasogie N, Chung F. Effect of return hospital visits on economics of ambulatory surgery. Curr Opin Anaesthiol 2001;14:573–78.

22.   Tong D, Chung F, Mezei G. Pre-existing medical conditions as predictors of adverse events in day case surgery. Br J Anaesth 1999;83: 262–70.

23.   Twersky R, Fishman D, Homel P. What happens after discharge? Return hospital visits after ambulatory surgery. Anesth Analg 1997;84: 319–24.

24.   Duncan PG, Cohen MM, Tweed WA, et al. The Canadian four-centre study of anaesthetic outcomes: are anaesthetic complications predictable in day surgical practice? Can J Anaesth 1992;39: 440–48.

25.   Chung F, Mezei G, Tong D. Adverse events in ambulatory surgery: a comparison between elderly and younger patients. Can J Anaesth 1999;46:309–21.

26.   Myles PS, Iacono GA, Hunt JO, et al. Risk of respiratory complications and wound infection in patients undergoing ambulatory surgery: smokers versus nonsmokers. Anesthesiology 2002;97:842–47.

27.   Tong D, Chung F, Mezei G. Which specific postoperative symptoms predict postoperative functional level in ambulatory patients? Anesthesiology 1997;87:A37.

28.   Jenkins K, Grady D, Wong J, et al. Post-operative recovery: day surgery patients' preferences. Br J Anaesth 2001;86:272–74.

29.   Beauregard L, Pomp A, Choiniere M. Severity and impact of pain after day-surgery. Can J Anaesth 1998;45:304–11.

30.   Rawal N, Hylander J, Nydahl P, et al. Survey of postoperative analgesia following ambulatory surgery. Acta Anaesthesiol Scand 1997; 41:1017–22.

31.   Rawal N. Analgesia for day-care surgery. Br J Anaesth 2001;87: 73–87.

32.   Tong D, Chung F. Postoperative pain control in ambulatory surgery. Surg Clin North Am 1999;79:401–30.

33.   McGrath B, Chung F, Elgendy H, et al. Pain 24 hours after ambulatory surgery. Can we do better? Canadian Anaesthetists' Society Annual Meeting Abstracts, June 2003.

34.   Chung F, Ritchie E, Su J. Postoperative pain in ambulatory surgery. Anesth Analg 1997;85:808–16.

35.   Jin F, Chung F. Postoperative pain—a challenge for anaesthetists in ambulatory surgery. Can J Anaesth 1998;45:293–96.

36.   Marshall SI, Chung F. Discharge criteria and complications after ambulatory surgery. Anesth Analg 1999;88:508–17.

37.   Pavlin J, Chen C, Penaloza D, et al. Pain as a factor complicating recovery and discharge after ambulatory surgery. Anesth Analg 2002;95:627–34.

38.   Crews JC. Multimodal pain management strategies for office-based and ambulatory procedures. JAMA 2002;288:629–32.

39.   Shang A, Gan T. Optimising postoperative pain management in the ambulatory patient. Drugs 2003;63:855–67.

40.   White PF. The role of non-opioid analgesic techniques in the management of pain after ambulatory surgery. Anesth Analg 2002;94: 577–85.

41.   Carrol NV, Miederhoff PA, Cox FM, et al. Postoperative nausea and vomiting after discharge from outpatient surgery centers. Anesth Analg 1995;80:903–9.

42. Sinclair D, Chung F, Mezei G. Can postoperative nausea and vomiting be predicted? Anesthesiology 1999;91:109–18.

43. Tong D, Chung F, Wong D. Predictive factors in global and anesthesia satisfaction in ambulatory surgical patients. Anesthesiology 1997;87:856–64.

44. Watcha MF, White PF. Postoperative nausea and vomiting: its etiology, treatment and prevention. Anesthesiology 1992;77:162–84.

45. Gan TJ, Meyer T, Apfel CC, et al. Consensus guidelines for the management of postoperative nausea and vomiting. Anesth Analg 2003;97:62–71.

46. Apfel CC, Laara E, Koivuranta M, et al. A simplified risk score for predicting postoperative nausea and vomiting: conclusions from cross-validations between two centers. Anesthesiology 1999;91:693–700.

47. Apfel CC, Kranke P, Eberhart LH, et al. Comparison of predictive models for postoperative nausea and vomiting. Br J Anaesth 2002;88:234–40.

48. Apfel CC, Kranke P, Katz MH, et al. Volatile anaesthetics may be the main cause of early but not delayed postoperative vomiting: a randomized controlled trial of factorial design. Br J Anaesth 2002;88:659–68.

49. Watcha MF. The cost-effective management of postoperative nausea and vomiting. Anesthesiology 2000;92:931–33.

50. Gan TJ. Postoperative nausea and vomiting—can it be eliminated? JAMA 2002;287:1233–36.

51. Higgins P, Chung F, Mezei G. Postoperative sore throat after ambulatory surgery. Br J Anaesth 2002;88:582–84.

52. McHardy FE, Chung F. Postoperative sore throat: cause, prevention and treatment. Anaesthesia 1999;54:444–53.

53. Wakeling HG, Butler PJ, Baxter PJC. The laryngeal mask airway: a comparison between two insertion techniques. Anesth Analg 1997;85:687–90.

54. Rieger A, Brunne B, Striebel HW. Intracuff pressures do not predict laryngopharyngeal discomfort after use of the laryngeal mask airway. Anesthesiology 1997;87:63–67.

55. Burgard G, Mollhoff T, Prien T. The effect of laryngeal mask cuff pressure on postoperative sore throat incidence. J Clin Anesth 1996;8:198–201.

56. Keller C, Sparr HJ, Brimacombe JR. Laryngeal mask lubrication—a comparative study of saline versus 2% lignocaine gel with cuff pressure control. Anaesthesia 1997;52:586–602.

57. Grady DM, McHardy F, Wong J, et al. Pharyngolaryngeal morbidity with the laryngeal mask airway in spontaneously breathing patients. Anesthesiology 2001;94:760–66.

58. Browne B, Adams CN. Postoperative sore throat related to the use of a Guedel airway. Anaesthesia 1988;43:590–91.

59. Wong SF, Chung F. Succinylcholine-associated postoperative myalgia. Anaesthesia 2000;55:144–52.

60. Melnick B, Chalasani J, Lim N, et al. Decreasing post-succinylcholine myalgia in outpatients. Can J Anaesth 1987;34:238–41.

61. Collins L, Prentice J, Vaghadia H. Tracheal intubations of outpatients with and without muscle relaxants. Can J Anaesth 2000;47:427–32.

62. Mikat-Stevens M, Sukhani R, Pappas A, et al. Is succinylcholine after pretreatment with d-tubocurarine and lidocaine contraindicated for outpatient anesthesia? Anesth Analg 2000;91:312–16.

63. Chung F, Un V, Su J. Postoperative symptoms 24 hours after ambulatory anaesthesia. Can J Anaesth 1996;43:1121–27.

64. Yogendran S, Asokumar B, Cheng D, et al. A prospective randomized double-blinded study of the effect of intravenous fluid therapy on adverse outcomes on outpatient surgery. Anesth Analg 1995;80:682–86.

65. Chung F. Are discharge criteria changing? J Clin Anesth 1993;5:64S–68S (suppl).

66. Pavlin DJ, Pavlin EG, Fitzgibbon DR, et al. Management of bladder function after outpatient surgery. Anesthesiology 1999;91:42–50.

67. Pavlin DJ, Pavlin EG, Gunn HC, et al. Voiding in patients managed with or without ultrasound monitoring of bladder volume after outpatient surgery. Anesth Analg 1999;89:90–97.

68. Mulroy MF, Salinas FV, Larkin KL, et al. Ambulatory surgery patients may be discharged before voiding after short-acting spinal and epidural anesthesia. Anesthesiology 2002;97:315–19.

69. Vaghadia H, Scheepers L, Merrick PM. Readmission for bleeding after outpatient surgery. Can J Anaesth 1998;45:1079–83.

70. Swan B, Maislin G, Traber K. Symptom distress and functional status changes during the first seven days after ambulatory surgery. Anesth Analg 1998;86:739–45.

71. Wu CL, Berenholtz SM, Pronovost PJ, et al. Systemic review and analysis of postdischarge symptoms after outpatient surgery. Anesthesiology 2002;96:994–1003.

72. Collins LM, Padda J, Vaghadia H. Mini-audits facilitate quality assurance in outpatient units. Can J Anaesth 2001;48:737–41.

EMERGING TECHNIQUES

Ambulatory Continuous Regional Anesthesia: Rationale, Logistics, and Organization

STEPHEN M. KLEIN   MARCY S. TUCKER   CHESTER C. BUCKENMAIER III

INTRODUCTION

Ambulatory surgery has grown dramatically in the past three decades. Today nearly 70% of all surgical cases in North America are performed on an ambulatory basis. Annually this accounts for over 31.5 million surgeries performed in over 2700 centers.[1] This trend continues with increasingly more complex surgery and a greater shift to office-based and minimally invasive procedures. Overall, the increase in ambulatory surgery has been a huge success economically without decreasing patient safety or satisfaction.

The development of short-acting sedatives and rapid elimination inhalational agents has aided in the growth and efficiency of ambulatory anesthesia. Despite this success, advances in pain management have not paralleled the increasing needs of ambulatory patients recovering in the home environment. Providing extended analgesia after painful surgery has limited the growth of appropriate ambulatory procedures. Chung and colleagues helped quantify the failure of outpatient pain management and noted that after some orthopedic, urologic, and plastic surgeries, the incidence of severe pain postoperatively was between 40% and 70%.[2]

Continuous peripheral nerve blocks (CPNBs) offer useful strategies for the management of postoperative pain. Not only do these techniques provide superior pain control,[3–6] but they decrease the stress response to surgery,[7] reduce intraoperative and postoperative blood loss,[8] reduce postoperative nausea and vomiting,[9] and reduce costs,[10] when compared to traditional treatments. Overall CPNBs have been associated with improved patient satisfaction.[11] This chapter will explore the advantages, logistics, and safety issues involved in using CPNBs in the ambulatory setting.

AMBULATORY CONTINUOUS CATHETERS

Single-injection peripheral nerve block (PNB) provides extended analgesia and an excellent side effect profile. However, a drawback to a perioperatively placed PNB is the regression of pain control provided by the long-acting local anesthetics after 12–24 hr.[12] Much of the analgesic benefit and opioid sparing is diminished when the block recedes in the postanesthesia care unit (PACU) or at home after discharge.[13] Relying on oral opioids alone is often insufficient to achieve the same level of analgesia provided by the PNB. Opioid use has been shown to increase with the recession of nerve blocks after major orthopedic surgery in ambulatory patients.[14]

CPNBs provide site-specific local anesthetic delivery, profound analgesia, minimal side effects, and avoidance of premature regression of an analgesic block. First described by Ansboro[15] in 1946, CPNBs have been increasingly utilized and refined. In the hospital, CPNB catheters have been shown to provide profound surgical anesthesia,[16] effective long-term postoperative analgesia,[17–19] reduced opioid requirements,[18,20,21] and improved rehabilitation.[5,19]

Since the landmark article by Rawal et al.[22] on the use of an elastometric balloon pump allowing patient self-administration of local anesthetic analgesia at home, interest in this technology has increased. Multiple studies and case reports have described the effective and safe management of postoperative analgesia using continuous home infusion systems.[11,21,23–28]

INDICATIONS

Discharging patients with a CPNB remains a new and evolving area of postoperative analgesia. As a result, most clinicians are highly selective of CPNB patients and still choose patients on a case-by-case basis based on the anticipated degree of postoperative pain and the ability of the patient to comply with postoperative instructions. There are no definitive insertion criteria. Major orthopedic surgeries of the upper extremity or lower extremity are ideal procedures for the CPNB techniques because an appropriately placed catheter often can provide substantial pain relief to the entire surgical site.

Successful applications

- Shoulder arthroplasty
- Open shoulder repairs
- Painful osteotomies or soft tissue dissection of the forearm and hand
- Breast cancer surgery
- Total knee arthroplasty
- Anterior cruciate ligament repair
- Ankle fusion or replacement
- Foot osteotomies

CONTRAINDICATIONS

Contraindications for CPNBs in the inpatient environment (infection at the site, patient refusal, evolving nerve injury) usually apply when evaluating patients for ambulatory applications. Performing an ambulatory CPNB should balance the risk of a continuous perineural infusion of local anesthetic in the home setting with the benefit of postoperative analgesia and recovery. Until more data are obtained, relative contraindications are determined based on a patient's inability to manage care at home (Table 45-1).

A NEW PERIOPERATIVE ROLE

The implementation of an outpatient continuous catheter program requires a multidisciplinary approach toward perioperative care. Managing postoperative pain after discharge from an outpatient surgery facility has traditionally been the responsibility of the surgeon. A continuous catheter program will involve an additional perioperative role for the anesthesia team requiring extended management beyond the recovery room and the day of surgery.[29] As more surgery is performed on an outpatient basis, the ambulatory anesthesiologist will need to develop mechanisms to address patient safety issues, pain and nausea concerns, and (along with the surgeon) postoperative complications in the patient's home environment. In addition, payment for this new effort will have to be available from third-party payers. Creating the infrastructure to support this endeavor will likely shift some resources designed for traditional inpatient care to more progressive outpatient uses. This represents a fundamental shift in philosophy.

OUTPATIENT MANAGEMENT

Initial guidelines for the use of peripheral nerve catheters in the home setting have been extrapolated from experience with managing CPNBs in the hospital. There are currently no data confirming the efficacy of these guidelines in outpatients. However, general safe practices regarding the use of CPNBs at home should include the following:

- Prior to discharge, peripheral nerve catheters should undergo careful testing for intravascular placement. This typically involves aspiration of the catheter to detect the presence of blood and performance of a test dose with local anesthetic containing epinephrine. It should be noted that these measures are designed to detect accidental intravascular placement but do not assure satisfactory catheter localization.
- Patient and accompanying caretaker education is an important component to achieving success. These instructions should include information on appropriate expectations, the pump function (stopping the infusion), and routine catheter care.[30]
- Patients should be given both verbal and written instructions on the warning signs and symptoms of local anesthetic toxicity and care of the blocked extremity.[14]
- Patients should be provided with written information so they can contact a physician or health care provider by telephone to answer questions during the infusion. A physician and follow-up infrastructure to handle problems should be available 24 hr to provide this service. Depending on the patient's needs, this resource is often utilized.[25]
- A daily telephone call should be made to monitor side effects from the infusion, determine efficacy, and inquire about the integrity of the insertion site. Based on answers to these issues, a determination should be made evaluating the effectiveness of continued therapy versus removing the catheter.

Written and verbal instructions should include:

Table 45-1   Relative Contraindications to Ambulatory Continuous Peripheral Nerve Blocks

- Contraindications to regional anesthesia
- Inability to comprehend instructions
- History of noncompliance with previous medical regimens
- Unable to accomplish activities of daily living with the continuous infusion
- Lack of an accompanying adult (to assist with care if necessary and appropriately monitor for side effects)
- Immunocompromise
- Severe hepatic disease or protein deficiency

- A warning to avoid bearing weight on the extremity (especially with lower extremity blocks) during the infusion.
- A warning that the protective reflex of pain will be absent from the blocked extremity and extra care should be taken to protect the limb (e.g., avoid contact with extremes of hot and cold).
- A warning that proprioception for the limb will be diminished and extra attention should be paid to the avoidance of potentially harmful positions.
- The patient is advised to begin taking scheduled oral acetaminophen and nonsteroidal anti-inflammatory drugs (NSAIDs) medications at discharge and to start oral opioids with the first onset of discomfort.
- A caution for the patient to avoid driving or operating hazardous equipment.

CATHETER REMOVAL

Whether a patient should remove the CPNB catheter at home or return to the hospital should be an individualized decision. This decision should be based on the comfort level of the patient and chaperone, the location of the insertion site, and the need for further physical examination. In contrast to epidural catheters, PNB catheters are rarely difficult or painful to remove. Initial data demonstrates that patients are comfortable with this practice, though extensive safety information does not yet exist.[21] Catheter removal by the patient at home is convenient for both the patient and physician, thus enhancing acceptance of CPNB. Most authors agree that catheters should not be advanced more than 3–5 cm beyond the tip of the needle during insertion to avoid kinking, coiling, or knotting below the skin. In general, the vast majority of patients are able to remove the catheter at home safely and easily with simple instructions (Table 45-2).

INFUSION PUMPS

A variety of home infusion pumps are currently available. Many initial designs focused on delivery of intravenous (IV) medications into the low-pressure peripheral venous

Table 45-2   Guidelines for Catheter Removal

- Wait until there is sensory block resolution before removal.
- Halt if there is pain or radiculopathy.
- After removing the dressing, slowly withdraw catheter.
- Never tug the catheter or pull against resistance.
- Document the integrity of the distal tip.
- Provide telephone guidance while the catheter is removed or access to a trained clinician in the event of difficulty.

system. In the last few years, these pumps have been adapted for use in home perineural infusions. Current models have improved accuracy, higher infusion pressure, larger reservoir volume, and bolus capabilities. In a series of articles by Ilfeld and colleagues[31,32] the authors examined the accuracy and consistency of many available portable infusion pumps and documented many of their attributes. They determined that several commercial models provided consistent accurate local anesthetic delivery. But, depending on the mechanism of pressure generation, accuracy could vary by as much as ±15%.[31,32] The accuracy was also affected by battery strength and temperature. Nevertheless, despite these variations, in most clinical situations these models would be capable of delivering an effective infusion rate. When used in extreme environments or for pediatric patients, additional scrutiny may be warranted.

Desirable characteristics of perineural home infusion devices include a large infusion reservoir (250–500 ml), constant infusion rate that is unaffected by extremes in temperature or pressure, and an uncomplicated infusion setting that is tamperproof, lightweight, transportable, inexpensive, and capable of supporting a patient-controlled bolus (PCB) function. All home infusion pumps must have a simple mechanism for infusion termination that is easily recognized and activated by the patient. Having a method to determine whether the pump is functioning and what volume has been delivered is also helpful.

LOCAL ANESTHETIC

The ideal local anesthetic for home infusion should provide profound analgesia, minimize motor block, resolve quickly, and have limited progression of motor block with continued infusion. This anesthetic would also provide a wide margin of safety if accidental intravascular delivery occurred. Unfortunately this ideal local anesthetic does not completely exist. To achieve these aims, full-concentration amide local anesthetics are typically used for single-injection PNBs, while dilute infusions of long-acting amide local anesthetics are typically utilized for home CPNB infusions. Numerous studies have documented the analgesic efficacy and safety of dilute bupivacaine (0.125–0.25%) when used for both upper[4,33–36] and lower extremity[19,30,37,38] continuous peripheral nerve infusions. More recently, dilute ropivacaine (0.2%) has also been shown to be effective for CPNBs. Because of the improved cardiovascular toxicity profile of ropivacaine[39,40] it may offer a safety advantage for home delivery when compared with bupivacaine. Levobupivacaine, a pure levorotatory enantiomer of bupivacaine, purportedly has similar potency but is less toxic than bupivacaine.[39,41,42] Data concerning its efficacy for continuous perineural infusions are limited, but given its identical structure and duration in PNBs one can hypothesize that it will perform similarly to bupivacaine when used for this purpose.

Another controversial issue concerning home perineural infusions involves the ideal infusion strategy. Numerous combinations of solutions and infusion rates have been used successfully for inpatient and outpatient CPNBs.

Differentiating between these strategies can be difficult because investigators often use different measures of success, such as best pain verbal analog scale (VAS) score, worst pain VAS over the time period, opioid consumption, and time until first analgesic use, and rarely is the accuracy of the catheter investigated. There are currently several studies underway that should provide additional guidance for outpatient infusions.

A simplified approach is to divide local anesthetic delivery into three basic strategies: continuous, intermittent bolus, and continuous with intermittent bolus. A continuous infusion technique is one of the more common methods employed for home peripheral nerve catheter infusion. The method is simple, reliable, and convenient for the anesthesiologist. It requires little patient participation and it facilitates the use of elementary and inexpensive pump technology. Unfortunately, this method does not allow for dosage adjustment or supplementation, leaving no treatment mechanism for breakthrough pain that may develop after resolution of the intense surgical block.[43] This drawback may require the use of a higher hourly local anesthetic dose, increasing the potential for local anesthetic accumulation.[35]

Intermittent bolus dosing of local anesthetic, as was demonstrated by Rawal et al.,[22,30] is another strategy for outpatient management. This approach gives the clinician and patient the greatest control and allows for differences in patient activity levels and perceptions of pain after surgery (e.g., some patients do not hurt all the time).[23] For femoral nerve blocks after major knee surgery, Eledjam and colleagues[44] determined that a large intermittent bolus of 10 mL of 0.2% ropivacaine every 60 min was as efficacious as an intermittent infusion of 0.2% ropivacaine 10 mL/hr or a continuous infusion of 5 mL/hr with a bolus of 5 mL every 60 min. Using their dosing strategy, the 10 mL bolus every 60 min also resulted in a lower consumption of local anesthetic. Despite the success of this strategy with inpatients, when there is the availability for supplemental IV analgesics, it is the authors' opinion that there remains a high potential in outpatients for breakthrough pain. This is especially true during periods of sleep when the patient's lack of response to the pain (pushing the intermittent bolus button) may result in complete analgesic resolution.

The final method, continuous infusion with intermittent bolus, affords the practitioner and patient the greatest flexibility and is the preferred method of the authors. The continuous basal infusion reduces the risk of breakthrough pain while allowing the patient to rapidly reinforce the analgesia with a bolus when needed. The advantages of this method compared to the previous methods mentioned were demonstrated by Singelyn et al.[35] in their study on continuous brachial plexus analgesia after open shoulder surgery. They found that a basal infusion combined with patient-controlled analgesia boluses to be as efficacious as a continuous technique and superior to an intermittent bolus technique. The basal infusion combined with a PCB resulted in the lowest total dose of local anesthetic, an important goal in outpatient administration. As with all general guidelines, adjustments for previous doses and duration of the infusion need to be individualized.

SAFETY CONCERNS

Discharge of the Patient with a Blocked Extremity

Discharging patients with an insensate extremity remains controversial. Though CPNBs offer clear advantages for early discharge and a low incidence of side effects following ambulatory surgery, many practitioners are concerned about patient injury if they are discharged with an insensate extremity. Concern has been raised that patients are at increased risk for limb injury without the protective reflex of pain or other bodily injury arising from falls, particularly with lower extremity blocks. Intuitively, there is merit in this concern, though few reports are available to support avoiding the use of long-acting PNBs. On the other hand, the traditional practice of sending patients home, immobilized, hobbling on a painful extremity, disoriented, and sedated on opioids might offer more risk.

Unfortunately, only a few large, prospective studies have examined this issue directly. Those that have addressed outpatient PNBs support the concept that regional anesthesia and discharge with an insensate limb may be done safely. In one study, Davis and colleagues[45] examined 543 brachial plexus blocks performed on 526 outpatients. In this study they demonstrated that axillary brachial plexus blocks could be utilized very effectively; only 7% of patients required a general anesthetic and no patients sustained a neurologic deficit. In another study, by Cooper et al.,[46] 1149 outpatients who had undergone an axillary brachial plexus block as part of their outpatient anesthetic were contacted postoperatively. They noted that the vast majority of patients (93%) would choose an axillary brachial plexus block again. Patients who were reluctant to choose the technique again generally had complications such as pain or bruising. Information about whether the limb was anesthetized at discharge was not presented.

To help further answer questions about discharging patients home with insensate limbs, the authors' group prospectively studied 2382 long-acting PNBs with ropivacaine in both the upper and lower extremity noting a low incidence of block failure, rare use of opioids in the recovery unit, and high rate of patient satisfaction.[14] This study reported a low incidence of block complications after discharge (0.2%), including one patient who accidentally fell while exiting a car. The vast majority of patients in the study appeared to protect themselves from further injury despite having a blocked extremity. The reason for the low incidence of problems is multifactorial. We suspect that some of the factors that may have contributed to this success were careful patient selection and detailed discharge instructions by the anesthesiologist and, more important, the PACU nurse just prior to leaving the ambulatory surgery facility.

Local Anesthetic Toxicity

Toxicity is a serious adverse event that is always possible when there is a continuous infusion of local anesthetic. While most commonly associated with large bolus injections during initial block placement, the possibility of toxicity occurring at home is still theoretically possible. To help reduce this risk, investigators have instituted several mechanisms to increase patient safety. Most clinicians have required study participants to display comprehension of the verbal and written instructions and require the presence of a chaperone. A common theme in the literature is the careful attention to avoid inadvertent vascular catheter placement. This is typically done by injecting a large test dose of local anesthetic with epinephrine via the catheter and monitoring for its effects prior to discharge to ensure the catheter tip is not misplaced. Perhaps more important is the use of dilute concentrations of local anesthetic that have already been found to be safe in inpatients. Ekatodramis and colleagues[47] recently provided a detailed analysis of serum ropivacaine concentrations when a 2 mg/mL concentration was infused for 48 hr in a continuous interscalene brachial plexus block. They demonstrated that after 6 and 9 mg/hr infusions, total and particularly free concentrations of ropivacaine were well below the limit shown to produce central nervous system effects in volunteers. Furthermore, the availability of a trained health care provider and physician to answer questions by telephone seems logical. Finally, daily telephone calls have been advocated to obtain efficacy data and to confirm safety, though the utility of this practice is hard to quantify.

Catheter Migration and Dislodgement

Accidental catheter dislodgement continues to be a problem for inpatient as well as outpatient catheters, particularly with freely mobile, superficial sites such as the neck and the axilla or the lumbar region, where perspiration is prominent. To address this issue several methods to fasten catheters have been advocated to avoid dislodgement. These have included suturing, retrograde subcutaneous tunneling,[48] cutaneous sutures,[13] medical adhesive, cynoacrylate glue,[49] and different methods of taping. In addition, selecting a more stationary insertion site such as a supraclavicular or infraclavicular region may be advantageous. Regardless of the selected method of securing or insertion site, proponents of CPNBs are usually meticulous when fastening catheters in an attempt to avoid this common point of failure.

While catheter dislodgement results in technique failure, it is otherwise not associated with complications. The risk of a CPNB catheter migrating from its initial insertion site into a blood vessel or other structure is more worrisome. This could conceivably result in local anesthetic toxicity or central neuraxial spread in an unmonitored environment. Furthermore, the risk should be minimized by selecting the minimally effective concentration of local anesthetic and providing detailed instructions on halting the infusion and obtaining help. Despite the obvious safety concern, only one case of peripheral nerve catheter migration has been reported in the literature.[50]

Insertion Site Infection

All percutaneous catheters are at risk of infection. However, the actual incidence of clinically relevant infections is generally considered very low. Contamination is most likely at the skin surface with either *Staphylococcus epidermidis* or *Enterococcus*. In a prospective trial conducted on hospitalized patients, Cuvillon and colleagues[51] performed semiquantitative bacteriologic cultures on the tips of femoral catheters after 48 hr of use. They documented a positive culture rate of 57%. Information on the risk of outpatient CPNB infection is currently unavailable but may be lower because of the absence of nosocomial acquired contamination at home. Despite this lack of data, it seems prudent to recommend careful attention to aseptic technique whenever continuous catheters are placed. In addition, some mechanism of insertion site examination may be beneficial if prolonged use (4–14 days) is planned.

ALTERNATIVES AND THE FUTURE

Though ambulatory CPNB holds great promise for the future, the continued development of this technology must be validated, with more studies examining outcome and risk. Additional comparative data with alternative infusion routes for postoperative pain management are also necessary. Examples include intra-articular,[6] subcutaneous,[52] and intrawound[53] infusion methods. Further promising research exploring the encapsulation of long-acting local anesthetics in inert polymers that can potentially provide days rather than hours of analgesia is being pursued.[54,55] The realization of this technologic breakthrough would dramatically potentiate the effects of single-injection blocks and could eliminate the need for perineural catheter infusions.

CPNB techniques are an exciting aspect of ambulatory anesthesia and acute pain management that has undergone rapid development in recent years. Successful application of these techniques will require a substantial educational investment by anesthesiologists and anesthesiologists in training. The rewards in reduced postoperative pain, improved patient satisfaction, and anesthesiologist professional development make this endeavor worthy of our attention.

REFERENCES

1. Hall MJ, Lawrence L. Ambulatory surgery in the United States, 1996. Adv Data 1998;(300):1–16.
2. Chung F, Ritchie E, Su J. Postoperative pain in ambulatory surgery. Anesth Analg 1997;85(4):808–16.
3. Selander D. Catheter technique in axillary plexus block: presentation of a new method. Acta Anaesthesiol Scand 1977;21(4):324–29.
4. Tuominen M, Haasio J, Hekali R, Rosenberg PH. Continuous interscalene brachial plexus block: clinical efficacy, technical problems and bupivacaine plasma concentrations. Acta Anaesthesiol Scand 1989;33(1):84–88.
5. Singelyn FJ, Deyaert M, Joris D, Pendeville E, Gouverneur JM. Effects of intravenous patient-controlled analgesia with morphine, continuous epidural analgesia, and continuous three-in-one block on postoperative pain and knee rehabilitation after unilateral total knee arthroplasty. Anesth Analg 1998;87(1):88–92.
6. Klein SM, Nielsen KC, Martin A, White W, Warner DS, Steele SM, et al. Interscalene brachial plexus block with continuous intraarticular infusion of ropivacaine. Anesth Analg 2001;93(3):601–5.

7. Mingus ML. Recovery advantages of regional anesthesia compared with general anesthesia: adult patients. J Clin Anesth 1995;7(7):628–33.

8. Chelly JE, Greger J, Gebhard R, Coupe K, Clyburn TA, Buckle R, et al. Continuous femoral blocks improve recovery and outcome of patients undergoing total knee arthroplasty. J Arthroplasty 2001;16(4):436–45.

9. Larsson S, Lundberg D. A prospective survey of postoperative nausea and vomiting with special regard to incidence and relations to patient characteristics, anesthetic routines and surgical procedures. Acta Anaesthesiol Scand 1995;39(4):539–45.

10. Nakamura SJ, Conte-Hernandez A, Galloway MT. The efficacy of regional anesthesia for outpatient anterior cruciate ligament reconstruction. Arthroscopy 1997;13(6):699–703.

11. Nielsen KC, Greengrass RA, Pietrobon R, Klein SM, Steele SM. Continuous interscalene brachial plexus blockade provides good analgesia at home after major shoulder surgery-report of four cases. Can J Anaesth 2003;50(1):57–61.

12. Tong D, Chung F. Postoperative pain control in ambulatory surgery. Surg Clin North Am 1999;79(2):401–30.

13. Klein SM, Greengrass RA, Gleason DH, Nunley JA, Steele SM. Major ambulatory surgery with continuous regional anesthesia and a disposable infusion pump. Anesthesiology 1999;91(2):563–65.

14. Klein SM, Nielsen KC, Greengrass RA, Warner DS, Martin A, Steele SM. Ambulatory discharge after long-acting peripheral nerve blockade: 2382 blocks with ropivacaine. Anesth Analg 2002;94(1):65–70.

15. Ansboro F. Method of continuous brachial plexus block. Am J Surg 1946;71:716–22.

16. Grant SA, Nielsen KC, Greengrass RA, Steele SM, Klein SM. Continuous peripheral nerve block for ambulatory surgery. Reg Anesth Pain Med 2001;26(3):209–14.

17. Sada T, Kobayashi T, Murakami S. Continuous axillary brachial plexus block. Can Anaesth Soc J 1983;30(2):201–5.

18. Borgeat A, Schappi B, Biasca N, Gerber C. Patient-controlled analgesia after major shoulder surgery: patient-controlled interscalene analgesia versus patient-controlled analgesia. Anesthesiology 1997;87(6):1343–47.

19. Capdevila X, Barthelet Y, Biboulet P, Ryckwaert Y, Rubenovitch J, d'Athis F. Effects of perioperative analgesic technique on the surgical outcome and duration of rehabilitation after major knee surgery. Anesthesiology 1999;91(1):8–15.

20. Serpell MG, Millar FA, Thomson MF. Comparison of lumbar plexus block versus conventional opioid analgesia after total knee replacement. Anaesthesia 1991;46(4):275–77.

21. Klein SM, Grant SA, Greengrass RA, Nielsen KC, Speer KP, White W, et al. Interscalene brachial plexus block with a continuous catheter insertion system and a disposable infusion pump. Anesth Analg 2000;91(6):1473–78.

22. Rawal N, Axelsson K, Hylander J, Allvin R, Amilon A, Lidegran G, et al. Postoperative patient-controlled local anesthetic administration at home. Anesth Analg 1998;86(1):86–89.

23. Klein SM, Greengrass RA, Grant SA, Higgins LD, Nielsen KC, Steele SM. Ambulatory surgery for multi-ligament knee reconstruction with continuous dual catheter peripheral nerve blockade. Can J Anaesth 2001;48(4):375–78.

24. Ilfeld BM, Morey TE, Wang RD, Enneking FK. Continuous popliteal sciatic nerve block for postoperative pain control at home: a randomized, double-blinded, placebo-controlled study. Anesthesiology 2002;97(4):959–65.

25. Ilfeld BM, Morey TE, Enneking FK. Continuous infraclavicular brachial plexus block for postoperative pain control at home: a randomized, double-blinded, placebo-controlled study. Anesthesiology 2002;96(6):1297–304.

26. Ganapathy S, Amendola A, Lichfield R, Fowler PJ, Ling E. Elastomeric pumps for ambulatory patient-controlled regional analgesia. Can J Anaesth 2000;47(9):897–902.

27. Chelly J, Gebhard R, Coupe K, Greger J, Khan A. Local anesthetic PCA via a femoral catheter for the postoperative pain control of an ACL performed as an outpatient procedure. Am J Anesthesiol 2001;28:192–94.

28. Buckenmaier CC, 3rd, Klein SM, Nielsen KC, Steele SM. Continuous paravertebral catheter and outpatient infusion for breast surgery. Anesth Analg 2003;97(3):715–17.

29. Rock P. The future of anesthesiology is perioperative medicine. Anesthesiol Clin North Am 2000;18(3):495–513, v.

30. Rawal N, Allvin R, Axelsson K, Hallen J, Ekback G, Ohlsson T, et al. Patient-controlled regional analgesia (PCRA) at home-controlled comparison between bupivacaine and ropivacaine brachial plexus analgesia. Anesthesiology 2002;96(6):1290–96.

31. Ilfeld BM, Morey TE, Enneking FK. The delivery rate accuracy of portable infusion pumps used for continuous regional analgesia. Anesth Analg 2002;95(5):1331–6.

32. Ilfeld BM, Morey TE, Enneking FK. Delivery rate accuracy of portable, bolus-capable infusion pumps used for patient-controlled continuous regional analgesia. Reg Anesth Pain Med 2003;28(1):17–23.

33. Tuominen M, Pitkanen M, Rosenberg PH. Postoperative pain relief and bupivacaine plasma levels during continuous interscalene brachial plexus block. Acta Anaesthesiol Scand 1987;31(4):276–78.

34. Borgeat A, Kalberer F, Jacob H, Ruetsch YA, Gerber C. Patient-controlled interscalene analgesia with ropivacaine 0.2% versus bupivacaine 0.15% after major open shoulder surgery: the effects on hand motor function. Anesth Analg 2001;92(1):218–23.

35. Singelyn FJ, Seguy S, Gouverneur JM. Interscalene brachial plexus analgesia after open shoulder surgery: continuous versus patient-controlled infusion. Anesth Analg 1999;89(5):1216–20.

36. Rosenberg PH, Pere P, Hekali R, Tuominen M. Plasma concentrations of bupivacaine and two of its metabolites during continuous interscalene brachial plexus block. Br J Anaesth 1991;66(1):25–30.

37. Singelyn FJ, Gouverneur JM. Extended "three-in-one" block after total knee arthroplasty: continuous versus patient-controlled techniques. Anesth Analg 2000;91(1):176–80.

38. Singelyn FJ, Aye F, Gouverneur JM. Continuous popliteal sciatic nerve block: an original technique to provide postoperative analgesia after foot surgery. Anesth Analg 1997;84(2):383–86.

39. Groban L, Deal DD, Vernon JC, James RL, Butterworth J. Cardiac resuscitation after incremental overdosage with lidocaine, bupivacaine, levobupivacaine, and ropivacaine in anesthetized dogs. Anesth Analg 2001;92(1):37–43.

40. Knudsen K, Beckman Suurkula M, Blomberg S, Sjovall J, Edvardsson N. Central nervous and cardiovascular effects of i.v. infusions of ropivacaine, bupivacaine and placebo in volunteers. Br J Anaesth 1997;78(5):507–14.

41. Huang YF, Pryor ME, Mather LE, Veering BT. Cardiovascular and central nervous system effects of intravenous levobupivacaine and bupivacaine in sheep. Anesth Analg 1998;86(4):797–804.

42. Mather LE, Huang YF, Veering B, Pryor ME. Systemic and regional pharmacokinetics of levobupivacaine and bupivacaine enantiomers in sheep. Anesth Analg 1998;86(4):805–11.

43. Klein SM, Steele SM, Nielsen KC, Pietrobon R, Warner DS, Martin A, et al. The difficulties of ambulatory interscalene and intra-articular infusions for rotator cuff surgery: a preliminary report. Can J Anaesth 2003;50(3):265–69.

44. Eledjam JJ, Cuvillon P, Capdevila X, Macaire P, Serri S, Gaertner E, et al. Postoperative analgesia by femoral nerve block with ropivacaine 0.2% after major knee surgery: continuous versus patient-controlled techniques. Reg Anesth Pain Med 2002;27(6):604–11.

45. Davis WJ, Lennon RL, Wedel DJ. Brachial plexus anesthesia for outpatient surgical procedures on an upper extremity. Mayo Clin Proc 1991;66(5):470–73.

46. Cooper K, Kelley H, Carrithers J. Perceptions of side effects following axillary block used for outpatient surgery. Reg Anesth 1995; 20(3):212–16.

47. Ekatodramis G, Borgeat A, Huledal G, Jeppsson L, Westman L, Sjovall J. Continuous interscalene analgesia with ropivacaine 2 mg/mL after major shoulder surgery. Anesthesiology 2003;98(1): 143–50.

48. Borgeat A, Tewes E, Biasca N, Gerber C. Patient-controlled interscalene analgesia with ropivacaine after major shoulder surgery: PCIA vs PCA. Br J Anaesth 1998;81(4):603–5.

49. Klein SM, Nielsen KC, Buckenmaier CC III, Kamal AS, Rubin Y, Steele SM. 2-octyl cyanoacrylate glue for the fixation of continuous peripheral nerve catheters. Anesthesiology 2003;98(2): 590–91.

50. Tuominen MK, Pere P, Rosenberg PH. Unintentional arterial catheterization and bupivacaine toxicity associated with continuous interscalene brachial plexus block. Anesthesiology 1991;75(2): 356–58.

51. Cuvillon P, Ripart J, Lalourcey L, Veyrat E, L'Hermite J, Boisson C, et al. The continuous femoral nerve block catheter for postoperative analgesia: bacterial colonization, infectious rate and adverse effects. Anesth Analg 2001;93(4):1045–49.

52. Vintar N, Pozlep G, Rawal N, Godec M, Rakovec S. Incisional self-administration of bupivacaine or ropivacaine provides effective analgesia after inguinal hernia repair. Can J Anaesth 2002;49(5): 481–86.

53. Pettersson N, Berggren P, Larsson M, Westman B, Hahn RG. Pain relief by wound infiltration with bupivacaine or high-dose ropivacaine after inguinal hernia repair. Reg Anesth Pain Med 1999;24(6): 569–75.

54. Holte K, Werner MU, Lacouture PG, Kehlet H. Dexamethasone prolongs local analgesia after subcutaneous infiltration of bupivacaine microcapsules in human volunteers. Anesthesiology 2002;96(6): 1331–35.

55. Masters DB, Domb AJ. Liposphere local anesthetic timed-release for perineural site application. Pharm Res 1998;15(7):1038–45.

Ambulatory Wound and Intra-articular Infusions

NARINDER RAWAL

INTRODUCTION

Effective management of pain may make the difference between surgery being performed on an inpatient or day-care basis. The potential cost saving of outpatient surgery may be negated by unanticipated hospital admission for poorly treated pain. Contrary to the common belief that ambulatory surgery is followed by mild pain, recent studies have shown that undertreatment of pain is common. About 30–40% of discharged outpatients may suffer moderate to severe pain during the first 24–48 hr.[1] This pain decreases with time but may be severe enough to interfere with sleep and daily functioning. Lengthy surgical procedures and certain types of operations (orthopedic, urologic, anorectal, hernia repair, breast augmentation, laparoscopic cholecystectomy, ear, nose, and throat, dental) tend to be associated with severe pain and therefore require more analgesia. The trend toward increasing ambulatory surgery and short or nonexistent hospital stay has led to a variety of analgesic techniques to treat postoperative pain. This chapter addresses pain management issues related to incisional and intra-articular techniques in the ambulatory setting with special emphasis on catheter techniques.

INCISIONAL, INTRA-ARTICULAR, OR PERINEURAL TECHNIQUES?

Perineural, incisional, and intra-articular catheter techniques are being used increasingly to manage postoperative pain in hospitalized and day surgery patients. Local anesthetic drugs can be delivered through such catheters as continuous infusions, on-demand self-administered bolus doses by patient-controlled regional analgesia (PCRA), or low-dose background infusions with possibility of on-demand bolus doses. Patients receiving local anesthetic by infusion or PCRA may achieve more vigorous postoperative physical therapy with improved analgesia than patients receiving only oral opioid analgesics. Improvement of physical therapy analgesia by ambulatory perineural

techniques has been reported when local anesthetic is delivered through interscalene, psoas compartment, femoral, infraclavicular and axillary brachial plexus, and popliteal sciatic nerve catheters.[2–7]

However, perineural techniques have a potential for significant complications.[8,9] They also have the disadvantage of requiring exact needle placement. Even in experienced hands there is a documented failure rate with peripheral nerve blocks,[10,11] and perineural catheter tip position may be unreliable in many patients.[12] Sensory and motor block of the entire extremity prevents postoperative neurologic assessment. In general, these risks are relatively infrequent, and perineural catheter techniques have a high risk-benefit profile for hospitalized patients; however, the use of some of these techniques in unsupervised patients at home requires a special organization because of potential risk of serious complications (Table 46-1). Although this author was the first to report the use of perineural (and incisional and intra-articular) catheter analgesia at home[13,14] and the perineural catheter technique is still used at our institution, the author's preference is for incisional and intra-articular catheter techniques because of their simplicity and safety, which are the two most important prerequisites for

Table 46-1 Concerns with Perineural Catheter Techniques at Home

- Risk of damage to extremity due to motor block
- Unpleasant numbness of entire extremity
- Risk of catheter migration
- Many peripheral nerves difficult to identify, catheter tip position unreliable (documented failure rates even in experienced hands)
- Potential risk for serious complications (up to 500–700 mL of local anesthetic infused in vicinity of blood vessels in unsupervised patients)

use of such techniques at home. Another reason for restrictive use of ambulatory perineural catheters is that in Sweden (and in most countries outside the United States) extensive joint surgery, which is one of the most important indications for perineural catheter techniques, is not an ambulatory procedure.

The use of incisional and intra-articular local anesthetic drugs to treat postoperative pain is an attractive technique because of its simplicity, safety, and low cost. Administration of local anesthetic in the wound or joint has several advantages over perineural techniques for postoperative analgesia (Table 46-2). Most of the literature is based on single-dose studies; however, in recent years catheter techniques are being increasingly used for inpatients and those at home after ambulatory surgery. Catheter techniques have greatly increased the usefulness and flexibility of incisional and intra-articular analgesia for several days after surgery. The technique is simple to perform; catheters can be placed under direct or arthroscopic visualization. This eliminates the risk of inadvertent penetration of vascular or neural structures. In addition, only the area of surgery is affected, allowing normal use of the extremity and early rehabilitation.[15] The incisional and intra-articular use of opioids and a variety of nonopioids alone or in combination with local anesthetics has also been studied.

LOCAL ANESTHETIC INCISIONAL INFILTRATION

Local anesthesia is an efficient, nonopioid pharmacologic approach to postoperative analgesia. Any pain management technique should be simple, safe, and inexpensive, and wound infiltration qualifies on these terms. It might be even more effective in outpatients with surgical procedures of less magnitude in which fewer tissue planes are crossed during the surgery.[16] Different infiltration techniques have been shown to be pain-reducing and opioid-sparing after cholecystectomy,[17] inguinal hernia repair,[18] breast surgery,[19] gynecologic laparotomies,[20] orthopedic,[21] anorectal,[22] and cardiac[23] surgery.

Table 46-2　Advantages of Incisional or Intra-articular Catheter Techniques (vs. Perineural Techniques)

- Catheters can be placed under direct vision or arthroscopic visualization
- Affects only the surgical area, thereby allowing normal use of extremity for early rehabilitation
- Eliminates unpleasant numbness of entire extremity due to sensory block
- Eliminates risk of damage to extremity due to motor block
- Eliminates risks due to vascular, neural, or pleural (interscalene block) placement of needle or catheter

A systematic review of over 90 studies showed that incisional techniques have analgesic effects in some but not all surgical procedures.[24] However, the systematic review was based on single-dose studies. The role of the technique used for local anesthetic administration may be crucial but it has been poorly studied. The relative contribution of different anatomic structures also needs to be evaluated; for example, there is some evidence that subfascial lidocaine may be more effective compared to subcutaneous administration after inguinal hernia surgery.[25] Also, improved pain relief has been noted if visceral structures are exposed to local anesthetic drugs in laparoscopic surgery.[26]

INCISIONAL CATHETER TECHNIQUES

Direct perfusion of surgical wounds with a solution of local anesthetic through an indwelling irrigation apparatus was first described by Capelle in 1936 and consisted of several large, thin, curved, hollow needles attached to a tube.[27] Blades and Ford evaluated the technique further in 1950. They placed small plastic tubes at the "inferior border of four ribs" and employed sutures to hold the tubes in place. The tubes were brought out at the anterior angle of the wound. The plastic tubes were placed over needles, which were then fitted through a cork. A sterile rubber cap was placed on the needles between injections. The authors used 2 mL of 1–2% procaine every 3 hr and demonstrated superior analgesia at rest and movement with a significant reduction in morphine requirement. There was no wound infection or any problem with wound healing. The authors concluded: "The method is easy and the results gratifying."[28] The technique was also used for postoperative analgesia after cholecystectomy[29] and gastric surgery.[30] However, the fear of potential infection and wound healing prevented the technique from becoming adopted as a routine method.

The introduction of longer-acting local anesthetic drugs and bacterial filters led to renewed interest in the 1980s in this modality of postoperative pain management,[31,32] but this interest was also short-lived. In 1997 the author described a technique that allowed self-administration of local anesthetic through incisional and perineural catheters for pain management at home after a variety of ambulatory surgical procedures.[13,14] This PCRA technique was made possible by disposable, elastomeric pumps (Fig. 46-1). The availability of safer elastomeric and other lightweight pump devices, improved catheters, and the preference for nonopioid analgesic techniques has led to the use of this technique for pain management after a variety of surgical procedures. Several studies have demonstrated that wound infusion with local anesthesia is effective after a number of surgical procedures. Incisional catheter techniques by intermittent boluses or continuous infusions have been used for postoperative analgesia after different surgical procedures such as hernia repair,[33] laparoscopic cholecystectomy,[34] cesarean section[33,36] cardiac surgery,[23] and sternal fracture.[37] They have been shown to be as effective as intravenous (IV) opioid patient-controlled analgesia (PCA) after laparotomy.[38] Significant reduction of postoperative opioid requirements and nausea has been reported after hysterectomy,[39] hip and knee joint re-

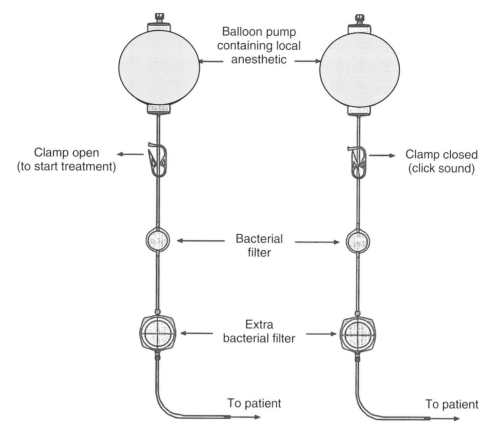

Figure 46-1 The elastomeric pump allows self-administration of local anesthetic. When the clamp is opened (left), the solution starts running into the catheter. After 6 min the patient closes the clamp to stop the infusion (right). (From Rawal N, Axelsson K, Hylander J, Allvin R, Amilon A, Lidegran G, Hallen J. Postoperative patient-controlled local anesthetic administration at home. Anesth Analg 1998;86(1):86–89. Reprinted with permission from Lippincott Williams and Wilkins.)

placement,[40] and anterior cruciate ligament (ACL) reconstruction.[41] The technique has also been used in the management of chronic pain[42] and cancer pain.[43] Catheters have been placed subcutaneously, subfascially, suprafascially, submuscularly, supraperiosteally, intra-articularly and intraperitoneally[14,23,34] (Fig. 46-2).

In the ambulatory setting incisional catheter techniques have been used for the following types of surgery: breast augmentation, maxillofacial surgery, bone harvesting from iliac crest,[14] laparoscopic cholecystectomy,[34] inguinal herniorrhaphy,[14,33] and hand surgery.[44] The type of procedure that qualifies as ambulatory surgery varies consider-

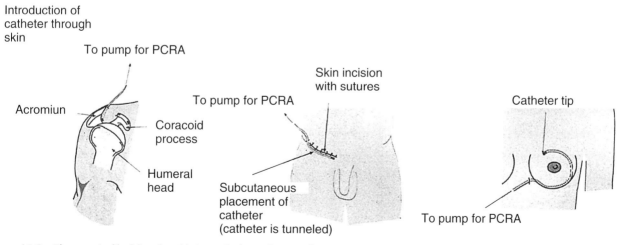

Figure 46-2 Placement of incisional and intra-articular catheters. The position of catheter placement following shoulder surgery (left), inguinal hernia surgery (center), and breast augmentation (right). All catheters are tunneled 3–4 cm subcutaneously for better fixation and reducing risk of infection. Catheters are taped and connected to elastomeric pumps.

ably in many countries depending on differences in health care systems and reimbursement policies. For example, inguinal hernia surgery is not an ambulatory procedure in many countries. The study by Vintar et al. showed that incisional catheter technique using ropivacaine through an elastomeric pump provides effective analgesia; however, it was not an ambulatory procedure in Slovenia at the time of the study.[33] Considering that incisional catheter techniques have been used successfully to treat pain after laparatomy, hysterectomy, cesarean section, hip and knee joint replacement, and ACL reconstruction, it can be expected that the role of these catheter techniques will increase when these procedures are performed on ambulatory basis. Some of these surgeries are already ambulatory surgical procedures in the United States.

A technique has been described in which immediate pain-free mobilization after tenolysis or tenosynovectomy is achieved by administration of bupivacaine instilled along the flexor sheath through a thin percutaneous catheter. Patients were sent home with their catheters; they self-administered 1–3 mL 0.5% bupivacaine before mobilization and exercises prescribed by the hand therapist. Mobilization was continued once daily in outpatients for 6 days during the first week. Catheters were removed when the patients could perform the exercises without pain. Difficulties in infiltrating all relevant structures, especially after major surgery, may limit the efficacy of wound infiltration.[47]

Since all nociceptive impulses do not originate from the surgical wound only, clearly there are limits to what incisional techniques can achieve. For many major surgical procedures epidural or perineural catheter techniques are still the gold standard. However, there is a need for studies that compare these simple, local-anesthesia-based techniques with IV opioid PCA and the much more invasive epidural and perineural techniques. Incisional catheter techniques in combination with balanced analgesic regimens using paracetamol and nonsteroidal anti-inflammatory drugs (NSAIDs) with or without judicious amounts of opioids may reduce or eliminate the need for IV opioid PCA and epidural techniques in some (but not all) major surgeries.

LOCAL ANESTHETIC INSTILLATION WITH AND WITHOUT CATHETERS

Instillation of local anesthetics without infiltration has also been proven efficacious. Topical analgesia with lidocaine aerosol has been found to be highly effective after inguinal herniorrhaphy,[45] and instillation of bupivacaine with epinephrine or lidocaine during laparoscopy reduces postoperative scapular pain. This technique has been used mainly for laparoscopic cholecystectomy and gynecologic surgery.

Contrary to the general belief, pain after laparoscopic surgery can be distressing. It is multifactorial and involves three different components with different intensity, time course, and pathophysiologic mechanisms. These include incisional pain (parietal pain), deep intra-abdominal pain (visceral pain), and shoulder pain (referred pain). For laparoscopic cholecystectomy there are conflicting reports

about the most painful component. Some studies show that incisional pain dominates over deep intra-abdominal and shoulder pain.[46] However, other studies report that visceral pain is the major component.[47] The rapid distension of the peritoneum leads to traction of nerves and release of inflammatory nociceptive mediators, and intra-abdominal surgical procedures add to tissue injury and produce visceral pain.[48] Several local anesthetic techniques have been employed to treat postlaparoscopy pain. Injection of local anesthetic into the subdiaphragmatic area has been shown to reduce shoulder pain for 48 hr.[49] The analgesic effect of intraperitoneal local anesthetics is unclear since available studies give conflicting data. Effective postoperative pain relief after intraperitoneal local anesthetic instillation and wound infiltration has been claimed[50] and denied.[51] The literature does not provide a clear relation between analgesia, dose of local anesthetic, and the site of application, and the evidence for improved analgesia with intraperitoneal local anesthetics remains inconclusive.[46] In a study comparing intraperitoneal 100 mg and 300 mg of ropivacaine with placebo it was demonstrated that both doses provided equally effective pain relief after laparoscopic cholecystectomy. As expected, the plasma concentrations were lower with smaller doses.[47] In a review of literature Bisgaard et al. report that publications support the routine use of incisional local anesthetics to reduce overall pain in patients having laparoscopic cholecystectomy.[46] Again, almost all literature is based on single-dose studies.

As with laparoscopic cholecystectomy, there are several components of pain after laparoscopic gynecologic surgery. Scapular pain secondary to peritoneal insufflation, especially when shoulder holders and exaggerated Trendelenburg position is used, tends to appear many hours after surgery, and hinders sleep. Infiltration of local anesthetics decreases scapular pain. Visceral pain has its maximal intensity during the first hours and is exacerbated by coughing, respiratory movements, and mobilization. It has been shown that intraperitoneal instillation of 100 mg of bupivacaine or 150 mg of ropivacaine at the end of laparoscopic gynecologic surgery can significantly reduce the need for morphine administration during the first 24 hr and also reduce the incidence of postoperative nausea and vomiting (PONV).[51]

In a recent study Gupta et al. have demonstrated that 10 mL of 0.5% ropivacaine bolus administered on demand through a catheter placed in the gallbladder bed reduced deep pain and pain on coughing in patients undergoing ambulatory laparoscopic cholecystectomy. The catheters were removed before the patients were discharged home at 20 hr after surgery. However, the analgesic effect was of short duration.[34]

The importance of the technique of intraperitoneal local anesthetic administration was demonstrated in a controlled study by Labaille et al. Local anesthetic or placebo solutions were given as follows: immediately after the creation of a pneumoperitoneum, the surgeon sprayed 10 mL of solution into the hepatodiaphragmatic space, 5 mL in the area of the gallbladder, and 5 mL into the space between liver and kidney. At the end of the operation, before the trocars were withdrawn, the surgeon sprayed an additional 20 mL of the solution onto the same areas. This study demonstrated that fractioned injection of 100 mg of intraperitoneal ropivacaine produces postoperative analgesia after laparoscopic cholecystectomy better than what was obtained with intraperitoneal placebo.[47] Increasing the dose to 300 mg did not improve efficacy but unsurprisingly led to excessively large plasma concentrations.

Although the efficacy of local anesthetic infiltration has been demonstrated in numerous studies in laparoscopic cholecystectomy, there is a lack of consensus regarding the dose, concentration, site, and manner of administration. Scheinin et al. failed to show efficacy; however, the entire dose of 150 mg of bupivacaine was instilled under the right hemidiaphragm.[52] In gynecology, decreased postoperative pain scores after local anesthetic administration have been reported. Here as well, however, the mode of administration lacks standardization, e.g., infiltration on the trajectory of the trocars, infiltration of the uterine tubes, and peritoneal instillation before and after insufflation.

ADJUVANTS TO LOCAL ANESTHETICS FOR INCISIONAL ANALGESIA

Several studies show that local infiltration with adjuvants such as opioids and nonopioids (NSAIDs) provides effective postoperative analgesia. NSAIDs have been used more frequently than opioids for wound infiltration. The most common indications have been inguinal hernia surgery, mastectomy, tonsillectomy, and hand surgery. Ketolorac and tenoxicam have been used most frequently. A literature review showed that the results of wound infiltration with NSAIDs are inconclusive.[53] Opioids have been administered close to nerve trunks and nerve endings to improve the efficacy of regional anesthesia and postoperative analgesia. The basis for this approach is the presence of opioid receptors and their endogenous ligands in the peripheral nervous system, and their effect on inflammatory pain.[54,55] Efficacy of peripheral opioids has been tested in experimental pain trials in volunteers, and in a large variety of surgical sites including incisional, dental, intrapleural, intraperitoneal, and intravenous regional anesthesia (IVRA). The technique has also been studied for perineural blocks such as intercostal, brachial plexus, femoral nerve, and ankle block.[55] Several opioids have been studied. A systematic review showed that morphine was the most commonly used opioid; the other opioids were fentanyl, alfentanil, buprenorphine, and butorphanol. Although no adverse effects were reported, the systematic review did not provide any evidence for a clinically relevant peripheral analgesic efficacy of opioids in acute pain.[55]

INTRA-ARTICULAR ANALGESIA

Many orthopedic surgeons commonly practice intra-articular administration of local anesthetic for diagnostic and some minor therapeutic procedures. The intra-articular technique has been used most frequently for knee and shoulder surgery, particularly for patients undergoing these surgeries on an outpatient basis. The technique has also been used for management of peri- and postoperative analgesia. Although arthroscopy of the knee decreases morbidity compared with open procedures, it does not eliminate pain.[56,57] Most of the intra-articular structures of the knee, including the joint capsule, synovial tissue, and anterior fat pad, have nerve endings and are capable of producing severe pain.[57,58] Inadequate pain relief and swelling may delay rehabilitation and return to work for up to 2 weeks after surgery.[59]

Pain management after major shoulder surgery remains challenging. Even minor arthroscopic shoulder surgery is often associated with severe postoperative pain.[60] Effective postoperative pain relief may be critical after shoulder surgery because pain restricts physiotherapy, which is crucial in preventing subsequent limitation of joint movement.[61] Systemic opioids are frequently used to treat postoperative pain after shoulder surgery; however, such techniques are associated with the well-known adverse effects such as nausea, vomiting, and respiratory depression.[61] In recent years peripheral nerve blocks such as interscalene, suprascapular, or axillary blocks as primary or supplemental anesthesia and to eliminate or decrease postoperative pain are increasingly used in some shoulder centers. Although effective, these blocks do have the potential for significant complications. Also, since needle and catheter placement has to be proximal to the operative area, it results in blockade of the nerve and muscle function in the entire arm, which prevents postoperative neurologic assessment.

Recent developments in intra-articular analgesia include study of best site of drug delivery, use of drug combinations, and use of catheter techniques. For example, it has been demonstrated that for some knee surgery procedures the effect of morphine is better if it is administered into the synovial tissue or the outer third of the meniscus rather than intra-articularly. For shoulder surgery, subacromial and intrabursal catheter techniques have been reported.

INTRA-ARTICULAR LOCAL ANESTHETICS

Intra-articular local anesthetics are frequently used in perioperative pain management; however, its analgesic efficacy is controversial. Analgesic effects have been claimed[57,62,63] and denied.[64,65] As some arthroscopic procedures can be successfully performed under intra-articular and incisional local anesthesia alone, it may be surprising that intra-articular local anesthetics do not consistently provide analgesia. These conflicting reports are due to problems with study designs. There is considerable variation in doses, volumes, and concentrations used in the various studies. Other confounding variables have been concomitant use of other analgesic methods or drugs such as NSAIDs, opioids, epinephrine, clonidine, cryotherapy, tourniquets, and infiltration of portals. Furthermore, in some investigations the pain intensity in the study groups and particularly control groups was relatively low.[64-66] A systematic review showed evidence of improved pain relief after intra-articular local anesthesia in 12 of 20 studies comprising almost 900 patients. The authors concluded that there was a weak evidence for reduction of postoperative pain and that the technique may be of clinical significance in ambulatory surgery.[67]

INTRA-ARTICULAR OPIOIDS

It is unclear why systematic reviews have shown some efficacy of morphine in the knee joint but no efficacy of opioids in peripheral sites outside the knee joint. This may be because the knee joint model better reflects the inflammatory process that is believed to be important in sensitizing peripheral opioid receptors.[68] It may also be related to inadequate opioid doses. Doses of morphine (0.5–5 mg) in the confined space of the knee joint can produce high local concentrations;[69] although similar doses injected into isolated limb or peritoneal or pleural cavity would produce much lower concentrations.[55] In general, adjuvants to local anesthetics have been much used only for single-bolus injection techniques.

The inflammatory response to surgery has been shown to be necessary to express the opioid receptors in the joint. Opioid receptors have been shown in synovial tissues under inflammatory conditions. Blood levels of opioids after intra-articular injection are quite low, suggesting that the effect of morphine is produced peripherally. The analgesic effect of intra-articular morphine and bupivacaine depends on the type of arthroscopic surgery performed. Intra-articular morphine has a better analgesic effect in surgeries with a higher inflammatory response while intra-articular bupivacaine has a better analgesic effect in surgeries such as diagnostic arthroscopies and partial meniscectomies with a lower inflammatory response. Bupivacaine seems more efficient when the synovial layer is intact.

It is generally accepted that locally administered opioids produce analgesia in the presence of inflammation and not in normal tissue. The possible reasons are: (a) inflammation induces a disruption of perineurium, which allows easier access of opioids to receptors, (b) previously inactive opioid receptors may be rendered active or become unmasked by inflammation, or (c) a combination of both mechanisms.[70] Intra-articular opioids provide pain relief by analgesic or anti-inflammatory effect or both.[71] Since the first report of intra-articular administration of morphine in humans in 1991,[72] numerous studies have confirmed that intra-articular morphine can provide effective and prolonged postoperative analgesia. However, in other studies the effects of intra-articular morphine have been less impressive. Various factors have been implicated in pain after arthroscopy and the effectiveness of intra-articular analgesia. These include preoperative pain scores, type and duration of surgery, experience of the surgeon, type of anesthesia (general or regional), dosage and volume of analgesic drug, use of epinephrine, and timing of intra-articular injection in relation to tourniquet release. Other confounding factors are day-case versus inpatient surgery, use of premedication and perioperative opioids, pain assessment on rest or on movement, and different methods of statistical analysis of pain scores.[73]

In a recent systematic review of studies available in the literature it was concluded that intra-articular morphine produces a definite but mild analgesic effect lasting up to 24 hr. This effect may be dose-dependent.[74] This long duration of a single dose of morphine was confirmed by a second systematic review by Kalso et al.[75] These authors separated sensitive and insensitive studies in the reviewed literature. Sensitive studies were those where the experienced pain intensity was ≥ 30% of a maximum of 100 on visual analog scale (VAS) in placebo groups. By including only sensitive studies, the authors could show that 5 mg intra-articular morphine in the knee joint provided up to 27 hr analgesia.[75]

Direct injection into the inflamed tissue of either the meniscus or the synovia may increase the period of tissue binding to opioids, creating a longer and stronger effect.[76] Kligman et al. compared the administration of morphine intra-articularly with its administration into the synovia or the outer third of the meniscus and demonstrated that direct injection of morphine into the synovial tissue or the outer third of the meniscus provides better pain relief than intra-articular morphine at 12 and 24 hr postoperatively.[76]

Intra-articular morphine is a better postoperative analgesic in those surgical procedures with more inflammation and pain. Intra-articular bupivacaine is a better postoperative analgesic in those procedures with less inflammation and pain, such as diagnostic arthroscopy and partial meniscectomy. Marchal et al. have shown that a different effect of intra-articular morphine and bupivacaine is found depending on the type of arthroscopic surgery performed. They included two groups of patients: low-inflammatory and high-inflammatory groups. The latter group underwent more extensive knee surgery (sinovial plicae removal, patellar shaving, lateral retinacular release, and ACL reconstruction).[77] These findings support the theory that inflammation is required for a peripheral analgesic effect of opioids. This analgesic effect was maximal 24 hr after surgery, as found by other authors. In patients subjected to "high-inflammatory" surgery, bupivacaine showed no analgesic effect. The long duration of intra-articular morphine analgesia (about 24 hr) may be explained by a large depot of drug being available for hours when inflammation in the knee joint slowly develops and activates silent opioid receptors and induces the transport of new opioid receptors into peripheral nerve endings. However, current evidence does not exclude a systemic effect or a local anesthetic effect.[75]

INTRA-ARTICULAR CATHETER TECHNIQUES

Intra-articular administration of local anesthetic has been used to provide surgical and postoperative pain relief for shoulder surgery. Most studies have focused on the shoulder joint because many patients experience moderate to severe pain after shoulder surgery. In recent years prolonged intra-articular analgesia has been achieved by continuous infusion of local anesthetic using disposable infusion pumps. The technique has the advantages of delivering local anesthetic to the surgical site, and ease and simplicity of catheter insertion and infusion device.[3] However, the literature so far is modest.

In a controlled trial of patients undergoing subacromial decompression, Savoie et al. demonstrated that 2 mL/hr 0.25% bupivacaine, infused into the subacromial area just beneath the resected edge of the acromion, provided significantly better analgesia than "saline." There was a significantly reduced need for postoperative rescue analgesics.[15] Klein et al. compared intra-articular infusion of 0.5% ropivacaine 2 mL/hr for 48 hr with placebo for pain management under interscalene brachial plexus block. The authors demonstrated that intra-articular infusion of local anesthetic resulted in prolonged analgesia (48 hr) and a 30% reduction in mean opioid consumption.[3]

At the author's institution Axelsson et al. evaluated the efficacy of PCRA during a 24-hr period after arthroscopic subacromial decompression. Catheters were introduced into the subacromial space under direct arthroscopic vision, ensuring that the holes of the catheter were beneath and close to the resected area of the rough subacromial bone surface (Fig. 46-2). The surgeon injected 25 mL of 1% ropivacaine (250 mg) via the catheter into the wound.[78] Self-administered boluses of 10 mL 0.5% ropivacaine provided effective analgesia in patients undergoing arthroscopic subacromial decompression. Morphine consumption was significantly reduced. Catheter tip cultures did not reveal any infection.[78] In another study of patients undergoing ambulatory open arthroscopic shoulder surgery (Bankart procedure) intra-articular ketolorac, morphine, and local anesthetic combination followed by intra-articular ropivacaine boluses on demand (PCRA) at home provided significantly better pain relief and reduced morphine consumption.[78]

In a controlled trial Barber and Herber have demonstrated that 0.5% bupivacaine infusion at a rate of 2 mL/hr for 48 hr provided effective analgesia after arthroscopic shoulder surgery. For subacromial and rotator cuff surgery the catheter was placed in the subacromial space. For glenohumeral surgery the catheter was placed in the glenohumeral joint. The outpatient surgical procedures also included rotator cuff repairs, superior labrum anterior-posterior lesion repairs, subacromial decompression, and capsular reefings.[79]

In another controlled study of pain management after ambulatory ACL reconstruction, Alford and Fadale compared intra-articular catheter technique using local anesthetic and saline versus no catheter (control group). All patients received a femoral nerve block. Group I received no catheter (control), group II received intra-articular catheter with saline (placebo), and group III received intra-articular catheter with 0.25% bupivacaine continuous infusion; catheters were placed in the anterior joint space and removed on day 4. The pain management protocol also included hydrocodone/acetaminophen, ibuprofen, cryotherapy, and leg elevation. The authors stratified their data on pain scores and demonstrated that median pain scores were better with both catheter techniques; however, bupivacaine infusion protected patients from the spikes of maximum pain.[41] It is conceivable that the results could have been even better if the authors had used a larger dose than the reported 200 mL for 3 days.

In most studies with wound or intra-articular catheter techniques the surgical procedure has been shoulder arthroscopy. However, Gottchalk et al. have used the technique for open shoulder surgery. After skin closure a sin-gle-dose wound infiltration was performed by a blinded orthopedic surgeon. Patients were randomly assigned to receive a total volume of 30 mL of saline or 30 mL of ropivacaine 7.5 mg/mL. Twenty milliliters of the respective study solution was injected after closure of the skin into the wound using the wound drain, which was then clamped for 20 min. An additional 10 mL was injected subcutaneously at both sides of the wound. Directly afterward the inserted catheter was connected to an elastomeric infusion pump, which contained 300 mL of saline, ropivacaine 2 mg/mL, or ropivacaine 3.75 mg/mL. With an insertion needle the catheters were placed in the subacromial space after subacromial and rotator cuff surgery and in the glenohumeral joint after glenohumeral surgery. With an infusion rate of 2 mL/hr mean pain scores were significantly lower during 7 postoperative days in the treatment group. Catheters were removed 48 hr after surgery.[80]

In contrast to the usually mild-to-moderate pain after diagnostic shoulder arthroscopy or minor arthroscopic shoulder surgery, pain after acromioplasty or rotator cuff reconstruction can be quite intense. The subacromial bursa presents a suitable compartment for drug delivery. Intrabursal administration of a combination of local anesthetic and opioid (e.g., oxycodone) offers an effective method of analgesia after shoulder surgery.[81] This technique has been developed further by Park et al., who studied the effect of a continuous infusion of intrabursal bupivacaine and morphine in patients undergoing subacromial arthroscopy. Patients with impingement syndrome, rotator cuff partial tear, acromioclavicular joint arthritis, and those with calcific tendonitis of the rotator cuff were studied. After stitching of the arthroscopic portal, a bolus of 5 mL of 0.5% bupivacaine and 2 mg of morphine was administered followed by subacromial infusion of 0.5 mL/hr for 3 postoperative days. The saline group received a subacromial intrabursal injection of 5 mL. In this controlled study continuous intrabursal infusion with morphine and bupivacaine for postoperative analgesia for 2 days after subacromial arthroscopy resulted in effective pain relief.[82]

Intra-articular catheter technique has also been used to treat pain after major knee surgery. In a double-blind, placebo-controlled study of pain management after ambulatory ACL reconstruction, Alford and Fadale compared intra-articular catheter technique using local anesthetic and saline versus no catheter (control group). All patients received a femoral nerve block. Group I received no catheter (control), group II received intra-articular catheter with saline (placebo), and group III received intra-articular catheter with 0.25% bupivacaine continuous infusion; catheters were placed in the anterior joint space and removed on postoperative day 4. The pain management protocol also included hydrocodone/acetaminophen, ibuprofen, cryotherapy, and leg elevation. In addition to analgesia and catheter function, patients also recorded range of motion and ability to perform straight-leg raises. To better study the analgesic effect of bupivacaine the authors stratified the pain ratings as maximum, minimum, and median. This study suggested some element of placebo effect from the presence of a catheter at lower pain levels, but also showed the protective effect of bupivacaine from spikes of maximum pain.[41]

Although the last three studies were in inpatients, they are included in this chapter because in many centers in the United States these surgical procedures are performed on an ambulatory basis. About 40% of patients undergoing knee arthroscopy have mild or no pain. Clearly this is a confounding factor because in the literature all patients are included in intra-articular morphine studies. Rosseland et al. used intra-articular catheter technique to improve the sensitivity of the study design. By leaving an intra-articular catheter in 57 patients and including only patients who developed moderate-to-severe pain within 1 hr after knee arthroscopy (n = 40), they could demonstrate that only 70% of patients had moderate-to-severe pain and that 10 mL intra-articular saline was as effective as 10 mL saline with 2 mg morphine. The analgesic efficacy of 10 mL saline may be due to a placebo effect or due to an antinociceptive effect by diluting algogenic substances in the newly traumatized knee joint. It is also possible that intra-articular saline has inherent pain-relieving effects in this model and therefore should not be regarded as an inactive placebo.[83]

RISK OF DELAYED WOUND HEALING AND INFECTION

Almost all clinical studies of local anesthetic infiltration have reported only general, subjective impression of wound healing over a relatively short time; their main focus has been the analgesic efficacy of wound infiltration. This short time period will miss incisional hernias, many of which are manifested only months or years after surgery. The reported incidence of early wound disruption is 0.5–3% and that of incisional hernia is about 1%; the risk increases considerably in the aged, diabetic, obese, and those with vascular disease.[84] Wound healing is a complex process that involves multiple cell types, cellular migration and contraction, extracellular protein synthesis, disposal of dead cells and debris, and modulation of inflammatory response to destroy pathogens without harming the wound. There are three stages of wound healing: (a) inflammatory, (b) granulation/proliferation, and (c) *remodelling*. Achievement of final strength (about 70% of original skin strength) requires 6–12 months via remodeling. Animal and in vitro studies have shown that inhibition of healing appears to be a general property of all local anesthetic drugs. This inhibition of wound healing is both time- and concentration-dependent, suggesting a concern with prolonged LA administration into the wound by catheter technique or sustained-release drug. Thus, there is a need for studies that measure wound strength and healing both at the end of the second stage (3–4 weeks) as well as at the end of the third stage (6–12 months), particularly in patients at a higher risk of wound complications.[84]

INTRA-ARTICULAR CATHETER TECHNIQUE AND INFECTION RISK

The incidence of infection after arthroscopic surgery is generally very low: 0–0.2%. Rosseland et al. reported no infection in over 150 patients treated with intra-articular catheter.[85] We have not seen any infection after subacromial catheters during the last 6 years. Park et al. did not report any infection in their study of intrabursal catheter technique for shoulder surgery.[82]

PATIENT-CONTROLLED REGIONAL ANESTHESIA OR CONTINUOUS INFUSION?

Local anesthetics can be delivered through perineural, incisional, and intra-articular catheters as continuous infusions, background infusions with possibility of on-demand boli, or on-demand boli only by PCRA. In most studies with ambulatory catheters, patients have been given fixed-dose, continuous-infusion local anesthetic until the contents of the elastomeric pumps are depleted. The electronic pumps allow the possibility of continuous infusion and PCRA; however, in general patients are uncomfortable with reprogramming of such pumps even if physicians provide instructions on the phone.[86] Given a choice, patients prefer the simplicity of elastomeric pumps.[87] This author prefers the PCRA bolus approach for the following reasons: it is well accepted that there is a great interindividual variation in analgesic requirements for postoperative pain. Since the duration of a single-dose local anesthetic varies considerably (3–12 hr), PCRA by intermittent on-demand bolus doses may be preferable to continuous infusion because it permits the patient to correct for individual variations in intensity and duration of postoperative pain. The authors' group studies have shown that the range of bolus administrations at home can vary from 0 to 10 (maximum allowed). The natural course after surgery is that pain decreases with time. Furthermore, it is well known that some patients do not need any analgesia after surgery.[83,88] The basal rate requirements can be highly variable and unpredictable. This was noted in a recent study of infraclavicular brachial plexus perineural infusion. The basal infusion rate of 8 mL/hr was optimal for about 21% of patients, 53% required a higher rate, and 26% required a lower rate.[89] There is no method to accurately predict individual patients' basal rate requirements, which may be influenced by patients' sensitivity to local anesthetics, surgical procedure, and accuracy of perineural catheter tip position.[89] Thus, with continuous-infusion catheter techniques many patients are overdosed because of the erroneous belief that every patient has severe, unremitting pain all the time.

Comparisons between intermittent-bolus and continuous-infusion techniques for epidural or perineural analgesia have shown that intermittent-bolus techniques, especially by PCRA, provide as good or better analgesia with significant dose reduction and consequently fewer side effects and better patient satisfaction.[90–94] PCRA is useful for ambulatory patients because it allows bolus dosing before physical therapy. PCRA permits patients to maintain adequate analgesia regardless of changes in pain intensity over time. A bolus of large volume by PCRA may provide a better quality of block owing to greater spread of local anesthetic solution. In an experimental study of subcutaneously placed catheter in pigs the author has seen that intermittent administration with 5 mL and 10 mL boluses resulted in a larger area of diffusion of dye compared to continuous infusions of 2 mL/hr and 5 mL/hr (unpublished observations). Furthermore, it has been demonstrated that intermittent bolus of local anesthetic in axillary brachial plexus catheters results in lower plasma bupivacaine levels compared with continuous infusion despite similar total doses.[95] However, this may or may not be applicable for incisional and for intra-articular catheter techniques. The psychologic benefit of self-pain management may also be important.

Extensive experience over more than two decades with IV opioid PCA has shown that patient satisfaction is very high when patients are allowed to manage their own pain. Local anesthetic incisional and intra-articular PCRA has been successfully used to provide postoperative analgesia after surgical procedures such as cesarean section,[35] hysterectomy,[39] hernia repair,[33] shoulder surgery,[14,77,78] hand surgery, bone harvesting from iliac crest, maxillofacial surgery, mastectomy, and breast augmentation surgery.[14] The technique has also been used to treat chronic pain and cancer pain.[42,43] However, the issue is controversial and further studies are needed to establish the pros and cons of continuous infusion, PCRA, or combination of these techniques.

WHICH PUMP—ELECTRONIC OR ELASTOMERIC?

Since these techniques are relatively new, there are only limited data about the performance of pumps. A large variety of pumps are available on the market (Figs. 46-3, 46-4). Many companies keep introducing new modifications and claiming improved performance; however, there are no controlled studies. To determine the optimal device for safe delivery of local anesthetic at home, factors that need to be considered are flow-rate accuracy, infusion flexibility, and total local anesthetic volume requirement. In general, there are two types of pumps: single-use elastomeric and multiple-use electronic pumps. It is beyond the scope of this chapter to go into details about the pros and cons of the multiple devices on the market.

If different rates of infusion, bolus volumes, and lockout times are desired, then an electronic pump will be necessary. The infusion can be tailored to provide a minimum basal rate and also allow bolus dosing for breakthrough pain and prior to physical therapy. The majority of nonelectronic pumps do not allow for both a basal rate and patient-controlled bolus and are exclusively single-use devices. Many elastomeric pumps have varying accuracy and consistency, and may have flow rates within ±15% of their expected rate. Infusion rates and infusion duration may be unpredictable. Some pumps regulate their infusion rate using a temperature-dependent device affixed to the patient. A change in the temperature of this regulator, for example due to change in skin temperature or the detachment of the regulator, may further decrease infusion accuracy considerably. However, elastomeric pumps are available whose flow varies little with time and temperature. Elastomeric pumps have reservoir volumes that are less than 300 mL (although some brands do provide up to 550 mL). If large

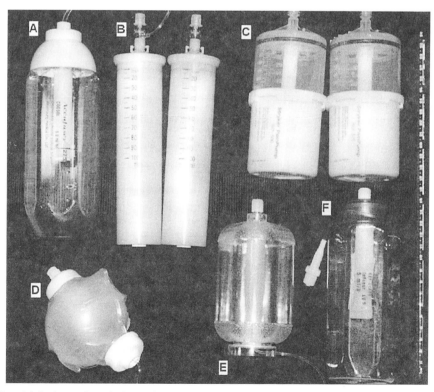

Figure 46-3   Portable basal-infusion-only or bolus-only nonelectronic pumps. (A) Accufuser, (B) Sgarlato, (C) Pain Pump, (D) C-Bloc, (E) Infusor, (F) Infusor LV5. (Reproduced by permission from Ilfield BM, Enneking K. Ambulatory perineural local anesthetic infusion. Tech Reg Anesth Pain Manag 2003;7:48–54.)

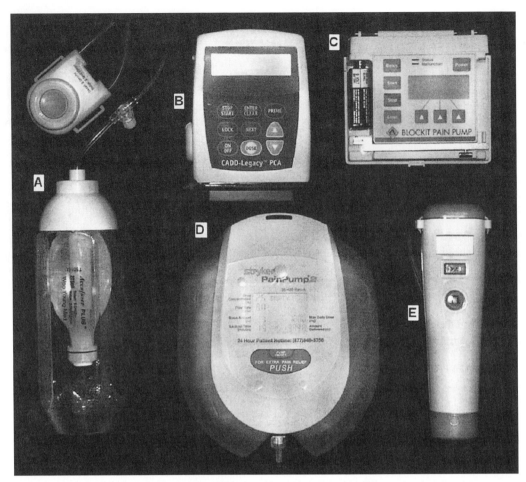

Figure 46-4 Portable pumps with basal infusion and possibility of bolus function. (A) Accufuser Plus, (B) Legacy, (C) Blockit, (D) Pain Pump 2, and (E) Palm Pump. (Reproduced by permission from Ilfield BM, Enneking K. Ambulatory perineural local anesthetic infusion. Tech Reg Anesth Pain Manag 2003;7:48–54.)

volumes of local anesthetic are prescribed as basal infusion, the total volume of the drug may not be adequate to last for the entire duration of 2–3 days generally necessary for surgical procedures with moderate-to-severe pain.

Most electronic pumps use an external bag and up to 1000-mL reservoirs. In general, electronic pumps are more expensive. This requires the patient to return the pump to the ambulatory surgery center; alternatively there has to be a system that ensures return of the pump by mail with a good organization for reuse of electronic pumps. Most of the cost data are available from the United States. In general, the cost of disposable elastomeric pumps is much higher in the United States (even for pumps made in the United States) than in Europe. Although the nonelectronic elastomeric pumps are not as accurate and as flexible as electronic pumps, studies show that patients prefer simple devices that avoid the need for reprogramming or the problems due to frequent alarms.[86,87] There is extensive experience with nonelectronic pumps providing safe and effective postoperative analgesia at home.

At the author's institution PCRA techniques have been used with an elastomeric pump (IFlow Corporation, Lake Forest, CA, USA) since 1997 (Fig. 46-1). Recently the author

has also introduced a new safer modification (Rawal pump) (Fig. 46-5). Several controlled trials at the author's institution[5,14,34,77] and the author's group experience with over 1000 patients suggest that the technique is effective and safe. These studies have also resulted in the increasing use of ropivacaine. The optimal equipment for perineural, incisional, or intra-articular ambulatory catheter techniques should be determined by controlled trials, and not merely by institutional preference or claims by device companies. Simplicity and safety are not mutually exclusive and the physician should ensure that the selected device provides the prescribed dose of local anesthetic within reasonable limits.

ORGANIZATIONAL ISSUES OF CATHETER TECHNIQUES AT HOME

All authors who have used ambulatory perineural incisional catheters emphasize the importance of a good organization as a prerequisite for the safe delivery of such analgesic techniques at home. However, there is no consensus on the requirements for such an organization. Some practitioners

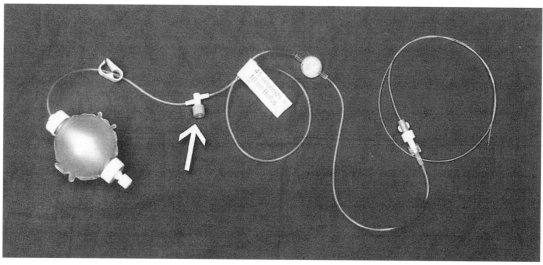

Figure 46-5   Recently a safer elastomeric pump has been introduced. This device (Rawal pump) has a bolus button (arrow), which the patient has to press for 45 sec to receive a 10-mL bolus. This is an improvement on the earlier elastomeric pumps where failure to close the clamp could result in the accidental delivery of the entire contents of the balloon pump.

have patients remove their catheters at home at the conclusion of their infusion; others prefer removing the catheters themselves. Some discharge patients with written instructions regarding catheter removal, and others give verbal instructions over the phone during removal. Some investigators have provided twice-daily home nursing visits, whereas others have relied on daily telephone contact.[86] Studies from the United States show that the organization is quite elaborate and includes: physician availability at all times, twice-daily home nursing visits in addition to telephone calls, catheter removal by health care provider or by patients caretaker with instructions on the phone by the anesthesiologist.[2,4] Our organization is quite simple and consists of verbal and written predischarge information about pump function and use of PCRA rescue analgesic medication, symptoms of local anesthetic toxicity, local hygiene, catheter removal, return of completed patient diary, and contact numbers in case of problems. A nurse from the postanesthesia care unit (PACU) calls the patient the day after surgery to confirm the proper functioning of the technique (Table 46-3).

Patient selection is important and before discharge the patients are expected to demonstrate that they have understood the technique by using the pump in the presence of a PACU nurse (Fig. 46-6). Our relatively simple approach is supported by the findings of a recent study that surveyed the use of ambulatory catheter techniques at home. The follow-up survey of patients who had undergone ambulatory perineural infusion showed that 98% of respondents reported feeling "safe" with infusion and felt comfortable removing their catheter at home. Only 4% would have preferred to return for a health care provider to remove the catheter, and 43% responded that they would have felt comfortable with exclusively written instructions and once-daily telephone contact. The main complaint consistently noted by the patients with ambulatory perineural infusions was leakage of clear fluid from the occlusive dressing. Only one-third of the patients felt

comfortable reprogramming their electronic pump at home.[86]

The patients also have the possibility of going to the nearest community health center to get the catheter removed by a nurse; however, very few patients utilize this service and less than 5% of patients return to the hospital to get their catheter removed. Some patients self-adminis-

Table 46-3   Patient Instructions for Postoperative Patient-Controlled Regional Analgesia at Home

Inform the patient about the technique and how the "balloon pump" works (oral and written information). Information should also include the following:

- Importance of opening and closing the clamp at prescribed times (use of a timer is encouraged). This is not necessary with the new "Rawal pump"; with the new pump the patient has to press the button for 45 sec to receive 10 mL—releasing the pressure stops the infusion

- Instructions for removal of catheter at the end of treatment

- Importance of good hygiene near the wound area

- Provide the name and telephone (and beeper) number(s) of the physician to be contacted in case of local anesthetic toxicity symptoms or other problems/concerns

- Ask the patient to return follow-up data about technique, satisfaction/dissatisfaction in a self-addressed envelope

- Telephone follow-up on the day after surgery by a nurse or physician

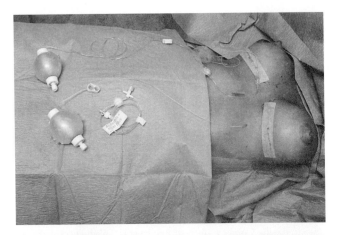
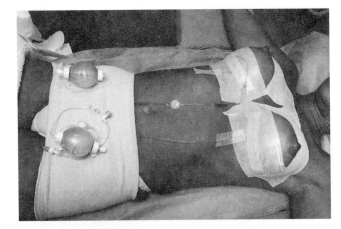
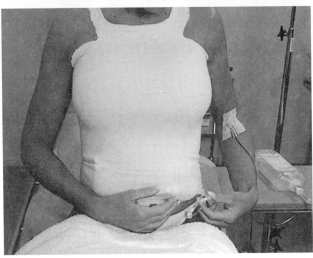
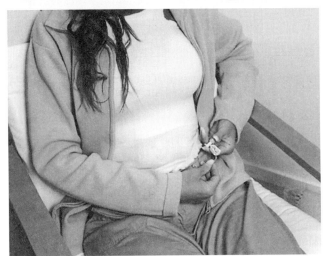

Figure 46-6   Incisional patient–controlled regional analgesia (PCRA) technique for breast augmentation surgery. Upper left: patient receives two elastomeric pumps (Rawal pump, I-Flow, Lake Forest, USA), one for each breast. Upper right: multiple-hole catheters are secured by tape. Lower left: patient demonstrates her understanding of pump function before discharge from hospital. Lower right: patient using device at home.

ter a bolus dose of local anesthetic before catheter removal. All the authors' group patients have 24-hr access to anesthesiology services. Since the introduction of this technique in 1997 we have had very high patient satisfaction rates and no major problems with infection, wound healing, or catheter removal by patients.

SUMMARY

As the number and complexity of ambulatory surgical procedures increase there will be greater demands on anesthesiologists to provide effective analgesia at home. Current methods are often inadequate. The relatively new technique of giving local anesthetic drugs through perineural, incisional, and intra-articular catheters has been shown to be feasible and to provide excellent dynamic analgesia with very few side effects. Recent developments in pump and catheter technology have led to the use of continuous infusions or PCRA techniques for superior pain management in inpatients and outpatients. Perineural catheter techniques have been used successfully for pro-

viding effective analgesia after extensive joint and extremity surgeries. However, sending patients home with 500–700 mL of local anesthetic to be delivered through catheters in the vicinity of large blood vessels requires an elaborate organization. Although the risk of catheter migration and toxic reactions are very low, it is still a matter of concern because the patients are unsupervised and may be far from a health care facility. Any pain management technique for unsupervised ambulatory surgery patients should be simple and safe. Incisional, intra-articular, and distal perineural techniques fulfill these criteria. Infiltration and intra-articular techniques have been shown to be effective for a variety of surgical procedures. The availability of elastomeric and electronic lightweight pumps, preloaded with local anesthetics, which allow self-administration on demand, or as continuous infusion, has led to the increasing use of incisional and intra-articular techniques. However, much work remains to be done to find the optimal catheter placement technique, dose-response studies, and relationship between volume and concentration of local anesthetics and the role of adjuvants. Studies are also necessary to identify the most appropriate techniques, i.e., incisional/intra-articular or perineural, for different surgical procedures.

ACKNOWLEDGMENT

The author wishes to acknowledge the assistance of Marianne Welamsson.

REFERENCES

1. Rawal N, Hylander J, Nydahl PA, et al. Survey of postoperative analgesia following ambulatory surgery. Acta Anaesthesiol Scand 1997;41:1017–22.

2. Klein SM, Grant SA, Greengrass RA, et al. Interscalene brachial plexus block with a continuous catheter insertion system and a disposable infusion pump. Anesth Analg 2000;91:1473–78.

3. Klein SM, Nielsen KC, Martin A, et al. Interscalene brachial plexus block with continuous intra-articular infusion of ropivacaine. Anesth Analg 2001;93:601–5.

4. Ilfeld B, Morey T, Kayser Enneking F. Continuous infraclavicular brachial plexus block for postoperative pain control at home: a randomized, double-blind, placebo-controlled study. Anesthesiology 2002;96:1297–1304.

5. Rawal N, Allvin R, Axelsson K, et al. Patient-controlled regional analgesia (PCRA) at home—controlled comparison between bupivacaine and ropivacaine brachial plexus analgesia. Anesthesiology 2002;96:1290–96.

6. Ilfeld B, Morey T, Wang D, et al. Continuous popliteal sciatic nerve block for postoperative pain control at home: a randomized, double-blind, placebo-controlled study. Anesthesiology 2002;97:959–65.

7. White P, Issioui T, Skrivanek G, et al. The use of continuous popliteal sciatic nerve block after surgery involving the foot and ankle: does it improve the quality of recovery? Anesth Analg 2003; 97:1303–9.

8. Benumof JL. Permanent loss of cervical spinal cord function associated with interscalene block performed under general anesthesia. Anesthesiology 2000;93:1541–44.

9. Borgeat A, Ekatodramis G, Kalberer F, et al. Acute and nonacute complications associated with interscalene block and shoulder surgery. Anesthesiology 2001;95:875–80.

10. Chan V. Nerve localizaton—seek but not so easy to find? Reg Anesth Pain Med 2002(3):27:245–48.

11. Hogan Q. Finding nerves is not simple. Reg Anesth Pain Med 2003;28:367–71.

12. Capdevila X, Biboulet P, Morau D, et al Continuous three-in-one block for postoperative pain after lower limb orthopedic surgery: where do the catheters go? Anesth Analg 2002;94:1001–6.

13. Rawal N. Postoperative patient-controlled regional analgesia at home. Reg Anesth 1997;22:A82.

14. Rawal N, Axelsson K, Hylander J, et al. Postoperative patient-controlled local anesthetic administration at home. Anesth Analg 1998; 86:86–89.

15. Savoie FH, Field LD, Jenkins N, et al. The pain control infusion pump for postoperative pain control in shoulder surgery. Arthroscopy 2000;16:339–42.

16. Rowlingson JC. How can local anesthetic in the wound not help? Anesth Analg 2001;92:3–4.

17. Moss G, Regal ME, Lichtig L. Reducing postoperative pain, narcotics, and length of hospitalization. Surgery 1986;99:206–10.

18. McLoughlin J, Kelley CJ. Study of the effectiveness of bupivacaine infiltration of the ilioinguinal nerve at the time of hernia repair for postoperative pain relief. Br J Clin Pract 1989;8:281–83.

19. Owen H, Galloway DJ, Mitchell KG. Analgesia by wound infiltra-

20. Patridge BL, Stabile BE. The effects of incisional bupivacaine on postoperative narcotic requirement, oxygen saturation and length of stay in the postoperative unit. Acta Anaesthesiol Scand 1990;34: 486–91.

21. Bourne MH, Johnson KA. Postoperative pain relief using local anesthetic instillation. Foot Ankle 1988;8:350–51.

22. Pryn SJ, Cross MM, Murison SC, et al. Postoperative analgesia for haemorrhoidectomy. Anaesthesia 1989;44:964–66.

23. White PF, Rawal S, Latham P, et al. Use of a continuous local anesthetic infusion for pain management after median sternotomy. Anesthesiology 2003;99:918–23.

24. Møiniche S, Mikkelsen S, Wetterslev J, et al. A qualitative systematic review of incisional local anaesthesia for postoperative pain relief after abdominal operations. Br J Anaesth 1998;81:377–83.

25. Yndgaard S, Holst P, Bjerre-Jepsen K, et al. Subcutaneously versus subfascially administered lidocaine in pain treatment after inguinal herniotomy. Anesth Analg 1994;79:324–27.

26. Alexander DJ, Ngoi SS, Lee L, et al. Randomized trial of periportal peritoneal bupivacaine for pain relief after laparoscopic cholecystectomy. Br J Surg 1996;83:1223–25.

27. Capelle W. Die Bedeutung des Wundschmerzes und seiner Ausschaltung für den Ablauf der Atmung bei Laparptomierten. Dtsch Ztschr Chir 1936;246:466–85.

28. Blades B, Ford WB. A method for control of postoperative pain. Surg Gynecol Obstet 1950;91:524–26.

29. Gerwig WH, Thompson CW, Blades B. Pain control after upper abdominal operations. Arch Surg 1951;62:678–81.

30. Lewis DC, Thompson WAL. Reduction of postoperative pain. Br Med J 1953;1:973–74.

31. Thomas DFM, Lambert WG, Lloyd-Williams K. The direct perfusion of surgical wounds with local anaesthetic solution: an approach to post-operative pain? Ann R Coll Surg Engl 1983;65:226–29.

32. Gibbs P, Purushotam A, Auld C, et al. Continuous wound perfusion with bupivacaine for postoperative wound pain. Br J Surg 1988;75: 923–24.

33. Vintar N, Rawal N, Požlep G, et al. Incisional analgesia by self-administration of local anaesthetic solution on demand after inguinal hernia repair: a comparison of bupivacaine and ropivacaine. Int Monitor Reg Anaesth Pain Ther 2000;12:A257.

34. Gupta A, Thörn SE, Axelsson K, Larsson LG, Ågren G, Holmström B, Rawal N. Postoperative pain relief using intermittent injections of 0.5% ropivacaine through a catheter after laparoscopic cholecystectomy. Anesth Analg 2002;95:450–56.

35. Fredman B, Shapiro A, Zohar E, et al. The analgesic efficacy of patient-controlled ropivacaine instillation after cesarean delivery. Anesth Analg 2000;91:1436–40.

36. Givens V, Lipscomb GH, Meyer NL. A randomized trial of postoperative wound irrigation with local anesthetic for pain after cesarean delivery. Am J Obstet Gynecol 2002;186:1188–91.

37. Duncan M, McNicholas W, O'Keeffe D, et al. Periosteal infusion of bupivacaine/morphine post sternal fracture: a new analgesic technique. Reg Anesth Pain Med 2002;3:316–18.

38. Cheong WK, Seow-Choen F, En KW, et al. Randomized clinical trial of local bupivacaine perfusion versus parenteral morphine infusion for pain relief after laparotomy. Br J Surg 2001;88:357–59.

39. Zohar E, Fredman B, Phillipov A, et al. The analgesic efficacy of patient-controlled bupivacaine wound instillation after total abdominal hysterectomy with bilateral salpingo-oophorectomy. Anesth Analg 2001;93:482–87.

40. Bvianconi M, Ferraro L, Traina GC, et al. Pharmacokinetics and efficacy of ropivacaine continuous wound instillation after joint replacement surgery. Br J Anaesth 2003;91:830–35.

41. Alford JW, Fadale P.D. Evaluation of postoperative bupivacaine infusion for pain management after anterior cruciate ligament reconstruction. J Arthroscop Rel Surg 2003(8)19:855–61.

42. Ganapathy S, Amendola A, Lichfield R, et al. Elastomeric pumps for ambulatory patient-controlled regional analgesia. Can J Anaesth 2000;47:897–902.

43. Douglas I, Bush D. The use of patient-controlled boluses of local anaesthetic via a psoas sheath catheter in the management of malignant pain. Pain 1999;82:105–7.

44. Kirchhoff R, Jensen PB, Nielsen NS, et al. Repeated digital nerve block for pain control after tenolysis. Scand J Plast Reconstr Hand Surg 2000;34:257–58.

45. Sinclair R, Cassuto J, Hogstrom S, et al. Topical anesthesia with lidocaine aerosol in the control of postoperative pain. Anesthesiology 1988;68:895–901.

46. Bisgaard T, Kehlet H, Rosenberg J. Pain and convalescence after laparoscopic cholecystectomy. Eur J Surg 2001:167:84–96.

47. Labaille T, Mazoit J.X., Paqueron X. The clinical efficacy and pharmacokinetics of intraperitoneal ropivacaine for laparoscopic cholecystectomy. Anesth Analg 2002;94:100–105.

48. Fong SY, Pavy TJG, Yeo ST, et al. Assessment of wound infiltration with bupivacaine in women undergoing day-case gynecological laparascopy. Reg Anesth Pain Med 2001;26:131–36.

49. Narchi P, Benhamou D, Fernandez H. Intraperitoneal local anaesthetic for shoulder pain after day-case laparoscopy. Lancet 1991; 338:1569–70.

50. Helvacioglu A, Weis R. Operative laparoscopy and postoperative pain relief. Fertil Steril 1992;57:548–52.

51. Goldstein A, Grimault P, Henique A, et al. Preventing postoperative pain by local anesthetic instillation after laparoscopic gynecologic surgery: a placebo-controlled comparison of bupivacaine and ropivacaine. Anesth Analg 2000;91:403–7.

52. Scheinin B, Kellokumpu I, Lindgren L, et al. Effect of bupivacaine on pain after laparoscopic cholecystectomy. Acta Anaesthesiol Scand 1995;39:195–98.

53. Rømsing J, Møiniche S, Østergaard D, et al. Local infiltration with NSAIDs for postoperative analgesia: evidence for a peripheral analgesic action. Acta Anaesthesiol Scand 2000;44:672–83.

54. Stein C. The control of pain in peripheral tissue by opioids. N Engl J Med 1995;332:1685–90.

55. Picard PR, Tramér MR, McQuay HJ, et al. Analgesic efficacy of peripheral opioids (all except intra-articular): a qualitative systematic review of randomized controlled trials. Pain 1997;72:309–18.

56. Convery PN, Milligan KR, Quinn P, et al. Efficacy and uptake of ropivacaine and bupivacaine after single intra-articular injection in the knee joint. Br J Anaesth 2001;87:570–76.

57. Chirwa SS, MacLeod BA, Day B. Intra-articular bupivacaine (Marcaine) after arthroscopic meniscectomy: a randomized double-blind controlled study. Arthroscopy 1989;5:352–53.

58. Smith I, Hemelrijck JV, White PF, et al. Effects of local anesthesia in recovery after outpatient arthroscopy. Anesth Analg 1991;73:536–39.

59. Heard SO, Edwards WT, Ferrrari D, et al. Analgesic effect of intra-articular bupivacaine or morphine after arthroscopic knee surgery: a randomized prospective double-blind study. Anesth Analg 1992;74:822–26.

60. Ritchie ED, Tong D, Chung E, et al. Suprascapular nerve block for postoperative pain relief in arthroscopic shoulder surgery: a new modality? Anesth Analg 1997;84:1306–12.

61. Horn E-P, Schroeder F, Wilhelm S, et al. Wound infiltration and drain lavage with ropivacaine after major shoulder surgery. Anesth Analg 1999;89:1461–66.

62. Geutjens G, Hambidge JE. Analgesic effects of intra-articular bupivacaine after day-case arthroscopy. Arthroscopy 1994;10:299–300.

63. Smith I, Van Hemelrijck J, White PF, et al. Effects of local anesthesia on recovery after outpatient arthroscopy. Anesth Analg 1991; 73:536–39.

64. Henderson RC, Campion ER, DeMasi RA, et al. Postarthroscopy analgesia with bupivacaine. A prospective, randomized, blinded evaluation. Am J Sports Med 1990;18:614–17.

65. Milligan KA, Mowbray MJ, Mulrooney L, et al. Intra-articular bupivacaine for pain relief after arthroscopic surgery of the knee joint in daycase patients. Anaesthesia 1988;43:563–64.

66. Reuben SS, Sklar J. Pain management in patients who undergo outpatient arthroscopic surgery of the knee. J Bone Joint Surg 2000;82-A:1754–66.

67. Møiniche S, Mikkelsen S, Wetterslev J, et al. A systematic review of intra-articular local anesthesia for postoperative pain relief after arthroscopic knee surgery. Reg Anesth Pain Med 1999;24:430–37.

68. Nagasaka H, Awad H, Yaksh T. Peripheral and spinal actions of opioids in the blockade of the autonomic response evoked by compression of the inflamed knee joint. Anesthesiology 1996;85:808–16.

69. Kalso E, Tramér MR, Carroll D, et al. Pain relief from intra-articular morphine after knee surgery: a qualitative systematic review. Pain 1997;71:127–34.

70. Stein C, Yassouridis A. Peripheral morphine analgesia. Pain 1997; 71:119–21.

71. Lawrence AJ, Joshi GP, Michalkiewicz A, et al. Evidence for analgesia mediated by peripheral opioid receptors in inflamed synovial tissue. Eur J Clin Pharmacol 1992;43:351–55.

72. Stein C, Comisel K, Haimerl E, et al. Analgesic effect of intra-articular morphine after arthroscopic knee surgery. N Engl J Med 1991; 325:1123–26.

73. Cook TM, Tuckey JP, Nolan JP. Analgesia after day-case knee arthroscopy: a double-blind study of intra-articular tenoxicam, intra-articular bupivacaine and placebo. Br J Anaesth 1997;78:163–68.

74. Gupta A, Bodin L, Holmström B, et al. A systematic review of the peripheral analgesic effects of intra-articular morphine. Anesth Analg 2001;93:761–70.

75. Kalso E, Smith L, McQuay, et al. No pain, no gain: clinical excellence and scientific rigour—lessons learned from IA morphine. Pain 2002;98:269–75.

76. Kligman M, Bruskin A, Sekliamser J, et al. Intra-synovial, compared to intra-articular morphine provides better pain relief following knee arthroscopy meniscectomy. Can J Anaesth 2002;49:380–83.

77. Marchal JM, Delgado-Martinez AD, Poncela M, et al. Does the type of arthroscopic surgery modify the analgesic effect of intra-articular morphine and bupivacaine? A preliminary study. Clin J Pain 2003;19-240–46.

78. Axelsson K, Johanzon E, Gupta A, et al. Intra-articular administration of ketorolac, morphine, and ropivacaine combined with patient-controlled regional analgesia (PCRA) for pain relief during shoulder surgery. Reg Anesth Pain Med 2001;26:A35.

79. Barber FA, Herbert MA. The effectiveness of an anesthetic continuous-infusion device on postoperative pain control. J Arthroscop Rel Surg 2002;18:76–81.

80. Gottschalk A, Burmeister M-A, Radtke P, et al. Continuous wound infiltration with ropivacaine reduces pain and analgesic requirement after shoulder surgery. Anesth Analg 2003;97:1086–91.

81. Muittari P, Kirvelä O. The safety and efficacy of intrabursal oxycodone and bupivacaine in analgesia after shoulder surgery. Reg Anesth Pain Med 1998;23:474–78.

82. Park J-Y, Lee G-W, Kim Y, et al. The efficacy of continuous intrabursal infusion with morphine and bupivacaine for postoperative analgesia after subacromial arthroscopy. Reg Anesth Pain Med 2002; 27:145–49.

83. Rosseland LA, Stubhaug A, Grevbo F, et al. Effective pain relief from intra-articular saline with or without morphine 2 mg in patients with moderate-to-severe pain after knee arthroscopy: a randomized, double-blind controlled clinical study. Acta Anaesthesiol Scand 2003;47:732–38.

84. Brower MC, Johnson ME. Adverse effects of local anesthetic infiltration on wound healing. Reg Anesth Pain Med 2003;28:233–40.

85. Rosseland LA, Stubhaug A, Sandberg L, et al. Intra-articular (IA) catheter administration of postoperative analgesics. A new trial design allows evaluation of baseline pain, demonstrates large varia-

tion in need of analgesics, and finds no analgesic effect of IA ketamine compared to IA saline. Pain 2003;104:25–34.

86. Ilfield B, Morey T, Kayser Enneking F. Portable infusion pumps used for continuous regional analgesia: delivery rate accuracy and consistency. Reg Anesth Pain Med 2003(5)28:424–32.

87. Capdevila X, Macaire P, Aknin P, Dadure C, Bernard N, Lopez S. Patient-controlled perineural analgesia after ambulatory orthopedic surgery: a comparison of electronic versus elastomeric pumps. Anesth Analg 2003;96(2):414–17.

88. McQuay HJ, Bullingham RE, Moore RA, et al. Some patients don't need analgesics after surgery. J R Soc Med 1982;75:705–8.

89. Ilfield B, Morey T, Kayser Enneking F. Continuous infraclavicular perineural infusion with clonidine and ropivacaine compared with ropivacaine alone: a randomized, double-blinded, controlled study. Anesth Analg 2003;97:706–12.

90. Singelyn FJ, Vanderelst PE, Gouverneur JM. Extended femoral nerve sheath block after total hip arthroplasty: continuous versus patient-controlled techniques. Anesth Analg 2001;92:445–49.

91. Ryckwaert Y, Branchereau S, Kaloulou R, et al. Postoperative analgesia by sciatic nerve block after foot surgery: continuous versus patient-controlled techniques. Reg Anesth Pain Med 2001:26: S130.

92. Collis RE, Platt FS, Morgan BM. Comparison of midwife top-ups, continuous infusion and patient-controlled epidural analgesia for maintaining mobility after a low-dose combined spinal-epidural. Br J Anaesth 1999;82:233–36.

93. Duncan LA, Fried MJ, Wildsmith JAW. Comparison of continuous and intermittent administration of extradural bupivacaine for analgesia after lower abdominal surgery. Br J Anaesth 1998;30: 7–10.

94. Vercauteren MP, Coppejans HC, ten Broecke PW, et al. Epidural sufentanil for postoperative patient-controlled analgesia (PCA) with or without background infusion: a double-blind comparison. Anesth Analg 1995;80:76–80.

95. Mezzatesta JP, Scott DA, Schweitzer SA, et al. Continuous axillary brachial plexus block for postoperative pain relief. Intermittent bolus versus continuous infusion. Reg Anesth 1997;22:357–62.

Multimodal Analgesia in the Ambulatory Setting

JAMES C. CREWS

INTRODUCTION

Office-based surgical procedures accounted for up to 25% of all elective surgical procedures performed in the United States in the year 2002, with steady growth in this segment expected over the coming years.[1] Ambulatory surgical procedures now make up more than 70% of the total volume of hospital-based elective surgical procedures.[2] More major surgical procedures are being performed on an ambulatory or 23-hr-hospital-stay basis, including intra-abdominal, intrathoracic, and major orthopedic procedures.

Postoperative pain and nausea/vomiting are the most common factors leading to delays in outpatient discharge and admissions to the hospital after ambulatory surgery.[2–4] In addition, several recent reviews have demonstrated that avoidance of postoperative incisional pain and avoidance of nausea/vomiting are among the highest priorities in perioperative management considerations from the surgical patient's perspective.[5–8] Despite an increased focus on pain management programs and the development of new standards for pain management, a recent survey published by Apfelbaum et al.[9] indicated that 80% of interviewed patients experienced pain after surgery. Of these patients, 86% reported moderate, severe, or extreme pain, with more patients experiencing pain after hospital discharge than before discharge. Experiencing postoperative pain was the most common concern (59%) of patients. In addition, almost 25% of patients who received pain medications experienced adverse effects.

An understanding of the pharmacologic concepts of analgesic drugs and pain management techniques for office-based and ambulatory surgical procedures is a crucial component in the perioperative anesthetic management of these patients. Tailoring of the perioperative anesthetic plan for patients with techniques to avoid or minimize postoperative pain, nausea/vomiting, and adverse effects of analgesic medications may play a significant role in improving patient satisfaction as well as postoperative rehabilitation.

Opioid analgesics are the historical choice of primary analgesic medications for postoperative pain. It has been well documented that opioid analgesics are commonly associated with nausea, vomiting, sedation, dysphoria, pruritus, constipation, urinary hesitancy, and respiratory depression.[10] Multimodal analgesia, or *balanced analgesia*, refers to the use of more than one medication or class of medication, or the use of more than one analgesic technique to produce analgesia through multiple mechanisms.[11] This strategy may be compared to the use of different classes of drugs in the treatment of hypertension or in cancer chemotherapy. Multimodal analgesic strategies for postoperative pain management, including the use of combinations of local anesthetic neural blockade techniques and nonopioid analgesic medications supplemented with opioid analgesics, have been shown to improve postoperative analgesia and reduce postoperative opioid requirements and opioid-related side effects.[12–14] Multimodal postoperative pain management is applicable and equally important in both the pediatric and adult patient populations.

PATIENT EDUCATION AND PREOPERATIVE CONSIDERATIONS

A multimodal strategy for postoperative analgesia should begin prior to the surgical procedure because patient preparation and education may improve postoperative outcome.[15] Patients should be educated on the importance and rationale for using the multimodal approach, including local anesthetic neural blockade, adjuvant analgesics, in addition to opioid analgesics. Patients may also benefit from an explanation of how much and what type of pain can be expected after their procedure. Patients should receive written, detailed instruction on the importance of coughing, deep breathing, and ambulation, as well as other specific instructions for postoperative rehabilitation issues related to their particular surgical procedure. Patient information on acute postoperative pain management is available from a number of public sources.[15,16]

Preemptive analgesia refers to the concept that an analgesic medication or intervention administered prior to surgical tissue injury may produce a greater effect than the same medication or intervention administered after surgical tissue injury.[17] This preemptive analgesic effect has been demonstrated for several different medications in animal models, but definitive clinical data in postoperative patients have been more challenging.[18,19] The theoretical basis for preemptive analgesia relates to the phenomenon of windup or hyperalgesia (increased pain response to subsequent stimulation) in response to acute tissue injury.[17] Prevention or reduction of this windup or hyperalgesic response by administration of analgesics prior to the tissue injury may reduce the overall pain response. Anti-inflammatory analgesic medications, local anesthetic wound infiltration or peripheral nerve block, or small doses of opioid analgesics are frequently administered prior to surgical incision to take advantage of this preemptive effect.[20,21]

NONOPIOID ANALGESICS

The nonopioid analgesics such as acetaminophen and nonsteroidal anti-inflammatory drugs (NSAIDs) are routinely used for minor surgical procedures. However, it is an important consideration to use these medications as adjuvant analgesics for even more major surgical procedures owing to their ability to produce analgesia through a nonopioid mechanism, reducing opioid analgesic requirement and reducing opioid-related side effects. Clinical trials have demonstrated an improvement in analgesic efficacy and a 30–40% reduction in opioid analgesic requirement with the perioperative coadministration of acetaminophen or NSAIDs.[22–24]

The routine perioperative use of NSAIDs has been limited perhaps in part due to concerns about their effects on platelet function and potential perioperative bleeding complications, and the incidence of gastroduodenal erosions and ulcerations associated with their use. The mechanism of activity of the NSAIDs involves inhibition of the cyclooxygenase-mediated pathways in the production of prostaglandin mediators of pain and inflammation.[25] This mechanism has been demonstrated to be active at the peripheral site of tissue injury as well as centrally in the spinal cord.[26] The discovery of a second isoform of the cyclooxygenase (COX) enzyme, known as COX-2, produced in most tissues only in response to tissue injury, pain, or inflammation, has led to the development of the COX-2-selective inhibitors or COXIBs.[25] These drugs (celecoxib, rofecoxib, and valdecoxib) have been demonstrated in multiple clinical trials to produce analgesic efficacy equal to that of the traditional nonselective NSAIDs without the COX-1-mediated side effects of inhibition of platelet aggregation or gastroduodenal ulceration.[27–29] Potential adverse effects of the nonopioid analgesics can include hepatic toxicity with high doses of acetaminophen, and exacerbation of hypertension, edema, heart failure, or renal insufficiency with the COXIBs in patients with these preexisting medical conditions or risk factors.

Due to their excellent analgesic efficacy, and ability to reduce opioid dose requirements and opioid-related side effects, the routine perioperative use of a COXIB, acetaminophen, or in some cases a nonselective NSAID should be considered in patients without contraindications to their use, as primary or adjuvant analgesics in the management of postoperative pain (Table 47-1).

Table 47-1   Dose Considerations for Nonopioid Analgesics for Healthy Adults as a Component of a Multimodal Strategy for Management of Postoperative Pain

Celecoxib	400 mg PO first dose, then 200 mg PO every 12 hr
Rofecoxib	50 mg PO every day for 5 days
Valdecoxib	40 mg PO first dose, then 20 mg PO every 12 hr
Acetaminophen	1000 mg PO every 6 hr
Ibuprofen	600 mg PO every 6 hr

LOCAL ANESTHETIC TECHNIQUES

Local anesthetic agents are the most powerful class of analgesic drugs in the management of localized postoperative pain. Local anesthetics block the transmission of neural impulses through a mechanism involving membrane sodium channel blockade. Sufficient local neural membrane sodium channel blockade inhibits propagation of the neural impulse in sensory, motor, and autonomic nerve fibers. Limitations of these drugs include a limited duration of action, limitations on the distribution of analgesic effect, and the relatively narrow therapeutic index of the drugs. Lidocaine (0.5–1%) and bupivacaine (0.25%) are the local anesthetic agents most commonly used for local anesthetic infiltration. The addition of epinephrine in a 1:200,000 concentration will prolong the duration of anesthetic effect.[30] Lidocaine has a relatively short duration of action. Bupivacaine, a more attractive drug from the standpoint of a longer duration of effect, is associated with profound cardiovascular (arrhythmias, cardiac arrest) and central nervous system (CNS) effects (seizures, CNS depression) in cases of unintentional intravascular injection or overdose.[30] Two new single-isomer local anesthetic agents, ropivacaine and levobupivacaine, provide moderate to long duration of action, equal to that of bupivacaine, and a better safety profile with respect to cardiovascular and CNS toxicity.[31,32] These two local anesthetics may be safer alternatives to bupivacaine for extending the duration of local anesthetic effect into the postoperative period.

For small-to-moderate and relatively superficial surgical procedures, infiltration of the surgical wound with a long-acting local anesthetic (bupivacaine 0.25%, ropivacaine 0.25–0.5%, or levobupivacaine 0.25%) produces up to 4 hr of pain relief.[30,31] This approach, in combination with a nonopioid analgesic such as COXIBs, acetaminophen, or nonselective NSAIDs, may produce adequate analgesia for minor surgical procedures and may be considered as the basal analgesic technique for all surgical procedures.

An attractive analgesic technique for ambulatory patients involves placement of small catheters into the surgical wound or near the local innervation of the surgical site and continuous infusion of 2–4 mL/hr of dilute concentrations of local anesthetic with disposable elastomeric (balloon-type) infusion devices.[33–35] This technique has demonstrated efficacy for minor peripheral surgical procedures[36] as well as major surgical procedures, including orthopedic shoulder surgery[34] and median sternotomy.[35]

In patients undergoing more extensive procedures, an anesthesiologist may use peripheral neural blockade or major plexus blockade to produce analgesia to a much wider tissue distribution and depth. The use of long-acting local anesthetics solutions (bupivacaine, ropivacaine, levobupivacaine) and dilute concentrations of epinephrine[30] can produce local anesthetic neural blockade for 12 hr or longer. Most neural blockade techniques for peripheral nerves or plexuses, which can be blocked with a single-injection local anesthetic technique, are also amenable to continuous catheter neural blockade techniques. The use of continuous local anesthetic neural blockade to extend local anesthetic analgesic effects for a period of 1–2 days or more after ambulatory surgical procedures has been described with brachial plexus blockade for major shoulder and upper-extremity procedures[34,37–39] and femoral and lumbar plexus blockade for major lower-extremity procedures.[40,41] The addition of low-dose clonidine to local anesthetic infusions for peripheral neural blockade has been demonstrated to improve analgesic efficacy and reduce local anesthetic and opioid dose requirements as compared to local anesthetic alone.[42]

Central neuraxial blocks, spinal (subarachnoid) or epidural local anesthetic neural blockade, are used to provide intraoperative anesthesia for some office-based and ambulatory procedures. Extension of analgesia into the postoperative period may be accomplished with the addition of spinal or epidural doses of opioid analgesics such as fentanyl. The duration of action for spinal or epidural fentanyl is on the order of about 4 hr. A longer-duration postoperative analgesia may be produced with continuous epidural infusion of dilute opioid or local anesthetic solutions. While used to continue postoperative analgesia during the inpatient phase of a postoperative stay, epidural infusions of opioids or local anesthetics are not frequently continued on an outpatient basis for postprocedural pain management in favor of more selective peripheral neural blockade infusions as previously described.

OPIOID ANALGESICS

For patients undergoing surgical procedures who are expected to require analgesic medication beyond the effect of the nonopioid adjuvant medications and local anesthetics, the use of intermittent doses of opioid analgesics such as oxycodone, morphine, or hydromorphone should be considered. Systemically administered opioid analgesics have a site of action primarily involving opioid-receptor binding in the brain, whereas spinally administered opioid analgesics have activity at opioid receptors in the spinal cord dorsal horn. The single-drug preparations of oxycodone (not the acetaminophen combination products), morphine, or hydromorphone may be added on a scheduled or an as-needed basis for moderate to severe levels of pain intensity. The morphine, hydromorphone, or plain oxycodone preparation offers advantages over the acetaminophen-opioid analgesic combination products in that dose adjustment to analgesic effect may be made without concern about exceeding the 4000 mg/day acetaminophen dose limit. A COXIB, acetaminophen or a nonselective NSAID is then dosed separately. Opioid analgesics, especially in higher doses, are likely to produce constipation. Consideration should be given to the coadministration of laxatives or stool softeners in patients receiving opioid analgesics.

While currently surrounded in controversy because of illegal diversion and misuse, the sustained-release opioid analgesics, such as OxyContin and MS Contin, offer a significant prolongation of the duration of effect and a reduction in the dosing frequency for opioid analgesics in patients with higher postoperative opioid analgesic requirements. A tapering dose of these sustained-release opioid analgesics administered in combination with a nonopioid analgesic and small intermittent doses of a shorter-acting opioid analgesic has been shown to improve postoperative sleep patterns and overall analgesic efficacy as compared to only shorter-acting opioid analgesic preparations.[43]

LADDER OF THERAPY FOR MULTIMODAL POSTOPERATIVE ANALGESIA

Similar to the ladder of therapy for cancer pain as developed by the World Health Organization (WHO), the multimodal strategy for the management of postoperative pain may be presented in a similar structure.[44] Minor superficial surgical procedures such as excisional biopsy are expected to have less postoperative pain, while larger or more extensive procedures, including orthopedic procedures, upper-abdominal, or thoracic surgical procedures, are generally associated with more postoperative pain. As with the WHO ladder of therapy, therapy for each patient begins at Step 1, with medications or interventions added in subsequent steps in response to increased pain intensity. Step 1 in this structural representation would include a nonopioid analgesic (COXIBs, acetaminophen, or nonselective NSAIDs) administered in a continuous, around-the-clock dosing regimen, and local anesthetic infiltration of the surgical wound for minor surgical procedures. Step 2 would include the addition of an opioid analgesic on an as-needed basis for surgical procedures with a moderate intensity of postoperative pain. Step 3 would include the addition of major peripheral neural blockade, plexus blockade, and sustained-release opioid analgesics as indicated for those patients undergoing more major surgical procedures, patients undergoing more painful procedures, or those patients who might otherwise be expected to have a high postoperative opioid dose requirement (Fig. 47-1).

STEP 3

STEP 1 + STEP 2 +
local anesthetic peripheral neural blockade
(with/without catheter) and the use of
sustained release opioid analgesics

STEP 2

STEP 1
intermittent doses of opioid analgesics

STEP 1

COXIBs, Acetaminophen, or NSAIDs
+
local anesthetic infiltration

Figure 47-1   Proposed ladder of therapy for multimodal postoperative pain management for ambulatory surgical procedures. COXIBs indicates selective cyclooxygenase-2 inhibitors; NSAIDs indicates nonsteroidal anti-inflammatory drugs. Step 1 therapy represents minor surgical procedures with Step 2–3 therapies added as the intensity of anticipated or actual degree of postoperative or postprocedural pain increases. (Used with permission from the *Journal of the American Medical Association*, August 7, 2002, Volume 288, No. 5, pp. 629–32. Copyright © 2002, American Medical Association, All rights reserved.)

ALTERNATIVE NONPHARMACOLOGIC THERAPIES

A variety of nonpharmacologic therapies have been described that either reduce postoperative pain, reduce postoperative analgesic requirements, reduce perioperative anxiety, or improve the patient's overall sense of well-being. These nonpharmacologic therapies include the application of heat or cold, massage, exercise, and transcutaneous electrical nerve stimulation (TENS).[15] Some patients have also demonstrated various postoperative benefits from relaxation, imagery, hypnosis, and biofeedback techniques.[15]

A recent study reported a 50% reduction in postoperative morphine requirement, a 20–30% reduction in postoperative nausea, and a 30–50% reduction in plasma cortisol and epinephrine with the use of preoperative intradermal acupuncture.[45] Another recent study reported the beneficial response to intraoperative music and therapeutic suggestions during general anesthesia. Patients exposed to relaxing music and soothing and encouraging therapeutic suggestion had a lower postoperative opioid dose requirement, better pain relief, and less postoperative fatigue at hospital discharge as compared to patients in the control group.[46] Nonpharmacologic therapies should be considered for any patient with interest or acceptance of these techniques as a component of a multimodal pain management strategy.

CONSULTATION OF A PAIN MANAGEMENT SPECIALIST

Patients with selected preprocedural indications may benefit from consultation with or evaluation and management by an anesthesiology pain management specialist. These patients may include those with a history of severe or unexpected adverse reactions to pain medications, or a history of difficulty with postoperative or postprocedural pain control, those patients scheduled to undergo more extensive or painful procedures, or those patients with a preprocedural history of chronic or recent opioid use. These patients may require special analgesic dosing considerations outside of those that could be commonly expected for office-based or ambulatory procedures. Patients with a history of preprocedural opioid use can be anticipated to have higher postprocedural analgesic requirements as compared to patients who are opioid-naïve. In general, perioperative patients presenting with a history of chronic opioid and nonopioid analgesic therapy should be maintained on those preoperative medications throughout the perioperative period, with additional doses of opioid and nonopioid medications as indicated for the additional anticipated postoperative pain stimulus. A consultation with an anesthesiology pain management specialist may be helpful in determining appropriate specialized pain management techniques or analgesic dosing recommendations for patients with these and other preprocedural considerations, or for patients who may present unusual postprocedural pain management problems.

FUTURE CONSIDERATIONS

There are several areas of pharmacologic research, which may add additional opioid and nonopioid analgesic alternatives for patients undergoing office-based and ambulatory surgical procedures. Clinical development of novel analgesic drugs, which act through nonopioid analgesic mechanisms including N-methyl-D-aspartate (NMDA) receptor antagonists, alpha-2 receptor agonists, and adenosine A_1-receptor agonists, among others, may provide additional nonopioid analgesic alternatives.[47] Propacetamol,[48] a prodrug of acetaminophen (paracetamol), and parecoxib,[49] a prodrug of the COXIB valdecoxib, are both in clinical development for perioperative intravenous administration. Patient-controlled electrophoretic transdermal drug delivery systems could allow postoperative ambulatory patient-controlled opioid analgesia without the requirement for intravenous access or infusion pumps.[50] Continued development in local anesthetic and opioid pharmacology with liposomal encapsulation techniques may allow selective neural blockade or peripheral or spinal opioid analgesia for a period of a few days with a single injection-technique.[51]

SUMMARY

The effectiveness of multimodal strategies for postoperative pain management has been demonstrated with a variety of medications and therapeutic interventions. Postoperative pain can delay the patient's discharge to home, impair the patient's ability to participate in early postoperative rehabilitation, and occasionally require hospital admission. The understanding that pain is more easily managed with a preventive approach as compared to a reactive treatment approach suggests initiation of appropriate therapy prior to, during, and immediately after the surgical procedure. The rational use of combinations of analgesic medications such as nonopioid analgesics, local anesthetic perineural infusion or infiltration of the surgical wound, and opioid analgesics, in addition to other nonpharmacologic therapeutic interventions, can improve pain relief, reduce postoperative side effects, and improve functional postoperative recovery for patients after office-based and ambulatory surgical procedures.

ACKNOWLEDGMENT

Portions of the text and figures in this chapter were previously published and are used with permission from the Journal of the American Medical Association, August 7, 2002, Vol. 288, No. 5, pp. 629–32. Copyright © 2002, American Medical Association, All rights reserved. (Crews JC. Contempo updates: multimodal pain management strategies for office-based and ambulatory procedures. JAMA 2002;288(5):629–32.)

REFERENCES

1. Laurito CE. The Society for Office-Based Anesthesia, Orlando, Florida, March 7, 1998. J Clin Anesth 1998;10:445–48.

2. White PF. Ambulatory anaesthesia and surgery: past, present and future. In: White PF (ed.), *Ambulatory Anaesthesia and Surgery.* London: WB Saunders, 1997.

3. Chung F, Ritchie E, Su J. Postoperative pain in ambulatory surgery. Anesth Analg 1997;85:808–16.

4. Fortier J, Chung F, Su J. Unanticipated admission after ambulatory surgery—a prospective study. Can J Anaesth 1998;45:612–19.

5. Jenkins K, Grady D, Wong J, et al. Post-operative recovery: day surgery patients' preferences. Br J Anaesth 2001;86:272–74.

6. Macario A, Weinger M, Carney S, Kim A. Which clinical anesthesia outcomes are important to avoid? The perspective of patients. Anesth Analg 1999;89:652–58.

7. Macario A, Weinger M, Truong P, Lee M. Which clinical anesthesia outcomes are both common and important to avoid? The perspective of a panel of expert anesthesiologists. Anesth Analg 1999;88:1085–91.

8. Waterman H, Leatherbarrow B, Slater R, Waterman C. Post-operative pain, nausea and vomiting: qualitative perspectives from telephone interviews. J Adv Nurs 1999;29:690–96.

9. Apfelbaum JL, Chen C, Mehta SS, Gan TJ. Postoperative pain experience: results from a national survey suggest postoperative pain continues to be undermanaged. Anesth Analg 2003;97:5347–40.

10. Gutstein HB, Akil H. Opioid analgesics. In: Hardman JG, Limbird LE, Gilman AG (eds.), *The Pharmacological Basis of Therapeutics.* New York: McGraw-Hill, 2001:569–620.

11. Kehlet H. Multimodal approach to control postoperative pathophysiology and rehabilitation. Br J Anaesth 1997;78:606–17.

12. Brodner G, Van Aken H, Hertle L, et al. Multimodal perioperative management—combining thoracic epidural analgesia, forced mobilization, and oral nutrition—reduces hormonal and metabolic stress and improves convalescence after major urologic surgery. Anesth Analg 2001;92(6):1594–2000.

13. Michaloliakou C, Chung F, Sharma S. Preoperative multimodal analgesia facilitates recovery after ambulatory laparoscopic cholecystectomy. Anesth Analg 1996;82:447–51.

14. Rosaeg OP, Krepski B, Cicutti N, et al. Effect of preemptive multimodal analgesia for arthroscopic knee ligament repair. Reg Anesth Pain Med 2001;26:125–30.

15. Acute Pain Management Guideline Panel. *Acute Pain Management: Operative or Medical Procedures and Trauma. Clinical Practice Guideline.* 1992. Rockville, MD, Agency for Health Care Policy and Research, Public Health Service, U.S. Department of Health and Human Services.

16. Pain control after surgery. American Academy of Family Physicians. 11-20-2001. Internet communication.

17. Woolf CJ, Chong MS. Preemptive analgesia—treating postoperative pain by preventing the establishment of central sensitization. Anesth Analg 1993;77:362–79.

18. Katz J. Pre-emptive analgesia: evidence, current status and future directions. Eur J Anaesthesiol Suppl 1995;10:8–13.

19. Dahl JB, Kehlet H. The value of pre-emptive analgesia in the treatment of postoperative pain. Br J Anaesth 1993;70(4):434–39.

20. Ejlersen E, Andersen HB, Eliasen K, Mogensen T. A comparison between preincisional and postincisional lidocaine infiltration and postoperative pain. Anesth Analg 1992;74:495–98.

21. Dahl JB, Hjortso NC, Stage JG, et al. Effects of combined perioperative epidural bupivacaine and morphine, ibuprofen, and incisional bupivacaine on postoperative pain, pulmonary, and endocrine-metabolic function after minilaparotomy cholecystectomy. Reg Anesth 1994;19:199–205.

22. Dahl JB, Kehlet H. Non-steroidal anti-inflammatory drugs: rationale for use in severe postoperative pain. Br J Anaesth 1991;66:703–12.

23. Etches RC, Warriner CB, Badner N, et al. Continuous intravenous administration of ketorolac reduces pain and morphine consumption after total hip or knee arthroplasty. Anesth Analg 1995;81:1175–80.

24. Korpela R, Korvenoja P, Meretoja OA. Morphine-sparing effect of acetaminophen in pediatric day-case surgery. Anesthesiology 1999;91:442–47.

25. Hawkey C, Kahan A, Steinbruck K, et al. Gastrointestinal tolerability of meloxicam compared to diclofenac in osteoarthritis patients. International MELISSA Study Group. Meloxicam Large-Scale International Study Safety Assessment. Br J Rheumatol 1998;37:937–45.

26. Yaksh TL, Dirig DM, Conway CM, et al. The acute antihyperalgesic action of nonsteroidal anti-inflammatory drugs and release of spinal prostaglandin E2 is mediated by the inhibition of constitutive spinal cyclooxygenase-2 (COX-2) but not COX-1. J Neurosci 2001;21:5847–53.

27. Clemett D, Goa KL. Celecoxib: a review of its use in osteoarthritis, rheumatoid arthritis and acute pain. Drugs 2000;59:957–80.

28. Matheson AJ, Figgitt DP. Rofecoxib: a review of its use in the management of osteoarthritis, acute pain and rheumatoid arthritis. Drugs 2001;61(6):833–65.

29. Desjardins PJ, Shu VS, Recker DP, et al. A single preoperative oral dose of valdecoxib, a new cyclooxygenase-2 specific inhibitor, relieves post-oral surgery or bunionectomy pain. Anesthesiology 2002;97:565–73.

30. Covino BG, Wildsmith JAW. Clinical pharmacology of local anesthetic agents. In: Cousins MJ, Bridenbaugh PO (eds.), *Neural Blockade in Clinical Anesthesia and Management of Pain*, 3rd ed. Philadelphia: Lippincott-Raven, 1998:97–128.

31. McClellan KJ, Spencer CM. Levobupivacaine. Drugs 1998;56:355–62.

32. Markham A, Faulds D. Ropivacaine: a review of its pharmacology and therapeutic use in regional anaesthesia. Drugs 1996;52:429–49.

33. Rawal N, Axelsson K, Hylander J, et al. Postoperative patient-controlled local anesthetic administration at home. Anesth Analg 1998;86:86–89.

34. Ilfeld BM, Morey TE, Wright TW, et al. Continuous interscalene brachial plexus block for postoperative pain control at home: a randomized, double-blinded, placebo-controlled study. Anesth Analg 2003;96:1089–95.

35. White PF, Rawal S, Latham P, et al. Use of a continuous local anesthetic infusion for pain management after median sternotomy. Anesthesiology 2003;99:918–23.

36. Barca F, Bertellini E, Siniscalchi A. Forefoot postoperative continuous pain control by nonelectronic device. J Foot Ankle Surg 1995;34:42–45.

37. Corda DM, Enneking FK. A unique approach to postoperative analgesia for ambulatory surgery. J Clin Anesth 2000;12:595–99.

38. Grant SA, Nielsen KC, Greengrass RA, et al. Continuous peripheral nerve block for ambulatory surgery. Reg Anesth Pain Med 2001;26:209–14.

39. Klein SM, Grant SA, Greengrass RA, et al. Interscalene brachial plexus block with a continuous catheter insertion system and a disposable infusion pump. Anesth Analg 2000;91:1473–78.

40. Klein SM, Greengrass RA, Gleason DH, et al. Major ambulatory surgery with continuous regional anesthesia and a disposable infusion pump. Anesthesiology 1999;91:563–65.

41. Klein SM, Greengrass RA, Grant SA, et al. Ambulatory surgery for multiligament knee reconstruction with continuous dual catheter peripheral nerve blockade. Can J Anaesth 2001;48:375–78.

42. Ilfeld BM, Morey TE, Enneking FK. Continuous infraclavicular perineural infusion with clonidine and ropivacaine compared with ropivacaine alone: a randomized, double-blinded, controlled study. Anesth Analg 2003;97:706–12.

43. Reuben SS, Connelly NR, Maciolek H. Postoperative analgesia with controlled-release oxycodone for outpatient anterior cruciate ligament surgery. Anesth Analg 1999;88:1286–91.

44. Ventafridda V, Tamburini M, Caraceni A, et al. A validation study of the WHO method for cancer pain relief. Cancer 1987;59:850–56.

45. Kotani N, Hashimoto H, Sato Y, et al. Preoperative intradermal acupuncture reduces postoperative pain, nausea and vomiting, analgesic requirement, and sympathoadrenal responses. Anesthesiology 2001;95:349–56.

46. Nilsson U, Rawal N, Unestahl LE, et al. Improved recovery after music and therapeutic suggestions during general anaesthesia: a double-blind randomised controlled trial. Acta Anaesthesiol Scand 2001;45:812–17.

47. Dahl V, Raeder JC. Non-opioid postoperative analgesia. Acta Anaesthesiol Scand 2000;44:1191–203.

48. Hernandez-Palazon J, Tortosa JA, Martinez-Lage JF, Perez-Flores D. Intravenous administration of propacetamol reduces morphine consumption after spinal fusion surgery. Anesth Analg 2001;92:1473–76.

49. Cheer SM, Goa KL. Parecoxib (parecoxib sodium). Drugs 1901;61:1133–41.

50. Gupta SK, Sathyan G, Phipps B, et al. Reproducible fentanyl doses delivered intermittently at different time intervals from an electrotransport system. J Pharm Sci 1999;88:835–41.

51. Grant GJ, Bansinath M. Liposomal delivery systems for local anesthetics. Reg Anesth Pain Med 2001;26:61–63.

Perioperative Information Systems: Customer–Driven Information Therapy for Sick Work Processes

TOM ARCHER · IAIN S. SANDERSON

THE BIG PICTURE

A Winter Day, Long Ago

In 1964 a young man returning to school after the Christmas holiday called American Airlines to make a plane reservation. In the past he had always made a reservation *request* and then would call back the next day to see if his request had been fulfilled. This time was different. The cheerful voice at the other end of the line was able to confirm his reservation within about 30 sec. The young man was amazed and delighted and vaguely realized that something fundamental had changed in the world. "You mean I don't have to call back tomorrow?" he asked incredulously. "No, it's all right here," the young lady replied. "We did it all by computer. We have a new system now."

Unbeknown to the young man, the SABRE system of computerized airline reservations had just been introduced. The world would never be the same. Over subsequent decades, the vision and practice of instantaneous information retrieval and real-time service became more and more pervasive. Expectations began to change. People began to assume that banks, insurance companies, travel agencies, and merchants would all have their data on file. When we called an institution we hoped that they would find us "in their system," and when they did, we were delighted and impressed. We felt that we belonged and that someone cared.

By the 1980s or the 1990s—depending on the industry—we *expected* to be "in the system." We learned to become indignant if the "system was down" or if the clerk couldn't find our information based on our name and street address alone. We began to penalize businesses that weren't good custodians and managers of our data. Information systems became a competitive business tool, a factor differentiating businesses that succeeded from businesses that failed. Spending for information technology soared.

When we drove in to have our oil changed, we expected that Jiffy Lube would know exactly what they did the last time, what they needed to do today, and what they should do 5000 miles from now. We learned that we didn't have to bring our service manual to Jiffy Lube because they kept our service records in their own information system. Keeping a customer's information on file became an important "value added" and by the end of the 1990s phrases like "real-time" and "seamless connectivity" became part of our conception of how the world should work.

Except, of course, in medicine.

"Isn't that all in my record? Shouldn't that all be in my record already?" How many times have we heard those plaintive queries from patients?

Medicine, like some tradition-bound medieval guild, remained relatively impervious to the information revolution. The signing of releases, the courtly, cadenced interchange of typewritten documents, the photocopying of charts—all of this pomp and circumstance continued unchanged for decades. To send a fax seemed like the height of technologic sophistication—a daring innovation. In medicine—the domain of diagnostic miracles and therapeutic triumphs—information technology (IT) would be introduced at an agonizingly slow pace.

In the 1980s and 1990s, we recognized that the world had entered the Information Age. Retailing and manufacturing invested massively in IT. Wal-Mart established its competitive advantage by means of its information systems and became known as the information-processing company that—incidentally—sold merchandise! With the Internet boom of the late 1990s this enthusiasm for IT became a feeding frenzy. The vision of seamless, real-time coordination of activities seized the public imagination. We began to seek information online, shop online, pay our bills online, and even date online.

What happened to medical information systems during the Internet revolution? They continued to evolve and improve, despite the fact that almost all of the Internet-based medical information start-ups failed in 2000 or 2001.

Nowadays, in medical IT, we are painfully "crossing the chasm," to use Geoffrey Moore's famous phrase: "The dormant dreams of the wild-eyed visionaries (whose start-ups failed) are slowly being poked, sifted through, resuscitated, and adapted by the Big Boys." The responsible adults have come on the scene. Actually they were always there, slowly making progress, but the media in the late 1990s were focused elsewhere—on the start-ups that flamed out so brilliantly.

The big companies, the men and women who want to make money rather than headlines, the university researchers with a long-term commitment—all of these "responsible adults" are slowly turning the youthful dreams of seamless interchange of medical information into reality.

Why Make Investments?

We invest in assets in order to increase *productivity*, or *value produced per quantity of time*. In the Middle Ages peasants invested in horses in order to be able to plow more land in the same amount of time. Later, farmers upgraded to tractors. Henry Ford invented the assembly line in order to increase productivity, to increase quality through standardization, and to decrease cost.

In short, all successful investments *change our ways of doing work*.

Why Invest in Information Technology?

IT is a general enabling technology,[1,2] similar to electric power. Like electric power, IT can be used to enhance our lives or to waste money.

The purpose of an investment in IT should be to *enable us to redesign our work processes in order to increase productivity*.

IT is no panacea and it frequently fails. IT should *not* be introduced because it is in fashion or because certain technology enthusiasts are fascinated by it.

The only legitimate use of IT is to *improve real-life work processes*.

For instance, with good Internet IT we can pull up the next day's surgery schedule or get a patient record from home—rather than having to call the operating room (OR), or drive in to the hospital. With the IT of the fax machine, we can review a consultation report within minutes, rather than having to wait for it to come in the mail. Because of tape recorders we can dictate a note and have someone else transcribe it, rather than having to type it out ourselves.

When IT enables us to *improve our work processes*, then we experience a productivity gain. We stop wasting our time.

These examples make another point: *IT does not have to be fancy in order to make a big difference*.

Don't Digitize Stupid Processes

On the other hand, keeping our work processes the same, but putting them in digital form, does nothing to increase our productivity. For example, if we have to copy the same information from one stupid form to another, it does not matter if we use a pen or a keyboard. To enhance our productivity (in this example) we would have to be able to *replicate* information automatically from one form to all other relevant forms, and thereby get rid of the need for a scribe. IT-based replication of basic data from one form to another would constitute a fundamental change in our work process of filling out innumerable, redundant, and stupid forms.

Do IT Investments Really Work?

The answer is "Yes, but with a time lag." Making IT work is a learning process that may take anywhere from 5 min to 20 years. It took American industry about 20 years to show macroeconomic evidence of the value of massive IT investment.

From the end of World War II until 1974, the productivity of American industry grew at almost 3% per year. From 1974 until 1995, however, the annual rate of productivity growth for the U.S. economy slumped to only 1.4%, despite the heavy IT investment of the 1970s and the 1980s.[3]

As late as 1987 one prominent economist saw no effect of IT investment on national productivity figures. In that year Robert Solow famously stated, "We see computers everywhere except in the productivity statistics."[4]

For the period 1996–2000 the rate of productivity growth finally increased to 2.5%, and Federal Reserve Board Chairman Alan Greenspan brought us the good news about IT and productivity in 1999 when he conjectured that IT might be contributing to a sustainable increase in the rate at which the economy could grow. Because of IT, he said, perhaps the economy could grow at 4% per year rather than at 3%. With this cautious support for the transformative power of IT, Mr. Greenspan helped to fuel the tech bonfire of the late 1990s.

So, IT finally received its vindication. After decades of increased IT spending, we were finally starting to see the payoff in the late 1990s. In these years, U.S. productivity revived, and its revival was most dramatic in the most IT-intensive industries.[5]

Health Care Information Technology—The Ugly Duckling

Health care IT spending has been about half of that in other industries, and has been much less successful. Failures have been frequent and massive. Many projects have been poorly thought out and have frequently lacked the full backing of top management.

Table 48-1   Thinking Outside the Computer Box: Questions to Ask Yourself *before* You Buy Information Technology

1. What are we REALLY trying to do?
2. What real-life clinical or business PROCESSES are we trying to improve?
3. Is there a SIMPLER way to improve the process?
4. Will PEOPLE use the technology?
5. Will people be THREATENED by the technology?
6. Why have past information technology projects FAILED here?
7. Is top management REALLY on board?

A frequent cause of health care IT failure is that projects are too ambitious or are poorly focused. Eager IT vendors, technology enthusiasts inside the organization, and naïve or inattentive managers conspire to sign up for "complete solutions" that frequently wind up in the dumpster. IT projects, if done at all, need to be of the *right size* and closely tied to improving everyday, real-life business activities.

Table 48-1 presents some of the nontechnical questions we need to ask ourselves before we invest in an IT "solution."

OBSTACLES TO THE REDESIGN OF WORK PROCESSES

Successful competition in a market economy (i.e., making money) requires ever-increasing quality at an ever-decreasing price. Increased quality and decreased price require reiterative rounds of business process redesign. Innumerable process changes occurred in the auto industry under Henry Ford and others, and this is why cars are no longer made by hand.

In medicine, of course, it's different, and we are still doing many things "by hand." It's true, the processes of medicine are more variable and uncertain than those of the auto industry, but many of us resist changing our work processes, no matter what business we are in.

Following are some of the reasons why people do not want to—or cannot—improve their work processes.

Suspicion of Business

Many people reject the idea that medicine should function as an efficient, moneymaking business. These are the people who proclaim, "Health care should be about people and not about profits!" This is like saying that human nutrition should be about carbon and not about nitrogen.

These people say that certain fields—usually health care and education—are too important to be left to the forces of the marketplace. They reject the idea that business and market forces improve human welfare. Since process im-

provement is a part of successful business practice, they reject process improvement. Or at best, they believe that disinterested bureaucrats can improve processes in the absence of market pressures.

Fear

Nobody likes to have his/her performance measured, and nobody likes to be told what to do. Best practices are adopted with glacial speed. We all fear that our shortcomings will be discovered. This is why medicine has not incorporated many of the practices of the auto industry. We fear scrutiny and criticism of our precious and comfortable work processes.

Change threatens people. People worry: Will I be able to adapt? Will I be able to learn the new system? Will I lose my job?

Organizational Pathology

Various types of organizational dysfunction also make it hard to redesign business processes.

Lip service: Key decision makers lack real commitment to constructive change, out of ambivalence or ignorance.

Lack of incentives for participants to work more efficiently. The rank and file often see a new IT project as just one more management fad. Sometimes the incentives are actually perverse. The ordinary employee gets the message that "Gee, if our wonderful new system works well enough we will be able to fire you!"

No clear goals for the new system: Do we want to make more money, have happier patients, make fewer mistakes, or publish more articles? What are we *really* trying to do?

We don't measure whether we are achieving our goals. Do we really want to know how we are doing? Usually not.

Unwillingness or inability to work together to transform work processes. (How many failed attempts have you seen to design a common anesthesia evaluation form?)

The not-invented-here syndrome: It is probably human nature to not want to admit that the other guy got there first. If management doesn't develop a system, management certainly doesn't want to borrow it from someone else. That would be an admission of defeat. The not-invented-here syndrome is especially prevalent in academia, where the profit motive is weak. When an enterprise is under economic pressure, decision makers are more willing to simply copy other people's streamlined work processes. But in the ivory tower, everyone wants to reinvent the wheel. Or at least they want to do further experiments to validate the wheel.

Medical Culture

Even if we think we can make a financial case for health care IT as a general enabler of clinical and business process redesign, we still have an uncomfortable, prickly factor in the equation: medical culture.

Doctors are individualistic. Their behavior often seems to say, "I am the boss and nobody is going to tell me how to care for my patients." In order to improve any process, we must start with some degree of standardization, and we must measure the process. Both standardization and measurement are anathema to many doctors, at least when it comes to their own activities.

Furthermore, medicine is not *supposed* to be easy! All of us—in our training and beyond—have spent countless hours poring through patient records, searching for hidden kernels of information that will help us make the diagnosis before the next physician does. In our heart of hearts perhaps we feel that it *should* hurt, at least a little, to dig out a patient's history—especially in the university setting. After all, isn't this search for information part of medical education? We may feel that there is something slightly *unmedical* about consulting the OR schedule or a patient's old chart from home. We make fun of radiologists who read CT scans from their bedside table.

Copying is another well-established medical tradition that stands in the way of streamlining work processes. During medical education we learn by copying. No one objects to the fact that medical students, interns, and residents record the same information in the chart over and over again. But later, after training, we never learn to *stop* copying! We copy and copy, until we feel like scribes rather than empathic and creative physicians. The copying and repetition that are part of medical training never stop.

If we try to redesign work processes in order to save time we run the risk of being seen as *lazy*. Medicine has not fully internalized the need to work *smart* as well as to work *hard*. This is another way of saying that medicine still has not come to terms with being a *business*.

Technology Worship

An enormous obstacle to good health care IT is the belief that patient information systems are primarily a technologic challenge. The technology is trivial in comparison to the human factors that make it hard for us to improve the ways in which we do our work.

DESPITE THE PROBLEMS, INFORMATION TECHNOLOGY IS COMING TO MEDICINE

As economic pressure increases in medicine and as IT becomes more prevalent and more understood, all these obstacles will be overcome. Here is why.

Everybody Wants More

Patients, as impatient consumers, want better, faster, and cheaper care. The patient—and society as a whole—want it all: They don't want to have to wait to see the doctor. They want their health care providers to have instant access to all relevant information. They want frequent updates on the progress of their loved one in surgery. They want total privacy of health care information and they want relevant and up-to-date educational material about their medical condition.

Physicians and nurses are demanding more too. Physicians and nurses want to get out from under the mountains of paper, the documentation requirements, and the need for entering the same data multiple times. They want to be able to spend more time with patients and less time chasing down information. They would like to stop playing phone tag with consultants. Physicians would like to be able to view schedules and patient information from home. They would like to get alerts on difficult patients. They would like to have best practices information at their fingertips. They would like to be paged when the patient arrives in the preoperative holding area. They would like to be informed when surgery will be delayed. They would like to have their billing done automatically.

Physicians are getting the IT idea. They have been "spoiled" by information technology in other industries. They want to start enjoying the benefits that IT offers for medicine. Even the government is starting to encourage the use of IT in medicine. The Centers for Medicare and Medicaid Services (CMS), the General Accounting Office (GAO), and even President Bush have all recently come out in favor of using IT in medical care.

So, if we *do* decide to try to improve work processes using IT, how would we go about it?

HOW TO USE INFORMATION TECHNOLOGY IN THE PERIOPERATIVE PERIOD

Market Research Comes First, Information Therapy Comes Later

First we must realize that IT must be subordinated to the improvement of concrete, everyday work processes. We do not want to fall into the trap of implementing an IT system and then trying to figure out what to do with it! In order to subordinate IT to work process redesign, we must do *market research* before we ever think about an IT "solution." Market research means that we have to discover *who our customers are* and *what their goals are*. Table 48-2 shows some perioperative customers and their goals.

The next step of market research is to identify *those work processes whose improvement might allow our customers to better achieve their goals*. Some perioperative work processes are shown in Table 48-3.

Our final market research question is: How could *information* improve our customers' work processes? In other words, how could we *prescribe IT for sick perioperative work processes?*

Prescribe Customer-Driven Information Therapy

Figure 48-1 illustrates the need to subordinate the use of IT to solving the problems that we identify in our market research. In Figure 48-1, information only enters the process on an "as-needed" basis, in step E, *after we have done our basic market research in steps A through D.*

Just like a medication, we need to think of administering the *right information* to the *right person*, at the *right place*, at the *right time*. Just as we would not give

Table 48-2   Perioperative Customers and Their Goals

1. Patients want to:
   a. Receive outstanding care.
   b. Save time and avoid repetition.
   c. Receive education and counseling.
   d. Receive emotional support.
   e. Keep their records private.
2. Physicians and nurses want to:
   a. Give outstanding care.
   b. Avoid busywork, copying, and repetition.
   c. Focus on the patient.
   d. Avoid errors.
   e. Receive timely clinical decision support.
   f. Do clinical research.
   g. Get paid as much as possible.
3. Medical leaders and hospital administrators want to:
   a. Improve clinical and business processes to increase quality of care, receive more income, and reduce labor and supply costs.
4. Third-party payers want to:
   a. Receive appropriate documentation of services performed.
   b. Reduce transaction costs through electronic data interchange (EDI).
   c. Receive population data for development of health care policies.
5. Government wants to:
   a. Assure public health and safety at minimal cost.
   b. Assure privacy and confidentiality of patients' data.
   c. Receive population data for development of health care policies.
6. Medical researchers and financial analysts want to:
   a. Have access to "clinical data repositories" and "data warehouses" in order to develop new medical and business knowledge.

Table 48-3   Perioperative Work Processes

Communication with surgeon's office.

Operating room (OR) staffing.

OR schedule preparation and dissemination.

Checking OR status.

Retrieval and interchange of patient information (history and physical examination, laboratory testing, consults, studies).

Communication between members of the surgical team.

Automated notification of perioperative events (patient arrival, surgical incision, etc.).

Checking patient location and status in preoperative holding area, OR, and postanesthesia care unit (PACU).

Creation of the anesthesia record.

Giving surgical updates to waiting family members.

Online logging of cases.

Accessing best practices information and other clinical decision support.

Creation of nursing documentation.

Creation and transcription of surgeon's operative report.

Maintenance of surgeon's preference card.

Accounting for medications.

Education of staff regarding medication and supply costs.

Writing orders.

Capturing and documenting charges and professional fees.

Bill preparation and delivery.

Materials management (inventory, reordering).

Personnel and facility performance evaluation (benchmarking).

Report generation.

Quality improvement.

Compliance with governmental regulations The Health Insurance Portability and Accountability Act of 1996 ([HIPAA], etc.).

any individual patient all of the medications in the pharmacy, the institution must not allow itself to be mesmerized or overwhelmed by technology. The institution must not invest in a "comprehensive IT solution" unless it has first gone through the basic market research to identify *exactly where* selective information therapy would be helpful.

Once bottlenecks have been identified, information can be supplied, as needed, to help facilitate work processes. For example, our market research might reveal that perioperative customers are crying out for the following work process improvements:

1. Better access to the OR schedule.
2. Better access to the preoperative evaluation.
3. Better access to old anesthesia records.
4. Better communication with the surgeon's office.
5. Less repetitive data entry.
6. Reduction in patient waiting times.

This process of identifying bottlenecks (areas of work process inefficiency) is the best way to attempt to find the elusive "return on investment" (ROI) for IT. If we attempt to provide an IT solution for work processes that do not need to be fixed, then we are probably wasting our time and money.

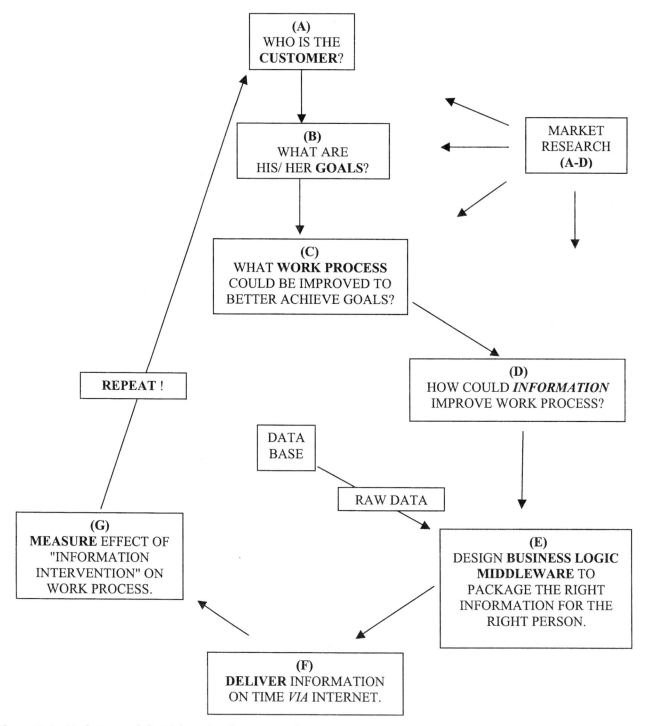

Figure 48-1 Market research first, information therapy second.

From a political and organizational point of view, as well, it makes sense to try to eliminate work process bottlenecks early on. If we can demonstrate "early wins" for our IT team, then we establish credibility, achieve momentum, and silence our critics. Concretely, using IT to improve work processes might have some of the following human and organizational benefits for many perioperative customers:

Increased Physician Job Satisfaction: Are physicians chasing down laboratory testing, electrocardiograms, and echocardiograms, and filling out multiple forms with the same information, or are they spending time with patients? Can they access the OR schedule, the preoperative evaluation, and the old anesthesia records from home? Can they automatically get a page when the patient arrives in the preoperative holding area?

Increased Patient Satisfaction: Is the patient waiting too long for care? Is the physician hurriedly flipping through the chart trying to get up to speed on a patient's history or is he/she looking at and listening to the patient? Is the patient getting all of the educational materials he/she might want?

Increased Income: Is the institution capturing all of its legitimate charges?

Recognize That Each Perioperative Environment Is Different

Each institution will have its own list of clinical and business priorities. Each institution will have certain festering problems, whose solution would bring a big sigh of relief from perioperative customers. Hence, information solutions need to be customized, particular, and focused. Not generic.

How do we achieve this customization of information therapy? Readymade systems that come from the various vendors cannot guess or anticipate the unique clinical and business needs of each institution.

In summary, customized information access and delivery are key for the *appropriate information therapy of sick work processes*.

THE PERIOPERATIVE INFORMATION SYSTEM AT DUKE

At Duke University Medical Center computerized perioperative information systems have existed for many years. As the system has evolved from a purely intraoperative record-keeping system to a more comprehensive perioperative information system, the IT team has had to do market research to see which perioperative processes needed improvement. They designed the information system to facilitate many basic, everyday work processes, such as the following:

1. OR schedule preparation and display.
2. Conveying alerts about critical patient conditions to members of the OR team.
3. Reviewing past anesthesia records.
4. Keeping a log of anesthesia cases.
5. Maintaining surgeon preference cards.
6. Picking instruments for cases.
7. Charge capture for pharmacy and anesthesia.
8. Quality improvement review of problem cases.

Demonstrating an ROI for the Duke University system is still controversial (as it is with many medical IT systems), but the Duke University IT team believes that they have the best chance of making a real difference in the lives of perioperative customers if they attempt to resolve real work process bottlenecks.

Figure 48-2 shows how the Duke University IT team is attempting to do this. Using the system architecture shown in Figure 48-2, the Duke team has come to the following conclusions:

1. Data should be entered once at the "point of care" and should then be replicated so as to populate data fields throughout the information system. This avoids the need to enter the same information multiple times.
2. Vendor-supplied data input systems are often very good at getting data *into* the system. The user interfaces are often well designed and easy to use, and, in general, they are superior to Internet-based data entry methods. Table 48-4 lists some online resources regarding commercial perioperative information systems.
3. Ergonomics are important. The specific technique of data entry makes significant difference. Touch screens generally work best. Avoid mouse and keyboard when possible. Touch screens need to be fluid-proof. Try to let the clinician maintain eye contact with the patient while he/she uses the data entry system. Tablet computers and handheld devices work well for this. Wireless devices will be required for many mobile perioperative customers.
4. Basic, raw data is stored in the database, but this raw data has only limited usefulness.
5. The key to the usefulness of the information system is the business logic middleware (a software layer), which is used to channel information from disparate sources into useful packages that are then sent to the appropriate location to facilitate the perioperative "supply chain." For example, the very act of scheduling a craniotomy initiates the process of picking the appropriate instruments and it transfers basic patient data to the Saturn perioperative information system.
6. Without middleware and the Internet, all we would be able to have as information output are the generic, vendor-supplied reports, and—hopefully—ad hoc queries of the database. It is true that "bolt-on" reporting tools such as "Crystal Reports" are available, but (in the opinion of the IT team at Duke University) these are awkward, expensive, and difficult to maintain.
7. Information access is best managed over the Internet, because of ease of access and low expense. The Internet "client" is very "thin" and hence needs little maintenance. Applications can be maintained and updated centrally, in the Web Application Server.
8. The Internet allows the Duke Anesthesiology staff to access information from anywhere, using any Internet-enabled computer, including handheld and other wireless devices.

The Department of Anesthesiology of Duke University has been monitoring the use of its Internet-enabled system, and the number of accesses has steadily increased from about 300 per day in January 2002 to about 1500 per day in May 2003.

Perioperative information systems, like business itself, will constantly evolve, but the focused and customer-driven application of information therapy to resolve work process bottlenecks is the best strategy for making IT relevant in the perioperative environment.

SUMMARY

In the last 30 years IT has transformed the work processes of many industries such as retailing, manufacturing, and

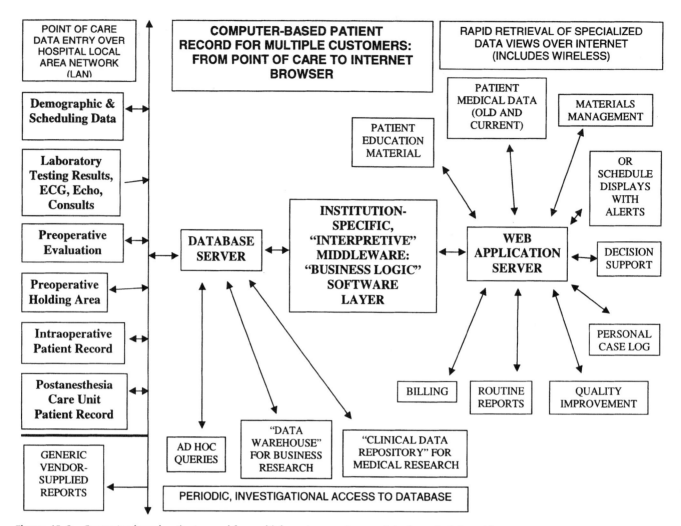

Figure 48-2   Computer-based patient record for multiple customers: From point of care to Internet browser.

Table 48-4   Online Resources for Perioperative Information Systems

> Cerner: http://www.cerner.com/aboutcerner/aboutcerner
> _4a.asp?id=2153
>
> Docusys: http://www.docusys.net/index.html
>
> GE Medical Systems: http://www.gemedicalsystems.com/
> inen/it_solutions/clinical/periop.html
>
> Healthcare IT Yellow Pages: http://www.health-infosys
> -dir.com/yphchis.asp
>
> HIMSS (Healthcare Information and Management
> Systems Society): http://www.himss.org/asp/
> abouthimss_homepage.asp
>
> Per-Se Technologies: http://www.per-se.com/solutions/
> index.asp
>
> Phillips Medical Systems: http://www.medical.philips
> .com/main/products/patient_monitoring/products/
> compurecord/
>
> PICIS: http://www.picis.com/index.asp
>
> Surgical Information Systems: http://www.orsoftware
> .com/products/index.cfm

transportation. We have come to expect "just-in-time" inventory management, "seamless connectivity," and "real-time responsiveness." We expect that successful companies will keep our information in their systems and that they will manage it well.

Medical care has lagged far behind other industries in its management of information. People in all industries fear changes in their work processes, but some aspects of medical culture make medical work processes particularly hard to change. Together, these human factors constitute formidable obstacles to the redesign of medical work processes. When IT solutions have been introduced in health care they have frequently failed. Two key (and related) reasons for failure are that the IT "solution" has not been sufficiently aligned with the institution's overall business strategy and that the "information therapy" has not been focused on specific work processes.

If we decide to introduce perioperative IT, then we need to make sure that it is subordinated to our general business purpose.[1] Organizations need to do market research in order to find out which work processes need information therapy. Perioperative market research involves these basic steps:

1. Identifying customers and their goals.
2. Identifying key work processes whose improvement might help the customers to better achieve their goals.
3. Asking how focused *information therapy* might help to improve those key work processes.

Each institution will have its own set of clinical and business priorities, its own areas of weakness and strength, and the IT solution has to be customized to meet each institution's needs. Subordination of IT to the improvement of problematic work processes implies that we can extract information from the system in a flexible and directed manner, just as we can give a specific medicine by a specific route, to a specific person at a specific time.

Based on the Duke experience, we believe that generic or raw perioperative information in the main database needs to be appropriately *packaged,* or *interpreted,* by business logic middleware. Once the data has been packaged and interpreted it can be disseminated to the appropriate recipient over the Internet. Our goal for a useful perioperative information system must be *to get the proper information to the proper person at the proper time.*

REFERENCES

1. Vogel LH. Finding value from IT investments: exploring the elusive ROI in healthcare. J Healthcare Inform Manag 2003;17(4):20–28.
2. Brynjolfsson E, Hitt LM. Beyond the productivity paradox: computers are the catalyst for bigger change. Commun ACM, 1998 Aug; 41:8.
3. McKinsey Global Institute. US Productivity Growth 1995–2000, Understanding the Contribution of Information Technology Relative to Other Factors. October 2001. Available at http://www.mckinsey.com/knowledge/mgi/feature.
4. Solow R. New York Times Book Review, July 12, 1987.
5. Stiroh KJ. Investing in information technology: productivity payoffs for U.S. industries. Curr Issues Econ Finance, Federal Reserve Bank of NY, 2001 June;7:1.

Imaging of Continuous Plexus Blockade–State of the Art: The Role of Fascias and Diffusion Spread Spaces in the Result of Continuous Peripheral Nerve Blocks

XAVIER CAPDEVILA · CLAUDIA COIMBRA

INTRODUCTION

The interest in peripheral nerve blocks (PNBs) has increased significantly in the last decade as postoperative analgesia has become a greater concern, and more importantly as the number of anticoagulated patients has increased. Furthermore, with economic issues becoming a greater consideration, the number of surgeries performed as ambulatory cases has been increasing progressively. With patients being discharged at home on the surgery day, postoperative pain management becomes a major challenge for anesthesia.

Single-injection PNBs, although efficient, provide only temporary postoperative analgesia. Continuous plexus and peripheral nerve blocks permit prolonged analgesia with fewer side effects related to opioids and faster functional recovery after surgery. Chung et al.[1] noted that after some orthopedic, urologic, and plastic surgeries, 40–70% of patients experienced moderate to severe pain at home. Orthopedic patients are the largest group to receive PNBs in ambulatory surgery. It has been reported that, despite the use of long-acting local anesthetics, 11% of patients report wound pain during the first 24–48 hr postoperatively, and 17–22% still require opioids 7 days after the surgery.[2] A number of investigations have shown the efficacy of continuous peripheral nerve blocks (CPNBs) in providing better analgesia, therefore limiting oral intake of opioids and

their associated side effects. However, this method of pain relief traditionally required cumbersome infusion pumps and hospital stay.

Recently, a number of studies have been undertaken to evaluate the feasibility and safety of CPNBs for postoperative pain control at home.[3–8] This has been possible with the introduction of ambulatory infusion pumps.[3] Ilfeld et al.[4–6] have demonstrated with randomized, double-blinded, placebo-controlled studies the reliability of these devices in providing adequate analgesia, after continuous blocks performed for upper as well as lower limb surgeries. Although no complications were reported in these studies, they include an insufficient number of patients to draw definitive conclusions.

Although good pain control is obtained with at-home perineural local anesthetic infusions, there are several potential inherent risks involving continuous catheters. These include catheter site infection, nerve injury, catheter migration, local anesthetic toxicity, and epidural or intrathecal anesthesia with interscalene brachial plexus or lumbar plexus blocks. Indeed, there have been numerous reports of unintentional, unsuspected inadequate catheterization of CPNBs.

Although CPNBs have been used efficaciously for over half a century, these techniques are not widely used. This can be explained by the lack of a simple and consistent method for plexus blocks, which in turn is responsible for the great variability in success rate. With the development of more precise imaging techniques, such as magnetic resonance imaging (MRI), we have been able to better understand the clinically relevant anatomy of the different plexuses and develop new techniques or improve old ones in order to improve the rate of successful blocks and decrease the associated risks of regional anesthesia. More recently, ultrasound has also been used as a guiding tool to the execution of upper limb as well as lower limb PNBs. Imaging has enabled anesthesiologists to explain objectively the clinical failure of certain blocks as well as the cause of some side effects. Furthermore, it has become a tool for better and quicker diagnosis of potentially dangerous side effects, such as epidural hematomas.

One can question the use of imaging techniques in the performance of CPNBs, which are already time consuming procedures. We know that success rates of continuous blocks are variable even when performed by experimented anesthesiologists. Reported success rates for the brachial plexus, using a nerve stimulator technique, are > 90% for the axillary approach and 75–100% for the interscalene approach.[9] No data are available for continuous infraclavicular brachial plexus blocks. As for the lumbar plexus, success rates using a femoral approach vary between 40 and 90%, around 70% for fascia iliaca approaches, and 85–100% for psoas compartment catheters.[9] For this reason, the unique aim of the techniques of medical imagery is to verify the spread of the local anesthetic solution or the location of the tip of the perineural catheter under the selected fascia or into the diffusion spread spaces. They do not replace anatomic knowledge. The first step for the anesthesiologist is the knowledge of anatomy, and imaging techniques should help him/her to understand the success or failures of CPNBs. For all these reasons, imaging seems to be a great asset in the execution of a more precise positioning of the catheter, or verifying the positioning of a catheter introduced using a nerve stimulator.

ANATOMY

The outer fascia is a loose layer of connective tissue situated just below the skin with cutaneous nerves running through it. The inner fascia is a dense layer of connective tissue situated just below the outer fascia and is attached to the muscles and intermuscular septa.

The cutaneous area that a nerve supplies is called a dermatome. The area innervated by each nerve at the surface varies from one person to another. The territories adjacent to these dermatomes overlap each other. Therefore, anesthetizing a single nerve requires a much smaller territory than the nerve's usual distribution area. All the muscles innervated by a single spinal nerve form a myotome. The osteo-articular region innervated by a nerve is called a sclerotome. Muscles with similar actions tend to be innervated by the same segments of the spinal cord. The fascia, intermuscular septa, and interosseous membranes determine these muscular groups.

For most PNBs, spreading the local anesthetic beyond the actual injection site makes it possible to block several nerve trunks and carry out plexus blockades. The concept

of a perineural sheath, which we owe to the work of Winnie et al.,[10] has given rise to several anatomic and clinical studies.

A given injection site corresponds to a common distribution pattern, which depends on the neighboring fatty and conjunctive tissue, and this is strangely marked out by the surrounding structures, notably the fascias. It has been shown that increasing the volume injected only slightly modifies the extension of the distribution corresponding to that particular injection site. In the same distribution area, each injection site corresponds to a preferential distribution of local anesthetic toward areas with less resistance.

DIFFUSION SPREAD SPACES OF THE UPPER LIMB AND IMAGERY

According to the type of block required, the approaches to the brachial plexus may be divided into two groups. Interscalene approaches bring about a radicular and thus metameric blockade, whereas all other approaches cause a nerve trunk block, which involves only the nerve trunks still present in the diffusion spread space corresponding to the injection site. This would explain, notably, the failings in anesthesia observed especially with single-injection axillary approaches to the brachial plexus.

The Interscalene Diffusion Spread Space

Interscalene and supraclavicular approaches to the brachial plexus are carried out within the interscalene diffusion spread space. This space, marked out by the cervical fascia, is in the shape of a tilted half-trapezoid egg timer, whose base would be up against the spinal column. The lower side corresponds to the upper orifice of the thorax and the pleural dome, the front and back edges are fascias of the middle and anterior scalene muscles, and the base is centered on the axillary artery. Emerging from between the scalene muscles, the brachial plexus is covered by a lateral extension of the prevertebral lamina of the cervical fascia, which continues along as far as the axillary fossa. At this level, the narrow retroclavicular passage represents an anatomic obstacle for the spread of local anesthetic from the subclavicular space to the axillary fossa. During a continuous interscalene block, the injection site situated in the lateral and median parts of the interscalene space gives excellent quality anesthesia of the upper roots of the brachial plexus, but does not involve the C8–T1 roots. During the injection, compression above the puncture point does not seem to favor caudal distribution of local anesthetics. The usual extension depends on the volume injected and the length of catheter inserted (Figs. 49-1, 49-2, and 49-3). These images may explain the results reported by Klein and coworkers in a recent preliminary report.[8] The authors have demonstrated the difficulties of ambulatory interscalene infusion of local anesthetics after rotator cuff surgery. Fifty to 70% of patients experienced intense pain after resolution of their initial surgical block. One of the causal factors may be the inaccurate position of the catheter.

On the contrary, for a supraclavicular brachial plexus blockade with the injection given in the lower part of the

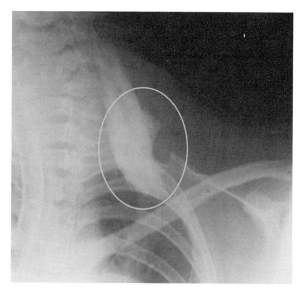
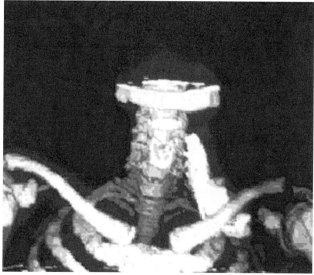

Figure 49-1   (Left) Single-injection interscalene brachial plexus block with 30 mL of local anesthetic solution. (Right) Three-dimensional computed tomographic scan of a single-injection interscalene brachial plexus block with 30 mL of local anesthetic solution.

interscalene space, the common distribution pattern remains localized there, without attaining its cephalic portion, as such anesthesia of the shoulder is often incomplete, particularly in the suprascapular nerve territory.

The Infraclavicular Diffusion Spread Space

Infraclavicular and axillary approaches to the brachial plexus are made within the infraclavicular diffusion spread space in the axillary fossa. The axillary fossa is shaped like a pyramid with a narrow summit, wide base, and three sides. It contains the axillary artery and its branches, the axillary vein and its tributaries, part of the brachial plexus,

and the axillary lymphatics found in the adipose and loose connective tissue between the root of the upper limb and the thoracic wall. The connective tissue becomes thicker to cover the axillary artery and each branch of the brachial plexus is brought together to form a bundle of blood vessels and nerves. The radial nerve leaves the axillary fossa with the deep brachial artery (arteria profunda braquii) passing under the teres major muscle, then between the humerus and the long head of the triceps. The medial cutaneous nerve of the arm leaves the brachial canal very high up, crossing the inner fascia to end up at the anteromedial aspect of the arm. The ulnar nerve initially goes along with the medial cutaneous nerve of the forearm at the medial edge of the

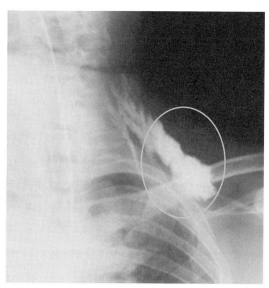
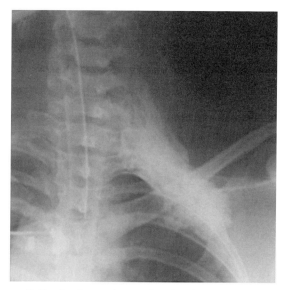

Figure 49-2   Continuous interscalene brachial plexus block: 2.5 cm of threaded catheter and 30 mL of local anesthetic solution. The result of the solution spread looks like a supraclavicular brachial plexus block.

Figure 49-3   Continuous interscalene brachial plexus block: 4 cm of threaded catheter and 30 mL of local anesthetic solution. The result of the solution spread looks like an infraclavicular brachial plexus block.

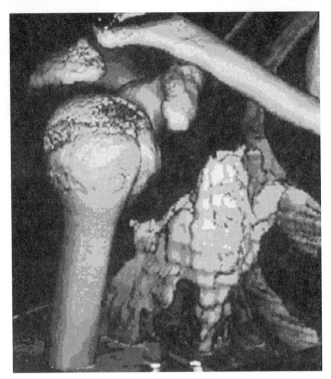

Figure 49-4   Three-dimensional computed tomographic scan of a continuous axillary brachial plexus block: 5 cm of threaded catheter and 30 mL of local anesthetic solution. The spread of the local anesthetic solution filled all the axillary space.

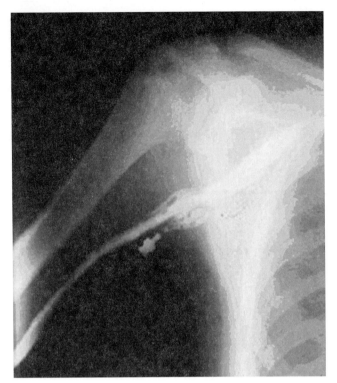

Figure 49-5   Continuous axillary brachial plexus block: 5 cm of threaded catheter and 30 mL of local anesthetic solution. The spread of the local anesthetic solution was only located along the median nerve.

brachial artery. The distribution of local anesthetic is limited by the fibrous tissue, which is roughly organized around each structure to form a neurovascular space divided into small compartments.[11] Because there are several nerves (axillary, radial, and musculocutaneous) spreading out from the bundle of vessels and nerves in the axillary fossa, the extension of anesthesia from an injection made with an infraclavicular approach is much better when made at the tip of the axillary fossa and in the center of the diffusion spread space, which would be situated within the median nerve (Figs. 49-4, 49-5). Likewise, a single injection via an axillary approach requires a large volume of local anesthetics and must be administered as high as possible in the axillary fossa with a catheter (Figs. 49-4, 49-5).[12] The frequency of sensorymotor anesthesia is over 90% in the distributions of median, radial, ulnar, and medial cutaneous nerves of the arm and forearm.

The concept of septa within the brachial plexus was first introduced in 1983 by Thompson and Rorie,[13] who examined the functional anatomy of the brachial plexus in cadavers as well as human volunteers by injecting radiopaque dye. They concluded that the brachial plexus sheath is a multicompartmental structure and that to obtain the highest success rate, an axillary brachial plexus block should be performed with separate injections. In 1987, Partridge et al.,[14] using a larger number of cadavers, confirmed this concept of interconnecting septa within the axillary sheath. Injection of methylene blue solution showed numerous small compartments of fluid, suggesting that the axillary sheath is made up of thin layers of ve-

lamentous fascia. However, they showed that these septa must be incomplete since a single injection of dye resulted in staining of all three nerves in the sheath. As the median and ulnar nerves are situated in the same diffusion spread space represented by the brachial canal at the root of the arm, a selective injection on the ulnar nerve is not indispensable during a continuous axillary brachial plexus blockade when the ulnar nerve is not specifically involved in the intervention.

Almost 20 years later, Klaastad et al.[15] examined the distribution of local anesthetics within the brachial plexus using MRI. They performed an axillary brachial plexus block by injecting the local anesthetic solution through a catheter inserted along the median nerve detected by nerve stimulator. They showed that, 30 min after the last local anesthetic injection, all but 1 of the 13 patients had some fluid in all quadrants. Five patients had complete filling of all quadrants whereas 8 patients lacked complete filling of at least one quadrant. However, only 2 patients (15%) had a surgical block of all three distal nerves 30 min after the last injection of local anesthetic. This suggests an inhibited cross-sectional spread. The MRI results confirm clinical findings by showing that in the majority of patients the full dose of local anesthetic did not completely surround the axillary artery. Although few patients were studied, this work shows once again the limits of regional anesthesia and how imaging can help us further understand not only the anatomy, but also the correlation with the clinical effects.

For a continuous axillary brachial plexus block, neither compression downstream from the puncture point nor adduction of the arm at the end of the procedure is effective in improving the quality of the blockade. The technique using multistimulation of the four nerves considerably reduces the need to use complementary anesthesia, as is common with a technique in which only one or two nerves are selected.

DIFFUSION SPREAD SPACES OF THE LOWER LIMB AND IMAGERY

Unlike the upper limb, it is impossible to completely anesthetize the lower limb with a single injection through a CPNB catheter. Indeed, the lower limb is innervated by two plexuses (lumbar and sacral) situated in two different anatomic areas. In most cases, it is necessary to block the lumbar plexus or its branches and the sciatic nerve separately. The fascia covering the anterior aspect of the psoas and iliac muscles forms a continuous strip. The psoas fascia joins at the top with the diaphragm fascia and at the bottom and sides with the fascia transversalis. The fascia iliaca covers the iliac muscle. At the top it adheres to the iliac crest, and at the bottom to the inguinal ligament, and continues on into the femoral trigone by covering the iliopsoas muscle. Laterally, it continues to form the fascia transversalis. Medially, it melts into the fascia covering the iliopsoas muscle. The fascia of the psoas muscle goes around the medial aspect and then the posterior aspect of the psoas muscle to join onto the periosteum of the linea arcuata of the pubis. In the rear part of the linea arcuata this fascia is in continuity with the fascia of the internal obturator muscle. Toward the front, it gradually separates from it and the continuity between the two fascias is represented by the periosteum of the pubis.

The lumbar plexus is situated in the main body of the psoas muscle. The diffusion spread space is bordered medially by the attachments of the psoas muscle onto the body of the vertebrae and on the transverse process. It is bordered ventrally by the fascia of the iliopsoas muscle. At the back, the distribution is limited by the quadratus lumborum and its fascia at the top and the iliac muscles in the iliolumbar fossa.

The extension of anesthesia for a continuous lumbar plexus block using a posterior approach is constant on the main branches of the plexus and involves the proximal third of the thigh; the femoral and obturator nerves appear to be blocked in nearly 100% of cases. Capdevila et al.[16] have shown the importance of estimating the depth of lumbar plexus using MRI before performing a continuous psoas compartment block. This type of block is not very popular, even among experienced anesthesiologists, due to the importance of potential adverse effects, such as epidural or intrathecal injection and visceral or kidney puncture. In this study, Capdevila has shown that the depth of lumbar plexus varies not only with weight but also between men and women. Before stimulation of the lumbar plexus and catheter insertion, localization of the L4 transverse process was obtained by MRI. Only 3 of the 80 patients studied had a catheter improperly positioned, one in the abdominal cavity, one in the retroperitoneum, and another in the L4–5 intervertebral disk. They were removed after opacification without any side effects. All reported good analgesia.

There are three types of imaging for the diffusion spread space after a psoas compartment block: (1) a shape like a spindle corresponding to the outline of the psoas muscle; (2) a wider and more blurred patch outlining the space between the psoas muscle and the quadratus lumborum muscle; (3) a vertical paravertebral opacity stretching from L2 to L5. The absence of epidural distribution must be sought as well as the absence of an abnormal catheter location: intraperitoneal, epidural, spinal, or outside the plexus (Figs. 49-6, 49-7).

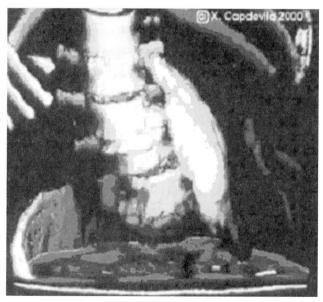 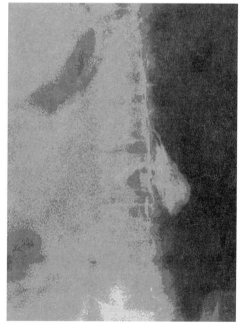

Figure 49-6   (Left) Three-dimensional computed tomographic scan of a continuous psoas compartment block: 3 cm of threaded catheter and 25 mL of local anesthetic solution. (Right) The spread of the local anesthetic solution was located in the psoas compartment and as a unilateral epidural anesthesia.

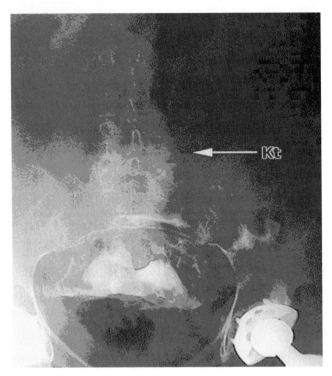

Figure 49-7 Continuous psoas compartment block: 3 cm of threaded catheter and 30 mL of local anesthetic solution. The spread of the local anesthetic solution was located into the peritoneal cavity.

The inguinal perivascular block is known as the "3-in-1" block as it can be used to simultaneously block the femoral nerve, the lateral femoral cutaneous nerve, and the obturator nerve with a single injection of at least 20 mL of local anesthetic or a continuous local anesthetic infusion. The authors claim to obtain 100% anesthesia on these three nerves, without specifying the method used to evaluate the different territories involved. Strangely, an increase of 20–40 mL in the volume injected does not improve the spread of cutaneous anesthesia.

Recent studies evaluated the efficacy of obturator nerve block (reduction in motor strength in the thigh adductors) as a result of the inguinal perivascular block. The femoral nerve is therefore blocked in almost 95% of cases; the lateral femoral cutaneous nerve is anesthetized in 70% of cases; however, the obturator nerve is only blocked in 4–10% of cases.

To complement these clinical studies, radiographic and anatomic studies show that the distribution of the solution injected using an anterior approach to the lumbar plexus is only made in a very inconsistent, incomplete, and unforeseeable way toward the obturator nerve. From the inguinal region, the liquid flows back under the fascia iliaca, at the surface of the iliopsoas muscle. The propagation is unpredictable, external on the iliac muscle and/or internal on the psoas muscle.[17,18] With an internal spread, the solution reaches the anterior aspect of the psoas muscle, then its lateral and internal aspects. The solution must spread throughout the fascia to reach the obturator nerve. The cephalic progression above L4 is low, not very strongly influenced by the increase in volume, and does not seem to reach the lumbar plexus in the heart of the psoas muscle. On a front-view X-ray after a perivascular or inguinal iliofascial block, lumbar opaqueness in respect to the plexus is rare (5.5% of cases); an internal diffusion spread with regard to the psoas muscle is more common. This proves that the solution has been diffused below the fascia iliaca, then at the surface of the psoas muscle but does not prove that it has reached the obturator nerve situated deeper down in the pelvic cavity.

Although successfully inserted, the clinical efficiency is not always related to the ease of the catheter insertion and the position of the catheter's tip is not always "ideal." It has been reported that peripheral nerve catheters result in up to 40% of secondary block failure. Using injected contrast media through the catheter, Capdevila et al.[19] have demonstrated that despite easy and successful insertion of the catheter, the direction of femoral catheters is unpredictable. Only 23% of the catheters were in the ideal position, meaning that the tip was near the lumbar plexus. Successful 3-in-1 block was observed in 91% of these patients. However, this percentage decreased to 52% when the catheter tip was placed medially under the fascia iliaca, which represented 33% of the catheters. In the majority of cases, 37%, the catheter coursed laterally under the iliacus muscle fascia. In these patients, only 27% had a successful 3-in-1 block. These findings, previously reported for single-injection 3-in-1 blocks, emphasize the fact that local anesthetic solution spreads under the fascia and often one or more nerves of the plexus are spared, resulting in incomplete analgesia.

Even when a catheter is used, the spread of local anesthetic to the lumbar plexus is difficult to obtain[17] with 3-in-1 blocks (Fig. 49-8). The quality of analgesia upon mobilization is significantly better after proximal surgery of the lower limb when the catheter is in the lumbar position; however, this ideal situation is rare and unforeseeable. These data were reinforced by MRI after an inguinal perivascular block in seven patients, which confirmed that the solution was diffused to the femoral and lateral femoral cutaneous nerves in the iliolumbar fossa, and slightly to the anterior branch of the obturator nerve at the proximal thigh, but reaches neither the lumbar plexus inside the psoas muscle nor the intrapelvic portion of the obturator nerve. When the fascia iliaca compartment block is used in infants the femoral nerve can be anesthetized in 100% of cases, the lateral femoral cutaneous nerve in 92% of cases, and the obturator nerve in 88% of cases. Unfortunately, these results have not been supported for adults. The anesthesia obtained with a fascia iliaca block, just as with an inguinal perivascular block in adults, is linked to diffusion spread below the fascia iliaca, anesthetizing the femoral and lateral femoral cutaneous nerves; an authentic lumbar plexus diffusion spread is exceptional.

The results of a block with an anterior approach to the lumbar plexus will vary between a 3.5-in-1 block (femoral nerve, lateral femoral cutaneous nerve, obturator and lumbosacral trunk nerves) and a less than 1-in-1 block (posterior branches of the femoral nerve).

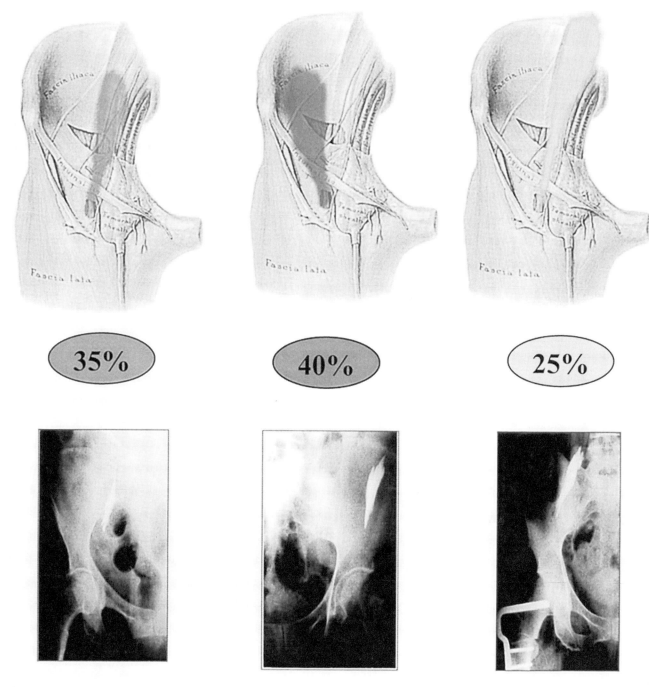

Figure 49-8 Spreads of local anesthetic solutions for continuous three-in-one blocks. Frontal radiographs of the pelvic region showing the spread of the 3 mL of contrast media. (Adapted from Capdevila X, Biboulet P, Morau D, Bernard N, Deschodt J, Lopez S, et al. Continuous three-in-one block for postoperative pain after lower limb orthopedic surgery: where do the catheters go? Anesth Analg 2002;94(4):1001–6.)

By blocking the sciatic nerve in the buttock the three main posterior cutaneous branches of the thigh, tibia, and common fibula can be blocked. A continuous parasacral block, performed using 10–15 mL of local anesthetic, constantly blocks the entire sacral plexus. The continuous popliteal sciatic nerve block is widely used for postoperative analgesia after foot or ankle surgery. The popliteal diffusion spread space allows a relatively predictable spread

of local anesthetics during single-injection blocks or continuous infusion.

OTHER TECHNIQUES

Since the mid-1990s, a number of studies using ultrasound to guide peripheral nerve or plexus blocks have emerged.

Several authors[20–22] have used ultrasound to identify new landmarks or validate currently used ones. They have used it to guide needle or catheter insertion. They have shown the safety of ultrasound-guided supraclavicular brachial plexus blocks in comparison to axillary brachial plexus blocks. They reported no pneumothorax and obtained a better sensory block of the musculocutaneus nerve in patients receiving a supraclavicular brachial plexus block compared to those undergoing an axillary brachial plexus block. The success of supraclavicular approaches to block the brachial plexus using ultrasound guidance was recently confirmed. Chan et al.[20] reported a 95% success rate after only one block attempt, and no complications in 40 patients. Other authors have reported success with this technique when performing infraclavicular brachial plexus blocks, although they have not used a control group. Chan has also demonstrated the advantage of real-time guidance with ultrasound for interscalene brachial plexus blocks. After several failed attempts with nerve stimulation, this author successfully blocked the brachial plexus with a single needle advancement and injection. Although this study involves a case report, it further emphasizes the potential benefit for ultrasound technology in regional anesthesia. Ultrasound guidance has also been used for blocks of the lower limb. Marhofer et al.[23] have shown that 3-in-1 blocks performed by ultrasonographic guidance require reduced amounts of local anesthetic to provide a good sensory block, actually of better quality, when compared to nerve stimulator techniques.

With the same objective of improving efficacy and safety of CPNBs, the use of stimulating catheters has recently been suggested as a potential means of immediately confirming correct catheter placement. Preliminary data by Pham-Dang and coworkers[24] suggest the potential clinical and economic impact of stimulating catheters for continuous perineural analgesia. Although literature concerning stimulating catheters is almost nonexistent, the concept of confirming the catheter's placement during its insertion is logical. Larger prospective controlled studies are necessary to determine the benefits of these more expensive catheters.

SUMMARY

All these studies suggest that imaging may improve the success of regional anesthesia and, more important, the safety of certain nerve blocks. This implication is significant in ambulatory surgery where the improvement of postoperative analgesia techniques will contribute to include a larger number of surgical procedures as ambulatory cases, therefore providing an important cost benefit. It is well known that pain is one of the leading causes of readmission following ambulatory surgery. Therefore, if the efficiency and safety of CPNBs can be improved, pain control in outpatients will also improve. Comparison of different CPNB techniques is only possible if optimal catheter tip position is verified, in order to prevent methodologic bias in interpretation of results. Stimulating catheters may represent an easy way to confirm catheter position and thereby enable comparison between different techniques of PNB.

REFERENCES

1. Chung F, Ritchie E, Su J. Postoperative pain in ambulatory surgery. Anesth Analg 1997;85(4):808–16.
2. Klein SM, Nielsen KC, Greengrass RA, Warner DS, Martin A, Steele SM. Ambulatory discharge after long-acting peripheral nerve blockade: 2382 blocks with ropivacaine. Anesth Analg 2002;94(1):65–70.
3. Capdevila X, Macaire P, Aknin P, Dadure C, Bernard N, Lopez S. Patient-controlled perineural analgesia after ambulatory orthopedic surgery: a comparison of electronic versus elastomeric pumps. Anesth Analg 2003;96(2):414–17.
4. Ilfeld BM, Morey TE, Wright TW, Chidgey LK, Enneking FK. Continuous interscalene brachial plexus block for postoperative pain control at home: a randomized, double-blinded, placebo-controlled study. Anesth Analg 2003;96(4):1089–95.
5. Ilfeld BM, Morey TE, Enneking FK. Continuous infraclavicular brachial plexus block for postoperative pain control at home: a randomized, double-blinded, placebo-controlled study. Anesthesiology 2002;96(6):1297–1304.
6. Ilfeld BM, Morey TE, Wang RD, Enneking FK. Continuous popliteal sciatic nerve block for postoperative pain control at home: a randomized, double-blinded, placebo-controlled study. Anesthesiology 2002;97(4):959–65.
7. Klein SM, Grant SA, Greengrass RA, Nielsen KC, Speer KP, White W, et al. Interscalene brachial plexus block with a continuous catheter insertion system and a disposable infusion pump. Anesth Analg 2000;91(6):1473–78.
8. Klein SM, Steele SM, Nielsen KC, Pietrobon R, Warner DS, Martin A, et al. The difficulties of ambulatory interscalene and intra-articular infusions for rotator cuff surgery: a preliminary report. Can J Anaesth 2003;50(3):265–69.
9. Liu SS, Salinas FV. Continuous plexus and peripheral nerve blocks for postoperative analgesia. Anesth Analg 2003;96(1):263–72.
10. Winnie AP, Radonjic R, Akkineni SR, Durrani Z. Factors influencing distribution of local anesthetic injected into the brachial plexus sheath. Anesth Analg 1979;58(3):225–34.
11. Sims JK. A modification of landmarks for infraclavicular approach to brachial plexus block. Anesth Analg 1977;56(4):554–55.
12. Retzl G, Kapral S, Greher M, Mauritz W. Ultrasonographic findings of the axillary part of the brachial plexus. Anesth Analg 2001;92(5):1271–75.
13. Thompson GE, Rorie DK. Functional anatomy of the brachial plexus sheaths. Anesthesiology 1983;59:117–22.
14. Partridge BL, Katz J, Benirschke K. Functional anatomy of the brachial plexus sheath: implications for anesthesia. Anesthesiology 1987;66:743–47.
15. Klaastad O, Smedby O, Thompson GE, Tillung T, Hol PK, Rotnes JS, et al. Distribution of local anesthetic in axillary brachial plexus block: a clinical and magnetic resonance imaging study. Anesthesiology 2002;96(6):1315–24.
16. Capdevila X, Macaire P, Dadure C, Choquet O, Biboulet P, Ryckwaert Y, et al. Continuous psoas compartment block for postoperative analgesia after total hip arthroplasty: new landmarks, technical guidelines, and clinical evaluation. Anesth Analg 2002;94(6):1606–13.
17. Capdevila X, Biboulet P, Bouregba M, Barthelet Y, Rubenovitch J, d'Athis F. Comparison of the three-in-one and fascia iliaca compartment blocks in adults: clinical and radiographic analysis. Anesth Analg 1998;86(5):1039–44.
18. Marhofer P, Nasel C, Sitzwohl C, Kapral S. Magnetic resonance imaging of the distribution of local anesthetic during the three-in-one block. Anesth Analg 2000;90(1):119–24.
19. Capdevila X, Biboulet P, Morau D, Bernard N, Deschodt J, Lopez S, et al. Continuous three-in-one block for postoperative pain after lower limb orthopedic surgery: where do the catheters go? Anesth Analg 2002;94(4):1001–6.

20. Chan VWS, Perlas A, Rawson R, Odukoya O. Ultrasound-guided supr-aclavicular brachial plexus block. Anesth Analg 2003;97:1514–17.

21. Chan V. Applying ultrasound imaging to interscalene brachial plexus block. Reg Anesth Pain Med 2003;28(4):340–43.

22. Sandhu NS, Capan LM. Ultrasound-guided infraclavicular brachial plexus block. Br J Anaesth 2002;89:254–59.

23. Marhofer P, Schrogendorfer K, Wallner T, Koinig H, Mayer N, Kapral S. Ultrasonographic guidance reduces the amount of local anesthetic for 3-in-1 blocks. Reg Anesth Pain Med 1998;23(6):584–88.

24. Pham-Dang C, Kick O, Collet T, Gouin F, Pinaud M. Continuous peripheral nerve blocks with stimulating catheters. Reg Anesth Pain Med 2003;28(2):83–88.

Ultrasonography and Peripheral Nerve Blocks

VINCENT W.S. CHAN   •   ANAHI PERLAS

INTRODUCTION

The use of regional anesthesia and analgesia has expanded significantly in the last few decades. Many regional techniques offer advantages for an ambulatory anesthesia setting, including better postoperative pain management and earlier hospital discharge.[1,2] However, to become widely accepted in an ambulatory setting, it is essential for these techniques to achieve consistent results with fast block onset, high success rates, and low complication rates. With these goals in mind, many imaging techniques have been explored in the past few years.

For the brachial plexus, magnetic resonance imaging (MRI) has the best definition and is currently the technique of choice for diagnostic imaging of the brachial plexus.[3] However, MRI is costly and not easily accessible for routine brachial plexus blocks. Computed tomography (CT) imaging is also useful but often reserved for selected cases with difficult anatomic landmarks.[4] CT scan likewise suffers from the same drawbacks as MRI in cost and portability. Fluoroscopy has been used to aid brachial plexus identification and performance.[5,6] This technique identifies bony anatomic landmarks but does not visualize neural structures. Most commonly, contrast dye is injected during fluoroscopy, which gives indirect evidence of accurate injection with dye spread along the course of the nerve within the plexus sheath. Finally, ultrasonography has been used successfully to define the anatomy of the brachial plexus in the interscalene, supraclavicular, infraclavicular, and axillary regions.[7] Among the techniques mentioned, ultrasound appears to be most attractive because it is available at the bedside, portable, noninvasive, and easily accessible in the operating room.

All the data published to date on ultrasound imaging of peripheral nerves are encouraging, but preliminary. There are few randomized controlled trials to prove that image-guided techniques are indeed more efficient, successful, or safer than blind techniques.

EQUIPMENT AND ULTRASOUND PRINCIPLES

Ultrasound is a sound wave with frequency greater than 20,000 cycles/sec (20 kHz). Ultrasound can direct as a beam, obeys the laws of reflection and refraction, and is reflected by objects of small size. However, the amount of ultrasound reflected depends on the acoustic mismatch. Propagation through dense objects, e.g., bone, is poor with nearly all of the ultrasound beam reflected. As a result, bone generates a hyperechoic (bright) image as a strong signal is returned to the emitting transducer. On the contrary, fat and tendon have low reflectivity; thus they form hypoechoic (dark) images. The outline of an object is generally best delineated when the ultrasound beam is at 90°. In the transverse (cross-sectional) view, nerves appear as round to oval-shaped nodular structures with internal punctuate echos. They may appear relatively hyper- or hypoechoic to the surrounding structures.

Because of the small size of peripheral nerves, it is essential to use high-quality ultrasound units that allow for high-resolution images. Compound imaging (several layers of ultrasound crystals as opposed to one) may be a desirable feature since it provides higher image resolution. Color Doppler is very helpful to differentiate vascular from neural structures, since many plexuses and peripheral nerves are in close proximity to vascular structures.

The choice of ultrasound probe depends on what anatomic area one wishes to scan, and is determined mainly by the depth required. A wide range of linear and curvilinear probes are available on the market. For most extremity blocks, linear probes are most suited, since they offer less image distortion than curvilinear array probes. When it comes to probes, there is an inverse relationship between the quality of image resolution and the depth; 12 or 15 MHz probes provide excellent resolution and image quality for peripheral nerve imaging, but the scanning depth is limited to 3 or 4 cm. They are well suited for superficial scans like the brachial plexus in the interscalene,

Table 50-1   Ultrasound Probes Best Suited for Imaging of Different Nerve Groups and Nerve Locations

Scanned Area	Linear or Curved	MHz
Interscalene	L	5–12
Supraclavicular	L	5–12 or 7–15
Infraclavicular	L	4–7
Axillary	L	5–12
Femoral nerve	L	5–12
Sciatic nerve	C or L	4–7
Popliteal fossa	L	4–7

supraclavicular, or axillary areas.[8,9] For deeper scans, like the brachial plexus in the infraclavicular area, or for sciatic nerve identification, one needs to use probes that allow for deeper penetration, accepting a lower-image resolution[10] (Table 50-1).

UPPER-EXTREMITY BLOCKS

As discussed above, linear probes of high resolution (12 or 15 MHz) seem to provide optimal image quality for most brachial plexus locations, since in most locations, the roots, trunks, or terminal nerves are very superficial, within 3 cm from the skin.[8,11] One possible exception is the infraclavicular area, where the brachial plexus divisions lie deep to the pectoralis major and pectoralis minor muscles, and therefore require deeper image penetration. For the infraclavicular area, probes between 7 and 10 MHz have been used succesfully.[10,12] When the probe is positioned perpendicular to the longitudinal nerve axis (cross-sectional view), the brachial plexus and its components typically appear as round-to-oval-shaped structures, with fine internal punctuate echos.[13]

Technique of Needle Placement

In most locations the authors recommend obtaining a transverse image of the plexus or its components before needle insertion. Once the nerves and surrounding structures are recognized, the needle is inserted at an angle, from one of the probe ends, and advanced in the same plane of the ultrasound beam, to optimize visualization of the needle shaft.[8] Nerve stimulation may or may not be used as further evidence of nerve localization. Once the needle is positioned in the desired location, local anesthetic can be injected slowly, and the spread is appreciated on the monitor. Sometimes, the bolus injected within the nerve cluster "pushes" the nerves to the periphery, and a "ballooning" effect of the nerve-containing compartment is seen. The needle can be repositioned, if necessary, to ensure spread of local anesthetic to all the neural structures

seen. Success rates reported at this early stage have been consistently around 95%.[9,10]

Interscalene Region

Scanning in the axial oblique plane one can obtain a transverse view of the brachial plexus in the interscalene location.[8] When scanning at the level of the cricoid cartilage (C6), one can quickly identify medial structures (e.g., the internal jugular vein anteriorly to the carotid artery). The sternocleidomastoid muscle is shaped like a triangle with the apex pointing laterally (Fig. 50-1). Deep to the sternocleidomastoid muscle, the brachial plexus is found in the interscalene groove between the scalenus anterior muscle medially and scalenus medius muscle laterally. Depending on the angle of the probe, one to three nerve roots or trunks are seen as nodular hypoechoic structures.

Sheppard et al.[13] scanned the brachial plexus in a coronal oblique view with 5–10-MHz probes. Nerve roots can be seen exiting the cervical neural foramina and roots and trunks can be followed from their origin to the clavicle with ultrasound. There is good correlation between ultrasound and MRI findings. Similarly, Martinoli et al.[14] examined the brachial plexus at the cervical root level and showed good correlation between ultrasound and CT imaging. For brachial plexus block, Yang et al.[11] placed catheters in the interscalene groove using ultrasound guidance and confirmed correct position with radiographic and CT examination. In our recent study,[8] we have developed an ultrasound-guided technique for needle placement in the interscalene region. By introducing the block needle from the end of the ultrasound probe and advancing in line with the plane of the beam, we can direct the needle to reach the brachial plexus under real-time guidance (Fig. 50-2). The needle can be visualized consistently and advanced with purposeful movement (Fig. 50-3). Once the needle is seen in contact with the desired root, local anesthetic is injected gradually in the usual fashion and the

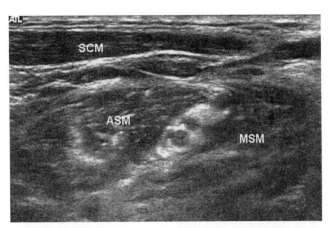

Figure 50-1   Anatomy of the brachial plexus at the interscalene groove as depicted by ultrasound. ASM = anterior scalene muscle, MSM = middle scalene muscle, SCM = sternocleidomastoid muscle. Note the brachial plexus roots in a transverse section, as hypoechoic, rounded structures, lying in an oblique plane between the anterior and middle scalene muscles.

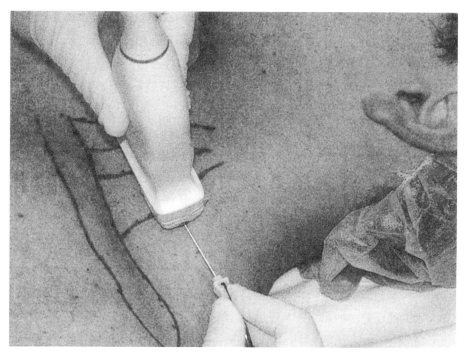

Figure 50-2   Ultrasound probe and needle position for the performance of interscalene brachial plexus block.

spread of the solution can be appreciated in the interscalene space (Fig. 50-4).

Supraclavicular Region

Ultrasound images in the supraclavicular region are best scanned in the coronal oblique plane in the authors' experience (Fig. 50-5). The subclavian artery, a round pulsatile hypoechoic structure, is consistently found lying immediately above the first rib. The brachial plexus can be found in grape-like clusters laterally, posteriorly, and often cephalad to the subclavian artery (Fig. 50-6). More medially, the subclavian vein, a pulsatile structure with valves, and the anterior scalene muscle are seen. Pleura

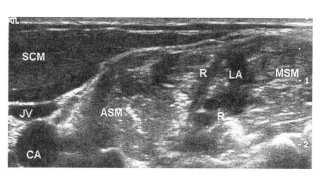

Figure 50-4   Same patient as in Figure 50-3. Local anesthetic solution has been injected and we can see it "bathing" the cervical roots. The needle has been withdrawn. ASM = anterior scalene muscle, MSM = middle scalene muscle, SCM = sternocleidomastoid muscle, R = nerve root, LA = local anesthetic, JV = jugular vein, CA = carotid artery.

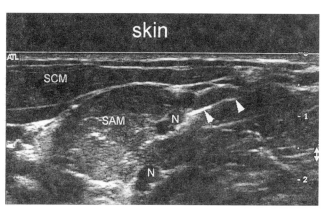

Figure 50-3   Nerve localization during ultrasound-guided interscalene brachial plexus block. Note the tip of the needle in direct contact with a cervical root. SAM = scalenus anterior muscle, SCM = sternocleidomastoid muscle, N = nerve roots; arrowheads indicate the needle shaft.

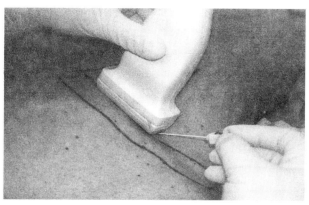

Figure 50-5   Ultrasound probe and needle position for the performance of supraclavicular brachial plexus block. Note the probe located parallel and immediately cephalad to the clavicle.

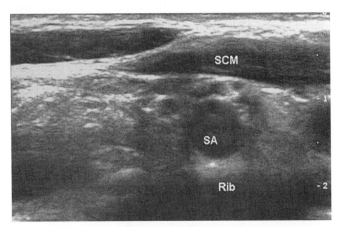

Figure 50-6 Anatomy of the brachial plexus in the supraclavicular fossa. Note the nerve trunks seen in a transverse plane, as rounded hypoechoic structures in close proximity to the subclavian artery. SCM = sternocleidomastoid muscle, SA = subclavian artery.

can be found on either side of the first rib. It is also hyperechoic and moves with respiration. Identification of the brachial plexus, vessels, lung, and first rib prior to needle insertion helps define the path of the block needle and improve safety.

Kapral et al.[9] performed ultrasound-guided supraclavicular brachial plexus block with catheter and compared it with ultrasound-guided axillary brachial plexus block. Catheter position in the plexus sheath was confirmed radiologically with contrast dye. Interestingly, block success was comparable (95%) in both groups. Pneumothorax did not occur. Yang et al.[11] also reported using ultrasound for placing supraclavicular brachial plexus catheters in four patients. In the authors' recently completed clinical series of ultrasound-guided supraclavicular brachial plexus blocks on 40 patients, 95% success rate was also obtained.[15] Needle movement could be tracked under ultrasound guidance, and local anesthetic spread was observed (Fig. 50-7).

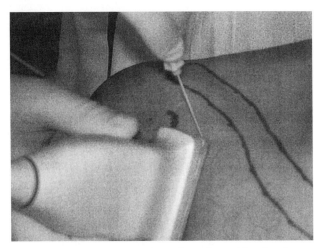

Figure 50-8 Ultrasound probe and needle position for the performance of infraclavicular brachial plexus block.

Infraclavicular Region

Several locations between the midclavicle (infraclavicular vertical approach)[16] and the coracoid process (coracoid approach)[17] are suitable for scanning the brachial plexus in the infraclavicular region. At midclavicle, one can visualize the subclavian artery and vein with the cords of the brachial plexus most commonly cephaloposterior to the subclavian artery.[12] When scanned in the parasagittal plane, 2 cm medially to the coracoid process, the cords of the brachial plexus are deep to the pectoralis major and pectoralis minor muscles and in close proximity to the axillary artery and vein (Figs. 50-8 and 50-9). For the infraclavicular region, the authors find that images are best obtained with a 7-MHz probe. Similarly to the previous approaches, the needle can be advanced and the local anesthetic injected under direct ultrasound guidance (Fig. 50-10).

Greher et al.[12] used ultrasound to assess topographic anatomy in the infraclavicular region and concluded that the

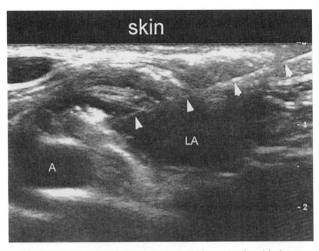

Figure 50-7 Nerve localization during ultrasound-guided supraclavicular brachial plexus block. Note the needle in close proximity to the nerve trunks, with the tip positioned just cephalad to the subclavian artery. A = subclavian artery, LA = local anesthetic solution; arrowheads indicate the needle shaft.

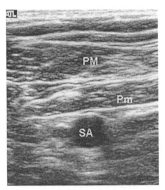

Figure 50-9 Anatomy of the brachial plexus in the infraclavicular region. In this frame three neural structures can be identified at the 2 o'clock, 5 o'clock, and 10 o'clock positions in relation to the subclavian artery. PM = pectoralis major muscle, Pm = pectoralis minor muscle, SA = subclavian artery.

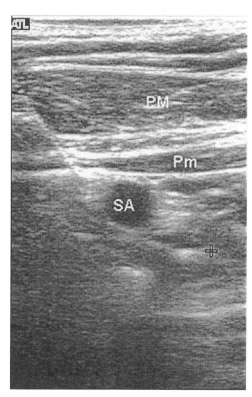

Figure 50-10   Needle localization during ultrasound-guided infraclavicular brachial plexus block. PM = pectoralis major, Pm = pectoralis minor, SA = subclavian artery.

surface landmarks suggested for the site of needle puncture by Kilka et al.[16] for the vertical approach is often too medial. Ootaki et al.[10] performed infraclavicular brachial plexus blocks guided by a 7-MHz probe. Needle and local anesthetic were placed adjacent to the subclavian artery without visualization of the brachial plexus. Local anesthetic injection generated a ring-shaped shadow around the artery and resulted in consistent success. Using a 2.5-MHz probe, Sandu and Capan[18] deposited local anesthetic in each of the three cords of the brachial plexus and accomplished 90% block success. Greher et al.[12] compared ultrasound-guided with nerve stimulator–guided infraclavicular brachial plexus block. Block success was higher and vascular puncture was less frequent with the ultrasound technique.

Axillary Region

When scanned at the axillary fold in a 90° outstretched arm (Fig. 50-11), terminal branches of the brachial plexus can be easily identified in close relationship to the axillary artery (commonly one) and veins (commonly one to two). Veins can be differentiated from the artery by their ease of compressibility and by color flow Doppler. Ultrasound imaging often shows two or three distinct hypoechoic nodules representing the median, ulnar, and radial nerves within 1 cm from skin surface (Fig. 50-12). Other structures commonly identified are the biceps, coracobrachialis, and triceps muscles. Figure 50-13 illustrates the ultrasound appearance of local anesthetic spread in the axillary area.

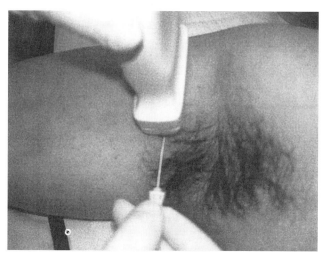

Figure 50-11   Ultrasound probe and needle position for the performance of axillary brachial plexus block.

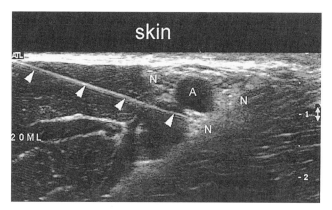

Figure 50-12   Anatomy and localization of the three main terminal nerves of the brachial plexus in the axillary area. Note the needle tip in close contact with the radial nerve. A = axillary artery, N = nerve; arrowheads indicate the needle shaft.

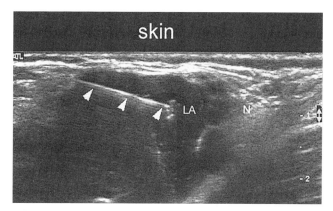

Figure 50-13   Neurovascular anatomy of the axilla during injection of local anesthetic. Note the nerves and the artery being "pushed away" by the local anesthetic solution. LA = local anesthetic solution, N = nerve.

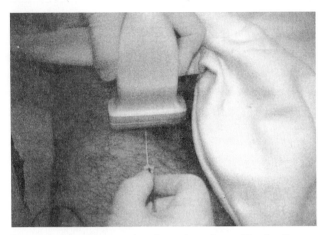

Figure 50-14 Ultrasound probe and needle position for the performance of femoral nerve block.

Using ultrasound, Retzl et al.[19] examined anatomic variations of the terminal branches of brachial plexus in the axilla. They found that at the usual level of axillary brachial plexus block, the radial nerve is most often located in the posterior and anterior lateral position in reference to the axillary artery. The median nerve is most commonly located in the anterior and posterior medial positions and the ulnar nerve in the posterior medial position. However, these nerves can be found in many other locations. Ultrasound guidance for axillary catheter placement has also been described.[20,21]

LOWER-EXTREMITY BLOCKS

At this time, there is a minimal amount of published data for ultrasound-guided lower-extremity blocks. We have used ultrasound guidance for the performance of femoral, sciatic, and popliteal sciatic nerve blocks (Figs. 50-14, 50-15, 50-16, 50-17, and 50-18). Note that as opposed to brachial plexus approaches, the authors frequently use a needle insertion perpendicular to the probe. The rationale behind this is that in the lower extremity, nerves tend to be more deeply localized, and a longitudinal needle approach may require a longer nee-

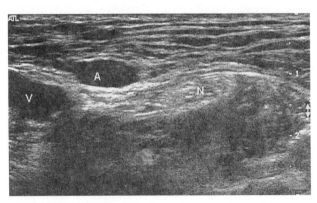

Figure 50-15 Imaging of the femoral nerve and vessels (left side). V = vein, A = artery, N = nerve.

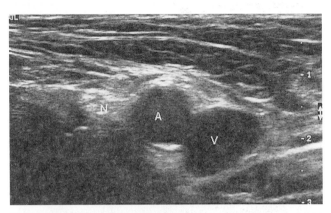

Figure 50-16 Imaging of the femoral nerve and vessels (right side). V = vein, A = artery, N = nerve.

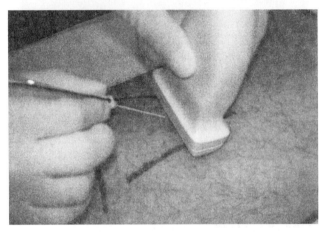

Figure 50-17 Ultrasound probe and needle position for the performance of popliteal sciatic nerve block.

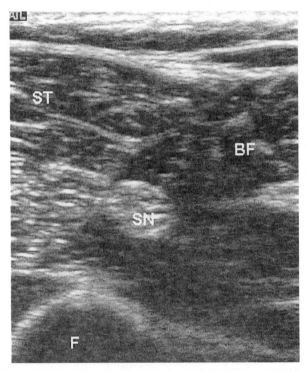

Figure 50-18 Ultrasound localization of the sciatic nerve block at midthigh. ST = semitendinosus, BF = biceps femoris, SN = sciatic nerve, F = femur.

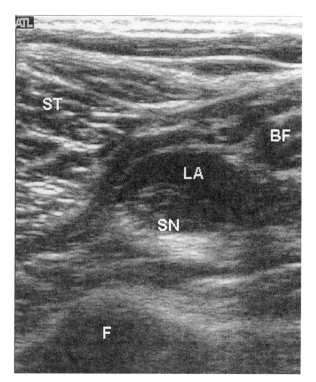

Figure 50-19   Local anesthetic spreading around the sciatic nerve at the midthigh level. ST = semitendinosus, BF = biceps femoris, SN = sciatic nerve, LA = local anesthetic solution, F = femur.

dle trajectory, making needle manipulation more difficult. Marhofer et al.[22] showed that ultrasound localization of the femoral nerve and its surrounding structures can reduce the onset time, improve the quality of sensory block, and minimize the risk of vascular puncture for the 3-in-1 block as compared with the nerve stimulator technique. For the posterior lumbar plexus approach, Kirchmair et al.[23] found ultrasound helpful in guiding the needle into the psoas compartment in cadavers. Although ultrasound could not identify nerves in this location, the psoas major muscle and adjacent structures (quadratus lumborum muscle, kidney, and vertebrae) were visualized, providing reference landmarks for needle placement.

Ultrasound identification of the sciatic nerve in the gluteal region proves difficult because of its deep location. Heinemeyer and Reimers[24] could not identify the sciatic nerve in the popliteal fossa in 26% of the subjects. A recent case report has been published of a sciatic nerve block in a child.[25] With a 7-MHz probe, the authors have identified the sciatic nerve in different locations between the subgluteal region and the popliteal fossa (Fig. 50-17). Although the sciatic nerve is sizable, the authors find visualization not always easy owing to the required depth of beam penetration and sometimes ill-defined interface between the sciatic nerve and surrounding fat in the lower extremity (Fig. 50-18). The local anesthetic solution usually spreads in a circumferential manner, surrounding the sciatic nerve with a ring shape, making the nerve more distinct (Fig. 50-19).

In summary, advanced ultrasound technology today can visualize nerves prior to needle insertion and is an im-

proved method of nerve localization. Observing needle advancement real time under ultrasound guidance can improve block accuracy and safety. Future studies are required to further define the clinical utility of ultrasound for peripheral nerve blocks.

REFERENCES

1. Pavlin DJ, Rapp SE, Polissar NL, Malmgren JA, Koerschgen M, Keyes H. Factors affecting discharge time in adult outpatients. Anesth Analg 1998;87:816–26.

2. Chan VW, Peng PW, Kaszas Z, Middleton WJ, Muni R, Anastakis DG, Graham BA. A comparative study of general anesthesia, intravenous regional anesthesia, and axillary block for outpatient hand surgery: clinical outcome and cost analysis. Anesth Analg 2001;93:1181–84.

3. Wong GY, Brown DL, Miller GM, Cahill DR. Defining the cross-sectional anatomy important to interscalene brachial plexus block with magnetic resonance imaging. Reg Anesth Pain Med 1998;23:77–80.

4. Mukherji S, Wagle A, Armao D. Brachial plexus nerve block with CT guidance for regional pain management. Radiology 2000;216:886–90.

5. Nishiyama M, Naganuma K, Amaki Y. A new approach for brachial plexus block under fluoroscopic guidance. Anesth Analg 1999;88: 91–97.

6. Moorty SS. Fluoroscopic imaging during supraclavicular lateral paravascular brachial plexus block. Reg Anesth Pain Med 2000;25: 327–28.

7. Peterson MK, Millar FA, Sheppard DG. Ultrasound-guided nerve blocks. Br J Anaesth 2002;88:621–24.

8. Perlas A, Chan VWS, Simons M. Brachial plexus examination and localization using ultrasound and electrical stimulation—a volunteer study. Anesthesiology 2003;99:429–35.

9. Kapral S, Krafft P, Eibenberger K. Ultrasound-guided supraclavicular approach for regional anesthesia of the brachial plexus. Anesth Analg 1994;78:507–13.

10. Ootaki C, Hayashi H, Amano M. Ultrasound guided infraclavicular brachial plexus block: an alternative technique to anatomical landmark-guided approaches. Reg Anesth Pain Med 2000;25:600–4.

11. Yang WT, Chui PT, Metreweli C. Anatomy of the normal brachial plexus revealed by sonography and the role of sonographic guidance in anesthesia of the brachial plexus. Am J Roentgenol 1998; 171:1631–36.

12. Greher M, Retzl G, Niel P, et al. Ultrasonographic assessment of topographic anatomy in volunteers suggests a modification of the infraclavicular vertical brachial plexus block. Br J Anaesth 2002;88: 632–36.

13. Sheppard D, Iyer R, Fernstermacher M. Brachial plexus: demonstration at ultrasound. Radiology 1998;208:402–6.

14. Martinoli C, Bianchi S, Santacroce E, Pugliese F, Graif M, Derchi LE. Brachial plexus sonography: a technique for assessing the root level. Am J Roentgenol 2002;179:699–702.

15. Chan VWS, Perlas A, Rawson R, Odukoya O. Ultrasound guided supraclavicular brachial plexus block. Anesth Analg 2003;97: 1514–17.

16. Kilka HG, Geiger P, Mehrkens HH. Infraclavicular vertical brachial plexus blockade: a new method for anesthesia of the upper extremity. An anatomical and clinical study. Anaesthesist 1995;44: 339–44.

17. Wilson JL, Brown DL, Wong GY, Ehman RL, Cahill DR. Infraclavicular brachial plexus block: parasagital anatomy important to the coracoid technique. Anesth Analg 1998;87:870–73.

18. Sandhu NS, Capan LM. Ultrasound-guided infraclavicular brachial plexus block. Br J Anaesth 2002;89:254–59.

19. Retzl G, Kapral S, Greher M, Mauritz W. Ultrasonographic findings of the axillary part of the brachial plexus. Anesth Analg 2001;92: 1271–75.

20. Ting PL, Sivagnanaratnam V. Ultrasonographic study of the spread of local anaesthetic during axillary brachial plexus block. Br J Anaesth 1989;63:326–29.

21. Guzeldemir ME, Ustunsoz B. Ultrasonographic guidance in placing a catheter for continuous axillary brachial plexus block. Anesth Analg 1995;81:882–83.

22. Marhofer P, Schrogendorfer K, Koinig H, Kapral S, Weinstabl C, Mayer N. Ultrasonographic guidance improves sensory block and onset time of three-in-one blocks. Anesth Analg 1997;85:854–57.

23. Kirchmair L, Entner T, Kapral S, Mitterschiffthaler G. Ultrasound guidance for the psoas compartment block: an imaging study. Anesth Analg 2002;94:706–10.

24. Heinemeyer O, Reimers CD. Ultrasound of radial, ulnar, median and sciatic nerves in healthy subjects and patients with hereditary motor and sensory neuropathies. Ultrasound Med Biol 1999;25:481–85.

25. Gray AT, Collins AB, Schafhalter-Zoppoth I. Sciatic nerve block in a child: a sonographic approach. Anesth Analg 2003;97:1300–302.

COLOR PLATES

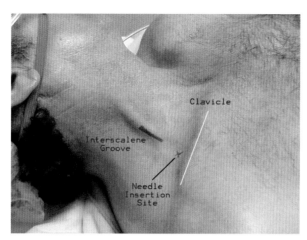

Plate 1 (p. 379) Supraclavicular brachial plexus block—subclavian perivascular technique landmarks.

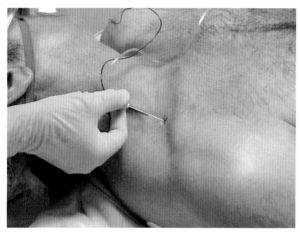

Plate 2 (p. 379) Needle direction during subclavian perivascular brachial plexus block placement.

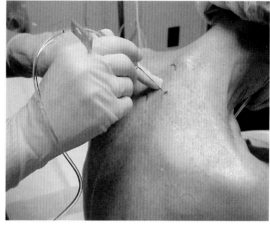

Plate 4 (p. 384) Needle direction during thoracic paravertebral block placement.

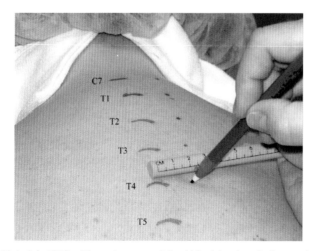

Plate 3 (p. 383) Thoracic paravertebral block landmarks for modified radical mastectomy. C7–T5 spinous processes are marked.

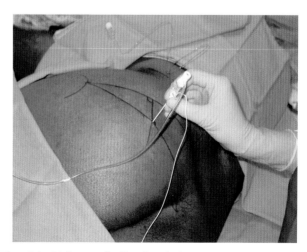

Plate 5 (p. 387) Needle direction during continuous sciatic nerve block placement (classic Labat's technique).

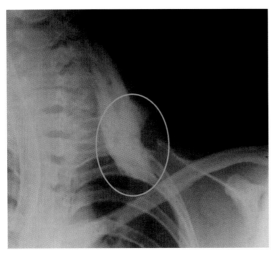

Plate 6 (p. 537)   Single-injection interscalene brachial plexus block with 30 mL of local anesthetic solution.

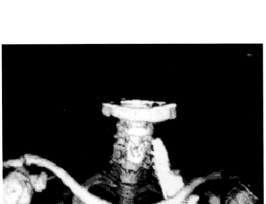

Plate 7 (p. 537)   Three-dimensional computed tomographic scan of a single-injection interscalene brachial plexus block with 30 mL of local anesthetic solution.

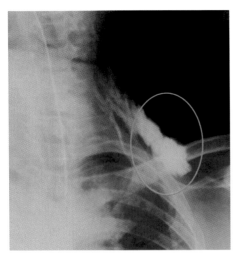

Plate 8 (p. 537)   Continuous interscalene brachial plexus block: 2.5 cm of threaded catheter and 30 mL of local anesthetic solution. The result of the solution spread looks like a supraclavicular brachial plexus block.

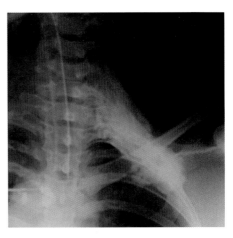

Plate 9 (p. 537)   Continuous interscalene brachial plexus block: 4 cm of threaded catheter and 30 mL of local anesthetic solution. The result of the solution spread looks like an infraclavicular brachial plexus block.

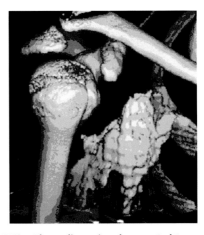

Plate 10 (p. 538)   Three-dimensional computed tomographic scan of a continuous axillary brachial plexus block: 5 cm of threaded catheter and 30 mL of local anesthetic solution. The spread of the local anesthetic solution filled all the axillary space.

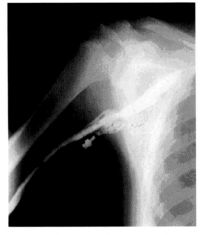

Plate 11 (p. 538)   Continuous axillary brachial plexus block: 5 cm of threaded catheter and 30 mL of local anesthetic solution. The spread of the local anesthetic solution was only located along the median nerve.

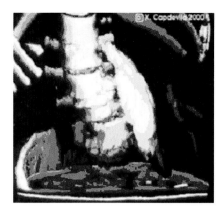

Plate 12 (p. 539) Three-dimensional computed tomographic scan of a continuous psoas compartment block: 3 cm of threaded catheter and 25 mL of local anesthetic solution.

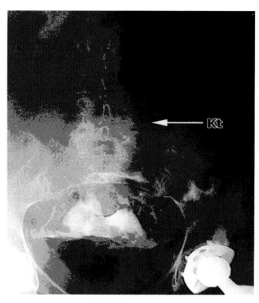

Plate 14 (p. 540) Continuous psoas compartment block: 3 cm of threaded catheter and 30 mL of local anesthetic solution. The spread of the local anesthetic solution was located into the peritoneal cavity.

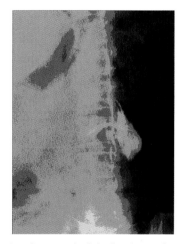

Plate 13 (p. 539) The spread of the local anesthetic solution was located in the psoas compartment and as a unilateral epidural anesthesia.

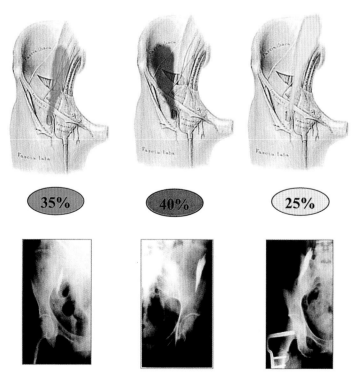

Plate 15 (p. 541) Spreads of local anesthetic solutions for continuous three-in-one blocks. Frontal radiographs of the pelvic region showing the spread of the 3 mL of contrast media. (Adapted from Capdevila X, Biboulet P, Morau D, Bernard N, Deschodt J, Lopez S, et al. Continuous three-in-one block for postoperative pain after lower limb orthopedic surgery: where do the catheters go? Anesth Analg 2002; 94(4):1001–6.)

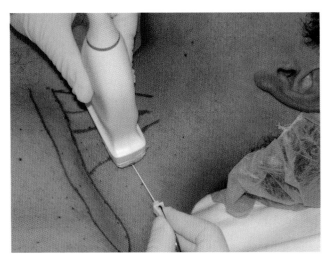

Plate 16 (p. 547)   Ultrasound probe and needle position for the performance of interscalene brachial plexus block.

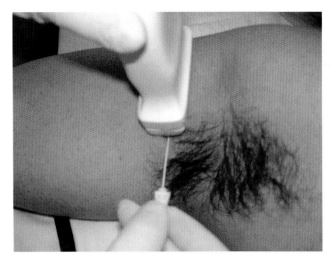

Plate 19 (p. 549)   Ultrasound probe and needle position for the performance of axillary brachial plexus block.

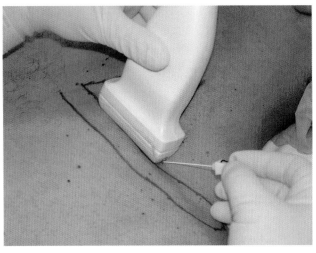

Plate 17 (p. 547)   Ultrasound probe and needle position for the performance of supraclavicular brachial plexus block. Note the probe located parallel and immediately cephalad to the clavicle.

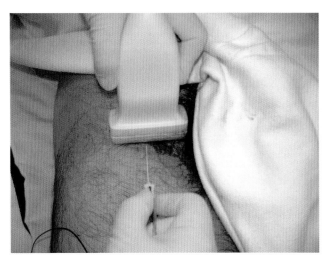

Plate 20 (p. 550)   Ultrasound probe and needle position for the performance of femoral nerve block.

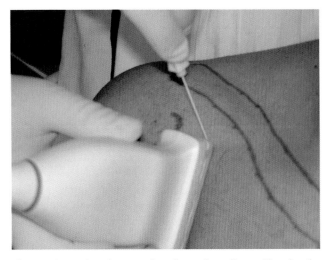

Plate 18 (p. 548)   Ultrasound probe and needle position for the performance of infraclavicular brachial plexus block.

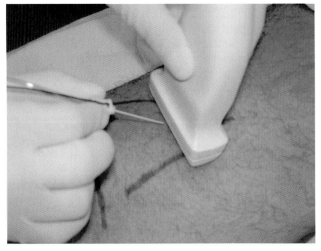

Plate 21 (p. 550)   Ultrasound probe and needle position for the performance of popliteal sciatic nerve block.

The Future of Ambulatory Surgery and Regional Anesthesia

SHRUTI SHAH • JERRY D. VLOKA • ADMIR HADZIC

INTRODUCTION

Ambulatory surgery in the United States continues to grow, at present comprising over 70% of all elective surgical procedures performed annually.[1] Significant recent advances in surgical techniques, such as endoscopic, laser, and minimally invasive arthroscopic procedures, have permitted many higher-risk patients to safely undergo a wide variety of procedures in an ambulatory setting.[2,3] This trend will likely persist as long as both patients and payers continue to reward improvements in surgical technology. The use of regional anesthesia and the ability to safely "fast-track" ambulatory surgery patients are becoming increasingly important elements in ambulatory surgery for both adults and children.[4,5] Conventional fast tracking allows patients who meet specific criteria before leaving the operating room (OR) to bypass the postanesthesia care unit (PACU) Phase 1 and proceed directly to the step-down unit (Phase 2). Such practice requires less monitoring, the patients can meet with family members immediately after the surgery, and they are permitted to ambulate, change into street clothes, and can be discharged home directly from the Phase 2 unit. The advances in surgical techniques, however, must be coupled with appropriate changes in anesthesia techniques to meet the growing demands for a cost-effective, safe, and pleasant recovery after ambulatory surgery. In this chapter, we discuss the current trends in ambulatory regional anesthesia and forecast the future of the field.

REGIONAL ANESTHESIA IN AN AMBULATORY SURGERY SETTING

A successful ambulatory surgical program depends on the appropriate and timely discharge of patients. Several studies have shown that after ambulatory surgery, rapid discharge protocols can be implemented for many patients and surgical procedures without significantly increasing the complications or side effects.[6] The key benefits of regional anesthesia, including less pain and emesis in the postoperative period, faster recovery and discharge, and improved patient satisfaction, all fit well within the modern framework of ambulatory surgery. The centerpiece of ambulatory anesthesia remains preemptive multimodal analgesia, antiemetic prophylaxis, and avoidance of general anesthesia (GA) with volatile agents.[7] In a review of 1200 consecutive patients, among patients who received peripheral nerve blocks for complex knee surgery, there was a lower incidence of nursing interventions and fewer unplanned hospital admission than in patients undergoing similar procedures without nerve blocks.[8] Indeed, the use of nerve blocks, particularly in patients undergoing orthopedic surgery, can optimize both surgical conditions and postoperative analgesia. The use of peripheral nerve blocks with avoidance of GA has been associated with less postoperative pain, nausea, vomiting, and unplanned hospital admissions after outpatient anterior cruciate ligament reconstruction.[9–11] Various regional anesthesia/analgesia strategies (peripheral nerve blocks, continuous perineural catheters for sensory-specific block, and the avoidance of GA with volatile agents) hold promise to result in a speedier and more pleasant recovery throughout the first 2–4 days after complex outpatient knee procedures.

As increasingly more complex surgery is performed on an outpatient basis, thromboprophylaxis will likely play an important role in decreasing the complications after outpatient surgery. The superiority of low-molecular-weight heparin (LMWH) to unfractionated heparin (UFH) for the treatment of acute thromboembolic events is supported by a recent meta-analysis of 13 well-designed, randomized trials conducted up to early 1998 (involving 4354 patients).[12]

In addition to better outcomes, the lower rates of recurrence and complications associated with LMWH translate into substantial cost savings. For instance, prevention of one recurrence yields a savings of $9337, prevention of one episode of pulmonary embolism reduces costs by $12,796, and prevention of one hemorrhage saves $1075.[13,14] In addition, the costs created by the side effects of recurrent thrombosis, including chronic venous insufficiency and postphlebitic syndrome, can also be substantial. In one study, patients assigned to outpatient treatment with LMWH had a 12.2% reduction in the rate of recurrence of deep venous thrombosis (DVT) and its complications.[15] Outpatient treatment of DVT with LMWH is at least as safe and effective as traditional inpatient treatment with UFH and quite practical, as 95% of eligible patients were able to complete a full course of LMWH treatment at home. The more widespread perioperative use of LMWH will likely cause a shift toward the selection of peripheral nerve blocks over central neuraxial blocks because of the risk of spinal and epidural hematoma in patients on LMWH.

CURRENT TRENDS IN REGIONAL ANESTHESIA FOR AMBULATORY SURGERY

The use of regional anesthesia in ambulatory surgery has significantly increased in the past decade, as predicted in earlier surveys.[16] The increase in the interest and use of regional anesthesia can be attributed to a number of causes: (1) a greater emphasis on perioperative analgesia, (2) a perceived improvement in outcome, (3) a wider availability of the training in regional anesthesia, (4) improved techniques, equipment, and drugs used for regional anesthesia, and (5) better patient education.[17]

Emerging Regional Anesthesia Techniques

The current emphasis on containment of health care costs has resulted in a rediscovery of anesthetic techniques that can facilitate outpatient surgical management and promote early discharge. For example, while central neuraxial anesthesia has often been used for outpatients undergoing inguinal herniorrhaphy, the delayed discharge and occurrence of orthostatic hypotension and urinary retention associated with these techniques limits their application in an outpatient setting. In contrast, paravertebral blocks produce excellent surgical conditions, while providing profound long-lasting analgesia with few undesirable side effects in the ambulatory setting.[18–22]

New techniques that allow extension of the benefits of peripheral nerve blocks in outpatients have emerged, such as continuous nerve blocks.[23–27] Several recent studies suggest that continuous perineural infusions have the potential to provide improved analgesia after outpatient shoulder surgery.[27–29] However, a successful localization of the brachial plexus and administration of local anesthetic via a perineurally inserted catheter does not always yield the expected analgesic results. In a study by Klein et al., the authors prospectively enrolled 17 patients undergoing outpatient rotator cuff surgery.[30] All patients received an interscalene brachial plexus block, followed by either a continuous *interscalene brachial plexus perineural* or *intra-articular* infusion through a catheter. In both groups, the infusion consisted of 0.2% ropivacaine at a rate of 10 mL/hr, supplemented by naproxen 500 mg, and acetaminophen 325 mg with oxycodone 5 mg. The authors stopped the study after 17 patients because 52% of the interscalene brachial plexus perineural infusion patients and 71% of the intra-articular infusion patients reported suboptimal analgesia. The authors concluded that both techniques failed to provide reliable analgesia and patient satisfaction. The most common problems were that many patients had pain, leakage from the catheter insertion site, and breakthrough pain, despite treatment with oral naproxen and acetaminophen with oxycodone for breakthrough pain. One patient even required hospitalization after treatment.

A methodologically similar study by another group[23] yielded more positive results, but excluded patients with failed blocks or patients with difficulty in inserting the catheters. In this study, the authors randomized 25 patients undergoing ambulatory shoulder surgery to receive a continuous infusion or placebo through a catheter placed perineurally in the interscalene groove. Using a continuous infusion of 0.2% ropivacaine at a rate of 8 mL/hr with a 2-mL patient-controlled analgesia (PCA) bolus dose every 15 min significantly decreased pain, opioid use, sleep disturbances, and other side effects compared to the placebo group and resulted in higher patient satisfaction and acceptance.

These two studies convey two important messages. First, intra-articular infusion of local anesthetic appears to be ineffective for postoperative pain relief, at least in patients having rotator cuff repair. Second, continuous perineural infusion of local anesthetic with PCA boluses does have the potential to provide excellent pain relief after shoulder surgery. However, more studies are clearly needed to determine optimal patient selection, technique,[31,32] equipment,[28,33,34] local anesthetic mixture and dosing regimen[35,36] to optimize the success rate and consistency of postoperative pain relief with continuous perineural techniques. This is particularly important in view of potential risks associated with the use of at-home perineural local anesthetic infusions, such as catheter site infection,[37] nerve injury,[38] catheter migration, local anesthetic toxicity,[39] and unintentional spread of the blockade epidurally or intrathecally.[40]

Nerve Localization

In recent years, there has been a growing interest in the development of imaging-guided nerve and plexus block techniques. Such trend is not surprising as localizing nerves prior to injection of local anesthetic is a crucial and perhaps the most challenging task for practitioners. Both magnetic resonance imaging[41] and computed tomographic scanning[42] provide excellent anatomic images of the brachial plexus, but they are expensive and inaccessible to the OR. Fluoroscopy is often used in pain management practice,[43,44] but its usefulness is limited to the utilization of bony landmarks and contrast-dye spread near to the neurovascular bundle within the plexus sheath. In addition, this technology is expensive and simply impractical in busy clinical practice.

Ultrasound is noninvasive, portable, more moderately priced, and has recently gained interest by some groups.[45] This real-time imaging technology can aid placement of brachial plexus blocks in the interscalene,[46] supraclavicular,[47] and infraclavicular regions.[48–50] Most previous ultrasound studies examining brachial plexus anatomy used scanning probes with a frequency in the range of 5–10 MHz. Advanced ultrasound technology today offers high-resolution probes (12–15 MHz) and compound imaging. High-frequency linear probes allow for the visualization of relatively small tissue structures, such as peripheral nerves close to the surface. By providing imaging of anatomic structures, ultrasound can potentially reduce the risks associated with nerve localization and increase the accuracy of the needle placement. Such new image-enhancing capability allows clear visualization of nerves and can potentially improve the technique of ultrasound-assisted brachial plexus block.[51,52]

The future of ultrasound in clinical anesthesiology will imminently focus on developing ever more portable, affordable, and high-image-quality units.

Our better understanding of the potential of nerve stimulators has led to their ubiquitous use for nerve localization.[53] This increase in clinical usage has undoubtedly resulted in a more objective approach to peripheral nerve blockade and a more clinician- and patient-friendly approach. Recent data suggest, however, that older units can be imprecise.[54] It is expected that newer models of nerve stimulators will be more accurate with standardized electrical features in order to obtain more consistent results.[54]

Pharmacologic Advances and Trends

While bupivacaine perhaps still remains as the most widely used long-acting local anesthetic, it has been associated with potentially fatal cardiotoxicity, particularly when accidentally given intravascularly.[55] The cardiotoxicity of bupivacaine stimulated interest in developing less toxic, long-lasting local anesthetics.[56] The development of *ropivacaine* and *levobupivacaine* is a direct result of that search. Ropivacaine, an enantiomer of 1-propyl-2', 6'-pipecolocylidide, was chosen because it has a lower toxicity than the R isomer. This is presumably because of slower uptake, resulting in lower blood levels for a given dose (5–7 hr, respectively). Dose-response data in volunteers and clinical studies have shown its potency to be approximately half of that of bupivacaine.[57,58] However, in concentrations of 0.5% and higher, it produces dense blockade with slightly shorter duration than bupivacaine. In concentrations of 0.75%, the onset of blockade is as fast as that of 1.5% mepivacaine or 3% 2-chloroprocaine, with reduced central nervous system (CNS) and cardiac toxicity potentials and a lower propensity for motor block. For these reasons, ropivacaine has become one of the most commonly used long-acting local anesthetics in peripheral nerve blockade.

Levobupivacaine contains a single enantiomer of bupivacaine hydrochloride, and is also similarly related chemically and pharmacologically to the amino amide class of local anesthetics. Few studies have examined the blocking properties of levobupivacaine in peripheral nerve blockade; however, the available studies suggest that they seem to parallel those of bupivacaine while having the benefit of a significantly lesser potential for cardiotoxicity.[55]

Limited duration of the analgesia and the recurrence of pain when the blocks resolve are some of the main limitations of regional anesthesia techniques. Ultralong-acting local anesthetic for nerve blocks or wound infiltration would theoretically be clinically very useful for patients undergoing ambulatory surgery that results in significant postoperative pain. Such a long-acting anesthetic agent would provide analgesia for several days, be free of local irritant effects, and result in mostly sensory blockade. Efforts have focused mostly on two types of compounds: liposomes and microspheres.

Liposomes are sealed sacs in the micron range that contain water-soluble drugs and can be slowly dispersed in an aqueous environment. They are biocompatible as a result of their biodegradability and low toxicity and quite convenient to administer as they can be administered via the intramuscular, subcutaneous, pulmonary, nasal, oral, topical, and intravenous (IV) routes,[59–63] in the vicinity of peripheral nerves,[64] and central neuraxially.[65] Studies examining the effectiveness of liposomes demonstrated encouraging results. Liposomes have been shown to significantly increase the duration of nerve blockade in comparison with free local anesthetic and provide analgesia up to 4 days.[66,67] Importantly, studies have also shown a reduction of CNS and cardiac toxicity of bupivacaine encapsulated in multilamellar liposomes when infused intravascularly, epidurally, and subcutaneously.[60–62]

Like liposomes, microspheres have the ability to deliver long-acting analgesia. Microspheres range from 10 to 150 microns in size and are thus larger than liposomes.[68] They are comprised of biodegradable polymers, whose varying properties can cause nerve blocks to last from 10 hr to 5.5 days. The addition of small amounts of dexamethasone to microspheres containing bupivacaine can significantly increase the duration of blockade in a safe manner, as plasma bupivacaine levels are far below those associated with systemic toxicity.[69] Controlled-release of bupivacaine and dexamethasone from microspheres has been shown to produce lengthy nerve block in sheep, up to 16 days.[70] Similarly, the research in humans also suggests that bupivacaine-loaded microspheres can be equally effective.[69,71]

Intravenous Sedation

Administration of regional anesthesia is most commonly coupled with IV sedation to provide patient comfort and supplement any unexpected intraoperative discomfort. As the recovery after intraoperative sedation is often a rate-limiting step in discharge of ambulatory surgery patients home, careful selection of drugs, dosages, and monitoring of the depth of sedation will play an increasingly important role. It has been well established that avoidance of airway instrumentation and administration of short-acting sedatives/hypnotic agents such as propofol constitutes the most appropriate intraoperative management of patients undergoing outpatient surgery.[72–74]

New techniques of administering drugs for IV sedation have been developed to better fit the ambulatory surgery setting. Patient-controlled sedation devices deliver a predefined bolus of IV drug during an established period of time with or without a lockout interval.[75] This method has been shown to result in better cooperation of patients and shorter awakening and discharge times, as well as higher levels of patient satisfaction, in comparison to anesthesiologist-controlled sedation. Patient target-controlled infusion (TCI) is an interesting new technique of continuous infusion in which pharmacokinetic models are used to predict the patient's plasma and affected site concentrations and allow the anesthesiologist to target a chosen concentration. Such devices calculate the appropriate infusion scheme to achieve the desired concentration.[76,77] Currently, TCI devices are approved in many countries, but only for propofol administration.

Monitoring the depth of sedation in anesthesia has undergone significant recent changes with the analysis of the bispectral index (BIS) of the electroencephalogram (BIS, Aspect Medical Systems, Newton, MA). BIS has demonstrated a significant correlation with the level of responsiveness and the loss of consciousness during anesthesia and sedation with various anesthetic agents.[78] BIS monitoring in outpatients having surgery under regional anesthesia may become an effective way to reduce anesthetic drug doses and delayed awakening.[79] The growing numbers of devotees of these monitors are convinced of their ability to assist in shorter, safer, and more cost-effective anesthesia, which, in the ambulatory realm, is often conducive to fast-tracking.[80] Clinical trials suggest that the use of rapid recovery techniques (such as BIS or lower-solubility inhaled anesthetics) may also allow patients to sufficiently fast-track from general anesthesia to permit bypass of the Phase 1 PACU.[81,82] However, further research is required to determine the cost-effectiveness of this rapidly emerging technology.[83]

Training in Regional Anesthesia

There is ample evidence that the current training in regional anesthesia leaves residents unprepared to implement the full breadth of regional anesthesia techniques. More than two decades ago, it was suggested that large discrepancies existed in the use of regional anesthesia among training programs (2.8–55.7% of total delivered anesthetics), and that some anesthesiology residency programs were failing to teach regional anesthesia adequately.[84] However, the reports also suggest that the use of regional anesthesia techniques is on the rise and that the overall use of regional anesthesia had increased to almost 30%, although the disparity among teaching programs still persists.[85] Several residents' surveys conducted nationally and internationally[16, 86, 87] have established that the number of peripheral nerve blocks performed during residency is indeed limited, and that residents lack confidence in their ability to perform such blocks.[88,89] A survey of exposure to regional anesthesia techniques indicated that 51%, 62%, and 75% of the graduating residents may not be confident in performing interscalene, femoral nerve, and sciatic nerve blocks, respectively.[90] These results are not surprising, as the survey also indicated that the residents surveyed had performed five or less of each block by the end of their residency training.

Regardless, American anesthesiologists clearly perceive a need to employ more peripheral nerve blocks in their practice, and it is predicted that the use of these techniques will increase in the future.[16,91] A similar trend has been seen in Europe, where, for example, French anesthesiologists utilize regional anesthesia in 23% of their cases, a 14-fold increase in comparison with the amount of regional anesthesia practiced in 1980.[92] Better-structured regional anesthesia rotation, a well-defined training curriculum, a dedicated team of mentors with training in regional anesthesia, and ample clinical volume are all prerequisites for the adequate training of residents. As the present training practices are being reevaluated and restructured in many residency training programs,[93] it is likely that a higher level of expertise in regional anesthesia will be attained by far more graduates.

Information Technology

While information technology is already being rapidly introduced in anesthesia clinical practice, many unforeseen great advances lie ahead. The developments in information technology will inevitably improve the safety of outpatient anesthesia and enable anesthesia providers to spend more time caring for the patient.[94] The current technology with bar code, voice, point and click, and pen-based or touch-screen systems is challenged to make information systems assist in clinical practice. This technology can provide simultaneous and universal access to data by multiple users at once.[95] For instance, the patient data can be accessed for administrative, clinical management, accounting, and research purposes. It is quite certain that in the near future the medical records of individual patients will be directly accessible online from the outpatient surgery facilities. This should help avoid unnecessary delays in receiving faxes or phone call to doctors' offices with various preoperative clinical and laboratory information.

FUTURE CHALLENGES

Reducing health care costs has been one of the principal forces in driving the development of ambulatory surgery since its inception. The origins of cost savings provided by ambulatory surgery, especially at the freestanding surgery center, are multiple. The facilities are designed to function more efficiently, personnel are used more efficiently, paperwork and overhead are kept to a minimum, and costs are controlled by minimizing auxiliary services.[96,97] However, the proliferation of ambulatory surgical facilities has in some places overwhelmed the market. On the other hand, the office-based surgery has expanded and it is estimated that as much as 65% of anesthesia practices provide some type of office-based anesthesia services.[98] Despite the well-documented higher risk of office-based surgery, the economic forces of customer convenience and cost containment will likely foster its growth.[99] Clearly, office-based anesthesia is another excellent opportunity to implement regional anesthesia techniques and demonstrate advantages they have to offer in this setting in facilitating quality anesthesia and recovery.

SUMMARY

It is difficult to accurately predict the future developments in ambulatory and regional anesthesia. However, the current financial and societal forces as well as rapid developments in regional anesthesia will likely continue to foster the growth of ambulatory anesthesia. New technology, new surgical techniques, and progress in anesthesiology will undoubtedly be financed and supported by society provided that ambulatory surgery continues to decrease the costs of health care. The relatively low cost, excellent recovery profile, and almost ubiquitous application of regional anesthesia are almost certain to expand its role in this setting, particularly as more centers offer the necessary training in various specific regional anesthesia techniques.

REFERENCES

1. Vital and health statistics: ambulatory and inpatient procedures in the US. Atlanta: Centers for Disease Control and Prevention, 1996.
2. Collins LM, Vaghadia H. Regional anesthesia for laparoscopy. Anesth Clin North Am 2001;19:43–45.
3. Pregler JL, Kapur PA. The development of ambulatory anesthesia and future challenges. Anesth Clin North Am 2003;21:207–28.
4. Patel RI, Verghese ST, Hannallah RS, Aregawi A, Patel KM. Fast-tracking children after ambulatory surgery. Anesth Analg 2001;92:918–22.
5. Watkins AC, White PF. Fast-tracking after ambulatory surgery. J Perianesth Nurs 2001;16:379–87.
6. McGrath B, Chung F. Postoperative recovery and discharge. Anesth Clin North Am 2003;21:367–86.
7. Williams BA, Kentor ML. Making an ambulatory surgery centre suitable for regional anaesthesia. Best Pract Res Clin Anaesthesiol 2002;20:175–94.
8. Brian W, Kentor M, Vogt M, Williams J, Chelly JE, Valalik S, Harner C, Fu FH. Femoral-sciatic nerve blocks for complex outpatient knee surgery are associated with less postoperative pain before same-day discharge: a review of 1,200 consecutive cases from the period 1996–1999. Anesthesiology 2003;98:1206–13.
9. Williams BA, Kentor ML, Williams JP, Figallo CM, Sigl JC, Anders JW, Bear TC, Tullock WC, Bennett CH, Harner CD, Fu FH. Process analysis in outpatient knee surgery: effects of regional and general anesthesia on anesthesia-controlled time. Anesthesiology 2000;93:529–38.
10. Williams BA, de Riso BM, Figallo CM, Anders JB, Sproul KA, Ilkin H, Harner CD, Fu FH, Nagarajan NJ, Evans JH III, Watkins WD. Benchmarking the perioperative process: II. Introducing anesthesia clinical pathways to improve processes and outcomes, and reduce nursing labor intensity in ambulatory orthopedic surgery. J Clin Anesth 1998;10:561–69.
11. Williams BA, de Riso BM, Figallo CM, Anders JB, Sproul KA, Ilkin H, Harner CD, Fu FH, Nagarajan NJ, Evans JH III, Watkins WD.

Benchmarking the perioperative process: III. Effects of regional anesthesia clinical pathway techniques on processes efficiency and recovery profiles in ambulatory orthopedic surgery. J Clin Anesth 1998;10:570–78.
12. Van den Belt AG, Prins MH, Lensing AW, et al. Fixed dose subcutaneous low molecular weight heparins versus adjusted dose unfractioned heparin for venous thromboembolism. (Cochrane Review) In: The Cochrane Library, Issue 2. Oxford:Update; 1998.
13. Medpar: The MedStat Group Outcome Analysis. Medpar, 1998 Inforum, Medistat, Nashville, TN, 1998.
14. Bergquist D, Lundbald B. Incidence of venous thromboembolism in medical and surgical patients. In: Bergquist D, Comerota A, Nicolaides A, Scurr J (eds.), *Prevention of Venous Thromboembolism.* London: Med-Orion Press,1994.
15. Bick RL. Low molecular weight heparins in the outpatient management on venous thromboembolism. Semin Thromb Hemost 1999; 25:97–99.
16. Hadžić A, Vloka JD, Kuroda MM, Koorn R, Birnbach DJ. The practice of peripheral nerve blocks in the United States: a national survey. Reg Anesth Pain Med 1998;23:241–46.
17. Wedel, DJ. Regional anesthesia and pain management: reviewing the past decade and predicting the future. Anesth Analg 2000;90:1244–45.
18. Klein SM, Bergh A, Steele SM, Georgiade GS, Greengrass RA. Thoracic paravertebral block for breast surgery. Anesth Analg 2002;90:1402–5.
19. Weltz CR, Klein SM, Arbo JE, Greengrass RA. Paravertebral block anesthesia for inguinal hernia repair. World J Surg 2003;27:425–29.
20. Klein SM, Steele SM, Greengrass RA. A clinical overview of paravertebral blockade. Internet J Anesthesiol 1999;3(1):[8 screens]. Available from http://www.ispub.com/ostia/index.php?xmlFilePath =journals/ija/vol3n1/block.xml. Accessed August 4, 2003.
21. Klein SM, Pietrobon R, Nielsen KC, Steele SM, Warner DS, Moylan JA, Eubanks WS, Greengrass RA. Paravertebral somatic nerve block compared with peripheral nerve blocks for outpatient inguinal herniorrhaphy. Reg Anesth Pain Med 2002;27:476–80.
22. D'Ercole FJ, Scott D, Bell E, Klein SM, Greengrass RA. Paravertebral blockade for modified radical mastectomy in a pregnant patient. Anesth Analg 1999;88:1351–53.
23. Ilfeld BM, Morey EM, Wang RD, Enneking FK. Continuous popliteal sciatic nerve block for postoperative pain control at home: a randomized, double-blinded, placebo-controlled study. Anesthesiology 2002;97:959–65.
24. Ilfeld BM, Morey EM, Wang RD, Enneking FK. Continuous interscalene brachial plexus block for postoperative pain control at home: a randomized, double-blinded, placebo-controlled study. Anesth Analg 2003;96:1089–95.
25. Rawal N, Allvin R, Axelsson K, Hellen J, Ekback G, Ohlsson T, Amilon A. Patient-controlled regional analgesia (PCRA) at home: controlled-comparison between bupivacaine and ropivacaine brachial plexus analgesia. Anesthesiology 2002;96:1290–96.
26. Grant SA, Nielsen KC, Greengrass RA, Steele SM, Klein SM. Continuous peripheral nerve block for ambulatory surgery. Reg Anesth Pain Med 2001;26:209–14.
27. Klein SM, Grant SA, Greengrass RA, Nielsen KC, Speer KP, White W, Warner DS, Steele SM. Interscalene brachial plexus block with a continuous catheter insertion system and a disposable infusion pump. Anesth Analg 2000;91:1473–78.
28. Tuominen M, Haasio J, Hekali R, Rosenberg PH. Continuous interscalene brachial plexus block: clinical efficacy, technical problems and bupivacaine plasma concentrations. Acta Anaesthesiol Scand 1989;33:84–88.
29. Rawal N, Axelsson K, Hylander J, et al. Postoperative patient–controlled local anesthetic administration at home. Anesth Analg 1998;86:86–89.
30. Klein SM, Steele SM, Nielsen KC, Pietrobon R, Warner DS, Martin A, Greengrass RA. The difficulties of ambulatory interscalene and intra-articular infusions for rotator cuff surgery: a preliminary report. Can J Anaesth 2003;50:256–69.

31. Pham-Dang C, Gunst JP, Gouin F, et al. A novel supraclavicular approach to brachial plexus block. Anaesth Analg 1997;85:111–16.

32. Boezaart AP, de Beer JF, du Toit C, van Rooyen K. A new technique of continuous interscalene nerve block. Can J Anaesth 1999;46:275–81.

33. Coleman MM, Chan VW. Continuous interscalene brachial plexus block. Can J Anaesth 1999;46:209–14.

34. Pham-Dang C, Kick O, Collet T, Gouin F, Pinaud M. Continuous peripheral nerve blocks with stimulating catheters. Reg Anesth Pain Med 2003;28:83–88.

35. Casati A, Vinciguerra F, Scarioni M, Cappelleri G, Aldegheri G, Manzoni P, Fraschini G, Chelly JE. Lidocaine versus ropivacaine for continuous interscalene brachial plexus block after open shoulder surgery. Acta Anaesthesiol Scand 2003;47:355–60.

36. Casati A, Borghi B, Fanelli G, Montone N, Rotini R, Fraschini G, Vinciguerra F, Torri G, Chelly J. Interscalene brachial plexus anesthesia and analgesia for open shoulder surgery: a randomized, double-blinded comparison between levobupivacaine and ropivacaine. Anesth Analg 2003;96:253–59.

37. Riberio FC, Georgousis H, Bertram R, Scheiber G. Plexus irritation caused by interscalene brachial plexus catheter for shoulder surgery. Anesth Analg 1996;82:870–72.

38. Borgeat A, Ekatodramis G, Kalberer F, Benz C. Acute and non acute complications associated with interscalene block and shoulder surgery: a prospective study. Anesthesiology 2001;95:875–80.

39. Tuominen MK, Pere P, Rosenburg PH. Unintentional arterial catheterization and bupivacaine toxicity associated with continuous interscalene brachial plexus block. Anesthesiology 1991;75:356–58.

40. Cook LB. Unsuspected extradural catheterization in an interscalene block. Br J Anaesth 1991;67:473–75.

41. Wong GY, Brown DL, Miller GM, Cahill DR. Defining the cross-sectional anatomy important to interscalene brachial plexus block with magnetic resonance imaging. Reg Anesth Pain Med 1998;23:77–88.

42. Mukherji S, Wagle A, Armao D. Brachial plexus nerve block with CT guidance for regional pain management. Radiology 2000;216;886–90.

43. Nishiyama M, Naganuma K, Amaki Y. A new approach for brachial plexus block under fluoroscopy guidance. Anesth Analg 1999;88:91–97.

44. Moorty SS. Fluoroscopic imaging during supraclavicular lateral paravascular brachial plexus block. Reg Anesth Pain Med 2000;25:327–28.

45. Kapral S, Marhofer P, Grau T. Ultrasound in local anesthesia. Part I. Technical development and background. Anaesthesist 2002;51:931–37.

46. Yang WT, Chuy PT, Metreweli C. Anatomy of the normal brachial plexus revealed by sonography and the role of sonographic guidance in anesthesia of the brachial plexus. Am J Roentogenol 1998;171:1631–36.

47. Kapral S, Krafft P, Eibenberger K. Ultrasound-guided supraclavicular approach for regional anesthesia of the brachial plexus. Anesth Analg 1994;78:507–13.

48. Ootaki C, Hayashi H, Amino M. Ultrasound-guided infraclavicular brachial plexus block: an alternative technique to anatomical landmark-guided approaches. Reg Anesth Pain Med 2000;25:600–604.

49. Sandhu NS, Kapan LM. Ultrasound-guided infraclavicular brachial plexus block. Br J Anaesth 2002;89:254–59.

50. Sandhu NS, Bahniwal CS, Capan LM. Ultrasound guidance reduces local anesthetic requirement for infraclavicular brachial plexus block. Anesthesiology 2001;95:851.

51. Anahi P, Chan V, Simons M. A brachial plexus examination and localization using ultrasound and electrical stimulation: a volunteer study. Anesthesiology 2003;99:429–35.

52. Kapral S, Marhofer P. Ultrasound in local anaesthesia. Part II. Ultrasound-guided blockade of peripheral nerve channels. Anaesthesist 2002;51:1006–14.

53. http://www.nysora.com, January 18, 2003.

54. Hadžić A, Vloka JD, Hadžić N, Thys DM, Santos AC. Nerve stimulators used for peripheral nerve blocks vary in their electrical characteristics. Anesthesiology 2003;98(4):969–74.

55. Girstwood RW. Cardiac and CNS toxicity of levobupivacaine: strengths of evidence for advantage over bupivacaine. Drug Safety 2002;25:153–63.

56. Mather LE, Chang DH. Cardiotoxicity with modern local anesthetics: is there a safer choice? Drugs 2001;61:333–42.

57. Gautier PE, de Kock M, van Steneberge A, et al. Intrathoracic ropivacaine for ambulatory surgery. Anesthesiology 1999;91:1239–45.

58. McDonald SB, Liu SS, Kopacz DJ, et al. Hyperbaric spinal ropivacaine: a comparison to bupivacaine in volunteers. Anesthesiology 1999;90:971–77.

59. Gesztes A, Mezei M. Topical anesthesia of the skin by liposome-encapsulated tetracaine. Anesth Analg 1988;67:1079–81.

60. Grant SA. The holy grail: long-acting local anesthetics and liposomes. Best Pract Res Clin Anaesthesiol 2002;16:345–52.

61. Boogaerts JG, Declercq A, Lafont N, et al. Toxicity of bupivacaine encapsulated into liposomes and injected intravenously: comparison with plain solutions. Anesth Analg 1993;76:553–55.

62. Boogaerts JG, Lafont ND, Declercq, et al. Epidural administration of liposome-associated bupivacaine for management of postsurgical pain: a first study. J Clin Anesth 1994;6:315–20.

63. Yu HY, Li SD, Sun P. Kinetic and dynamic studies of liposomal bupivacaine and bupivacaine solution after subcutaneous injection in rats. J Pharm Pharmacol 2002;54:1221–27.

64. Boogaerts JG, Lafont ND, Luo H, Legros FJ. Plasma concentrations of bupivacaine after brachial plexus administration of liposome-associated and plain solutions to rabbits. Can J Anaesth 1993;40:1201–4.

65. Mashimo T, Uchida I, Pak M, et al. Prolongation of canine epidural anesthesia by liposome encapsulation of lidocaine. Anesth Analg 1992;74:827–34.

66. Mowat JJ, Mok MJ, MacLeod BA, Madden TD. Liposomal bupivacaine: extended duration nerve blockade using large unilamellar vesicles that exhibit a proton gradient. Anesthesiology 1996;85:635–43.

67. Hall RJ. Hydrochlorate of cocaine. NY Med J 1984;40:643–44.

68. Curley J, Castillo J, Hotz J. Prolonged regional nerve blockade: injectable biodegradeable bupivacaine/polyester microspheres. Anesthesiology 1996;84:1401–10.

69. Holte K, Werner M, Lacouture P, Kehlet H. Dexamethasone prolongs local analgesia of subcutaneous bupivacaine microcapsules in human volunteers. Anesthesiology 2002;96:1331–35.

70. Drager C, Benziger D, Gao F, Berde CB. Prolonged intercostal nerve blockade in sheep using controlled-release of bupivacaine and dexamethasone from polymer microspheres. Anesthesiology 1998;89:969–79.

71. Estebe JC, Le Corre P, Chevanne F. Effects of dexamethasone on motor brachial plexus block with bupivacaine and with bupivacaine-loaded microspheres in sheep model. Anesthesiology 2001;95:A911.

72. Kern C, Weber A, Aurilio C, Forster A. A patient evaluation and comparison of recovery profile between propofol and thiopentone as induction agents in day surgery. Anesth Intens Care 1998;26:156–61.

73. Ghouri AF, Ruiz MA, White PF. Effect of flumazenil on recovery after midazolam and propofol sedation. Anesthesiology 1994;81:333–39.

74. White PF, Negus JB. Sedative infusions during local and regional anesthesia: a comparison of midazolam and propofol. J Clin Anesth 1991;3:32–39.

75. Ng J, Kong CF, Nyam D. Patient-controlled sedation with propofol for colonoscopy. Gastrointest Endosc 2001;54:8–13.

76. Passot S, Servin F, Allary R, et al. Target-controlled versus manually-controlled infusion of propofol for direct laryngoscopy and bronchoscopy. Anesth Analg 2002;94:1212–16.

77. Van den Nieuwenhuyzen MC, Engbers FH, Vuyk J, Burm AG. Target-controlled infusion systems: role in anaesthesia and analgesia. Clin Pharmacokinet 2001;38:181–90.

78. Glass PS, Bloom M, Kearse L, et al. Bispectral analysis measures sedation and memory effects of propofol, midazolam, isoflurane and alfentanil in healthy volunteers. Anesthesiology 1997;86:836–47.

79. Sandlar NA. The use of bispectral analysis to monitor outpatient sedation. Anesth Prog 2000;47:72–83.

80. Ahmad S, Yilmaz M, Marcus RJ, Glisson S, Kinsella A. Impact of bispectral index monitoring on fast tracking of gynecologic patients undergoing laparoscopic surgery. Anesthesiology 2003;98:849–52.

81. Gan TJ, Glass PS, Windsor A. Bispectral index monitoring allows faster emergence and improved recovery from propofol, alfentanil and nitrous oxide anesthesia. Anesthesiology 1997;87:808–15.

82. Song D, Joshi G, White P. Fast-track eligibility after ambulatory anesthesia: a comparison of desflurane, sevoflurane and propofol. Anesth Analg 1998;86:267–73.

83. Yli-Hankala A, Vakkuri A, Annila P, Korttila K. EEG bispectral index monitoring in sevoflurane or propofol anaesthesia: analysis of direct costs and immediate recovery. Acta Anaesthesiol Scand 1999;43:545–49.

84. Bridenbaugh L. Are anesthesia resident programs failing regional anesthesia? Reg Anesth 1982;7:26–28.

85. Kopacz DJ, Bridenbaugh LD. Are anesthesia residency programs failing regional anesthesia? The past, present, and future. Reg Anesth 1993;18:84–87.

86. Bouaziz H, Mercier FJ, Narchi P, et al. Survey of regional anesthesia practice among French residents at time of certification. Reg Anesth 1997;22:218–22.

87. Epstein RM, Kitz RJ, Larson CP Jr, Stoelting RK. A modification in the training requirements in anesthesiology: requirements for the third clinical year. Anesthesiology 1985;62:175–77.

88. Bridenbaugh L. Are anesthesia residency programs failing regional anesthesia? Reg Anesth 1982;7:26–28.

89. Chelly JE, Greger J, Gebhard R, Hagberg CA, Al-Samsam T, Khan A. Training of residents in peripheral nerve blocks during anesthesiology residency. J Clin Anesth 2002;14:584–88.

90. Smith M, Sprung J, Zura A, et al. A survey of exposure to regional anesthesia techniques in American anesthesia residency training programs. Reg Anesth Pain Med 1999;24:11–16.

91. Horlocker TT. Peripheral nerve blocks—regional anesthesia for the new millennium. Reg Anesth Pain Med 1998;23:237–40.

92. Clergue F, Auroy Y, Pequignot F, et al. French survey of anesthesia in 1996. Anesthesiology 1999;91:1509–20.

93. Hadžić A. Vloka JD, Koenigsamen J. Training requirements for peripheral nerve blocks. Curr Opin Anesthesiol 2002;15:669–73.

94. Raeder JC. Anaesthesiology into the new millennium. Acta Anaesthesiol Scand 2000;44:3–8.

95. Higgins MS. Data management for a perioperative medicine practice. Anesthesiol Clin North Am 2000;18:647–61.

96. Henderson JA. Ambulatory surgery: past, present, and future. In: Wetchler BV (ed.), Anesthesia for Ambulatory Surgery, 2nd ed. Philadelphia: Lippincott; 1991:1–27.

97. Reed WA, Ford JL. Development of an independent outpatient surgical center. Int Anesth Clin 1976;14:113–30.

98. Koch ME, Giannuzzi R, Goldstein RC. Office anesthesiology: an overview. Anesthsiol Clin North Am 1999;17:395–405.

99. Kopp VJ. Preoperative preparation: value, prospective, and practice in patient care. Anesthesiol Clin North Am 2000;18:551–74.